THE THEATRE OF DON JUAN

The Theatre of

Don Juan

A Collection of Plays and Views, 1630-1963

Edited with a commentary

by

OSCAR MANDEL

UNIVERSITY OF NEBRASKA PRESS • LINCOLN AND LONDON

For, and with, Adriana

Acknowledgments for permission to reprint and translate copyrighted material begin on page 730. The original of the title-page decoration is a bas-relief on the monument to Tirso de Molina in Ciudad-Trujillo, Dominica. The sculptor is Federico Coullaut Valera.

Third paperback printing: 1993

Library of Congress Cataloging-in-Publication Data
The Theatre of Don Juan.
  Bibliography: p.
  1. Don Juan—Drama. 2. Drama—Collections.
I. Mandel, Oscar.
[PN6120.D7T48   1986]   808.82'9351   86-1491
ISBN 0-8032-8137-4 (pbk.)

∞

Contents

Part III: *THE MOLECULAR DON JUAN*

Contents

Illustrations

The Legend of Don Juan

"The speaking in a perpetual hyperbole is comely in nothing but love," Francis Bacon wrote more than three centuries ago in his essay upon that inexhaustibly bemusing subject. As though to show how right the Englishman was, and just possibly in the very year in which the words were written, a Spanish monk was bringing Don Juan into the world: the most hyperbolical of lovers, destined to place one thousand and three of his own countrywomen on an immortal list.

The great adorer—and satirist—of women performed so well that many persons think of him to this day as a man who lived and created his legend out of his own deeds. In 1835, an imaginative or negligent historian, Louis Viardot, even advanced the claim that the story of Don Juan Tenorio could be be read in an old chronicle of Seville. This Tenorio, member of an illustrious family and companion of Don Pedro the Cruel (1350–1369), was supposed to have carried off the daughter of the Commander of the Order of Calatrava and to have murdered the latter, who was barring his way. For this and for similar crimes the powerful monks of the Convent of San Francisco in Seville lured him into the church, arrested him, tried him, and secretly executed him. They allowed the rumor to be spread that Don Juan had been cast into Hell by the memorial statue of the Commander.[1] Viardot's report was credited, or at least respected, for almost a century. But Spanish investigators, rummaging among the archives of Seville and other cities, could find no trace of the story, and today all scholars agree that Don Juan—in English, plain Sir John—and his adventures are fictions as pure as the fiction of Don Quixote. There was once an important family in Seville called Tenorio, but the only possible conclusion to be drawn from this lone fact is that Don Juan's creator borrowed the ancient name to give his tale the appearance of truth.

The man who created Don Juan was a monk and dramatist of the first half of the seventeenth century, Gabriel Téllez, better known as Tirso de Molina, and considered today one of the four best playwrights of Spain's Golden Age. In 1630 a play entitled *El Burlador de*

1. See Louis Viardot, *Études sur l'histoire des institutions, de la littérature, du théâtre et des beaux-arts en Espagne* (1835).

3

Sevilla y convidado de piedra (The Jester of Seville and the Stone Guest) appeared under his name in a collection of works by Lope de Vega "and other authors." [2] No one knows when the play was written, or on what occasion it was first performed. The only certainty is that Tirso began to write plays around 1605 and that, as the result of an official rebuke, he virtually ceased to do so in 1625. A possible date of composition is 1616, when Tirso is known to have been in Seville.

Since we will be much concerned with the *story* of Don Juan, as distinguished from the significance of the Don Juanesque character, it may be useful to begin with a summary of the basic account, that of Tirso's *El Burlador*.

The play opens in the palace of the King of Naples. It is late at night. Don Juan, his face muffled, enters with the Duchess Isabela. When she manages to see his face, Isabela realizes that she has been tricked—this is not her fiancé, the Duke Octavio, but a stranger who has impersonated the Duke to ravish her. Her calls for the guard bring on the King and the Spanish Ambassador. The Ambassador is charged with the stranger's arrest. When the two are left alone, the Ambassador discovers that the interloper is his nephew. He allows Don Juan to escape, and holds his tongue when Duchess Isabela avers to the King that Duke Octavio is the guilty man.

The scene changes to the Spanish coast near Tarragona. En route back to Seville, Don Juan and his servant Catalinón (the name means *coward*) have been shipwrecked but have managed to swim ashore. Don Juan is tended by a beautiful fisher-girl, Tisbea. Hitherto wholly uninterested in lovemaking, she takes fire on seeing the handsome cavalier. Don Juan promises marriage, enjoys her for one night, and travels on to Seville.

There, at the court of King Alfonso of Castile, he encounters Duke Octavio, who has fled Naples to avoid arrest. Although Octavio has no idea that it was Don Juan who tricked his way into the Duchess Isabela's bed, King Alfonso has learned the truth of the affair. The King has kept silent to protect Isabela's good name, but he plans to see that justice is done. He decrees that Don Juan must marry Isabela as soon as she arrives from Naples; in the meanwhile he is to be banished to Le-

2. There is no single perfect equivalent in English for the word *burlador. Joker, jester, trickster, rogue, prankster,* and *seducer*—all of these are adequate approximations. The translation used in this volume accepts *playboy* as a modern rendering. For a fuller discussion of the play, the question of its authorship, and the textual problems, see pages 37 ff.

brija. As consolation to Octavio for his loss of Isabela, the King promises him the hand of Doña Ana, daughter of the illustrious Commander of the Order of Calatrava. But Ana is in love with the Marquis de Mota, one of Don Juan's cronies—a circumstance which gives Don Juan the opportunity for another masquerade. On the eve of his banishment he contrives to enter Ana's bedchamber disguised as the Marquis. This time, however, his intended victim is not deceived. She cries out; her father comes to her rescue; and Don Juan kills him with a sword thrust. Again the trickster manages to escape, and again an innocent person gets the blame for his crime: the Marquis de Mota is arrested for killing the Commander.

On his way to exile in Lebrija Don Juan happens upon a rustic wedding feast. The bride, Arminta, takes his eye. By pretending he had long ago promised her marriage he succeeds in seducing her and, of course, when he has enjoyed her for a night he promptly takes off. Somewhat unaccountably he decides to return to Seville.

Throughout the play Don Juan has brushed aside good advice and laughed off warnings that sooner or later he must pay the piper. Now it begins to appear that the day of reckoning is at hand. From Catalinón, whom he meets in a church, Don Juan hears that Octavio and the Marquis have discovered that he is the man for whose crimes they have been blamed, and that Isabela and Tisbea too are hot on his trail. He is confronted by another grim reminder of his evil-doing when he enters a chapel in the church: before him is the tomb of the murdered Commander, with the Commander's statue standing above an inscription threatening vengeance. Characteristically, Don Juan jeers at the threat; despite the terrified Catalinón's remonstrances, he tweaks the stony beard of the Statue and invites it to sup with him.

The Statue duly appears at the meal. It exacts from Don Juan a solemn promise that he will be its guest at a banquet in the chapel the next night. Determined to exhibit his courage, Don Juan keeps the engagement. The Statue grasps his hand and flings him down to Hell, heedless of his cry for a priest. Catalinón is spared to report the miracle. Now Octavio will marry Isabela after all, and Doña Ana, her father avenged, is reunited with the Marquis.[3]

Tirso's play can be characterized as average Spanish tragicomedy of

3. *Isabela* and *Ana* become *Isabella* and *Anna* in the English spelling. The spelling used in the discussion of characters in a particular translation will follow that of the translator. In general discussion of the Don Juan matter, the English form will be used.

the Golden Age. Most of its episodes could have been invented by any professional dramatist of the epoch, or pulled out of the file. A few seductions (Tirso lazily duplicated his episodes: two ladies, two rustic damsels), disguises and mistaken identities, the theme of honor, a humorous servant, a couple of pastoral episodes in the flowery rhetoric of Arcadia—this was the regular diet of the Spanish theatre-goer. It would be idle, therefore, to look for sources for most of these episodes.

The scenes that did distinguish *El Burlador* from other plays—those concerning the Statue—are the only ones which can be traced beyond the possibility of doubt to older materials. The motif of an offense to the dead, a macabre invitation and counter-invitation, and the dead man's revenge is common to the folklore of Spain and other European countries. Thus most of *El Burlador* is Renaissance fiction; but Tirso drew on folklore to finish off his play with a sensationally stageworthy "machine."

Many variants of the basic tale have been unearthed in Europe; here I give one of the Spanish ballads in a prose translation, keeping the crudity and stiffness of the original *romance:*

A spark [*un galán*] was on his way to church to attend Mass. He didn't go for the sake of Mass, but to look at the young and pretty girls. In the middle of the road he saw a skull. He looked at it long and gave it a great kick. The skull bared its teeth as though laughing. "Skull, I invite you to my feast tonight." "Don't jest, good knight, for I pledge you my word." The spark went home astounded. All day he was melancholy. When the night arrived he ordered supper. He had not eaten a mouthful when somebody knocked at the door. He sent one of his pages to see who it might be. "Servant, ask your master whether he remembers his promise." "Servant, tell him I do; let him come in and be welcome." He gave him a golden chair for his body, and gave him many dishes, but he refused to eat. "I did not come to see you or to eat your supper. I came to bid you to walk with me to church at midnight." At midnight the cocks were singing; at midnight they went to the church. In the middle of the church there was an open grave. "Knight, go in, go in, go fearless to the grave. There you'll sleep with me, and eat my supper too." "I will not go in; God has not allowed it." "Were it not there is a God, were it not you called on God, were it not these relics hang on your chest, you'd enter here alive whether you wanted to or not. Go home now, low-born villain, and if you meet another skull, bow to it and say for it a *pater noster,* and throw it into the charnel-house. You will want this done to you when you leave this world." [4]

4. This *romance* was recited to Juan Menéndez Pidal by a woman of the people in the province of León in 1885. It can most conveniently be found, along with all the other collected versions, in Dorothy B. MacKay, *The Double Invitation in the Legend of Don Juan* (Palo Alto: Stanford University Press, 1943).

In some of the versions of the folktale, the rascal pays for his frivolity with his life. In several the skull is replaced by a hanged man. A few times a statue appears (but Tirso could have found his Statue in one of Lope's plays or in other strictly literary works). Sometimes the young sinner is on his way to his own wedding, and this is what suggests the invitation to him. In one account the idea occurs to him because the hanged man's mouth is open—he must be hungry! But in every case the tale is made to perplex. Why *two* offenses, the kick (or some other taunt) and the invitation? Why—unless the "hero" is going to a banquet—an invitation to a meal? And why does the prankster accept the return invitation?

I am not satisfied that the story can be linked, as Said Armesto has affirmed, to the ritual of eating a meal once a year (usually on All Souls' Day) over the grave of the departed.[5] None of the versions allude to this ritual; the invitation occurs on any day of the year; and it is almost always a casual taunt, not a malicious perversion of a holy ceremony. What we feel increasingly as we read from version to version is simply that the storytellers themselves were puzzled, and that the variants are usually attempts to rationalize or to mitigate the monstrous original tale. I should say the *two* original tales; for it is clear that the folktale which Tirso knew and used is a blending of two stories. The first is that of a perfectly accidental injury done to the dead (a skull kicked by an unwary pedestrian) which the spirit savagely avenges by killing the offender; the second deals with a conscious and consciously sarcastic invitation to a dead man to a supper, again avenged by the spirit but this time at a fatal meal offered in return. Both tales, it will be recalled, are represented in Tirso's last act: Don Juan pulls the Statue's beard, an act similar to the kicking of the skull, before launching his dinner invitation. And in the play as in all the folktales the two ghostly vengeances are fused into one.

The first of the two tales presents no difficulty to our imagination. We think of respect to the dead (or to the spirits, or to the gods, or to God) as due in the normal scheme of things, and stories of blasphemy and punishment are too common among us to require an explanation. But the second tale is troublesome, for the scamp's invitation looks like an unmotivated eccentricity. Why, of all things, a meal? A reason must be concealed somewhere, for an eccentricity would not have persisted in popular tradition.

The existence of so many tales on this bizarre subject points to a significant experience, perhaps a rite, which time effaced—or, rather, converted into a hallucinatory tale made to frighten naughty children. I believe that the legend which has come down to us is a mitigation of a grim and yet intelligible motif, that of the eating of the dead, possibly as a religious rite. In the evolution of this theme, when the ritualistic significance had already faded, the next step might well have been to consider such a meal an offense and a horror (thus the tale of Thyestes), which would be avenged by the dead in kind. We catch a glimpse of this stage in the following tale:

> A woman disinters a corpse, removes its entrails [asadura], cooks them, and serves them to her husband for supper. That night the dead man comes to the house crying for his "asaúra." He approaches the terrified woman, snatches her by the hair, and drags her to the cemetery, where he kills her, removes her "asadura," puts them in himself, and buries himself again.[6]

Is it not likely that the legends of the Double Invitation were at one time more gruesome tales, and that Don Juan's ancestors had made a feast of, and not with, the dead?

In its later stages the once savage motif was softened even more. Instead of being eaten the hero was simply killed, though for no very clear reason. Eventually he was let off with a warning. The same spirit of justice and mercy also palliated the first tale, that of the accidental kick. True, a few of the surviving versions are old and merciless: the kick is unintentional yet the offender must perish. Here is a reaction of the dead which is as impersonal, in a sense, as our own natural laws. To the primitive mind intentions do not count in sacred matters. A profanation is like a false turn over the edge to the abyss: you die whether or not you meant to take the step. However, most of the extant versions moralize the episode by making the kick, or whatever taunt is recorded, a premeditated one. Others add motivation at every point of the tale. Gradually hearts grow softer and the death penalty is reduced to a severe warning. Finally the story is Christianized: the offender is protected by prayers, relics, and virtuous deeds, and his fright is salutary.

Tirso, as might be expected from a professional playwright, made the old folktale as plausible as he could. In El Burlador the dead man is not only an acquaintance of the offender (that in itself is an important step toward reason) but also a victim. And next, the offender is

6. MacKay, *The Double Invitation in the Legend of Don Juan*, p. 16.

given a reason for his taunt—he is irked by the menacing inscription. The taunt is no longer an accident involving an unknown departed spirit, but a premeditated and motivated insult to a dead victim. Now, too, the offender has a reason for keeping his appointment—his Spanish desire to exhibit his daring. Finally, instead of being killed for a trifling offense (how could a Renaissance gentleman, unable to consult Carl Jung, sense the archetypal significance of a kicked skull murdering the kicker?), the sinner is paying for a life of levities and crime.

A bearding, a kick, or a biting remark—nothing could be more natural in *El Burlador*. But just why the inscription under the Statue should prompt the angry and scornful Don Juan to ask it to supper rather than to a dance or for a game of cards is more than Tirso or anyone else could explain. A challenge to a duel would have been more in keeping with Don Juan's code, and in fact Don Juan alludes to the possibility in his first encounter with the Statue (Act III, Scene 3). But even though the supper made no sense, Tirso was not about to omit it. He made the most of its theatrical value, and asked no questions.

Tirso could have done without the Statue—he could have killed off Don Juan in a duel with Octavio, delivered him over to the authorities for execution, or struck him down with a lightning bolt—but the Statue gave him a conclusion agreeable both to the instincts of a popular playwright and the piety of a Mercedarian monk. For though Master Tirso might wink, Brother Gabriel would have insisted on the seriousness of the Statue. It did not descend from its pedestal and grasp the sinner's hand to amuse the ladies in the gallery, but—ostensibly, at least—to preach the doctrine of timely repentance. Tirso put the best of his passion into the last act. It might have disconcerted him to know that Don Juan was to be remembered for his splurge of seductions, and not for his neglect of the sacraments.

The history of Tirso's Statue is rich in ironies. *El Burlador* made an impression not because the Statue was meaningful but because it was good theatre. Moreover, the Statue which was intended to elevate the tale was the cause of its coming to be regarded as a vulgar farce. Finally, when times and tastes changed and Don Juan was treated as serious drama once more, the very Statue which had given the play its seriousness to begin with, and which was responsible for its survival, was the first object to be dismissed. And yet the best versions of the Don Juan play are still those which have remained somehow true to the folktale. Today in Ingmar Bergman's *The Devil's Eye* and Max

Frisch's *Don Juan, or the Love of Geometry* the aggrieved Statue stalks again, affording modern audiences quite as much satisfaction as it gave the spectators of the seventeenth century.

II

For most people Don Juan is forever the Don Giovanni whom Mozart set to music. He is seen and heard with his servant (now called Leporello), and with Elvira, Anna, and Octavio—pursued, philandering, giving a feast, serenading, masquerading, and defying the Statue— as Mozart's librettist, Lorenzo da Ponte, saw fit to move him. But Da Ponte's libretto is no sport: it is a true child of Tirso's play, descending in a direct and legitimate line from *El Burlador* by way of a whole series of French, Italian, and Spanish successors. We are therefore justified in speaking of a distinct Don Juan Tenorio story or legend, invented by Tirso de Molina, living on in full vigor until the end of the neoclassical era and more precariously since. In the nineteenth century the story was given a new direction by its encounter with the legend of the sinful but redeemed hero, Miguel Mañara.[7] But while occasionally rerouted, Tirso's original has by no means been abandoned.

The plot of *El Burlador* consists, as we have seen, of two easily distinguishable layers: the amorous adventures of Don Juan—Renaissance fiction, *ad hoc* invention—and the episodes with the Statue, drawn from folklore. Disregarding the separate origin of the two layers, I will speak of Tirso's entire story and of the stories which it begot in turn as the *legend* of Don Juan. But Don Juan is not legend only. In our world he is also *myth:* he has become for us the permanent symbol of a particular human passion, activity, or aspiration. He is not and never was a god; his life does not explain cosmic phenomena; and yet, like Faust, he has almost the stature of one of the immortals of the classical pantheon because he is the incarnation of a fundamental human drive.

We will turn presently to the significance of Don Juan as symbol or

7. Miguel Mañara lived in the seventeenth century and is said to have tried as a youth to emulate the fictitious Don Juan. Later he was converted and lived out his days in virtuous contrition. Many legends grew up around him, but they did not impinge on the Don Juan matter until the nineteenth century, when the two stories were interfused. See page 452 in this volume.

myth. Here it is enough to say that the myth requires him to pursue and win women as inevitably as he breathes. Don Juan without women is like Prometheus without fire. But this is a general requirement, allowing for any plot obedient to it which the author may choose to exploit or invent. We cannot separate Oedipus from the specific legend concerning him which Sophocles has retold; but if Don Juan is detached from the episodes through which Tirso and his successors conducted him, if he is given instead an entirely new set of women to seduce, he is still the same symbolic being. Tirso's legend created the myth, but it *is not* the myth. There is after all no limit to the stories that can be told about men who have a greater amorous success than their neighbors, and such a theme bores few men and fewer women. Our literature is replete with heroes who more or less resemble Don Juan. Indeed, the editor of a collection of plays on the subject is likely to turn melancholic over his problems. Shall he include any play concerning *a* Don Juan, that is to say a notable seducer of women? Must the hero's name be Don Juan? Should the play retell or adapt Tirso's story? Can it consist wholly of new adventures for the hero? Must the significant myth underlie the play?

For the purpose of this collection, a Don Juan play is one which uses, adapts, or alludes to the original legend and the very Don Juan Tenorio created by Tirso de Molina. We do not ask the playwright to use the legend so as to express the mythical essence—the true meaning—of Don Juan. In eighteenth-century puppet plays, Don Juan is not amorous; in nineteenth-century musical comedy, he is an oaf; in the twentieth-century conceptions of Shaw and Frisch, he distrusts and even dislikes women. These are aberrations from the myth (for if Don Juan is not the great lover, he does not exist as myth); but they perpetuate the legend all the same. Our discussion cannot ignore the myth, but our history and our collection of plays revolves around the sheer fiction itself.

Nor are we concerned with the numerous analogues of Don Juan. I call *analogues* narratives concerning great seducers which do not treat in any manner whatsoever the Don Juan Tenorio episodes of the legend: for example, Richardson's *Clarissa*, Laclos' *Les Liaisons dangereuses*, Chekhov's *Platonov*, or Christopher Fry's *Venus Observed*. Another analogue is Byron's *Don Juan*, since it is perfectly possible to use the name without the matter—I can call a fierce dog Achilles if I wish! Some of the analogues are far greater works of art than are plays in the "true" line, and there is no reason for not assembling a collection of plays concerning great lovers. But that is another book—and ten thousand pages long.

Tirso's legend has adapted itself to a surprising variety of purposes and moods, and every age has found something in it to amuse, mystify, or instruct. At least one critic, Hoffmann, denied that the bare story has any intrinsic merit, but were this true it would not have survived for nearly three and a half centuries and be alive at this very moment. Tirso's formula is elementary but deeply satisfying: the blood-red verve of love in the gold of palaces and the green of open fields, followed by black retribution in the ghostly recess of a church. Love and death: this is Don Juan's primary poetry. Granted we cannot point to a Don Juanesque masterpiece in literature which compares with *Don Quixote* or *Faust*. But the legend has produced a store of minor riches and major curiosities. The number of retellings and adaptations in existence is in itself cause for wonder. *El Burlador* has been, in Ortega y Gasset's words, a quarry to which anyone could go for materials. No play of the Renaissance has so vast a progeny as this undated piece which its author, not even identified beyond all possibility of doubt, did not bother to include in his own collected works.

III

When Don Juan took shape in that Renaissance which equaled the ancient world in fecundity of myth-making, he embodied, probably beyond his author's guess or intention, an aspect of being forever interesting to mankind. Don Juan became a myth representing the *triumph of sensuality*. But this triumph should not be understood as a triumph in the world. Eventually, to be sure, Don Juan was to become the type of the irresistible lover, *l'homme fatal;* but in his early, his classical career, he had not by any means found a way of pleasing all women. Some he pleased, but others he had to rape, and others to dazzle with his position in the world. No; the triumph is an inward one; triumph in the self. With him, sensuality is no longer one element in his character, nor is the pursuit of women simply an absorbing occupation to be set beside several other occupations; rather it is his life's only business; whatever else he may be or do is incidental.

This fact makes him a symbol. Pure sensuality is an abstraction, as is pure gluttony, or pure miserliness. Religion and literature have often offered to the imagination these embodiments of a single passion or a single activity. Is this not, actually, the religious and aesthetic equivalent of the scientist's isolation of an element he wishes to study? When the object is isolated and inserted into a given situation, we know that any alteration in the latter is caused by the object, and thereby we see the nature and the intensity of the object's effect on the situation. This abstract statement fits the world of art as well as it does the laboratory. Don Juan is really the incarnation of a given "humour." When we see him in action, we see the action of sensuality uncontaminated by any other passion. The significance of this act of isolation is plain. Isolation gives dramatic force. We owe to it some of the most memorable "monsters" in literature—Achilles, Medea, Creon, or Uriah Heep and Pecksniff. For isolation aggrandizes the object. We see it unnaturally but more distinctly. Cleared of the complications and counterforces of reality, it works on our senses with satisfying absoluteness and with forceful simplicity. As soon as Achilles haggles with his shoemaker or Don Juan lectures his bailiff about the crops of his estate, the dramatic directness and beauty are gone. Bacchus drinks forever; Achilles fights forever; Don Quixote tilts forever; and Don Juan loves forever. The maturest mind delights in these hypertrophies. Reality is seen standing on stilts and speaking through a megaphone. We lose its details, but we see it to remember.

Not all the details are lost, of course. Don Juan is in each play a particular and individual embodiment of the abstraction. Each author gives him a particular accent, a distinct coloration, a peculiar habit or two. We require the illusion of conversing with a real protagonist even when we most keenly feel the literal absurdity of his character and of his actions. After all, our human symbol must do something in the world (unless, indeed, he is to be restricted to conversation with other symbols, as in those tedious allegorical masques); and as soon as he acts he must take on certain characteristics of a real human being. He must be given a name and an address. What struts in Tirso's play is not Amor, but Don Juan in the streets of Seville. It is a delicate business for the artist, to hold his balance so that he can animate his symbolic figure in a real street without falling into the ludicrous.[8]

8. The union of the abstract and the individual (Coleridge makes much of it in the *Biographia Literaria*) has this effect in the case of Don Juan, that, among other things, he *must* be an idle aristocrat. If the idea of sensuality is to be embodied in a man for literary purposes, this man must be at perfect leisure. He cannot be working in a factory or in an office, or writing books, or making agricultural experiments. As soon as this happens, he descends (or rises) into the realm of realistic, complex, ambiguous literature; he ceases to be a universal symbol. The pure idea of sensuality in a concrete setting can meet the laws of likelihood only in the shape of a man whose time is entirely his own.

I repeat that no writer is compelled to accept or, even if he accepts it, to use this interpretation of the legend. He can, as some have done, rework it to make Don Juan a misogynist. Might not a wit turn Faust into an ignoramus? Conversely, a writer can invent his own hero and endow him with hyperbolical lust. But as long as Don Juan is remembered, he will be remembered as the great lover; and as long as great lovers are known, they will be called Don Juans. Even the aberrant versions of the legend will count on our knowledge and acceptance of the myth as a fixed point of departure for themselves.

The question has often been raised, why did Don Juan fail to get himself born until the seventeenth century? I doubt whether a satisfactory answer has ever been given, and I should not like to discount the possibility of mere accident. (Because so much literature has been lost, we cannot, in fact, guarantee that a true Don Juan never was invented before, but it is certain that no such figure ever became a type.) The answer may be that Don Juan was born when a career of sensuality became a possible serious occupation for a dignified man. For we must remember that even when the adventures of Don Juan are surrounded by comedy or farce, his own enterprise is basically serious. Pleasure is no joke. Before the Renaissance this triumph of sensuality could never have been conceived of as a serious matter.

In antiquity (I speak only of Graeco-Roman antiquity; it may be that other cultures have other Don Juans to show) we find Zeus the philanderer or the god Priapus—the latter, incidentally, has been suggested as Don Juan's true ancestor—but both are comic in their sexual role. Among mortal heroes, great lovers were Theseus, Jason, and Paris. Theseus, however, takes his women as booty, just as Agamemnon and any warrior did. Jason takes his out of policy; he is the ancestor of all the princes who love politically. And Paris, the true lover, is an object of contempt and derision. Quite significantly, his fondness for women is equated with his bad soldiering. Preoccupation with women does not suit a great man. It is not envied. It has little status. Women are not important enough to make their seduction, whether by flattery or by trickery, a serious achievement. But Don Juan is strong; walks with his head high; is feared and admired: and only under these conditions can he be begotten as hero.

In Rome, too, the wholesale pursuit of women seems to have been regarded as a subject for comedy. When Catullus is serious, it is because he addresses the *one* woman. The love poems of other writers of the time, from Ovid down, are seldom free of irony, sarcasm, or plain good fun. The art of seducing a thousand and three women is still a comic art. The great serious lover in Roman literature, the lover in whom love is not even remotely humorous, is Aeneas; but Aeneas never loved anyone but Dido; and had he given up the empire for her sake, he would have become as ridiculous a figure as Paris—or Mark Antony. Indeed, Antony holds our key. To the Romans he could never be anything but weak, pathetic, despicable. But in Shakespeare's time he was already glorious; the possibility that Rome was really worth losing for a woman could be seriously envisaged. Racine's Antony—his Titus—could consider in all gravity giving up the realm for the sake of Berenice. Dryden but carried this romantic childishness (which has caused incalculable damage to Western literature) to its conclusion:

> My queen is dead.
> I was but great for her; my pow'r, my empire,
> Were but my merchandise to buy her love,
> And conquered kings, my factors,

says his hero with sublime foolishness. In a world which glorified Antony, Don Juan was willing to alight.

What was true in Rome continued to be true throughout the Middle Ages. In serious love, Aeneas was the only possible model. The seriously sensual man loved only once, and loved faithfully: thus the troubadour, thus the fictive image Dante and Petrarch created of themselves, thus Tristram, Lancelot, Abelard, Paolo. The lechers and adventurers were confined to the comic once more. We find them in Boccaccio, in Chaucer, and in a hundred fabliaux, and usually with the same emphasis on the prank which still survives in Tirso and in the *commedia dell' arte*. The comic triumph of sensuality is forever fixed in the grandiose appetites of the Wife of Bath.

In the Middle Ages the "real man" must still show his prowess in war or in chivalric love—a love utterly faithful and partly spiritual. But gradually the warrior became a courtier, *un galant homme,* whose sword was only an ornament, and whose advancement often depended on the elegance of his addresses to women.[9] Here is where the Cid makes way for Don Juan. He becomes a glamorous predator. When he robs men of their women, he also robs them of their honor—a feat he had once been forced to perform on the battlefield. When a man can obtain in the boudoir glory, victory, admiration, in addition to erotic pleasure, the times are ripe for Don Juan.

Still, the famous list, or the number one thousand and three, reminds

9. Note the semantic advance in the very word *gallantry,* from military to sexual accomplishment.

us that the comic element will seldom be absent from Don Juan's kind of glory. His lapse from a royal *corral* in Madrid to the puppet-box of strolling players in a German province is no accident. For our response to sex remains ambivalent. One day sex is our most agonizing concern; the next, a subject of simple jokes. We regard nakedness and the sexual act much as Homer's audience did: at best it seems undignified. "And the blessed gods roared with inextinguishable laughter" when they saw Mars and Venus caught in the net. We are still ashamed, and shame is the curious emotion which breeds both laughter and tears, the first in defense, the other in consequence. All careers, all ambitions, all postures are vulnerable to satire and laughter; but in our world at least none is so exactly poised between the comic and the tragic as the passion of love. To be civilized means to be *dressed;* and we continue to view the state of undress with tremulous humor, with eagerness, with shame, with solemnity, with slyness.

Uneasily comic or wholly tragic, I take this *triumph of sensuality* to be the irreducible character of the mythical Don Juan. He is many things besides as we follow him from text to text, for sensuality can be looked at a hundred ways, but he is not any one of these things all the time. Here Don Juan is an atheist; there a Christian. At one time he is a thinker; at another a fool. Now he is a joyous bibber of all pleasures, then again he is the despondent seeker of an elusive ideal. Here virile, there effete; here ever victorious and irresistible, there rebuffed and defeated; here young, there old. One time he adores women, another time he despises them. He can be a gentleman or a ruffian. And he may appear as hero, villain, or—often—as both. All this means, very simply, that these categories are the "accidents" of Don Juan. They are the attributes which give him his individual humanity while he pursues his symbolic career of pure sensuality. For without the "genius of sensuality," as Kierkegaard calls it, and *only* without this, the myth of Don Juan does not exist.

IV

In the vast body of critical literature which surrounds and sometimes smothers Don Juan, one of the commonest views expressed is that the essence of his character does not lie in his sensuality but in his rebellion. "He represents," says Gendarme de Bévotte, "the philosophy of the self, the independent morality raised against the old rule of submission." Denis de Rougemont compares Don Juan to Nietzsche, and

Stefan Zweig compares Nietzsche to Don Juan. And Madariaga asks, "What would Don Juan do without walls to scale, without virginities to violate? What would he do without religious, moral and social laws to transgress?"[10] Gendarme de Bévotte adds that if Don Juan did not appear in the ancient world, it was because the ancient world countenanced the flesh. As long as indulgence in the flesh did not constitute rebellion against the religious or social law, Don Juan had no need to be invented.

As far as this last argument is concerned, it can be countered that the ancient world, though it did not ask that the flesh be mortified, nevertheless had the power to conceive of a vital conflict between private pleasure and political responsibility. The story of Dido and Aeneas demonstrates this point. If the essence of Don Juan had been rebellion, he could easily have appeared in antiquity. Perhaps an Alcibiades would have furnished the living example. Again in the Middle Ages, a rebel very much like Tirso's could have been the hero of a morality play. I have already suggested another solution to the problem of Don Juan's late appearance. The point here is that the idea of Don Juan as *essentially*, or *primarily*, a rebel is a shade away from the truth. To believe that his sexual vagaries are the expression of his revolt against God or Society is to believe that the revolt came first and the sexual adventures second, and that the second would not exist without the first. I wonder if critics and scholars have not been guilty of a desire to "elevate" their hero's character. The spirit still enjoys a better reputation than the flesh, and there is perhaps a surreptitious profit to be made by promoting Don Juan to a Promethean position.[11]

The truth is that, just as Malvolio had greatness thrust upon him, so is rebellion thrust upon Don Juan. Nowhere is this clearer than in Tirso's play. His is, in a sense, the most innocent of all Don Juans. He is incapable of arguing. He feels no hostility toward society or religion; in fact, he has no connection with either until the connection is

10. See Georges Gendarme de Bévotte, *La Légende de Don Juan* (Paris: Hachette, 1911), I, 8; Denis de Rougemont, "Don Juan," *Nouvelle Revue Française*, LIII (1959), 62–68; and Salvador de Madariaga, *Don Juan y la Don-Juanía* (Buenos Aires: Editora Espasa-Calpe, 1950), p. 18.

11. "Don Juan is not an atheist in the progressive sense of the word. His unbelief is not militant, i.e. productive of human actions. It is simply a lack of belief. What is present is not another conviction, but no conviction. . . . He uses any argument—without believing in it—that will win a woman, as he uses any that will rid him of her." Thus Bertolt Brecht, in his Notes to an adaptation of Molière's play, presented by the Berliner Ensemble in 1954. See *Stücke* (Frankfurt-am-Main: Suhrkamp, 1959), XII, p. 190.

forced on him. He loves tricks and he loves to make love to women. He is this element of you and me and the next person abstracted from us to make a mythical man who shall be *only* this sensuality. But when he goes into action, he finds himself—almost unaccountably, as far as he is concerned—opposed by Authority. He tries to brush it aside. He is far from wanting to overthrow it. He does not even want to think about it. "Just leave me alone till I'm old," he tells God. This is Tirso's Don Juan. But even the reasoning Don Juans of Molière, Rosimond, and Shadwell use concepts only to justify themselves. They do not preach an attack on society; they only explain why society should not attack them.

A myth does not exist to give recondite entertainment to a handful of scholars. It is the concrete expression of great general concerns— almost, one is tempted to say, of human instincts. Now what would the man in the street say if we asked him for the meaning of Don Juan? He would be surprised that the question needed to be asked; the answer is obvious. Don Juan is a great lover, irresistible to women. Don Juan an atheist? a nonconformist? a left-winger? "Well, I never thought about it," our average citizen might say. "Could be." In short, on second thought—perhaps. But on first thought, is there a doubt? Don Juan is a Don Juan, and no mistake. And in this, we can—we must—trust the people, because myths are made for them and about them. The Statue which was so memorable for popular audiences—more so than Don Juan himself—punished a sexual offender, not a philosophical and political radical.

Rebels are represented often enough in myth and literature: if a rebel is wanted, why choose a professional hunter of women? Better reach at once for Prometheus, Julien Sorel, Stephen Dedalus. As a rebel, Don Juan cuts a shabby and trivial figure compared to them; as a sensualist, we feel immediately that he is "in his element"—his turn to teach! The trouble is that many critics and writers are so accustomed to being in the Opposition that they have all but lost the conception of loyalty to one's society, and so they see rebels and iconoclasts, nonconformists and radicals, under every literary bed.

Nevertheless, Don Juan the sensualist does find himself opposed, not only by injured fathers, husbands, and fiancés, but by the Law and by God. (This is of course as true of the comic medieval scamps as it is of the serious Don Juan.) And by simple aesthetic calculus the more opposed he is, the more interesting. Give him a husband or a rival to jump over, and that is something. Raise the obstacle by adding the police: better still. Then set Society against him; the King; the Church; and finally God in person: each time the hero's prowess is greater, and his fall more calamitous. We are not surprised, therefore, to see Don Juan born not only when he can be taken seriously, but also where the forces set against him are the greatest: in Renaissance Spain. I do not know that this birthplace is as inevitable for him as Spanish critics assert; but he certainly appears at his most interesting and at his greatest where women are kept, though vainly kept, indoors; where they are the repositories of men's most precious possession, their honor; where adultery is scandal and scandal the destruction of a woman; where chastity is a woman's greatest virtue; and where the law of man and the law of God alike forbid sensuality.

The inward triumph of sensuality exists any time and anywhere; but who would mention it—who would make stories of it—if it did not make trouble either for the seduced or for the seducer? The mythological Don Juan is always opposed. He is not necessarily invented just because he would be opposed if he were invented; but if he *is* invented, we may be sure that he has, and is, an enemy. In societies friendly to promiscuity his enemies might be mere rivals in Don Juanism, in which case the literature would be merely psychological and domestic. But in Western civilization promiscuity is opposed by institutions, and this turns Don Juan into a rebel against society, willy-nilly. It is an easy next step for a writer to make him *first of all* a rebel. One more step, and the writer, holding on to the rebel, rids him (as Shaw and Frisch do) of his lust for women altogether. It is a curious evolution.

Setting aside the question of what is first and what is second, we recognize that the typical Don Juan does satisfy more than our erotic ambitions. But instead of invoking the fact of his rebellion, I invoke that of his strength. The original Don Juan, and the Don Juan of the entire classical period, is a powerful man. He shows this by being so often successful in his tricks, by an extraordinary adeptness with the sword, by (and this is usually overlooked) his wonderful luck, even by his excellent connections and his noble birth, and by his thrilling defiance of the forces of the supernatural, which the common man is always told to adore but which he does not mind having flouted—by somebody else. Finally, our hero demonstrates his power by abandoning every woman he has possessed—and if nothing else takes strength, this does. For if God is a fist, woman is glue: she "sticks" to a man. He touches her, and from that time she considers herself his, she follows him—even if it is only to cry for revenge, she enslaves him by calling him her master. Surely, many who followed Don Juan's adventures on the stage must have chuckled more over his victorious farewells than they panted over the sexual adventures, especially since the latter were usually handled with reticence. Sex is sweet to man, but victory is sweeter.

I do not call this power or victory essential to the figure of Don Juan any more than I accept his posture of rebellion as central to the myth, partly because in the nineteenth century Don Juan was domesticated by the women (and then we see him faithfully in love) and in our own he has been demoralized: our age does not believe in captains of their own souls. But Tirso's Don Juan is one of the authentic strong men of fiction. Had he begun as wobble-kneed as he has ended, he would have died after his first appearance.

Erotic and powerful, Don Juan was the kind of figure made to order for the Renaissance. The Spanish stage of the Golden Age was as fertile in violent inventions as the contemporaneous English theatre, or the American film of our own times. Perhaps the autocratic regime sensed, in some cellar of its collective mind, that the stage provided the people with a safe and efficient outlet for its dangerous passions. Discipline in the nation, but an orthodox uproar in the theatre. Even this uproar, however, unpolitical as it had to be, must come to an end, and the audience must be sent home sober once more under the umbrella of the official superego. And this the action of *El Burlador* accomplishes to perfection. It offers in three acts a rampaging instinct in episodes of pleasure and power, after which it claps on the lid and through the Statue (which Otto Rank not inappropriately interprets as the father image) satisfies the need for—or at any rate the expectation of—reestablished order. The blood has had its fling, yet the conscience is appeased.

Early in his history Don Juan picks up the doctrine of atheism, but once again this position of revolt is incidental, not essential. A play about an atheist was hardly possible in Spain, and Tirso's hero is merely indifferent. But when Molière and Shadwell took up the theme of atheism, they were actually walking on an old track. Long ago the Church, as well as the literary defenders of the faith, had learned to preach the convenient and still popular doctrine that atheism is a direct cause of immoral behavior. The Renaissance is full of pictures of monstrous atheists. If it happened that a scoundrel did his worst in a play or a novel without being an unbeliever, the next writer could easily supply the missing doctrine. The age could imagine a kindly

Turk or an amiable Indian, but not—at least overtly—an innocent atheist. We should note, however, that Don Juan flaunts his atheism with the very reverse of today's "anguish" and "nausea." It gives him a liberty he craves with all his soul. He joyously embraces his own absurdity and faces death—and presumably annihilation—with the bravura of an indomitable hidalgo. The classical Don Juan is not acquainted with the "sense of the abyss."

V

One could write a useful literary history of Western Europe by citing for illustrations nothing but Don Juan texts. Don Juan never created a climate; he always responded to it, and in fact responded to it with almost academic perfection. With Tirso, he is duly baroque; with Molière, a courtly libertine whom the wits at a small distance from Louis XIV could wink at (one critic has remarked that he is a precursor of the Encyclopaedists). Da Ponte's hero is all eighteenth-century Italy, that is to say philosophically vacant and utterly refined. With Grabbe he thickens into Romanticism—a late example of *Sturm und Drang* at its stormiest and most pressing. With Montherlant he is old, disabused, and analytic, as becomes our times. Always he beats with the pulse of his epoch, and the reason is that not one literary work concerning him is great enough to have forced a new note on its times or to have deviated into eccentric splendor. The fact must be faced: Don Juan as a type of man remains in the end more interesting than any of the plays, poems, or novels which gave him life. The two masterpieces which use his name—Byron's and Shaw's—do not treat the traditional legend at all, and it is curious that England, which has not distinguished itself in its treatment of the Tenorio matter, should have brought forth two offspring with the bar sinister, both superior to any of the true line. In the true line, only Mozart's score is imperishable; but is that score in its very being an expression of the Don Juan theme? Could it not, with minor changes and casual revisions, have been adapted to an entirely different libretto?

Don Juan's mythical life readily divides itself into three acts, the Classical, the Romantic, and what I shall call the Molecular, with some overlapping between the second and third of these. Two works mark the boundaries: Hoffmann's little essay very clearly, Rostand's play a little less so. These three phases can also be expressed in terms of blood, soul, and intellect—at first Don Juan is sheer energy, then he aspires to an ideal, and finally he thinks about himself. It would not be fanciful to correlate the evolution of even so humble a subject with that of our civilization itself, and to trace in both the gradual decay of vital enthusiasm in favor of disabused analysis.

In his classical career, Don Juan is a frank and joyous libertine. He does not think too much about the world, and he worries very little indeed about himself. He is, besides, an outright scoundrel, who may snatch from us something of fondness or admiration, but who can lay no formal claim to either. He is childlike and even childish; philosophically, he seems rather thin; yet he is perfectly strong as a man. He stays of a piece from start to finish; he and his antagonists and victims are moved by simple and single purposes; and he is flatly damned at the end. Theatrically the action is bustling, episodic, haphazard, improbable.

The Romantic Don Juan is more adult and less naïve. He still has tremendous energy, but that energy is channeled by the consciousness of an ideal, or at least of a defined goal. It is unfortunate that in the creation of Don Juan fables, Romanticism showed something of its worst side, its inclination to multiply the emotional voltage of old situations. Or perhaps it is more accurate to say that the romantic writers arbitrarily lowered their own resistance to emotional currents. They practically invented sensitivity. True, they rediscovered the abyss thereby; but they also had a way of manufacturing an abyss at every turn of the street. As a result, neoclassicism is less profound, but also less silly. If it has not the sublimity of Dostoievsky, it also is free of the claptrap of Hugo and Dumas and Balzac at their worst. Bach and Mozart would never release a fortissimo unless it was imperiously called for; Tchaikovsky and Mahler felt entitled to vociferate and call to witness the eternal and the infinite and the universal any hour of the day. The new Don Juan is of necessity a titan. He is also, of course, the conscious rebel. He had always been an outcast, but now this is accounted a virtue. "Classicism judges its hero in the name of society; Romanticism judges society in the name of its hero." [12] He longs, he is sad, he meditates, he is cursed and haunted, his crime is noble, and his stance heroic. He had been a kind of playboy once, a juvenile delinquent with a lineage; now he is kin to Faust and to Prometheus. By the same token, his antagonists, who had carried all the dignity of the State and God, now turn into pasty-faced philistines. Our Octavio, in

12. André Maurois, "Don Juan," *L'Illustration*, CCI (December 3, 1938), n.p.

particular, becomes a ridiculous weakling, who, as Grabbe's Leporello points out, wears gloves and speaks grammatically. Soon, too, our Don Juan, the ruffian who once was unceremoniously clobbered by Lucifer in the puppet-box, is brought to the feet of God by a Pure Woman and a chorus of angels.

At the same time, the theatrical action is unified and rationalized. The action, though operatic, obeys the laws of reasonable time and place, due progress, orderly pacing, and psychological and historical verisimilitude. We are informed of Don Juan's background—often down to his childhood—and of his motives. Simple types make way for ambiguous dispositions. Characteristically we are told (Hoffmann was first guilty of spreading the report) that Anna does not hate Don Juan, but is torn by love and hate; she must pursue him, yet success will kill her. Also, the Romantic versions of Don Juan are far more serious. Not only the farce but the comedy too is often dismissed, and the Leporello-type recedes. Finally, the Romantic Don Juan is capable, or would like to be capable, of love. His dissipations are no longer motivated by his love for dissipation but by his ardent longing for the perfect woman who eludes him. If she does manifest herself, he falls at her feet and is saved. However, he keeps one important quality from the older days—his dash, his fire. The Don Juans conceived by Mérimée, by Dumas, by Zorrilla, by Lenau are all full of Spanish zest, even when the Spanish in them smells a little of the paintbrush. At least they are still looking for something—usually the undiscoverable Ideal Woman. The nineteenth century had a strong sense of direction. Tirso's hero is slapdash, our own protagonists aimless; but a century ago the hero aspired, and his needle pointed staunchly north.

Even when the Romantic Don Juan is sad, he is grandly miserable:

> le calme héros, courbé sur sa rapière,
> Regardait le sillage et ne daignait rien voir.

Such is Baudelaire's hero, still proud and capable of the proud man's primary emotion: disdain. But in our own time—poor Don Juan! The priapic follies are over, and the Pure Woman is forgotten too. Don Juan is shriveled, old, nauseated, and rather disgusting. Little girls laugh at his senile attempts. But he thinks a great deal, chiefly about himself. He even knows he is a Myth. He talks about Absurdity. Indeed, he talks endlessly. The reader does not deserve to be wearied with his conversation, but a characteristic fragment may be salutary: "I drown every day . . . I don't even feel the days running away. With the days run the months, run the years, runs my life. I remain standing with my arms open, my hands open: I can't catch anything. . . . I am alone. . . . Whatever interests men—love, money, glory, the idea—leaves me as cold as marble. . . . I don't believe in anything. . . ." And so forth.[13] Or another: "Look Beatrice, I am not what you think; I lied that afternoon; I am tied to a crime, linked to a sad yesterday. My past once appeared to me and I saw myself in a mirror soiled with blood. I was evil, and I didn't know, Beatrice, that evil existed. I was ugly and I had thought I was handsome and dashing. I was old as vice, old as crime, and I was looking for my youth in that mirror. I thought I was valiant and yet I trembled when I saw myself. For my cowardice is such, Beatrice, that I am frightened by my own company."[14] When Don Juan appears on stage, we are not surprised to have him described in words like these: "Enter Don Juan, gentleman of the 18th century, clothes worn thin under the gold braid, flabby hat, socks dubiously white, and shoes with elastics. A sorry gentleman! We will see, a little later, that he is blond, curly, thin, small, sallow, nervous."[15]

Don Juan nervous! To this, in truth, he has come. Psychiatric doctrine finishes him off by turning him into the abject victim of a complex. "Don Juan's behavior," writes Otto Fenichel, "is no doubt due to his Oedipus complex. He seeks his mother in all women and cannot find her." The peculiarity in his complex is that "it is dominated by the pre-genital aim of incorporation [psychologese for eating or swallowing], pervaded by narcissistic needs and tinged with sadistic impulses." His exaggerated sexual activity is "an unsuccessful attempt to use the genital apparatus for discharging some nongenital, warded-off, and dammed-up need."[16] The most telling word here is "unsuccessful." One might have supposed that Don Juan's discharge of nongenital needs through the genital apparatus would be a singularly successful one, but in these times success is out of the question. Western civilization is haunted by loss of control and by failure. While existentialists speak of the built-in failures of life, and artists inspect the defeated and the helpless, colonies are lost, empires shrink, and politicians steal frightened glances in the

    13. André Obey, *L'Homme de cendres*, produced in 1949 and printed in *Opéra*, supplément théâtral, No. 16 (January, 1950). The speech is on pp. 21–22.
    14. Manuel and Antonio Machado, *Juan de Mañara*, in *La Duquesa de Benameji* (Madrid: Colección Austral, 1942), p. 238. The play dates from 1927.
    15. Michel de Ghelderode, *Don Juan*, in his *Théâtre* (Paris: 1955), IV, 34. The play was first printed in 1928.
    16. *The Psychoanalytic Theory of Neuroses* (New York: W. W. Norton, 1945), pp. 243–244.

direction of the East, where muscles bulge and the trumpets bellow. In such an atmosphere it is evident that Don Juan, humiliated, browbeaten, ridiculous, and superannuated, will go syphilitic or drink out his old age in a sodden tavern, talking metaphysics.

For this perhaps final stage of the legend of Don Juan, the name Realistic naturally suggests itself at first. But is it a fair label? There is a rather simple habit among us of calling any denigration an instance of realism. Yet is it not immodest to be so sure what reality is? Are mean things always real, and are real things always mean? Quite possibly; but not so surely that we should feel easy in calling ourselves realists, and everybody before us, by implication, dreamers. I had rather call this third stage of Don Juan's evolution his Molecular stage, for ours might well be known as the Molecular age. The name points to the science which dominates our lives; to our habit of analyzing all things down to their indivisible minimum; to the dehumanization of life; to our sense of isolation and fragmentation; to the virtual abandonment of the idea of human progress; and to our small helplessness.

The last Don Juan is Molecular in several of these respects, but especially so in his helplessness. In his older incarnations he satisfied more than our concealed sexual lust; he also elated by his force, his freedom, his control. He was his own master; he succeeded so well in knocking down obstacles that only God could stop him; he dashed headlong into the history he made for himself. And such is the very spirit of the Renaissance. He did not even, like a modern existentialist, pause to "choose himself." Explicitly in Shadwell and implicitly everywhere else, he is simply satisfied with the nature he has. As for Tirso's play, its errors, naïvetés, and blots can almost be forgotten for the sense of impetuous motion and furious advance it gives us. The Classical Don Juan has no time to fall in love. Ramiro de Maeztu is right when he says that Don Juan must not fall in love because he is irresistible force. To fall in love is to pause, to submit. At that point the career is broken, and Don Juan loses control—or rather the sense of control—over his destiny. He becomes, in the words of the Quintero brothers, "a slave to his slave-girl." The man in love is ripe for disappointment and failure. The scene darkens. Don Juan becomes modern.

And here is by all odds the most important event in the dramatic life of Don Juan. *He ceases to enjoy himself.* I put this simply and baldly because there is no better way of letting in the resonances of this stupendous change—stupendous, for here again what happened to Don Juan also happened in the fiber of our whole culture. The irrepressible child of the Renaissance, who seems to have enjoyed even the scene of his damnation—what a chance for bravado!—crumbles into a shabby and uneasy psychological case. It was in a Rostand play, curiously enough, that Don Juan was dragged off the pedestal.[17] Rostand's hero has his eyes opened by the devil. He discovers that he never really knew the women he seduced. Then he finds out that he did not even dominate them; it is they who chose him: "C'est quand je t'eus choisi que tu m'as regardée." But surely at least he pleased them! No—he pleased them for such trivial reasons that he is quite humiliated. Was he bold? Not even that. He ran like a coward from love and suffering. Romeo and Tristram, not Don Juan, are the real heroes for a woman. "Tu n'as eu que toutes les femmes—mais pas une!" Well then, at any rate he made them suffer. Not so. The tears were only a part of the amorous program in which the women luxuriated. As a last resort, Don Juan claims that once he gave a man a piece of gold in the name of humanity. He was the first to use this word. From the libertine sprang the Revolution. Whereupon Molière's Pauper enters and throws the coin back at Don Juan. When the moment of judgment arrives, Don Juan is even denied the fire of the damned. He is condemned to be an eternal marionette.

In this clever critique, full of witty couplets, only one thing is forgotten, namely, that Don Juan had enjoyed himself. It does not occur to him to bring this forward in answer to the devil's ridicule. A world lies in the omission. Don Juan has forgotten what he has. He only knows what he has not. His nerves are shattered.

VI

Neither the myth nor the legend of Don Juan has required that a single and necessary principle govern the treatment of his women.

17. Although the Portuguese poet Guerra Junqueiro preceded him in the attack. Here is Don Juan in a poem entitled "The Last Moments": "Stinking, barefoot, with a laugh like that of an old parasite. . . . His peeled white skull reminds one of an ostrich egg or a billiard ball. The torn cassock which serves him as a coat is so to speak a greasy map of all the shreds of misery: silk, wool, cotton, lace, remnants of an auction. . . . His hideous dark mouth looks like an inkwell; he frightens one when he laughs. A stench of manure or spoiled fruit issues from that hole. . . . He goes on living in lost alleyways showing people his burning sores and his bestial, obscenely swollen legs, the color of lilies and gangrene." This unfortunate picture appeared in 1874 in the collection *A Morte de D. João*. Long before, Stendhal and Gautier had already represented Don Juan growing old and weary. The transition from the second to the third acts of Don Juan's career is a gradual one.

In Tirso's *El Burlador de Sevilla*, the women are shadowy and conventional. We really do not know who they are; only Isabela's sly remark that as long as Octavio is thought to be the guilty party she does not mind her seduction brings her to life for a moment. As for Tisbea, she is little more than an exercise in pastoral *culteranismo*, the Spanish equivalent of euphuism. As is to be expected, the delineation of women, or the statement of their point of view, improves as time passes. Charlotte, the peasant girl in Molière's play, is one of the master's richest creations. The scornful shepherdess and the distraught swain, subjects of thousands of insipid poems and romances in the sixteenth century, are here so humanized, so freshened, so realized, that we forget that Tisbea and Amaryllis are Charlotte's mothers, and Damon and Corydon, Pierre's fathers. I do not know that Molière ever drew the portrait of a woman with more grace and truth than in his *Dom Juan*. But his Elvire, who receives most of the critics' attention and praise, is a pathetic dish whose many sisters in elegant romances of the seventeenth century have been justly forgotten.

In general, Don Juan's women are portrayed with great sympathy, often with indignant pity. The sentimental author sees them as innocent victims; their love is pure, their disappointment heartbreaking. But the Don Juan story also allows for anti-feminist satire. There is more than a hint of this in Tirso's play. Goldoni's heroine is a social climber; even a duke does not satisfy her. As for Da Ponte's Zerlina, she is a little hussy who can readily be persuaded to ditch poor Masetto, as the latter well knows. Pushkin's Anna is as consolable a widow as the Matron of Ephesus. Predictably, in modern versions Don Juan is often harried by a pack of lustful women who all but force him into his role.[18]

While Don Juan is still the aggressor—in his early days especially—he is far from irresistible. He finds himself obliged to impersonate true lovers, to promise marriage, to tempt with his social position, or simply to rape. Presently, however, a few of the women—they are summarized in the figure of Elvira—really fall in love with him, even when they understand his treachery. He will be exposed by two sisters he has been wooing simultaneously, and yet return an hour later and find a

18. Hence the anti–Don Juan type, the man who would gladly be rid of his charms. There is, however, a middle point. Here women desire Don Juan, but they do not assault him, they only give their own subtle signal of "consent." It still remains for Don Juan to respond, that is to say to act, to initiate the sensual pact which both will call a conquest. Henri-René Lenormand's *L'Homme et ses fantômes* (1924) illustrates the point in two vivacious acts.

passionate welcome in the arms of one.[19] Eventually, he is able to scorn trickery altogether, and to rely entirely on his invincible charms. In Claude-André Puget's *Echec à Don Juan* (1941), five women, all but one of whom have been "mistreated" by Don Juan, stand waiting for him at the dock in attitudes of fatal longing. He is their all. An hour with Don Juan is worth a lifetime of subsequent misery.[20] It is easy for a witty author to exploit this fascination of Don Juan to show what weak vessels women are; but others allow this weakness to take a tragical turn. Mérimée's Sister Teresa dies for Don Juan, mourning only that he did not violate her. Even Puget's heroine, who has coldly set out to make him fall in love with her, fatally succumbs to him.

Among the many modes of handling Don Juan's effect on women, the motif of the irresistible hero is worth singling out, for it illustrates a curious change in our sensibility. Don Juan did not become irresistible to women until the Romantic age, and I am disposed to think that it is a trait of the female imagination to make him so. When the female voice began to assert itself and even, perhaps, to dominate in literature, Don Juan evolved to become the woman's, rather than the man's ideal. I do not mean that more women were writing in the Romantic age and thereafter, although this happened to be the case, but rather that the audience, and indeed Western culture, became somewhat feminized—acquired emotions and views which we regard as feminine. The emotional inflation which I spoke of before as a Romantic trait is also a feminine trait. Don Juan is now the woman's dream of the perfect lover, fugitive, passionate, daring. He gives her the one unforgettable moment, the magnificent exaltation of the flesh which is too often denied her by the real husband, who thinks that men are gross and women spiritual. To be the fatal Don Juan may be the dream of a few men; but to meet him is the dream of many women. Musset—feminine genius par excellence—hinted this much in an analogue to the Don Juan matter, *A Quoi rêvent les jeunes filles:*

> A girl of fifteen dreams of her lovers
> Coming in summer nights on slender ladders,
> Sword in hand, and cloak up to the eyes—

and again, this time through a father's words,

> No! You drop from the sky like a tragedy,
> You thrash my lackeys, you force my locks,

19. Jacinto Grau, *El Burlador que no se burla* (1930), Act II.
20. See Gregorio Martinez Sierra, *Don Juan de España* (1921), Act II.

You stroke the dog, you ravish my daughter,
You make a perfect havoc in the family:
That is what they look for in a husband.

Is not what we call Classicism a male tendency, and Romanticism a leaning to the feminine? Music exemplifies this even better than literature. What happened from Mozart to Schubert (compare their songs) was, in a sense, a feminizing of the sensibility. This is a subject we cannot pursue further here. In Don Juan, at any rate, the male and classical imagination that invented him saw *a conqueror of obstacles*— tricking, lying, compelling, jilting; and the female, romantic imagination conceived him as himself capable of love, and above all, as irresistible to every woman, a supreme prize to win (from other women?), and a supreme satisfaction to possess, however briefly.

VII

I have perhaps suggested already that the first Don Juan, the one who was born with Tirso and who died, sublimely elegant and immortally trivial, singing to Mozart's music his fiery

Finch'han dal vino
Calda la testa,

is a creature altogether superior to what his second and third incarnations made him. He was probably guillotined during the French Revolution, and the gentleman Hoffmann met was an impostor. I will go farther and claim that Don Juan in the puppet-box is aesthetically a more pleasing object than the Don Juan who aspires to the infinite, or who falls at the feet of a convent girl, or who has a bucket of slop emptied on his aging head. Needless to say, the critics have been far from kind to the puppet plays. "From a literary viewpoint, their value is nil," says Gendarme de Bévotte, and no one, as far as I know, has quarreled with him. The latest book in English— Professor Weinstein's—does not mention these farces at all. The fact is that we are still led by the nose to admire whatever can lay a claim to "profundity" and to disdain whatever merely amuses. The pompous harangues in, say, the Don Juan versions of Milosz, Machado, or Obey appeal to certain readers on the lookout for "significant statements." But simple folly is still preferable to philosophical bombast.

The puppet plays of the eighteenth century, one of which is reprinted in this collection, share with the versions of Tirso, Shadwell, and Da Ponte an open and naïve verve and a lustiness for which Grabbe's philosophical apparatus or Montherlant's disabused tirades are insufficient compensation. But the marionette theatre aside, pre-Romantic versions of the Don Juan matter had a decisive superiority over all later ones: they eschewed realism. Realism broke the delicate balance between the abstract and the individual in favor of the latter. In a fine passage, Kierkegaard points out that as soon as the thousand and three mistresses of Don Juan leave their musical existence to become verbal, the literal absurdity of the whole idea leaps to the eye. This is near the mark. The obvious unrealities in drama as conceived by Tirso and Shadwell among others are enough to induce in us a suspension of the critical function similar to that which we experience in reading a fantasy or a fairy tale, or in listening to an opera. They prepare us for symbolic drama, and specifically for Don Juan as a symbol (elegantly attired, of course), a force, an element, rather than a given Mr. John Tenorio. The realists are too busy with *trompe-l'oeil*. Lavedan's Marquis de Priola (a Don Juan type) runs into his Elvira at the soirée of an ambassador, where they are very likely to meet. We see the fine drawing room, the buffet, the chandeliers, then the entrance of Elvira (I use the name for convenience) with a friend, her startled fright, and eventually her precipitate exit through a distinct door. In contrast, Molière's Elvire pops out of nowhere, a servant materializes in the middle of a wood to give Don Juan a warning, suddenly the tomb of the Commander appears, and so forth. Lavedan, furthermore, knows that people make small talk before great subjects are brought up. Each event is a platform that must be climbed to on a staircase of other events, all given due time and all duly located. Tirso's Don Juan, instead, is washed ashore after a shipwreck and seduces a fishergirl (who talks in *concetti* at him) the moment he sinks down on the beach. What! still drenched? Must he not be revived, dried, fed, put to bed? Surely a doctor must be called; the police must be alerted. The charming girl nurses him back to life, gradually love is awakened in her, and the scoundrel schemes to make the most of her innocence. Thus the realist, or the sentimental realist—it does not matter. But Tirso and the other classicists leap into the heart of things with sovereign unconcern for all that we consider elementary likelihood. Only recently, in fact, have playwrights like Beckett, Ionesco, and others rediscovered the uselessness of dramatic decorum.

The artists who emended all the "crudities" of the early versions were of course convinced that they had greatly improved the literary scene. They must have felt as I take it the painters of the Renaissance did (with as little justification) when they compared their handiwork with the incomprehensible naïvetés of medieval art. It would be foolish to deny the several advantages of realism. But the pre-Realistic plays did better justice to the Don Juan theme. In their fantastic world,[21] where the laws of normality and likelihood are flouted, Don Juan becomes superhuman: incredibly strong, incredibly successful, incredibly potent, incredibly courageous. Our minds, diverted from meticulous inquiry, are ready to accept this creature, for when we accept a lover who flirts with two girls simultaneously on stage by dancing from one to the other, we also accept the man who has seduced a thousand and three women in Spain and whom the voice of God himself cannot dissuade from his course (for God has asked the impossible: if Don Juan ceases to be sensual, he also ceases to be). True poets concerned with the typical, the central, the symbolic, our pre-Realists skipped the tiresome preliminaries of realistic art and introduced Don Juan into the company of the other fantasms: Achilles fought with a river, Prometheus was gnawed by a vulture, Oedipus outsmarted the Sphinx, and Don Juan had his thousand and three. The law is simple: because a symbolic figure gathers in himself the thoughts, purposes, actions, desires, and destinies of a multitude of human beings, he must be human in order still to be a *figure,* but other than human and greater than human in order to be *symbol.* This law only the classical versions of Don Juan consistently, if innocently, obeyed.

VIII

The subject of Don Juan still does not seem to be exhausted. He continues to give men ideas for plays, novels, poems, and (especially) essays. Since the absolute masterpiece on this theme has not yet appeared, the race is, in a sense, more open than it is for another Faust or another Don Quixote. I admit I share with several other critics a degree of skepticism in this regard, and find it discouraging that after three and a half centuries we still await the immortal word. Has the opportunity slipped, and have we become incapable of doing much more than analyzing the hero in discursive plays? Indeed, a collection

21. The world of Molière fantastic? We hear nothing except what a great realist Molière was. But he was nothing of the kind. He isolated and exposed true human passions in perfectly beautiful and absurd plays, in which there are not twenty lines together which could ever have occurred in reality.

of plays and documents such as this one has a sad testamentary air about it. Perhaps the times are not suited to Don Juan. "A few quick words on the telephone," says one of the Spanish critics, "and the swift career of an automobile to the suburbs constitute the entire procedure for what was once mysterious intrigue and heroic adventure."[22] One of the conditions for Don Juan still exists: we take the career of a sensualist seriously and we can imagine the conquest of women as an enviable achievement. But is the contemporary Don Juan too feebly opposed? Has he no rivals? Does he find no reluctant maidens? Is society amiable with him? Does ease demolish his glory? The answer is always no. I think that it is too early to bury Don Juan. After all, mass seduction today is not so easy as all that. There are still husbands, brothers, and boy friends keeping watch. There is still the nation urging young men to the graver duty of slaughtering the enemy. There are businessmen, tax collectors, and old aunts ready to frown on a career of heedless pleasure. And there are young women still whose hearts are broken by false promises. Why not another Don Juan? But I should like to see him done next time in the spirit of *Les Caves du Vatican* or *Felix Krull*. Perhaps he will be gloriously and infamously dodging responsible employment, military duty, public service, and personnel questionnaires when we see him again in the fragrant company of willing girls.

We may hope that the new Don Juan will not be plaguing us with his search for the ideal woman. In the two best literary interpretations of this century—Shaw's flirtation with the legend in *Man and Superman* (1903) and Max Frisch's *Don Juan, or the Love of Geometry* (1953)—the hero is flatly a misogynist. Although philosophically speaking this means that he is no longer a true Don Juan, the reversal does point the way toward a treatment suitable for a critical age like ours. The author's stance, or the hero's own, should be ironic. But irony is a weapon of the weak; it is the weapon Thersites uses against Ajax; and it is doubtful, therefore, whether we can expect Don Juan to be as strong, as satisfied with his life, as firmly in control of his destiny, and as proud of himself as he was in his heyday. He need not lose his dignity—again, both Shaw and Frisch have proved this—but he will no longer be able to take it for granted. He will be struggling to assert it.

In our age, lethal to rhetoric and sentiment, and growing weary, too, of psychological verisimilitude, the way up is the way down: to be

22. Gregorio Marañón, *Don Juan* (Colección Austral; Buenos Aires: Editora Espasa-Calpe, 1944).

great, Don Juan must become simpler; to say much, he must talk less; to mean more, he must be relieved of elaborate motives; and to be taken more seriously, he must amuse better. By means of cold wit, ironical fantasy, and pregnant levity, we can recapture something of the vigor and above all the manliness of the Classical Don Juan, without sacrificing the intellectual opportunities his adventures suggest.

Part I
THE CLASSICAL
DON JUAN

Vivan le femmine!
Viva il buon vino!
Sostegno e gloria
D'umanità!

DA PONTE

Long live women!
Long live good wine!
Glory and support
Of all mankind!
            DA PONTE

Don Juan in Spain (1616?-1630)

Tirso de Molina and *El Burlador de Sevilla y convidado di piedra*

Gabriel Téllez, the friar who wrote under the name of Tirso de Molina, was born of unknown parents in Madrid around 1583.[1] Nothing is known about his earliest years, and we first meet him in Guadalajara in 1601, taking his vows in the Order of Nuestra Señora de la Merced (Our Lady of Ransom). The members of this order, founded in 1223 during the Crusades, were pledged to offer their own persons as hostages to redeem Christians captured by the Moslems—but this was not the kind of sacrifice likely to be demanded of monks in the age of Philip III. The religious life seems to have provided Fray Gabriel with many comforts and considerable liberty; it gave him a home, and, to judge from his plays, it did not keep the pleasures and the passions of the world a secret from him.

Except for trips on the business of his order and perhaps an interval for study at the University of Salamanca, Tirso lived in Toledo from 1605 to 1615, the decade of his greatest creative exuberance. Toledo in those years was also the home of Lope de Vega, and as Tirso was his acknowledged disciple it is attractive to suppose that from their association in Toledo came the incentive and encouragement which launched the younger genius on his writing career.

The first printed mention of Tirso as one of the "comic poets" of the day occurs in 1610. Other references and documents as well as his own words prove that by then and for at least twenty years to come, he was a popular playwright whose works were eagerly bought and produced by well-known acting companies. From the documents pertaining to

1. For the best summary in English of the little that is known about Tirso, see Gerald E. Wade, "Tirso de Molina," *Hispania (A Teachers' Journal)*, XXXII (May 1949), 131–140. The most ardent—and imaginative—of Tirso's biographers is Blanca de los Ríos, who has collected and discussed all the documents in the three volumes of the Aguilar edition of Tirso's works (Madrid: 1946, 1952, 1958).

moneys owed him for his plays, it appears—rather surprisingly—that Tirso was able to transact business on his own behalf. But there is no evidence that theatrical activities as such offended his superiors; in fact, the chronicler of the Merced, to whose duties Tirso succeeded in 1632, was a rival playwright. It was a time when everyone—noblemen and plebeians, churchmen and laymen—ran to the plays; a time when performances were given in private houses, in the king's palace, and in convents as well as in the theatres of the city. Since the *corrales,* as the latter were called, were leased by pious confraternities to finance hospitals for the poor, grumbling moralists suffered from a disadvantage unknown to English puritans.

In 1616 Tirso crossed the Atlantic to work and lecture for his order on the Caribbean island of Santo Domingo. After his return to Spain in 1618, he was given the theological title of *presentado* and the post of *definidor,* an elective responsibility of middling importance. Later we hear of him in Madrid, figuring in its literary life and publishing his first book (1621), and in various other towns in Spain and probably Portugal. But his plays may have been in greater demand than was good for him, for in 1625 an act of the Council of Castile ordered "Maestro Téllez, por otro nombre Tirso, que hace comedias," to cease writing his wicked plays forthwith and to retire to a place remote from Madrid. Scholars are unanimous in ascribing this prohibition and banishment to personal and political reasons rather than to a sudden burst of moral indignation. Tirso's plays were often lewd and ribald; but they had been so for twenty years. Although no precise information as to the nature of his offense has been discovered, Tirso, according to Gerald E. Wade, "found it impossible to refrain from attacking his enemies in print, from giving advice to people in high places, including the King himself, from using his plays as propaganda for his friends."[2] Presumably an injured party was able to strike back.

Tirso's *faux pas,* whatever it was, marks a turning point in his life. Inconclusive evidence suggests that he continued to dabble in playwriting, but essentially his career as a working dramatist was over. In the years which followed he published five volumes of his plays (not including *El Burlador*) and wrote the chronicle of the Merced. He continued to rise with decent regularity in the hierarchy of his order, and his last post was the honorable one of Superior to the convent of Soria. He died near that city in 1648. Of the 400-odd plays which he

---

2. Wade, "Tirso de Molina," p. 139. In a series of outstanding articles, Ruth L. Kennedy has demonstrated in Tirso's plays of the 1620's his intimate concern with the doings and tattles of his day. See *Hispanic Review,* X, XI, XII (1942–1944), *passim.*

may have written, eighty-six survive—not all of them necessarily his. It may be surmised that the near oblivion into which he was to sink had already begun to cover him during his last years in the world.

It has already been noted that *El Burlador de Sevilla* appeared in 1630 in a collection of plays by Lope de Vega "and other authors." The date of composition is unknown, but the period from 1612 to 1616 (the year of Tirso's departure for Santo Domingo) has recommended itself to the most knowledgeable Tirsists. *El Burlador* is given as Tirso's work in the 1630 volume, and we are told on the title page that the actor Figueroa, a man of good reputation in his craft, performed in the play. But not a single record exists of a specific performance of *El Burlador* during the seventeenth century. Did the audience which applauded Figueroa—or so we hope—realize that it was witnessing the birth of a "significant myth"? It would be rash to suppose so.[3]

To this day *El Burlador* is reprinted in both scholarly and popular editions as the authentic play composed by Gabriel Téllez, though the text presents difficulties: minor gaps, prosodic irregularities, obscurities of meaning (some of them beyond clarification), and logical incoherences in the action. To correct this text, editors have resorted to another version of the play, printed in Seville without date (though probably after Tirso's death) and only discovered in 1878. Its title, *Tan largo me lo fiáis*—roughly "The Day of Settlement Is Far Off Yet!" —is Don Juan's favorite reply to those who try to warn him of God's approaching wrath. The play appeared as a *suelta,* or loose copy, with Calderón named as the author—an ascription which no one has taken seriously.

The one surviving copy of this edition has sorely puzzled the scholars. *Tan largo* offers many departures from *El Burlador*—some minute, some substantial—and yet it is plainly the same drama: its "plot outline" would differ little from that of *El Burlador,* and half of the lines of the two plays are identical, or nearly identical. Does it represent an earlier or a later version of Tirso's play? Is it by Tirso or by a rehandler, a *refundidor?* Or is *El Burlador* itself the clumsy reworking of the authentic play? *Tan largo* has been reprinted several times since its

3. A few scholars, among them Arturo Farinelli and Ludwig Pfandl, have questioned Tirso's authorship of *El Burlador.* Their opinion must be treated with respect, but neither they nor any other scholars have proposed another candidate as the begetter of Don Juan, and nothing in the play itself, not even its crudity, is either above or below Tirso's range. Most scholars—and the Spaniards sometimes with a touch of ferocity—reaffirm Tirso's right of paternity, which had gone unchallenged for two and a half centuries.

discovery (it has never been translated), and almost from the beginning a few students have argued for its authenticity and its priority. But only recently have several American scholars presented virtual proof that *Tan largo,* though the existing copy is a late printing, represents the version closer in time and accuracy to Tirso's original drama.[4] It now appears that neither *Tan largo* nor *El Burlador* has final authority as Tirso's true play. An earlier text—or more than one—stands behind both. Each has passages or entire scenes which are preferable to corresponding passages and scenes in the other. *Tan largo* is distinctly more logical, more coherent, more the *pièce bien faite* than *El Burlador,* but the latter has in many places a greater poetic brilliance, more verve, a bolder rhythmical freedom, and more, if grosser, comic incident. In my opinion both versions show the hand of a master poet, but also that of a careless copyist or printer.

Which of the two versions ought to be printed in future editions? The problem is more than familiar to editors of Shakespeare, and we can imitate their methods in dealing with it. Where two versions of a play exist, neither of which is identifiable beyond doubt as the authentic text, both of which have imperfections, and both of which have preferred readings by linguistic, logical, or aesthetic criteria, a composite text may be constructed from the elements of these versions. This, it must be stressed, is a *best* text rather than a conjecturally genuine one. Not only is it impossible to reconstruct a warranted authentic *Burlador* (or a warranted authentic *Hamlet,* for that matter), but we do not even know if Tirso ever wrote a draft of the play which he considered the master or final version.

I dwell on these problems of the editorial shop because the translation which follows is the first attempt in any language, including Spanish, to present a conflated text of Tirso's play. The title of *El Burlador de Sevilla,* too famous and too good to be dropped, has been devoutly preserved even though *Tan largo* is the more important of the two texts. Other editors have used *Tan largo* to clear up specific

4. For a discussion, see J. Casalduero, "Contribución al estudio del tema de Don Juan en el teatro español," *Smith College Studies in Modern Languages,* XIX (1938), 3, 4; the second volume in Blanca de los Ríos' edition of Tirso, already cited; G. E. Wade and E. J. Mayberry, "Tan Largo Me Lo Fiáis and El Burlador . . .," *Bulletin of the Comediantes,* XIV (Spring 1962), 1–16; and M. R. Lida de Malkiel, "Sobre la prioridad de ¿Tan largo me lo fiáis?," *Hispanic Review,* XXX (October 1962), 275–295. At this point, I wish to express my particular gratitude to Professor Wade, whose erudite advice has been of great help in guiding me into the difficult byways of Tirso scholarship. If not all my conclusions agree with his, he has nevertheless led me to several important reconsiderations and to the correction of several errors.

difficulties in the text of *El Burlador;* here *Tan largo* dominates, with generous levies upon *El Burlador.* But because *El Burlador* is the stronger version in the final scenes—perhaps Tirso took a second look and saw some possibilities he had overlooked in his earlier draft—the closing portions of the present translation lean heavily on the traditional text.[5]

The reader must not imagine that we are tampering with a play of rousing popularity, either on the stage or in the library. Tirso himself failed to include *El Burlador* in his collected works. It was reprinted twice in the seventeenth century and a few times in the eighteenth;[6] but no one before the nineteenth century would have dreamed of calling it a masterpiece. In the theatre, as we have seen, one looks in vain for early records of its performance. During the eighteenth and nineteenth centuries *El Burlador* was displaced from the stage by its more sophisticated offsprings, and today the Spanish-speaking world knows Don Juan chiefly through Zorrilla's version of 1844. Far from damaging a consecrated text, our conflation (or perhaps that of a wiser future editor, for the door is open) might actually encourage performances by its offer of a more rational, a more stageworthy play.

In "The Legend of Don Juan," I noted that Tirso's play consists of two easily separable parts: Don Juan's amorous career and divine punishment meted out to him through the Statue. Although I doubt that Tirso began with the folkloric Double Invitation, the first part of the play does answer the question which the ballads neglected: Who is the

5. And yet a reasonable case can be made out for sticking to *Tan largo* even in the final scenes. They lack much of the farce which was injected into *El Burlador* and imitated by later Italian and French writers. It would be rash, however, to infer from the presence of farce that the play was rehandled by a hack. The fun is good; Spanish drama is notoriously mixed; and there is no ground for supposing that Tirso would have been unwilling to spice several scenes whose success may have come as a surprise even to him. The fact that *El Burlador* does extend the scenes with the Statue, as well as the revenge of the injured maidens, strongly suggests such a success.

6. Everett W. Hesse, *Catálogo bibliográfico de Tirso de Molina* (Madrid: Publicaciones de la Revista Estudios, 1949), gives six reprintings of *El Burlador* (always as Tirso's unquestioned work) between 1720 and 1769, but none from that date to 1838. The latter half of the eighteenth century was a time of fervid gallicism in Spain. Critics and writers, supported by noble patrons and royalty itself, sought to correct or drive away the "irregular" plays of the Golden Age. *El Burlador* was one of forty-two old plays prohibited in a short-lived "reform" in 1800–1801. This, together with the notice that Moratín, the eminent Spanish playwright of that time, had seen a performance of Tirso's play in Naples proves that *El Burlador* had not quite vanished. Its precarious survival is traced also in Alice H. Bushee, *Three Centuries of Tirso de Molina* (Philadelphia: University of Pennsylvania Press, 1939).

offender? In answering it, he performed upon the ballad the same operation which Molière was to perform on the bare *commedia dell' arte* scenarios. Molière revolutionized the *commedia* by taking a stock character—say, the old father who opposes his daughter's marriage—and giving him so much life that the play in effect exists only for him: thus Harpagon or Monsieur Jourdain. Tirso did not go so far—in *El Burlador* the Double Invitation is as important as ever; but he immortalized the old *romance* by giving the nameless scamp of the ballad a face, a personality, a name, an ambition, a career.

I have shown, too, that the episode of the Statue does not partake of the inevitability which we admire in great drama. Don Juan must be punished; and he must be punished by the hand of God—so much is understood. But this does not mean that the instrument must be the monument of one of his victims; a lightning bolt would have served God as well. And even less were two dinners called for. In short, a showman's flair, not an aesthetic or a religious imperative, led Tirso to the popular ballad. Moreover, cunningly though the invented episodes of Don Juan's wicked life and the traditional tale of the Double Invitation are sewn together, the stitches show. As Don Juan pursues his infamous career, breaking hearts and heads, the victims and their friends and relatives collect to harass him. They plot their vengeance; they are ready to strike. Whereupon the Statue interposes and nullifies all their work. An action carefully prepared for fails to materialize. This is the error of false anticipation committed by Tirso and all those who used his plot. In Tirso's case the critics have covered the mistake with a patch. The dramatist, they assure us, is saying that human vengeance is out of place or is ineffective, and that God himself, setting aside human attempts, must mete out a just retribution. But it would have been better if Tirso rather than the critics had made this point. For Tirso's Statue does not lift a finger to stop the mortals. It goes about its business, and at the end the victims are amazed (and a little disappointed?) to find that nothing is left for them to do.[7]

7. It is amusing to think that the actor who played the Stone Guest was a live person impersonating the kind of automatic figure which traditionally represented a live person. In antiquity priests astonished the populace with nodding, moving, walking, and even speaking statues of gods, and the Christian clergy continued the practice. Everybody was familiar with animated figures—of Christ, the Madonna, the saints, devils, and secular or fantastic personages—in church, processions, or at street corners. Tirso's Statue does not nod its head or reply when first addressed, but the trick was perfectly available to the playwright, and his successors made free use of it. See Charles Magnin, *Histoire des marionettes en Europe* (Paris: 1862), pp. 1–74.

All the same, the play's pious intention—sincere or ostensible—should be underlined. *El Burlador* deals with a man who neglects the Church and its offer of salvation; it does not deal with an atheist. And yet precisely because Don Juan's libertinism is opposed by the Church, and because he is unmindful of the Church until the last moment, we can say that he is predestined for a more accented skepticism. "Tirso," says Angel Valbuena Prat, "intuits the formidable historical contrast between the inherited medieval morality, and the hedonistic rebellion of the Renaissance."[8] From the carefully untheoretical hedonism of Renaissance Spain and Italy to the programmed license of the conscious atheist there is only a step, which Don Juan was to take with the first breath of freedom.

To extract from *El Burlador* a notable theological lesson concerning repentance and grace, and to involve the play as a document in the religious controversies of Tirso's time is, I think, to do it a disservice, for philosophy is the merest down on its surface. Modern readers remember the play for its sheer vitality and movement—Madariaga speaks of "waves of energy"—and for the headlong character of Don Juan himself. The hero is quite the Spaniard whom Stendhal describes in the forty-seventh chapter of *De l'Amour:* "hard, abrupt, not very elegant, full of fierce pride, never concerned about anyone else." Pí y Margall notes Don Juan's perfect egotism too, and further defines Tirso's hero as a man who neither loves nor hates. The ardor he feels for lovely women has nothing to do with spiritual passion; when he kills, he kills in self-defense. Self-reliant to the end, his weapons are his own sword, not daggers of hirelings, his eloquence, his cleverness. He is intrepid and incorrigible. His only serious passion is for his honor. Pí y Margall justly points out that it is the blemish on his honor which offends him in the inscription at the base of the statue. "Honor y placer": these are his two gods.[9]

Tirso's Don Juan stands equidistant from the vulgar prankster of the fabliau and the refined courtier of High Renaissance comedy. Undoubtedly he is what used to be called a man of parts: noble in speech, arrogant but dignified in his demeanor, and utterly dauntless. But at the same time he has a primitive fondness for the jest itself; he is the

8. *Historia de la literatura española* (sixth ed.; Barcelona: Gustavo Gili, 1960), VI, 405. Valbuena also indicates the deeper conflict and tension: "the spirit of life and sex in its struggle with death" (p. 404), and sees in this the secret of the story's success.

9. F. Pí y Margall, "Observaciones sobre el carácter de D. Juan Tenorio," in *Colección de Libros españoles raros y curiosos* (Madrid: 1878), XII, xi ff.

burlador,. and boasts of it. He uses no flattery on the two high-born ladies he seduces, and although his tongue wags freely when he is working on the two humble girls, he is busier bribing them than flattering them. Nor does he sigh or study the labyrinths of the mind. How far we are from the world of *Les Liaisons dangereuses!* Obviously the women here are still the property of the menfolk. They have not yet forced their wooers to perfume the paths of seduction.

These women are drawn with a rough hand. Tirso does not go out of his way to attack them, but so much the worse: he simply takes their little duplicities for granted. Isabela is thoroughly unscrupulous, Ana brazenly invites her cousin into her room though her father has bestowed her on Don Juan, Arminta forgets her husband in a trice, and when Tisbea attempts suicide, she does so not because her tender heart is broken, but because her reputation is lost. The type of Elvira, cheated, abandoned, yet still in love, is missing altogether. Don Juan's victims know how to hit back.

But the ancestor of Leporello is already present: Catalinón, the eternal confidential servant, the voice of prudence and reason, the ambulant critic, the very slave who whispered, "Hominem te memento"—*thou art but a man*—into the ear of Roman generals riding in their triumph, and the jester of many princes. Tirso also invented Octavio, the loser, whom Shaw has captured with unexcelled suavity in *Man and Superman;* and Ana, innocent but combative. But chiefly Tirso was the first and last to present the Statue with a conviction which convinces in turn. Only Mozart's Commendatore is grander; and only these two are not farcical or ridiculous.

El Burlador de Sevilla—the old text—is a spirited though crude and faulty piece of entertainment. Properly restored (for it is unjust to blame Tirso for textual faults), the play is an excellent romp, a tough morality play, more play than morality. Many Spanish critics speak of it (of the old text, that is) with gusts of exaltation. A few frankly despise it. I venture to say, at all events, that Tirso *happened* on a character who had the power to become an immortal type. It was a magnificent accident, but magnificent accidents may occur in secondary works. To praise *El Burlador* as a masterpiece of the human intellect is to make the mistake of ascribing the significance of the mythical hero to the vehicle which first carried him. Unlike Hamlet, but like Faust, Don Juan was not born in a work as important as his own person.

This importance, we should recall, does not seem to have impressed itself on the first audiences. Don Juan probably did not look memorably different from other seducers in other plays. As far as I know, there is no record of the expression "a Don Juan" in the seventeenth century. The spectator paid his money, not primarily to watch a great lover at work, but to gawk at the stone figure (often on horseback), the macabre banquet, the terrified flunkey, the dauntless skeptic, the fiery handclasp, and the swallowing up of the enviable villain with generous effects of fire and smoke and even voices from the cellarage. That is why the early Don Juan plays are not really erotic. They are replete with violence, trickery, revenge, and retribution, not with the languors and intimacies which titillate.

TIRSO DE MOLINA

The Playboy of Seville

or

Supper with a Statue

(1616?)

Translated by Adrienne M. Schizzano
and Oscar Mandel

TRANSLATORS' NOTE

El Burlador, like most Spanish and English plays of its epoch, moves its actors rapidly from place to place. The shifts from Naples to Tarragona, from Tarragona to Seville, from Seville to Dos Hermanas, as well as the shifts within Seville—a square, a street, another street, the palace, a church—are all made without interruption in the playing. The stage of city theatres was usually bare (a simple prop or two occasionally appeared), there was no curtain to separate it from the audience, and actors marked a change of scene by vanishing through one door and reappearing through another, or by informing the audience of their whereabouts in so many words. As in the English theatre, an inner room at the back of the stage, curtained off from the main platform, could be used for interior scenes. (It is there, no doubt, that the Statue of the Commander was revealed.) An upstairs gallery over the inner room was used for scenes requiring altitude. The female parts, incidentally, were performed by actresses, and not, as in England, by boy actors. For a full account, see Hugo A. Rennert, *The Spanish Stage in the Time of Lope de Vega* (New York: Hispanic Society of America, 1909).

TEXTS

¿Tan largo me lo fiáis? in *Comedias de Tirso de Molina,* vol. II. Edited by Emilio Cotarelo y Mori. Madrid: Bailly-Baillere, 1907. *El Burlador de Sevilla y Convidado de piedra* in *Tirso de Molina: Obras,* vol. I. Edited by Américo Castro. Clásicos Castellanos. Madrid: Espasa-Calpe, 1932.

Persons in the Play

The King of Castile
The King of Naples
Don Diego Tenorio
Don Juan Tenorio, *his son*
Don Pedro Tenorio, *brother of Don Diego; Spanish Ambassador at the court of Naples*
Duke Octavio
Duchess Isabela
Marquis de la Mota
Don Gonzalo de Ulloa, *Commander of the Order of Calatrava*
Doña Ana, *his daughter*
Tisbea, *a fishergirl*
Anfriso, *her admirer*

Tirseo
Alfredo
Salucis   } *fishermen*
Coridon
Belisa, *a rustic maiden*
Arminta, *a shepherdess*
Batricio, *her betrothed*
Gaceno, *her father*
Catalinón, *servant to Don Juan*
Ripio, *servant of Duke Octavio*
Fabio, *companion to Duchess Isabela*
A Woman

Fishermaids, fishermen, shepherds and shepherdesses, servants, musicians, guards of the palace, courtiers

Synopsis of Scenes

Act I

1. A hall in the palace of the King of Naples.
2. Duke Octavio's palace, Naples.
3. A beach near Tarragona.
4. A room in the Alcázar, the palace of the King of Castile, Seville.
5. Near the cottage of Tisbea, Tarragona.

Act II

1. A room in the Alcázar, Seville.
2. The city of Seville.
3. Near the village of Dos Hermanas.

Act III

1. Gaceno's house, Dos Hermanas.
2. Near Tarragona.
3. Inside a church, Seville.
4. An inn, Seville.
5. A room in the Alcázar.
6. The Fortress of Triana.
7. Before the church.
8. A room in the Alcázar.

ACT I

Scene 1

Night. A hall in the palace of the King of Naples. Enter Don Juan Tenorio *and the* Duchess Isabela. *His face is hidden.*

Isabela: Leave quietly, Duke Octavio.

Don Juan: I'll be light as a feather.

Isabela: Still—I'm afraid you'll be heard. You know it's a crime to enter the palace at night.

Don Juan [*in the act of leaving*]: At another time, Duchess, I will express my gratitude for your favors.

Isabela: You've given me your hand in marriage.

Don Juan: The gainer is myself.

Isabela: I ventured my honor because of your pledge to be my husband.

Don Juan: I am your husband, and I give you my hand again.

Isabela: Wait! Here is a light. I want to see my good fortune. Oh God!

Don Juan: Put out that light!

Isabela: I'm ruined. Who are you?

Don Juan: A man who has enjoyed you.

Isabela: You're not the Duke?

Don Juan: No.

Isabela: Who are you? Speak!

Don Juan: A man.

Isabela: Your name?

Don Juan: I have no name.

Isabela: A trickster has seduced me. Help! Help!

Don Juan: Wait.

Isabela: Take your hand away! Villain!

Don Juan: Don't scream.

Isabela: Help! Guards! Guards!

[*Enter* King of Naples.]

King of Naples: What is it?

Isabela: The King! Everything is lost!

King of Naples: Who is there?

Don Juan: Can't you see? A man and a woman.

51

KING OF NAPLES [*Aside.*]: This calls for caution. I'll try to smooth things over.

[*Enter* DON PEDRO, *the Spanish Ambassador, and* SOLDIERS.]

DON PEDRO: My lord, I heard voices. What is the matter?

KING OF NAPLES: Have these two arrested and punished.

DON PEDRO: Who are they?

KING OF NAPLES: It's better for me not to know. Don't arouse me. I'm trying to control myself, and I know their guilt as it is. Don Pedro Tenorio, I charge you to make the arrest. Find out who these two are, and see to everything else.

[*Exit* KING OF NAPLES.]

DON PEDRO: Give yourself up, sir.

DON JUAN: If anybody touches me, I'll kill him.

DON PEDRO [*to soldiers*]: Kill him!

DON JUAN: You're giving them poor advice. Tell them to put up their swords. If I have to die, I'll take all of you along for consolation. I warn you!

SOLDIER: Die, villain!

DON JUAN: Fool! I'm a gentleman.

DON PEDRO: This is too much!

DON JUAN: Stop! Leave me with the Spanish Ambassador. I'll surrender to him alone.

DON PEDRO: Now you're speaking sensibly. Leave, all of you, and take this woman along.

ISABELA [*Aside.*]: How can one man be so vicious! I have lost my honor and lost Octavio.

[*Exeunt* ISABELA *and soldiers.*]

DON PEDRO: Show your courage and strength now that we're alone.

DON JUAN: I have strength, Uncle, but I never used it against you.

DON PEDRO: Who are you?

DON JUAN: Don Juan.

DON PEDRO: Don Juan?

DON JUAN: Yes, my lord.

DON PEDRO: And you say it just like that?

DON JUAN: End my life and with it all my misery.

DON PEDRO: Traitor. A man without honor can't be my nephew. You with a woman in the King's palace? And you dare outrage my name with this crime?

DON JUAN: Uncle, I don't want you to delay—arrest me if you must. But remember, it was love that drove me to this. A man who loves is blind. I am young. You were young once.

DON PEDRO: Who is the lady?

DON JUAN: The lady is—

DON PEDRO: Who? Speak!

DON JUAN: Isabela.

DON PEDRO: The Queen's lady-in-waiting?

DON JUAN: I duped her by pretending to be Duke Octavio.

DON PEDRO: Worse! Your father sent you from Castile to Naples for committing the same crime against a noblewoman there. Italy gave you asylum, but still you continue your scandalous life, sparing neither single nor married women. And now, with a duchess, in the palace itself! I would have killed you on the spot. But you're the blood of my blood, and I must let you go. Where to now?

DON JUAN: Here is a balcony.

DON PEDRO: Climb over it and down.

DON JUAN: It's high but I'll use my cape.

DON PEDRO: Just don't startle the King again. I'll tell him you escaped through a window.

DON JUAN: It's almost day.

DON PEDRO: The only thing you can do is leave Naples and go back to Spain. If I can convince the King with my story, I'll try to marry you to Isabela and force you to wipe off this blot.

DON JUAN: Sir, you honor me.

DON PEDRO: You'll have letters from me about this sad affair.

DON JUAN [Aside.]: Not so sad for me.

DON PEDRO: Go now. But don't forget that punishment, death, and Hell await people like you.

DON JUAN: Plenty of time for that.

DON PEDRO: Still presumptuous. Come, over the balcony.

DON JUAN [Aside.]: I'm off for Spain—quite satisfied with myself.

[Exeunt DON JUAN TENORIO and DON PEDRO TENORIO. Enter KING OF NAPLES.]

KING OF NAPLES: Men envy the king's crown but they don't know its price. They know only how to complain about having to live under its law. But I envy simple cattle herders and tillers of the land. They live by their sweat but they don't suffer injustice nor do they rule nations. For let a king have a thousand eyes and still he must be all ears, must listen to complaints and avenge the wrongs of the country.

[Enter DON PEDRO TENORIO.]

DON PEDRO: My lord, while I was carrying out your orders, the man—

KING OF NAPLES: Died?

DON PEDRO: Escaped.

KING OF NAPLES: What?

DON PEDRO: Who would believe it? The guards and I attacked him. Like a desperate man, judging us weak, he began to strike back ferociously. I cried, "Kill him!" He tied his cape to the railing of the balcony and fell like Lucifer. I ran and saw him in the moonlight writhing like a snake on the ground. I cried for help, but by the time I had gone to the door he had vanished. I thought it best to pursue no further in order to prevent a scandal.

KING OF NAPLES: You're a wise man, Ambassador. But I am very sorry the man wasn't killed. Do you know who the lady is?

DON PEDRO: My lord, it is the Duchess Isabela.

KING OF NAPLES: What did you say?

DON PEDRO: What you heard.

KING OF NAPLES: Then the offence is more serious and the man of more importance. Send for her.

[*Enter* ISABELA.]

ISABELA [*Aside.*]: How can I look at the King?

KING OF NAPLES [*Aside.*]: I am ashamed to see her.

ISABELA [*Aside.*]: Love, give me courage.

KING OF NAPLES: Duchess!

ISABELA: My lord, I confess. Let my punishment be my shame in your presence. Yes, I violated your palace. After Duke Octavio had given me his hand in marriage, he gained admission to the palace, to my soul, and to my dearest possession. My chastity, my honesty are lost.

KING OF NAPLES: You're saying it was Duke Octavio?

ISABELA: Yes, my lord.

KING OF NAPLES: What good are guards, servants, walls, and fortifications against Love, which is a child and yet breaks through them all! Don Pedro, arrest the Duke—and this woman too.

ISABELA: My lord, turn your face to me.

KING OF NAPLES: You offended me when my back was turned. Justice demands that now I turn mine to you.

[*Exit* KING OF NAPLES.]

DON PEDRO: The King is justly offended with my lady.

ISABELA [*Aside.*]: The offence will be slight if Duke Octavio makes amends.

DON PEDRO: Come, my lady. [*Aside.*] If I can, I'll have the innocent Duke acquitted—and I'll see my nephew married to Isabela.

[*Exeunt* DON PEDRO *and* ISABELA.]

Scene 2

Duke Octavio's palace in Naples. Morning. Enter DUKE OCTAVIO *and* RIPIO.

RIPIO: Up so early, sir!

OCTAVIO: To a man in love, rest is impossible. Have you seen a wretch struggling among the waves until the foaming sea engulfs him? My bed is that sea. I drown under the cold sky, I suffer at night, and only daylight rescues me from my torment.

RIPIO: Forgive me. But I find your love impertinent.

OCTAVIO: You're a fool.

RIPIO: I think it's impertinent to love as you do. May I go on?

OCTAVIO: All right—continue.

RIPIO: Does Isabela love you?

OCTAVIO: How can you doubt it?

RIPIO: Just an academic question. You love her too?

OCTAVIO: I do!

RIPIO: Well, wouldn't I be a fool to lose my senses for a woman who loves me and whom I love in return? Now if she did not love you, it would be reasonable to persist, adore her and shower her with gifts and wait patiently for her surrender. But if you love each other equally, what prevents you two from marrying?

OCTAVIO: Fool! You expect me to marry like a lackey or a washer-woman?

RIPIO: What's wrong with a washerwoman? She scrubs and gossips and jokes as she spreads her wash out to dry. As for giving—she is very generous. And if Isabela doesn't feel like giving, see if she will take. [*Enter* SECOND SERVANT.]

SECOND SERVANT: The Spanish Ambassador has just arrived accompanied by the King's guard. He is asking with rough words to speak to you, as though he had come to arrest you.

OCTAVIO: Arrest me? For what? I have nothing to fear. Show him in. [*Enter* DON PEDRO *and others.*]

DON PEDRO: Only an innocent man can sleep so late.

OCTAVIO: Your visit honors me, Your Excellency. My crime is not to have met a gentleman like you at the door.

DON PEDRO: I was forced to come.

OCTAVIO: I know that only force would prevail upon a man of your rank to enter this house. But humble as it is, I place it at your disposal.

DON PEDRO: After kissing your hand, my lord, I should like to speak with you alone about a certain affair.

OCTAVIO [to Servants]: Leave us alone.

RIPIO: Yes, sir.

OCTAVIO: Clear out the room.

SECOND SERVANT [to Ripio]: This means prison.

RIPIO [to Second Servant]: I think you're right.

SECOND SERVANT: Envy's at the bottom of this.

[Exeunt RIPIO and SECOND SERVANT.]

OCTAVIO: We're alone.

DON PEDRO: Excellency, look at this paper.

OCTAVIO [reads]: "Arrest Duke Octavio, and if he resists, let him die. The King." Arrest! What have I done?

DON PEDRO: You know better than I. Last night there was a scandalous disturbance at the palace, offensive to the King and to the people. As the shadows of the night folded their tents and, stumbling against each other, fled before the coming of dawn, I was discussing with His Majesty certain problems of state (great matters are enemies of the sun). Suddenly we heard a woman's cries echo through the dark halls: "Help, help!" The King rushed out with a light—bold as always—and in the great hall he saw the cause of the uproar. I joined him with the Captain of the Guards and other gentlemen. "Arrest this man and this woman," said the King, and left us. The man blew out the light before we could recognize him. We threw ourselves on him, but he escaped from us like a Libyan tiger and fled over a balcony. We decided not to pursue him for fear of alarming the court. We reported to the King. The lady, whose name is Isabela—I say it to confound you—was brought into the presence of the King and confessed with tears and sobs that Duke Octavio had enjoyed her as her husband. The King ordered her arrest and yours. Listen to me. I am your friend: run away or hide in a safe place.

OCTAVIO: Either you're jesting or I'm dreaming. A man with Isabela in the Palace? I'll go mad. Before I believe that Isabela deceived me, salamanders will inhabit the lowest depths of the stormy seas and fish will seek fire instead of water. I am ashamed to listen to you. A man with Isabela in the Palace? I have gone mad.

DON PEDRO: As there are birds in the wind; fish in the sea; four elements for all creatures to share, and saints in heaven; as there is loyalty in a good friend, deceit in the enemy, darkness at night, light in the day—so what I have told you is true.

OCTAVIO: Enough! Tell me no evil against Isabela. And yet—if her love was a lie, you are right to speak out. Speak, speak! Your tongue draws my blood, but this is a gentle death, a blessing for my grief. With another man and not with me? But why wait?—Let me kill my enemy. What am I saying? This is madness. But what consolation is sanity to me? My friend, a man with Isabela in the palace? I have gone mad. Nothing astonishes me. The most faithful of women is, after all, only a woman. The affront is clear and I want to know no more.

DON PEDRO: You seem both prudent and wise. Choose the best way out.

OCTAVIO: I'll leave.

DON PEDRO: But quickly, Duke Octavio.

OCTAVIO: I'll sail for Spain to end all my troubles.

DON PEDRO: I suggest the door of the garden.

OCTAVIO: Oh weathervane! A feeble reed that bends before the softest wind! Come, I'm pouring oil on my fire. Away from this nest of deceit to another land. Farewell, my country! A man with Isabela? I have gone mad!

Scene 3

A beach near Tarragona. A young woman, TISBEA, *enters with a fishing pole.*

TISBEA: Of all the girls whose rosy feet the waves kiss on these shores, I alone am not ruled by love. I sail in my little boat with my companions. I like to catch the little fish lashed by the waves. I wander free from the prisons which love fills with fools. My only pleasure is to give the fish my baited line. Others suffer and mourn, but I spend my youth without a care. I let the silly fish leap into my net, and I alone do not fall into the snares of love. Meantime Anfriso is my slave, a fisherman, the most generous and gentle man in the land. All the women would die for him; I instead kill him with disdain. This is the game of love: to love those who hate you, and to despise those who adore you. In the cold night Anfriso keeps watch about my hut, and every morning, even in cold weather, my threshhold is adorned with fresh boughs which he has cut from the elms. He sere-

nades me sweetly with flute or guitar. But nothing impresses me because I live beyond the reach of love. But all this silly talk is taking me away from my favorite pastime and my one desire—to cast my line to the wind and waves. Look! A boat foundering in the sea! And two men leaping off! It struck the reef and now it's sinking!
[*Voice off stage: "Help, I'm drowning!"*]

A man is carrying the one who screamed. He is carrying his friend on his back and bravely saving him as Aeneas saved Anchises. But there's no one on the beach to help. Anfriso, Tirseo, Alfredo, help! I see some fishermen looking at me—I hope they hear me. What a miracle! They've touched shore! And now the man who was swimming is out of breath and the one who cried out has gained strength.
[*Enter* CATALINÓN, *carrying* DON JUAN *in his arms. Both are wet.*]

CATALINÓN: Ugh! So much salt in that sea! Near the beach a man can swim and save himself, but farther out it's deathly dangerous. How could God put together so much water and not add a little wine? And if he had to fill the sea with water, why all that salt? That's too much for somebody like me who doesn't even fish. If fresh water is bad for a man's health, imagine what all that salt will do to me! I really need a bit of wine now.

If I survive all the water I drank today, I make a vow to abstain from it forever; I'll even refrain from looking at the holy water. Master, you're cold and stiff! Are you dead? The sea is responsible but they'll naturally blame me for it. Cursed be the man who first sowed pine trees in the sea and the man who first sailed in the fragility of wood. And curses on Jason and Tiphys! He's dead. Unbelievable! Catalinón, Catalinón, where can you go now?

TISBEA: What's the matter, my good man?

CATALINÓN: Ah, fishermaid, much evil and little good. My master died trying to save me. Look for yourself. What shall I do?

TISBEA: You're wrong. He's still breathing.

CATALINÓN: Where? Here?

TISBEA: Naturally; where else?

CATALINÓN: He might be breathing out in another place.

TISBEA: Fool.

CATALINÓN: I want to kiss your snowy hands.

TISBEA: Why don't you call the fishermen in that hut over there?

CATALINÓN: Will they come if I call?

TISBEA: Of course. Who is this gentleman?

CATALINÓN: He is the son of the King's Chamberlain. He's going to make me count as soon as we get to Seville—if the King agrees, that is.

TISBEA: What's his name?

CATALINÓN: Don Juan Tenorio.

TISBEA: Go and call my people.

CATALINÓN: Right away.

[*Exit* CATALINÓN. TISBEA *places* DON JUAN's *head in her lap.*]

TISBEA: Wake up, handsomest of all men, and be yourself again.

DON JUAN: Where am I?

TISBEA: In the arms of a woman.

DON JUAN: If the sea gives me death, you give me life. But the sea really saved me only to be killed by you. Oh the sea tosses me from one torment to the other, for I no sooner pulled myself from the water than I met its siren—yourself. Why fill my ears with wax, since you kill me with your eyes? I was dying in the sea, but from today I shall die of love.

TISBEA: You have abundant breath for a man who almost drowned. You suffered much, but who knows what suffering you are preparing for me? Perhaps you're my Trojan horse, come out of the sea. I found you at my feet all water, and now you are all fire. If you burn when you are so wet, what will you do when you're dry again? You promise a scorching flame; I hope to God you're not lying.

DON JUAN: Dear girl, God should have drowned me before I could be charred by you. Perhaps love was wise to drench me before I felt your scalding touch. But your fire is such that even in water I burn.

TISBEA: So cold and yet burning?

DON JUAN: So much fire is in you.

TISBEA: How well you talk!

DON JUAN: How well you understand!

TISBEA: I hope to God you're not lying.

[*Enter four fishermen*—ANFRISO, TIRSEO, ALFREDO, *and* SALUCIO—*and* CATALINÓN.]

CATALINÓN: They've come.

TISBEA: Your master is alive.

DON JUAN: Your presence has given me the life I lost.

ANFRISO: What do you want, Tisbea? You have only to speak. Those who worship you are ready to satisfy your least desire: We are ready to furrow the earth, plow the sea, tread the fire, and arrest the wind.

TISBEA [*Aside.*]: Only yesterday these tender words sounded ridiculous to me, but today I understand that they may be true. [*Aloud.*]

Friends, I was fishing here when I saw a ship sink and these two men swim clear. I called for help but no one heard me. One of them lay lifeless on the sand. It was this gentleman whom his servant had carried out of the water. I was distressed and called for your help.

TIRSEO: We are all at your command.

TISBEA: Take them to my cottage. There we'll dry their clothes and look after them. Our kindness will please my father.

CATALINÓN [to Don Juan]: She is a marvelous woman.

DON JUAN [to Catalinón]: Listen to me.

CATALINÓN: Yes.

DON JUAN: If she asks my name, tell her you don't know me.

CATALINÓN: Are you trying to tell me what to do?

DON JUAN: I'm dying with love for her. I must enjoy her tonight.

CATALINÓN: How?

DON JUAN: Just follow me and listen. . . . [DON JUAN draws CATALINÓN aside.]

ALFREDO: Salucio, the dancing must begin within the hour.

SALUCIO: Tonight we'll dance and sing till we drop.

[Exeunt ANFRISO and other fishermen.]

DON JUAN: I'm dying.

TISBEA: But you're walking.

DON JUAN: You can see how painful it is.

TISBEA: How well you talk!

DON JUAN: How well you understand!

TISBEA: I hope to God you're not lying.

[Exeunt.]

Scene 4

A room in the Alcázar, the palace of the King of Castile, Seville. The KING OF CASTILE *enters with* DON GONZALO DE ULLOA.

KING OF CASTILE: Was your embassy successful, Don Gonzalo?

DON GONZALO: In Lisbon I found your cousin preparing thirty vessels to leave for Goa. He received me well indeed.

KING OF CASTILE: He fears the sword in the brave hand of an Ulloa. Your strength has threatened the Moor many times. Did you like Lisbon?

DON GONZALO: It's the eighth marvel of the world. Indeed, sir, it deserves to be your capital.

KING OF CASTILE: Is it larger than Seville?

DON GONZALO: No city can equal Seville.

KING OF CASTILE: Don Gonzalo, do you have children?

DON GONZALO: One daughter, my lord, whose beauty comforts my old age and encourages my efforts.

KING OF CASTILE: I intend to marry her well.

DON GONZALO: Who can possibly deserve her?

KING OF CASTILE: I know of a young gentleman in Italy of noble blood and reputation. He is the son of Don Diego, my Chamberlain, the brother of the famous Don Pedro, who represents me so well at the Neapolitan court. Your son-in-law shall be Count of Lebrija, a city his father subdued for me. I know your daughter deserves even better, but now your mind can be at ease. When we are old, peace of mind has the power to slow the galloping horse of time.

DON GONZALO: You honor me too much, my lord.

KING OF CASTILE: Go and let the good news be known.

DON GONZALO: May your life never touch the gates of oblivion.

KING OF CASTILE: Notable merit deserves an equal reward.

DON GONZALO: All Seville will know my happiness.

KING OF CASTILE: Return to me later.

DON GONZALO: Enjoy your immortal Kingdom.

[*Exeunt* KING OF CASTILE *and* DON GONZALO *in different directions.*]

Scene 5

Near the cottage of Tisbea, Tarragona. DON JUAN *enters with* CATALINÓN.

DON JUAN: Saddle the two mares while the fishermen are having their feast. When I'm in trouble I rely on flying hooves.

CATALINÓN: You've decided to seduce Tisbea?

DON JUAN: You don't think I've reformed?

CATALINÓN: I know you're the scourge of women.

DON JUAN: She's a lovely girl and I'll die without her.

CATALINÓN: You're the perfect guest.

DON JUAN: Fool! I'm as good a guest as Aeneas was to the Queen of Carthage.

CATALINÓN: You and the others like you who cheat and seduce women will pay for your pleasure with your lives.

DON JUAN: Plenty of time for that.

CATALINÓN: Here comes the lamb.

DON JUAN: Go quickly and saddle the mares.

CATALINÓN: Poor girl! You're about to be repaid for your generosity.
[*Exit* CATALINÓN. *Enter* TISBEA.]

TISBEA: I can't stay away from you.

DON JUAN: If only I could believe your words.

TISBEA: Why not?

DON JUAN: Because if you loved me, you would be kind to me.

TISBEA: I'm yours.

DON JUAN: But if that's so—why wait? Why doubt? Why hesitate?

TISBEA: Because I think that my love for you is a punishment for my indifference of old.

DON JUAN: So is mine. For I have loved none other than you. But now I give you my word, and the hand of a husband.

TISBEA: You're a nobleman.

DON JUAN: Don't speak of such things, Tisbea. I am in your house, and I had rather be a humble fisherman here, enjoying the favors of your beautiful person, than possess all the treasures of the world.

TISBEA: I would like to believe you, but you men are all deception.

DON JUAN: Look into my eyes. Come into my arms. Kiss me, and give me your soul in that kiss.

TISBEA: I surrender to you. You are now my husband.

DON JUAN: By your beautiful and fatal eyes! I swear!

TISBEA: Remember, my love, there is hell and death.

DON JUAN [*Aside*.]: Plenty of time for that! [*Aloud*.] While I live, I am your slave.

TISBEA: Take my hand.

DON JUAN: And here is mine to set your mind at rest.

TISBEA: Our wedding bed is prepared in my cottage. Wait for me among the reeds till the time comes.

DON JUAN: And how do I enter?

TISBEA: I'll show you the way.

DON JUAN [*Aside*.]: She is blind—but satisfied.

TISBEA: May my love bind yours. If not, may God punish you.

DON JUAN [*Aside*.]: Plenty of time for that.
[*Exeunt* DON JUAN *and* TISBEA. *Enter* CORIDON, ANFRISO, BELISA *and musicians*.]

CORIDON: Call Tisbea and the others so the guests can enjoy our performance.

ANFRISO: She must be very busy with them. They're lucky men!

CORIDON: Everybody is envious of Tisbea. Here's her house.

BELISA: This spot is better for dancing. Let's call her and the others from here: Tisbea, Lucinda, Antandra.

ALL [*singing*]: A girl went out to sea,
         She cast her net so wide
         She found, instead of fish,
         My dying soul inside.

[*Enter* TISBEA.]

TISBEA: Fire! Fire! And madness! I'm burning! My hut is burning! Sound the alarm my friends, for my soul is on fire. My own house, an instrument of my dishonor! Fire! Burning stars have kindled my tresses and winds have fanned the flames. I laughed at other girls for falling in love and now love is laughing at me. A man deceived me with a promise of marriage and violated my honesty and my bed. He enjoyed me, and I even supplied the mares for his escape to cap his joke and my disgrace. He came like a cloud from the sea to drown me. But I believed his words—and I deserve nothing better. Friends, follow him. No, I'll ask vengeance from the King. I'll go to him myself. Fire! Fire! Water! Water! Have mercy, love, my heart is in flames!

[*Exit* TISBEA.]

CORIDON: Follow her; she is so desperate she might fling herself into the sea.

BELISA: Her pride ruined her.

ANFRISO: To this her blind confidence brought her. She's running to the sea! Tisbea, wait! Listen!

BELISA: She is coming back. Hold her, don't let her run away. Hold her tight.

[*Enter* TISBEA.]

TISBEA: Fire! Fire! Have mercy, love, my heart is in flames!

[*Exeunt.*]

ACT II

Scene 1

A room in the Alcázar, Seville. Enter KING OF CASTILE *and* DON DIEGO TENORIO.

KING OF CASTILE: What are you saying?

DON DIEGO: It's true, my lord. My brother, your Ambassador, wrote it in this letter. They found my son in the King's palace with a beautiful lady. She, however, accused Duke Octavio of the crime.

KING OF CASTILE: Who is she? A lady of rank?

DON DIEGO: Duchess Isabela.

KING OF CASTILE: Isabela? The audacity! And where is your son now?

DON DIEGO: I don't want to conceal the truth from Your Majesty. He arrived in Seville last night with a servant.

KING OF CASTILE: Tenorio, you know my great esteem for you. I will send a letter immediately to the King of Naples, marry the young scamp to Isabela, and pacify the innocent Duke Octavio. But I want Don Juan banished from here at once.

DON DIEGO: Where to, my lord?

KING OF CASTILE: He must leave Seville for Lebrija tonight. I am making the sentence light only out of consideration for your merits, Don Diego. But what shall we tell Gonzalo de Ulloa? I promised your son to his daughter. How can we solve that problem?

DON DIEGO: My lord, I am ready to do whatever is called for. Don Gonzalo's high distinction—

KING OF CASTILE: I see one way of appeasing his anger: I'll make him majordomo of the palace.

[Enter a Servant.]

SERVANT: A gentleman is here from abroad. My lord, he says he is the Duke Octavio.

KING OF CASTILE: Duke Octavio?

SERVANT: Yes, my lord.

KING OF CASTILE: I wonder if he discovered your son's impudent trick. If so, no doubt he'll ask permission to challenge him.

DON DIEGO: My life is in your hands, Your Highness, for my real life is that of my disobedient son. Young as he is, he is already strong and courageous. Indeed, his friends call him the Hector of Seville because of his many heroic actions. Your Highness, reason with Octavio; prevent a duel.

KING OF CASTILE: Enough, Tenorio. A father's honor—

[To Servant] Show the Duke in.

DON DIEGO: Allow me to kiss your feet. How can I repay your favors?

[Enter OCTAVIO in traveling clothes.]

OCTAVIO: My lord, I come before you as a wretched exile and wanderer. Let me embrace your feet. Your presence mends all the miseries of my journey.

KING OF CASTILE: Duke Octavio. . . .

OCTAVIO: I have fled the rank frivolity of a woman and the unintentional injustice of a king; though I should not say so, for the law shines clear in the mirror of kings. A woman lightly deceived the King, accusing me of seduction in the palace. But I trust in time to disabuse him and to make my innocence clear.

KING OF CASTILE: Duke, I know you are innocent. I will ask the King of Naples to restore your possessions and to make amends for the losses you are suffering during your absence. Moreover, I will marry you in Seville if you wish, and if the King of Naples agrees. Though Isabela may seem an angel of beauty, she is ugly beside the wife I shall be giving you. She is the daughter of Don Gonzalo de Ulloa, Grand Commander of Calatrava, the terror of the Moors. Her virtue, which is second only to her beauty, would be a sufficient dowry in itself. And this sun among the stars of Castile shall be your wife.

OCTAVIO: My lord, you have made my journey my happiness. Your wish is my command.

KING OF CASTILE [to Don Diego]: Lodge the Duke comfortably.

OCTAVIO: The man who trusts in you, my lord, is well rewarded. Though you are Alfonso the Eleventh, you are truly the first Alfonso. [Exeunt all.]

Scene 2

The City of Seville. DUKE OCTAVIO *and his servant* RIPIO *enter from different sides.*

RIPIO: Well, what happened?

OCTAVIO: I am too happy to speak.

RIPIO: Any success?

OCTAVIO: Much gained and little lost. His Highness received me with the most loving condescension. His favors have ended my troubles. He asks me to remain in Seville, and I am madly anxious to please him.

RIPIO: And did he find you a wife?

OCTAVIO: Yes, my friend; a native of Seville. You are surprised, but Seville produces not only the strongest and liveliest men, but also the most graceful women. In short, you see me perfectly consoled.

RIPIO: I take it Isabela no longer keeps you awake.

OCTAVIO: Right.

[*Enter* DON JUAN *and* CATALINÓN.]

CATALINÓN: Wait. The Duke. Isabela's Sagittarius—or rather her Capricorn.*

DON JUAN: Don't give us away.

CATALINÓN [Aside.]: He'll flatter him after stabbing him in the back.

DON JUAN [to Octavio]: Octavio! Forgive me for not taking leave of you. I was called away from Naples suddenly on business of the King.

OCTAVIO: And you find me here, my friend, for the same reason.

DON JUAN: Who would have thought we'd meet again in Seville? And that you'd leave the lovely coast of Naples?

OCTAVIO: Naples is beautiful, but Seville is a fair match for it.

DON JUAN: When did you arrive?

OCTAVIO: Yesterday.

DON JUAN: Splendid! I want you to savor all the beauties of Seville. Twelve gates, ramparts with magnificent views over the countryside, a river—the Guadalquivir—next to which your Tiber is a teardrop— and alongside the river charming sirens no one stops his ears against. One look at our Alcázar would have made the Trojans forget Troy and the Babylonians their hanging gardens. The Hall of the Kings is so rich you'd think Jupiter held court there in his shower of gold. Its fifty-four pillars grunt under the weight. Did I say pillars? I should have said towers, and even towers are like twigs compared to them. As for the cathedral, it is so huge that only a lynx can see from one portal to another. Every day two hundred masses are sung at its two famous altars. Where is Heaven served more majestically? Neither in Rome nor in Toledo, if Toledo will forgive my saying so. Its tower is surmounted by a bronze weathervane representing Faith. We call it La Giralda—that is to say, "The Fickle Woman." During Holy Week you will see the most astounding processions—sixty of them—pouring rubies over God like floods of blood. Seville also has more than a hundred convents, two of them so large they are cities in themselves, and twelve hospitals for the poor. A genuine Ribera hangs in one of them.

In the streets the traders scramble and compete, major guilds, minor guilds—a perpetual come-and-go. Ships that have seen the boundary of dawn and the kingdom of night unload their pearls, coral, amethysts, embroideries, brocades, the finest fabrics—and everything the sun, the earth, and the sea engender for man to enjoy and squander. Besides this, the women are handsome, spirited, and

*Octavio, who was once Isabela's protector (in the Zodiac, Sagittarius is the Archer), has become a cuckold (Capricorn is the Goat). [Translator's note.]

proud—sorceresses when they talk, but constant, chaste, and firm in their actions—except when they are riding in their closed carriages. Curses on Pharaoh who invented them! . . . Well, such is Seville, and believe me I have been too brief in my praises.*

OCTAVIO: If I had heard your description in Naples before I came here, I would have laughed at you. But now that I see it, I must confess I don't think any praise of Seville exaggerated. But who is the man coming this way?

DON JUAN: The Marquis de la Mota.

OCTAVIO: Well, allow me to take my leave.

DON JUAN: If you need me, my sword is at your command.

CATALINÓN [Aside.]: And he'll take your name if he needs it to seduce another woman, like the scoundrel he is.

OCTAVIO: I am obliged to you.

[Exit OCTAVIO.]

CATALINÓN [to Ripio]: If I can be of any use to you, you'll always find me ready for you.

RIPIO: Where are you staying?

CATALINÓN: At the Sign of the Sparrow—a tavernacle of wine, my friend.

[Exit RIPIO. Enter MARQUIS DE LA MOTA accompanied by his SERVANT.]

MARQUIS [to Don Juan]: I have been looking for you all day without finding you. Don Juan! You are in Seville, and here's your friend pining away in your absence.

*A kind of guided tour of Seville, more than 650 lines long, is condensed in this speech, which replaces Ulloa's equally long and even more extraneous description of Lisbon in El Burlador.

In a private communication, Professor Gerald E. Wade refers to the Cuadros viejos of Julio Monreal for an explanation of the passage concerning the carriages: "The Spanish thought that the carriage was invented by the Germans, and hence it was for a time looked upon as a foreign thing and a sort of Lutheran devil, a vicio infernal that caused men to loll at their decadent ease rather than ride on horseback as he-men should, and that caused women to lose their chastity. The coche was accused of being a frequent place for love-trysts, much like the automobile today. Tirso cracks in Desde Toledo a Madrid

> que hay hembra que una noche
> no se acostó, por solo andar en coche—

there was a woman who couldn't go to bed one night, she was too sore from lying down in a coach. The coche became a status symbol of great importance, and—when the owner's means permitted—was decorated in every extravagant way possible, something like a deluxe convertible with us. The traffic problem in the center of cities became acute. . . ." [Translator's note.]

DON JUAN: By God, my friend, you do me great honor.

CATALINÓN [*Aside.*]: If it doesn't concern women or anything that interests him, you can trust him to act like a gentleman.

DON JUAN: What's new in Seville?

MARQUIS: Things have changed at court.

DON JUAN: And the women?

MARQUIS: The women too.

DON JUAN: What about Inès?

MARQUIS: Going to Vejel.

DON JUAN: Good resort for a great lady like her.

MARQUIS: The years are driving her there.

DON JUAN: To die. And her sister?

MARQUIS: She's a sorry sight: her head and brows completely bald. But she still thinks everybody admires her, and affects to mistake even an insult for a compliment.

DON JUAN: And Theodora?

MARQUIS: This summer she cured herself of the French disease by sweating it out. And now she is so affectionate that day before yesterday she pulled a tooth of mine—whispering gentle words all the time.

DON JUAN: And Julia of Candle Street?

MARQUIS: Fights on, armed with her cosmetic box.

DON JUAN: Still thinks of herself as caviar?

MARQUIS: No; just plain cod by now.

DON JUAN: And the Catarranas district: still crowded?

MARQUIS: Yes. With harpies.

DON JUAN: Are those two sisters still alive?

MARQUIS: Yes, also that monkey of Tolù and their mother Celestina, who teaches them all her tricks.

DON JUAN: The old witch! What about the older daughter?

MARQUIS: Blanca? Penniless. But she found a saint for whom she can fast.

DON JUAN: Vigils and all?

MARQUIS: Oh, she's a holy woman now.

DON JUAN: And the other?

MARQUIS: More practical; she doesn't reject any rubbish.

DON JUAN: Like a good builder. Tell me, Marquis, have you played any tricks lately?

MARQUIS: Last night Esquivel and I made terrors of ourselves. For tonight we've got two little adventures planned.

DON JUAN: I'll come along. However, I also want to visit a little nest where I left a few eggs hatching for us. But what about your love affairs?

MARQUIS: I've forgotten all about them. I have higher cares these days.

DON JUAN: How so?

MARQUIS: I desire the impossible.

DON JUAN: Ah. She's not interested.

MARQUIS: That's not it. She loves me.

DON JUAN: Who is she?

MARQUIS: My cousin Doña Ana, who arrived recently in Seville.

DON JUAN: From where?

MARQUIS: Lisbon. Her father is the Ambassador.

DON JUAN: Is she beautiful?

MARQUIS: Extremely. Nature excelled itself in creating Doña Ana.

DON JUAN: That beautiful! By God, I must see her.

MARQUIS: You will see the greatest beauty under the sun.

DON JUAN: Marry her, if she is so beautiful.

MARQUIS: The King has given her away already, nobody knows to whom.

DON JUAN: Does she love you?

MARQUIS: She writes to me. . . .

CATALINÓN [*Aside*.]: Say no more—the greatest scoundrel of Spain is about to trick you.

DON JUAN: Why be miserable if you are completely satisfied with her? Bring her out, woo her, write to her, seduce her, and the consequences be damned!

MARQUIS: I am waiting to hear her final resolution now.

DON JUAN: Don't waste more time—find out—I'll look for you here later.

MARQUIS: Good-bye then.

CATALINÓN [*to the Marquis' servant*]: Master Square, or rather Round, farewell.

SERVANT: Good-bye.

[*Exeunt* MARQUIS DE LA MOTA *and servant.*]

DON JUAN [*to Catalinón*]: Follow the Marquis.

CATALINÓN: He has just entered the Alcázar.

DON JUAN: Follow him.

[*Exit* CATALINÓN. *A* WOMAN *speaks behind a barred window.*]

WOMAN: Pst!

DON JUAN: Who's there?

WOMAN: If you are discreet, courteous, and a friend of the Marquis, give him this letter immediately. A lady's happiness depends on it.

DON JUAN: I'll give it to him. I am his friend and servant.

WOMAN: Farewell, stranger.

[*The* WOMAN *disappears.*]

DON JUAN: The voice is gone. Isn't this a fairy tale? The wind was my courier for this letter. Could it be a message from the woman the Marquis was sighing over just now? The playboy of Seville is in luck again! Playboy of Seville! That is what all Spain calls me. The man whose greatest pleasure is to play a woman for a fool and abscond with her honor. By God, now that I've walked away from the square I'll open this! Can she be another Isabela? How delightful! The letter is open. It's hers! Signed, "Doña Ana, your cousin." [*Reads the letter.*] "My cruel father tells me that he has given me away, but not to you. Now as you have given me your pledge of marriage, I entrust myself to you. Come tonight at eleven. You will find a door open. Wear a colored cape. Leonora and my other two servants will let you in, my love. Farewell." Poor lover! Did anyone ever see the likes of this? [*Laughing.*] What a joke. By God, I'll enjoy her through the same lie I used on Isabela in Naples.

[*Enter* CATALINÓN.]

CATALINÓN: The Marquis is coming.

DON JUAN: We have business tonight.

CATALINÓN: A new trick?

DON JUAN: The best!

CATALINÓN: I don't approve. We can't go on like this. One of these days you'll be tricked by your own tricks.

DON JUAN: You've become a preacher, have you?

CATALINÓN: Right makes me valiant.

DON JUAN: Fear will make you a coward. Since when does a servant have a will of his own? Your duty is to act and keep your mouth shut. And that's my last warning to you.

CATALINÓN: From now on I'll do as I am told. Say the word and I'll tame a tiger or an elephant.

DON JUAN: Quiet, the Marquis is coming.

CATALINÓN: To be tamed?

[*Enter* MARQUIS DE LA MOTA.]

DON JUAN: Marquis, I was entrusted with a charming message for you through a grill. I couldn't see anyone, but by the voice I understood it was a woman. You are to appear at a certain door at midnight.

The door will be open and all your amorous hopes will be rewarded. But you must wear a colored cape in order to be recognized by little Leonora, the maid.

MARQUIS: What are you saying?

DON JUAN: That I received this message from a window—without seeing a soul.

MARQUIS: Beautiful message! My friend, I owe heaven to you. Let me kiss your feet.

DON JUAN: Remember, I am not your cousin! [Aside.] I'm going to make love to her, and you're kissing my feet!

MARQUIS: I'm so happy I've lost my wits. Sun, rush me to her arms!

DON JUAN: It's getting dark already.

MARQUIS: I'm going home at once to get dressed for tonight. I'm absolutely wild.

DON JUAN: Just wait. You'll be even wilder at midnight.

MARQUIS: Best of all cousins—you want to reward my faith and love!

CATALINÓN [Aside.]: Christ be my witness, I wouldn't give a penny for his cousin.

[Exit MARQUIS DE LA MOTA. Enter DON DIEGO TENORIO.]

DON DIEGO: Don Juan.

CATALINÓN: Your father is calling you.

DON JUAN: My lord, what can I do for you?

DON DIEGO: You can become more settled, wiser, and more honorable. Why are you trying to kill me?

DON JUAN: Why do you come to me this way?

DON DIEGO: Because of your behavior, your madness. The King has ordered me to throw you out of the city because of one of your pranks. You concealed it from me, but the King has been informed. Your crime is so serious I hardly dare talk about it. To betray a friend in the royal palace! May God punish you according to your deserts. You fancy that He winks at your crimes, but I say your punishment is at hand. Profaner of God's name, God will be a terrible judge on the day of your death.

DON JUAN: The day of my death? Plenty of time for that. It's a long journey till then.

DON DIEGO: It will seem very short to you then.

DON JUAN: But the journey His Highness requires of me right now, is that a long one too?

DON DIEGO: The King sends you to Lebrija for your treachery—not punishment enough, in my opinion. You will remain there until Duke Octavio is satisfied and the talk in Naples about Isabela has subsided.

CATALINÓN [*Aside.*]: If the old man knew about the poor fishergirl, he'd really foam at the mouth.

DON DIEGO: Since I can't chastize you, say or do what I will, I leave you in the hands of God.

[*Exit* DON DIEGO TENORIO.]

CATALINÓN: The old man was almost crying.

DON JUAN: That's how old people are. Come, it's dark already; let's call on the Marquis.

CATALINÓN: If we must. You've made up your mind to seduce his woman?

DON JUAN: This trick will go down in history.

CATALINÓN: I hope we survive it!

DON JUAN: You're a coward.

CATALINÓN: And you're a regular bluebeard. When you arrive in a town a sign should be posted: "Beware of the great deceiver of women, the playboy of Spain."

DON JUAN: "The playboy of Spain." I like that name.

[*Enter the* MARQUIS DE LA MOTA *and* MUSICIANS, *singing. It is evening.*]

MUSICIAN: Oh what is Love's delight? To hurt each where
       He cares not whom, with darts of deep desire:
       With watchful jealousy, with hope, with fear,
       With nipping cold, and secret flames of fire.*

DON JUAN: What's this?

CATALINÓN: A serenade.

MARQUIS: The words of this song seem meant for me.

DON JUAN: Who is there?

MARQUIS: A friend. Don Juan?

DON JUAN: Is it you, Marquis?

MARQUIS: Who else?

DON JUAN: As soon as I saw your cape I knew it was you.

MARQUIS: Sing, Don Juan is here.

[*The* MUSICIANS *repeat the song.*]

DON JUAN: What's the house you're gazing at?

*From Thomas Watson's "The Shepherd's Solace," in *England's Helicon* (1600). [*Translator's note.*]

MARQUIS: That of Don Gonzalo de Ulloa.

DON JUAN: Well, it's early yet.* Where shall we go?

MARQUIS: To Lisbon.

DON JUAN: But we're in Seville!

MARQUIS: Didn't you know that half the whores of Lisbon live in the best part of Seville?

DON JUAN: Where do they live?

MARQUIS: In Serpent Alley, where the Portuguese Eves tempt our Adams with apples that cost a great deal of money.

CATALINÓN: I don't like the idea of wandering through that street. It's honey in the day but dirt at night. And what Portuguese dirt is like I experienced once when it was slopped over me from a window.

DON JUAN: While you're going to Serpent Alley, I'll have some fun on my side.

MARQUIS: Actually, I've another enterprise waiting for me nearby.

DON JUAN: Why don't you leave that one to me? I'll take care of it for you.

MARQUIS: Good idea. Put on my cape and take my place.

DON JUAN: Excellent. Show me the house.

MARQUIS: Change your voice and accent while you're about it. Do you see that lattice?

DON JUAN: Yes.

MARQUIS: Go up to it, call "Beatrice," and go in.

DON JUAN: What is she like?

MARQUIS: Fresh and plump.

CATALINÓN: Like a water jar.

MARQUIS: We'll meet later by the church.

DON JUAN: Goodbye, Marquis.

[*Exit* MARQUIS DE LA MOTA.]

CATALINÓN: Where to now?

DON JUAN: To my trick.

CATALINÓN: Nobody gets away from you.

DON JUAN: I love these disguises!

CATALINÓN: You threw a cape at the bull.

DON JUAN: No, the poor bull threw it at me!

[*Exeunt* DON JUAN *and* CATALINÓN. *Reenter* MARQUIS DE LA MOTA, *his* SERVANT, *and Musicians.*]

*This sentence, not in the original, has been supplied for the sake of clarity. [*Translator's note.*]

MARQUIS: Beatrice will think it's I calling on her!

SERVANT: Very clever of you.

MARQUIS: I love these errors!

SERVANT: Everything in this world is error.

MARQUIS: My heart beats with the clock. Each quarter of the hour is a step to supreme fulfillment. Oh, it's a cold and frightening night! Come soon, midnight, but after that, let it never be day!

SERVANT: Where is the next party?

MARQUIS: In Serpent Alley.

MUSICIAN: And what shall we sing?

MARQUIS: Anything to flatter my hopes.

MUSICIANS: No sweeter life I try
            Than in her love to die.

[*Exeunt all.*]

DOÑA ANA [*from within*]: Traitor, you are not the Marquis! I'm deceived!

DON JUAN: But I am the Marquis!

DOÑA ANA: Enemy! You lie! You lie!

[*Enter* DON GONZALO, *half-dressed, sword in hand.*]

DON GONZALO: Ana's voice!

DOÑA ANA: Help! Somebody—kill this traitor—he killed my honor!

DON GONZALO: Who could dare? Killed her honor! My God! And her tongue tolling it to the world!

DOÑA ANA: Kill him!

[*Enter* DON JUAN, *sword in hand, and* CATALINÓN.]

DON JUAN: What's here?

DON GONZALO: A gate to the tower of honor, closing in your face.

DON JUAN: Let me pass!

DON GONZALO: First through my sword!

DON JUAN: Listen to me!

DON GONZALO: Don't waste your breath.

DON JUAN: Listen, I say!

DON GONZALO: The cries I heard told me enough.

DON JUAN: I am your nephew!

DON GONZALO: You're lying. The Marquis de la Mota is no traitor. Villain! Your death for my honor!

DON JUAN: I tell you I am the Marquis!

DON GONZALO: And if you are, the offence is all the greater. Traitor, die!

DON JUAN: This is how I die!

[*They fight.*]

CATALINÓN: If I survive this time, no more tricks for me.

DON GONZALO: Oh! You've killed me.

DON JUAN: Blame yourself.

DON GONZALO: What good is life without honor?

DON JUAN [*to Catalinón*]: On our way.

[*Exeunt* DON JUAN *and* CATALINÓN.]

DON GONZALO: Wait! This blood lends me strength. No, he needn't wait. My wrath will follow him. Villainous coward!

[DON GONZALO *is carried off. Enter* MARQUIS DE LA MOTA, *his Servant, and Musicians.*]

MARQUIS: Midnight will be striking soon. It seems to me that Don Juan is taking uncommonly long with Beatrice. Oh the torments of impatience!

[*Reenter* DON JUAN *and* CATALINÓN.]

DON JUAN: Marquis?

MARQUIS: Don Juan?

DON JUAN: Yes. Take back your cape.

MARQUIS: How was the game?

DON JUAN: Sad. Somebody died.

CATALINÓN: And we'd better run away from him.

MARQUIS: But did you trick her?

DON JUAN: Yes, I did.

CATALINÓN [*Aside.*]: And you too, into the bargain.

DON JUAN: But it was a costly joke.

MARQUIS: I'll pay for it, Don Juan, because the woman will blame me for it.

DON JUAN: It's almost twelve.

MARQUIS: May this night last forever the moment I am in Ana's arms.

DON JUAN: Goodbye, Marquis.

CATALINÓN [*Aside.*]: The poor man's due for a surprise.

DON JUAN [*to Catalinón*]: Let's go.

CATALINÓN: I'll be quicker than an eagle.

[*Exeunt* DON JUAN *and* CATALINÓN.]

MARQUIS: You can all go home. I have to proceed alone now.

SERVANT: Night was made for sleep.

[*Exeunt Musicians.*]

VOICES [*Within.*]: Unheard of! Horrible! A calamity!

MARQUIS: God help me! Voices from the Alcázar. At this time? What can it be? I seem to be looking at another burning Troy. Torches like giants of flames. The lights are coming near! Why are they burning like the sun and dividing into squadrons? I must find out before—

[*Enter* DON DIEGO TENORIO *and the Guard.*]

DON DIEGO: Who is there?

MARQUIS: Somebody who wants to know the reason for all this clamor.

DON DIEGO: This is the cape the Commander spoke about in his last words. Arrest him.

MARQUIS: Arrest me? How dare you! I am the Marquis de la Mota!
[*Draws his sword.*]

DON DIEGO: Put up your sword. You can show your courage without using it. The King has ordered your arrest.

MARQUIS: God in heaven!
[*Enter* KING OF CASTILE, *attended.*]

DON DIEGO: My lord, here is the Marquis.

MARQUIS: Your Highness has ordered my arrest?

KING OF CASTILE: Take him and remove him from my presence. I want to see his head on a stake. What! You dare look at me?

MARQUIS: Your highness—my innocence—

KING OF CASTILE: Enough. To the dungeon!

MARQUIS: Oh the tyrannical glories of love, so quick in passing and yet so long in coming. "There's many a slip 'twixt the cup and the lip," says the wise proverb. But why is the King offended? Why am I being arrested?

DON DIEGO: Who knows the answer to that better than you, my lord?

MARQUIS: Than I?

DON DIEGO: Let's go.

MARQUIS: Strange confusion.

KING OF CASTILE: Try the Marquis at once, and off with his head in the morning. As for the Commander's burial, it must be conducted with all the solemnity and dignity he deserves. At my own expense he will be given a tomb and a statue of bronze and matching stone. An inscription in gothic letters will cry out for vengeance. But where did Doña Ana go?

DON DIEGO: To the Queen, my lord, for sanctuary.

KING OF CASTILE: Castile and the rest of the kingdom will mourn this loss; Calatrava will weep the death of a great Commander.
[*Exeunt all.*]

Scene 3

A wedding feast near the village of Dos Hermanas. Enter BATRICIO *and* ARMINTA, GACENO, BELISA, *other* SHEPHERDS *and* MUSICIANS.

MUSICIANS [*singing*]:

> O who can sing her beauties best,
>   or what remains unsung?
> Do thou Apollo tune the rest,
>   unworthy is my tongue.
> To gaze on her, is to be blest,
>   so wondrous fair her face is;
> Her fairness cannot be exprest
>   in Goddesses nor Graces.*

GACENO: Batricio, in giving you my Arminta, I am giving you my soul and my being.

BATRICIO: The meadow puts on its brightest colors for us. I won her with my desires. I deserved her by my labors.

MUSICIANS: A thousand years of union for such a wife and such a husband!

[*They repeat the song.*]

GACENO: Well sung. The Kyrie never sounded better.

BATRICIO: The sun that rises in the east does not rise like the sun of my soul. There is no sun like the sun of her eyes and her brow. My sun shines brighter than the noontide sun. Sing therefore to my sun thousands of sweet melodies.

[*The Musicians repeat the song.*]

ARMINTA: Batricio, I am grateful but you are quite a flatterer. From now on you will be my sun and I will be your moon, and grow by your light alone.

[*Enter a* SHEPHERD.]

SHEPHERD: Gentlemen, you are about to have guests at your wedding feast.

GACENO: Let the whole world participate in our joy.

BATRICIO: Who's coming?

SHEPHERD: Don Juan Tenorio.

BATRICIO: It's an ill wind when a gentleman appears at a feast. I foresee spoiled pleasure and jealousy. How did he hear of my wedding?

SHEPHERD: Traveling on the road to Lebrija.

---

*From "Theorello: A Shepherd's Idyll" in *England's Helicon*. [*Translator's note.*]

BATRICIO: The devil must have sent him. But why should I worry? Everybody can join us who will. And yet—a gentleman at my wedding—an ill wind for me.

GACENO: Let the whole court of Alfonso the Eleventh come, along with the Colossus of Rhodes, the Pope, and Prester John. They'll find royal entertainment with Gaceno. We have mountains of bread, Guadalquivirs of wine, Babylons of bacon, and larders bursting with birds and doves and basted hens. The presence of this great nobleman among us will be an honor bestowed on my grey head.

SHEPHERD [to Batricio]: Careful. He is the son of the Chamberlain.

BATRICIO: An ill wind for me. They must seat him next to my bride. My pleasure is spoiled and I am jealous already. I'll have to love, suffer, and be still.

[Enter DON JUAN and CATALINÓN in traveling clothes.]

DON JUAN: I heard on the highway of a wedding here. I should like to join in your festivities, since I was fortunate enough to hear about them.

GACENO: You have come to honor and magnify them.

BATRICIO [Aside.]: I am in charge here and I still say you've come in an evil hour.

GACENO: Give the gentleman a seat.

DON JUAN: If you allow me, I'll sit here.

[He sits next to ARMINTA.]

BATRICIO: But if you sit before me, sir, you'll be taking the bridegroom's place.

DON JUAN: That doesn't sound too bad.

GACENO: He is the bridegroom, sir.

DON JUAN: Forgive my error and ignorance.

BATRICIO [Aside.]: Why must I always be the loser?

CATALINÓN [Aside.]: Poor fellow, he's fallen into Lucifer's hands.

DON JUAN [to Arminta]: Is it possible, madam, that I should be so fortunate? I really envy your husband.

ARMINTA: You seem to be a flatterer.

BATRICIO [Aside.]: I was right. Nobility at a wedding is an ill wind that blows no good.

DON JUAN: Your hands are too delicate to grant to a peasant.

CATALINÓN [Aside.]: Give him your hand in game and you'll lose your hand in earnest.

BATRICIO [Aside.]: Jealousy will kill me.

GACENO: Let's eat now to give our new friend a chance to rest.

DON JUAN [*to Arminta*]: Why do you hide your hand?

ARMINTA: It doesn't belong to me.

GACENO: Sing, everybody!

DON JUAN [*to Catalinón*]: What do you think of all this?

CATALINÓN [*to Don Juan*]: These bumpkins may massacre us yet.

DON JUAN: Beautiful eyes and delicate hands—they have set me on fire.

CATALINÓN: Time to brand another lamb. This makes four.

DON JUAN: Come, they're watching me.

BATRICIO [*Aside.*]: Didn't I say it was an ill wind?

GACENO: Sing! Sing!

BATRICIO [*Aside.*]: I'm dying!

CATALINÓN: Sing now, cry later.

[*The Musicians repeat the song.*]

ACT III

Scene 1

Gaceno's house in the village of Dos Hermanas. Enter BATRICIO, *deep in thought.*

BATRICIO: Oh Jealousy, my death and my hell, spare me! I am worn out with rage and grief. And he, the great man, why does he torment me? What does he want? I was right when I cried, "It's an ill wind" after seeing him. Not only must he sit next to my wife, but he wouldn't allow me to dip a finger into my own plate! He brushed my hand aside every time I tried to taste a dish. "Tut, tut, such bad manners!" he said. And he stuck so close to Arminta that people began to think he was her husband, and I his best man. When I wanted to speak with my own bride, he growled, "Such bad manners" again and shoved me aside. And when I appealed to the others they just smiled and answered, "You have no reason to complain. It really is nothing. What are you afraid of? Keep quiet, it must be a custom at court." Custom devil! It may have been a custom in Sodom for a stranger to eat of the bridal dish while the bridegroom went hungry! And the other rascal, each time I got my hands on something to eat, he'd say, "You don't like this? You really have no taste for finer things," and suddenly take it away from me. I'm simply furious! Is this a wedding or a practical joke? Am I among Christians? Now that supper is over, I suppose he will follow us to bed too. And when I hug my wife, he'll say, "Tut, tut, such bad manners!" Here he comes. What shall I do? I can't stand it—I'll hide. Too late—he saw me.

[*Enter* DON JUAN.]

DON JUAN: Batricio.

BATRICIO: At your service, sir.

DON JUAN: When love rages in the soul, Batricio, it will speak out. I must tell you—

BATRICIO [*Aside.*]: Another calamity for me?

DON JUAN: Some time ago I gave my heart to Arminta, and I enjoyed . . .

BATRICIO: Her honor?

DON JUAN: Yes.

BATRICIO [*Aside.*]: This confirms what my own eyes have seen. If Arminta didn't love him she would never have allowed me to be insulted so.

DON JUAN: I have been her promised husband, and have enjoyed her favors, these six months. I tell you this because I see no other way out. But I speak the truth, Batricio. Our engagement and our friendship were kept secret because of the King and my father. But neither reason nor law can keep two loving souls apart. Don't stand in the way of our marriage, my friend. Either I must be satisfied, or else, by God, I'll kill whoever has given me trouble.

BATRICIO: Since you're allowing me to choose, my lord, I'll do as you like. Gossip is the ruin of honor and women. A woman's reputation is like a bell; one crack in it, and it's broken for good. Enjoy her, my lord, enjoy her a thousand years. I'd rather die with the truth than live with a lie.

[*Exit* BATRICIO.]

DON JUAN: I vanquished him by appealing to honor. These peasants are always consulting their honor, as though they carried it in their hands. And no wonder. After so many deceptions, honor has fled from the city to the countryside. So then: I twisted him around my little finger, and now I can enjoy the girl without fear. Night is falling, and I have yet to hoodwink her father. Stars in the sky, look down upon me and, if I am not to be punished till the day of my death, grant me luck in this hoax!

[*Exit* DON JUAN. *Enter* ARMINTA *and* BELISA.]

BELISA: Arminta, your bridegroom is coming. Time to go into the house and get undressed.

ARMINTA: Belisa, I don't know what to think of this unhappy wedding. Who is this gentleman who deprives me of my joy? My poor Batricio was drowning in melancholy all day; I saw him jealous and perplexed. So much misfortune! I hate the man who separates me from my love. Shameless impudence has become a mark of nobility in Spain. Leave me now, Belisa; I don't know what to think. I feel lost. Go now. I hate the man who separates me from my love. . . .

BELISA: Go in; I think I hear Batricio coming. It couldn't be anyone else in the house of newlyweds.

ARMINTA: Good night, my dear Belisa.

BELISA: Comfort him in your arms.

ARMINTA: God, turn my sighs into words of love, my tears into caresses.

[*Exeunt* BELISA *and* ARMINTA. *Enter* DON JUAN, GACENO *and* CATALINÓN.]

DON JUAN: God be with you, Gaceno.

GACENO: I'd like to come with you to inform my daughter of her good fortune.

DON JUAN: That can wait till tomorrow.

GACENO: You're right. In giving you my daughter, Don Juan, I am giving my soul away.

DON JUAN: Your daughter is now my wife.

[*Exit* GACENO.]

DON JUAN: Saddle the mares, Catalinón.

CATALINÓN: When do we leave?

DON JUAN: At dawn, and dying with laughter after this trick.

CATALINÓN: Master, another wedding is waiting for us in Lebrija, so hurry with this one.

DON JUAN: This is going to be my most refined hoax.

CATALINÓN: Excellent; but see we don't get hoaxed right back, and that we come out of this merrymaking alive.

DON JUAN: What are you afraid of? Isn't my father the Chief Justice, and isn't he the King's favorite?

CATALINÓN: God punishes favorites too when they wink at evildoing. And at the gambling table it can happen that those who just look on also get hurt. God knows I've looked on at your games, but I don't care to be reduced to cinders by a bolt from heaven, not me!

DON JUAN: Enough—saddle the mares. Tomorrow we'll sleep in Seville.

CATALINÓN: In Seville?

DON JUAN: Yes.

CATALINÓN: You're joking! Think of what you did in Seville! Remember there's only a little step from the longest life to death, and from death to hell.

DON JUAN: If you give me that much time, come, deceits, come, pranks!

CATALINÓN: Sir . . . !

DON JUAN: Go on, your cowardice bores me.

[*Exit* CATALINÓN.]

DON JUAN: Night spreads out its dark silence, and the Pleiades tread the highest pole among clusters of stars. Now is the time for adventure. Love, whom no man can resist, be my guide to her bed. Arminta!

ARMINTA: Who's calling me? My Batricio?

DON JUAN: I am not Batricio.

ARMINTA: Then who is it?

DON JUAN: Look carefully, Arminta.

ARMINTA: My God, I am ruined! In my room at this hour!

DON JUAN: This hour is mine, Arminta.

ARMINTA: Leave at once, or I'll shout for help. You owe Batricio some courtesy. We too in our village have our Emilias and our Lucretias.

DON JUAN: Arminta, two words! Listen to me and conceal your warm, your precious blush in your heart.

ARMINTA: Leave me, my husband is coming.

DON JUAN: I am your husband. Are you surprised?

ARMINTA: Since when?

DON JUAN: Since now.

ARMINTA: Who settled this?

DON JUAN: My good fortune.

ARMINTA: Does Batricio know?

DON JUAN: Yes; he has forgotten you.

ARMINTA: Forgotten me?

DON JUAN: Yes, because I adore you.

ARMINTA: Adore me?

DON JUAN: In these two arms.

ARMINTA: Leave!

DON JUAN: How can I? I would die without you.

ARMINTA: You lie!

DON JUAN: Arminta, listen to the truth—for are not women friends of truth? I am a nobleman, heir to the ancient family of the Tenorios, the conquerors of Seville. After the King, my father is the most powerful and considered man at court. His lips hold power of life and death. By chance I happened on this road and saw you. Love sometimes behaves in a manner that surprises even himself. I saw you, adored you, and love burns in me so, that I must marry you. Let the King disapprove, my father forbid and threaten, and the whole kingdom murmur, yet I will be your husband. Batricio has foregone his rights, and your father has sent me here to give you my hand in marriage. Speak to me now, Arminta.

ARMINTA: I don't know if what you're saying is truth or lying rhetoric. I am married to Batricio, everybody knows it. How can the marriage be annulled, even if he abandons me?

DON JUAN: When the marriage is not consummated, whether by malice or deceit, it can be annulled.

ARMINTA: You are right. But, God help me, won't you desert me the moment you have separated me from my husband? With Batricio all was simple truth.

DON JUAN: Come! Give me your hand and confirm your pledge to me.

ARMINTA: You're not deceiving me?

DON JUAN: To deceive you would be to deceive myself.

ARMINTA: Then swear that you will carry out your promise.

DON JUAN: By your white hand: I swear.

ARMINTA: Call on God to damn you if you are untrue.

DON JUAN: If I do not keep my word, let God send a man to ensnare and kill me. [*Aside.*] A dead man, of course. God forbid he should be alive.

ARMINTA: With this oath, I am your wife.

DON JUAN: My soul is yours.

ARMINTA: Yours are my soul and my life.

DON JUAN: Arminta, light of my eyes, tomorrow your beautiful feet will slip into polished silver slippers with buttons of the purest gold. And your alabaster throat will be imprisoned in beautiful necklaces; on your fingers, rings set with amethysts will shine like stars, and from your ears will dangle oriental pearls.

ARMINTA: I am yours.

DON JUAN [*Aside.*]: Little you know the playboy of Seville!
[*Exeunt.*]

Scene 2

Near Tarragona. Enter DUCHESS ISABELA *and* FABIO, *her companion.*

FABIO: Isabela, what good is sadness? It is true that love is a deceiver; he attacks those who were laughing at him; and presently they weep.

His gifts are torment, fear, suffering, and scorn. And when you left Naples, your suffering was understandable. But now you can exchange grief for joy. A new day is breaking for you. You lost Octavio, but Don Juan awaits you to take your beautiful hand, and your happiness will not be long delayed. Hold back your tears and your complaints—his house is one of the best of Castile.

ISABELA: I do not grieve because I am to marry Don Juan. The whole world knows his rank. What I weep, and must weep forever, is my lost reputation, the tale of which has spread wherever I go.

FABIO: Soon you'll be in his arms, tenderly entwined, like the ivy and the elm.

ISABELA: Even in my bridal bed I will remember my honor lost and my reputation ruined.

FABIO: Isabela, look at that fishergirl. She is sitting on a rock, gazing at the sea, crying softly and addressing her complaints to the sky. Listen! She is asking for vengeance; she is mourning the loss of something precious, and of hope. I'll ask her to keep you company while I look after the rest of our escort. Tell her your griefs. Take ease together with sweet laments.

[He leaves.]

ISABELA: A traitor robbed me of my beloved master and my dearest treasure. Oh bitter night, mask of the sun and mask of truth!

[Enter TISBEA.]

TISBEA: Violent Spanish sea—torrents of water and flying waves, carrying to the coast now innocent shells, now bitter deceit. You know my lament, for you bore my miseries. I cry into your deaf ears. You destroyed my honor—the honor of Tisbea, known for her cruelty to men!

ISABELA: Beautiful fishermaid, why do you complain so bitterly of the sea?

TISBEA: It nursed my ruin. You who are fortunate can look on it and smile.

ISABELA: I, too, weep because of the sea.

TISBEA: Why? Has a ravisher forced you with him across it, like a second Europa?

ISABELA: They are taking me to Seville to be married against my wishes.

TISBEA: Then you will understand my plight and pity my tears. Listen. The waters washed ashore a man named Don Juan Tenorio; victim of a shipwreck, and dying. I nursed him back to health and made him a guest in my house. But the guest turned viper in my nest, lied to me, deceived me, gave me his pledge of marriage, and with sweet false words robbed me of my honor, and left me after enjoying me.

ISABELA: Enough! Cursed woman! Out of my sight! Oh, you have killed me. No, wait, if it was grief that moved you, you are not to blame. Continue. Is it all true?

TISBEA: True as life and death.

ISABELA: Evil strike the woman who believes the words of a man! It was God who brought me to this hut. You have revived my determination to seek revenge. Evil strike the woman who believes the words of a man!

TISBEA: I beg you to take me with you, my lady, and my poor old father as well. He wants to ask the King for justice and satisfaction. And Anfriso, the man I should have married and loved forever, and who wants me even now, let him come with us too.

ISABELA: You may all come with me.

TISBEA: Evil strike the woman who believes the words of a man!

[*Exeunt.*]

Scene 3

Inside a church in Seville. Enter DON JUAN *and* CATALINÓN.

CATALINÓN: Everything is going wrong.

DON JUAN: Why?

CATALINÓN: Octavio has found out about the matter in Italy. The Marquis is complaining to the King that you fooled him with a false message from his cousin and that you borrowed his cape to ruin him. They say that Isabela is coming over to be your wife. They say—

DON JUAN [*cuffing him*]: Enough!

CATALINÓN: You broke one of my teeth!

DON JUAN: Tattler! Who told you all this nonsense?

CATALINÓN: Nonsense?

DON JUAN: Yes, nonsense.

CATALINÓN: It's all true.

DON JUAN: I don't care. Let Octavio try to kill me. Am I dead? Don't I have two good hands? Come, where did you find us a room?

CATALINÓN: In a secluded street.

DON JUAN: Fine.

CATALINÓN: Meantime this church can be your sanctuary.

DON JUAN: Why don't you tell me next they'll kill me here in broad daylight? Come—did you see the bridegroom of Dos Hermanas?

CATALINÓN: Yes. Full of anguish, too.

DON JUAN: Arminta won't discover our hoax for two weeks.

CATALINÓN: She is so blind to it that she calls herself Doña Arminta.

DON JUAN: This is going to be delicious.

CATALINÓN: Of course. But she'll cry for it.

[*They see the tomb of Don Gonzalo de Ulloa.*]

DON JUAN: Whose tomb is this?

CATALINÓN: Don Gonzalo's.

DON JUAN: The man I killed! Quite a tomb!

CATALINÓN: That's how the King ordered it. What does the inscription say?

DON JUAN [*reading*]: "Here the most loyal of knights expects God's vengeance on a traitor." [*He laughs. To the Statue*] So you want vengeance, old boy, stone-beard!

[DON JUAN *pulls the Statue's beard.*]

CATALINÓN: You can't pluck it—he has a powerful beard.

DON JUAN [*to the Statue*]: Join me tonight for supper at my inn. We can fight it out there and then, if you're still hungry for vengeance. Of course, I can't promise you a good scuffle if you carry a stone sword in your hand.

CATALINÓN: Well, if he's coming to dine with us, let's go order a meal.

DON JUAN [*to the Statue*]: You've been waiting a long time for this vengeance. If you still want it, you'd better wake from your sleep. Or are you waiting for me to die? If you are, give up hoping, because I've plenty of time till then, plenty of time.

[*Exeunt* DON JUAN *and* CATALINÓN.]

Scene 4

An inn in Seville. Enter two SERVANTS. *They set a table.*

FIRST SERVANT: Let's prepare supper. Don Juan should be coming soon.

SECOND SERVANT: The table is ready. But what made him order an early supper? He usually comes in at dawn.

FIRST SERVANT: I suppose he wants more time for his gallivanting tonight.

[*Enter* DON JUAN *and* CATALINÓN.]

DON JUAN [*to Catalinón*]: Did you lock the door?

CATALINÓN: Just as you ordered.

DON JUAN [*to the Servants*]: Quick! Fetch my dinner!

SECOND SERVANT: It is here already.

DON JUAN: Catalinón, sit down!

CATALINÓN: I really prefer to eat alone.

DON JUAN: I told you: sit down.

CATALINÓN: I am sitting.

FIRST SERVANT [*Aside.*]: He must think he's on the road, to eat with his valet.

[*A knock.*]

CATALINÓN: Quite a knock!

DON JUAN: See who's at the door.

FIRST SERVANT: I'll open.

CATALINÓN: It could be the constables, master.

DON JUAN: Let them come; no reason to worry.

[*The* FIRST SERVANT *runs back in fright.*]

FIRST SERVANT: My God, what I've seen!

DON JUAN [*to First Servant*]: Speak, what happened? What did you see?

CATALINÓN: He looks a little scared.

DON JUAN: Did you see a devil or what? I'm getting angry.

[*More knocks.*]

CATALINÓN: They're knocking again!

DON JUAN [*to Catalinón*]: You'd better go see who it is.

CATALINÓN: Who? Me?

DON JUAN: Yes, you. Move!

CATALINÓN: Listen, master. My grandmother was found hanging like a bunch of grapes—and since then they say she wanders over the earth like a soul in pain. That's why I don't like all this knocking.

DON JUAN: Enough!

CATALINÓN: Master, you know I am a coward.

DON JUAN: The door!

CATALINÓN: I'm sick.

DON JUAN: Still standing?

CATALINÓN: Who has the keys?

SECOND SERVANT: The door is only bolted.

DON JUAN: What's wrong? Why don't you go?

CATALINÓN: This marks the end of Catalinón. The seduced women have come to take their revenge on the two of us.

[CATALINÓN *goes to the door and comes running back.*]

DON JUAN: What now?

CATALINÓN: God help me! They're killing me; they caught me!

DON JUAN: Who's caught you? And who's killing you? What did you see?

CATALINÓN: Master, when I . . . got there . . . I saw . . . I ran back . . .

Who grabbed me? Who pulled me? I arrived . . . I was blinded
. . . When I saw him . . . I swear to God! He spoke and said, "Who
are you? . . ." he answered . . . and I answered . . . and then . . . I
ran into and saw . . .

DON JUAN: Saw what?

CATALINÓN: I don't know.

DON JUAN: Is this what wine does to you? Give me the light, chicken,
and I'll see for myself.

[DON JUAN *takes the candle and moves toward the door. The* STATUE
OF DON GONZALO *comes to meet him.* DON JUAN *falls back, dismayed,
his hand on his sword. Slowly, the* STATUE *comes closer to* DON JUAN,
*who retreats until the two are standing face to face at the center of
the stage.*]

DON JUAN: Who are you?

THE STATUE: It is I.

DON JUAN: Who?

THE STATUE: The man you invited to dinner.

DON JUAN: To dinner, then! And if you brought friends they'll find
plenty to eat too. The table is set. Sit down.

CATALINÓN: Angels protect me!

DON JUAN: Catalinón, sit next to the dead man.

CATALINÓN: I already had supper. You go ahead with your guest. I
don't think I can eat a thing just now.

DON JUAN: You're a fool. Are you afraid of a dead man? What would
you do if he were alive? Base and stupid fear!

CATALINÓN: I am really bloated.

DON JUAN: I'll get angry, watch out!

CATALINÓN: Excuse me, sir, but I smell bad.

DON JUAN: Sit down! I'm waiting for you.

CATALINÓN: I can't. My—uh—posterior has died on me.

DON JUAN [*to the Servants*]: And you fools, why do you stand there
trembling?

CATALINÓN: I never liked to eat with foreigners. And now you force
me to eat with a guest made out of stone.

DON JUAN: What can a man of stone do to you?

CATALINÓN: Break my head, for instance.

DON JUAN: Why don't you speak to him? Politely, now.

CATALINÓN [*to the Statue*]: How are you? Are you well lodged—in the
great beyond? Does it have many mountains or is it flat? Do they appreciate poetry there?

FIRST SERVANT: He nods to everything.

CATALINÓN: Are there many taverns? There must be, if Noah lives there.

DON JUAN [to the Servants]: You there, something to drink!

CATALINÓN: Sir Dead Man, in this country of yours, do they mix their drinks with ice? [The STATUE nods.] With ice. Good country.

DON JUAN [to the Statue]: If you'd like some singing, they'll sing. [The STATUE nods.]

SECOND SERVANT: He said yes!

DON JUAN: Sing!

CATALINÓN: Sir Deadly has good taste. He is a nobleman, and fond of merriment.

[Singing within.]

> Lady, take me as I am,
>   A man of rich desires.
> Youth is mine, and I shall live
>   To light a thousand fires.

CATALINÓN: This Sir Corpse isn't eating much. It's either the summer weather or simply that he is a man with a small appetite. I can't keep my hands from shaking. They must drink little over there—but I'll drink for two. [He drinks.] A toast to stone! By God, I feel better already.

[Singing within.]

> Lady, take me as I am,
>   A man of rich desires.
> Youth is mine, and I shall live
>   To light a thousand fires.
>
> Do not speak of death to me,
>   Lady, I shall never learn.
> Life is long, my credit sound,
>   I must love before I burn.

CATALINON: Which one of your seduced ladies are they singing about, master?

DON JUAN: Tonight I laugh at them all. Back in Naples, Isabela—

CATALINÓN: That one isn't really cheated now, master, since she is to be your wife, as is right. But you cheated the fishergirl who saved you from the sea, and paid her with counterfeit coin for her hospitality. Next you seduced Doña Ana—

DON JUAN: Quiet! Here's her would-be avenger who suffered for her.

CATALINÓN: Of course, he is a very brave man. And he is made of stone, and you of flesh and blood. Not a pleasant situation.

[*The* STATUE *signals that it wants to be alone with* DON JUAN.]

DON JUAN: You two, clear the table! He wants to remain alone with me.

CATALINÓN: Bad sign! Don't stay with him. Dead people can often kill a giant with a single bite.

DON JUAN: Out, all of you! I'm not Catalinón! Go, he is coming closer to me.

[*Exeunt* SERVANTS *and* CATALINÓN.]

DON JUAN: The door is shut. I'm waiting. What do you want, oh shadow, phantom, or vision? If you walk in torment or if you are seeking satisfaction, tell me, and I give you my word that I shall do whatever you command. Do you enjoy God's grace, or is your soul damned? Did I kill you in a state of mortal sin? Speak, I am anxious to hear you.

THE STATUE [*speaking slowly as if from another world*]: Will you keep your word as a gentleman?

DON JUAN: I am a man of honor and I keep my word.

THE STATUE: Give me your hand, then. Don't be afraid.

DON JUAN: What? I afraid? Were you Hell itself, I would give you my hand.

THE STATUE: I have your hand and your word. I shall look for you to-morrow night. I will offer you supper at ten o'clock. Will you come?

DON JUAN: I expected something more challenging. Tomorrow I'll be your guest. Where do we meet?

THE STATUE: In my chapel.

DON JUAN: Shall I come alone?

THE STATUE: No, both of you come. But keep your word as I have kept mine.

DON JUAN: I will keep it. I am a Tenorio.

THE STATUE: And I, Ulloa.

DON JUAN: I shan't fail.

THE STATUE: I believe you. Adieu.

[*It moves toward the door.*]

DON JUAN: Wait, I'll give you a light.

THE STATUE: I need no light. I am in grace.

[*The* STATUE *leaves very slowly, watching* DON JUAN. DON JUAN *remains alone and shaken.*]

DON JUAN: God help me! My body is soaked with sweat and my heart is frozen in my body. When he took my hand, he burnt it with a hellish heat unlike any living warmth. And as he spoke, his breath blew like an infernal wind. Pah! I must be imagining all this: fear of the dead is the basest of all fears. If I don't cower before the noblest men alive, powerful men, reasonable and endowed with souls, why should I tremble before a dead body? Tomorrow I shall be his guest in the chapel. All Seville will be terrified and astounded by my courage. [*Exit* DON JUAN.]

Scene 5

A room in the Alcázar in Seville. Enter the KING OF CASTILE *and* DON DIEGO TENORIO.

KING OF CASTILE: Has Isabela arrived?

DON DIEGO: Yes, but dissatisfied.

KING OF CASTILE: Isn't she happy about this marriage?

DON DIEGO: Her reputation is ruined.

KING OF CASTILE: But her anguish stems from something else, surely. Where is she?

DON DIEGO: At the convent of the Carmelites.

KING OF CASTILE: Let her leave the convent at once. I want her here at the palace. She will wait on the Queen.

DON DIEGO: If she is to marry Don Juan, Your Highness should command his presence at court.

KING OF CASTILE: Let him come. I want the news of their marriage to be spread to the whole world. Tomorrow Don Juan will be Count of Lebrija. He will own it and rule it. Isabela loved and lost a duke but gained a count.

DON DIEGO: We all acknowledge your bounty.

KING OF CASTILE: I owe you so many favors that even with this I remain behind in my payments. Don Diego, what do you think of marrying Doña Ana today as well?

DON DIEGO: To Octavio?

KING OF CASTILE: No, Duke Octavio cannot be the one to undo the wrong. Doña Ana has pleaded with me by intermediary of the Queen to forgive the Marquis. Now that her father is dead she wants a husband. In the Marquis she will find both a husband and a father. Don Diego, go quietly with a few people to speak with him at the Fortress of Triana, and inform him that I pardon him for the welfare and security of his cousin.

DON DIEGO: Again, I see my wishes fulfilled.

KING OF CASTILE: You can tell him they will be married tonight.

DON DIEGO: All ends well. It will be easy to persuade the Marquis—he is devoted to his cousin.

KING OF CASTILE: You should also inform Octavio. The Duke has no luck with women. Poor man, they are only interested in appearances and talk. By the way, I hear that he is very angry with your son.

DON DIEGO: I daresay he found out that he owes his misfortunes to Don Juan. Look—here he is.

KING OF CASTILE: Don't leave my side. Your son's crime touches you too. [*Enter* OCTAVIO.]

OCTAVIO: Unconquerable King, allow me to kiss your feet.

KING OF CASTILE: Rise, Duke, and cover your head. What is your wish?

OCTAVIO: I have come to kneel at your feet with a just suit, worthy of being granted.

KING OF CASTILE: Duke, if it is just, I give you my word: it will be granted. Speak!

OCTAVIO: My lord, you have learned by letters from your Ambassador, and the rumor has reached everyone, that one night in Naples—an evil night for me—Don Juan Tenorio used my name with Spanish arrogance to violate the honor of a lady.

KING OF CASTILE: Enough! I know your disgrace. What is it exactly you want?

OCTAVIO: Permission to prove him a traitor in the field.

DON DIEGO: You will not! His blood is noble—

KING OF CASTILE: Don Diego!

DON DIEGO: My lord.

OCTAVIO: Who are you to speak like this to the King?

DON DIEGO: One who keeps silent at the King's command. Or I would answer you with this sword.

OCTAVIO: You're old.

DON DIEGO: In Italy I was young once—as you Italians found out to your sorrow. My sword was familiar to Naples and Milan.

OCTAVIO: But now your blood is frozen. *Is* is what matters, not *was*.

DON DIEGO: I *was* and I *am*.

KING OF CASTILE: Stop! Enough! Be still, Don Diego! You are showing little respect for my person. And you, Duke Octavio, you will be able to speak at your leisure after the weddings. Don Juan is a gentleman of my house, and of my making, and [*pointing to* DON DIEGO] he is a branch of that venerable trunk. Respect him as such.

OCTAVIO: My lord, I will do as you say.

KING OF CASTILE: Follow me, Don Diego.

DON DIEGO [*Aside.*]: Oh, my son! How poorly you have repaid the love I have given you.*

[*Exeunt* KING OF CASTILE *and* DON DIEGO.]

OCTAVIO: Is there a man as wretched as I in this world? I trusted in a treacherous friend. I was accused in his place by Isabela because she had lost her dearest jewel, her reputation. But if the King will not avenge her, I, Octavio, will.

[*Enter* GACENO *and* ARMINTA.]

GACENO: This gentleman will tell us where to find Don Juan Tenorio. [*To Octavio*] Sir, could you tell us where to find a Don Juan whose name, I am sure, is well known at court?

OCTAVIO: I suppose you mean Don Juan Tenorio?

ARMINTA: Yes, that's the one.

OCTAVIO: He is here. Do you want to see him?

ARMINTA: I do. He is my husband.

OCTAVIO: What?

ARMINTA: You haven't heard about it here at the Alcázar?

OCTAVIO: Don Juan hasn't said anything to me.

GACENO: Is that possible?

OCTAVIO: I assure you.

GACENO: Doña Arminta is an honorable woman. We are an old family, Christian to the bones. Besides, she is the sole heir to our farm, better than a count or a marquis. Don Juan promised to marry her, and took her away from Batricio.

ARMINTA: Tell him I was a virgin when Don Juan took me.

GACENO: That's beside the point.

OCTAVIO [*Aside.*]: Here is another of Don Juan's pranks. And I'll be able to use what they've told me for my vengeance. [*Aloud.*] What can I do for you?

GACENO: Well, the days are going by, and I would like the ceremony to be performed. If not, I'll take the matter to the King.

OCTAVIO: Your demands are just.

GACENO: Also reasonable and lawful.

OCTAVIO [*Aside.*]: This couldn't have fallen out better! [*Aloud.*] A wedding is being prepared in the Alcázar just now.

---

*Three lines are omitted here, in which the King promises Octavio that his marriage will take place tomorrow. As Ana has been promised to the Marquis, and Isabela to Don Juan, either the King is soothing Octavio with a regal lie, or—more likely—Tirso slipped. [*Translator's note.*]

ARMINTA: Maybe it's mine!

OCTAVIO [*Aside.*]: A little stratagem is called for at this point. [*Aloud.*] Come, my lady. You shall be dressed as befits a lady of the court, and then I myself shall lead you into the King's apartment.

ARMINTA: And take me by the hand to Don Juan, too.

OCTAVIO: A cunning idea.

GACENO: I like your plan, sir.

OCTAVIO [*Aside.*]: With these two, my revenge is set. Isabela, you shall be satisfied.

[*Exeunt all.*]

Scene 6

The Fortress of Triana. Enter DON DIEGO TENORIO *and* MARQUIS DE LA MOTA.

DON DIEGO [*to a Guard*]: Release the Marquis.

MARQUIS: If I am going to my death, I wish to thank you.

DON DIEGO: The King has ordered your release.

MARQUIS: Does he know my innocence? Has he recognized the man who is really guilty—and whose name I refrain from speaking for your sake?

DON DIEGO: For my sake! First you kill your uncle and then you blame me!

MARQUIS: I blame you for accusing me. Your son killed him. I gave Don Juan my cape. False villain! I was about to die for nothing.

DON DIEGO: What are you saying?

MARQUIS: Nothing but the truth. Don Juan took a message from my cousin, addressed to me. It was an invitation—to enjoy her at eleven o'clock that night. But the villain told me midnight, and at eleven he entered her room in my place. I mourn for my uncle, but oh, the greater misery is that Don Juan took my cousin from me, and held her in his arms!

[*Exeunt.*]

Scene 7

Before the church. Enter DON JUAN *and* CATALINÓN.

CATALINÓN: How did the King receive you?

DON JUAN: More affectionately than my father.

CATALINÓN: Did you see Isabela?

Don Juan: Yes.

Catalinón: How is she?

Don Juan: Like an angel.

Catalinón: Did she receive you well?

Don Juan: She turned pale, and then she blushed—like a rose bursting out of its petals at dawn.

Catalinón: Is the wedding set for tonight?

Don Juan: Without fail.

Catalinón: Had you married before, master, you wouldn't have had time to seduce so many women. As it is, you're taking a wife with troubles on all sides.

Don Juan: Again talking like a fool?

Catalinón: Why can't you get married tomorrow? Today is a bad day.

Don Juan: Why?

Catalinón: It's Tuesday.*

Don Juan: Fool. The only bad day for me is when I'm short of cash. Everything else is nonsense.

Catalinón: Come sir, you have to get dressed. It's late and they'll be waiting for you.

Don Juan: First we have another business to settle.

Catalinón: Like what?

Don Juan: Dining with the dead man.

Catalinón: Folly of all follies!

Don Juan: I gave my word.

Catalinón: What if you break it! I don't see what recourse a man of stone has.

Don Juan: He could slander me.

Catalinón: The church is closed anyway.

Don Juan: Knock.

Catalinón: I don't see why. Who's going to open? The sacristans are asleep.

Don Juan: Knock at this little door.

Catalinón: It's open!

Don Juan: Well, go in.

Catalinón: Let a monk sprinkle the place first with holy water.

Don Juan: Be quiet and follow me.

Catalinón: I should be quiet?

*Tuesdays and Fridays were considered bad days for traveling or getting married. [Translator's note.]

DON JUAN: Yes.

CATALINÓN: God deliver me from these dinners.

[*They enter through a door.*]

CATALINÓN: How dark the church is and yet so large! Oh God! Master, hold me, somebody is pulling me by the cape!

[*Enter the* STATUE OF DON GONZALO.]

DON JUAN: Who is there?

THE STATUE: It is I.

CATALINÓN: Now I'm done for.

THE STATUE: I am the dead man; don't be afraid. I did not think you would keep your word, Don Juan—since you make a joke of everything.

DON JUAN: You consider me a coward?

THE STATUE: Yes, I do, for on a certain night you fled after killing me.

DON JUAN: Only because I didn't want to be recognized. But now I am here. What do you want?

THE STATUE: I want to invite you to supper.

CATALINÓN: You must excuse us. We have no taste for cold dishes, and I don't even see a kitchen.

DON JUAN: I accept.

THE STATUE: But first you must lift the lid of this tomb.

DON JUAN: I will lift these pillars too, if you like.

THE STATUE: You are very brave.

DON JUAN: I'm full of life and strength.

CATALINÓN: A black table! Don't you have anyone to wash it?

THE STATUE: Sit down.

DON JUAN: Where?

CATALINÓN: Here come two black servants with stools.

[*Enter two Figures in black carrying stools. They set the table.*]

THE STATUE [*to Catalinón*]: Sit down, too.

CATALINÓN: Excuse me, sir, I have already eaten. Dine with your guest.

DON JUAN: Stop your chatter.

CATALINÓN: I stop. God, help me out of this broil. What kind of dish is this?

THE STATUE: Vipers and scorpions.

CATALINÓN: Such delicacies!

THE STATUE: These are our specialties. [*To Don Juan*] Aren't you eating?

DON JUAN: I would eat if you fed me all the vipers of hell.

CATALINÓN: What kind of wine do you drink in the hereafter?

THE STATUE: Try some!

CATALINÓN: Pah! Gall and vinegar!

THE STATUE: Such is the wine from our cellars. Now listen to a song.

VOICES: Fool, think not that Heaven
                             Can forget a crime.
                       God exacts full payment
                             In his own due time.
                       There shall no sinner boast,
                             While mocking God's command,
                       "Life is long, there's time to pay."
                             Sinner, judgment is at hand!

CATALINÓN: A foul song, by Jesus! Did you hear it, master? It was meant for you.

DON JUAN: My blood is freezing up.

CATALINÓN: Try a little of this ragout.

DON JUAN: I have eaten. Tell them to take away the table.

THE STATUE: Give me your hand. Never fear; give me your hand.

DON JUAN: Fear? Take it! . . . Ai, I'm burning alive! Burning, burning!

THE STATUE: This is little compared to the fire you were looking for. The wonders of God, Don Juan, are unfathomable. His justice demands that a dead man exact the payment of your crimes. As a man sows, so shall he reap.

DON JUAN: I'm burning, let my hand go! [DON JUAN *draws his dagger with his free hand.*] I'll stab you to death. . . . Useless! I'm stabbing the empty air!

THE STATUE: Don Juan! You are paying for the women you cheated.

DON JUAN: I didn't harm your daughter! She saw the hoax in time.

THE STATUE: No matter! Your intention condemns you.

DON JUAN: Let me send for a priest at least; I want to confess and be absolved!

THE STATUE: It cannot be. You thought of that too late.

DON JUAN: I'm burning, burning! I'm dying!

[DON JUAN *dies.*]

CATALINÓN: No escaping. I see I'm going to die too for following you about.

THE STATUE: This is the justice of God. As a man sows, so shall he reap.

[*A great noise. The tomb sinks with* DON JUAN *and* STATUE OF DON GONZALO. CATALINÓN *crawls on the ground.*]

CATALINÓN: God in heaven! What's happening? The whole chapel is burning; and I'm left here for the wake. If I can crawl out of here I'll tell his father. Saint George, Saint Agnus Dei, get me out into the street alive!

Scene 8

A room in the Alcázar in Seville. Enter KING OF CASTILE, DON DIEGO, *and courtiers.*

DON DIEGO: My lord, the Marquis wishes to kiss your royal feet.

KING OF CASTILE: Let him come in, and go notify Don Juan that he need wait no longer.

[*Enter* BATRICIO *and* GACENO.]

BATRICIO: My lord, why are such enormities allowed? Your own servants outrage the poor people of the land.

KING OF CASTILE: What are you saying?

BATRICIO: Don Juan Tenorio, detestable traitor that he is, stole my wife from me the night of my marriage, before its consummation. I have brought witnesses with me.

[*Enter* TISBEA *and* ISABELA.]

TISBEA: If Your Highness does not bring Don Juan to justice, I will complain to God and to men as long as I live. The sea cast him adrift; I gave him life and hospitality; and to reward my kindness he lied to me with the name of husband.

KING OF CASTILE: What are you saying?

ISABELA: She is telling the truth.

[*Enter* ARMINTA *and* OCTAVIO.]

ARMINTA: Where is my husband?

KING OF CASTILE: Whom do you mean?

ARMINTA: Don't you know? My husband is Don Juan Tenorio. I am here to be married to him. So he swore to me. He is a nobleman and cannot forswear. My lord, give orders for my wedding.

[*Enter* MARQUIS DE LA MOTA.]

MARQUIS: It is time, my lord, to bring the truth to light. Know that Don Juan Tenorio is guilty of the crime imputed to me. Though he was my friend, he brutally deceived me. I have two witnesses to bear me out.

KING OF CASTILE: Is this shamelessness possible? Don Juan must be arrested and executed.

DON DIEGO: Yes, let him be arrested and punished. I ask it as a reward for my services to the crown, lest heaven punish me for the wickedness of my son.

KING OF CASTILE: This is how my favorites behave!

[*Enter* CATALINÓN.]

CATALINÓN: Gentlemen, listen to the strangest event the world has ever witnessed. Listen! and kill me afterward if you wish. Don Juan was mocking the statue of the Commander the day before yesterday. To insult the dead man, he pulled the Statue's beard and invited him to supper. Fool that he was! The Statue came, and returned the invitation. We went to the church, and there, when supper was over, after a thousand horrible signs, the Statue grasped his hand and squeezed it till he died, and said, "God commands me to kill you thus in punishment for your crimes. As a man sows, so shall he reap."

KING OF CASTILE: What are you saying?

CATALINÓN: It's the truth. And before he died, my master cried out that he had not touched Doña Ana's honor, because she recognized him in time.

MARQUIS: I could kiss you for this news!

KING OF CASTILE: Heaven is just! Now then, Don Juan is dead; there is no impediment to a marriage between Isabela and Duke Octavio.

OCTAVIO: I receive her with gratitude, my lord, now that she is a widow.

MARQUIS: And I shall marry my cousin.

BATRICIO: And we'll marry our own girls in order to bring the true story of the guest of stone to an end.

KING OF CASTILE: And let the tomb be carried to the church of St. Francis in Madrid where it will be revered as it deserves.

Don Juan in Italy, France, and England (1625-1676)

The *Commedia dell' Arte;* Dorimon and Villiers

The Kingdom of Naples, in which Tirso placed the opening scenes of *El Burlador de Sevilla,* had been ruled by the Spaniards since 1435. We are not surprised, therefore, to hear of a performance of his play, or a play based on his, in Naples in 1625 and 1626, probably in Spanish.[1] It is known, too, that the actor Roque de Figueroa, who had originally played Tirso's Burlador, was repeating the work in Naples in 1636–1637. But Don Juan did not stay confined to Spanish territory for very long. In 1641 an Italian poetaster refers to the *Convitato di pietra* as a "vulgarissima tragedia," that is to say an extremely popular tragedy. Two specific Italian plays are spoken of in the 1650's: one, lost, by a certain Onofrio Giliberto, and another which appeared under the name of Jacinto Andrea Cicognini, though it has since been shown not to be his work.[2]

The pseudo-Cicognini is clearly derived from Tirso's play, which it conscientiously eviscerates. As will happen in many later versions, the part of the servant has been magnified to overshadow that of Don Juan. Passarino, the successor to Catalinón, is going to miss the macaroni of Naples when he is in Seville, and farts for a jest: such is the humor in this play. Still, flat as it is, it has a few bright inventions (or are they inventions?) which will be used again and again in later versions: the Tisbea sings of the joys of rustic life—a probable source for the Pilgrim's meditation; Passarino is a glutton; Passarino throws the list of his master's women at the audience; Don Juan tests Passarino to see

---

1. J. G. Fucilla, "El Convidado de Piedra in Naples in 1625," *Bulletin of the Comediantes,* X (Spring 1958), 5–6.

2. By Benedetto Croce in his *Aneddoti di varia letteratura* (Naples: 1943), vol. II Croce modestly but decisively confirms a correction made in 1668 by a friend of the deceased Cicognini but either unnoticed or unheeded by later scholars.

whether the latter would betray him to the police and discovers that indeed he would; Don Juan reflects on the vanity of those who build large monuments for their bones; and Passarino cries out for his wages after the devils have swallowed his master.

Benedetto Croce has argued for the close relationship between the pseudo-Cicognini and *commedia dell' arte* farces dealing with the same subject. For Don Juan had found his true home, not in the formal Italian theatre, but among the wandering actors who gave to the Western world the masked and motley figures of Arlecchino (Harlequin), Columbina, Il Capitano, Il Dottore, Pantalone, Pulcinello, and a confetti-spray of others—characters developed from generous hints in Roman comedy, but who, like Hans Wurst in Germany, Arlequin in France, Hans Pickelheering in Holland, and Punch in England, adapted themselves so genially to every country that they seemed everywhere to be immemorial native figures.

The term *commedia dell' arte* was given to this popular yet consummately professional drama in the eighteenth century, when the art was in fact dying out. These tightly-knit companies had begun to be active in the middle of the sixteenth century, setting up their trestles, stretching their curtain, tuning up their guitars, and beating their drums in every city and village of the Italian peninsula. We might look upon this theatre as, in a sense, the Italian people's answer to the revivals or imitations of Seneca, Plautus, and Terence, the courtly pastorals and the mythological pageants with which the upper classes and the high clergy, with their retinue of scholars, entertained themselves throughout the sixteenth century.

The small *commedia dell' arte* companies—typically they consisted of seven male and three female comedians—specialized, naturally enough, in broad comedy. Even when they drew upon tragic subjects, they turned them into farces dominated by the antics (or *lazzi*, as they were called) of Arlecchino. No wonder, then, that in their versions of our tale and in the puppet plays which these in turn spawned all over Europe, the character of Don Juan recedes, making way for his servant Arlecchino and, of course, the Statue of the Commander.[3]

So profuse are the contemporary records and illustrations for the

3. Several Don Juan farces have survived among the hundreds of scenarios still extant. In one of these, preserved in the Biblioteca Nazionale of Naples, Tirso's play is improved in several places. Most notably, the character of the Marquis disappears and his place is taken by Octavio himself, who is thus tricked for the second time by Don Juan. The scenario is printed in E. Petraccone (ed.), *La Commedia dell' arte* (Naples: 1927).

commedia wherever it traveled, and so numerous are the modern accounts, that it would be idle to add yet another. Here, instead, is a vivacious description by Philippe Monnier, written in *The Mask* of January 1911:

. . . They had only to receive a scenario which someone had scribbled on his knee, to meet the stage manager in the morning to arrange the outlines of the plot, and to hang the paper within easy reach of the wings; the rest they could invent themselves. Familiarity with the stage and their profession and their art had taught them a whole bundle of tricks and quips. They had a store of proverbs, sallies, charades, riddles, recitations, cock-and-bull stories, and songs jumbled together in their heads. They knew all sorts of metaphors, similes, repetitions, antitheses, cacophonies, hyperboles, tropes, and pleasant figures; and besides they had a volume of tirades, which they had learnt by heart, of soliloquies, exclamations of despair, sallies, conceits of happy love, or jealousy, or prayer, or contempt, or friendship, or admiration, always on the tips of their tongues, ready to utter when they were out of breath. They raised their scaffolding high into the air, and then gave themselves up to their own fertile genius and their amazing caprice. . . . They seized opportunity by the forelock and turned the least accident to profit. They drew inspiration from the time, the place, the color of the sky, or the topic of the day, and established a current between their audience and themselves out of which the mad farce arose, the joint product of them all. It varied at each representation, seemed different every evening, with all the spirit and warmth and alertness of spontaneous creation, a brilliant ephemeral creature born of the moment and for the moment.

The pieces went with the speed of lightning and the noise of Pandemonium. The house was consumed with shrieks of laughter, like the tumult of a whirlwind. It was all lover's intrigue, complicated by disguises, kidnappings, unexpected returns, impersonations and supposititious infants. Retorts, misunderstandings, character-sketches, jests, caricatures, blows, and kicks were their stock in trade. They groped about in the dark and ran into one another and fell down. They mutilated words. They put out their tongues, rolled their eyes, made grimaces. They boxed their ears with their feet. They sang songs and recited, and poured forth proverbs, quotations, precedents. There were scenes of tumult and uproar and inexpressible confusion, in which they were knocked down and got up again, supporting themselves as they could, tripped each other up, got in each other's way, and ran off in the midst of the clatter.

They passed the word around, for instance, to make Pantaloon believe that his breath smelt. Pantaloon blows his horn from the window to proclaim the opening of the chase. Gratiano appears holding a cock, Burattino with a monkey on a chain, and a child on the back of a bear is leading a lion. Harlequin, armed with a blacksmith's tools, draws four of Pantaloon's soundest teeth. He waits on Don Juan at table and wipes the plates on the seat of his breeches before he hands them, or produces his cap, full of cherries, from the same place, and cracks the stones with his teeth and pretends to spit them on the ground. He keeps hissing some tune through his lips or pursues a fly in the air and catches it. He counts his coat-buttons, saying, "She loves me, she loves me not, she loves me." There is only one plate of macaroni between three of them, and they eat it in floods of tears. . . . Dreams were grafted on mistakes, marvels on absurdities. Pirouettes, repartees, music, dances, jests, acrobatic feats, grimaces and dumb-show, pantomime and drama, peals of laughter and peals of thunder followed in quick succession.[4]

Partly because none of the companies maintained a resident playwright or a professional poet, they failed to produce a Shakespeare or a Molière or even a Goldoni. They could and did influence these men (American audiences for which the Piccolo Teatro di Milano performed a few Goldoni plays in 1960 will not soon forget these sophisticated reworkings of *commedia* farces), and they influenced countless writers and composers down to our own day; but they were too successful ever to feel the need for more "literary" material. Perhaps we can add a deeper reason for their failure: by the seventeenth century it was too late for an Italy which had surrendered itself to foreign powers and the calculated rigors of the Counter Reformation to bring forth a great literature.

In this period Italians were exporting themselves, with their thousand and one skills, in a human movement which resembles the diffusion of Greek intellectuals in the Roman Empire and of German intellectuals under Hitler. The *commedia dell' arte* companies were part of an amazing tide of statesmen, scientists, musicians, painters, architects, and impresarios who were finding employment in nations more powerful than their own. And indeed our comedians were welcomed (except by the pious) wherever they went. Already in the late sixteenth century they were playing in Bavaria, Austria, Spain, France, even England; and both at home and abroad they appear no longer only as tatterdemalion vagabonds but often as respected, admired, sometimes adulated court entertainers. While some of them continue to caper before the audience of the market place, others are embraced by kings, princes, and prelates, weary at last of pastoral artifice or of the bookish plays served up by grammarians. Among the players were men and women of the highest intellectual, moral, and physical caliber; and the best companies, playing as part of the festivities for a royal progress, a marriage, a victory,

4. Quoted by Sheldon Cheney, *The Theatre* (London: Longmans, Green, 1929), pp. 233–234.

and sometimes granted a "permanent" theatre to perform in, combined the topical, the salacious, and the lyrical veins with a delicacy and a brio designed to appeal to the most refined tastes.

In 1653, when the Italian Cardinal Mazarin was ruling France during the minority of Louis XIV, a company of Italian players was installed at the theatre of the Petit-Bourbon. Paris by then had known the *commedia* for some seventy or eighty years, and this troupe, like the others, performed in its own language without any inconvenience to the public, which knew how to interpret a pratfall when it saw one. The players at the Petit-Bourbon are of prime interest to us because in 1658 they gave the first known performance in Paris of a Don Juan play—their own version of the old *Convitato di pietra*. Their success with the play was prodigious, and soon a couple of French companies complimented them— and cashed in on the play's popularity—with imitations.

Just at this time, as it happened, the Italians were required to make room at the Petit-Bourbon for Molière's company, newly returned from a twelve-year tour of the provinces. Since the foreigners played on Sundays, Tuesdays, and Fridays, and Molière's company on the other days, there is no mystery about the manner in which Molière became acquainted with the Don Juan story—if, indeed, he had not read or seen versions of it at an earlier date. Luckily, part of the scenario of the Italian play has been preserved. It consists of notes by and for Biancolelli, the actor who impersonated Arlecchino after 1662. As the scenarios were used over and over, there is no doubt that this one represents substantially the farce which Parisians—and surely Molière—saw in 1658. The little piece is an amusing hodgepodge of slapstick, indecencies, and irrelevancies, and it seems to have given Molière a few bad ideas. Here is a humorous sample: "While my master is at table, I tell him that I served a doctor who told me that a certain dish is hard to digest. He gives it to me; I eat it hungrily; he refers to what the doctor told me; I reply that the dish is what is hard to digest; not what is in it." Arlecchino throws the long scroll of women's names into the audience, inviting the gentlemen to read and see whether one of their relations is listed there.

The French imitations were more serious, partly because they derived from the pseudo-Cicognini and probably Giliberto, partly because the *commedia*'s light touch was inimitable. The playwrights were Dorimon and Villiers (or de Villiers)—their first names are unknown—obscure actors and poetasters who survive only as sources for Molière. But so low had Don Juan fallen in the estimate of polite society that even a self-acknowledged hack like Villiers approached his task with fastidious disgust. His fellow actors at the Hôtel de Bourgogne, he wrote in his Dedication to Corneille, had demanded the play of him "in the belief that the ignorant, who are far more numerous than those who understand the theatre, would take a greater pleasure in the figure of Dom Pierre [the Commander] on his horse than in the verse or the management of the play." Their company, he continued, had been *reduced* to treating this subject; he had written it only to make money for them. He was painfully aware of the irregularity of the play, which violated every rule of classical decorum, and he gladly disclaimed any originality, stressing—perhaps in all honesty, perhaps to save his reputation—that he had but translated from the Italian.

Actually, the Dorimon play is not without interest. In this version Don Juan is rather softhearted. His misdeeds are all given to us by report out of the past. His murder of the Commander is unpremeditated, and he is generally courteous. Furthermore, the hero begins to reason. In a remarkable soliloquy, Don Juan decides to meet the Statue because he has seen everything else on earth—Les Esprits fors, les Grands, les Scavans, et la Guerre—and now divine curiosity leads him to desire an interview with the dead (V, 7). It is a curious anticipation of the Faustian element which Romantic writers were to infuse in the Don Juan matter.

In both Dorimon's and Villiers' plays, a new episode occurs: Don Juan meets a Pilgrim, or a Hermit, and forces him to exchange clothes. When Octavio arrives looking for his enemy, Don Juan, disguised as the holy man, easily disarms and kills him. No one knows the origin of this highly effective scene, but an almost identical episode takes place in an *Ateista fulminato* discovered not long ago, but unfortunately not dated.[5]

The Villiers and Dorimon plays bear identical titles: *Le Festin de Pierre ou le fils criminel (Peter's Banquet or the Criminal Son)*. The subtitle is sensational rather than accurate: Don Juan merely strikes his father, who later dies of grief. As for the main title, it results from a

5. This is an interesting *commedia dell' arte* scenario, which might have influenced the Don Juan plays—unless it was itself influenced by them. The little play also has an avenging Statue which carries the bandit-hero to Hell. Thomas Shadwell, who was to write his own Don Juan (see p. 167), claimed in his Preface of 1676 that a "worthy gentleman" had informed him that the *Ateista fulminato* had been performed on Sundays for many a year in Italian churches. But Shadwell had not read it or seen it; and despite the similarities, two of which I have mentioned, the play is not even a Don Juan analogue. Discovered and first printed by Simone-Brouwer, the scenario has been reprinted in Petraccone's book, cited in note 3 *supra*.

mistranslation of the Italian *pietra,* meaning *stone.* Perhaps Dorimon (whose play came first) had read it *pietro* in his haste, and not caring much one way or the other decided that the Commander's name must be Peter. This bit of slovenliness speaks volumes for the contempt into which the whole subject had fallen. Neither Villiers nor Molière noticed, or felt like noticing, Dorimon's error.

Along with the pseudo-Cicognini, Molière, and the *commedia dell' arte* farces, the plays of Dorimon and Villiers provided the materials for scores of popular plays, puppet plays, vaudevilles, and operas, when Tirso's original had become nothing but a title to be mentioned in a preface or glimpsed in a catalogue.

I reproduce three scenes from the Dorimon and Villiers plays. In the first of them—Act III, Scene 5 of the Villiers—Don Philippe is in pursuit of Don Juan, who has seduced his bride and killed her father. Don Juan has disguised himself as a pilgrim.

DON JUAN: No one will recognize me in these clothes. But isn't that Don Philippe I see? Yes, it's my enemy.

DON PHILIPPE: I see a pilgrim. My friend, could you show me the way?

DON JUAN: Where do you want to go? [*Aside.*] Here I am without a sword; my wishes are foiled. I'll disguise my voice as best I can.

DON PHILIPPE: You're a pilgrim?

DON JUAN: Yes, thanks to the kindly gods.

DON PHILIPPE: Do you always live here?

DON JUAN: Usually.

DON PHILIPPE: You don't travel?

DON JUAN: I do when I've nothing else to do.

DON PHILIPPE: You're ill at ease, running about and staying in one place!

DON JUAN: I seek rest when I'm tired of roaming.

DON PHILIPPE: Do you see people sometimes? Hermits are allowed visitors, I believe.

DON JUAN: They are.

DON PHILIPPE: Have you by any chance come across a young man of about—

DON JUAN: No, on my conscience.

DON PHILIPPE: I haven't finished; be patient; a young man of about my carriage, my appearance; and his complexion—

DON JUAN: No, sir.

DON PHILIPPE: Do let me speak!

DON JUAN: I'm not stopping you, but I haven't seen anyone. [*Aside.*] I mustn't say too much, or he may suspect me.

DON PHILIPPE: What! Shall I be always pursuing, and never find the criminal whom my ill fortune shields from punishment? What! The tears of a daughter and the death of a father shall remain unavenged? Ye gods, do not allow the murderer to escape death. I owe this victim to my dear Amaryllis.

DON JUAN: You might find news of him in town.

DON PHILIPPE: The traitor has just left it; but let him be sure that I'll be avenged before the day is over.

DON JUAN: You know that the gods forbid vengeance. To obtain their help one must supplicate them with due humility.

DON PHILIPPE: I do supplicate them, and with all my soul. Great gods, if you deliver the blackguard into my hands—

DON JUAN: Sir, forgive me for interrupting you, but you are too violent, and the indecency of your prayers undoubtedly shocks the gods. They must be addressed humbly, and never with arms at one's side. Remove them.

DON PHILIPPE: Willingly, and I declare that I will pour out my blood, and never hold a sword again, if I am not avenged. Give me, great gods—

DON JUAN: Madman, you came this way to murder a man, but look at me and see who I am: I am the very Don Juan you're pursuing up and down the countryside. I disguised myself only to seize this sword, and would dispatch you this instant if something didn't move me to postpone—

DON PHILIPPE: Assassin, traitor, blackguard, what! I've found you and cannot kill you? Villain, parricide, impudent seducer, with my bare hands—

DON JUAN: This is too much eloquence; go find your father-in-law in Hell. [*Kills him.*]

DON PHILIPPE: Help, friends, help, I'm dead! Adorable Amaryllis, alas, weep over me.

The second scene, also from Villiers (IV, 5), finds Don Juan and his servant Philipin on the shore, having just escaped drowning in a shipwreck. Don Juan has sworn to mend his ways, but even as he is spelling out his good intentions, two charming girls, Oriana and Belinda, come on the scene.

DON JUAN: Yes, my dear Philipin, I'm resolved, and shall henceforth require this of myself.

PHILIPIN: Require what?

DON JUAN: To detest vice, run from violence, and abhor injustice; if Beauty itself dared appear this minute before my penitent heart, you would see— you would see whether I can be tempted—ye gods! What beauties are these?

PHILIPIN: Sir, remember—

DON JUAN: Hold your tongue. What are the jewels of the land doing here?

ORIANA: Good God, let's leave this place.

DON JUAN: Stay!

BELINDA: Are you offering violence to us?

PHILIPIN: Have you forgotten your repentance?

DON JUAN: No, but I want to satisfy my curiosity.

ORIANA: Our time is limited, sir, and we must return to the village.

DON JUAN: Oh, how easily a heart is lost when it is unexpectedly struck by so much beauty.

BELINDA: Is that all, sir? These are idle tales. Come, Oriana.

PHILIPIN: Sir, the sailors, the reefs, the shipwreck?

DON JUAN [to Oriana]: Yours are the loveliest eyes I have ever seen.

PHILIPIN: The winds—

DON JUAN [to Belinda]: Oh how yours pierce the soul!

PHILIPIN: The tempest—

DON JUAN [to Oriana]: Your waist is the most charming in the world.

PHILIPIN: The thunders—

DON JUAN [to Belinda]: I can't resist you.

PHILIPIN: The elements—

DON JUAN: Shut your mouth and be damned!

ORIANA: Do you need so many of us, sir?

DON JUAN: Another word. Adorable creatures—

PHILIPIN: So this is the fear of God, to worship the devils?

DON JUAN: This is too much. One more insolent word and your last hour has struck.

BELINDA: To conclude, sir, what did you wish to tell us?

DON JUAN: That you must end my torment, be favorable to me, and repay my love this very day.

ORIANA: Great gods, what do I hear?

BELINDA: Heaven, come to our help!

ORIANA [calling her sweetheart]: Evander!

BELINDA [the same]: Dear Damon!

ORIANA: Father, help! Never will I yield to you!

PHILIPIN [Aside]: You'll have to be mighty clever. [Aloud]: Good grief! Sir!

DON JUAN: What now?

PHILIPIN: I hear a noise.

DON JUAN: Are you running away, cruel girls? But you must satisfy my lust.

[Exeunt. Presumably Don Juan succeeds in raping Belinda.]

And finally, here is the Statue scene from Dorimon's version (IV, 8). Don Juan and his servant—here called Briguelle—have just read the inscription on the Statue's base.

BRIGUELLE: I must tell you that I find this epitaph frightening. It's aimed straight at us.

DON JUAN: Well, if I have to die, this sword of mine will do for others as well.

BRIGUELLE: Sir! the statue struck me with a wink.

DON JUAN: Since you're frightened, I'll smash it for you.

BRIGUELLE: You're ill-tempered. Why trouble the dead in their graves?

DON JUAN: At least I'll raze the inscription. Spirit whose bones lie in the sepulchre, come and avenge yourself without delay.

BRIGUELLE: Spirit whose bones lie under this statue, stay where you are. I humbly beg you, virtuous ghost, not to believe my master, whose mind is wandering.

DON JUAN: These threats don't frighten me.

BRIGUELLE: You ought to thank him, sir. If he wanted to rise out of this monument, he'd frighten you to death.

DON JUAN: Weakling and coward, when the soul has withdrawn from the body, do you think it cares about, or even remembers, the flesh it lived in once?

BRIGUELLE: But you killed this dead man and he wants vengeance.

DON JUAN: Do you suppose he'll rise up against me? This corpse is too dead ever to return. Those who believe otherwise are ignorant fools.

BRIGUELLE: I don't understand all this philosophy, sir, but I'm afraid of ghosts and don't trust them.

DON JUAN: Well, if he is really capable of re-entering his body and of conversing with the living, ask him to be good enough to sup with me tomorrow.

BRIGUELLE: Me? Have the courage? I'll do nothing of the kind; you can ask him yourself. Heavens! Did you ever see the likes of him?

DON JUAN: Go ask him.

BRIGUELLE: Ha!

DON JUAN: Do as I say.

BRIGUELLE: Not if you knocked me down or killed me.

DON JUAN: Do it, or I'll bury you with him.

BRIGUELLE: If you mean it, I'm a dead man.

DON JUAN: Stop arguing and do my bidding.

BRIGUELLE: But—

DON JUAN: No more buts.

BRIGUELLE: Well, if I must. [*To the Statue*]: Ghost, Spirit, Statue, Ornament of the dead, in a word, whoever you are—*I* don't know you—I know that alive you were a gentleman—but I believe that you are now Spirit and Ghost—but, amiable Spirit and spotless Ghost, I have come to ask you—but you won't do it—on behalf of my master, who esteems you and who, whatever he may say, regrets his crime—to share a very bad meal with him. [*The Statue nods.*] Ah, sir!

DON JUAN: What's the matter?

BRIGUELLE: I'm frightened.

DON JUAN: Why?

BRIGUELLE: Didn't you see it? Don't pretend.

DON JUAN: What? What didn't I see?

BRIGUELLE: The statue—

DON JUAN: Well?

BRIGUELLE: Replied with a nod of the head, and this means it will come to our house.

DON JUAN: How amusing! You're so scared that you can't see straight.

BRIGUELLE: Well, go look for yourself whether it's an illusion.

DON JUAN: I will—not to encourage you in your extravagance, but to dare the shade in its grave. Shade, I conjure you.

[*The Statue nods again.*]

BRIGUELLE: Again!

DON JUAN: Yes, come, I'll expect you. This is a novelty. Well, I'm glad. Follow me, Briguelle, follow me.

BRIGUELLE: I'm no longer scared, and I'm reasonable again—how could he come without knowing where we live?[6]

In sum, neither the Dorimon nor the Villiers lacks ideas (though we never can tell how original they are, inasmuch as the Giliberto and probably a few scenarios are lost to us); but in the original French their style is for the most part so insipid, their versification so stiff, their tone so flat, that they can serve only to put into relief the brilliance of the master who rewrote the play.

Molière and *Dom Juan ou Le Festin de Pierre*

Few of the episodes which Molière threw into his *Dom Juan* are entirely of his own invention. Furthermore, the play is an anarchy of unrelated scenes, false anticipations, loose ends, and unexplained matters. What are we to say? The versions of Villiers, Dorimon, and the pseudo-Cicognini hang together yet they are anemic; Molière's would be laughed out of a graduate class in playwriting, but it is a masterpiece. It has vitality, its prose is forceful, its dialogue is superbly intelligent, and its humor thrusts home.

The play's history is as checkered as its structure. *Dom Juan* stands between two giants, *Tartuffe* (1664) and *Le Misanthrope* (1666), and the three together—all onslaughts on hypocrisy—may be called the dark plays of Molière's comic career. From the moment *Tartuffe* appeared on the stage, it brought down on its proprietor's head libels, interdictions, hatreds, and intrigues against which he fought for five years—

6. The scenes from Dorimon and Villiers are translated by the editor from G. Gendarme de Bévotte (ed.), *Le Festin de Pierre avant Molière* (Paris: Connely et Cie., 1907).

attaching Louis XIV himself to his side—to partial victory. *Dom Juan* shows Molière's preoccupation not only with the theme of hypocrisy but also with the accusations of freethinking often made against him —as, for example, that he was a monster who deserved burning on earth before tasting the fires of hell. There were, it must be confessed, some grounds for these accusations, for this son of the bourgeoisie who might have succeeded his father, the estimable M. Poquelin, in the post of Upholsterer to the King, had thumbed his nose at the cozy title, had adopted the name of Molière (no one knows why), joined a company of actors of dubious morality, organized performances in Paris, and landed in jail as a bankrupt. Bailed out by his father, Molière had vanished into the provinces with his band of players, not to be seen again in Paris for twelve years. His early activities might have been dismissed as the indiscretions of youth, but since his return to Paris his plays, if not subversive, had been at least satirical enough to awaken alert consciences. Molière became known as a *libertin*—an Epicurean and a skeptic. He consorted with persons of the scantest piety, and it was rumored that the young actress in his company whom he had married was his natural daughter. Worst of all, he was outrageously popular—no blasphemer muttering in a corner, but an infidel in a position to seduce a city. And so when the hue-and-cry against *Tartuffe* began, it may be said that the attack had already been five years in the mounting.

Modern scholars have made the most of the figure of Molière as a Rebel. But we must beware of daubing over our favorite authors with the ideals of our own time. Molière was as faithful a servant of the king as the next man, and the next man in this case was anybody. In Molière's day Louis XIV was young, happy, and loved; he had made himself the orb around which the whole nation and much of Europe revolved. With unfailing courtesy and patience, and with the assurance of divine power, he invoked the services of artists as earnestly as those of generals and ministers. In exchange he gave money, encouragement, compliments, jobs, and protection. He was, I should say, a perfect patron of the arts: a man who read no books himself (he preferred dancing), but who appreciated those who wrote them. We do not like to admit into our field of vision the spectacle of art—especially literature, its most dangerous form—thriving under a dictatorship; but if we ask which authors of the Grand Siècle were creating works of genius underground, which men of letters were compelled to flee to express themselves, the answer is—none at all. It is true that French writers were allowed no political, religious, or metaphysical audacities; but then in the seventeenth century it had not yet been decided that the artist has a sacred mission, that he is prophet to the nation at large, the voice chosen to disclose the deepest truth to his blind fellow citizens. Undeniably, there was much Molière would have added to, or altered, in his plays had he lived in a democracy. Though his works do not record them, we can be sure that free conversations took place at certain intimate reunions over a companionable bottle of wine; and he strove long and hard to obtain the repeal of the ban placed on *Tartuffe*. But meantime he continued to entertain the king and the people; he was glad to accept pensions, honored to have Louis as a godfather to his first son, and not above wangling interdictions against his rivals. Nor did he hesitate to tone down *Tartuffe* ("to compromise his integrity," as we would say) in order to see it on the boards once more. As the head of the Troupe de Monsieur, the company patronized by the king's only brother, as a favorite both *à la cour et à la ville,* and even as a pure intellectual, Molière was willing to make compromises. Granted, then, he and his contemporaries were less than perfectly honest in their art—there were no Célines and Sartres under Louis XIV; but if compromise can beget the works of Corneille, Molière, Racine, La Fontaine, Boileau (to name only a handful among dozens), what use, we may dare wonder, is integrity?

Dom Juan was exhibited fifteen times at the Palais-Royal, the theatre to which Molière's company had moved in 1661. But coming as it did nine months after *Tartuffe* had been prohibited, the new play only made more trouble for the embattled Molière. After the first performance he was forced to suppress the scene with the beggar (III, 2) and to soften other passages. But this failed to appease his opponents, the pious faction which, besides pursuing skeptics like Molière, campaigned unceasingly against the stage itself. "Who can endure," wrote a pamphleteer, "the boldness of a clown [Molière] who makes a joke of religion, who preaches libertinism, and who makes the majesty of God fair game on stage for a master and a servant—for an atheist who laughs at it, and for a servant, even more impious than his master, who makes the audience laugh at it?" Whether Molière felt that *Dom Juan* was not worth a fight, or whether he decided he could not sustain his counteroffensive on two fronts, we have no way of knowing; but he took the king's benevolent advice (and a pension with it), withdrew the play, and never saw it thereafter either in print or on stage. In 1674 Dutch booksellers printed Dorimon's version as his. In 1682, nine years after Molière's death, a badly censored but genuine text appeared in France. Before then

The arrival of the Stone Guest *(Dom Juan ou Le Festin de Pierre,* Act IV, Scene 8). Frontispiece after P. Brissart engraved by J. Sauvé for a 1682 edition of the works of Molière.

Thomas Corneille (younger brother of the illustrious Pierre) had written an inoffensive, rhymed *Festin de Pierre* (1677) in a kind of collaboration with the dead man, and this version held the stage until the nineteenth century. But a 1683 Dutch edition of the uncensored play was eventually discovered, and in 1841 the real *Dom Juan* was restored to the theatre at last.

The obvious haste and negligence with which Molière composed his play suggest that he too wanted his share of the profits which Don Juan commanded at the box office. He had no particular interest in the type of the seducer or the professional ladies' man. When he explored promiscuity at all, it was that of women, not of men. Does not his Don Juan anticipate the Célimène of *Le Misanthrope?* But if he does, what pretext was there for consigning him to eternal damnation? Dorimon and Villiers had solved this problem by adding the crime of parricide —or indirect parricide—to his seductions. But Molière had reasons for keeping his hero relatively clean. Besides rejecting parricide, he omitted the murder of the Octavio type and in fact reversed the situation, so that we see Don Juan saving the life of the character who most nearly resembles Octavio. Moreover, having eliminated Anna altogether, he could not even provide Don Juan with the basic murder, that of the girl's infuriated father. A Commander is mentioned in the play, but we do not know who he is or why Don Juan killed him; we are told only that he was killed in accordance with the laws of dueling, long before the play's opening action. When the Statue finally appears, neither we nor Molière can say exactly why it is there.

The only conclusion possible is that Molière did not *want* to damn Don Juan. That, of course, was no crime in itself; but what was an audience to think when this noble rogue, for whom the playwright seemed to be making excuses, turned out to be an arrant and vocal atheist? Molière's Don Juan is unforgettably the man who believes that "two plus two equals four, and four plus four equals eight," a statement Cartesian in its impeccable clarity, but revolutionary in its omissions. Was Molière writing an open defense of atheism?

So it seemed to his enemies; and so it seems to us. But Molière must have thought otherwise, for while he patted his hero with one hand, he was careful to slap him with the other. In the opening scene Sganarelle calls Don Juan "un grand seigneur méchant homme"; and certainly he is cynical, frivolous, and unreliable throughout the play. He cruelly mistreats Elvire, taunts and hoodwinks his father (whom he wishes in his grave), and fools an honest if simple-minded creditor. However, the case to be made in his favor is even stronger. No one in the play is capable of refuting his skepticism; he behaves honorably toward Elvire's brother; he has the last and significant word in the encounter with the beggar; and he plainly speaks for Molière on the question of medicine. Even his hypocrisy represents as much an attack on the society which almost exacts this vice as a criticism of Don Juan himself; and it is worth remembering that Byron considered turning *his* hero into a Methodist for the same reason.

It is an error to seek to unify the play. Its ambiguity was intended. In all his other dramatic pieces except *Le Misanthrope*,[1] Molière provided the audience with a totally reliable character who carries the point of view; but in *Dom Juan* no such character appears. Molière was using the play to toss off a number of his pet ideas—on medicine, honor, hypocrisy, religious disputation, even on tobacco—but he dodged responsibility by making Don Juan here his mouthpiece (perhaps) and there his butt (perhaps).

The impression he finally gives—or gives to one reader, for the critics are sorely divided on this singular play—is that he would have used Don Juan as the spokesman for his own radicalism as frankly as Byron was to do, had he but dared. But he knew that the king would not protect him beyond a given point and therefore remained irresolute, pushing with his opinions and pulling with his fears. This leaves us with a remarkable human document, in which the raw, unresolved struggle between individual free thought and official decency is, for once, caught and immortalized in the work itself rather than in private letters or notebooks. Unverifiable as my hypothesis is, it has at least the merits of being consonant with what we know of Molière and of accounting for the play's philosophical come-and-go.

Dom Juan is so much a play about irreligion that it almost forgets to be a play about sex. Anna is missing; there are no abductions (only a thwarted attempt, dramatically worthless, to carry off a girl from a boat); no irruptions into a lady's bedroom; no interrupted weddings. But taking a hint from Tirso's Isabela—there is some evidence that he knew *El Burlador*—Molière tried to raise the character of Elvire to a tragic pitch, though he seems to have confused rhetoric with true emotion. For the rest, the play is full of sudden and fugitive beauties. Its disorganization is almost as attractive as that of *Tristram Shandy*

1. I have discussed the similar ambiguity of this play in "Molière and Turgenev: The Literature of No-Judgment," *Comparative Literature*, XI (Summer 1959), 233–249.

and Byron's *Don Juan*. I wish it had been far longer rather than much more coherent, for the sketches and the hints tantalize. The famous scene with the beggar vanishes before one has done questioning it. The touch of Don Juan's aroused lust on hearing the prayers of Elvire beckons and is lost. Fortunately, we do have in full a few scenes on which Molière imprinted his whole genius—the episodes concerning Pierrot, Charlotte, and Mathurine. They are quite the best painting in this genre after *A Midsummer Night's Dream*. Molière rescued the noble rustics of the previous versions from literary convention and introduced them to humanity with a comic tenderness which no writer has ever surpassed.

MOLIÈRE

Don John; or, The Libertine

A Comedy

(1665)

Translated by John Ozell,
revised and augmented by Oscar Mandel

EDITOR'S NOTE

John Ozell's English version of *Dom Juan, ou Le Festin de Pierre* was first printed in 1714. Without having anything like the genius of Dryden to bring to his translations, Ozell had one resource denied even to the best modern translator (and who has done Molière justice?)— namely the English language of 1700, not only most suitable for Molière, but strong, flexible, pure, and elegant in itself. I did not hesitate to prefer his version to any of those which have followed, even though Ozell knew only the mutilated text. In the present text the gaps are filled with as little trace of repair work as possible, and a number of lapses are, I hope, corrected. Where eighteenth-century printing style might inconvenience the reader I have modernized Ozell's text, but chiefly with respect to punctuation, paragraphing, and to such typographical features as italicized proper names and place names. For the most part the original spelling has been retained, and in other details the text follows the 1714 edition.

TEXTS

The Works of Monsieur Molière, vol. VI. London: Lintot, 1714.
Molière, *Oeuvres*, vol. V. Edited by Despois and Mesnard. Paris: 1912.

DRAMATIS PERSONAE

Men

Don Louis, *Father to Don John*
Don John, *his Son*
Don Carlos, ⎫
Don Alonso, ⎭ *Brothers to Elvira*
The Statue of the Governor
Francisco, *a poor Man*
Mr. Sunday, *a Tradesman*
Sganarelle, *Servant to Don John*
Pierrot, *a Countryman*
Gusman, *Usher to Elvira*
Violette, ⎫
Ragotin, ⎭ *Lacquies to Don John*
Ramee, *a Hector*
A Pauper*
Don John's Followers
Don Carlos' and Don Alonso's Followers
A Ghost

Women

Donna Elvira, *Wife to Don John*
Charlotta, ⎫
Mathurina, ⎭ *Countrywomen*

Scene *lyes in Sicily.*

*This character did not appear in the version followed by Ozell. [*Editor's note.*]

119

ACT I

Scene 1

Sganarelle, Gusman

SGANARELLE [*with a Tobacco-Box in his Hand*]: Let Aristotle and all the Philosophers in the World say what they will, nothing is like Tobacco; 'tis the Darling of all Men of Honour, and he that lives without Tobacco is not worthy of Life. It not only gladdens and purges Man's Brain, but it likewise puts him in the way to Virtue, and one learns with it to become an honest Man. Don't you see that as soon as ever one takes it, with what an obliging Manner one uses everybody, and how glad one is to give it on all sides, be one where he will? We don't so much as stay till 'tis ask'd for, but prevent People's wishes; so true it is that Tobacco inspires all those that take it with Sentiments of Generosity and Virtue. But enough of this; let's resume the Thread of our Discourse. So your Mistress, dear Gusman, Donna Elvira, surprised at our Departure, set out after us; and her Heart, which my Master has pierced too deeply, cannot live, you say, without coming hither to him? Shall I give you my Opinion? I'm afraid that she'll be but ill rewarded for her Love; and that her Journey to this City will produce but little Fruit. You'd as good ha' stay'd at home.

GUSMAN: And pray, Sganarelle, tell me, what can inspire you with such an ill Augury? Has your Master open'd his Heart to you upon that Subject, and has he told you that some Coldness for her made him leave us?

SGANARELLE: No; but by what I see I can guess how things are, and tho' he has not yet told me anything, I could lay a Wager that there the Shoe pinches. Perhaps I may be deceived, but yet in such cases Experience has given me some knowledge.

GUSMAN: What! Could this sudden Departure proceed from Don John's Infidelity? Could he so far abuse Elvira's chaste Flame?

SGANARELLE: No, but he is young and fears—

GUSMAN: Could a Man of his Quality do so base an Action?

SGANARELLE: His Quality! A fine Reason truly! Why 'tis not that will prevent him.

GUSMAN: But the sacred Tyes of Marriage engage him.

SGANARELLE: Ah! Friend Gusman, you're but little acquainted with Don John, I see.

GUSMAN: 'Tis true, I am not, if he be so perfidious to us; and I can't imagine how after so much Love and Impatience, so many pressing Homages, Vows, Sighs, Tears, so many passionate Letters, burning Protestations, reiterated Oaths; so many Transports, and so much Warmth as he testify'd, even to force the sacred Obstacle of a Nunnery to put Donna Elvira in his Power; I say, I can't imagine how, after all this, he can have the Heart to break his Word.

SGANARELLE: I don't find it so difficult to imagine; and if you knew the Spark thoroughly, you'd think it no such hard thing. I don't say he has changed his Sentiments for Donna Elvira, I am not yet sure on't. You know I set out before him by his Order, and since his Arrival he has not yet talk'd to me, but by way of forewarning I must tell you (under the Rose) that you behold in my Master, Don John, the greatest Libertine that the Earth ever bore, a Madman, a Dog, a Devil, a Turk, an Heretick, that believes neither Heaven nor Hell, nor Devil; who lives like a downright Brute-Beast, one of Epicurus' Swine, a true Sardanapalus, that stops his Ears to every Christian Remonstrance that can be made to him, and esteems all we believe as idle Trash. You tell me he has marry'd your Mistress; he'd ha' done more to ha' satisfy'd his Passion, and besides her would have marry'd you, her Cat, and her Dog. A Marriage don't cost him much, it is his accustom'd Snare to entrap the fair Sex; and he's a Marryer at all Adventures; Damsel, Gentlewoman, Citizen's Wife, Country-lass, nothing's too hot or too cold for him; and if I were to tell you the Names of all those he has marry'd in several Places, 'twould be a Chapter that would last till Night.

You are surprised and change Colour at what I tell you; yet this is only a Sketch of him; and there's need of other strokes of the Pencil to finish his Picture. 'Tis enough to tell you that Heav'n must needs overwhelm him some Day or other, that I had better belong to the Devil than to him, and that he makes me Witness of so many Horrors that I could wish he were I know not where. But a wicked Lord is a terrible thing; I must be faithful to him in spite of my Teeth*; Fear performs in me the Duty of Zeal, bridles my Thoughts, and often obliges me to applaud what in my Heart I detest.

Here, he's coming to walk in the Palace; let's part. I have told you

*In spite of myself. [Editor's note.]

all this freely, and it came a little hastily out o' my Mouth; but if ever any on't comes to his Hearing, I'll promise you I shall be so free as to tell you you lye in your Throat.

Scene 2

Don John, Sganarelle

DON JOHN: What Man was that? He look'd like Donna Elvira's Gusman.

SGANARELLE: Something like him, indeed.

DON JOHN: What! Was't he?

SGANARELLE: He himself.

DON JOHN: How long has he been in this City?

SGANARELLE: Ever since yesterday Evening.

DON JOHN: What brings him hither?

SGANARELLE: I believe you may guess what disturbs him.

DON JOHN: Our Departure, I suppose.

SGANARELLE: The good Man is sadly mortify'd with it, and ask'd me the Cause of't.

DON JOHN: And what Answer did you give?

SGANARELLE: I said you had not told me anything about it.

DON JOHN: But what do you think of it? What do you imagine about this Affair?

SGANARELLE: Why, I believe, without wronging you, there's some new Love in the Case.

DON JOHN: You believe it?

SGANARELLE: Yes.

DON JOHN: Faith, you're not deceiv'd; I must confess another Object has driven Elvira out of my Head.

SGANARELLE: O, Don John, I know at my Finger's Ends that your Heart is the greatest Wanderer in the World; it loves to ramble from Bonds to Bonds, and hates to stay long in a Place.

DON JOHN: And, tell me, do you not think I am in the right to do what I do?

SGANARELLE: Ha, Sir!

DON JOHN: Speak.

SGANARELLE: Yes, to be sure you're in the right. If you have a Mind to it, nobody can contradict it. But if you have not a Mind to't, it may be the Case is alter'd.

DON JOHN: Well, I give you leave to speak, and to tell me your Thoughts.

SGANARELLE: Why then, Sir, I must freely tell you I don't approve of your Method, and I think it a very ill thing to make Court to every-body, as you do.

DON JOHN: What! Wou'd you have me stick to the first Object that takes me, to renounce the World for that, and have no more Eyes for anybody? A fine thing indeed to pique oneself on a false Honour of being faithful, to bury oneself for ever in one Passion, and to be dead from one's very Youth to all other Beauties that may strike our Eyes. No, no, Constancy is fit for none but Fools, all the Fair Sex have a right to Charm us, and the Advantage of being first met with ought not to deprive the others of the just Pretensions they all have upon our Hearts. For my part, Beauty ravishes me wherever I meet with it; and I easily give way to the sweet Violence with which it hurries us along. Though I am engaged, my Love for one Belle does not engage me to do Injustice to all the rest; I have Eyes for the Merit of all, and render to every one the Homage and Tribute to which we're oblig'd by Nature. However it be, I can't refuse my Heart to any that I think amiable, and when a handsome Face de-mands it of me, if I had Ten Thousand I shou'd give 'em all. Rising Inclinations, after all, have inexpressible Charms, and all the Pleas-ure of Love lies in Variety. One tastes an extreme delight in reduc-ing by an hundred Contrivances the Heart of a young Beauty; to see the Progress we daily make in it; to combat by Transports, Sighs, and Tears the innocent Virtue of a Soul, which can hardly prevail with itself to yield; to demolish Inch by Inch all the little Resistances that oppose us; to vanquish the Scruples on which she prides herself, and to lead her gently whither we would have her go. But when one is once Master there is nothing further to be said nor wish'd for; all the Charms of the Passion are over, and we sleep in the Tranquility of such a Love unless some new Object come to awaken our Desires and present to our Heart the attracting Charms of another Conquest to undertake. In short, nothing is so sweet as to triumph over the Resistance of a beautiful Person; and in that I have the Ambition of Conquerors, who fly perpetually from Victory to Victory and can never prevail with themselves to put a bound to their Wishes. Noth-ing can restrain the Impetuosity of my Desires; I have an Heart for the whole Earth; and like Alexander, I cou'd wish for new Worlds wherein to extend my Amorous Conquests.

SGANARELLE: Body o' me, how you talk! One wou'd think you had learn't this by Heart; you speak like a Book.

DON JOHN: What have you to say to't!

SGANARELLE: Faith, I have to say—I don't know what I have to say; for you turn things in such a Manner that one wou'd believe you are right, and yet you are not. I had the finest Thoughts in the World, and your Discourse has put 'em all out o' my Head, but another time I'll write down my Arguments to dispute with you.

DON JOHN: Do so.

SGANARELLE: But, Sir, wou'd it be included in the Permission you have given me if I told you that I am a trifle scandaliz'd with the Life you lead?

DON JOHN: How! What Life do I lead?

SGANARELLE: A very good one. But to marry every Month as you do—

DON JOHN: Can there be anything more agreeable?

SGANARELLE: 'Tis true, I believe it may be very agreeable and very diverting; I myself cou'd swallow it if there were no harm in't. But, Sir, to make a Jest of a holy Sacrament, which—

DON JOHN: Come, come, 'tis a Question between Heaven and me, which we'll resolve without troubling your Head.

SGANARELLE: Faith, Sir, I've heard it said 'tis but a scurvy Jest to Jest with Heaven, and that Libertines never come to a good End.

DON JOHN: Have not I told you, Mr. Fool, that I did not love Remonstrances?

SGANARELLE: God forbid I shou'd say this to you, you best know what you have to do; and if you believe nothing, you have your Reasons for't; but there are some little impertinent People in the World who are unbelievers without knowing why, who pretend to be Freethinkers because they imagine it fits well upon 'em, and if I had such a Master I wou'd plainly say to him, looking in his Face: Are you bold enough to mock Heaven? Do you not tremble to scoff as you do against the most sacred things? It agrees mighty well for you indeed, little Worm, little Shrimp (I speak to the Master I mention'd), it agrees mighty well with you indeed to turn into Jest what other Men revere. Do you think that because you're a Man of Quality, have a fair well-curl'd Wig, a Feather in your Hat, a laced Suit of Cloaths and flame-colour'd Ribbans (I don't speak to you but to t'other), do you think, quo' I, that you're e'er the wiser, that everything's lawful for you to do, and that you are not to be put in your place? Know from me that am your Servant that Heaven sooner or later punishes the Impious, that a wicked Life leads to a wicked Death, that—

DON JOHN: Peace.

SGANARELLE: Why, what's to be done?

DON JOHN: I must tell you that a Beauty sticks in my Heart, and that attracted by her Charms I have follow'd her quite to this City.

SGANARELLE: And Sir, have you no Terror upon your Spirits for the Death of the Governor you kill'd here Six Months ago?

DON JOHN: Why Terror? Did not I kill him well?

SGANARELLE: Very well, extraordinary well; he has no Cause to complain on't.

DON JOHN: I have had my Pardon for this Affair.

SGANARELLE: Ay, but perhaps this Pardon don't extinguish the Resentment of Relations and Friends, and—

DON JOHN: Oh, don't let's think of the harm that may happen to us, but only of what may give us Pleasure. The Person I speak of is a young Gentlewoman (the most agreeable in the World) newly betroth'd, and brought hither by the Man that's to marry her. Chance shew'd me these two Lovers three or four Days before their Voyage. Never did I see two Persons so satisfy'd with one another, and shew so much Love. The visible Tenderness of their mutual Ardour disturb'd me; it struck me to the Heart, and my Love began by Jealousy. Yes, I cou'd not bear to see 'em so content together, Indignation allarm'd my Desires, and I thought it wou'd be an extreme Pleasure to spoil their Accord and break that Affection, the Delicacy whereof offended my Heart. But hitherto all my Endeavours have been in vain, and I now have recourse to the last Remedy. The intended Husband is today to take the air with his Mistress on the Sea. I have, without letting you know anything of the matter, already prepared everything to satisfy my Love, and I have a little Bark and Men ready, with whom I may very easily run away with the Fair One.

SGANARELLE: Ha! Sir—

DON JOHN: What!

SGANARELLE: You do very well; there's nothing like contenting oneself.

DON JOHN: Then be ready to go along with me, and take care to get all my Arms, that—[He perceives Donna Elvira.] O unhappy meeting! Traitor, you did not tell me that she herself was here.

SGANARELLE: Sir, you did not ask me.

DON JOHN: Sure she is mad not to change her Dress, but to come hither in her country Suit.

Scene 3

Donna Elvira, Don John, Sganarelle

DONNA ELVIRA: Will you do me the Favour, Don John, to recognize me? May I at least hope you'll turn your Face this way?

DON JOHN: Madam, I must confess I am surprised, and did not expect
you here.

DONNA ELVIRA: Yes, I see you did not expect me, and you are indeed
surpriz'd, but quite otherwise than I hoped for; and the manner of
your Surprise fully satisfies me in what I before refused to believe.
I marvel at my Simplicity and the Weakness of my Heart to doubt a
Treason which so many Appearances confirm'd me in. I confess I
was very good, or rather very foolish, to try to deceive myself and
contradict my Eyes and Judgment. I search'd for Reasons to excuse
to my Tenderness the Remissness of Friendship it perceived in you,
and I forged an hundred lawful Causes for so hasty a Departure, to
justify you from the Crime which my Reason accused you of. In vain
my just Suspicion daily advised me. I rejected its Voice, which represented you as criminal, and I listen'd with Pleasure to an hundred
ridiculous Chimeras which described you innocent to my Heart. But
now this Reception gives no further room for Doubt, and the Look
you receiv'd me with teaches me many more things than I wou'd
willingly know. Yet I shou'd be very glad to hear from your own
Mouth the Cause of your Departure. Pray speak, Don John, and let
me see with what Air you are able to justifie yourself.

DON JOHN: Madam, there's Sganarelle can tell you why I came away.

SGANARELLE: I, Sir? By your leave, I know nothing of the Matter.

DONNA ELVIRA: Well then, Sganarelle, speak; it don't signify from
whose Mouth I hear his Reasons.

DON JOHN [making Signs to Sganarelle to go nearer]: Come, speak to
the Lady.

SGANARELLE: What wou'd you have me say to her?

DONNA ELVIRA: Come nearer, since he'll have it so, and tell me the
Cause of so sudden a Journey.

DON JOHN: Why don't you answer?

SGANARELLE: I have nothing to answer; you are pleas'd to be merry
with your Servant.

DON JOHN: Will you answer, I say?

SGANARELLE: Madam—

DONNA ELVIRA: What?

SGANARELLE [turning to his Master]: Sir—

DON JOHN [threatening him]: If—

SGANARELLE: Madam, the Conquerors, Alexander, and the new Worlds
caused our Departure. This is all I can say, Sir.

DONNA ELVIRA: Pray do you, Don John, explain these fine Mysteries.

DON JOHN: Madam, to tell you the Truth—

DONNA ELVIRA: You a Courtier, accustom'd to these things, and defend yourself no better? I pity you to see you in this Confusion; why don't you arm yourself with a noble Impudence? Why don't you swear that you have still the same Sentiments for me, that you still love me with an unparallel'd Ardour, and that nothing can unbind you from me but Death? Why don't you tell me that Affairs of the utmost Consequence obliged you to depart without my Knowledge? That in spite of your Teeth you must remain here for some time, and that I may return from whence I came, assur'd that you'll follow my steps as soon as may be? That you burn to be at home, and that being absent from me you endure the Pains of a Body separated from its Soul? Thus you ought to defend yourself, and not be so Thunderstruck.

DON JOHN: I must confess, Madam, I have not the Talent of Dissimulation, and wear a sincere Heart. I won't tell you that I've still the same Sentiments for you, and that I burn to be with you, since 'tis certain I came away only to avoid you; not for the Reasons you imagine, but out of a pure Motive of Conscience, and because I did not think I could live with you any longer but in Sin. Scruples took me, Madam, and I open'd the Eyes of my Soul to what I was doing. I reflected that to marry you I had forced the Gate of a Convent, that you broke the Vows which engaged you elsewhere, and that Heav'n is very jealous of such Things. Repentance seiz'd me, and I fear'd the Wrath of Heav'n. I thought our Marriage was but a disguis'd Adultery, that it would bring some disgrace from above upon us, and that I ought to endeavour to forget you, and give you an Opportunity of returning to your former Obligations. Wou'd you oppose so holy a Design, Madam? I'd have Heaven upon my hands by keeping you; and—

DONNA ELVIRA: O impious Wretch, 'tis now that I know you thoroughly; and to my Misfortune I know you too late. Such a Knowledge can only serve to make me run mad. But your Crime shall not long remain unpunish'd; and the same Heav'n you mock will revenge me of your Perfidiousness.

DON JOHN: Heaven, Sganarelle!

SGANARELLE: Forsooth! We care not a straw for that, we two.

DON JOHN: Madam—

DONNA ELVIRA: 'Tis enough, I'll hear no more, and I am sorry I have heard so much. 'Tis a Meanness to hear one's Shame express'd too plain; and in such Cases a noble Heart should take its Resolution at the first Word. Don't expect that I'll break out into Reproaches and Abuses; no, no, my Wrath is not one that will exhale in vain Words; all its Heat is reserved for Revenge. I tell you again, Heav'n will punish you, perfidious Wretch, for this Deed; and if Heav'n has nothing in it that terrifies you, be at least afraid of an offended Woman.

SGANARELLE: If he should be touch'd with Remorse now!

DON JOHN [after a little Consideration]: Come, let's about our amorous Enterprize.

SGANARELLE: O what an abominable Master am I obliged to serve!

ACT II

Scene 1

Charlotta, Pierrot

CHARLOTTA: 'S Bodykins, Pierrot, yau ceame thither just i' th' nick.

PIERROT: Marry, they weare within eames eace of being drawn'd, boath of 'um.

CHARLOTTA: What, the high Wind that was i' th' Morning overturn'd 'um into th' Sea?

PIERROT: I'll tell it yau all, just as't fell out; for, as the saying is, I first spy'd 'um, 'twas mea that first spy'd 'um. I and fat Lucas was on the Sea shoar, and was amusing ourselves with throwing Clods of Yearth at one another's Heads; for you know, fat Lucas loves to be pleaying, and sometaimes I pleay too. Therefore as we were pleaying, for pleaying we was, I spy'd a huge weay off something that stirr'd in the Weater, and which ceame towards us, shake, shake. I look'd steadfastly on't, and all of a sudden I saw that I saw nought any longer. O Lucas, says I, I think I see two Men swimming dawn thear. Marry, says he, your Sight's dimm. 'Sdeath, says I, my Sight ben't dimm, they're Men. Not at all, say's he, you are purblind. Will you lay a Weager, says I, that I ben't purblind, says I, and that they be two Men, says I, that are swimming this weay, says I? 'Znigs, says he, I lay a Weager, no! Will you lay ten Pence, says I. With all my Heart, says he; and to sheaw yau, there's the Mony dawn, says he. I was neither Fool nor Dunce, I breavely throaws dawn four Pieces with Marks, and five Pence in Doubles; by th' Mass, as boldly as if I had drank oaff a Gleass of Wine; for I am ventersom and dash at a Venture. Yet I kneaw what I dud, to be sure. I had scant leay'd, but I saw the two Men pleain, who made a sign to us to goa fetch 'um, and I teakes up the Steakes. Come, Lucas, says I, you see theay call us; come quickly and help 'um. Noa, says he, they ha' made me lose. To cut shoart my Tale, I rattled soa that wea got into a Boat, and then we meade such ado that we got 'um out o' th' Weater, and then I carry'd 'um hoame to our House, before the Fire, and then they pull'd oaff all their Cloaths to dry 'umselves, and then two moare of the seame Gang ceame, who seaved 'umselves, and then Mathurina ceame, and he ogled her. This is all that was done, Charlotta.

CHARLOTTA: Did not yau tell me, Pierrot, that one of 'um is handsomer than the rest?

PIERROT: Yea, that's the Master; he is some great great Gentleman to be sure, for he has Gold upon his Cloaths from top to bottom, and those that serve'n are Gentlefolk themselves; and yet, as great a Mon as he is, by th' Mass, he'd been drawn'd if I had not come as I dud.

CHARLOTTA: Good lack!

PIERROT: 'Twas certainly so.

CHARLOTTA: Is he still naked at your House, Pierrot?

PIERROT: No, they dress'd 'umselves before us. Lord, I never beheld People dress themselves so in my born; the whim whams thoase Courtiers put on! I shou'd be confounded to do't, for my part, and I was ameaz'd to see't. Why, Charlotta, they had Heare which didn't grow to their Heads, and they put it on like a Cap. They have Shirts which have Sleeves as you and I might easily get into. Instead of Breeches, they wear a Wardrobe as big as from hence to Easter; instead of Doublets, they wear little tiny Wastecoats that doant reach dawn to their Arse; and instead of Cravats, great Neck-Handkerchiefs with four huge Tufts of Linnen which hang dawn o' their Breasts. They ha' other little Cravats too about their Arms, and great swathes o' lace at their Legs; and among all this, soa many Ribbans, soa many Ribbans, that 'tis a downraight pity. The very Shoas are stuff'd with 'um from one end to t'other, and they are meade in such a foarm that I shud break my Neck with 'um.

CHARLOTTA: Faith, Pierrot, I mun go sea this.

PIERROT: O steay a little, Charlotta, I ha' something to say t'ye.

CHARLOTTA: Well, what is't?

PIERROT: Do you see, Charlotta, as the saying is, I mun leay open my Heart to yau. I love ye, you know it, and we are to be marry'd; but by th' Mass, I e'nt satisfy'd with ye.

CHARLOTTA: Why, what's the matter?

PIERROT: The Matter is that you make me plaguy mad.

CHARLOTTA: How!

PIERROT: By th' Mass, you don't love me.

CHARLOTTA: O, is that all?

PIERROT: Yea, that's all, and enough too.

CHARLOTTA: Law, Pierrot, yau always tell ma the seame thing.

PIERROT: I always tell yau the seame thing, because 'tis always the seame thing; and if it was not always the seame thing, I shud not always tell yau the seame thing.

CHARLOTTA: But what wou'd you have?

PIERROT: Marry, I'd ha' yau love me.

CHARLOTTA: Why? Doa'nt I?

PIERROT: Noa, you doan't love me, and yet I do all I con to meake yau. I buy you—no offence—Ribbans of all the Men that go by, I go venture my Neck o' th' Rocks to get you Shells, I make those that play upon the Cymbal play for you when 'tis your Birthday, and I might as well run my Head against the Wall. Do you see, 'tis not honest not to love thoase that love us.

CHARLOTTA: Why I do love you.

PIERROT: Aye, mightily indeed!

CHARLOTTA: How wou'd you ha' ma do?

PIERROT: I'd ha' yau do as People do when they love as they ought.

CHARLOTTA: Why, don't I love yau as I ought?

PIERROT: No; People play an hundred little Tricks when they love heartily. Do you see fat Thomassa, how fond she is of young Robin? She's always about him to provoke'n, and never lets'n be at quiet. She's always putting some Trick or other upon him, or always cuffing him as she goes by; and t'other Day as he was sitting on a Joint-Stool, she pull'd it from under'n, and made him fall all along. See how People do when they love; but you ne'er speake a Word to ma, yau always stand like a Block, and I may goa by yau twenty times and you never gi' me the least Blow, nor speak the least Word to me. By th' Mass, this is not feair, you're too caud.

CHARLOTTA: What wou'd yau ha' ma do? I can't alter myself.

PIERROT: Yes yau can. When one loves anybody, one always give some Token or other that a Body loves.

CHARLOTTA: I love yau as much as I can; and if that doan't satisfie you, you may love somebody else an you will.

PIERROT: I say'd so. If you lov'd ma, wou'd you talk thus?

CHARLOTTA: Why do you come to plague a body then?

PIERROT: Why, what harm do I do you? I only desire a little Friendship from you.

CHARLOTTA: Well, let me alone and don't be so heasty; perhaps it may come all of a sudden, when we think nothing o' th' matter.

PIERROT: Shake Hands then, Charlotta.

CHARLOTTA: Well, there.

PIERROT: Promise me, then, to try to love ma more.

CHARLOTTA: I'll do all I con, but it must come of itself. Pierrot, is that the Gentleman?

PIERROT: Yea, that's he.

CHARLOTTA: Lord, how pretty he is! What a pity it wou'd ha' been if he had been drawn'd.

PIERROT: I'll be back presently; I'll go teake a Pint to refresh myself for the trouble I've had.

Scene 2

Don John, Sganarelle, Charlotta

DON JOHN: We have miss'd our Aim, Sganarelle, and that sudden Storm has, together with our Bark, o'erthrown the Project we had form'd. But to tell you the truth, the Countrywoman I just now left makes amends for this Misfortune, and I have observed in her Charms which efface from my Mind all the Spleen that the ill Success of our Enterprise gave me. That Heart must not escape me, and I have already so dispos'd it that it won't need many Sighs.

SGANARELLE: Sir, I must confess it, you amaze me; we're scarce escap'd from the danger of Death when, instead of thanking Heaven for the Pity it was pleased to take on us, you labour anew to incur its Anger by your old Fancies; and your Amours incr—peace, Knave, you don't know what you say; your Master best knows what he has to do. Come.

DON JOHN [perceiving Charlotta]: Whence comes this other Lass? Sganarelle, did you ever see anything prettier? Tell me, don't you think this as good as t'other?

SGANARELLE: Certainly. [*Aside.*] Another Piece!

DON JOHN: Well met, pretty Lass! What! Are there such handsome Creatures as you amongst these Fields, these Trees, and Rocks?

CHARLOTTA: I am as you see, Sir.

DON JOHN: Are you of this Village?

CHARLOTTA: Yes, Sir.

DON JOHN: And live here?

CHARLOTTA: Yes, Sir.

DON JOHN: What's your Name?

CHARLOTTA: Charlotta, Sir, at your Service.

DON JOHN: Ah what a fine Person 'tis! What piercing Eyes!

CHARLOTTA: Sir, you make me ashamed.

DON JOHN: O don't be ashamed at the Truth. Sganarelle, what do you say to her? Can anything be more agreeable? Pray turn a little; what a fine Shape! Hold up your Head a little; and what a pretty Face! Open your Eyes quite; O how fine they are! Pray let me see your Teeth; how amorous they are; and those provoking Lips. For my part I am ravish'd, and never beheld so charming a Person.

CHARLOTTA: Sir, you are pleas'd to say all this; I can't tell whether you make a Jest of me or no.

DON JOHN: I make a Jest of you! God forbid! I love you too well for that; I speak from the bottom of my Heart.

CHARLOTTA: If it be so, I'm oblig'd to you.

DON JOHN: Not at all; you are not at all oblig'd to me for what I say; you owe it to your Beauty alone.

CHARLOTTA: Sir, these are too fine Words for me. I have not wit to answer you.

DON JOHN: Sganarelle, look on her Hands.

CHARLOTTA: Fie, Sir, they're as black as I don't know what.

DON JOHN: Ha! What say you; they are the finest in the World; pray let me kiss 'em.

CHARLOTTA: Sir, you do me too much Honour; if I had dreamt of this, I would not ha' fail'd to ha' wash'd 'em with Bran.

DON JOHN: Pretty Charlotta, you are not marry'd, are you?

CHARLOTTA: No, Sir, but I am soon to be, with Pierrot, Son to Goody Simonetta.

DON JOHN: What! Shou'd such a one as you be Wife to a Peasant! No, no; that's a Profanation of so much Beauty. You was not born to live in a Village. You certainly deserve a better Fortune, and Heaven,

which knows it well, brought me hither on purpose to hinder this
Marriage and do justice to your Charms; for in short, fair Charlotta,
I love you with all my Heart, and if you'll consent I'll deliver,you
from this miserable Place, and put you in the Condition you deserve.
This Love is doubtless sudden, but 'tis an Effect of your great Beauty.
I love You as much in a quarter of an Hour as I shou'd another in
six Months.

CHARLOTTA: Truly, Sir, I don't know what to do when you speak. Your
Words make me glad, and I shou'd be mighty desirous to believe
you; but I was always told that one shou'd never believe Gentlemen,
and that you Courtiers are Sharpers, who think of nothing but
abusing Maidens.

DON JOHN: I am none of those sort of People.

SGANARELLE: [Aside.] No, to be sure!

CHARLOTTA: Do you see, Sir, there's no Pleasure in suffering oneself to
be abused. I am a poor Countrywoman, but I value my Reputation,
and had rather be dead than dishonour'd.

DON JOHN: What! Do you think me so wicked as to abuse such a one
as you, and so base as to dishonour you! No, no: I have too much
Conscience to do any such thing. I love you, Charlotta, virtuously
and honourably, and to shew you that I speak the Truth, know that
I have no other Design than to marry you. Wou'd you desire a
greater Testimony of it? I am ready to do it when you will, and I
take that Man to be witness of the Promise I make you.

SGANARELLE: Never fear; he'll marry you as much as you will.

DON JOHN: Ah, Charlotta! I plainly perceive you are not yet acquainted with me. You do me wrong to Judge of me by others, and
if there are Cheats in the World, Men who think of nothing but
abusing Maidens, you ought to scratch me out of the Number, and
not to question my Sincerity. Besides, your Beauty may be a sufficient
Assurance to you. When a Woman's made like you, she need never
have such Fears. Believe me, you have not the Air of one that's to
be abus'd, and for my part, I confess, I'd pierce my Heart with a
thousand Wounds if I had the least Thought of betraying you.

CHARLOTTA: Lord, I can't tell whether what you say is true or no, but
you make a Body believe you.

DON JOHN: When you believe me, you'll certainly do me Justice, and
I again repeat the Promise I have made. Do you accept it? Won't you
consent to be my Wife?

CHARLOTTA: Yes, if my Aunt will.

DON JOHN: Give me your Hand then, Charlotta, since I have your Consent.

CHARLOTTA: But pray, Sir, don't deceive me now; 'twou'd be a Sin; and you see I do what I do Innocently.

DON JOHN: What, do you still doubt my Sincerity? Will you ha' me swear frightful Oaths? May Heav'n—

CHARLOTTA: Lord, don't swear; I believe you.

DON JOHN: Give me a little Kiss then, in earnest of your Word.

CHARLOTTA: Oh, Sir, stay 'till I be marry'd; then I'll kiss you as much as you will.

DON JOHN: Well, Charlotta, I'll do whatever you please; only give me your Hand, and let me by a thousand Kisses express the Rapture I am—

Scene 3

Don John, Sganarelle, Pierrot, Charlotta

PIERROT [*getting between 'em, and pushing away Don John*]: Soft and fair, Sir, if you please; you heat yourself too much; you may hap' get a Purisie.

DON JOHN [*pushing away Pierrot roughly*]: Who sent for this Impertinent?

PIERROT: Be at quiet, and don't be caressing our Brides.

DON JOHN [*continuing to thrust him away*]: The noisy Fellow!

PIERROT: S'heart, People aren't to be push'd thus.

CHARLOTTA [*taking Pierrot by the Arm*]: Let him alone, Pierrot.

PIERROT: How do you mean, let'n alone? I woan't, not I.

DON JOHN: What!

PIERROT: 'Znigs, because you're a Gentleman, you come to tickle our Wives under our Noses; go and tickle your own.

DON JOHN: Hey day!

PIERROT: Ay, and hey day too! [DON JOHN *gives him Box on the Ear.*] 'Sbodykins, don't strike me. [*Another.*] 'Sdeath. [*Another.*] 'Zblood. [*Another.*] 'Sheart, 'tis not Fair to beat Folk thus. Is this my Reward for saving you from being drawn'd?

CHARLOTTA: Pierrot, don't be angry.

PIERROT: I will be angry; and you're a Hussy to let yourself be cuddled.

CHARLOTTA: O Pierrot, there's more in the cease than you think for; the Gentleman will marry me, and you ought not to put yourself into a Passion.

PIERROT: Aye! When you're engaged to me?

CHARLOTTA: That's nothing, Pierrot; if you love me, shou'd not you be glad to see me a Gentlewoman?

PIERROT: No; I'd rather see you hang'd than another's.

CHARLOTTA: Go, go, Pierrot, don't trouble yourself; if I am a Gentlewoman you shall get something by 't, and you shall serve us with Butter and Cheese.

PIERROT: S'death, I won't, tho' you peay'd me double for't. Do you hearken thus to what he says? 'Sheart, if I had Thought of this before, he might ha' drawn'd for me; I'd ha' given 'n a Blow on his Head with my Oar.

DON JOHN [coming up to Pierrot to strike him]: What's that you say?

PIERROT [getting behind Charlotta]: I fear no a Man.

DON JOHN [going to him]: Let me lay Hands on you—

PIERROT [gets on t'other side Charlotta]: I doan't ceare, not I.

DON JOHN [running after him]: We'll try that.

PIERROT [escapes behind Charlotta again]: I ha' seen Gentlefolk before now.

DON JOHN: Ha' ye.

SGANARELLE: Lord Sir, let the poor Fellow alone. 'Tis a pity to beat him. Go, honest Man, and don't speak to him.

PIERROT [gets by Sganarelle and speaks boldly to Don John]: I will speak to 'en.

DON JOHN [Lifts up his Hand to give Pierrot a Blow, who Pops down his Head, and Sganarelle receives the Blow.]: I'll teach you to—

SGANARELLE [looking upon Pierrot, who stoop'd to avoid the Blow]: Plague take the Booby!

DON JOHN: You're rewarded for your Charity.

PIERROT: Faith, I'll go tell her Aunt all this.

DON JOHN: In short, I shall be the happiest of Mankind, and I wou'd not change my Fortune for all the things in the World. What Pleasure shall I have when you're my Wife! and—

Scene 4

Don John, Sganarelle, Charlotta, Mathurina

SGANARELLE [perceiving Mathurina]: Ah ha!

MATHURINA [to Don John]: Sir, what are you doing with Charlotta there? Are you talking to Her of Love too?

DON JOHN [Aside to Mathurina.]: No, on the contrary she testifies a desire to be my Wife, and I tell her I'm engag'd to you.

CHARLOTTA: What is't you want, Mathurina?

DON JOHN [*Aside to Charlotta.*]: She is jealous of my speaking to you and wou'd fain have me marry her, but I tell her 'tis you I would have.

MATHURINA: What! Charlotta—

DON JOHN [*Aside to Mathurina.*]: All you can say to her will be in vain. She has got that Fancy into her Head.

CHARLOTTA: What then, Mathurina—

DON JOHN [*Aside to Charlotta.*]: Your Words wou'd be in vain; you'd never get her off that Whim.

MATHURINA: Do you—

DON JOHN [*Aside to Mathurina.*]: She won't hear Reason.

CHARLOTTA: I'd—

DON JOHN [*Aside to Charlotta.*]: She's as Obstinate as the Devil.

MATHURINA: Truly—

DON JOHN [*Aside to Mathurina.*]: Say nothing to her; she's a mad Woman.

CHARLOTTA: I think—

DON JOHN [*Aside to Charlotta.*]: Let her alone; she's an extravagant Wretch.

MATHURINA: No, no, I must speak to her.

CHARLOTTA: I'll hear her Reasons.

MATHURINA: What—

DON JOHN [*Aside to Mathurina.*]: I'll lay you a Wager she tells you I promis'd to Marry her.

CHARLOTTA: I—

DON JOHN [*Aside to Charlotta.*]: I'll lay a Wager she affirms that I promised to take her for my Wife.

MATHURINA: 'Tis not well, Charlotta, to meddle with other Folks' Merchandise.

CHARLOTTA: 'Tis not fit, Mathurina, that you shou'd be Jealous because the Gentleman speaks to me.

MATHURINA: 'Twas me that the Gentleman first saw.

CHARLOTTA: If he saw you First, he saw me Second, and has promised to marry me.

DON JOHN [*Aside to Mathurina.*]: Well, did not I tell you so?

MATHURINA: I beg your Pardon, 'twas me and not you that he promised to Marry.

DON JOHN [*Aside to Charlotta.*]: Did not I guess this?

CHARLOTTA: You must tell that Tale to others; 'twas me he promised.

MATHURINA: Do you make a Jest of People? Once more, 'twas me.

CHARLOTTA: There he is; he'll tell you whether I'm in the right or no.

MATHURINA: There he is to contradict me if I tell a Lye.

CHARLOTTA: Sir, did you promise to marry her?

DON JOHN [*Aside to Charlotta.*]: You jest sure!

MATHURINA: Is it true, Sir, that you have given your Word to be her Husband?

DON JOHN [*Aside to Mathurina.*]: Cou'd you have such a Thought?

CHARLOTTA: You see she affirms it.

DON JOHN [*Aside to Charlotta.*]: Let her alone.

MATHURINA: You see how positive she is.

DON JOHN [*Aside to Mathurina.*]: Let her say what she will.

CHARLOTTA: No, no, we must know the Truth.

MATHURINA: We must have it decided.

CHARLOTTA: Yes, Mathurina, I'll ha' the Gentleman prove you a Noddy.

MATHURINA: Charlotta, I'll ha' the Gentleman prove you a Goose.

CHARLOTTA: Sir, pray decide the Quarrel.

MATHURINA: Satisfie us, Sir.

CHARLOTTA: You shall see.

MATHURINA: Ay, and you shall too.

CHARLOTTA [*to Don John*]: Speak.

MATHURINA [*to Don John*]: Speak.

DON JOHN [*being perplex'd, addresses himself to both*]: What wou'd you have me say? You both equally affirm that I promised to marry you. Does not each of you know the Truth without my explaining myself any farther? Why wou'd you oblige me to Repetitions? Has not she that I really promis'd wherewithal in herself to Laugh at what t'other says, and ought she to be disturb'd, provided I accomplish my Promise? Words are nothing, Deeds are all. Therefore by them only will I satisfie you, and when I marry, you shall see which of the two possesses my Heart. [*Aside to Mathurina.*] Let her believe what she will. [*Aside to Charlotta.*] Let her flatter herself in her Imagination. [*Aside to Mathurina.*] I adore you. [*Aside to Charlotta.*] I am entirely yours. [*Aside to Mathurina.*] All Faces are ugly in your Presence. [*Aside to Charlotta.*] One cannot bear others when one has seen you. I have some Commands to give; I'll return in a Quarter of an Hour.

CHARLOTTA [*to Mathurina*]: I am she he loves, however.

MATHURINA: 'Tis me he'll Marry.

SGANARELLE: Poor Girls! I pity your Innocence, and can't endure to see you run thus to your Destruction. Take my Advice, both of you: don't let his Stories fuddle you, and stay in your Village.

DON JOHN [*returning*]: I'd fain know why Sganarelle don't follow me.

SGANARELLE [*to the Girls*]: My Master is a Knave; his Design is only to abuse you, as he has several others; he is a Marryer of the whole Sex, and— [*Perceives Don John*] 'Tis false, and whosoever tells you so, you shou'd tell him he Lies. My Master is not the Marryer of the whole Sex; he's no Knave; he has no Design to abuse you, and never abused any others. O, there he is, ask him himself.

DON JOHN: Yes.

SGANARELLE: Sir, as the World is full of Backbiters, I was beforehand with 'em, and told 'em that if anybody shou'd tell 'em any Harm of you, that they shou'd not believe it but tell him he ly'd.

DON JOHN: Sganarelle.

SGANARELLE: Yes, my Master is a Man of Honour; I'll maintain it.

DON JOHN: Hemp!

SGANARELLE: They are Impertinents.

Scene 5

Don John, Ramee, Charlotta, Mathurina, Sganarelle

RAMEE: Sir, I come to inform you that you are not safe here.

DON JOHN: How so?

RAMEE: Twelve Men on Horseback are searching for you, and will be here in a Moment. I can't tell how they cou'd follow you, but I heard it of a Countryman whom they enquired of, and to whom they described you. The Affair presses, and the sooner you get from hence the better.

DON JOHN [*to Charlotta and Mathurina*]: An important Affair obliges me to be gone, but pray remember the Word I have given you, and believe you shall hear from me before tomorrow Night— [*Exeunt* MATHURINA *and* CHARLOTTA.] As the Match is unequal, I must use Stratagem, and the better to avoid the Misfortune that threatens me, Sganarelle shall dress in my Cloaths, and I—

SGANARELLE: A good Jest, to expose me to be kill'd in your Cloaths, and—

DON JOHN: Come quickly, I do you too much Honour, and happy is the Servant that can have the Glory of dying for his Master.

SGANARELLE: I thank you for your Glory. O Heav'ns, since Death is in the Case, grant me the Favour not to let me be taken for another.

ACT III

Scene 1

Don John in a Campaign Dress, Sganarelle dress'd like a Physician

SGANARELLE: Come, Sir, confess that I was in the right, and that we're both disguised to a Miracle. Your first Design was not at all proper; this conceals us much better than what you would ha' done.

DON JOHN: 'Tis true you're very well disguised; but I can't imagine where you discover'd that ridiculous Equipage.

SGANARELLE: 'Tis the Dress of an old Physician, which was left in Pawn in the Place where I had it; and it cost me Mony to get it. But do you know, Sir, that this Garment makes me a considerable Man? That I am saluted by those I meet with, and that I am consulted as if I were a skilful Man?

DON JOHN: How so?

SGANARELLE: Five or six Country People, seeing me go by, came to ask my Advice upon several Diseases.

DON JOHN: You answer'd 'em that you knew nothing of the Matter, ha?

SGANARELLE: No, not at all. I had a Mind to maintain the Honour of my Habit. I argued upon the Illness, and gave 'em a Prescription.

DON JOHN: And what Remedies did you prescribe?

SGANARELLE: Faith, Sir, I order'd 'em hap nap at a Venture, and 'twould be a comical Thing if the Patients should recover and come to thank me for't.

DON JOHN: And why not? Why should not you have the same Privilege as all other Physicians? They have no greater Share than you in the Cures of our Diseases, and all their Art is pure Grimace. They do nothing but receive the Glory of accidental Success, and you, like them, may make profit of the Fortune of the Patient, and see all that may proceed from the Favours of Chance or the Force of Nature attributed to your Remedies.

SGANARELLE: What, Sir, are you impious in Physick too?

DON JOHN: 'Tis one of greatest Errors that are amongst Men.

SGANARELLE: What! Have you no belief in Sena, Cassia, nor Emetic Wine?

DON JOHN: And why would you have me believe in 'em?

SGANARELLE: You have a heretick Soul. Yet you see what a Noise Emetic Wine has lately made in the World. Its Miracles have converted the most Incredulous, and 'tis not three Weeks ago since I, I that speak to you, beheld a wonderful Effect of it.

DON JOHN: And what was it?

SGANARELLE: There was a Man who for six Days lay a-dying. They could not tell what to give him, and all the Remedies did no good 'till at length they gave him Emetic.

DON JOHN: So he recover'd, ha?

SGANARELLE: No, he dy'd.

DON JOHN: Admirable Effect!

SGANARELLE: Why he could not die for six Days together, and that made him die 'pon the Spot. Would you have anything more effectual?

DON JOHN: You're in the Right.

SGANARELLE: But enough of Physick, which you ha' no belief in. Let's speak of other things, for this Habit inspires me with Wit, and I find myself in a Humour to dispute with you. You know you allow me to dispute, and forbid me nothing but Remonstrances!

DON JOHN: Well?

SGANARELLE: I'd fain know the bottom of your Thoughts, and be better acquainted with you than I am. Is't possible you have no Belief in Heaven at all?

DON JOHN: Leave this Matter.

SGANARELLE: You don't, in short. And in Hell?

DON JOHN: Eh!

SGANARELLE: The same. And in the Devil, if you please?

DON JOHN: Yes, yes.

SGANARELLE: As little. Have you no Belief in the Life hereafter?

DON JOHN: Ha! ha! ha!

SGANARELLE: Here's a man I will not easily convert. And tell me, what of the Bogy Man? Have you faith in him? Eh?

DON JOHN: A Plague on the Fool!

SGANARELLE: This is more than I can endure; for nothing is surer than the Bogy Man, and I wou'd go to the Stake for him. But a Man must have a Belief in this World. What is yours?

DON JOHN: What I believe?

SGANARELLE: Yes.

DON JOHN: I believe that two and two make four, Sganarelle, and four and four make eight.

SGANARELLE: A fine Creed! Handsome Articles of Faith! Your Religion, I see, is Arithmetik. It must be confess'd strange Follies enter the Heads of Men, and for all their Study they are often less wise than before. For my part, Sir, I have not study'd like you, thank

God, and no Man can boast he taught me anything; yet with my
little Sense, my small Judgment, I see things better than all the
Books, and I understand very well that the World which we see is
not a Toadstool that came of itself one Night. Let me ask you who
made those Trees, those Rocks, this Earth, and the Sky above you?
Did it all come built of itself? Here, for example, you are yourself:
did you make yourself alone? Was not your Father needed to beget
you upon your Mother? Can you behold all the Inventions of which
the human Machine consists without admiring how they conform
together? These Nerves, these Bones, these Veins, these Arteries, this
Heart, this Liver, this—these Lungs, and all the other Ingredients
which—zounds, will you not interrupt me? I cannot dispute if I a'nt
interrupted. You say nothing on Purpose, and allow me to speak
from very Malice.

DON JOHN: I am waiting for the End of your Argument.

SGANARELLE: My Argument is that Man has something admirable,
whate'er you may say, which all the learned Heads cannot explain.
Is't not a Prodigy I shou'd be here, and have that in my Head which
thinks a thousand different things in a Moment, and does with my
Body all that it will? I want to clap my Hands, lift my Arm, raise my
Eyes to the Sky, encline my Head, move my Feet, go to the right,
to the left, forward, backward, turn—

[*He turns and falls.*]

DON JOHN: Good! There's your Argument with a broken Nose.

SGANARELLE: 'Sblood! I'm a Fool to reason with you. Believe what you
will; 'tis nothing to me whether you be damn'd or no.

DON JOHN: While you reason'd, we lost our Way. Call that Man yonder and ask the Way of him.

Scene 2

Don John, Sganarelle, a Pauper

SGANARELLE: Ho there! Fellow! Ho! Mate! Ho! Friend! A little Word
with you, if you please. Where lies our Way to the City?

PAUPER: Follow this Path, Gentlemen, and turn on your right Hand
when you come to the Forest's end. But I warn you to be upon your
Guard, for Robbers have been lurking of late in these Parts.

DON JOHN: I'm obliged to you, Friend, and thank you with all my
Heart.

PAUPER: Will you help me, Sir, with a small Charity?

DON JOHN: So! I see your Advice is selfish.

PAUPER: Sir, I am a poor Man, retired for ten Years in the Solitude of this Forest, and I will not fail to pray that Heaven bestow upon you all Manner of Goods.

DON JOHN: Eh! Ask Heaven for a Coat, without troubling yourself about other Men's Affairs.

SGANARELLE: You don't know this Gentleman, my good Man; he believes only that two and two make four, and four and four make eight.

DON JOHN: What is your Occupation amidst these Trees?

PAUPER: To pray Heaven all Day that the kind Persons who succour me may thrive.

DON JOHN: It cannot be, then, but you live comfortably here.

PAUPER: Alas, Sir, I am as poor as can be.

DON JOHN: Surely you jest. A Man who prays to Heaven all Day must be well furnish'd.

PAUPER: I assure you, Sir, that I have often not a Crust to put into my Mouth.

DON JOHN: Here is a strange thing, and your Efforts are but ill rewarded. Go to, I'll give you a Piece of Gold forthwith if you curse.

PAUPER: Oh, Sir, wou'd you have me commit such a Sin?

DON JOHN: Think only whether you wou'd earn a Piece of Gold or no. Here is one I'll give you if you curse. Here—but you must curse.

PAUPER: Sir—

DON JOHN: You shall not have it otherwise.

SGANARELLE: Marry, swear a little; there's no Harm in't.

DON JOHN: Take it, here, take it, I say; but curse away.

PAUPER: No, Sir, I had rather starve.

DON JOHN: Begone, I'll give it you for the love of Mankind. But what do I see? One Man set upon by three; the Match is too unequal, and I must not suffer so base a thing.

[*Runs to the place of Battle.*]

Scene 3

Don John, Don Carlos, Sganarelle

SGANARELLE: Sure my Master is mad to run into a Danger he might have kept out of; but Faith, his help has done't, and the two have driven away the three.

DON CARLOS [*with his Sword in his Hand*]: The flight of these Thieves

shews of what Consequence the help of your Arm is; let me return
you Thanks for so generous an Action, Sir, and—

DON JOHN: I have done nothing, Sir, but what you'd ha' done in my
Place. Our own Honour is concern'd in such Adventures, and the
Action of those Rogues was so base that not to have opposed 'em
would ha' been siding with 'em. But how came you to fall into their
Hands.

DON CARLOS: I lost my Brother and all our Followers by chance, and
as I was trying to get 'em again, I met with these Robbers, who
presently kill'd my Horse, and were it not for your Valour would
have done the same by me.

DON JOHN: Do you design to go towards the City?

DON CARLOS: Yes, but without going into it. My Brother and I are
obliged to travel for one of those troublesome Affairs which reduce
Gentlemen to sacrifice themselves and their Families to the Severity
of their Honour, since the best Success is always fatal, and since, if
they don't leave this Life, they're obliged to leave the Kingdom; and
in this I think the Condition of a Gentleman unfortunate, not to
be secure in the Prudence and Honesty of his own Conduct, but to
be subjected by the Laws of Honour to the Irregularity of another's,
and to see his Life, Repose and Estate depend upon the Whim of
the first rash Fellow that takes it in his Head to do him one of those
Injuries which an honest Man must perish for.

DON JOHN: We have the Advantage of making others run the same
Risk, and to give those who take a Fancy to offend us as much
Uneasiness. But would it not be an Indiscretion to ask what your
Affair may be?

DON CARLOS: The thing is to be made a Secret no longer, and when an
Injury is once publish'd, our Honour does not oblige us to conceal
our Shame, but rather to make our Revenge known and disclose our
Design of taking it. Therefore, Sir, I shall not scruple to tell you that
the Offence we seek Revenge for is a Sister's being seduced and
stol'n from a Nunnery, and that the Author of this Offence is one
Don John Tenorio, Son to Don Louis Tenorio. We have search'd
him for some Days, and we follow'd him this Morning upon the
Report of a Servant, who told us that he set out on Horseback accompany'd by four or five, and that he went by this Coast; but all
our Diligence was in vain, and we could not discover what's become
of him.

DON JOHN: Do you know this Don John whom you speak of, Sir?

DON CARLOS: I myself don't. I never saw him, and only heard him described by my Brother; but Report don't give him any of the best Characters, and 'tis a Man whose Life—

DON JOHN: Hold, Sir; he's one of my Friends, and 'twould be a kind of Baseness in me to hear any ill said of him.

DON CARLOS: For your sake, Sir, I'll say nothing of him; and the least thing I owe you, after you have saved my Life, is to say nothing in your Presence of one you are acquainted with when I can't speak well of him. But as much his Friend as you are, I hope you won't approve of his Action, nor think it strange that we seek Revenge for't.

DON JOHN: On the contrary, I'll serve you in it, and save your Labour; I am Don John's Friend, I can't help being so, but it is not reasonable that he should offend Gentlemen with Impunity; I'll engage myself to make him give you Satisfaction.

DON CARLOS: What Satisfaction can be done for such Injuries?

DON JOHN: All that your Honour can desire, and without giving you the Trouble to make any further search for Don John, I'll promise to bring him where and when you please.

DON CARLOS: This is very pleasant News, Sir, to offended Hearts; but after what I owe you, I should be uncommonly sorry if you were to be of the Party.

DON JOHN: There is that Intimacy between Don John and me that he can't fight but what I must fight too; but I answer for him as for myself, and you have no more to do than to tell me when you'd have him meet you and give you Satisfaction.

DON CARLOS: How cruel is my Destiny! Must I owe my Life to you, and Don John be one of your Friends?

Scene 4

Don Alonso and three Servants, Don Carlos, Don John, Sganarelle

DON ALONSO: Water my Horses, and bring 'em after us. I'll walk a little. O Heav'ns! What do I see! What! Brother, are you talking with our mortal Enemy?

DON CARLOS: Our mortal Enemy!

DON JOHN [*retiring back fiercely, laying his Hand upon his Sword*]: Yes, I myself am Don John, and the Advantage of Number shall not oblige me to conceal my Name.

DON ALONSO: Ah, Traitor, you must perish, and—

Don Carlos: Hold, Brother, I owe my Life to him; without the Help of his Arm I should have been kill'd by some Thieves I met with.

Don Alonso: Would you have that Consideration put a stop to our Revenge? The Services of an Enemy do not engage our Soul, and if you measure the Obligation against the Injury, your Gratitude is here ridiculous; and as Honour is infinitely more precious than Life, 'tis properly no Obligation to be obliged for Life to one that deprives us of our Honour.

Don Carlos: I know the Difference, Brother, which a Gentleman ought always to make between one and t'other, and the Acknowledgement of the Obligation does not blot out my Resentment of the Injury. But let me now repay him what he has lent me. Let me acquit my-self upon the Spot for the Life I owe him by delaying our Revenge, and give him the Liberty of enjoying for a few Days the Fruit of his Kindness.

Don Alonso: No, 'tis hazarding our Revenge to defer it, and the Opportunity of taking him may not come again; Heaven now offers it, and we ought to improve the Occasion. When Honour is mortally wounded, one ought to keep no Measure, and if you are not willing to lend your Arm to the Action, you may begone, and leave to my Hand the Glory of such a sacrifice.

Don Carlos: Pray, Brother—

Don Alonso: All you can say's superfluous; he must die.

Don Carlos: Hold, I say, Brother. I won't see his Life attack'd and I swear I'll defend him against anyone, be it who it will, and will guard him with the same Life he has saved. To address your Blows, you must kill me first.

Don Alonso: What! Do you side with our Enemy against me, and in-stead of being seized at his Aspect with the same Transports that I am, do you shew Sentiments full of Mercy for him?

Don Carlos: Brother, let's be moderate, and not Revenge our Honour with so much Rage. Let's have an Heart that we can master, a Valour without Savageness, and which does things by a pure Deliberation of our Reason, and not by the Instigation of a blind Passion. I won't remain obliged to my Enemy; I must acquit myself of my Obligation to him before I do anything else. Though our Revenge be defer'd, it will be ne'er the less exemplary; on the contrary 'twill be the greater, and this Opportunity, not taken, will make it appear the juster in the Eyes of the whole World.

Don Alonso: O strange Weakness! Thus to hazard the Interests of your Honour for the ridiculous Thought of a chimerical Obligation!

DON CARLOS: No, Brother, don't disturb yourself. If I commit a Fault I am able to repair it, and I take upon me the whole Care of our Honour; I know what that obliges us to do, and the Delay of a Day, which my Gratitude imposes, will but augment my Impatience to satisfy it. Don John, you see how careful I am to restore you the Good I have received from you, and by that you may imagine that I shall acquit myself of my Duty with the same Warmth, and that I shall be no less exact to repay you the Injury than the Kindness. I won't oblige you now to express your Sentiments, and I give you the Liberty to think at your leisure of the Resolutions you are to take. You are sufficiently acquainted with the greatness of the Offence you have committed, and I make you yourself Judge of the Reparations it requires. There are peaceful Means to satisfy us; there are likewise violent and bloody ones. But make what Choice you will, you have given me your Word to make Don John satisfie me; pray take care to do it, and remember that, away from this Place, I owe no Obligation except to my Honour.

DON JOHN: I required nothing of you, and shall keep my Promise.

DON CARLOS: Come, Brother, a Moment's Forbearance does not injure the Severity of our Duty.

Scene 5

Don John, Sganarelle

DON JOHN: So ho, Sganarelle.

SGANARELLE: Anon!

DON JOHN: What, Knave, do you run away when I'm attack'd?

SGANARELLE: I beg your Pardon, Sir, I was hard by; I believe this Dress is Purgative, and that to wear it is as good as a Potion.

DON JOHN: Plague take your Insolence! Cover your Cowardice with a more honourable Veil at least. Do you know who he is whose Life I saved?

SGANARELLE: No, not I.

DON JOHN: 'Tis a Brother of Elvira's.

SGANARELLE: A—

DON JOHN: He is a good honest Man; he was not ungrateful, and I'm sorry I have a Quarrel with him.

SGANARELLE: 'Twou'd be easy for you to pacifie things.

DON JOHN: Yes, but my Passion for Donna Elvira is worn out, and the

Engagement does not at all agree with my Humour. I am for Liberty in Love, you know it, and cannot bear to confine my Heart within four Walls. I have told you twenty times that I have a natural Inclination to give way to whatever attracts me. My Heart belongs to all the Fair Sex, and they're to take it by turns, and keep it as long as they can. But what lofty Edifice do I see amongst those Trees?

SGANARELLE: Don't you know?

DON JOHN: No, truly.

SGANARELLE: Why 'tis the Tomb the Governor was making when you kill'd him.

DON JOHN: You're in the right. I did not know that 'twas hereabouts. Everybody speaks Wonders of this Work, as well as of the Governor's Statue; I have a mind to go see it.

SGANARELLE: Sir, don't go.

DON JOHN: Why not?

SGANARELLE: 'Tis not civil to go see a Man that you kill'd.

DON JOHN: On the contrary, 'tis a Visit I'll make him out of Civility, and which he ought to receive graciously if he's a Gallant Man. Come, let's go in.

[*The Tomb opens, and on the inside is a stately Mausoleum and the* STATUE OF THE GOVERNOR.]

SGANARELLE: O how fine this is! Fine Statues! Fine Marble! Fine Pillars! How fine this is! What do you think on't, Sir?

DON JOHN: That the Ambition of a dead Man cou'd not reach further; and what I think most wonderful is that a Man who in his Lifetime took up with a simple Habitation shou'd desire so magnificent a house when he can no longer enjoy it.

SGANARELLE: Here's the Governor's Statue.

DON JOHN: Zoons, there he is with the Habit of a Roman Emperor.

SGANARELLE: Faith, Sir, 'tis finely made. It looks as if it were alive and were going to speak. He gives us such Looks as wou'd frighten me if I were alone; I think he e'nt pleas'd to see us.

DON JOHN: He's in the wrong then, and 'twou'd be an ill Reception of the Honour that I bestow upon him. Ask him if he'll come and Sup with me.

SGANARELLE: 'Tis a thing he has no need of, I think.

DON JOHN: Ask him, I tell you.

SGANARELLE: Do you Jest? 'Twou'd be a piece of Folly to speak to a Statue.

DON JOHN: Do as I bid you.

SGANARELLE: What Extravagance this is! Sir Governor—I can't help laughing at my Folly, but my Master makes me do it—Sir Governor, my Master Don John desires to know if you'll do him the Honour to come and Sup with him. [*The* STATUE *nods.*] Ha!

DON JOHN: What's the matter? What ails you? Speak.

SGANARELLE [*makes the same Sign the Statue had made to him, and nods*]: The Statue—

DON JOHN: What do you mean, Villain?

SGANARELLE: I tell you the Statue—

DON JOHN: What of the Statue? I'll break your Bones unless you speak.

SGANARELLE: The Statue nodded to me.

DON JOHN: Plague take the Knave!

SGANARELLE: He nodded to me, I tell you; nothing's more certain. Go speak to him yourself, and see—

DON JOHN: Come, Rogue, come, I'll shew you your Cowardice. Watch me. Will the Lord Governor come and Sup with me?

[STATUE *nods again.*]

SGANARELLE: I'd give ten Pounds for this. Well, Sir?

DON JOHN: Come, let's be gone.

SGANARELLE: These are your Free-thinkers that will believe nothing.

ACT IV

Scene 1

Don John, Sganarelle, Ragotin

DON JOHN: Be it as it will, no more of that. 'Tis a Trifle, and we might have been deceived by a false Light, or surprized by some Vapour which disturb'd our Eyes.

SGANARELLE: O, Sir, don't try to contradict that which we have seen with these very Eyes. Nothing can be more certain than the Nod of the Head, and I don't doubt but Heaven, offended with your Life, produced this Miracle to convince you, and to reclaim you from—

DON JOHN: Do you hear? If you trouble me any more with your foolish Morality, if you say the least Word to me about it, I'll call somebody, get a Bull's Pizzle, have you held by three or four, and break your Bones. Do you hear me?

SGANARELLE: Very well, Sir, mighty well, you express yourself plain enough; that's one good thing in you, you never seek for Shifts, you say things with an admirable Clearness.

DON JOHN: Come, let me have my Supper as soon as possible. A Chair, Boy.

Scene 2

Don John, Violette, Sganarelle, Ragotin

VIOLETTE: Sir, here's your Tradesman, Mr. Sunday, wants to speak with you.

SGANARELLE: Ay, we wanted a Creditor's Compliment. What cou'd put it in his head to come to ask us for Mony; and why did not you tell him that my Master was not at home?

VIOLETTE: I have told him so for these three Quarters of an Hour; but he wou'd not believe it and sat down without to wait.

SGANARELLE: Let him wait as long as he will.

DON JOHN: No, on the contrary, bid him come in; 'tis very ill Politicks to conceal oneself from Creditors. 'Tis good to pay 'em with something, and I have the Art of sending 'em away satisfy'd without giving 'em a Farthing.

Scene 3

Don John, Mr. Sunday, Sganarelle, Servants

DON JOHN [*with a great deal of Civility*]: O Mr. Sunday, come hither. How glad am I to see you, and how angry I am with my People for not letting you come in before! I order'd 'em, indeed, to deny me to everybody, but that Order did not extend to you; you have a right always to find my Door open.

MR. SUNDAY: Sir, I'm very much obliged to you.

DON JOHN [*to his Lacquies*]: Rascals, I'll teach you to leave Mr. Sunday in an Antichamber; I'll make you know People.

MR. SUNDAY: Sir, 'tis nothing.

DON JOHN: What, to deny me to Mr. Sunday, the best of my Friends?

MR. SUNDAY: Sir, I'm your Servant. I came to—

DON JOHN: Come, a Chair for Mr. Sunday, quickly.

MR. SUNDAY: Sir, I'm very well as I am.

DON JOHN: No, no, I'll have you sit down by me.

MR. SUNDAY: There's no need on't.

DON JOHN: Take away that Stool, and bring an Armchair.

MR. SUNDAY: Sir, you jest, and—

DON JOHN: No, no, I know what I owe you, and will make no Difference between us two.

MR. SUNDAY: Sir—

DON JOHN: Come, sit down.

MR. SUNDAY: There's no need on't, Sir: I have but one word to say to you. I was—

DON JOHN: Sit down, I say.

MR. SUNDAY: No, Sir, I am very well; I came to—

DON JOHN: No, I won't hear you unless you sit down.

MR. SUNDAY: Sir, I do as you'll have me. I—

DON JOHN: Faith, Mr. Sunday, you look very hearty and jolly.

MR. SUNDAY: Yes, Sir, at your Service. I come—

DON JOHN: You have an admirable Constitution, fresh Lips, a cherry Colour, and brisk Eyes.

MR. SUNDAY: I wou'd fain—

DON JOHN: How does Madam Sunday your Wife do?

MR. SUNDAY: Very well, Sir, thank God.

DON JOHN: She's a fine Woman.

MR. SUNDAY: She's your Servant, Sir. I came to—

DON JOHN: And how does your little Daughter Claudine?

MR. SUNDAY: Mighty well.

DON JOHN: What a pretty little Girl 'tis! I love her with all my Heart.

MR. SUNDAY: You do her too much Honour, Sir. I—

DON JOHN: And does little Colin make a Noise with his Drum still?

MR. SUNDAY: Yes, Sir. I—

DON JOHN: And your little Dog, Basquet? Does he bark as he us'd to do, and bite People's Legs?

MR. SUNDAY: More than ever, Sir, and we can't break him of it.

DON JOHN: Don't wonder if I inquire so much about your Family, for I concern myself mightily in it.

MR. SUNDAY: We're infinitely obliged to you, Sir. I—

DON JOHN [holding his Hand to him]: Give me your Hand, Mr. Sunday. Are you my Friend?

MR. SUNDAY: Sir, I'm your Servant.

DON JOHN: Faith, I'm yours with all my Heart.

MR. SUNDAY: You Honour me too much. I—

DON JOHN: There's nothing that I wou'd not do for you.

MR. SUNDAY: Sir, you have too much Goodness for me.

DON JOHN: I hope you'll believe it's without Selfishness too.

MR. SUNDAY: I have not deserved this Favour; but, Sir—

DON JOHN: Hark, Mr. Sunday, will you sup with me? Come, no Compliments.

MR. SUNDAY: No, Sir, I must be gone presently. I—

DON JOHN [*rising*]: Come, a Torch, quickly, to light Mr. Sunday, and let four or five of my People take Musketoons to guard him.

MR. SUNDAY [*rising too*]: Sir, there's no need on't; I can go very well alone. But—

[SGANARELLE *takes away the Chairs hastily.*]

DON JOHN: What? You shall be guarded; I interest myself in your Person, and am both your Servant and Debtor.

MR. SUNDAY: O Sir—

DON JOHN: 'Tis a thing I won't conceal, and I tell it the whole World.

MR. SUNDAY: If—

DON JOHN: Give me leave to wait upon you to the Door.

MR. SUNDAY: O Sir, you're pleas'd to be merry. Sir—

DON JOHN: Embrace me then; I beg you once more to be persuaded that I am entirely yours, and that there's nothing that I wou'd not do to serve you.

[*Exit.*]

SGANARELLE: I must own you have in my Master a Man that has a great Kindness for you.

MR. SUNDAY: 'Tis true he uses so much Civility and Ceremony that I can never ask him for my Money.

SGANARELLE: I assure you he'd destroy his whole Family for you, and I wish something wou'd but happen to you, that somebody wou'd cudgel you, you shou'd see how—

MR. SUNDAY: I believe it; but Sganarelle, pray put him in mind of my Money.

SGANARELLE: O don't be disturb'd about it. He'll pay extreamely well.

MR. SUNDAY: But you, Sganarelle, owe me something yourself.

SGANARELLE: Fie, don't speak of it.

MR. SUNDAY: Why, I—

SGANARELLE: Don't I know what I owe you?

MR. SUNDAY: Yes, but—

SGANARELLE: Come, Mr. Sunday, I'll light you.

MR. SUNDAY: But my Money—

SGANARELLE [*taking Mr. Sunday by the Arm*]: You jest.

MR. SUNDAY: I will—

SGANARELLE [*pulling him*]: Eh!

MR. SUNDAY: I mean—

SGANARELLE [*pushing him*]: Trifles!

MR. SUNDAY: But—

SGANARELLE [*pushing him*]: Fie.

MR. SUNDAY: I—

SGANARELLE [*pushing him quite off the Stage*]: Fie, I say.

Scene 4

Don Louis, Don John, Violette, Sganarelle

VIOLETTE: Sir, here's your Father.

DON JOHN: This Visit is all that was wanting to make me mad.

DON LOUIS: I see I disturb you, and that you cou'd very gladly have
dispensed with this Visit. 'Tis true we're strangely troublesome to
each other, and if you are uneasie at my Sight, I am very uneasie at
your Conduct. Alas, how little do we know what we do when we do
not leave to Heaven the Care of what is necessary for us, when we
would be wiser than it, and importune it by our blind Wishes and
inconsiderate Requests! I wish'd for a Son with unparallel'd Ardour;
I incessantly pray'd for one with incredible Transports; and the Son
which Heaven has granted me is the Grief and Punishment of this
same Life which I thought he must comfort and rejoice. With what
Eye do you think I can behold that Series of unworthy Actions which
we have much ado to show the World with a fair Countenance; that
continual Train of wicked Affairs which daily reduces us to tire the
Goodness of our Sovereign, and which has exhausted the Merit of
my Services and the Credit of my Friends? O what Baseness is this!
Do you not blush to be so little deserving of your Birth? Do you
think you have any right now to boast of it? What have you done
in the World to be call'd a Gentleman? Do you believe 'tis enough to
bear the Name and Arms of one, and that 'tis a Glory to be sprung
of noble Blood when a Man lives like an infamous Wretch? No, no,
Birth is nothing where Virtue is wanting. We have no further share
in the Glory of our Ancestors than as we endeavour to resemble
them, and the Lustre of their Actions, which they spread over us,
impose on us a Duty to do them the same Honour, to follow the
Examples they give us, and not to degenerate from their Virtues if
we would be esteem'd their true Descendants. Thus in vain you descend from the Ancestors you spring from; they disown you for their
Blood, and all their illustrious Actions give you no Advantage. On
the contrary, their Fame is your Dishonour, and their Glory lights to
everyone's Eyes the Shame of your Actions. In short, know that a
Gentleman that lives ill is a Monster in Nature; that Virtue is the

first Degree of Nobility; that I esteem a Name much less than Actions, and that I should have more regard for the Son of a Porter that was an honest Man than the Son of a Monarch that should live like you.

DON JOHN: Sir, if you'd sit down you might talk with greater ease.

DON LOUIS: No, Insolence, I won't sit down, nor speak any more; I see that all my Words have no effect upon you. But know, unworthy Son, that a Father's tenderness is spent by your Actions, that, sooner than you imagine, I shall put a stop to your Irregularities, prevent the Wrath of Heaven upon you, and by your Punishment wash away the Shame of having begotten you.

[*Exit.*]

Scene 5

Don John, Sganarelle

DON JOHN: Die as soon as you can; that's the best thing you can do. Every Dog must have his Day, and it makes me mad to see Fathers live as long as their Sons.

[*Sits down in his Chair.*]

SGANARELLE: O Sir, you're in the wrong.

DON JOHN: In the wrong?

SGANARELLE: Sir—

DON JOHN [*Rising*]: In the wrong?

SGANARELLE: Yes, Sir, you were in the wrong to hear him; you ought to have turn'd him out by Neck and Shoulders. Was ever anything more Impertinent? A Father to make Remonstrances to his Son, and to bid him correct his Actions, remember his Birth, lead the Life of a Man of Honour, and an hundred other Follies of the like Nature? Is that to be borne by such a Man as you, who knows how to live? I admire your Patience, and had I been in your Place, I should ha' sent him packing. [*Aside.*] O damn'd Compliance, to what dost thou reduce me!

DON JOHN: Is Supper ready?

Scene 6

Don John, Donna Elvira, Ragotin, Sganarelle

RAGOTIN: Sir, here's a Lady in a Veil that comes to speak with you.

DON JOHN: Who can it be?

SGANARELLE: We must see.

DONNA ELVIRA: Don't be surpris'd, Don John, to see me at this Hour, and in this Equipage. A pressing Motive obliges me to make this Visit, and what I have to say to you will admit of no delay. I don't now come in the Anger that I shew'd before; I am changed from what I was this Morning. 'Tis no more that Donna Elvira who pray'd against you, and whose irritated Soul utter'd nothing but Threats and breathed Revenge only. Heaven has banish'd from my soul all the unworthy Ardour I had for you, all the tumultuous Transports of a criminal Affection, all the shameful Passions of a gross and earthly Love, and it has left in my Heart a Flame refined from all commerce of the Senses, a Tenderness entirely holy, a Love abstracted from everything, and acting not for itself but for your Interest only.

DON JOHN [to Sganarelle]: You weep, I think?

SGANARELLE: Excuse me.

DONNA ELVIRA: 'Tis that perfect and pure Love which brings me hither for your Good, to impart to you an Advice from Heaven, and try to preserve you from the Precipice you are running into. Yes, Don John, I am acquainted with all the Irregularities of your Life, and that same Heav'n which has touch'd my Heart and made me consider the Errors of my Conduct, inspired me to come to you and to tell you on its behalf that your Offences have exhausted its Mercy; that its terrible Indignation is ready to fall upon you; that it lies in your Power to prevent it by a speedy Repentance, and that perhaps you have not a Day longer to save yourself from the greatest of Misfortunes. For my part, I am not ty'd to you any longer by any worldly Affection. Thank Heav'n, I am recover'd from foolish Thoughts; my Retreat is resolv'd upon, and I only desire Life enough to expiate the Fault I have committed, and merit by an austere Penance a Pardon for the Blindness into which the Transports of a blameable Passion plunged me. But in this Retreat I should be extremely sorry that a Person whom I had cherished so tenderly should become a fatal Example of Heaven's Justice, and 'twould be an incredible Joy to me if I could prevail upon you to ward off the terrible Blow that threatens you. Pray, Don John, grant me as the last Favour this sweet Comfort; don't refuse me your Salvation which I request with Tears, and if you yourself are not concern'd for your own Interest, yet be so for my Desires at least. Don't let me have the cruel Mortification of seeing you condemn'd to eternal Punishments.

SGANARELLE: Poor Woman!

DONNA ELVIRA: I have loved you with an extream Tenderness; nothing

in the World was so dear to me as you have been. I forgot my Duty
for you, I have done everything for you, and all the Recompence I
desire is that you'd correct your Life and prevent your Destruction.
I beg you to save yourself, either for your own sake or mine. Once
more, Don John, I desire it with Tears, and if the Tears of a Person
you have loved be not sufficient, I conjure you to do it by all that
is most capable of touching you.

SGANARELLE [*Aside.*]: Tyger!

DONNA ELVIRA: Now I am gone; this is all I had to say to you.

DON JOHN: Madam, 'tis late, stay here; we'll get as good a Lodging
for you as we can.

DONNA ELVIRA: No, Don John, don't keep me any longer.

DON JOHN: Madam, I assure you you'd oblige me if you'd stay.

DONNA ELVIRA: No, I tell you, don't let us lose time in superfluous
Discourse; let me go quickly, don't wait upon me, and think of
nothing but profiting by my Advice.

Scene 7

Don John, Sganarelle; Don John's Servants

DON JOHN: Do you know that I still felt a little Emotion for her; that
I found this whimsical Novelty agreeable, and that her negligent
Habit, her languishing Air, and her Tears awaken'd in me some
few Remains of an extinguish'd Flame?

SGANARELLE: That's as much as to say her Words had no effect upon
you?

DON JOHN: Come; Supper, quickly.

SGANARELLE: Very well.

DON JOHN [*sitting down to Table*]: Still, Sganarelle, we must think of
reforming.

SGANARELLE: Ay, marry, we must.

DON JOHN: Yes, Faith, we must reform; we'll live thus for twenty or
thirty Years longer, and then we'll take care of ourselves.

SGANARELLE: Oh!

DON JOHN: What do you say to't?

SGANARELLE: Nothing; here comes Supper.

[*He takes a bit out of one of the Plates, before it comes to Table,
and claps it in his Mouth.*]

DON JOHN: Your Cheek seems to be swell'd. What is't? Speak, what's
i' your Mouth?

SGANARELLE: Nothing.

DON JOHN: Let's see; Zoons, 'tis a Fluxion that's fallen into his Cheek; quick, a Lancet to cut it. The poor Fellow can't live long, and this Impostume may choak him; stay, let's see whether 'tis ripe. Ah Sirrah!

SGANARELLE: Faith, Sir, I had a mind to taste if your Cook had not overseason'd it.

DON JOHN: Come, sit down and eat. I have something for you to do after Supper. I see you are hungry.

SGANARELLE [*Sits down.*]: 'Tis true, Sir; I han't eat since Morning. Taste this; it's mighty good. [*A Lacquey takes away Sganarelle's Plate so soon as ever he has put anything upon it.*] My Plate, my Plate. Soft and fair, if you please. Faith, Brother, how skilful you are in giving me empty Plates; and you, little Violette, how well you know when to give Drink. [*Whilst one Lacquey gives Sganarelle Drink, t'other takes away his Plate again.*]

DON JOHN: Who knocks so hard?

SGANARELLE: Who the Devil comes to trouble us at our Meals?

DON JOHN: I'll sup in quiet; let nobody come in.

SGANARELLE: Let me see to it. I'll go to the Door myself.

DON JOHN: What's the Matter? Who's there?

SGANARELLE: The—[*He nods as the Statue did.*]—is there.

DON JOHN: I'll see him, and shew that nothing can shake me.

SGANARELLE: O poor Sganarelle, where wilt thou hide thyself!

Scene 8

Don John, the GOVERNOR'S STATUE *which goes and sits down to Table; Sganarelle, and Servants.*

DON JOHN: A Chair and a Plate, quickly. [*To Sganarelle.*] Come, sit down.

SGANARELLE: Sir, I e'nt a hungry now.

DON JOHN: Sit you down, I say. Drink here. Here's the Governor's Health, Sganarelle. Give him some Wine.

SGANARELLE: Sir, I'm not thirsty.

DON JOHN: Drink, and sing your Song to make the Governor merry.

SGANARELLE: I have a Cold, Sir.

DON JOHN: 'Tis no matter, come. Do you there come and join his Voice.

STATUE: Don John, 'tis enough. I invite you to come and sup with me tomorrow. Shall you be bold enough?

DON JOHN: Yes, I'll come accompany'd by none but Sganarelle.

SGANARELLE: I thank you, but I fast tomorrow.

DON JOHN [to Sganarelle]: Here, take this Torch.

STATUE: Those that are conducted by Heav'n have no need of Light.

ACT V

Scene 1

Don Louis, Don John, Sganarelle

DON LOUIS: What, Son, is it possible that Heav'n's Goodness has heard my Prayers? Is what you tell me true? Don't you abuse me with a false Hope, and may I believe the surprizing Novelty of such a Conversion?

DON JOHN [playing the Hypocrite]: Yes, I am return'd from all my Errors. I am not the same as I was Yesterday Evening, and Heav'n has all of a sudden work'd a Change in me which will surprize everybody. It has touch'd my Heart and open'd my Eyes, and with Horror I look back upon the long Blindness I have been in and the disorderly Life I have led. I consider all the Abominations of it, and am amaz'd how Heav'n cou'd so long endure 'em, and has not twenty times let fall upon my Head the Blows of its terrible Justice. I see the Favour its Goodness has done me in not punishing me for my Crimes, and I intend to profit as I ought; to shew the World a sudden Alteration of my Life, thereby to repair the Scandal of my past Actions, and to endeavour to obtain of Heav'n a full Forgiveness. This I'll go about, and I beg you, Sir, to contribute to the Design and to help me yourself to a Person that may be my Guide, and under whose Conduct I may walk securely into the Journey I am undertaking.

DON LOUIS: O Son, how easily is a Father's Tenderness recall'd, and how a Child's Offences are immediately wash'd away by the least mention of Repentance. I now forget all the Uneasiness you have given me, and all is effaced by the Words you have spoken. I confess I am not myself. I shed Tears for Joy, all my Desires are satisfy'd, and I have no more to ask of Heav'n. Embrace me, my Son, and

I conjure you, persist in this laudable Resolution. I'll immediately go tell this happy News to your Mother, share with her the sweet Transports of the Rapture I am in, and thank Heav'n for the holy Thoughts it has been pleased to inspire you with.

Scene 2

Don John, Sganarelle

SGANARELLE: O, Sir, how glad am I to see you converted! I have long expected this, and now, thank Heav'n, all my Wishes are accomplish'd.

DON JOHN: Plague take the Ass!

SGANARELLE: How! The Ass!

DON JOHN: What; do you take all I said for current Coyn, and do you think that my Mouth is in Concert with my Heart?

SGANARELLE: What, is not—don't you—your—O what a Man this is! What a Man this is!

DON JOHN: No, no, I'm not at all changed, and my Sentiments are still the same.

SGANARELLE: Don't you yield to the surprising Marvel of that Statue, both moving and speaking?

DON JOHN: There's something in that indeed which I don't comprehend; but be it as 'twill, that is not capable either to convince my Mind or shake my Soul; and if I said I would mend my Conduct and lead an exemplary Life, 'twas a Design I form'd out of pure Policy, a useful Stratagem, a necessary Grimace which I'll constrain myself to, to manage a Father whom I have need of, and to be secure from an hundred Accidents which may happen to me from Men. I entrust you with this Secret, Sganarelle, and I'm glad that I've a Witness of the real Motives which instigate me to do Things.

SGANARELLE: What! Still an Unbeliever, and yet pretend to Godliness?

DON JOHN: And why not? There are a great many besides me that practice that Trade, and who make use of the same Mask to abuse the World.

SGANARELLE: Oh! What a Man! What a Man!

DON JOHN: There's no shame in this now; Hypocrisie is a fashionable Vice, and all fashionable Vices pass for Virtues. The Part of an honest Man is the best a Man can play. The Profession of an Hypocrite has wonderful Advantages today. 'Tis an Art whose Imposture is always respected, and tho' 'tis discover'd, nobody dares speak against it. All Men's other Vices are exposed to Censure, and each has the Liberty of attacking them openly; but Hypocrisie is a privileged Vice which with its Hand stops everyone's Mouth and enjoys in quiet an absolute Impunity. One contracts, by means of this Grimace, a strict Friendship with all the Professors of it. He that offends one, pulls 'em all upon him; and those who act sincerely in it, and whom everyone knows to be really touch'd, those, I say, are generally the Dupes to the others; they are easily gull'd by the Grimacers, and blindly support the Apes of their Actions. How many are there who by this Stratagem have cunningly to my Knowledge made up for the Disorders of their Youth, who make a Shield of Religion's Coat, and under a respectful Outside have Liberty to be the wicked'st Fellows in the World? 'Tis no matter if their Intrigues be publish'd and they be known for what they are; they are ne'er the less in Credit, and a little hanging down of the Head, a mortify'd Groan, and two Turnings up of the Eyes set all to rights again. Under this favourable Covert I intend to secure my Affairs. I won't leave off my beloved Customs, but I'll take care to conceal myself and take Diversion privately. But if I come to be discover'd, my Part will be taken by all the League without my stirring in it, and I shall be defended by them against everybody. In short, this is the true way to do all I have a Mind to with Impunity. I'll set up for a Censor of the Actions of others, judge ill of all the World, and have a good Opinion of none but myself. If anyone offends me ever so little, I'll never forgive, but demurely preserve an irreconcileable Hatred. I'll be the Avenger of Heaven's Interests, and under that commodious Pretence I'll pursue my Enemies, accuse 'em of Impiety, and halloo at 'em the indiscreet Zealots, who without knowing the Reason will cry out against 'em, load 'em with Injuries, and by their own private Authority pronounce Damnation against 'em. Thus Men's Weakness must be profited by, and thus a wise Man will accommodate himself to the Vices of his Age.

SCANARELLE: O Heav'ns! What do I hear! Hypocrisie was all that was wanting to finish you quite, and this is the full Measure of Abominations. Sir, this last Stroke provokes me, and I can't help speaking. Do what you please to me, beat me, break my Bones, murther me if you will, I must disburthen my Heart, and like a faithful Servant tell you what I ought. Know, Sir, that a Pitcher never goes so often to the Well but it comes home broke at last, and as that Author, tho' I don't know who 'tis, very well says, Man in this World is like a Bird on a Bough; the Bough is fix'd to the Tree; he that is fix'd to the Tree follows good Precepts; good Precepts are better than fair Words; fair Words are found at Court; at Court are Courtiers; the Courtiers follow the Fashion; Fashion proceeds from the Fancy; the Fancy is a Faculty of the Soul; the Soul is what gives us Life; Life ends in Death; Death puts us in Mind of Heaven; Heaven is above the Earth; the Earth is not the Sea; the Sea is subject to Storms; Storms torment Vessels; Vessels need a good Pilot; a good Pilot is prudent; Prudence is not in the Young; the Young must obey the Old; the Old love Riches; Riches make rich Men; rich Men are not poor; the Poor are in Need; Need hath no Law; whoever has no Law lives as a brute Beast; and, in consequence, you shall be damn'd to all the Devils.

DON JOHN: A fine Argument, truly!

SGANARELLE: If this won't convince you, so much the worse for you.

Scene 3

Don Carlos, Don John, Sganarelle

DON CARLOS: Don John, I meet you very seasonably, and had rather speak to you here than at your Lodgings to ask you your Resolutions. You know that Care concerns me, and I in your Presence took this Affair upon me. For my Part, I don't conceal it, I should be glad if things could be adjusted peaceably, and there's nothing I wou'd not do to prevail with you to take that Course, and to see my Sister publickly confirm'd by you in the Title of your Wife.

DON JOHN [in a canting Tone]: Alas! I would with all my Heart give you the Satisfaction you desire, but Heaven directly opposes it; it has inspired my Soul with a Desire to change my Life, and I have now no other Thought than to quit entirely all worldly Things, to lay aside as soon as possible all manner of Vanity, and henceforth to correct, by an austere Conduct, all the criminal Irregularities which the Heat of blind Youth hurry'd me into.

DON CARLOS: This design, Don John, does not run counter with what I say, and the Company of a lawful Wife may be very agreeable to the laudable Thoughts Heav'n inspires you with.

DON JOHN: Alas! not at all; 'tis a Design your Sister too has form'd; she is resolved to retire, and we were both touch'd at the same time.

DON CARLOS: Her Retirement cannot satisfie us because it may be imputed to your Contempt of her and our Family, and our Honour requires that she should live with you.

DON JOHN: I assure you, it cannot be. I was very desirous of it, and this very Day consulted Heav'n about it; but when I consulted it, I heard a Voice which told me that I ought not to think of your Sister, and that I could never work out my Salvation in her Company.

DON CARLOS: Do you think these fair Excuses will blind us, Don John?

DON JOHN: I obey the Voice of Heav'n.

DON CARLOS: What! Would you have me be contented with such a Story?

DON JOHN: Heav'n will have it so.

DON CARLOS: Did you take my Sister out of a Nunnery to leave her at last?

DON JOHN: Heav'n ordains it so.

DON CARLOS: Shall we bear this Blot upon our Family?

DON JOHN: Blame Heaven for it.

DON CARLOS: What? Nothing but Heav'n?

DON JOHN: Heav'n will have it so.

DON CARLOS: 'Tis enough, Don John, I understand you; I won't take you here, the Place won't admit of it; but before long I shall meet with you.

DON JOHN: You may do as you please. You know I don't want a Heart, and that I can make use of my Sword when there's need for't; I'll go walk presently in that little bye Street which leads to the Convent; but for my Part, I declare that 'tis not I that wou'd fight; Heav'n forbids that I should have such a Thought, and if you attack me, we shall see what will be the Consequence.

DON CARLOS: 'Tis true, we shall see, we shall see.

Scene 4

Don John, Sganarelle

SGANARELLE: What a dev'lish Stile do you use, Sir! This is worse than all the rest, and I'd rather have you as you were before. I always had

Hopes of your Salvation, but now I despair of it, and I believe that Heav'n, which hitherto has endured you, cannot bear this last Abomination.

DON JOHN: Pish, Heav'n is not so strict as you imagine, and if as often as Men—

SGANARELLE [*Seeing the Ghost*]: Oh Sir, 'tis Heav'n that speaks to you; and 'tis a Warning it gives you.

DON JOHN: If Heav'n gives me Warning, it must speak plainer if 'twou'd have me understand it.

Scene 5

Don John, Sganarelle, a Ghost in the form of a Woman veil'd

GHOST: Don John has but a Moment's time to lay hold on the Mercy of Heav'n, and if he do not repent now, his Destruction is certain.

SGANARELLE: Do you hear, Sir?

DON JOHN: Who dares to say this? I think I know the Voice.

SGANARELLE: Oh, Sir, 'tis a Ghost, I know it by its walking.

DON JOHN: Ghost, Phantom, or Devil, I'll see what 'tis.

[*The* GHOST *changes its Figure, and represents Time with a Scythe in its Hand.*]

SGANARELLE: O Heav'ns! Do you see this Metamorphosis, Sir?

DON JOHN: No, no, nothing is capable of terrifying me, and with my Sword I'll try whether 'tis a Body or a Spirit.

[*The* SPIRIT *vanishes when Don John offers to strike it.*]

SGANARELLE: O Sir, yield to so many Proofs, and fall to Repentance quickly.

DON JOHN: No, no, come what will, it shall never be said that I was capable of Repentance. Follow me.

Scene 6

The Statue, Don John, Sganarelle

STATUE: Stay, Don John. Yesterday you gave me your Word to come and eat with me.

DON JOHN: I did; where must I go?

STATUE: Give me your Hand.

DON JOHN: There 'tis.

STATUE: Don John, Obstinacy in Wickedness brings on a fatal Death; and Heaven's Mercy rejected opens away for its Thunder.

DON JOHN: O Heav'ns, what do I feel! An invisible Flame consumes
me; I can bear it no longer; all my Body is a burning Firebrand.
Oh—

[*Thunder and Lightning, with a great noise, fall upon* DON JOHN,
*the Earth opens and swallows him up, and Great Flames rise from
the Place he sunk into.*]

SCANARELLE: Ha! My Wages! My Wages! Now is everybody satisfy'd
by his Death. Offended Heav'n, violated Laws, seduced Daughters,
dishonour'd Families, abused Parents, Wives reduced to Misery,
Husbands to Desperation, ev'rybody is contented; I alone am miserable. My Wages, my Wages, my Wages!

Rosimond and Shadwell

In early seventeenth-century England, playwrights like Beaumont and Fletcher would have understood and appreciated the Italian or French Don Juan. Fletcher's *The Wild-Goose Chase* (1621) has a vanquisher of female hearts who brazenly shows his Elvira (Oriana by name) a list of the women he has seduced. But the Puritan element was powerful in England, and in 1642 it forced the closing of the playhouses. They remained dark throughout the Civil Wars of the '40's and the Commonwealth period which followed the deposition and execution of King Charles I; and the genuine Don Juan did not cross the Channel until Charles II, no slouch with women himself, had restored the rule of the Stuarts.

Neither the English yeoman nor the English burgher had turned into a fashionable rake, but the official Restoration spirit was wanton and elegant, godless and gay. At court, and in the circles influenced by court life, the rule was merriment; and to assume an air of responsible gravity, smacking as it would of Puritanism, was almost an act of lèse-majesté. John Richard Green, though hostile to Toryism, has probably done justice to the spirit of the times:

The whole face of England was changed in an instant. All that was noblest and best in Puritanism was whirled away with its pettiness and tyranny in the current of the nation's hate. Religion had been turned into a system of political and social oppression, and it fell with that system's fall. Godliness became a byword of scorn; sobriety in dress, in speech, in manners was flouted as a mark of the detested Puritanism. Butler in his "Hudibras" poured insult on the past with a pedantic buffoonery for which the general hatred, far more than its humour, secured a hearing. Archbishop Sheldon listened to the mock sermon of a Cavalier who held up the Puritan phrase and the Puritan twang to ridicule in his hall at Lambeth. Duelling and raking became the marks of a fine gentleman; and grave divines winked at the follies of "honest fellows" who fought, gambled, swore, drank, and ended a day of debauchery by a night in the gutter. Life among men of fashion vibrated between frivolity and excess. One of the comedies of the time tells the courtier that "he must dress well, dance well, fence well, have a talent for love-letters, an agreeable voice, be amorous and discreet—but not too constant." To graces such as these the rakes of the Restoration added a shamelessness and a brutality which passes belief. Lord Rochester was a fashionable poet, and the titles of his poems are such as no pen of our day could copy. Sir Charles Sedley was a fashionable wit, and the foulness of his words made even the porters of Covent Garden pelt him from the balcony when he ventured to address them. The Duke of Buckingham is a fair type of the time, and the most characteristic event in the Duke's life was a duel in which he consummated his seduction of Lady Shrewsbury by killing her husband, while the Countess in disguise as a page held his horse for him and looked on at the murder.[1]

The royal master of the revels, Charles II, had spent much of his exile in France. His mother, Queen Henrietta Maria, was the daughter of the French king Henry IV. Charles himself sympathized with Roman Catholicism and died a Catholic. As king, he depended upon French gold to implement his Tory policies. In a word, the Restoration became the French period of England as the Enlightenment was to become the English period of France. Poets and playwrights imported, adapted, translated, and imitated the work of Frenchmen, though never attaining the polish which the latter acquired, as it were, with their mothers' milk. On the other hand, if Congreve was not quite up to Molière, and if Otway was far down from Racine, both Dryden and Pope were to beat Boileau at his own satires and epistles and to make the heroic couplet in English outshine the French. Furthermore, while the English comedy of the Restoration lacks the humanity of Molière, its cold and rapid wit, so alarming to those who seek reassurance in the arts, is an achievement without parallel in the France of that epoch.

Thomas Shadwell, to whom we are modestly indebted for bringing Don Juan to England, used as his sources not only the French plays we have discussed and exhibited, but also—and most notably—a later play, *Le nouveau Festin de Pierre, ou l'Athée foudroyé* (1669), by Claude La Rose, Sieur de Rosimond. Rosimond was an actor at the Théâtre du Marais who took over several of Molière's comic roles after the master's death, and who, although he wrote a devout life of the saints, grew fat with drinking and died in a tavern in 1686.

The weakness of *Le nouveau Festin* as a work of art is the same mortal stiffness of language which mars the work of Villiers and Dorimon, but the treatment of the subject has a certain originality, and this version became the prime source for Shadwell's far superior play. Rosimond transformed the two brothers of Elvira—Molière's least happy contribution—into two companions who share in the debauches as well as in the punishment of Don Juan. More important, he developed Don Juan into a figure still more philosophical than Molière's

1. *History of the English People* (New York and London: Harper, n.d.), Book VIII, Ch. 1, pp. 328–329.

Thomas Betterton as Don Juan in *The Libertine*. Frontispiece by Paul Rotha for volume V of *The Complete Works of Thomas Shadwell*, published in 1927 by the Fortune Press.

character, here again paving the way for Shadwell. Rosimond's hero is a reasoning hedonist who sees nothing in the universe which has authority to trammel the instincts of man. "What," cries his virtuous servant, "you commit crimes without horror?" And Don Juan replies, "Learn that there is no crime for a courageous man; only the cowardice of men gives it its odious name. If all hearts were great and magnanimous, what is called crime would be crime no longer. It is all cowardice and timidity passing for virtue. A great man need not deny himself anything, and crime is virtue for whoever dares commit it."[2]

Out of Rosimond's play and helpings from several other French versions, Thomas Shadwell concocted (in less than a month, according to his own boast) the strangest and wildest and most ferocious Don Juan of them all. No Frenchman of the court of Louis XIV could have made so barbarous a play, but none could have written quite such an interesting one either. Shadwell was understating the case when he declared in his Preface, "I had rather try new ways to please, than to write on in the same Road, as too many do." Although he obeyed the letter of several preceding versions, he infused an altogether original spirit into the matter. *The Libertine* is a seventeenth-century *Ubu roi*. Philosophically, it makes explicit the systematic hedonism which animates the typical comedies of the period. At the same time, Shadwell has anticipated, in the manner of a circus, the final dream of Raskolnikov in *Crime and Punishment*, namely, the vision of Atheism unleashing the brute passions of man. His play is as consciously the enactment of a philosophical doctrine as is *The Stranger*, and its hero is no more and no less incredible than the cold hero of Camus' work. Both are types of the Absurd Man, that is to say of man living in his person the metaphysics of universal inanity—with this important difference, however, that Don Juan swills life with roars of laughter: " 'Tis a sign I am not weary of my life, that I make so much use on't!" he cries. Freedom can go no farther than it does in the soul of Don Juan. Hence Shadwell's world goes berserk with evil. No one can take seriously the damnation scene, his nod to decency. Innocence here is helpless, reason overthrown, order abolished. But only pedantic dullness would criticize Don Juan's character on the ground that it does not exist.[3] Only sentimentalism could be revolted by the farcical crowding-up of outrages. We are looking at a metaphysical puppet play. Coleridge's words are

2. *Le nouveau Festin de Pierre, ou l'Athée foudroyé*, Act I, Scene 2. The play can be found in V. Fournel (ed.), *Les Contemporains de Molière* (Paris: 1875), vol. III.

3. See August Steiger's trifling *Thomas Shadwell's "Libertine"* (Berne: 1904), p. 57.

just: "The play is thoroughly imaginative. Nothing of it belongs to the
real world, but the names of the places and persons. The comic parts,
equally with the tragic; the living, equally with the defunct characters,
are creatures of the brain; as little amenable to the rules of ordinary
probability, as the Satan of Paradise Lost or the Caliban of The Tempest, and therefore to be understood and judged of as impersonated
abstractions." And again: "The very extravagance of the incidents . . .
prevents the wicked from shocking our minds to any painful degree."[4]

Saintsbury, who edited several of Shadwell's plays for the Mermaid
series, conceded to their author a certain "command of comic incident
and situations" and "direct power of dramatic observation of actual
life," but—strangely enough—found him dull, and confirmed Dryden's
verdict that he could do anything but write. Dryden pulverized Shadwell's reputation through his famous attacks; but in sober truth
Shadwell is one of the sounder playwrights of the Restoration, not
elegant, not very witty, and by his own admission lacking polish and
"correctness"; but he wrote with force and high comic verve. In an
Allusion to Horace, Rochester praised Shadwell and Wycherley, whom
he thought the two best comic dramatists of the day:

> Of all our *Modern Wits* none seems to
> Once to have toucht upon true *Comedy*,
> But hasty *Shadwel*, and slow *Wicherley*.
> Shadwells unfinish'd works do yet impart
> Great proofs of force of *Nature*, none of Art;
> With just bold strokes he dashes here, and there,
> Shewing great *Mastery* with little Care,
> And scorns to varnish his good Touches o're
> To make the *Fools* and *Women* praise 'em more.[5]

Shadwell's weapon was a bludgeon, but I am persuaded that a stage
which welcomes Ionesco is once more ready for Shadwell's bizarre
comedy, which I do not hesitate to call one of the most impressive plays
of its epoch. Producers are invited to read the play with commercial
attention.

4. *Biographia Literaria*, ch. 23. John Austen calls this an "outrageously extravagant
estimate," and refers to Shadwell's play as "this monstrous concoction." See his *Story
of Don Juan* (London: Martin Secker, 1939), pp. 176 and 185. In the quarrels concerning the immorality of the stage which followed Jeremy Collier's *Short View*
(1698), several defenders of the theatre cited *The Libertine* as an outstanding example
of high morality because Don Juan is punished at the end. Small wonder Collier's
side won that memorable battle.

5. See Vivian de Sola Pinto, *Enthusiast in Wit: A Portrait of John Wilmot Earl of
Rochester, 1647–1680* (Lincoln: University of Nebraska Press, 1962), pp. 135–136.

Thomas Shadwell (1642?–1692) is known chiefly as the victim of Dryden's most triumphant invectives, *MacFlecknoe* and a portion of the second part of *Absalom and Achitophel*.[6] The two had been squabbling since the beginning of Shadwell's career in 1668, when the momentous question between them was whether Ben Jonson had Wit and used it, or had it but did not use it. Only the most spiritless writers of the Restoration failed to enlist in three or four simultaneous quarrels, but in this case animosity was fanned by religious and political differences—Dryden was a high Tory and Shadwell a "true-blew Protestant." The absence of the latter's work from the stage for a period of seven years has been ascribed to Dryden's malevolence. But for the most part Shadwell was an active and successful dramatist whose plays—*The Libertine* among them—made money for the Duke's Company, with which he was affiliated, and whose companionship was sought by such wits and men of fashion as Etherege, Wycherley, and the Earl of Rochester. Dryden could not find much to say against him and was forced to dwell on such forgivable sins as his dullness, his fatness and conviviality, the circumstance that his patron, the Duke of Newcastle, lived in the North, and his poverty.

On the accession of William and Mary, Shadwell replaced his enemy as poet laureate and wrote some very bad poems. Illness obliged him to resort to opium, an overdose of which is said to have killed him in the fourth year of his laureateship. That he was indeed poor is shown by his touching testamentary request "to bee buryed in Flannel with the least charge that may be."

6. A. S. Borgman, *Thomas Shadwell: His Life and Comedies* (New York: New York University Press, 1928) is authoritative, but it has no discussion of *The Libertine*, which Shadwell called a tragedy on the technicality of its bloodletting.

THOMAS SHADWELL

The Libertine

A Tragedy in Five Acts

(1676)

EDITOR'S NOTE

The following text is based on that of 1676 reproduced in facsimile in *The Complete Works of Thomas Shadwell,* edited by Montague Summers. There is no fully authoritative text. Summers himself supplies variants—all of them negligible—from editions published in Shadwell's lifetime. A number of errors have been tentatively corrected here. A few passages remain garbled—a number which were obviously written as prose were carelessly set as verse — and it may be that several lines or brief speeches, present in Shadwell's manuscript, are lost forever. Scene divisions have been supplied, and in some cases scene descriptions and stage directions have been amplified. Punctuation and spelling have been slightly modernized, more with an eye to the reader's convenience than to consistency. Incorrect descriptions in the cast list have been amended, and omitted roles have been added.

TEXT

The Complete Works of Thomas Shadwell, vol. III. Edited by Montague Summers. London: The Fortune Press, 1927.

The Persons Represented

Don John, *the Libertine; a rash, fearless man, guilty of all vice*
Don Antonio, ⎫
Don Lopez, ⎬ *his three friends*
Don Octavio, ⎭
Jacomo, *Don John's valet*
Leonora, *Don John's mistress, abused by him, yet follows him for love*
Maria, *beloved by Don Octavio*
Flora, *her maid*
Maria's Brother
Don Francisco, *father to Clara and Flavia*
Clara, ⎫ *his daughters*
Flavia, ⎭
Six Women, *all wives to Don John*
Hermit
Two Bridegrooms, *intended for husbands to Clara and Flavia*
Captain of the Ship
Master of the Ship
Ghosts
Shepherds, Shepherdesses, and Nymphs
Four or Five Country Fellows
Old Woman
Officer and Soldiers
Sailors, Fiddlers, Servants, Attendants, Nuns, and Devils

Synopsis of Scenes

Act I

Scene 1. A Street in Seville.
Scene 2. Another part of Seville.
Scene 3. Maria's chamber.

Act II

Scene 1. Don John's town house.
Scene 2. The street outside Don John's town house.

Act III

Scene 1. Aboard a ship.
Scene 2. The shore, near a hermit's cave.
Scene 3. A wood, near Don Francisco's.

Act IV

Scene 1. A hall at Don Francisco's.
Scene 2. A delightful grove.
Scene 3. A church.
Scene 4. The dining room at Don John's country house.

Act V

Scene 1. Town square, near a convent.
Scene 2. A church (same as Act IV, Scene 3).

PROLOGUE

Our Author sent me hither for a Scout,
To spy what bloody Critics were come out,
Those Picaroons in Wit, wh' infest this Road,
And snap both Friend and Foe that come abroad.
This Savage Party crueller appears
Than in the Channel Ostend Privateers;
You in this Road or sink or plunder all;
Remorseless as a Storm on us you fall:
But as a Merchant, when by Storms distress'd,
Flings out his bulky Goods to save the rest,
Hoping a calm may come, he keeps the best,
In this black Tempest which o'er us impends,
Near Rocks and Quicksands, and no Ports of Friends,
Our Poet gives this over to your rage,
The most irregular Play upon the Stage,
As wild, and as extravagant as th' Age.
Now, angry Men, to all your spleens give vent;
When all your fury has on this been spent,
Elsewhere you with much worse shall be content.
The Poet has no hopes you'll be appeas'd,
Who come on purpose but to be displeas'd;
Such corrupt judges should accepted be
Who can condemn before they hear or see.
Ne'r were such bloody Critics yet in fashion;
You damn by absolute Predestination.
But why so many to run one man down?
It were a mighty triumph when y'have done.
Our scarcity of Plays you should not blame
When by foul poaching you destroy the Game.
Let him have but fair play, and he may then
Write himself into Favour once again.
If after this your Anger you'll reveal,
To Caesar he must make his just appeal;
There Mercy and Judgment equally do meet,
To pardon Faults, and to encourage Wit.

ACT I

Scene 1

A street in Seville. Enter Don John, Don Lopez, Don Antonio, *and* Jacomo, *Don John's valet.*

Don John: Thus far without a bound we have enjoy'd
  Our prosp'rous pleasures, which dull Fools call Sins,
  Laugh'd at old feeble Judges, and weak Laws,
  And at the fond, fantastic thing call'd Conscience
  Which serves for nothing but to make men Cowards,
  An idle fear of future misery,
  And is yet worse than all that we can fear.
Don Lopez: Conscience made up of dark and horrid thoughts,
  Rais'd from the fumes of a distemper'd Spleen.
Don Antonio: A senseless fear would make us contradict
  The only certain Guide, Infallible Nature,
  And at the call of Melancholy Fools
  (Who style all actions which they like not, Sins),
  To silence all our Natural appetites.
Don John: Yet those conscientious Fools that would persuade us
  To I know not what, which they call Piety,
  Have in reserve private delicious Sins,
  Great as the happy Libertine enjoys,
  With which, in corners, wantonly they roll.
Don Lopez: Don John, thou art our Oracle; thou hast
  Dispelled the Fumes which once clouded our Brains.
Don Antonio: By thee we have got loose from Education
  And the dull slavery of Pupillage,
  Recover'd all the liberty of Nature;
  Our own strong Reason now can go alone
  Without the feeble props of splenatic Fools
  Who contradict our common Mother, Nature.
Don John: Nature gave us our Senses, which we please;
  Nor does our Reason war against our Sense.
  By Nature's order, Sense should guide our Reason,

176

Since to the mind all objects Sense conveys.
But Fools for shadows lose substantial pleasures,
For idle tales abandon true delight,
And solid joys of day for empty dreams at night.
Away, thou foolish thing, thou colic of the mind,
Thou Worm by ill-digesting stomachs bred:
In spite of thee, we'll surfeit in delights,
And never think aught can be ill that's pleasant.

JACOMO: A most excellent sermon, and no doubt, Gentlemen, you have edifi'd much by it.

DON JOHN: Away! thou formal phlegmatic Coxcomb, thou
Hast neither courage, nor yet wit enough
To sin thus. Thou art my dull conscientious Pimp.
And when I am wanton with my Whore within,
Thou with thy Beads and Pray'r-Book keep'st the door.

JACOMO: Sir, I find your worship is no more afraid to be damn'd than other fashionable Gentlemen of the Age: but, methinks, Halters and Axes should terrify you. With reverence to your Worships, I've seen civiler men hang'd, and men of as pretty parts too. There's scarce a city in Spain but is too hot for you, you have committed such outrages whereso'er you come.

DON LOPEZ: Come, for diversion, pray let's hear your Fool preach a little.

JACOMO: For my part, I cannot but be troubled that I shall lose my Honour by you, Sir; for people will be apt to say, *Like Master, Like Man.*

DON JOHN: Your honour, Rascal, a Sow-gelder may better pretend to it.

JACOMO: But I have another scruple, Sir.

DON JOHN: What's that?

JACOMO: I fear I shall be hang'd in your company.

DON JOHN: That's an honour you will ne'er have courage to deserve.

JACOMO: It is an honour I am not ambitious of.

DON LOPEZ: Why does the Fool talk of hanging? We scorn all Laws.

JACOMO: It seems so, or you would not have cut your elder brother's throat, Don Lopez.

DON LOPEZ: Why, you Coxcomb, he kept a good Estate from me, and I could not Whore and Revel sufficiently without it.

DON ANTONIO: Look you, Jacomo, had he not reason?

JACOMO: Yes, Antonio, so had you to get both your Sisters with Child; 'twas very civil, I take it.

DON ANTONIO: Yes, you fool, they were lusty young handsome Wenches, and pleas'd my appetite. Besides, I sav'd the Honour of the Family by it, for if I had not, somebody else would.

JACOMO: O horrid villany!
But you are both Saints to my hopeful Master;
I'll turn him loose to Belzebub himself;
He shall outdo him at his own Weapons.

DON JOHN: I, you Rascal.

JACOMO: Oh no, Sir, you are as innocent. To cause your good old Father to be kill'd was nothing.

DON JOHN: It was something, and a good thing too, Sirra: his whole design was to debar me of my pleasures: he kept his purse from me, and could not be content with that, but still would preach his sense-less Morals to me, his old dull foolish stuff against my pleasure. I caus'd him to be sent I know not whither. But he believ'd he was to go to Heaven; I care not where he is, since I am rid of him.

JACOMO: Cutting his throat was a very good return for his begetting of you.

DON JOHN: That was before he was aware on't; 'twas for his own sake; he ne'r thought of me in the business.

JACOMO: Heav'n bless us!

DON JOHN: You Dog, I shall beat out your brains, if you dare be so impudent as to Pray in my company.

JACOMO: Good Sir, I have done, I have done—

DON LOPEZ: Prithee let the insipid Fool go on.

DON ANTONIO: Let's hear the Coxcomb number up your crimes, The patterns we intend to imitate.

JACOMO: Sir, let me lay your horrid crimes before you:
The unhappy minute may perhaps arrive
When the sense of 'em may make you penitent.

DON ANTONIO: 'Twere better thou wer't hang'd.

DON LOPEZ: Repent! Cowards and Fools do that.

DON JOHN: Your valiant well-bred Gentlemen never repent: But what should I repent of?

JACOMO: After the Murther of your Father, the brave Don Pedro, Governour of Seville, for whom the Town are still in grief, was in his own house barb'rously kill'd by you.

Don John: Barbarously! you lie, you Rascal, 'twas finely done; I run him through the Lungs as handsomely, and kill'd him as decently, and as like a Gentleman as could be. The jealous Coxcomb deserv'd death; he kept his Sister from me; her eyes would have kill'd me if I had not enjoy'd her, which I could not do without killing him. Besides, I was alone, and kill'd him hand to fist.

Jacomo: I never knew you go to Church but to take Sanctuary for a Murder, or to rob Churches of their Plate.

Don John: Heav'n needs not be serv'd in Plate, but I had use on't.

Jacomo: How often have you scal'd the Walls of Monasteries? Two Nuns, I know, you ravish'd, and a third you dangerously wounded for her violent resistance.

Don John: The perverse Jades were uncivil, and deserv'd such usage.

Jacomo: Some thirty Murders, Rapes innumerable, frequent Sacrilege, Parricide; in short, not one in all the Catalogue of Sins have scap'd you.

Don John: My bus'ness is my pleasure; that end I will always compass without scrupling the means; there is no right or wrong but what conduces to or hinders pleasure. But you tedious insipid Rascal, if I hear more of your Morality, I will Carbonado you.

Don Antonio: We live in the life of Sense, which no fantastic thing call'd Reason shall control.

Don Lopez: My reason tells me I must please my Sense.

Don John: My appetites are all I'm sure I have from Heav'n, since they are Natural, and them I always will obey.

Jacomo: I doubt it not, Sir; therefore I desire to shake hands and part.

Don John: D'ye hear, Dog, talk once more of parting, and I will saw your Windpipe. I could find in my heart to cut your Rascal's Nose off, and save the Pox a labour: I'll do't, Sirra; have at you.

Jacomo: Good Sir, be not so transported; I will live, Sir, and will serve you in anything; I'll fetch a Wench, or anything in the world, Sir. [*Aside.*] O how I tremble at this Tyrant's rage.

Don Antonio: Come, 'tis night, we lose time to our adventures.

Don Lopez: I have bespoke Music for our Serenading.

Don John: Let's on, and live the noble life of Sense.

To all the powers of Love and mighty Lust
In spite of formal Fops I will be just.
What ways soe're conduce to my delight,
My Sense instructs me, I must think 'em right.

On, on my Soul, and make no stop in pleasure;
They're dull insipid Fools that live by measure.
[*Exeunt all but Jacomo.*]

JACOMO: What will become of me? if I should leave him, he's so revengeful he would travel o'r all Spain to find me out and cut my throat. I cannot live long with him neither: I shall be hang'd, or knock'd o' th' head, or share some dreadful Fate or other with him. 'Tis between him and me as between the Devil and the Witch who repents her bargain and would be free from future ills, but for the fear of present durst not venture.

[*Enter* LEONORA.]

Here comes Leonora, one of those multitudes of Ladies he has Sworn, li'd to, and betray'd.

LEONORA: Jacomo, where is Don John? I could not live to endure a longer absence from him. I have sigh'd and wept myself away: I move, but have no life left in me. His coldness and his absence have given me fearful and killing apprehensions. Where is my Dear?

JACOMO: Your Dear, Madam! he's yours no more.

LEONORA: Heav'n! What do I hear? Speak, is he dead?

JACOMO: To you he is.

LEONORA: Ah me, has he forgot his Vows and Oaths?
Has he no Conscience, Faith, or Honour left?

JACOMO: Left, Madam, he ne'r had any.

LEONORA: It is impossible; you speak this out of malice, sure.

JACOMO: There's no man knows him better than I do.
I have a greater respect for you than for any he has betray'd, and will undeceive you: he is the most perfidious Wretch alive.

LEONORA: Has he forgot the Sacred Contract which was made privately betwixt us, and confirm'd before the altar during the time of holy Mass?

JACOMO: All times and places are alike to him.

LEONORA: Oh how assiduous was he in his passion! How many thousand vows and sighs he breath'd! What tears he wept, seeming to suffer all the cruel pangs which Lovers e'r endur'd! How eloquent were all his words and actions!

JACOMA: His person and his parts are excellent, but his base vices are beyond all measure: why would you believe him?

LEONORA: My own love brib'd me to believe him: I saw the man I lov'd more than the world oft on his knees, with his eyes up to Heav'n, kissing my hand with such an amorous heat, and with such ardor, breathing fervent vows of loyal love, and venting sad complaints of extreme sufferings. I, poor easy Soul, flattering myself to think he meant as I did, lost all my Sex's faculty, Dissembling; and in a month must I be thus betray'd?

JACOMO: Poor Lady! I cannot but have bowels for you: your sad Narration makes me weep in sadness: but you are better us'd than others. I ne'r knew him constant a fortnight before.

LEONORA: Then, then he promis'd he would marry me.

JACOMO: If he were to live here one month longer, he wou'd marry half the Town, ugly and handsome, old and young: nothing that's female comes amiss to him—

LEONORA: Does he not fear a thunderbolt from Heav'n?

JACOMO: No, nor a Devil from Hell. He owns no Deity but his voluptuous appetite, whose satisfaction he will compass by Murders, Rapes, Treasons, or Aught else. But pray let me ask you one civil question: Did you not give him earnest of your Body, Madam?

LEONORA: Mock not my misery. Oh! that confounds me. Ah! I thought him true, and lov'd him so, I could deny him nothing.

JACOMO: Why, there 'tis; I fear you have, or else he wou'd have marri'd you: he has marri'd six within this month, and promis'd fifteen more, all whom he has enjoy'd and left, and is this night gone on some new adventure, some Rape, or Murder, some such petty thing.

LEONORA: Oh Monster of Impiety!
Oh false Don John! wonder of cruelty!
[She swoons.]

JACOMO: What a pox does she swoon at the news! Alas! poor Soul, she has mov'd me now to pity, as she did to love. Ha! the place is private—if I should make use of a Natural Receit to refresh her, and bring her to life again, 'twould be a great pleasure to me, and no trouble to her. Hum! 'tis very private, and I dare sin in private. A deuce take her, she revives, and prevents me.

LEONORA: Where is the cruel Tyrant! inhuman Monster! but I will strive to fortify myself. But Oh my misfortune! Oh my misery! Under what strange Enchantments am I bound? Could he be yet a thousand times more impious, I could not choose but love his Person still.

JACOMO: Be not so passionate; if you could be discreet, and love yourself, I'd put you in a way to ease your grief now, and all your cares hereafter.

LEONORA: If you can now ease an afflicted Woman who else must shortly rid herself of life, employ your Charity: 'twas never plac'd yet on a Wretch needed it more than I.

JACOMO: If Loyalty in a Lover be a Jewel! say no more, I can tell you where you may have it—

LEONORA: Speak not of truth in man, it is impossible.

JACOMO: Pardon me, I speak on my own knowledge.

LEONORA: Is your Master true then? and have you happily deceiv'd me? Speak.

JACOMO: As true as all the power of Hell can make him.

LEONORA: If he be false, let all the world be so.

JACOMO: There's another-guess man than he, Madam.

LEONORA: Another! Who can that be? [Aside.] No, no, there's no truth found in the Sex.

JACOMO: He is a civil, virtuous, and discreet, sober person.

LEONORA: Can there be such a man? What does he mean?

JACOMO: There is, Madam, a man of goodly Presence too—
Something inclining to be fat, of a round plump face, with quick and sparkling eyes, and mouth of cheerful overture—
His nose, which is the only fault, is somewhat short, but that's no matter; his hair and eyebrows black, and so forth.

LEONORA: How, he may perhaps be brib'd by some other man, and what he said of his Master may be false.

JACOMO: How she surveys me! [Sings and struts about.] Fa-la-la.

LEONORA: Who is this you speak of?

JACOMO: A man who, envy must confess, has excellent parts, but those are gifts, gifts—mere gifts—thanks be to Heav'n for them.

LEONORA: But shall I never know his name?

JACOMO: He's one whom many Ladies have honour'd with their affection; but no more of that. They have met disdain, and so forth. But he'll be content to marry you. [Sings.] Fa-la-la-la.

LEONORA: Again I ask you who he is?

JACOMO: Lord, how inapprehensive she is! Can you not guess?

LEONORA: No.

JACOMO: Your humble Servant, Madam.

LEONORA: Yours, Sir.

JACOMO: It is myself in person; and upon my honour, I will be true and constant to you.

LEONORA: Insolent Varlet! Am I fall'n so low to be thy scorn?

JACOMO: Scorn! As I am a Christian Soul I am in earnest.

LEONORA: Audacious Villain! Impudence itself!

JACOMO: Ah, Madam! your Servant, your true Lover must endure a thousand such bobs* from his Mistress; I can bear, Madam, I can.

LEONORA: Because thy Master has betray'd me, am I become so infamous?

JACOMO: 'Tis something hard, Madam, to preserve a good reputation in his company; I can scarce do't myself.

LEONORA: Am I so miserable to descend to his man?

JACOMO: Descend, say you: Ha, ha, ha!

LEONORA: Now I perceive all's false which you have said of him. Farewell, you base ungrateful Fellow.

JACOMO: Hold, Madam; come in the Morning and I will place you in the next room, where you shall overhear our discourse. You'll soon discover the mistake, and find who 'tis that loves you. Retire, Madam, I hear somebody coming.

[*Exeunt* JACOMO, LEONORA.]

Scene 2

Another part of Seville. Enter DON JOHN *in the Street.*

DON JOHN: Let me see, here lives a Lady: I have seen Don Octavio haunting about this house, and making private signs to her. I never saw her face, but am resolv'd to enjoy her because he likes her; besides, she's another Woman.

[*Enter* DON ANTONIO.]

DON ANTONIO: Welcome to our place of rendezvous. Well, what game! what adventure! [*Enter* DON LOPEZ.] Come, dear Lopez.

DON ANTONIO: I have had a rare Adventure.

DON LOPEZ: What, dear Antonio?

DON ANTONIO: I saw at a Villa not far off a grave, mighty, bearded Fool, drinking Lemonado with his Mistress; I mislik'd his face, pluck'd him by the Whiskers, pull'd all one side of his Beard off, fought with him, run him through the thigh, carri'd away his Mistress, serv'd her in her kind, and then let her go.

DON JOHN: Gallantly perform'd, like a brave Soldier in an Enemy's Country: When they will not pay Contribution, you fight for Forage.

DON LOPEZ: Pox on't, I have been damnably unfortunate; I have

*Bobs = taunts. [*Editor's note.*]

neither beat man nor lain with Woman tonight, but fall'n in love most furiously: I dogg'd my new Mistress to her Lodging; she's Don Bernardo's Sister, and shall be my Punk.

Don John: I could meet with no willing Dame, but was fain to commit a Rape to pass away the time.

Don Antonio: Oh! A Rape is the joy of my heart; I love a Rape, upon my Clavis, exceedingly.

Don John: But mine, my Lads, was such a Rape it ought to be Registered; a Noble and Heroic Rape.

Don Lopez: Ah! dear Don John!

Don Antonio: How was it?

Don John: 'Twas in a Church, Boys.

Don Antonio: Ah! Gallant Leader!

Don Lopez: Renown'd Don John!

Don Antonio: Come, let's retire, you have done enough for once.

Don John: Not yet, Antonio, I have an Intrigue here. [*Enter Fiddlers.*] Here are my Fiddlers; Rank yourselves close under this Window, and sing the Song I prepar'd.

SONG

Thou joy of all hearts, and delight of all eyes,
Nature's chief Treasure, and Beauty's chief Prize,
  Look down, you'll discover
Here's a faithful young vigorous Lover,
  With a Heart full as true
  As e'r languish'd for you;
Here's a faithful young vigorous Lover.

The Heart that was once a Monarch in's Breast
Is now your poor Captive, and can have no rest;
    'Twill never give over,
  But about your sweet bosom will hover.
    Dear Miss, let it in;
    By Heav'n 'tis no sin;
Here's a faithful young vigorous vigorous Lover.

Don John: Now Fiddlers, be gone.

[*Window opens,* Maria *looks out, and flings a Paper down.*]

Maria: Retire, my dear Octavio; read that Note. Adieu.

[*Exit* Maria.]

Don John: Good, she takes me for Octavio. I warrant you, Boys, I shall succeed in this adventure. Now my false Light assist me.

The Libertine   185

[*Reads by a dark Lanthorn.*] "Go from this Window; within eight minutes you shall be admitted to the Garden door. You know the Sign." Ha, the Sign! Gad, she lies; I know not the Sign.

DON ANTONIO: What will you do? you know not the Sign. Let's away, and be contented this night.

DON JOHN: My friends, if you love me, retire. I'll venture, though Thunderbolts should fall upon my head.

DON LOPEZ: Are you mad? As soon as she discovers the deceit, she'll raise the house upon you, and you'll be murder'd.

DON JOHN: She'll not raise the House for her own sake, but rather grant me all I ask to keep her counsel.

DON ANTONIO: 'Tis very dangerous: be careful of yourself.

DON JOHN: The more danger the more delight: I hate the common road of pleasure. What! Can I fear at such a time as this! The cowardly Deer are valiant in their Rutting time, I say. Be gone—

DON ANTONIO: We'll not dispute your commands. Good luck to you.

[*Exeunt* DON ANTONIO *and* DON LOPEZ.]

DON JOHN: How shall I know this devilish Sign?

[*Enter* OCTAVIO *with Fiddlers, and stands under Maria's Window.*] Ha! Whom have we here? Some Serenading Coxcomb. Now shall we have some damn'd Song or other, a Cloris, or a Phillis at least.

SONG

When you dispense your Influence,
　Your dazling Beams are quick and clear;
　You so surprize and wound the Sense,
　So bright a Miracle y'appear,
Admiring Mortals you astonish so,
　No other Deity they know,
But think that all Divinity's below—

One charming Look from your illustrious Face
　Were able to subdue Mankind;
　So sweet, so powerful a Grace
　Makes all men Lovers but the blind:
Nor can they freedom by resistance gain,
　For each embraces the soft Chain,
And never struggles with the pleasant pain.

DON OCTAVIO: Begone! begone! the Window opens.

DON JOHN: 'Sdeath! This is Octavio. I must dispatch him, or he'll spoil all; but I would fain hear the Sign first.

MARIA: What strange mistake is this? Sure he did not receive my Note, and then I am ruin'd!

DON OCTAVIO: She expects the Sign. Where's my Whistle? O here.
[*He whistles.*]

DON JOHN: I have found it, that must be the Sign—

MARIA: I dare not speak aloud, go to the Garden Door.
[DON JOHN *rushes upon* OCTAVIO, *and snatches the Whistle out of his hand.*]

DON OCTAVIO: 'Sdeath, what Ruffian's this?

DON JOHN: One that will be sure to cut your throat.

DON OCTAVIO: Make not a promise to yourself of what you can't perform.
[*They fight.*]

DON JOHN: I warrant you. Have at you.

MARIA: O Heav'n! Octavio's Fighting! Oh my heart!

DON OCTAVIO [*falls*]: Oh! I am slain.—

DON JOHN: I knew I should be as good as my word. I think you have it, Sir—Ha!—he's dying—Now for the Lady—I'll draw him farther off, that his groans may not disturb our pleasure—Stay—by your leave, Sir, I'll change Hat and Cloak with you; it may help me in my design.

DON OCTAVIO: O barbarous Villain!
[*He dies.*]

MARIA: They have done fighting, and I hear no noise. Oh unfortunate Woman! my dear Octavio's kill'd—

FLORA: Perhaps, Madam, he has kill'd the other. I'll down to the Garden door; if he be well, he'll come thither, as well to satisfy his appointment, as to take refuge. Your Brother's safe, he may come in securely—
[*Exit to the door.*]

MARIA: Haste! Haste! Fly! Fly! Oh Octavio. I'll follow her.
[*She follows.*]

DON JOHN: Now for the Garden Door. This Whistle will do me excellent Service. Now good luck.
[*Goes to the Door and Whistles.*]

FLORA: Octavio?

DON JOHN: The same.

FLORA: Heav'n be prais'd, my Lady thought you had been kill'd.

DON JOHN: I am unhurt: let's quickly to her.

FLORA: Oh! She'll be overjoy'd to see you alive.

DON JOHN: I'll make her more overjoy'd before I have done with her. This is a rare adventure!

[*Enter* MARIA *at the Door.*]

FLORA: Here's your Jewel, Madam, speak softly.

MARIA: Oh my dear Octavio! I have got you within these arms?

DON JOHN: Ah, my Dear, unpierc'd by anything but by your eyes.

MARIA: Those will do you no hurt. But are you sure you are not wounded?

DON JOHN: I am. Let me embrace my pretty Dear. [*Aside.*] And yet she may be a Blackamore for aught I know—

MARIA: We'll retire to my Chamber. Flora, go out, and prepare us a Collation.

DON JOHN: O admirable adventure! Come, my Delight.

[*Exeunt. Enter* DON LOPEZ, DON ANTONIO *and* JACOMO.]

JACOMO: Where's my pious Master?

DON ANTONIO: We left him hereabouts. I wonder what he has done in his adventure: I believe he has had some bustle.

DON LOPEZ: I thought I heard fighting hereabout.

JACOMO: Gad forgive me! fighting! where! where!

DON ANTONIO: O thou incorrigible Coward!

DON LOPEZ: See, here's some of his handy-work; here's a man kill'd.

JACOMO: Another murder. Heav'n, what will become of me? I shall be hang'd, yet dare not run away from him.

[*Enter an* OFFICER *with a Guard, going the Round.*]

OFFICER: Stand! who are there?

DON LOPEZ: We do stand, Rascal, we never use to run.

JACOMO: Now shall I be taken hang'd for my Master's murder.

[*Offers to run.*]

DON ANTONIO: Stand, you Dog! offer once more to run, and I'll put Bilbow in your guts.

JACOMO: Gad forgive me! what will become of me?

OFFICER: What's here? A Man murder'd? Yield, you are my prisoners.

JACOMO: With all my heart! but as I hope to be saved, we did not kill him, Sir.

OFFICER: These must be the murderers; disarm 'em.

DON ANTONIO: How now, Rascal! Disarm us!

DON LOPEZ: We are not us'd to part with our Swords.

JACOMO: I care not a farthing for my Sword; 'tis at your service.

DON ANTONIO: Do you hear, Rascal; keep it and fight, or I'll swear the murder against you.

DON LOPEZ: Offer to flinch, and I'll run you through.

OFFICER: Take their Swords, or knock 'em down.

[*They fight.* JACOMO *offers to run, some of the Guards stop him.*]

JACOMO: A pox on't; I had as good fight and die as be taken and be hang'd.

[*Guards are beaten off.*]

DON LOPEZ: Are you gone, you Dogs? I have pinck'd some of you.

JACOMO: Ah Rogues! Villains! I have met with you.

DON ANTONIO: O brave Jacomo! you fought like an imprison'd Rat. The Rogue had conceal'd Courage, and did not know it.

JACOMO: O Cowards! Rascals! a man can get no honour by fighting with such Poltroons! but for all that, I will prudently withdraw; this place will suddenly be too hot for us.

DON LOPEZ: Once in your Life you are in the right, Jacomo.

JACOMO: O good Sir, there is as much to be ascribed to Conduct as to Courage, I assure you.

[*Exeunt.*]

Scene 3

Maria's chamber. Enter DON JOHN *and* MARIA.

MARIA: Speak softly, my Dear; should my Brother hear us, we are ruin'd.

DON JOHN: Though I can scarce contain my joy, I will. [*Aside.*] O she's a rare Creature in the dark; pray Heav'n she be so in the light.

[*Enter* FLORA *with a Candle; as soon as they discover Don John, they shriek out.*]

MARIA: O Heaven! I am ruin'd and betrayed.

FLORA: He has Octavio's clothes on.

MARIA: O he has murder'd him. My Brother shall revenge it.

DON JOHN: I will cut his throat if he offers it.

MARIA: ⎫
FLORA: ⎭ Thieves! Murder! Murder! Thieves.

DON JOHN: I will stop your shrill windpipes.

[*Enter Maria's* BROTHER, *with his Sword drawn.*]

BROTHER: 'Sdeath! A man in my Sister's Chamber! Have at you. Villain.

DON JOHN: Come on, Villain.

[DON JOHN *kills the* BROTHER.]

FLORA: Murder! Murder!

MARIA: O Villain, thou hast kill'd my Brother, and dishonour'd me. [*Enter five or six Servants, with drawn Swords.*] O your Master's murdered!

DON JOHN: So many of you; 'tis no matter. Your Heroes in Plays beat five times as many. Have at you, Rogues. [MARIA *runs away shrieking, and* DON JOHN *beats the Servants off, and stops* FLORA.] Now give me the Key of the Garden, or I'll murder thee.

FLORA: Murder! Murder! There, take it—

[*She runs away.*]

DON JOHN: So, thus far it is well; this was a brave adventure.

'Mongst all the Joys which in the world are sought,

None are so great as those by dangers bought.

[*Exit.*]

ACT II

Scene 1

Don John's town house. JACOMO *alone.*

JACOMO: What will this lewd Master of mine do? this Town of Seville will not much care for his company after his last night's Achievements. He must either fly, or hang for't. Ha! methinks my blood grows chill at the naming of that dreadful word *Hang.* What will become of me? I dare not leave him, and yet I fear that I shall perish with him. He's certainly the first that ever set up a Religion to the Devil.

[*Enter* LEONORA.]

LEONORA: I come to claim your promise; is Don John within?

JACOMO: No, Madam, but I expect him every minute. You see, Madam, what honour I have for you, for I venture my ears to do this.

LEONORA: You oblige me extremely; so great is the present pain of doubt that we desire to lose it, though in exchange of certainty that must afflict us more.

JACOMO: I hear him coming; withdraw quickly.

[*She withdraws. Enter* DON JOHN.]

DON JOHN: How now, sir, what wise thoughts have you in your Noddle?

JACOMO: Why, Sir, I was considering how well I could endure to be hang'd.

DON JOHN: And why so, Buffle?*

JACOMO: Why you will force me to wait upon you in all your fortunes, and you are making what haste you can to the Gallows—

DON JOHN: Again at your reproofs. You insipid Rascal; I shall cut your ears off, Dog—

JACOMO: Good Sir, I have done; yet I cannot but admire, since you are resolv'd to go to the Devil, that you cannot be content with the common way of travelling, but must ride post to him.

DON JOHN: Leave off your idle tales, found out by Priests to keep the Rabble in awe.

JACOMO: Oh horrid wickedness! If I may be bold to ask, what noble exploits did your Chivalry perform last night?

DON JOHN: Why, Sir, I commited a Rape upon my Father's Monument.

JACOMO: Oh horror!

DON JOHN: Do you start, you Villain? Hah!

JACOMO: I, Sir, who, I, Sir? not I, Sir.

DON JOHN: D'hear, Rascal, let me not see a frown upon your face; if I do, I will cut your throat, you Rogue.

JACOMO: No Sir, no Sir, I warrant you; I am in a very good humor, I assure you—Heav'n deliver me!

DON JOHN: Now listen and learn. I kill'd a Lady's Lover, and suppli'd his place, by stratagem enjoy'd her. In came her foolish Brother and surprized me, but perished by my hand; and I doubt not but I maul'd three or four of his Servants.

[JACOMO starts.]

JACOMO [Aside.]: Oh horrid fact!

DON JOHN: Again, Villain, are you frowning?

JACOMO: No Sir, no Sir; don't think so ill of me, Sir. Heav'n send me from this wicked Wretch! What will become of us, Sir? We shall be apprehended.

DON JOHN: Can you fear your Rascally Carcass when I venture mine? I observe always, those that have the most despicable persons are most careful to preserve 'em.

---

*Buffle = nincompoop. [Editor's note.]

JACOMO: Sir, I beg your pardon; but I have an odd humor, makes me something unfit for your Worship's service.

DON JOHN: What's that, Sirra?

JACOMO: 'Tis a very odd one, I am almost asham'd to tell it to you.

DON JOHN: Out with it, Fool—

JACOMO: Why Sir, I cannot tell what is the reason, but I have a most unconquerable antipathy to Hemp. I could never endure a Bell-rope. Hanging is a kind of death I cannot abide. I am not able to endure it.

DON JOHN: I have taken care to avoid that; my friends are gone to hire a Vessel, and we'll to Sea together to seek a refuge, and a new Scene of pleasure.

JACOMO: All three, Sir?

DON JOHN: Yes, Sir.

JACOMO: Three as civil, discreet, sober persons as a man wou'd wish to drink with.

[*Enter* LEONORA.]

LEONORA: I can hold no longer!

DON JOHN: 'Sdeath, you Dog, how came she here?

JACOMO: I don't know, Sir; she stole in.

LEONORA: What Witchcraft do I suffer under that when I abhor his vices, I still love his person? Ah, Don John! have I deserv'd that you should fly me? Are all your Oaths and vows forgotten by you?

DON JOHN: No, no; in these cases I always remember my Oaths, and never forget to break them.

LEONORA: Oh impiety! Did I, for this, yield up my Honour to you? After you had sigh'd and languished many months, and shew'd all signs of a sincere affection, I trusted in your truth and constancy, without the Bond of Marriage, yielded up a Virgin's Treasure, all my Innocence, believed your solemn Contract, when you invok'd all the Pow'rs above to testify your Vows.

DON JOHN: They think much of us; why don't they witness 'em for you? —Pish, 'tis nothing but a way of speaking which young amorous Fellows have gotten.

LEONORA: Did you not love me then? What injury had I e'r done you that you shou'd feign affection to betray me?

DON JOHN: Yes, 'faith, I did love you, and shew'd you as frequent and as hearty signs of it as I could; and i'gad y'are an ungrateful Woman if you say the contrary.

LEONORA: O heav'n! Did you and do not now? What crime have I committed that could make you break your Vows and Oaths, and banish all your passion? Ah! with what tenderness have I receiv'd your feign'd affection, and ne'r thought I liv'd but in your presence; my love was too fervent to be counterfeit—

DON JOHN: That I know not, for since your Sex are such dissemblers, they can hold out against and seem to hate the men they love; why may they not seem to love the men they hate?

LEONORA: O cruel Man! Could I dissemble? Had I a thousand lives, I ventur'd all each time I saw your face; nay, were I now discover'd, I should instantly be sacrific'd to my raging Brother's fury; and can I dissemble?

DON JOHN: I do not know whether you do or no; you see I don't; I am something free with you.

LEONORA: And do you not love me then?

DON JOHN: Faith, Madam, I lov'd you as long as I could for the heart and blood of me, and there's an end of it; what a Devil wou'd you have more?

LEONORA: O cruel man! how miserable have you made me!

DON JOHN: Miserable! use variety as I do, and you'll not be miserable. Ah! there's nothing so sweet to frail human flesh as variety.

LEONORA: Inhuman Creature! what have I been guilty of that thou shouldst thus remove thy Affections from me?

DON JOHN: Guilty, no: but I have had enough of you, and I have done what I can for you, and there's no more to be said.

LEONORA: Tigers would have more pity than thou hast.

DON JOHN: Unreasonable Woman! would you have a man love after enjoyment? I think the Devil's in you.

LEONORA: Do you upbraid me with the rash effects of Love which you caus'd in me? And do you hate me for what you ought to love me for? Were you not many months with Vows and Oaths betraying me to that weakness? Ungrateful Monster!

DON JOHN: Why the Devil did you not yield before? you Women always rook in Love; you'll never play upon the square with us.

LEONORA: False Man! I yielded but too soon. Unfortunate Woman!

DON JOHN: Your dissembling Arts and jilting tricks, taught you by your Mothers, and the phlegmatic coldness of your constitutions make you so long in yielding that we love out almost all our love before you begin, and yet you would have our love last as long as yours. I got the start of you a long way, and have reason to reach the Goal before you.

LEONORA: Did you not swear you wou'd forever love me?

DON JOHN: Why there 'tis; why did you put me to the trouble to swear it? If you Women wou'd be honest and follow the Dictates of Sense and Nature, we shou'd agree about the business presently, and never be forsworn for the matter.

LEONORA: Are Oaths so slighted by you, perfidious Man?

DON JOHN: Oaths! Snares to catch conceited Women with; I wou'd have sworn all the Oaths under the Sun. Why I wou'd have committed Treason for you, and yet I knew I should be weary of you—

LEONORA: I thought such love as mine might have deserv'd your constancy, false and ungrateful man!

DON JOHN: Thus your own vanity, not we betray you. Each Woman thinks though men are false to others that she is so fine a person none can be so to her. You shou'd not take our words of course in earnest.

LEONORA: Thus Devils do in Hell, who cruelly upbraid whom they have tempted thither.

DON JOHN: In short, my constitution will not let me love you longer: and whatever some Hypocrites pretend, all mankind obey their constitutions, and cannot do otherwise.

LEONORA: Heav'n, sure, will punish this vile treachery.

DON JOHN: Do you then leave it to Heav'n, and trouble yourself no farther about it.

LEONORA: Ye Sacred Pow'rs who take care of injur'd innocence, assist me.

[*Enter* JACOMO.]

JACOMO: Sir, Sir! Stand upon your guard.

DON JOHN: How now! What's the matter?

JACOMO: Here's a whole Battalion of courageous Women come to charge you.

[*Enter* SIX WOMEN.]

DON JOHN: Keep 'em out, you Villain.

JACOMO: I cannot, they overrun me.

DON JOHN: What an inundation of Strumpets is here?

LEONORA: O Heav'n! I can stay no longer to be a witness of his falsehood—

[*Exit* LEONORA.]

FIRST WOMAN: My Dear, I desire a word in private with you.

DON JOHN: 'Faith, my Dear, I am something busy, but I love thee dearly. [*Aside.*] A pox on thee!

SECOND WOMAN: Don John, a word: 'tis time now we should declare our marriage; 'tis now about three weeks.

DON JOHN: Ay, we will do it suddenly.

THIRD WOMAN: Prithee, Honey, what bus'ness can these idle Women have? Send them packing, that we may confer about our affairs.

FOURTH WOMAN: Lord! How am I amaz'd at the confidence of some Women! Who are these that will not let one converse with one's own Husband? By your leave, Ladies.

JACOMO: Now it works! tease him, Ladies, worry him soundly.

FIFTH WOMAN: Nay, by your leave, good Madam; if you go to that. [*Pulls* DON JOHN *from the other.*]

SIXTH WOMAN: Ladies, by all your leaves; sure none of you will have the confidence to pretend an interest in this Gentleman—

DON JOHN: I shall be torn in pieces: Jacomo, stand by me.

FIRST WOMAN: Lord, Madam, what's your meaning? none ought to claim a right to another Woman's Husband, let me tell you that.

SECOND WOMAN: You are in the right, Madam. Therefore prithee, Dear, let's withdraw, and leave them; I do not like their company.

DON JOHN: Ay, presently, my Dear. What an excellent thing is a Woman before Enjoyment, and how insipid after it!

FOURTH WOMAN: Come, prithee, put these Women out of doubt, and let them know our marriage.

DON JOHN: Tomorrow we'll declare and celebrate our Nuptials.

SIXTH WOMAN: Ladies, the short and the long on't is, you are very uncivil to press upon this Gentleman. Come, Love, e'en tell 'em the truth of the story.

FOURTH WOMAN: Uncivil, Madam, pardon me; one cannot be so in speaking to one's own.

THIRD WOMAN: That's true; she little thinks who that is.

SIXTH WOMAN: To their own! Ha, ha, ha, that's true—Come, Honey, keep 'em no longer in Ignorance.

FOURTH WOMAN: Come, Ladies, I will undeceive you all; think no further of this Gentleman, I say, think no further of him—

FIRST WOMAN: What can this mean?

DON JOHN: Hold, for Heav'n's sake; you know not what you do.

FOURTH WOMAN: Yes, yes, I do; it shall all out: I'll send 'em away with Fleas in their Ears. Poor silly Creatures!

DON JOHN: Now will Civil Wars arise—

FOURTH WOMAN: Trouble yourselves no longer about Don John; he is mine—he is mine, Ladies.

ALL: Yours!

DON JOHN: Pox on't, I must set a good face upon the bus'ness; I see murder will out—

SIXTH WOMAN: Yours, that's pleasant; he's mine—

FIFTH WOMAN: I have been too long patient; he is my Husband.

FIRST WOMAN: Yours, how can that be? I am sure I am his Wife.

THIRD WOMAN: Are you not asham'd, Ladies, to claim my Husband?

SECOND WOMAN: Are you all mad? I am sure I am marri'd to him.

ALL: You!

DON JOHN: Look you, Ladies, a Man's but a Man! Here's my Body, take't among you as far as 'twill go. The Devil can't please you all—

JACOMO: Pray, Ladies, will you dispatch; for there are a matter of fifteen more that are ready to put in their claims, and must be heard in their order.

DON JOHN: How now, Rogue, this is your fault, Sirra.

JACOMO: My fault, Sir, no; the Ladies shall see I am no Traitor. Look you, Ladies—

DON JOHN: Peace, Villain, or I will cut your Throat. Well, Ladies, know then, I am marri'd to one in this company; and tomorrow morning, if you will repair to this place, I will declare my marriage, which now for some secret Reasons I am oblig'd to conceal—Now will each Strumpet think 'tis her I mean.

FIRST WOMAN: 'That's well enough.

FOURTH WOMAN: I knew he would own me at last.

THIRD WOMAN: Now they will soon see their errors.

FIFTH WOMAN: Now we'll conceal it no longer, Dearest.

DON JOHN: No, no, I warrant you—

SIXTH WOMAN: Lord, how blank these Ladies will look.

SECOND WOMAN: Poor Ladies—

JACOMO: Ladies, pray let me ask a question, which of you is really marri'd to him?

ALL: I, I, I.

DON JOHN: 'Sdeath, you Son of a Baboon. Come, Pox on't, why should I dally any longer! Why should I conceal my good actions! In one word, I am married to every one of you, and have above four score more; nor will I ever give over till I have as many Wives and Concubines as the Grand Signior.

JACOMO: A very modest civil Person truly—

FOURTH WOMAN: O horrid Villain!

SIXTH WOMAN: Perfidious Monster!

[*Enter* DON LOPEZ *and* DON ANTONIO.]

DON ANTONIO: How now, Don John. Hah; you are a ravenous Bird of prey indeed; do you fly at no less than a whole Covey of Whores at once? you scorn a single Strumpet for your Quarry.

DON LOPEZ: What, in Tears too! Fie, Don John; thou art the most ungenteel Knight alive: Use your Ladies civilly for shame.

DON JOHN: Ah, before the Victory, I grant you; but after it, they should wear Chains, and follow the Conqueror's Chariot.

DON LOPEZ: Alas, poor Harlots!

DON JOHN: Peace, peace, good words; these are certain Animals call'd Wives, and all of 'em are my Wives. Do you call a Man of Honour's Wives, Harlots? out on't.

FIRST WOMAN: Perfidious Monster!

DON ANTONIO: Excellent!

DON JOHN: Come on, you are come very opportunely, to help to celebrate my several and respective Weddings. Come, my Dears; 'faith, we will have a Ballad at our Weddings. Where are my Fiddlers?

SIXTH WOMAN: O savage Beast!

FOURTH WOMAN: Inhuman Villain! Revenge shall follow.

DON JOHN: Pox on Revenge, call in my Minstrels. [*Enter* FIDDLERS.] Come, Sing my Epithalamium.

SONG

Since Liberty, Nature for all has design'd,
A pox on the Fool who to one is confin'd.
   All Creatures besides
   When they please change their Brides.
All Females they get when they can,
Whilst they nothing but Nature obey.
   How happy, how happy are they!
   But the silly fond Animal, Man,
Makes Laws 'gainst himself, which his Appetites sway;
      Poor Fools, how unhappy are they!
CHORUS: Since Liberty, Nature for all has design'd,
         A pox on the Fool who to one is confin'd.

At the first going down, a Woman is good,
But whene'er she comes up, I'll ne'r chew the Cud,
   But out she shall go.
   And I'll serve 'em all so.
When with One my Stomach is cloy'd,
Another shall soon be enjoy'd.

Then how happy, how happy are we!
Let the Coxcomb when weary, drudge on,
And foolishly stay when he wou'd fain be gone.
Poor Fool! How unhappy is he!
CHORUS: At the first going down, &c.

Let the Rabble obey; I'll live like a Man,
Who by Nature is free to enjoy all he can:
Wise Nature does Teach
More truth than Fools Preach;
They bind us, but she gives us ease.
I'll revel, and love where I please.
She, she's my infallible Guide.
But were the Bless'd freedom deni'd
Of variety in the things we love best,
Dull Man were the slavishest Beast.
CHORUS: Let the Rabble obey, &c.

DON JOHN: Come, how do you like this? Let's be merry, my Brides.

FOURTH WOMAN: O monstrous Traitor! Do you mock our Misery?

DON JOHN: Good Spouse, be not passionate—faith, we'll have a Dance.
Strike up—
[*They Dance.*]

DON LOPEZ: Be comforted, good Ladies; you have Companions in your
misfortunes.

DON ANTONIO: He has been marri'd in all the Cities of Spain; what a
breed of Don Johns shall we have!

DON JOHN: Come, Sweethearts; you must be civil to these Gentlemen;
they are my Friends, and men of Honour.

SIXTH WOMAN: Men of Honour! They are Devils if they be your
Friends.

DON JOHN: I hate unreasonable, unconscionable fellows who when
they are weary of their Wives will still keep 'em from other Men.
Gentlemen, ye shall command mine.

FOURTH WOMAN: Thinkest thou I will outlive this affront?

DON JOHN: I'll trust you for that, there's ne'r a Lucrece nowadays; the
Sex has learnt Wit since. Let me see, Antonio, thou shalt have for
thy present use, let me see, my sixth Wife—'faith, she's a pretty
buxom Wench, and deserves hearty usage from thee.

SIXTH WOMAN: Traitor, I'll be reveng'd on all thy treachery.

DON ANTONIO: A mettl'd Girl; I like her well. She'll endure a Rape gallantly. I love resistance; it endears the pleasure.

DON JOHN: And Lopez, thou shalt have, let me see, ay, my fourth Spouse; She's a brave Virago; and Gad if I had not been something familiar with her already, I would venture my Life for her.

FOURTH WOMAN: Vile Wretch! Think'st thou I will outlive this affront? Impious Villain! Though thou hast no sense of Virtue or Honour left, thou shalt find I have.

DON JOHN: Virtue and Honour! There's nothing good or ill but as it seems to each man's natural appetite. If they will not consent freely, you must ravish, friends: that's all I know, you must ravish.

FIRST WOMAN: Unheard-of Villany! Fly from this Hellish place.

DON ANTONIO: Ladies, you shall fly, but we must ravish first.

DON LOPEZ: Yes, I assure you we must ravish—

FOURTH WOMAN: No, Monster, I'll prevent you.
    [*Stabs herself.*]

DON ANTONIO: S'death, she's as good as her word.
    The first time I e're knew a Woman so.

DON LOPEZ: Pox on't, she has prevented me; she's dead.

DON JOHN: Say you so? well, go thy ways, thou wer't a Girl of pretty parts, that's the truth on't; but I ne'r thought this had been in thee.

SECOND WOMAN: These sure are Devils in the shape of men.

DON JOHN: Now see my providence; if I had been marri'd to none but her, I had been a Widower.

FIRST WOMAN: O horror! horror! fly! fly!

SIXTH WOMAN: No, I'll be reveng'd first on this barbarous Wretch.

DON JOHN: Why look you, here's a Wench of mettle for you; go ravish quickly—

SIXTH WOMAN: Let's fly, and call for help, some in the street may help us—
    [*They all run off, crying: Help, murder, murder.*]

DON ANTONIO: Let 'em go; they are confin'd, they can't get out.

DON JOHN: It shall ne'r be said that a Woman went out of this House *Re intacta;* but after that, 'twill be time for to fly.

DON LOPEZ: We have a hir'd Vessel; the Master is a brave Rogue of my acquaintance; he has been a Bandit.

DON ANTONIO: A brave, honest, wicked Fellow as heart can wish; I have ravish'd, robbed, and murdered with him.

DON JOHN: That's well. Hey, where are my Rogues? Hey! [*Enter* SERVANT *and* JACOMO.] Here, Sirrah, do you send my Goods on Board.

Don Antonio: My Man will direct you.

[*Exit* Servant.]

Don John: Come, Sirra, do you remove this Body to another Room—

Jacomo: Oh horrid fact! What, another Murder! What shall I do?

Don John: Leave your complaints, you Dog; I'll send you after her.

Jacomo: Oh! I shall be hang'd, I shall be hang'd.

Don John: Take her up, Rascal; or I'll cut your throat.

Jacomo: I will, Sir. Oh mercy upon me! I shall be hang'd—

Don John: Now, Sirrah, do you run into the streets and force in the next Woman you meet, or I'll cut your Windpipe; and let nobody out—

Jacomo: What hellish act will he now commit?

Don John: Take her up, you Hen-hearted compassionate Rascal.

Jacomo: Heaven! what will become of me? [*Carries her off.*] Oh! Oh—

Don John: Now, Gentlemen, you shall see I'll be civil to you; you shall not ravish alone: indeed I am loath to meddle with mine old acquaintance, but if my Man can meet with a Woman I have not lain withall, I'll keep you company; let her be old or young, ugly or handsome, no matter.

Don Lopez: Faith, I will ever say you are a well bred man.

Don Antonio: A very civil person, a man of Honour.

[*Enter* Servant, *forcing in an ugly* Old Woman, *who cries out.*]

Don John: This unlucky Rogue has made but a scurvy choice, but I'll keep my word. Come, Bawd, you must be ravish'd, Bawd.

Old Woman: O murder! murder! help! help! I was never ravish'd in my life.

Don John: That I dare swear; but to shew I am a very vigorous Man, I'll begin with you. But you Rascal, Jackal, I'll make you Cater better next time.

Servant: Indeed, Sir, this was the first I met.

Don John: Come on, Beldam, thy face shall not protect thee.

Old Woman: Oh my Honour! my Honour! help, help, my Honour!

Don John: Come, to our business.

[*Enter* Jacomo.]

Jacomo: O Sir! Sir! shift for yourself; we shall all be hang'd; the house is beset. Oh what shall we do?

Don John: Away, Coward: were the King of Spain's Army beleagu'ring us, it should not divert me from this Exploit.

Don Antonio: Nor me.

Don Lopez: Nor me. Let's on.

DON JOHN: Keep the doors fast, Sirra. Come on.

JACOMO: Oh what will become of me! Oh Heav'n! mercy on me! Oh
Oh!

[*Exeunt.*]

Scene 2

A street outside Don John's town house. Enter MARIA, *in nun's
habit, with* FLORA.

MARIA: Thus I have abandoned all my Fortune and laid by my Sex,
Revenge, for thee. Assist me now,
You Instruments of Blood, for my dear Brother's
And for my much more dear Octavio's sake.
Where are my Bravos?

FLORA: They have beset the Villain's House,
And he shall ne'r come out alive.

MARIA: O let 'em shew no more remorse
Than Hungry Lions o'r their prey will.
How miserable am I made by that
Inhuman Monster! No savage Beast
Wild deserts e'r brought forth, provoked
By all its hunger and its natural rage,
Could yet have been so cruel.
Oh my Octavio! whether art thou fled
From the most loving and most wretched
Creature of her Sex? What Ages of delight
Each hour with thee brought forth!
How much, when I had thee, was all the world
Unenvied by me! Nay, I piti'd all my Sex
That cou'd have nothing worth their care,
Since all the treasure of Mankind was mine.
Methought I cou'd look down on Queens when he
Was with me: but now, compared to me,
How happy is the Wretch whose sinews
Crack upon the merciless Engine
Of his torture! I live with greater torments than he dies.

FLORA: Leave your complaints. Tears are no Sacrifice for blood.

MARIA: Now my just grief, to just revenge give place.
I am ashamed of these soft Tears till I've
Revenged thy horrid Murder. Oh that I could

Make the Villain linger out an Age in
Torments! But I will revel in his blood: Oh
I could suck the last drop that warms the
Monster's heart. That might inspire me with
Such cruelty as vile Man, with all his horrid
Arts of power, is yet a stranger to;
Then I might root out all his cursed Race.

FLORA: I'll follow all your fortunes, my dear Lady;
Had I ten thousand lives, in this cause I'd
Venture one by one to my last stake.

MARIA: Thou art my dear and faithful Creature;
Let not thy fortunes thus be wrack'd with mine.
Be gone, and leave thy most unhappy Mistress,
One that has miseries enow to sink the Sex.

FLORA: I will not leave you till death takes me from you.

MARIA: Oh that I had been some poor lost Mountain Girl,
Nurs'd up by Goats, or suckl'd by wild Beasts,
Exposed to all the rage of heats and killing colds.
I ne'r cou'd have been abandoned to such fury.
More savage cruelty reigns in Cities
Than ever yet in Deserts among the
Most venomous Serpents and remorseless
Ravenous Beasts could once be found.
So much has barbarous Art debauch'd
Man's innocent Nature.

FLORA: Lay by your tears till your revenge be finish'd;
Then, then, you may have leisure to complain.

MARIA: I will; 'tis blood I now must spill or
Lose my own in the attempt. But if I can
Have the fortune, with my own hand, to reach
The Dog's vile heart, I then shall die
Contented, and in the other World I'll
Torture him so, Devils shall learn of me to
Use the Damn'd.

FLORA: Let's to our Sacred Instruments of revenge.

MARIA: Come on. So just a cause would turn the
Vilest Ruffian to a Saint.
[Exeunt. Bravos watch at Don John's house. MARIA and FLORA
re-enter.]

MARIA: Come, friends, let once a Woman preach courage

To you; inspired by my just rage, this Arm
Shall teach you wonders. I'll shew you now
What Love with just Revenge can do.

FIRST BRAVO: We are so practised in the trade of death,
We need no teaching.

MARIA: There's Gold good store; if you dispatch the Dog,
I'll give you yet much more; if not,
If all the wealth I have can buy your lives,
I'll have 'em instead of his.

FIRST BRAVO: For half the Sum, I'd kill a Bishop at the Altar.
[*They retire. Enter* DON JOHN, DON ANTONIO, DON LOPEZ, *and*
JACOMO.]

DON JOHN: Now we have finished our design; let's make a Sally, and
raise the Siege.

DON ANTONIO: Jacomo, do you lead the Van.

DON LOPEZ: Lead on, Jacomo, or we are sure to lose you; you are not
good at bringing up the Rear.

JACOMO: Nay, good Gentlemen, I know myself better than to take
place of Men of Quality, especially upon this occasion.

DON JOHN: Sirra, go on: I'll prick him forward. Remember, if you do
not fight, I am behind you.

JACOMO: Oh Heaven! Oh Jacomo! what will become of thy dear person? Is this your Courage, to put me forward to what you dare not
meet yourselves?

DON JOHN: No words; Rogue; on, on, I say—

JACOMO: Oh I shall be murdered! murdered! Oh! Oh!

DON JOHN: On, on, you Dog.

JACOMO: Inhuman Master! It must be so! Heaven have mercy on my
better part.
[*Enter* MARIA.]

MARIA: Fall on, fall on, that's the Villain! have at you, Dog—

DON JOHN: Courage, Jacomo.

JACOMO: Oh! Oh!
[*They fight, and are driven off, but* MARIA *and* FLORA *remain.*]

MARIA: Oh Cowardly Villains! The Traitor will escape their hands.
Oh Dogs! More feeble than the feeblest of our Sex. Let's after him,
and try our strength. [*Enter* DON JOHN.] He is return'd—Fall on.

DON JOHN: Ha! Must I encounter Boys?
[*He kills* FLORA.]

FLORA: Oh I am slain—

MARIA: At thy heart, base Villain.

[DON JOHN *disarms* MARIA.]

DON JOHN: There, take your Sword: I'll not nip Roguery in the bud; thou may'st live to be as wicked as myself.

MARIA: Poor Flora! But, Dog, I'll be reveng'd on thee yet ere I die.

[*Exit* MARIA. *Enter* DON LOPEZ, DON ANTONIO, JACOMO.]

JACOMO: What! no thanks! no reward!

DON JOHN: What's the matter, Sirra?

JACOMO: What, no acknowledgment? You are but an ungrateful man, let me tell you that, to treat a man of my prowess thus.

DON JOHN: What has your valour done?

JACOMO: Nothing, nothing; sav'd your life only, that's all. But men of valour are nothing nowadays. 'Tis an ungrateful Age. I fought like a Hero—

DON ANTONIO: Call'd a Stag at Bay.

DON LOPEZ: You can fight, when there's no way of escape, without it.

JACOMO: Oh! What's here! Another murder! Fly, fly; we shall be hang'd!

DON JOHN: Come on! let's now to Sea to try our fortunes.

JACOMO: Ay, make haste; I've laid Horses, and will shift by Land. Farewell, Sir; a good Voyage—

DON JOHN: I will murder you if you refuse to go to Sea—.

JACOMO: O, good Sir, consider, do but consider; I am so Seasick always: that wicked Element does not agree with me.

DON JOHN: Dare you dispute! Go on, I say.

JACOMO: O, good Sir, think, think a little; the merciless Waves will never consider a man of parts. Besides, Sir, I can swim no more than I can fly.

DON JOHN: I'll leave you dead upon the place if you refuse.

JACOMO: O Sir, on my knees I beg you'l let me stay. I am the last of all my Family; my Race will fail if I should fail.

DON JOHN: Damn your Race—

DON ANTONIO: Do not we venture with you?

JACOMO: You have nothing but your lives to venture, but I have a whole Family to save; I think upon Posterity. Besides, Gentlemen, I can look for no safety in such wicked company.

DON JOHN: I'll kill the Villain. His fear will else betray us.

JACOMO: O hold! hold! For Heav'ns sake hold—

[GHOST OF DON JOHN'S FATHER *rises*.]

GHOST: Hold! hold!

JACOMO: Ay, hold, hold. Oh Heav'n! your Father's Ghost; a Ghost! a Ghost! a Ghost! Oh! Oh!

[*Falls down and roars.*]

DON JOHN: 'Sdeath! What's here? My Father alive!

GHOST: No, no; inhuman Murderer, I am dead.

DON JOHN: That's well; I was afraid the old Gentleman had come for his Estate again; if you wou'd have that, 'tis too late; 'tis spent—

GHOST: Monster! behold these wounds.

DON JOHN: I do; they were well meant, and well perform'd, I see.

DON ANTONIO: This is strange! How I am amaz'd!

DON LOPEZ: Unheard of Wonder!

GHOST: Repent, repent of all thy Villanies;

My clamorous Blood to Heav'n for vengeance cries.

Heav'n will pour out his judgments on you all;

Hell gapes for you, for you each Fiend does call,

And hourly waits your unrepenting Fall.

You with eternal horrors they'll torment,

Except of all your crimes you suddenly repent.

[GHOST *sinks*.]

JACOMO: Oh! Oh! Heav'n deliver me from these Monsters.

DON JOHN: Farewell, thou art a foolish Ghost. Repent, quoth he! What could this mean? our senses are all in a mist sure.

DON ANTONIO: They are not; 'twas a Ghost.

DON LOPEZ: I ne'r believ'd those foolish Tales before.

DON JOHN: Come, 'tis no matter; let it be what it will, it must be natural—

DON ANTONIO: And Nature is unalterable in us too.

DON JOHN: 'Tis true, the nature of a Ghost cannot change ours.

DON LOPEZ: It was a silly Ghost, and I'll no sooner take his word than a Whore's.

DON JOHN: Thou art in the right. Come, Fool, Fool, rise; the Ghost is gone.

JACOMO: Oh! I die, I die; pray let me die in quiet.

DON ANTONIO: Oh! If he be dying, take him up; we'll give him burial in the Sea. Come on.

JACOMO: Hold, hold, Gentlemen; bury me not till I am dead, I beseech you—

DON JOHN: If you be not, Sirra, I'll run you through.

JACOMO: Hold, hold, Sir, I'll go, I'll go—

Don Lopez:
Don Antonio: } Let's on.

Don John: Should all the Bugbears Cowards feign appear,
  I would urge on without one thought of fear.
Don Antonio: And I.
Don Lopez: And I.
  [*Exeunt all.*]

ACT III

Scene 1

Aboard a ship. Enter Don John, Don Lopez, Don Antonio,
Jacomo, Captain of the Ship, Master, *and Sailors.*

Master: Mercy upon us! What sudden dreadful storm is this? We are
  all lost; we shall split upon the Rocks. Luff, luff—
Jacomo: Oh! Oh! Mercy! Oh I was afraid of this! See what your
  wickedness has brought me to? Mercy! Mercy!
Don John: Take away thy Cowardly face; it offends me, Rascal.
Captain: Such dreadful claps of Thunder I never yet remember'd.
Don John: Let the Clouds roar on and vomit all their Sulphur out;
  they ne'r shall fright me.
Don Antonio: These are the Squibs and Crackers of the Sky.
Don Lopez: Fire on, fire on; we are unmov'd.
Captain: The Heav'ns are all on fire; these unheard-of Prodigies
  amaze me.
Don John: Can you that have stood so many Cannons, be frighted at
  the farting and the belching of a Cloud?
Master: Bless me, Captain! six of our Foremast men are even now
  struck dead with Lightning.
Sailor: O that clap has rent our Masts in sunder.
Jacomo: O we are lost! You can swim, Sir; pray save me, Sir, for my
  own and Family's sake—
Don John: Toss these cowardly Rogues overboard. Captain, Courage!
  Let the Heav'ns do their worst, 'tis but drowning at last.
Jacomo: But—in the name of Heav'n, but drowning, quoth he; your
  drowning will prepare you for burning, though. Oh, Oh, Oh—
Sailor: Captain, Captain, the Ship's on fire in the Forecastle—

CAPTAIN: All hands to work upon the Forecastle. Heav'n! How it blazes already!—

[*Exit* CAPTAIN.]

JACOMO: Oh! Oh! We burn, we drown, we sink. Oh! We perish, we are lost, we are lost. Oh, Oh, Oh.

MASTER: O horrid Apparitions! Devils stand and guard the Fire, and will not suffer us to quench it. We are lost.

[*Enter* CAPTAIN.]

CAPTAIN: In all the dangers I have been, such horrors I never knew; I am quite unmann'd.

DON LOPEZ: A Man and fear: 'tis but dying at last.

DON JOHN: I never yet could know what that foolish thing Fear is.

CAPTAIN: Help, help, the fire increases. What horrid sights are these? where'r I turn me, fearful Spirits appear.

[*Exeunt* CAPTAIN *and Sailors.*]

DON JOHN: Let's into the Boat, and with our Swords keep out all others.

DON ANTONIO: While they are busy about the fire we may 'scape.

DON LOPEZ: If we get from hence, we certainly shall perish on the Rocks—

DON JOHN: I warrant you—

JACOMO: O good Gentlemen, let us shift for ourselves, and let the rest burn or drown, and be damn'd an they will.

DON JOHN: No, you have been often leaving me: now shall be the time we'll part. Farewell.

JACOMO: Oh! I'll stand by you while I live. Oh the Devil, the Devil! What horrors do I feel? Oh I am kill'd, I am dead!

[*A Thunderclap strikes* DON JOHN *and* JACOMO *down.*]

DON JOHN: 'Sdeath! Why this to me? You paltry foolish bugbear Thunder, am I the mark of your senseless Rage?

DON LOPEZ: Nothing but accident. Let's leap into the Boat.

DON ANTONIO: The Sailors all make towards us; they'll in and sink it.

DON JOHN: Sirra, if you come on, you run upon my Sword.

JACOMO: O cruel Tyrant! I burn, I drown, I sink! Oh I die, I am lost.

CAPTAIN: All shift aboard; we perish, we are lost.

MASTER: All lost, all lost.

[*A great shriek, they all leap overboard.*]

Scene 2

The shore, near a hermit's cave. Enter an old HERMIT.

HERMIT: This forty years I've liv'd in this neighb'ring Cave, and from these dreadful Cliffs which are always beaten by the foaming Surges of the Sea beheld the Ocean in its wildest Rage, and ne'r yet saw a storm so dreadful: such horrid flashes of lightning, and such claps of thunder, never were in my remembrance. Yon Ship is all on fire, and the poor miserable Wretches must all perish. The dreadful object melts my Heart, and brings a flood of tears into my eyes. It is prodigious, for on the sudden all the Heavens are clear again, and the enraged Sea is become more patient.

[*Enter* DON FRANCISCO.]

DON FRANCISCO: Oh Father, have you not been frighted at this prodigious storm, and at yon dreadful spectacle?

HERMIT: No man that has an apprehension but wou'd have been mov'd with horror.

DON FRANCISCO: 'Twas the most violent Tempest I ever saw. Hold, yonder are some coming in a small Vessel, and must necessarily split upon the Rock; I'll go and help to succour 'em.

HERMIT: Here are some this way, just come in a small Boat:
Go you to those, and these I will assist—

DON FRANCISCO: I'll haste to their relief—

[*Exit* DON FRANCISCO.]

HERMIT: Hah! these are come safe to Land, three men, goodly men they seem to be; I am bound in charity to serve them: they come towards me.

[*Enter* DON JOHN, DON ANTONIO, *and* DON LOPEZ.]

DON JOHN: Much ado, we are safe, but my Man's lost; pox on him, I shall miss the Fool; it was a necessary Blockhead.

DON ANTONIO: But you have lost your Goods, which were more necessary.

DON LOPEZ: Our Jewels and Money we have all about us.

DON JOHN: It makes me laugh to think how the Fools we left behind were puzzl'd which death to choose, burning or drowning.

DON ANTONIO: But how shall we dispose of ourselves? We are plaguy wet and cold. Hah! What old Fool is that?

DON LOPEZ: It is a Hermit, a fellow of mighty Beard and Sanctity.

DON JOHN: I know not what Sanctity he may have, but he has Beard enough to make an Owl's Nest, or stuff a Saddle with.

HERMIT: Gentlemen, I see you are shipwrack'd, and in distress; and my Function obliges me in charity to succour you in what I may.

DON ANTONIO: Alas! what canst thou help us to? Dost thou know of ever a house near hand, where we may be furnished with some necessaries?

HERMIT: On the other side of this vast Rock there is a fertile and a pleasant Valley where one Don Francisco, a rich and hospitable Man, has a sweet Dwelling; he will entertain you nobly. He's gone to assist some shipwrack'd Persons, and will be here presently. In the meantime, what my poor Cave can afford you shall be welcome to.

DON LOPEZ: What can that afford? You oblige yourself to fasting and abstinence.

HERMIT: I have studied Physick for the relief of needy people, and I have some Cordials which will refresh you; I'll bring one to you— [Exit HERMIT.]

DON JOHN: A good civil old Hypocrite: but this is a pleasant kind of Religion that obliges 'em to nastiness and want of meat. I'll ha' none on't—

DON ANTONIO: No, nor of any other, to my knowledge.

[Enter HERMIT with a Cordial.]

HERMIT: Gentlemen, pray taste of this Vial; it will comfort your cold stomachs.

DON JOHN: Ha! 'tis excellent, 'faith. Let it go round.

HERMIT: Heav'n bless it to you.

DON LOPEZ: Ha! it warms.

DON ANTONIO: Thank thee, thou art a very honest old fellow, i'faith.

DON JOHN: I see thou art very civil; but you must supply us with one necessary more, a very necessary thing, and very refreshing.

HERMIT: What's that, Sir?

DON JOHN: It is a Whore, a fine young buxom Whore.

DON ANTONIO: ⎫
DON LOPEZ: ⎭ A Whore, Old Man, a Whore.

HERMIT: Bless me, are you Men or Devils?

DON JOHN: Men, men, and men of lust and vigor. Prithee, old Sot, leave thy prating, and help me to a Strumpet, a fine salacious Strumpet; I know you Zealots have enough of 'em. Women love your godly Whoremasters.

HERMIT: Oh Monsters of impiety! are you so lately scap'd the wrath of Heaven, thus to provoke it?

DON ANTONIO: How! by following the Dictates of Nature. Who can do
otherwise?

DON LOPEZ: All our actions are necessitated, none command their own
wills.

HERMIT: Oh horrid blasphemy! would you lay your dreadful and
unheard of Vices upon Heaven? No, ill men, that has given you
free-will to good.

DON JOHN: I find thou retir'st here, and never read'st or think'st.
Can that blind faculty the Will be free
When it depends upon the Understanding?
Which argues first before the Will can choose;
And the last Dictate of the Judgment sways
The Will, as in a Balance, the last Weight
Put in the scale, lifts up the other end,
And with the same Necessity.

HERMIT: But foolish men and sinners act against
Their Understandings, which inform 'em better.

DON ANTONIO: None willingly do anything against the last
Dictates of their Judgments; whatsoe'r men do,
Their present opinions lead 'em to.

DON LOPEZ: As fools that are afraid of sin are by the thought
Of present pleasure, or some other reason,
Necessarily byass'd to pursue
The opinion they are of at that moment.

HERMIT: The Understanding yet is free, and might persuade 'em
better.

DON JOHN: The Understanding never can be free;
For what we understand, spite of ourselves we do:
All objects are ready form'd and plac'd
To our hands; and these the Senses to the Mind convey,
And as those represent them, this must judge:
How can the Will be free, when the understanding,
On which the Will depends, cannot be so.

HERMIT: Lay by your devillish Philosophy, and change the dangerous
and destructive course of your lewd lives.

DON ANTONIO: Change our natures; go bid a Blackamore be white; we
follow our Constitutions, which we did not give ourselves.

DON LOPEZ: What we are, we are by Nature; our reason tells us we
must follow that.

DON JOHN: Our Constitutions tell us one thing, and yours another; and which must we obey? If we be bad, 'tis Nature's fault that made us so.

HERMIT: Farewell. I dare no longer hear your impious discourse. Such hardened Wretches I ne'r heard of yet.
[*Exit* HERMIT.]

DON ANTONIO: Farewell, old Fool.

DON JOHN: Thus Sots condemn what they can never answer. [*Enter* DON FRANCISCO.] This I believe is Francisco, whom he spoke of; if he has but a handsome Wife, or Daughters, we are happy.

DON LOPEZ: Sir, we are shipwracked men, and if you can direct us to a place where we may be furnished with some necessaries, you will oblige us—

DON FRANCISCO: Gentleman, I have a House hard by; you shall be welcome to it. I even now endeavoured to succour a Youth and beauteous Woman who, with two Sailors in a Boat, were driven towards these Rocks, but were forced back again, and I fear are lost by this time. I desire nothing more than to assist men in extremes, and am o'rjoy'd at the opportunity of serving you.

DON JOHN: We thank you.

DON FRANCISCO: You shall command my House as long as you please: I see you are Cavaliers, and hope you will bear with some inconvenience. I have two young and, though I say it, handsome Daughters, who are tomorrow morning to be marri'd; the Solemnity will bring much company together, which I fear may incommode my house and you—

DON ANTONIO: You pose* us with this kindness.

DON JOHN: Whatever pleases you cannot be inconvenient to us.

DON LOPEZ: On the contrary, we shall be glad to assist you at the Ceremony, and help to make up the joyful Chorus.

DON FRANCISCO: You shall command my house and me;
I'll shew you the way to it.

DON JOHN: Your humble Servant. We'll follow you.
[*Exit* DON FRANCISCO.]
This is an admirable adventure.
He has Daughters, Boys, and to be marri'd too:
If they have been so foolish to preserve those
Toys they call Maidenheads, their senseless

*Pose = confuse, perplex. [*Editor's note.*]

Husbands shall not be troubled with them:
I'll ease them of those. Pox, what should those dull
Drudging Animals call'd Husbands do with such Treasures:
No, they are for honest Whoremasters, Boys.

DON ANTONIO: Well said, Don; we will not be wanting in our endeavors to succeed you.

DON LOPEZ: To you alone we must give place. *Allons.*

[*Exeunt. Enter* HERMIT, MARIA *in Man's habit, and* LEONORA.]

HERMIT: Heaven be praised, you are safely now on Land.

MARIA: We thank you, Reverend Father, for your assistance.

LEONORA: We never shall forget the obligation.

HERMIT: I am happy to be so good an Instrument.

LEONORA: We followed a Vessel which we saw fired with Lightning, and we fear that none of 'em escaped.

MARIA: I hope the Villain I pursue has scap'd. I would not be revenged by Heaven, but my own hand; or if not by that, by the Hangman's.

LEONORA: Did any come to land? for I most nearly am concern'd for one, the grief for whom, if he be lost, will soon, I fear, destroy me.

HERMIT: Here were three of that company came safe to Land; but such impious Wretches as did not deserve to escape, and such as no virtuous person can be concerned for, sure; I was stiff with fear and horror when I heard 'em talk.

MARIA: Three, say you?

LEONORA: By this sad description it must be Don John and his two wicked Associates; I am asham'd to confess the tenderness I have for him. Why should I love that Wretch? Oh my too violent passion hurries me I know not whither! Into what fearful dangerous Labyrinths of misery will it conduct me?

MARIA: Were they Gentlemen?

HERMIT: By their outside they seemed so, but their insides declared them Devils.

MARIA: Heaven! it must be the Villain and his barbarous
Companions. They are reserved for my revenge:
Assist me, Heaven, in that just cause.
Oh, Villain, Villain! inhuman Villain!
Each minute is, methinks, a tedious Age
Till I have dipt my hands in thy heart's blood.

HERMIT: You seem'd o'rjoy'd at the news of their safe arrival. Can any have a kindness for such dissolute abandon'd Atheists?

MARIA: No; tis revenge that I pursue against the basest of all Villains.

HERMIT: Have a care; Revenge is Heaven's, and must not be usurped by Mortals.

MARIA: Mine is revenge for Rapes and cruel murders, and those Heaven leaves to Earth to punish.

HERMIT: They are horrid crimes, but Magistrates must punish them.

LEONORA: What do I hear? Were he the basest of all men, my love is so headstrong and so wild within me, I must endeavour to preserve him, or destroy myself. To what deplorable condition am I fall'n? What Chains are these that hold me? Oh that I could break them! and yet I wou'd not if I cou'd. Oh my heart!

HERMIT. They are gone to one Don Francisco's house. That Road will bring you to it; 'tis on the other side of this Rock, in a pleasant Valley. I have not stirr'd these forty years from these small bounds, or I wou'd give him notice what Devils he harbours in his house. You will do well to do it.

JACOMO [within]: Help, help, murder! I am drown'd, I am dead. Help, help!

HERMIT: Hah! What voice is that? I must assist him—

MARIA: Father, farewell. Come, Madam, will you go to this house? Now, Monster, for my revenge.

LEONORA: I will; but for different ends we go;
'Tis Love conducts me, but Revenge brings you.
[Exeunt MARIA, LEONORA.]

JACOMO: Oh help, help! I sink, I sink!

HERMIT: Poor man, sure he is almost drown'd.

JACOMO: No, not yet; I have only drunk something too much of a scurvy unpleasant Liquor.

HERMIT: Reach me your hand—
[He pulls him out.]

JACOMO: Ay, and my heart too; Oh! Oh! Sir, a thousand Thanks to you: I vow to Gad, y'are a very civil person, and, as I am an honest man, have done me the greatest kindness in the world, next to the piece of the Mast which I floated upon, which I must ever love and honour; I am sorry it swam away; I wou'd have preserv'd it, and hung it up in the Seat of our ancient Family.

HERMIT: Thank Heaven for your deliverance, and leave such vain thoughts.

JACOMO: I do with all my heart; but I am not settled enough to say my prayers yet. Pray, Father, do you for me: 'tis nothing with you; you are us'd to it; it is your Trade.

HERMIT: Away, vain Man; you speak as if you had drunk too deeply of another Liquor than Sea-water.

JACOMO: No, I have not, but I wou'd fain. Where may a man light of a Glass of good Wine? I would gladly have an Antidote to my poison. Methinks, Pah! these Fishes have but a scurvy time; I am sure they have very ill drinking.

HERMIT: Farewell, and learn more devotion and thankfulness to Heav'n—

[*Exit* HERMIT.]

JACOMO: Ha! 'tis uncivilly done to leave a Man in a strange Country. But these Hermits have no breeding. Poor Jacomo, Dear Jacomo, how I love thy person, how glad am I to see thee safe. For I swear, I think thou art as honest a fellow as e'r I met with. Well, farewell, thou wicked Element; if ever I trust thee again—Well, Haddocks, I defy you, you shall have none of me, not a Collop; no, no, I will be eaten by Worms, as all my Ancestors have been. If Heaven will but preserve me from the Monsters of the Land, my Master and his two Companions (who, I hope, are drown'd), I'll preserve myself from those of the Sea. Let me see, here is a path—this must lead to some house. I'll go, for I am plaguy sick with this Salt water. Pah—

[*Exit* JACOMO.]

Scene 3

A wood near DON FRANCISCO's. *Enter* CLARA *and* FLAVIA *with her two Maids.*

CLARA: Oh, Flavia, this will be our last happy night; tomorrow is our Execution day; we must marry.

FLAVIA: Ay, Clara, we are condemn'd without reprieve. 'Tis better to live as we have done, kept from all men, than for each to be confin'd to one whom yet we never saw, and a thousand to one shall never like.

CLARA: Out on't, a Spanish Wife has a worse life than a coop'd Chicken.

FLAVIA: A singing Bird in a Cage is a Princely Creature compar'd to that poor Animal call'd a Wife here.

CLARA: Birds are made tame by being cag'd, but Women grow wild by confinement, and that, I fear, my Husband will find to his cost.

FLAVIA: None live pleasantly here but those who should be miserable, Strumpets. They can choose their Mates, but we must be like Slaves condemn'd to the Gallies; we have not liberty to sell ourselves, or venture one throw for our freedom.

CLARA: O that we were in England! There they say a Lady may choose a Footman and run away with him, if she likes him, and no dishonour to the Family.

FLAVIA: That's because the Families are so very Honourable that nothing can touch them: their Wives run and ramble whither and with whom they please, and defy all censure.

CLARA: Ay, and a jealous Husband is a more monstrous Creature there than a Wittol here, and wou'd be more pointed at. They say if a Man be jealous there, the Women will all join and pull him to pieces.

FLAVIA: Oh happy Country! we ne'r touch Money; there the Wives can spend their Husband's Estate for 'em. Oh Bless'd Country!

CLARA: Ay, there they say the Husbands are the prettiest, civil, easy, good-natur'd, indifferent persons in the whole world; they ne'r mind what their Wives do, not they.

FLAVIA: Nay, they say they love those men best that are kindest to their Wives. Good men! poor hearts. And here, if an honest Gentleman offers a Wife a civility by the by, our bloody, butcherly Husbands are cutting of Throats presently—

CLARA: Oh that we had these frank civil Englishmen instead of our grave, dull, surly Spanish Blockheads, whose greatest Honour lies in preserving their Beards and Foreheads inviolable.

FLAVIA: In England if a Husband and Wife like not one another, they draw two several ways and make no bones on't; while the Husband treats his Mistress openly in his Glass Coach, the Wife, for Decency's sake, puts on her Vizar, and whips away in a Hackney with a Gallant, and no harm done.

CLARA: Though of late 'tis as unfashionable for a Husband to love his Wife there as 'tis here, yet 'tis fashionable for her to love somebody else, and that's something.

FLAVIA: Nay, they say Gentlemen will keep company with a Cuckold there as soon as another man, and ne'r wonder at him.

CLARA: Oh happy Country! there a Woman may choose for herself, and none will into the Trap of Matrimony unless she likes the Bait; but here we are tumbled headlong and blindfold into it.

FLAVIA: We are us'd as they use Hawks, never unhooded or whistled off till they are just upon the Quarry.

CLARA: And 'tis for others, not ourselves, we fly, too.

FLAVIA: No more, this does but put us in mind of our misery.

CLARA: It does so. But prithee let's be merry one night; tomorrow is our last. Farewell all happiness.

FLAVIA: O that this happy day would last our lives-time. But prithee, my Dear, let's have thy Song, and divert ourselves as well as we can in the meantime.

CLARA: 'Tis a little too wanton.

FLAVIA: Prithee let's be a little wanton this evening; tomorrow we must take our leaves on't.

CLARA: Come on then; our Maids shall join in the Chorus: Here they are.

SONG

Woman, who is by Nature wild,
  Dull bearded men encloses;
Of Nature's freedom we're beguil'd
  By Laws which man imposes:
Who still himself continues free,
Yet we poor Slaves must fetter'd be.

CHORUS: A shame on the Curse
    Of, For better for worse;
'Tis a vile imposition on Nature:
    For Women should change,
    And have freedom to range,
Like to every other wild Creature.

So gay a thing was n'er design'd
  To be restrain'd from roving.
Heav'n meant so changeable a mind
  Should have its change in loving.
By cunning we could make men smart,
But they by strength o'ercome our Art.

CHORUS: A shame on the Curse
    Of, For, &c.

How happy is the Village Maid
  Whom only Love can fetter;
By foolish Honour ne'r betray'd,

She serves a Pow'r much greater:
That lawful Prince the wisest rules,
Th' Usurper's Honour rules but Fools.

CHORUS: A shame on the Curse,
　　　　Of, For, &c.

Let us resume our ancient right;
　Make man at distance wonder;
Though he victorious be in fight,
　In love we'll keep him under.
War and Ambition hence be hurl'd,
Let Love and Beauty rule the World.

CHORUS: A shame on the Curse
　　　　Of, For better, &c.

FLAVIA: Oh, dear Clara, that this were true! But now let's home, our Father will miss us.

CLARA: No, he's walk'd abroad with the three Shipwrack'd Gentlemen.

FLAVIA: They're proper handsome Gentlemen; but the chief, whom they call Don John, exceeds the rest.

CLARA: I never saw a finer person; pray Heaven either of our Husbands prove as good.

FLAVIA: Do not name 'em. Let the Maids go home, and if my Father be there, let him know we are here.

[*Exeunt Maids.*]

CLARA: In the meantime, if he be thereabouts, do you go down that Walk and I'll go this way, and perhaps one of us shall light on him.

FLAVIA: Agreed.

[*Exeunt both. Enter* DON JOHN, DON LOPEZ, *and* DON ANTONIO.]

DON JOHN: Where have you left the old man, Don Francisco?

DON LOPEZ: He's very busy at home, seeing all things prepar'd for his Daughters' Weddings tomorrow.

DON JOHN: His Daughters are gone this way: if you have any friendship for me, go and watch the old man; and if he offers to come towards us, divert him, that I may have freedom to attack his Daughters.

DON ANTONIO: You may be sure of us, that have serv'd you with our lives: besides, the justice of this cause will make us serve you. Adieu.

[*Exeunt* DON LOPEZ *and* DON ANTONIO.]

DON JOHN: Now for my Virgins. Assist me, Love. Fools, you shall have no Maidenheads tomorrow night. Husbands have Maidenheads! No, no—poor sneaking Fools.

[*Enter* JACOMO.]

JACOMO: I have lost my way; I think I shall never find this house. But I shall never think myself out of the way unless I meet my impious Master; Heaven grant he be drown'd.

DON JOHN: How now, Rascal, are you alive?

JACOMO: Oh Heaven! He's here. Why was this lewd Creature sav'd? I am in a worse condition than ever; now I have scap'd drowning, he brings hanging fresh into my memory.

DON JOHN: What, mute, Sirra?

JACOMO: Sir, I am no more your Servant; you parted with me, I thank you, Sir, I am beholding to you. Farewell, good Sir, I am my own man now—

DON JOHN: No. Though you are a Rogue, you are a necessary Rogue, and I'll not part with you.

JACOMO: I must be gone; I dare not venture further with you.

DON JOHN: Sirra, do you know me, and dare you say this to me? Have at your Guts; I will rip you from the Navel to the Chin.

JACOMO: O good Sir, hold, hold. He has got me in his clutches; I shall never get loose—Oh! Oh!

DON JOHN: Come Dog, follow me close, stinking Rascal.

JACOMO: I am too well pickl'd in the Salt water to stink, I thank you, I shall keep a great while. But you were a very generous Man to leave a Gentleman, your Friend, in danger as you did me. I have reason to follow you: but if I serve you not in your kind, then am I a sous'd Sturgeon.

DON JOHN: Follow me, Sirra; I see a Lady.

JACOMO: Are you so fierce already?

[*Enter* CLARA *singing*, A shame on the Curse, &c.]

CLARA: Ha! This is the Stranger;
What makes him here?

DON JOHN: A delicate Creature. Ha! This is the Lady.
How happy am I to meet you here—

CLARA: What mean you, Sir?

DON JOHN: I was undone enough before, with seeing your Picture in the Gallery; but I see you have more Excellencies than Beauty; your Voice needed not have conspir'd with that to ruin me.

CLARA: Have you seen my Picture?

DON JOHN: And lov'd it above all things I ever saw, but the Original. I am lost beyond redemption, unless you can pity me.

JACOMO [Aside.]: He has been lost a hundred times, but he always finds himself again—and me too; a pox on him.

DON JOHN: When Love had taken too fast hold on me ever to let me go, I too late found you were tomorrow to be marri'd.

CLARA: Yes, I am condemn'd to one I never saw, and you are come to rally me and my misfortunes.

JACOMO: Ah, Madam, say not so; my Master is always in earnest.

DON JOHN: So much I am in earnest now that if you have no way to break this marriage off and pity me, I soon shall repent I ever came to Land; I shall suffer a worse wrack upon the Shore; here I shall linger out my life in the worst of pains, despairing Love; there I should have perish'd quickly—

JACOMO: Ah poor man! he's in a desperate condition; I pity him with all my heart—

DON JOHN: Peace, Rascal. Madam, this is the only opportunity I am like to have. Give me leave to improve it.

CLARA: Sure, Sir, you cannot be in earnest.

DON JOHN: If all the Oaths under the Sun can convince you, Madam, I swear—

JACOMO: O Sir, Sir, have a care of Swearing, for fear you should, once in your life, be forsworn—

DON JOHN: Peace, Dog, or I shall slit your Windpipe.

JACOMO: Nay, I know if he be forsworn, 'tis the first time, that's certain.

CLARA: But, Sir, if you be in earnest, and I had an inclination, 'tis impossible to bring it about; my Father has dispos'd of me.

DON JOHN: Dispose of yourself. I'll do well enough with him, and my Fortune and Quality are too great for him for whom you are intended to dispute with me.

CLARA: If this be true, wou'd you win a Woman at first sight?

DON JOHN: Madam, this is like to be the first and last; tomorrow is the fatal day that will undo me.

JACOMO: Courage, Don, matters go well.

CLARA [Aside.]: Nay, I had rather have a Peasant of my own choosing than an Emperor of another's. He is a handsome Gentleman, and seems to be of Quality. Oh that he could rid me of my intended slavery. Sir, talk not of impossible things; for could I wish this, my Father's Honour will not suffer him to dispense with his promise.

DON JOHN: I'll carry you beyond his power, and your intended Husband's too.

CLARA: It cannot be; but I must leave you, I dare not be seen with you—

DON JOHN: Remember the short time you have to think on this: will you let me perish without relief? if you will have pity on a wretched man, I have a Priest in my company; I'll marry you, and we'll find means to fly early in the morning before the house are stirring.

CLARA: I confess I am to be condemn'd to a Slavery, that nothing can be worse; yet this were a rash attempt.

DON JOHN: If you will not consent to my just desires, I am resolv'd to kill myself, and fall a Sacrifice to your disdain. [*Holds his Sword to his breast.*] Speak, speak my doom!—

CLARA: Hold, hold—

JACOMO: Ay, hold, hold: poor foolish Woman, she shou'd not need to bid him hold.

CLARA: I'll find a means this night to speak with you alone; but I fear this is but for your diversion.

JACOMO: Yes, 'tis for diversion indeed; the common diversion of all the world.

DON JOHN: By all that's great and good, my Intentions are honourable.

CLARA: Farewell, Sir, I dare not stay longer.

DON JOHN: Will you keep your word, Madam?

JACOMO: You'll keep yours, no doubt—

CLARA: I will; anything rather than marry one I cannot love, as I can no man of another's choosing.

DON JOHN: Remember, Madam, I perish if you do not; I have only one thing to say: Keep this Secret from your Sister till we have effected it; I'll give you sufficient reason for what I say. [*Exit* CLARA.] Victoria, Victoria; I have her fast, she's my own.

JACOMO: You are a hopeful man; you may come to good in time.

[*Enter* FLAVIA.]

DON JOHN: Here is the other Sister; have at her.

JACOMO: Why, Sir, Sir; have you no conscience?
Will not one at once serve your turn?

DON JOHN: Stand by, Fool. Let me see, you are the Lady.

FLAVIA: What say you Sir?

DON JOHN: You have lately taken up a stray heart of mine; I hope you do not intend to detain it without giving me your own in exchange.

FLAVIA: I a heart of yours? Since when, good Sir? You are but this day shipwrack'd on this Coast and never saw my face before.

DON JOHN: I saw your Picture, and I saw your motion, both so charming I could not resist them; but now I have a nearer view, I see plainly I am lost.

FLAVIA: A goodly handsome man! but what can this mean?

DON JOHN: Such killing Beauties I ne'r saw before; my heart is irrevocably gone.

FLAVIA: Whither is it gone, Sir? I assure you I have no such thing about me, that I know of.

DON JOHN: Ah, Madam, if you wou'd give me leave to search you, I should find it in some little corner about you that shall be nameless.

FLAVIA: It cannot be about me; I have none but my own, and that I must part with tomorrow to I know not whom.

DON JOHN: If the most violent love that man e'r knew can e'r deserve that treasure, it is mine; if you give that away, you lose the truest Lover that e'r languished yet.

JACOMO: What can be the end of this? Sure Blood must follow this dishonour of the Family, and I, unfortunate, shall have my throat cut for company.

FLAVIA: Do you know where you are?

DON JOHN: Yes, Madam, in Spain, where opportunities are very scarce, and those that are wise make use of 'em as soon as they have 'em.

FLAVIA: You have a mind to divert yourself; but I must leave you; I am disposed to be more serious.

DON JOHN: Madam, I swear by all—

JACOMO: Hold, hold; will you be forsworn again?

DON JOHN: Peace, Villain, I shall cut that tongue out.

FLAVIA: Farewell, I cannot stay.

[Exit FLAVIA.]

DON JOHN: I'll not leave her; I'll thaw her if she were Ice, before I have done with her.

JACOMO: There is no end of this lewdness. Well, I must be kill'd or hang'd once for all, and there's an end on't.

[Exeunt. Enter MARIA and LEONORA.]

LEONORA: I am faint with what I suffered at Sea, and with my wandring since; let us repose a little; we shall not find this house tonight.

MARIA: I n'er shall rest till I have found Don Francisco's house; but I'll sit down awhile.

LEONORA: I hope he will not find it till I have found means to give

Don John warning of his cruel intentions: I would save his life who,
I fear, would not do that for me. But in the miserable case that I
am in, if he denies his love, death would be the welcom'st thing on
earth to me.

MARIA: Oh my Octavio! how does the loss of thee perplex me with
despair! the honour of Mankind is gone with thee. Why do I whine?
grief shall no longer usurp the place of my revenge. How could I
gnaw the Monster's heart. Villain! I'll be with you. When I have
reveng'd my dear Octavio's loss, I then shall die contented.

[*Enter* DON LOPEZ *and* DON ANTONIO.]

DON LOPEZ: Th' old man's safe; I long to know Don John's success.

DON ANTONIO: He's engag'd upon a noble cause. If he succeeds, 'twill
be a victory worth the owning.

DON LOPEZ: Hah! whom have we here? a young man well habited,
with a Lady too; they seem to be strangers.

DON ANTONIO: A mischief comes into my head that's worth the doing.

DON LOPEZ: What's that, dear Antonio?

DON ANTONIO: We are in a strange Country, and may want money: I
would rob that young Fellow. We have not robb'd a good while;
methinks 'tis a new wickedness to me.

DON LOPEZ: Thou art in the right. I hate to commit the same dull sin
over and over again, as if I were marri'd to it: variety makes all
things pleasant.

DON ANTONIO: But there's one thing we'll ne'r omit. When we have
robb'd the Man, we'll ravish the Woman.

DON LOPEZ: Agreed; let's to't man. Come on, young Gentleman, we
must see what riches you have about you.

MARIA: O Villains! Thieves! Thieves! these are the inhuman Companions of that bloody Monster.

LEONORA: Have pity on poor miserable Strangers.

DON ANTONIO: Peace; we'll use you kindly, very kindly.

DON LOPEZ: Go you carry that young Gentleman, bind him to a Tree,
and bring the money, while I wait upon the Lady.

DON ANTONIO: Will you play me no foul play in the meantime then?
For we must cast Lots about the business you wot of.

DON LOPEZ: No, upon my honour.

MARIA: Honour, you Villain?

DON ANTONIO: Come, young Gentleman, I'll tame you.

MARIA: Help! help!

[*Exit* DON ANTONIO *hauling* MARIA.]

LEONORA: Have you no humanity in you? Take our money, but leave us liberty; be not so barb'rously cruel.

[*Re-enter* DON ANTONIO.]

DON ANTONIO: Come, I have made haste with him; now let us draw Cuts who enjoys the Lady first.

LEONORA: O heav'n assist me! what do I hear? help! help!

[*Enter four or five Countrey Fellows, coming from work.*]

FIRST COUNTRY FELLOW: What, two men a robbing of a Lady! Begone, and let her alone, or we have sower Cudgels shall wasle* your bones, I tell you that.

DON ANTONIO: How now, Rogues?

[*They fight off the Stage.*]

LEONORA: Thanks to Heav'n. I fly! I fly! where shall I hide myself.

[*Exit* LEONORA. *Enter* DON JOHN *and* JACOMO.]

DON JOHN: I shall conquer 'em both. Now, Sirrah, what think you?

JACOMO: Why I think you manage your business as discreetly, and take as much pains to have your throat cut, as any man in Spain.

DON JOHN: Your fear o'errules your sense; mine is a life Monarchs might envy.

JACOMO: 'Tis like to be a very short one at this rate.

DON JOHN: Away, Fool, 'tis dark, I must be gone; I shall scarce find the way home.

[*Enter* LEONORA.]

LEONORA: Heaven guard me from these wicked Wretches. Help! help! they are here.

DON JOHN: How now, Madam? what, afraid of a Man!

LEONORA: Don John, no, not of you; you are the man i' th' world I would have met.

DON JOHN: Leonora, you are the woman i' th' world I would have avoided. 'Sdeath! she will spoil my new designs; but I have a trick for her. What miracle brought you hither?

LEONORA: Love, that works the greatest miracles, made me follow you; and the same Storm drove me on this shore on which you were thrown, and thus far I've wander'd till I have found you.

DON JOHN: This is the most unreasonable unsatiable loving Lady that ever was abus'd by man; she has a kind of Spaniel love; the worse you use her, the more loving she is. Pox on her, I must be rid of her.

LEONORA: I am very faint and weary, yet I was resolved not to rest till I had found you.

---

*Wasle = to beat down. [*Editor's note.*]

DON JOHN: Your unwearied love has o'ercome and convinc'd me; there is not such a Woman breathing.

LEONORA: This is a Sovereign Medicine for all my sorrows; I now, methinks, am happier than ever. But I am faint and ill.

DON JOHN: Here, Madam, I have an excellent Cordial; 'twill refresh you; and I'll conduct you where you shall never be unhappy more.

LEONORA: From that dear hand 'tis welcome—[*Drinks.*]
To your health.

DON JOHN: And to your own destruction; you have drunk your last.

LEONORA: What means my Love?

DON JOHN: Y'have drunk the subtilest poison that Art e'r yet invented.

JACOMO: O murder! murder! what have you done?

DON JOHN: Peace, Villain, leave your unseasonable pity—
You cannot live two minutes.

LEONORA: O ungrateful Tyrant! thou hast murdered the only Creature living that cou'd love thee. Heaven will revenge it, though to me 'tis kindness. Here all my sorrows shall forever cease.

DON JOHN: Why would you persecute me with your love?

LEONORA: I could not help it. I came to preserve you, and am destroyed for't.

JACOMO: Oh horrid fact!

DON JOHN: To preserve me! I wear my safety by my side.

LEONORA: Oh I faint! Guard yourself. There's a young gentlemen pursues your life. Have a Care—
I came to tell you this, and thus I am rewarded.
Heav'n pardon you. Farewell. I can no more.
[*She dies.*]

JACOMO: This object sure will strike your heart! Tigers would melt at this. Oh the Earth will open and swallow you up, and me for company. There's no end of your murders.

DON JOHN: This is the first time I ever knew compassion.
Poor Fool, I pity her, but tis too late—
Farewell all senseless thoughts of a remorse,
I would remove what e'r wou'd stop my course.
[*Exeunt.*]

ACT IV

Scene 1

A hall at Don Francisco's. Enter DON JOHN, DON LOPEZ, DON
ANTONIO, *and* JACOMO.

DON JOHN: This night's success exceeded all my hopes. I had admittance to their several Chambers, and I have been contracted to both
the Sisters, and this day resolve to marry 'em, and at several times
enjoy them; and in my opinion I shall have a brace of as pretty
Wives as any man in Spain.

DON ANTONIO: Brave Don John, you are Master of your Art; not a
Woman in Spain can stand before you.

DON LOPEZ: We can but envy you, and at a distance imitate; but both
their Maids shall to pot, I assure you.

JACOMO: How far will the Devil hurry you?

DON JOHN: 'Tis not the Devil, 'tis the Flesh, Fool.

JACOMO: Here will be fine cutting of throats. Poor Jacomo, must thou
be cut off in the flower of thy Age?

[*Enter* DON FRANCISCO.]

DON FRANCISCO: Gentlemen, your Servant; I hope you rested well this
night.

DON LOPEZ: We thank you, Sir; never better.

DON ANTONIO: We never shall requite this obligation.

JACOMO: I warrant you my Master will; he's a very grateful civil person indeed.

DON JOHN: The favour is too great to be suddenly requited; but I
shall study to deserve it.

JACOMO: Good man, you will deserve it.

[*Enter* TWO BRIDEGROOMS.]

DON FRANCISCO: Gentlemen, you are come, you are early.

FIRST BRIDEGROOM: This joyful occasion made us think it late.

SECOND BRIDEGROOM: The expectation of so great a blessing as we this
day hope to enjoy would let us have but little rest last night.

FIRST BRIDEGROOM: And the fruition will afford us less tonight.

DON JOHN: Poor Fools! you shall be bob'd. How it tickles my Spleen
to think on't.

DON FRANCISCO: These are to be my Sons-in-law.

DON JOHN: And my Cuckolds beforehand.

DON FRANCISCO: Pray know 'em, Gentlemen; they are Men of Honour.

DON JOHN: I shall be glad to serve them; [*Aside.*] But first I'll serve their Ladies.

DON FRANCISCO: Come, Gentlemen, I'll now conduct you to my Daughters; and beg your pardon for a moment, I'll wait on you again.

[*Exit* DON FRANCISCO *and* BRIDEGROOMS.]

DON ANTONIO: These Fools will spoil your design.

DON JOHN: No, poor Sots; I have persuaded the Ladies to feign sickness, and put off their marriage till tomorrow morning, to gain time; as the meanwhile I have 'em safe, Boys.

DON LOPEZ: But will not the Sisters betray you to one another?

DON JOHN: No, I have wheedled each into a jealousy of the other, and each believes that if the other knows it, she in honour will reveal it to the Father.

JACOMO: Sir, if you be so very weary of your life, why don't you make use of a convenient Beam? 'tis the easier way; so you may die without the filthy pother you keep about it.

DON JOHN: Away, Coward; 'tis a sign I am not weary of my life that I make so much use on't!

JACOMO: Oh Jacomo! Thou art lost. 'Tis pity a Fellow of thy neat spruce parts should be destroy'd.

[*Enter* DON FRANCISCO.]

DON FRANCISCO: Come, Gentlemen, will you not refresh yourselves with some cool Wines this morning?

DON LOPEZ: We thank you, Sir, we have already.

[*Enter a* SERVANT.]

SERVANT: Sir, here's a young Gentleman, a Stranger, desires to speak with you.

DON FRANCISCO: Admit him. [*Enter* MARIA *in Man's Habit.*] Your humble Servant.

MARIA: Sir, when I've told you what I come for, I doubt not but I shall deserve your thanks. I come to do you service.

DON FRANCISCO: You have 'em, Sir, already—

MARIA: You have lodg'd within your house some ship-wrack'd men who are greater Villains than the Earth e'r bore; I come to give you warning of 'em, and to beg your power to revenge such horrid actions as heart could never yet conceive, or tongue could utter. Ha! they are these—Revenge, Revenge cruel, unnatural Rapes and Murders. They are Devils in the shapes of Men.

DON FRANCISCO: What say you, Sir?

JACOMO: Now the snare is fall'n upon me; methinks I feel cold Steel already in my Body. Too well I know that face.

DON JOHN: I know that Face. Now, Impudence, assist me. What mad young man is that?

DON FRANCISCO: These, by their habits and their miens, are Gentlemen, and seem to be men of Honour.

MARIA: By these two last night I was robb'd and bound to a Tree, and there have been all night, and but this morning was reliev'd by Peasants—I had a Lady with me whom they said they would ravish, and this Morning I saw her dead; they must have murder'd her.

DON FRANCISCO: Heav'n! What do I hear?

JACOMO: Oh! I am noos'd already; I feel the knot, methinks, under my left ear.

DON ANTONIO: The youth raves; we never saw his face; we never stirr'd from the bounds of this house since we came hither.

DON LOPEZ: 'Sdeath, let me kill the Villain. Shall he thus affront men of our quality and honour?

DON FRANCISCO: Consider I am a Magistrate.

DON JOHN: The Youth was robb'd, and with the fright has lost his wits. Poor Fool! let him be bound in's bed.

DON FRANCISCO: Do not persist in this, but have a care.

These injuries to men of Honour shall not go unpunished.

MARIA: Whither shall injur'd Innocence fly for succour if you so soon can be corrupted? Monster, I'll revenge myself; have at thy heart.

DON FRANCISCO: What means the Youth? Put up your Sword.

DON ANTONIO: We told you, Sir, he was mad.

MARIA: Oh impudent Villains! I ask your pardon, Sir; my griefs and Injuries transport me so, I scarce can utter them. That Villain is Don John, who basely murdered the Governor of Seville in his house, and then dishonoured his fair Sister.

DON JOHN: Death and Hell! this injury is beyond all sufferance.

DON FRANCISCO: Hold, Sir, think in whose house you are.

JACOMO: O Lord! what will this come to? Ah Jacomo! thy line of life is short.

MARIA: This is the Villain who kill'd the Lover of Antonio's Sister, deflow'rd her, and murder'd her Brother in his own house.

DON JOHN: I'll have no longer patience.

DON ANTONIO: Such a Villain should have his throat cut, though in a Church.

DON LOPEZ: No man of honour will protect those who offer such injuries.

DON JOHN: Have at you, Villain.

DON FRANCISCO: Nay then. Within there: Ho! I will protect him, or perish with him.

[*Enter two* BRIDEGROOMS.]

FIRST BRIDEGROOM: What's the matter?

DON JOHN: This rashness will spoil my design upon the Daughters; if I had perfected that, I would have own'd all this for half a Duccatoon. [*To* DON FRANCISCO] I ask your pardon for my ill manners; I was provok'd too far; indeed the accusations are so extravagant and odd, I rather should have laughed at 'em. Let the young Fool have a vein open'd; he's stark staring mad.

DON ANTONIO: A foolish Impostor. We ne'r saw Seville till last night.

MARIA: Oh Impudence!

JACOMO: No, not we; we never were there till yesterday. Pray, Sir, lay that young Fellow by the heels for lying on us men of Honour.

DON FRANCISCO: What is the matter, Friend, you tremble so?

DON LOPEZ: 'Sdeath, the Dog's fear will betray us.

JACOMO: I tremble, Sir? no, no, Sir: I tremble—Though it would make anyone tremble to hear one lie as that young Gentleman does. Have you no conscience in you?

MARIA: Heav'n can witness for me, I speak not false. Octavio, my dear Octavio, being dearest to me of all the world, I would in Seville have revenged his murder but the Villain there escaped me; I followed him to Sea, and in the same Storm in which their Ship perish'd I was thrown on shore. Oh my Octavio! if this foul unnatural murther be not reveng'd, there is no Justice left among mankind. His Ghost, and all the rest whom he has barbarously murder'd, will interrupt your quiet; they'll haunt you in your sleep. Revenge, revenge!

SECOND BRIDEGROOM: This is wonderful.

DON FRANCISCO: There must be something in this; his passion cannot be counterfeited, nor your man's fear.

JACOMO: My fear? I scorn your words; I fear nothing under the Sun. I fear? Ha, ha, ha—

DON JOHN: Will you believe this one false Villain against three who are Gentlemen and men of honour?

JACOMO: Nay, against four who are Gentlemen and men of honour.

MARIA: O Villain, that I had my Sword imbru'd in thy heart's blood.

Oh my dear Octavio! Do Justice, Sir, or Heaven will punish you.
[*Enter* CLARA.]

DON FRANCISCO: Gentlemen, he is too earnest in his grief and anger
to be what you wou'd have him, an Impostor. My house has been
your Sanctuary, and I am obliged in honour not to act as a Magistrate, but your Host; no violence shall here be offer'd to you, but
you must instantly leave this house, and if you would have safety,
find it somewhere else. Be gone.

DON JOHN: This is very well.

MARIA: Oh! will you let 'em go unpunish'd?
Whither shall I fly for vengeance?

DON FRANCISCO: Pray leave this place immediately.

JACOMO: Ah, good Sir, let's be gone—Sir, your most humble Servant.

CLARA: Oh, Sir, consider what you do; do not banish Don John from
hence.

FIRST BRIDEGROOM: Ha! what means she?

DON FRANCISCO: What say you?

CLARA: Oh, Sir, he is my Husband, we were last night contracted.

DON FRANCISCO: Oh! what do I hear?

FIRST BRIDEGROOM: I am dishonoured, abus'd. Villain, thou diest.

DON JOHN: Villain, you lie; I will cut your throat first.

DON FRANCISCO: Hey, where are my people here?
[*Enter Servants and* FLAVIA.]

FLAVIA: Oh, Sir, hold; if you banish Don John, I am lost forever.

DON FRANCISCO: Oh Devil! what do I hear?

FLAVIA: He is my Husband, Sir; we were last night contracted.

CLARA: Your Husband! Heaven! what's this?

SECOND BRIDEGROOM: Hell and Damnation!

DON FRANCISCO: Oh! I have lost my senses.

MARIA: Oh Monster! now am I to be believ'd?

JACOMO: Oh spare my life! I am innocent as I hope to live and breathe.

DON JOHN: Dog, you shall fight for your life, if you have it.

DON FRANCISCO: First I'll revenge myself on these.

DON JOHN: Hold, hold, they are both my Wives, and I will have them.
[DON FRANCISCO *runs at his Daughters; they run out.*]

DON FRANCISCO: Oh Devil! fall on—

MARIA: Fall on, I will assist you.
[*They fight. Maria and Don Francisco are killed, the two Bridegrooms are hurt,* JACOMO *runs away.*]

DON JOHN: Now we've done their business.

Ah, cowardly Rogue! are not you a Son of a Whore?

JACOMO: Ay, Sir, what you please. A man had better be a living Son of a Whore than a dead Hero, by your favour.

DON JOHN: I could find in my heart to kill the Rascal; his fear, some time or other, will undo us.

JACOMO: Hold, Sir, I went, Sir, to provide for your escape. Let's take Horses out of the Stable and fly; abundance of Company are coming, expecting the Wedding, and we are irreparably lost if we take not this time. I think my fear will now preserve you.

DON ANTONIO: I think he counsels well. Let's fly to a new place of pleasure.

DON JOHN: But I shall leave my business undone with the two Women.

DON LOPEZ: 'Tis now scarce feazible. Let's fly; you'll light on others as handsome where we come next.

DON JOHN: Well, dispose of me as you please; and yet it troubles me.

JACOMO: Haste, haste, or we shall be apprehended.

[*Exeunt. Enter* CLARA *and* FLAVIA.]

FLAVIA: O that I ever liv'd to see this day!
This fatal day! 'Twas our vile disobedience
Caus'd our poor Father's death, which Heaven
Will revenge on us. So lewd a Villain
As Don John was never heard of yet.

CLARA: That we should be so credulous! Oh dreadful
Accident. Dear Father, what Expiation can
We make? our crimes too foul for
Tears to wash away, and all our lives will
Be too short to spend in penitence for this
Our levity and disobedience. He was the
Best of Fathers, and of Men.

FLAVIA: What will become of us, poor miserable Maids,
Lost in our Fortunes and our Reputations?
Our intended Husbands, if they recover of their
Wounds, will murder us; and 'tis but Justice:
Our lives too now cannot be worth the keeping.
Those Devils in the shapes of men are fled.

CLARA: Let us not waste our time in fruitless grief;
Let us employ some to pursue the murderers.
And for ourselves, let's to the next Monastery,
And there spend all our weary life in penitence.

FLAVIA: Let's fly to our last Sanctuary in this world,

And try, by a Religious life, to expiate this Crime:
There is no safety or no hope but there.
Let's go, and bid a long farewell to all the
World, a thing too vain, and little worth our care.
CLARA: Agreed; farewell to all the vanity on Earth,
Where wretched Mortals, toss'd 'twixt hope and fear,
Must of all fix'd and solid joy despair.
[*Exeunt.*]

Scene 2

A delightful Grove. Enter TWO SHEPHERDS *and* TWO NYMPHS.

FIRST SHEPHERD: Come Nymphs and Shepherds, haste away
To the happy Sports within these shady Groves;
In pleasant lives time slides away apace,
But with the wretched seems to creep too slow.
FIRST NYMPH: Our happy leisure we employ in joys,
As innocent as they are pleasant. We,
Strangers to strife, and to tumultuous noise,
To baneful envy, and to wretched cares,
In rural pleasures spend our happy days,
And our soft nights in calm and quiet sleeps.
SECOND SHEPHERD: No rude Ambition interrupts our rest,
Nor base and guilty thoughts how to be great.
SECOND NYMPH: In humble Cottages we have such contents,
As uncorrupted Nature does afford,
Which the great, that surfeit under gilded Roofs,
And wanton in Down Beds, can never know.
FIRST SHEPHERD: Nature is here not yet debauch'd by Art;
'Tis as it was in Saturn's happy days:
Minds are not here by Luxury invaded;
A homely Plenty, with sharpe Appetite,
Does lightsome health and vigorous strength impart.
FIRST NYMPH: A chaste, cold Spring does here refresh our thirst
Which by no feverish surfeit is increas'd;
Our food is such as Nature meant for Men
Ere with the Vicious, Eating was an Art.
SECOND NYMPH: In noisy Cities riot is pursu'd,
And lewd luxurious living softens men,
Effeminates Fools in Body and in Mind,

Weakens their Appetites, and decays their Nerves.
SECOND SHEPHERD: With filthy steams from their excess of Meat,
  And cloudy vapours rais'd from dangerous Wine,
  Their heads are never clear or free to think;
  They waste their lives in a continual mist.
FIRST SHEPHERD: Some subtle and ill men choose Temperance,
  Not as a Virtue, but a Bawd to Vice,
  And vigilantly wait to ruine those
  Whom Luxury and Ease have lull'd asleep.
SECOND SHEPHERD: Yes, in the clamorous Courts of tedious Law,
  Where what is meant for a relief's a grievance;
  Or in Kings' Palaces, where Cunning strives
  Not to advance Kings' Interests, but its own;
FIRST NYMPH: There they in a continual hurry live,
  And seldom can, for all their subtle Arts,
  Lay their foundations sure; but some
  Are undermin'd, others blown down by storms.
SECOND NYMPH: Their subtilty is but a common Road
  Of flattering great men, and oppressing little,
  Smiling on all they meet, and loving none.
FIRST SHEPHERD: In populous Cities, life is all a storm;
  But we enjoy a sweet perpetual calm:
  Here our own Flocks we keep, and here
  I and my Phillis can embrace unenvi'd.
SECOND SHEPHERD: And I and Celia without jealousy.
  But hark, the Pipes begin; now for our sports.
  [A Symphony of Rustic Music.]

> Nymphs and Shepherds, come away;
> In these Groves let's sport and play,
> Where each day is a Holy-day,
> Sacred to Ease and happy Love,
> To Dancing, Music, Poetry:
> Your Flocks may now securely rove
> Whilst you express your jollity.

[Enter SHEPHERDS and SHEPHERDESSES, singing in Chorus.]

> We come, we come, no joy like this.
> Now let us sing, rejoice, and kiss.
> The Great can never know such bliss.

1. As this.
2. As this.
3. As this.
ALL: As this.

 The Great can never know such bliss.

  1. All th' Inhabitants o'th' Wood
   Now celebrate the Spring
  That gives fresh vigour to the blood
   Of every living thing.
CHORUS: The Birds have been singing and billing before us,
   And all the sweet Choristers join in the Chorus.

  2. The Nightingales and jugging throats
   Warble out their pretty Notes,
   So sweet, so sweet, so sweet:
   And thus our Loves and Pleasures greet.
CHORUS: Then let our Pipes sound, let us dance, let us sing
   Till the murmuring Groves with loud Echoes shall ring.
 [*Dance begins.*]

  3. How happy are we,
   From all jealousie free;
  No dangers or cares can annoy us:
   We toy and we kiss,
   And Love's our chief bliss;
  A pleasure that never can cloy us.
CHORUS: Our days we consume in unenvied delights,
   And in love and soft rest our happy long nights.

  4. Each Nymph does impart
   Her love without Art
  To her Swain, who thinks that his chief Treasure.
   No envy is fear'd,
   No sighs are e'r heard
  But those which are caus'd by our pleasure.
CHORUS: When we feel the bless'd Raptures of innocent Love,
   No joys exceed ours but the pleasures above.

   In these delightful fragrant Groves,
   Let's celebrate our happy Loves.
   Let's pipe, and dance, and laugh, and sing;
   Thus every happy living thing
   Revels in the chearful Spring.

[*Dance continues. Enter* DON JOHN, DON LOPEZ, DON ANTONIO, *and* JACOMO.]

DON JOHN: So, thus far we are safe; we have almost kill'd our Horses with riding cross out of all Roads.

JACOMO: Nay, you have had as little mercy on them as if they had been Men or Women. But yet we are not safe; let us fly farther.

DON JOHN: The house I lighted at was mine during my life, which I sold to that fellow; he, since he holds by that tenure, will carefully conceal us.

JACOMO: 'Tis a Tenure I will not give him two months purchase for.

DON JOHN: Besides, our Swords are us'd to conquest.

DON ANTONIO: At worst, there is a Church hard by; we'll put it to its proper use, take refuge in't.

DON LOPEZ: Look here, here are Shepherds, and young pretty Wenches; shall we be idle, Don?

DON ANTONIO: By no means; 'tis a long time, methinks, since we were vicious.

DON JOHN: We'll serve 'em as the Romans did the Sabines; we'll rob 'em of their Women; only we'll return the Punks again when we have us'd them.

JACOMO: For Heaven's sake, hold.

DON JOHN: Sirra, no more; do as we do, ravish, Rascal, or by my Sword, I'll cut thee into so many pieces, it shall pose an Arithmetician to sum up the fractions of thy body.

JACOMO: I ravish! Oh, good Sir! my Courage lies not that way; alas, I, I am almost famish'd, I have not eat today.

DON JOHN: Sirra, by Heaven, do as I bid thee, or thou shalt never eat again. Shall I keep a Rascal for a Cypher?

JACOMO: Oh! What will become of me? I must do it.

DON JOHN: Come on, Rogue, fall on.

DON ANTONIO: Which are you for?

DON JOHN: 'Tis all one; I am not in Love but in Lust, and to such a one, a Bellyfull's a Bellyfull, and there's an end on't.

FIRST SHEPHERDESS: What means this violence?

SECOND SHEPHERDESS: Oh! Heav'n protect us.

JACOMO: Well, I must have one too; if I be hang'd, I had as good be hang'd for something.

[*Everyone runs off with a Woman.*]

DON LOPEZ: Rogues, come not on; we'll be in your guts.

ALL SHEPHERDESSES [*They cry out.*]: Help, help.

FIRST SHEPHERDESS: What Devils are these?

[*Exeunt. Three or four Shepherds return with* JACOMO.]

FIRST SHEPHERD: Here's one Rogue. Have we caught you, Sir? We'll cool your courage.

JACOMO: Am I taken prisoner? I shall be kept as an honourable Hostage at least—

SECOND SHEPHERD: Where are these Villains, these Ravishers?

JACOMO: Why you need not keep such a stir, Gentlemen, you will have all your Women again, and no harm done. Let me go, I'll fetch 'em to you.

FIRST SHEPHERD: No, you libidinous Swine; we'll revenge the Rapes on you.

JACOMO: Good kind civil people, pass this by. 'Tis true my Master's a very Tarquin; but I ne'r attempted to ravish before.

SECOND SHEPHERD: I'll secure you from ever doing of it again. Where's your Knife?

JACOMO: Heav'n! What do you mean? Oh spare me! I am unprepar'd; let me be confest.

FIRST SHEPHERD: We will not kill you, we'll but geld you. Are you so hot, Sir?

JACOMO: Oh bloody Villains! have a care, 'tis not a season for that, the Signs in Scorpio.*

SECOND SHEPHERD: Down with him—

JACOMO: O help help! murder! murder! Have a care what you do. I am the last of all my Race—Will you destroy a whole Stock and take away my Representers of my Family?—

FIRST SHEPHERD: There shall be no more of the Breed of you—

JACOMO: I am of an ancient Family. Will you cut off all hopes of a Son and Heir? Help! Help! Master, Don John Oh! Oh! Oh!

[*Enter* DON JOHN, DON LOPEZ, *and* DON ANTONIO.]

DON JOHN: How now, Rogues? do you abuse my Man?

[*The* SHEPHERDS *fly.*]

JACOMO: O Sir, this is the first good thing you ever did. If you had not come just in the Nick, I had lost my Manhood.

DON ANTONIO: 'Tis no matter for the use you make on't.

DON LOPEZ: But come, let's now to Supper.

JACOMO: Come on, I am almost starv'd.

[*Exeunt.* SHEPHERDS *return.*]

---

*Scorpio is the fruitful sign and governs man's sexual organs. [*Editor's note.*]

First Shepherd: Let's not complain, but Dog the Rogues, and when
we have Hous'd 'em, we will to the next Magistrate, and beg his
pow'r to apprehend 'em.
[*Exeunt.*]

Scene 3

A Church, with the Statue of Don Pedro *on Horseback in it.*

Don John: Let's in and see this Church.

Jacomo: Is this a time to see Churches? But let me see whose Statue's
this? Oh Heav'n! this is Don Pedro's, whom you murder'd at Seville.

Don John: Say you so? Read the Inscription.

Jacomo: *Here lies Don Pedro, Governour of Seville, barbarously murder'd by that impious Villain Don John, 'gainst whom his innocent
blood cries still for vengeance.*

Don John: Let it cry on. Art thou there, i' faith? Yes, I kill'd thee, and
wou'd do't again upon the same occasion. Jacomo—invite him to
Supper.

Jacomo: What, a Statue! Invite a Statue to Supper? Ha, ha—can
Marble eat?

Don John: I say, Rascal, tell him I would have him Sup with me.

Jacomo: Ha, ha, ha! who the Devil put this whimsey into your head?
Ha, ha, ha! Invite a Statue to Supper?

Don John: I shall spoil your Mirth, Sirra; I will have it done.

Jacomo: Why, 'tis impossible; wou'd you have me such a Coxcomb,
invite Marble to eat? Ha, ha, ha. [*He goes several times towards the
Statue and returns laughing.*] Good Mr. Statue, if it shall please your
Worship, my Master desires you to make Collation with him pres-
ently—[*The* Statue *nods his head,* Jacomo *falls down and roars.*]
Oh I am dead! Oh, Oh, Oh.

Don John: The Statue nods its Head; 'tis odd—

Don Antonio: 'Tis wonderful.

Don Lopez: I am amaz'd.

Jacomo: Oh I cannot stir! Help, help.

Don John: Well, Governour, come, take part of a Collation with me,
'tis by this time ready; make haste, 'tis I invite you. [Statue *nods
again.*] Say you so? Come on, let's set all things in order quickly.

Jacomo: Oh fly, fly.

Don Antonio: This is prodigious.

[*Exeunt* Don John, Don Lopez, Don Antonio, *and* Jacomo.]

Scene 4

At Don John's country house; a Dining Room, a Table spread, Servants setting on Meat and Wine.

DON JOHN: Come, our meat is ready, let's sit. Pox on this foolish Statue; it puzzles me to know the reason on't. Sirra, I'll give you leave to sit.

DON ANTONIO: Let's eat; ne'r think on't.

JACOMO: Ay, come, let's eat; I am too hungry now to think on the fright—

[JACOMO *eats greedily.*]

DON JOHN: This is excellent Meat. How the Rogue eats. You'll choke yourself.

JACOMO: I warrant you, look to yourself

DON ANTONIO: Why, Jacomo, is the Devil in you?

JACOMO: No, no; if he be, 'tis a hungry Devil.

DON LOPEZ: Will you not Drink?

JACOMO: I'll lay a good foundation first.

DON JOHN: The Rascal eats like a Cannibal.

JACOMO: Ay, 'tis no matter for that.

DON JOHN: Some Wine, Sirra.

JACOMO: There, Sir, take it; I am in haste.

DON ANTONIO: 'Sdeath, the Fool will be strangl'd.

JACOMO: The Fool knows what he does.

DON JOHN: Here's to Don Pedro's Ghost; he should have been wel-come.

JACOMO: O name him not.

DON LOPEZ: The Rascal is afraid of you after death.

JACOMO: Oh! Oh! [*Almost chok'd*] Some Wine, give me some Wine.

DON ANTONIO: Take it.

JACOMO: So, now 'tis down.

DON ANTONIO: Are you not satisfi'd yet?

JACOMO: Peace, peace; I have but just begun. [*One knocks hard at the door.*] Who's there? come in, I am very busy.

DON JOHN: Rise, and do your duty.

JACOMO: But one morsel more, I come. [*Knocks again.*] What a pox, are you mad? [*Opens the door. Enter* GHOST.] Oh! the Devil, the Devil.

DON JOHN: Hah! It is the Ghost; let's rise and receive him.

DON ANTONIO: I am amaz'd.

DON LOPEZ: Not frightened, are you?

DON ANTONIO: I scorn the thoughts of fear.

[*They salute the* GHOST.]

DON JOHN: Come, Governour, you are welcome; sit there; if we had thought you would have come, we wou'd have stay'd for you. But come on, Sirra, give me some Wine.

[*The* GHOST *sits.*]

JACOMO: Oh! I am dead; What shall I do? I dare not come near you.

DON JOHN: Come, Rascal, or I'll cut your Throat.

JACOMO: I come, I come, I come. Oh! Oh!

[*Fills Wine, his hand trembles.*]

DON JOHN: Why do you tremble, Rascal? Hold it steadily—

JACOMO: Oh! I cannot.

[JACOMO *snatches meat from the Table, and runs aside.*]

DON JOHN: Here, Governour, your health. Friends, put it about. Here's excellent Meat; taste of this Ragout. If you had had a body of flesh, I would have given you *chair entière*—but the Women care not for Marble. Come, I'll help you. Come, eat, and let old quarrels be forgotten.

GHOST: I come not here to take Repast with you;
Heaven has permitted me to animate
This Marble Body, and I come to warn
You of that Vengeance is in store for you,
If you amend not your pernicious lives.

JACOMO: Oh Heav'n!

DON ANTONIO: What, are you come to preach to us?

DON LOPEZ: Keep your Harangues for Fools that will believe 'em.

DON JOHN: We are too much confirm'd. Pox o' this dry discourse, give me some Wine. Come, here's to your Mistress; you had one when you were living: not forgetting your sweet Sister. Sirra, more Wine.

JACOMO: Ay, Sir—Good Sir, do not provoke the Ghost; his Marble Fists may fly about your ears, and knock your brains out.

DON JOHN: Peace, Fool.

GHOST: Tremble, you impious Wretches, and repent;
Behold, the Pow'rs of Hell wait for you.

[*Devils rise.*]

JACOMO: Oh! I will steal from hence. Oh the Devil!

DON JOHN: Sirra, stir not; by Heav'n, I'll use thee worse than Devils can do. Come near, Coward.

JACOMO: Oh I dare not stir; what will become of me?

DON JOHN: Come, Sirra, eat.

JACOMO: O, Sir, my Appetite is satisfied.

DON JOHN: Drink, Dog, the Ghost's Health: Rogue, do't, or I'll run my Sword down your throat.

JACOMO: Oh! Oh! Here, Mr. Statue, your Health.

DON JOHN: Now, Rascal, sing to entertain him.

JACOMO: Sing, quoth he! Oh! I have lost my voice: I cannot be merry in such company. Sing—

DON ANTONIO: Who are these with ugly shapes?

DON LOPEZ: Their manner of appearing is something strange.

GHOST: They're Devils, that wait for such hard impious
Men. They're Heaven's Instruments of eternal vengeance.

DON JOHN: Are they some of your Retinue? Devils, say you? I am sorry I have no Burnt Brandy to treat 'em with; that's Drink fit for Devils—[*They sink.*] Hah! they vanish.

GHOST: Cannot the fear of Hell's eternal tortures
Change the horrid course of your abandon'd lives?
Think on those Fires, those everlasting Fires,
That shall without consuming burn you ever.

DON JOHN: Dreams, Dreams, too slight to lose my pleasure for.
In spite of all you say, I will go on,
Till I have surfeited on all delights.
Youth is a Fruit that can but once be gather'd,
And I'll enjoy it to the full.

DON ANTONIO: Let's push it on: Nature chalks out the way that we should follow.

DON LOPEZ: 'Tis her fault, if we do that we should not. Let's on, here's a Brimmer to our Leader's health.

JACOMO: What hellish Fiends are these?

DON JOHN: Let me tell you, 'tis something ill bred to rail at your Host that treats you civilly. You have not yet forgot your quarrel to me.

GHOST: 'Tis for your good; by me Heaven warns you of its wrath, and gives you a longer time for your repentance. I invite you this night to a repast of mine.

DON JOHN: Where?

GHOST: At my Tomb.

DON ANTONIO: What time?

GHOST: At dead of night.

DON JOHN: We'll come.

GHOST: Fail not.

DON LOPEZ: I warrant you.

GHOST: Farewell, and think upon your lost condition.

DON JOHN: Farewell, Governour, I'll see what Treat you'll give us.

DON ANTONIO: ⎫
DON LOPEZ: ⎬ And I.

JACOMO: That will not I. Pox on him, I have had enough of his company, I shall not recover it this week. If I eat with such an Host, I'll
be hang'd.

DON JOHN: If you do not, by Heaven, you shall be hang'd.

JACOMO: Whither will your lewdness carry me? I do not care for
having a Ghost for my Landlord. Will not these Miracles do good
upon you?

DON JOHN: There's nothing happens but by Natural Causes,
Which in unusual things Fools cannot find,
And then they style 'em Miracles. But no Accident
Can alter me from what I am by Nature.
Were there
Legions of Ghosts and Devils in my way,
One moment in my course of pleasure I'd not stay.
[*Exeunt all.*]

ACT V

Scene I

Town square near a convent. Enter JACOMO, *with Back, Breast, and
Head-piece.*

JACOMO: Well, this damn'd Master of mine will not part with me; and
we must fight five or six times a day, one day with another, that's
certain. Therefore thou art wise, honest Jacomo, to arm thyself, I
take it. Sa, sa, sa—Methinks I am very valiant on the sudden. Sa, sa,
sa. Hah! there I have you. Paph—Have at you. Hah—there I have
you through. That was a fine thrust in tierce. Hah—Death! what
noise is that?
[*Enter* DON JOHN.]

DON JOHN: How, now Sirrah, what are you doing?

JACOMO: Nothing but practising to run people through the bodies,
that's all; for I know somebody's throat must be cut before midnight.

DON JOHN: In Armour too! why, that cannot help you, you are such a
cowardly Fool; fear will betray you faster within than that can
defend you without—

JACOMO: I fear nobody breathing, I; nothing can terrify me but the Devilish Ghost. Ha! who's that coming? [*Leaps back.*] O Heaven!

DON JOHN: Is this your courage? You are preparing for flight before an Enemy appears.

JACOMO: No, no, Sir, not I; I only leapt back to put myself upon my guard—Fa, la, la—

[*Enter* DON LOPEZ *and* DON ANTONIO.]

DON JOHN: Whom have we here?

JACOMO: Oh where! where! who are they?

DON JOHN: Oh my Friends! where have you been?

DON ANTONIO: We went to view the stately Nunnery hard by, and have been chatting with the poor sanctifi'd Fools till it's dark; we have been chaffering for Nuns-flesh.

DON LOPEZ: There I made such a discovery, if you do not assist me, I am ruin'd for ever. Don Bernardo's Sister, whom I fell in love with in Seville is this day plac'd there for probation; and if you cannot advise me to some way or other of getting her out for some present occasion I have for her, I am a lost man, that's certain.

DON ANTONIO: The business is difficult, and we resolved to manage it in council.

JACOMO: Now will they bring me into some wicked occasion or other of shewing my prowess: a pox on 'em.

DON JOHN: Have you so long followed my fortunes to boggle at difficulty upon so honourable an occasion? Besides, here is no difficulty.

DON LOPEZ: No? the Walls are so high, and the Nunnery so strongly fortifi'd, 'twill be impossible to do it by force; we must find some stratagem.

DON JOHN: The stratagem is soon found out—

DON ANTONIO: As how, Don John?

DON JOHN: Why, I will set fire on the Nunnery; fire the Hive, and the Drones must out or be burnt within: then you may, with ease, under pretence of succour, take whom you will.

DON LOPEZ: 'Tis a gallant design.

DON ANTONIO: I long to be about it. Well, Don, thou art the bravest Fellow breathing.

JACOMO: Gentlemen, pray what became of that brave Fellow that fir'd the Temple at Ephesus? Was he not hanged, Gentlemen, hum—

DON ANTONIO: We are his Rivals, Fool; and who would not suffer for so brave an action?

DON JOHN: He's a Scoundrel and a Poltroon that would not have his Death for his Fame.

Don Lopez: That he is, a damn'd Son of a Whore, and not fit to drink with.

Jacomo: 'Tis a rare thing to be a Martyr for the Devil. But what good will infamy do you when you are dead? when Honour is nothing but a vapour to you while you are living. For my part I'd not be hang'd to be Alexander the Great.

Don Antonio: What a phlegmatic dull Rascal is that who has no Ambition in him.

Jacomo: Ambition! What, to be hang'd? Besides, what's the intrinsic value of honour when a man is under ground? Let 'em but call me honest Jacomo, as I am, while I live, and let 'em call me, when I am dead, Don John if they will.

Don John: Villain, dare you profane my name?

Jacomo: Hold, Sir, think what you do; you cannot hurt me; my Arms are Pistol proof.

[*Enter a* Servant.]

Servant: I come to give you notice of an approaching danger. You must fly; an Officer with some Shepherds have found you were at our house, and are come to apprehend you for some outrage you have commited; I came to give you notice, knowing our Family has a great respect for you.

Don John: Yes, I know your Family has a great respect for me, for I have lain with everyone in it but thee and thy Master.

Jacomo: Why look you now, I thought what 'twou'd come to. Fly, Sir, fly; the darkness of the night will help us. Come, I'll lead the way.

Don John: Stay Sirra, you shall have one occasion more of shewing your valour.

Don Antonio: Did ever any Knight Errant fly that was so well appointed?

Don Lopez: No; you shall stay and get Honour, Jacomo.

Jacomo: Pox of Honour; I am content with the Stock I have already.

Don John: You are easily satisfied. But now let's fire the Nunnery.

Don Antonio: Come on.

Don Lopez: I long to be at it.

Jacomo: O Jacomo! Thy Life is not worth a piece of Eight. 'Tis in vain to dissuade 'em, Sir; I will never trouble you with another request if you'll be graciously pleas'd to leave me out of this adventure.

Don John: Well, you have your desire.

Jacomo: A thousand Thanks, and when I see you again, I will be humbly content with a Halter.

DON JOHN: But do you hear, Fool? Stand Sentinel here, and if any-thing happens extraordinary, give us notice of it.

JACOMO: O, good Sir! What do you mean? That's as bad as going with you.

DON JOHN: Let me find you here when I come again, or you are a dead man—

[*Exeunt* DON JOHN, DON LOPEZ, *and* DON ANTONIO.]

JACOMO: I am sure I am a dead man, if you find me here. But would my Armour were off now, that I might run the lighter. Night, assist me. Heaven! what noise is that? To be left alone in the dark, and fear Ghosts and Devils, is very horrible. But Oh! Who are these?

[*Enter* OFFICER, *Guards, and Shepherds.*]

FIRST SHEPHERD: We are thus far right; the Ravishers went this way.

SECOND SHEPHERD: For Heaven's sake take 'em dead or alive; such des-perate Villains ne'r were seen.

JACOMO: So; if I be catch'd I shall be hang'd; if not, I shall be kill'd. 'Tis very fine. These are the Shepherds. I'll hide myself.

[*He stands up close against the Wall.*]

FIRST SHEPHERD: If we catch the Rogues we'll broil 'em alive; no death can be painful enough for such Wretches.

JACOMO: O bloody-minded Men—

SECOND SHEPHERD: O impious vile Wretches! that we had you in our clutches! Open your dark Lanthorn, and let's search for 'em.

JACOMO: What will become of me? My Armour will not do now.

FIRST SHEPHERD: Thus far we hunted them upon a good scent, but now we are at a fault.

JACOMO: Let me see; I have one trick left; I have a Disguise will fright the Devil.

SECOND SHEPHERD: They must be hereabouts.

JACOMO: I'll in amongst them, and certainly this will fright 'em.

FIRST SHEPHERD: Oh Heaven! What horrid Object's this?

JACOMO: The Devil.

SECOND SHEPHERD: Oh fly, fly! The Devil, the Devil! fly—

[*Exeunt Shepherds and others, frightened.*]

JACOMO: Farewell, good Gentlemen. This is the first time my face e'r did me good. But I'll not stay, I take it. Yet whither shall I fly? Oh! What noise is that? I am in the dark, in a strange place too; what will follow? There lie. Oh! my Arms. Hah! Who's there? Let me go this way—Oh the Ghost! the Ghost! Gad forgive me, 'twas nothing but my fear. [*A noise within:* "Fire, fire, the Nunnery's on fire."] Oh vile Wretches! they have done the deed. There is no flying; now the place will be full of People, and wicked Lights that will discover me if I fly.

[*Within.* Fire, fire, fire; the Nunnery's on fire; help, help—*Several people cross the Stage, crying* Fire.]

JACOMO: What shall I do? there's no way but one, I'll go with the Crowd. [*More people cross the Stage; he runs with them.*] Fire Fire —Murder! help! help! fire! fire—

[*Enter* DON JOHN, DON ANTONIO, DON LOPEZ, *and* FOUR NUNS.]

DON JOHN: Fear not, Ladies, we'll protect you.

FIRST NUN: Our Sex and Habits will protect us.

DON LOPEZ: Not enough, we will protect you better.

FIRST NUN: Pray leave us; we must not consort with men.

DON ANTONIO: What, would you run into the fire to avoid Mankind? You are zealous Ladies indeed.

DON JOHN: Come, Ladies, walk with us; we'll put you in a place of safety.

FIRST NUN: We'll go no further; we are safe enough; be gone, and help to quench the fire.

DON JOHN: We have another fire to quench; come along with us.

DON LOPEZ: Ay, come, you must go.

DON ANTONIO: Come along, we know what's good for you; you must go with us.

FIRST NUN: Heaven! What violence is this? what impious men are these? Help! Help!

[*All cry* Help. *Enter* FLAVIA *and* CLARA, *in the habit of Probationers.*]

FLAVIA: Here are the bloody Villains, the causes of our misery.

CLARA: Inhuman Butchers! now we'll have your Lives.

DON JOHN: Hah! here are a brace of my Wives. If you have a mind to this Fool, take her betwixt you; for my part, I'll have my own. Come, Wives, along with me; we must consummate, my Spouses, we must consummate.

CLARA: What Monsters are these?

ALL NUNS: Help! help!

DON ANTONIO: 'Sdeath! these foolish Women are their own Enemies.

DON LOPEZ: Here are so many people, if they cry out more, they'll interrupt us in our brave design.

DON JOHN: I warrant you; when they cry out, let us out-noise 'em. Come, Women, you must go along with us.

FIRST NUN: Heaven! What shall we do? Help! help!

DON JOHN: Help! help! Fire! fire! fire!

DON LOPEZ:
DON ANTONIO: } Help! help!

[*They hale the Women by the hands, who still cry out, and they with them. Enter several people, crying out* Fire, JACOMO *in the rear.*]

JACOMO: Fire! fire! fire! Help! help!

'Sdeath! here's my Master.

DON JOHN: Sirra, come along with me, I have use of you.

JACOMO: I am caught.

DON JOHN: Here, Sirra, take one of my Wives, and force her after me. Do you refuse, Villain?

[*Enter Shepherds, with* OFFICER *and Guards.*]

NUNS: Help! help! good people, help! rescue us from these Villains.

FIRST SHEPHERD: Who are you, committing violence on Women?

SECOND SHEPHERD: Heavens! they are the Villains we seek for.

JACOMO: Where is my Armour now? Oh my Armour.

OFFICER: Fall on.

[*They fight, Women fly,* JACOMO *falls down as kill'd, Two Shepherds and the* OFFICER *are kill'd.*]

DON JOHN: Say you so, Rogues?

DON LOPEZ: So, the Field's our own.

DON JOHN: But a pox on't, we have bought a Victory too dear; we have lost the Women.

DON ANTONIO: We'll find 'em again. But poor Jacomo's kill'd.

JACOMO [*Aside.*]: That's a lie.

DON LOPEZ: 'Faith, let's carry off our dead.

DON JOHN: Agreed; we'll bury him in the Church; while the Ghost treats us, we'll treat the Worms with the body of a Rascal.

JACOMO [*Aside.*]: Not yet a while.

DON LOPEZ: Come, let's take away the Fool.

JACOMO: No, the Fool can take up himself. 'Sdeath! you resolve not to let me alone dead or alive—

Here are more Murders, Oh!

DON LOPEZ: Oh counterfeiting Rascal! Are you alive?

[*The Clock strikes Twelve.*]

DON ANTONIO: The Clock strikes Twelve.

DON JOHN: 'Slife, our time's come; we must to the Tomb. I would not break my word with the Ghost for a thousand Doubloons—

JACOMO: Nor I keep it for ten times the Money.

DON JOHN: But you shall keep your word, Sir.

JACOMO: Sir, I am resolv'd to Fast tonight; 'tis a Vigil. Besides, I care not for eating in such base company.

[*Within.* Follow, follow, follow—]

DON LOPEZ: D'hear that noise? The remaining Rogues have rais'd the Mobile, and are coming upon us.

JACOMO: Oh! let's fly—fly—What will become of me?

DON ANTONIO: Let's to the Church, and give the Rogues the Go-by.

DON JOHN: Come on, since 'tis my time, and I have promis'd the Governour, I'll go—You had best stay, Sirra, and be taken.

JACOMO: No. Now I must go to the Church whether I will or no. Away, away, fly!

[*Enter Two Shepherds with a great Rabble.* Here they went; follow, follow—*Exeunt all.*]

Scene 2

The Church, the STATUE *of* DON PEDRO *on Horseback; on each side of the Church,* DON JOHN'S [FATHER'S] GHOST, MARIA'S, DON FRAN-CISCO'S, LEONORA'S, FLORA'S, MARIA'S BROTHER'S [GHOSTS]; [*devils*] *and others, with torches in their hands. Enter* DON JOHN, DON ANTONIO, DON LOPEZ, *and* JACOMO.

JACOMO: Good Sir, let's go no farther; look what horrid Attendants are here. This wicked Ghost has no good meaning in him.

DON JOHN: He resolves to treat us in State; I think he has robb'd all the Graves hereabouts of their Dead to wait upon us.

DON ANTONIO: I see no Entertainment prepar'd.

DON LOPEZ: He has had the manners to light off his Horse, and enter-tain us.

DON JOHN: He would not sure be so ill bred to make us wait on him on foot.

JACOMO: Pox on his Breeding, I shall dye with fear; I had as good have been taken and hang'd. What horror seizes me!

DON JOHN: Well, Governour, you see we are as good as our words.

DON ANTONIO: Where's your Collation?

DON LOPEZ: Bid some of your Attendants give us some Wine.

[STATUE *descends.*]

STATUE: Have you not yet thought on your lost condition?
Here are the Ghosts of some whom you have murder'd
That cry for vengeance on you—

FATHER'S GHOST: Repent, repent of all your horrid crimes:

Monsters, repent, or Hell will swallow you.

DON JOHN: That's my Old man's voice. D'y hear Old Gentleman, you talk idly.

JACOMO: I do repent; O spare me. I do repent of all my sins, but especially of following this wicked Wretch.

[*He kneels.* DON ANTONIO *kicks him.*]

DON ANTONIO: Away, Fool.

DON FRANCISCO'S GHOST: My blood cries out upon thee, barbarous Wretch.

DON JOHN: That's my Host Francisco; 'faith, thou wert a good honest Blockhead, that's the truth on't—

FLORA'S GHOST: Thou shalt not escape Vengeance for all thy crimes.

DON JOHN: What Fool's that? I am not acquainted with her.

LEONORA'S GHOST: In time lay hold on mercy, and repent.

DON JOHN: That was Leonora, a good-natur'd silly Wench, something too loving, that was all her fault.

MARIA'S GHOST: Villain, this is the last moment of thy life.
And thou in flames eternally shalt howl.

DON JOHN: Thou li'st; this is the young hot-headed Fool we kill'd at Francisco's. Pox on him, he disappointed me in my design upon the Daughters. Would thou wert alive again that I might kill thee once more.

DON LOPEZ: No more of this old foolish stuff; give us some Wine to begin with.

DON ANTONIO: Ay, Give us some Wine, Governour.

DON JOHN: What, do you think to Treat us thus? I offer'd you a better entertainment. Prithee trouble us no more, but bid some of your Attendants give us some Wine; I'll drink to you and all the good company.

STATUE: Give 'em the Liquor they have most delighted in.

[*Two of the Ghosts go out, and bring four Glasses full of blood, then give 'em to* DON JOHN, DON ANTONIO, *and* DON LOPEZ.]

DON LOPEZ: This is something.

DON JOHN: This is civil.

DON LOPEZ: I hope a good desert will follow.

[GHOST *offers a Glass to* JACOMO, *who runs round* DON JOHN, DON ANTONIO, *and* DON LOPEZ, *roaring.*]

JACOMO: Are you stark distracted? Will you drink of that Liquor? Oh Oh! What d'you mean? Good sweet Ghost, forbear your civility. Oh, I am not dry, I thank you—

DON JOHN: Give it to me. Here, take it, Sirra.

JACOMO: By no means, Sir; I never drink between meals. Oh Sir—

DON JOHN: Take it, Rascal.

JACOMO: Oh Heav'ns!

DON JOHN: Now, Governour, your Health; 'tis the reddest drink I ever saw.

DON LOPEZ: Hah! pah! 'tis blood.

DON ANTONIO: Pah! it is—

JACOMO: Oh! I'll have none of it.

[*They throw the Glasses down.*]

DON JOHN: 'Sdeath, do you mean to affront us?

STATUE: 'Tis fit for such bloodthirsty Wretches.

DON JOHN: Do you upbraid me with my killing of you? I did it, and would do it again: I'd fight with all your Family one by one, and cut off root and branch to enjoy your Sister. But will you Treat us yet no otherwise?

STATUE: Yes, I will, ye impious Wretches.

[*Makes a Flourish.*]

DON LOPEZ: What's here? Music to treat us with?

DON ANTONIO: There is some pleasure in this.

SONG OF DEVILS

FIRST DEVIL: Prepare, prepare, new Guests draw near,
    And on the brink of Hell appear.

SECOND DEVIL: Kindle fresh Flames of Sulphur there.
    Assemble, all ye Fiends,
    Wait for the dreadful ends
    Of impious Men, who far excel
    All th' Inhabitants of Hell.

CHORUS OF DEVILS: —Let 'em come, Let 'em come,
    To an eternal dreadful Doom,
    Let 'em come, Let 'em come.

THIRD DEVIL: In mischiefs they have all the damn'd outdone;
    Here they shall weep, and shall unpiti'd groan,
    Here they shall howl, and make eternal moan.

FIRST DEVIL: By Blood and Lust they have deserv'd so well
    That they shall feel the hottest flames of Hell.

SECOND DEVIL: In vain they shall here their past mischiefs bewail,
    In exquisite torments that never shall fail.

THIRD DEVIL: Eternal Darkness they shall find,
                And them eternal Chains shall bind,
                To infinite pain of sense and mind.

CHORUS OF   } —Let 'em come, Let 'em come,
DEVILS: } To an eternal dreadful Doom
                } Let 'em come, Let 'em come.

STATUE: Will you not relent and feel remorse?

DON JOHN: Cou'dst thou bestow another heart on me, I might; but
with this heart I have, I cannot.

DON LOPEZ: These things are prodigious.

DON ANTONIO: I have a kind of grudging to relent, but something
holds me back.

DON LOPEZ: If we could, 'tis now too late; I will not.

DON ANTONIO: We defy thee.

STATUE: Perish, ye impious Wretches; go and find
The punishments laid up in store for you.
[It thunders, DON LOPEZ and DON ANTONIO are swallow'd up.]
Behold their dreadful Fates, and know that thy last moment's come.

DON JOHN: Think not to fright me, foolish Ghost; I'll break your
Marble body in pieces, and pull down your Horse.

JACOMO: If fear has left me my strength, I'll steal away.
[Exit.]

DON JOHN: These things I see with wonder, but no fear.
Were all the Elements to be confounded,
And shuffl'd all into their former Chaos,
Were Seas of Sulphur flaming round about me,
And all Mankind roaring within those fires,
I could not fear or feel the least remorse.
To the last instant I would dare thy power.
Here I stand firm, and all thy threats contemn;
Thy Murderer stands here; now do thy worst.
[It Thunders and Lightens, Devils descend and sink with DON JOHN,
who is cover'd with a Cloud of fire as he sinks.]

STATUE: Thus perish all
Those men who by their words and actions dare
Against the will and power of Heav'n declare.
[Scene shuts.]

EPILOGUE

Spoken by Jacomo

Through all the Perils of the Play I've run,
But know not how your fury I may shun;
I'm in new dangers now to be undone—
I had but one fierce Master there,
But I have many cruel Tyrants here
Who do most bloodily my life pursue;
Who takes my Livelihood may take that too.
'Gainst little Players you great factions raise,
Make Solemn Leagues and Cov'nants against Plays.
We who by no Allies assisted are,
Against the Great Confederates must make War.
You need not strive our Province to o'er-run;
By our own stratagems we are undone.
We've laid out all our Pains, nay, Wealth for you,
And yet, hardhearted men, all will not do.
'Tis not your Judgments sway, for you can be
Pleas'd with damn'd Plays (as heart can wish to see);
'Ounds, we do what we can, what wou'd you more?
Why do you come, and rant, and damn, and roar?
'Sdeath, what a Devil would you have us do?
Each take a Prison, and there humbly sue,
Angling for single Money with a Shoe?
What, will you be Don Johns? have you no remorse?
Farewell then, bloody men, and take your course.
Yet stay—
If you'll be civil, we will treat of Peace,
And the Articles o'th' Treaty shall be these:
"First, to the men of Wit we all submit;
The rest shall swagger too within the Pit,
And may roar out their little or no Wit.
But do not swear so loud to fright the City,
Who neither care for wicked men, nor witty;
They start at ills they do not like to do,
But shall in Shops be wickeder than you.
"Next you'll no more be troubl'd with Machines.
Item, you shall appear behind our Scenes,
And there make love with the sweet chink of Guineas,

The unresisted eloquence of Ninnies.
Some of our Women shall be kind to you,
And promise free ingress and egress too.
But if the Faces which we have won't do,
We will find out some of Sixteen for you.
We will be civil when nought else will win ye;
We will new bait our Trap, and that will bring ye.
"Come, faith, let all old breaches now be heal'd,
And the said Articles shall be Sign'd and Seal'd."

DON JUAN

in ITALY, GERMANY,

and AUSTRIA (1736-1787)

Don Juan in the Eighteenth Century

Throughout the eighteenth century, managers of popular theatres could count on Don Juan, the Commander, the Servant, and the Devil to bring in the gawkers. In spite of this fact, or because of it, new plays about the Burlador were scarce, and good new plays scarcer still. The old plots bequeathed by the *commedia dell' arte* companies, as well as the reworkings of Villiers and Dorimon, served the unlettered public. Our information about the popular stage—often ambulant, fly-by-night, improvised and disreputable—is spotty. We can be sure that many performances of the *Festin de Pierre* or the *Convitato di pietra* have left no record, and that many an improvised script on stray sheets of paper has been lost. But enough evidence exists to show that Don Juan was thriving in Italy, in Germany, in Holland, and in France.[1] We know, for example, that he was a familiar hero of melodramatic farces, pantomimes, and vaudevilles at the fairs of Paris. At one run of a *Grand Festin de Pierre ou l'Athée foudroyé*, we are given a glimpse of the director making his pitch to the crowd: "This way! This way! Mister Pompey will change costumes twelve times. He will carry off the Commander's daughter in a frogged jacket and will be struck down by lightning in a spangled coat!"[2]

The history of Don Juan in the eighteenth century—or rather, up to 1787, the year of Mozart's *Don Giovanni*—unfolds chiefly in the market

---

1. I can find no information about Don Juan on the popular Spanish stage in that epoch. Tirso's piece, however, was reprinted a few times, and Zamora's play, of which more below, achieved great popularity.

2. E. Campardon, *Les Spectacles de la foire* (Paris: 1877), II, 243.

places of Europe; but a few words should be said about his career in
the "respectable" theatre.

In England Shadwell's play remained extremely popular until the
third decade of the eighteenth century. A French *Festin de Pierre*
seems to have satisfied audiences at the New Haymarket as well, for it
returned five times between 1721 and 1735. At Drury Lane Shadwell's
work was produced several times together with *Harlequin Doctor
Faustus*, but we need not suppose that the managers cunningly fore-
saw the extraordinary union of these two personages which was to
be made less than a century later.[3]

Only two "literary" plays created before 1787 require mention. The
first is Carlo Goldoni's *Don Giovanni Tenorio* (1736), a play no one
admires, but which was, after all, written by the best playwright Italy
produced between Tasso and D'Annunzio. As if to signify his contempt
for the vulgar *commedia*, Goldoni dropped the part of the servant
altogether. But at the same time—in eighteenth-century Venice intellectual daring was out of the question—he robbed his hero of all
intellectual interest. Goldoni's Don Juan is a painfully attenuated
character. Deprived of his folk vigor, his humor, and his intelligence,
he is merely a weak, duped, unenthusiastic Neapolitan fop. It is a
gauge of his fatuity that he tries to rape Anna at dinner when her
father, the Commander, leaves them for a moment to speak with
someone outside. And what is more, he makes this attempt knowing
that he is in deep trouble (Isabella is pursuing him) and that he needs
the Commander's friendship. I mention this episode only to give the
reader a glimpse into the ineptness of Goldoni's effort. Shall I add
that Isabella, disguised in male clothes—they deceive no one at any
time—challenges Don Juan to a duel which the poor fellow is not even
able to bring to an end with a few flicks of his rapier? (The Commander steps in, and—for all we know—saves Don Juan's life.) In the
end, Don Juan is not even allowed to die in the Statue's grasp. Although it is present, the Statue disgusted Goldoni; he disposes of
his polite lecher with a more dignified lightning bolt. We wonder
idly why a fine or a month in jail would not have sufficed.

But worse than the weaknesses in plot and character are those in the

3. See *The London Stage 1660–1800*, Parts 2 and 3 (1700–1729 and 1729–1747), an
exhaustive compilation being issued by Southern Illinois University Press. Only the
two parts just mentioned have been published at this writing. For the period between
1747 and Mozart, Allardyce Nicoll in his *History of English Drama 1660–1900* (Cambridge: Cambridge University Press, 1952), III, 325 mentions only a farce at Drury
Lane in 1782.

An eighteenth-century conception of the "Double Invitation" scene. Engraving by Laurent Carr after François Boucher for a 1734 edition of the works of Molière.

verse. Goldoni was writing a serious play, and he used the pale, ele-vated language whose English equivalent we find, say, in Johnson's *Irene* or Addison's *Cato*. The only amusing episodes concern Elisa, the rustic maiden (inherited from Molière and anticipating Da Ponte's Zerlina) whom Don Juan seduces. Goldoni was avenging himself on an unfaithful mistress in portraying Elisa as an ambitious vixen who jilts her sweetheart to fall in Don Juan's arms. When Don Juan deceives her in turn, she tries to win back Carlino. Carlino advises her to stick to Don Juan, and Don Juan politely returns her to Carlino. Deserted by both, the little hussy takes comfort from her charms, which she is sure will give her the last word, after all.

Goldoni's comedy is not calamitously bad. The worst neoclassic art, whether it be literature, music, or painting, is only dull; and so is this play. The great catastrophes of taste were to occur in the Romantic era, when men flew, or tried to fly, higher.

A somewhat more interesting play than Goldoni's is Antonio de Zamora's *No hay plazo que no se cumpla ni deuda que no se paga* (1744), which might be translated as "Bills fall due and debts must be paid." Zamora figures among the writers whose sad lot it was to close the great age of the Spanish theatre. It would be hard to offer more than a modest defense of his version of Don Juan. The Statue inter-rupts an avenger about to empty his pistol at Don Juan; Ana coarsely plots a murder of her seducer; there is a brawl with students, a gypsy, an attempted rape on stage, and dozens of other titillating episodes which explain why the play held the stage until the next century, when Zorrilla's work thrust it into oblivion, and which explain, too, why serious critics never could stomach it. The play is, however, several degrees better than most melodrama. To us, it is remarkable chiefly because it seems to end with the hero's redemption. The text is equivo-cal at this point, and Zamora's humane attempt cursory at best. But already a new wind is blowing; soon it will be discovered that Don Juan has a soul.[4]

4. Another play, *La Venganza en el sepulcro* by Alonso de Córdoba y Maldonado, seems to have been composed in the late seventeenth century under the partial influ-ence of French models. The play, which was never printed, is noteworthy chiefly because Don Juan is shown as being faithfully in love with Ana, a curious if obscure anticipation of his nineteenth-century character.

The Puppet Theatre and *Don Juan und Don Pietro oder das Steinerne-Todten-Gastmahl*

Except for Goldoni and Zamora, Don Juan in the pre-Mozartean eighteenth century was left mostly to the rough care of vagabond comedians, vaudeville performers, shadow-players, and puppeteers, who often caused great alarm in decent circles and official quarters. Still, the folk theatre occasionally was able to secure the approval of the bureaucracy, and even to settle permanently in a village or city provided the shows were clean. As in the great days of the *commedia dell' arte,* actors and managers connected with the the folk theatre were sometimes men of the best reputation: thus, for example, the great Johann La Roche, who created the figure of Kasperle, a refined successor to the clownish Hans Wurst, and whom Mozart probably saw as Don Juan's servant at the Leopoldstädter Theater in Vienna.

Alongside the folk theatre there flourished what was really a branch of it, the puppet theatre. Its history, which parallels that of the "real" theatre, begins in the churches, where the miracle plays and other festive theatricals were sometimes performed by moving statuettes and dolls. Congregations were familiar with animated crucifixes, Marys, and saints. Eventually the dolls left the churches (sometimes by sudden ejection) and conquered the streets and the fairs. At all times they imitated, and often they rivaled, both the live folk theatre and the legitimate stage. They exhibited the same characters (for instance, Pulcinella and Arlecchino), exploited the same subjects, and followed the same fashions, although of course they tended to introduce farce into the tragedies which they adopted. When the stage degenerated through over-lavish visual effects, the puppets followed suit. But they had one advantage: when the theatre was persecuted, as under Cromwell and in Germany a few decades later, the puppets were usually left alone, and in certain years the whole burden of theatrical history fell on their wooden shoulders.

It is easy to forget that up to the end of the last century puppets entertained people of any age and condition. Philosophers (with perhaps a blush) sought recreation in the frolics of Hans Wurst, Hans Pickelheering, Arlecchino, or Punch; the wealthy hired puppets for private performances; good burghers flocked to the fairs to enjoy them; and villagers everywhere clapped them. A number of clever puppeteers are fondly cited by poets and chroniclers. Theatrical companies less fondly petition kings or councils for their repression. Charles V of Spain toyed with them in his retirement; Haydn wrote music for them. Their subtle engineering made them a worthy object of attention for "projectors"—the scientists of the early days—and, in the Middle Ages, of occasional suspicion by the Church. Their language was not always suitable for children either, and they were often terrible little satirists.

The closeness of the puppet drama to whatever was in vogue at the time is clearly seen in typical repertories. The great warehouse of plots and characters was the *commedia dell' arte,* which gave Don Juan to the puppets; but folktales and traditional legends like *Cinderella* and *Bluebeard* also flourished, and so did the old chivalric romances, tales of Charlemagne and his peers or of Rinaldo and Armida. Playwrights like Gozzi, Goldoni, and Molière were amiably ransacked. Operas and ballets were copied, or rather adapted (for Arlecchino and Pierrot had to accompany Pamina and Papageno); and always the figures of ancient Greece and Rome reappeared—the last time that they took part in the popular culture of Europe. Thus *Polichinelle-Perseus,* or *Aeneas' Descent into Hell,* or *Ulysses in Phaeacia,* or *The Forsaken Dido.* At the same time, the mystery and miracle plays of the Middle Ages were breathing a lively last breath on the puppet stage—stories taken from the Scriptures or from various Lives of the Saints. This was particulary the case in Spain, where sacred or profane miracles formed the backbone of the puppets' repertory. These puppets *(titeres)* took over the established theatres during Lent, when the regular drama was suspended, and offered in miniature the same fare which could be had in flesh and bone the rest of the year.

Although many tragedies and melodramas were performed straight, the characteristic folk or puppet play allowed the clown to upstage the serious characters, as in the *commedia dell' arte.* An audience was likely to mark time (and for good reason) as long as Polichinelle or Hans Wurst was absent from the stage. So again in the Don Juan puppet plays the hero yields to the funny servant, and the love interest is neglected for tomfoolery—some of it very crude. But the humor belongs to any time and any nation. Here, for instance, is what happens when Don Juan tells his Servant to repeat after him his words to the Statue:

> DJ: Don Pietro.
> S: Don Pietro.
> DJ: My Master Don Juan.
> S: My master Don Juan.
> DJ: Who has had the honor of murdering you.

S: You mean it's a honor when you kill a body?

DJ: Peace, rascal, and go on.

S: Peace, rascal, and go on.

DJ: What are you saying, dog?

S: What are you saying, dog?

And so forth.[1]

I know of no separate study of the fortunes of Don Juan as a puppet, but his popularity is well authenticated. "The noble Don Juan Tenorio appears in an incredible number of puppet and marionette texts," we are told. "It can be said that no repertory worthy of our respect—especially in the remoter past—exists without its *Convitato di pietra* or its *Don Giovanni il Dissoluto*."[2] Like the live folk plays, the puppet versions of Don Juan drew freely on the French and Italian versions which we have recorded already, but they left out the old touch of philosophy. The spectators were adults, but they hardly looked to puppet plays for exhibitions of atheism. Don Juan's sins spoke for themselves.

The puppet plays are brief, full of casual non sequiturs, coarse, rich in dialect, and, I repeat, gay. They are not worth the spilling of critics' blood, but I submit that Don Juan was to see worse days than those he spent in the puppet-box.

Translated here is a puppet play performed in the eighteenth century in Augsburg. For the scene in which Don Juan kills Don Philippo, I have substituted a more elaborate one (based on the old French versions) from a kindred play staged in Strasburg. While the Augsburg play is cruder and more naïve, it is more direct and, I think, closer to the typical puppet-farce atmosphere. But much of the humor is strictly visual and is undoubtedly lost in the text. And much of it depends on Hans Wurst's juicy dialect, which the reader's imagination will also have to supply.

1. R. M. Werner (ed.), *Der Laufner Don Juan* (Hamburg and Leipzig: 1891), p. 128. This is a Bavarian folk comedy which may date back to the first half of the eighteenth century.

2. Roberto and Renata M. Leydi, *Marionette e burattini* (Milan: Collana del "Gallo Grande," 1958), p. 257. It is, however, likely that Don Juan was more popular —perhaps a great deal more—in Italy than elsewhere in Europe. George Speaight in his *History of the English Puppet Theatre* (London: Harrap, 1955) does not mention any performance of a Don Juan play in eighteenth-century England. Neither is Don Juan mentioned in J. E. Varey's pioneering *Historia de los Titeres en España* (Madrid: Revista de Braganza, 1957), which takes us up to the mid-eighteenth century. As only a handful of titles seem to have been preserved, however, it cannot be asserted that Don Juan was an alien to the Spanish puppet stage. More evidence, positive or negative, is needed.

A PUPPET PLAY FROM AUGSBURG

Don Juan and Don Pietro

or

The Dead Stone's Banquet

(Before 1787)

Translated by Marion Sonnenfeld

EDITOR'S NOTE

The fourth scene in Act II of the original text has been replaced by Act IV, Scene 7 of a Don Juan puppet play performed in Strasburg. See the preceding commentary.

TEXT

Don Juan und Don Pietro, oder das Steinerne-Todten-Gastmahl and *Don Juan oder der Steinerne Gast* in J. Scheible, *Das Kloster,* vol. III. Stuttgart: 1846.

Persons in the Play

Don Juan

Don Pietro, *the Governor of the city*

Don Philippo, *betrothed to Donna Marillis*

Hans Wurst, *servant to Don Juan*

Donna Marillis, *daughter of Don Pietro*

Lippel, *a messenger*

The Devil

Two Guards

A Hermit

First Landlady

Second Landlady

The Statue [A Ghost]

Synopsis of Scenes

Part the First

Act I. A vaulted hall.
Act II. A street.
Act III. A garden.

Part the Second

Act I. A street.
Act II. A woods, near a cavern.
Act III. An inn.

Part the Third

Act I. A street.
Act II. A room in the inn.
Act III. A churchyard.

ACT I

A vaulted hall. Present are DON JUAN, DON PIETRO, *and* DON PHILIPPO.

DON PIETRO: Well, my friends, since the King has given me this position, I inform you in his Majesty's name, Don Juan, that you are to leave the Court and its vicinity within the next twenty-four hours.

DON JUAN: That I can do, Governor; but I hope, Don Pietro, that you do not intend to deprive me of the hand of your daughter, Donna Marillis.

DON PIETRO: The King has ordered that too.

DON JUAN: Why so? What has the King to say about your daughter? Aren't you her father? Did you not give me your promise? Will you break it now?

DON PIETRO: Stop, Juan! Since you have lost the King's favor through your bad behavior, let me tell you that I am bestowing my daughter's hand, not on you, but on Don Philippo.

DON PHILIPPO: What's this, my dear Don Pietro? How do I come to obtain my heart's desire when I least expect it?

DON PIETRO: The King wishes it, and I must obey him.

DON JUAN: Well, you've become governor now, and the job suits you well, since it requires a hypocrite.

DON PIETRO: But you, dear Don Philippo, hurry to my daughter and hasten with her to the King so that you both can express your gratitude to him.
[*Exits.*]

DON PHILIPPO: I'll go at once to perform this pleasant duty.
[*Exits. Enter* HANS WURST.]

DON JUAN: Heaven and earth, what did I hear! Did I understand correctly? So I'm not to possess Donna Marillis!

HANS WURST: Are you there, master? Folks is saying as how you're a bridegroom without a bride.

DON JUAN: What are you saying? What must I hear? Has this hateful tale spread among the lowest servants?

HANS WURST: That it has. Bridegroom without a bride. Well, go and trust a skirt if you want to be bamboozled.

262

DON JUAN: No, my Hans Wurst, I don't believe it possible that Donna Marillis can forget me.

HANS WURST: You don't believe it possible, does you? Well, pots and kettles, here comes Don Philippo with Donna Marillis! You'll see what you'll see.

DON JUAN: Let's get out of their way, Hans Wurst, so we can hear what they're saying.

[*Exeunt. Enter* DON PHILIPPO *and* DONNA MARILLIS.]

DON PHILIPPO: Dearest Donna Marillis, it is your father's desire and command that I am to call for you.

DONNA MARILLIS: Dearest, best Don Philippo, my heart is full of joy! What a pleasant change after unmannerly Don Juan.

HANS WURST [*behind the scene*]: Did you hear that, master? Are you getting an earful?

DON PHILIPPO: Let us go then, Donna Marillis. Let us hasten to express our gratitude to the King.

DONNA MARILLIS: Quite right, dearest Don Philippo. Let us go; follow my steps.

[*Exeunt.* HANS WURST *and* DON JUAN *return.*]

HANS WURST: Did you see that, master? Women are as changeable as the weather in April.

DON JUAN: I've seen only too clearly. "What a pleasant change after the unmannerly Don Juan!" That went through my heart like a dagger. No, Hans Wurst, no; Donna Marillis must be mine, even if the destruction of half the world would be the price!

HANS WURST: Come, come. Don't be an idiot; I wouldn't puzzle my head about that female.

DON JUAN: There is only one Donna Marillis, and I cannot forget her. But I recall I have some other business to attend to. Follow me soon. [*Exits.*]

HANS WURST: My master is an idiot. He'll worry her and pester her, and what for? He won't get her anyway. Nowadays men don't bawl like puppies over a female. Plenty of women around; they're cheaper than beef.

ACT II

A street. DON JUAN *and* HANS WURST *are talking.*

DON JUAN [*leaving*]: No, Hans Wurst, no, I can't forget Donna Marillis; just look at her pretty clothes! Her charming figure has been captivating me for a long time. Look at her bright, sparkling eyes, her pretty red lips. No—never, never, can I forget her.

HANS WURST: Ow! What's all that yammering over a girl? Button yourself to a new one. Plenty of girls around.

DON JUAN: You're right, Hans Wurst, but I'll never get another Donna Marillis. Just look at her pretty linen and her beautiful pink cheeks! Her whole appearance is just made for loving.

HANS WURST: So you like her pretty linen. You shouldn't look just at that, you know. There's some what has pretty petticoats, and ribbons and laces, and what struts around town in 'em. But if you looked below the surface, you'd find nothing but pimples and—holes.

DON JUAN: When it comes to girls of your class, you may be right, Hans Wurst, but you're not right about Donna Marillis.

HANS WURST: Why not? One female's like another.

DON JUAN: Her pretty pink cheeks!

HANS WURST: Her pretty pink cheeks! Many's the beauty I know goes around as hot as a fire. But catch her in the morning and she looks like a slate with the chalk erased all over it.

DON JUAN: Quiet, Hans Wurst. Who's that coming toward us?

HANS WURST: It's a peasant.

DON JUAN: I wonder what he wants.

[Enter LIPPEL.]

LIPPEL: I've got a letter here and I don't know who it's for. The wind has blowed through it and mixed up all the letters for me, and now I can't read it any more. Say, you there in the red jacket, can you read to who this letter is addressed to?

HANS WURST: Sure, I'll read it to you. Hey, look, master—the letter belongs to Don Philippo.

LIPPEL: What did you say his name was?

HANS WURST: You stupid ass! His name's Don Philippo.

LIPPEL: That's right—Don Philililippo.

DON JUAN: Move over, Hans Wurst. Let me see.

HANS WURST: Just look; you'll see.

DON JUAN: You are a lucky messenger. You must have gotten up on the right side of your bed today.

LIPPEL: How's that? Don't tell me you're Don Philililippo! That would be my luck.

DON JUAN: Indeed I am; and now I'll save you some trouble. Come to the nearest inn with me, and I'll relieve you of the letter and give you your reward.

HANS WURST: But you ain't Don Philippo.

DON JUAN: Yes, I am. Come with me, messenger.

[*Exeunt.*]

HANS WURST: That's a fine lookout! Now he has to be Don Philippo! That is one desperate trick, I tell you. Let's see what else my master will do.

[DON JUAN *returns.*]

DON JUAN: Hans Wurst, what do you suppose is in this letter?

HANS WURST: Well, I don't know. What does it say?

DON JUAN: It says that Don Philippo is to call for Donna Marillis at eleven tonight to take her to the ball.

HANS WURST: How's that? Don Philippo wants to take Donna Marillis to the ball and you have the letter?

DON JUAN: He won't take her. I'll tell you right now that I'm going to take over.

HANS WURST: How will you do that?

DON JUAN: I'll use a rope ladder, climb up the garden wall, and take Donna Marillis away.

HANS WURST: That is not decent; but to take her from under his nose is still less decenter.

DON JUAN: Shut up! I see Don Philippo coming toward me. Now, rascal, you'll have to be the one who opened up the letter.

HANS WURST: But I didn't open it!

DON JUAN: You have to have opened it!

HANS WURST: But I didn't. That's a dirty lie.

DON JUAN: Blasted idiot, how dare you open other people's letters, letters not meant for your master!

[*Enter* DON PHILIPPO.]

DON PHILIPPO: Dear Don Juan, why are you so enraged at your servant?

DON JUAN: Dearest Don Philippo, just listen: this blasted idiot dares open other people's mail—namely, a letter from your beloved Donna Marillis' tender hand to you.

DON PHILIPPO: It doesn't really matter, my dear Don Juan. The letter got into worthy hands.

HANS WURST: So it did. No worthier sharpster could have laid hands on it.

DON PHILIPPO: As for you, varlet, don't you dare ever again open mail that isn't addressed to you.

HANS WURST: I didn't open it.

DON PHILIPPO: Say that again. You did not open it?

HANS WURST: I did not. It isn't true.

DON JUAN: Don't waste your time with this fool. Follow me to the inn. I'll hand the letter over to you there.
[*Exeunt.*]

HANS WURST: Go, you two. Each of you is a worse hooligan than the other. Look, there's the messenger. I'll talk to him.
[*Enter* LIPPEL.]

LIPPEL: Is that you? Your master sent me to you to collect for delivering his letter. He said because he didn't have no money on him.

HANS WURST: So you're the clever messenger boy that delivers mail so well.

LIPPEL: Yus, that's me. I done did a good job, didn't I?

HANS WURST: Sure, you brought the letter to the right place. So my master said I had to pay you?

LIPPEL: That's what your master said: pay him!

HANS WURST: What do you usually get for a letter?

LIPPEL: Usually I gets a penny; but being that your master wears a doublet all glittery with gold, I hope he'll give me six.

HANS WURST: Don't be silly. Only six pennies? I'll give you more because you're such a clever messenger.

LIPPEL: All the better. The more, the better I likes it.

HANS WURST: Just wait. I'll pay you in dollar pieces.

LIPPEL: Come on, that be too much.

HANS WURST: Not at all. It's not too much for me.
[*He shoves him around.*]

ACT III

A garden with arbors and lanterns. Enter DON JUAN *and* HANS WURST.

DON JUAN: Quiet now, Hans Wurst, don't make a sound. Every moment is precious; it's already time for Don Philippo to call for Donna Marillis to take her to the ball, and I must be there first.

HANS WURST: But if you're going to do some dirt, why do you have to take me along, poor orphan child that I am, so that we'll both hang?

DON JUAN: Be quiet; I'll compensate you for all the harm you come to.

HANS WURST: Thanks! You'll compensate me for hanging, will you? Come on, master, don't go on with this tomfoolery.

DON JUAN: Stay here and keep watch. If you see someone coming, give me a signal.

HANS WURST: So if I see someone, I have to let you know?

DON JUAN: Yes, you'll call me.

HANS WURST: I'll go *ho, ho, pst, pst!*

DON JUAN: Just so I don't get interrupted.

[*He wants to leave.*]

HANS WURST: If someone comes now, I'll go *ho, ho!*

DON JUAN: Hans Wurst, is someone there?

HANS WURST: No, I'm just practicing to see if I can do it right. Ho, ho! Ho, ho! Ho, ho!

DON JUAN: That's enough now; don't detain me any longer.

[*He exits.*]

HANS WURST: Well, see to it that you hurry back. Now, let me see, I don't want to kill myself standing up; it makes more sense to sit over there.

[*He sits down. The* DEVIL *enters.*]

HANS WURST: What's that? Well, I guess I'll sit down on the other side.

DEVIL: Who's there?

HANS WURST: Oh, damn it all! He's back again. I guess I'd better leave, I don't care where my master is.

[*He exits. Enter* DON JUAN, DONNA MARILLIS, *and* DON PIETRO.]

DON JUAN: Come, dearest Donna Marillis.

DONNA MARILLIS: Help, father! I'm being abducted! Help!

DON PIETRO: Who is the abductor of my daughter?
Ah, so it's you, Don Juan!

DON JUAN [*kills him with his sword*]: To hell you go!

DONNA MARILLIS: Oh, Don Juan, what have you done? You've killed my dearest father so that you can ravish me.

[*She struggles with Don Juan. At approach of Don Philippo he relinquishes her and runs away. Enter* DON PHILIPPO.]*

DON PHILIPPO: What's the matter, Donna Marillis? Why do I discover you lying thus upon the ground?

DONNA MARILLIS: Look, just look, Don Philippo; my father has been killed by the wicked Don Juan!

DON PHILIPPO: God, what audacity! However, dearest Donna Marillis, do not grieve too much about the death of your dearly beloved father; I shall now convey his lifeless body to your domicile and then pursue Don Juan in order to bind him over to Justice.

*Direction supplied. [*Editor's note.*]

DONNA MARILLIS: Do so, dearest Don Philippo. But all my life I shall grieve for you, my dearest father.

[*Exeunt. Enter* DON JUAN *and* HANS WURST.]

DON JUAN: Come, Hans Wurst; don't make a sound.

HANS WURST: Yes, I'm coming. But why do I have to be so quiet?

DON JUAN: I've killed Don Pietro.

HANS WURST: Pots and kettles! This is going to make fireworks for us!

DON JUAN: Follow me!

HANS WURST: If I only escape the rope this time!

[*They Exit.*]

PART THE SECOND

ACT I

A street. DON PHILIPPO *and* DONNA MARILLIS *are talking.*

DON PHILIPPO: Dearest Donna Marillis, I have done my uttermost to find the wicked Don Juan and deliver him to the authorities; but I have failed.

DONNA MARILLIS: I thank you for your zeal, and I shall reward you with my hand in marriage. But come with me now to attend to the burial of my father.

[*Exeunt. Enter* DON JUAN *and* HANS WURST.]

HANS WURST: What did you put these clothes on me for?

DON JUAN: So you can safely escape out of Barcelona.

HANS WURST: Oh! You mean because nobody knows me in this get-up?

DON JUAN: Not exactly. It's the carnival season, and no one in a mask may be stopped.

HANS WURST: Just let me take care of myself. I'll lie my way out of any hole.

DON JUAN: Well then, off with you. I'm going to climb over the city wall with my trusty rope ladder.

HANS WURST: Master, where do we meet again?

DON JUAN: I'll wait for you near the tall oak tree outside the city.

[*Exits.*]

HANS WURST: All right, I get it. Now I'll be going. [*Sees guards.*] Oh, there's the police; I'll leave this way instead. [*Sees guards there too.*] Oh, they're calling, I'll have to get out over there and fast.

[*Enter a* GUARD.]

GUARD: Halt! Who goes there? Who is the gentleman?

HANS WURST: Who I am? Oh, Christ! What now?

[*Another* GUARD *enters.*]

HANS WURST: Oh Christ! Two guards!

GUARDS: Now then. Furnish your name, sir. Who are you?

HANS WURST: Who am I? I'm who I am, period.

GUARDS: That's not enough. We want to know who you are, sir.

HANS WURST: Just wait. I'll lie my way out of this one. Tell me, how long have you served this post?

FIRST GUARD: I've only been here for four days.

HANS WURST: All the better for me if you haven't been here long. [*To the other Guard*] And since when have you been here?

SECOND GUARD: A week.

HANS WURST: Well then, I'll tell you who I am: I am the Commander of the garrison and you didn't recognize my mug. Don't you know it's the carnival season?

GUARDS: Forgive us; we didn't know.

HANS WURST: What are you doing anyway? What do you want in the city?

GUARDS: We're looking for Don Juan and his servant.

HANS WURST: How's that? You're looking for Don Juan and his servant, and you stand around like stupid fools? I've just seen him walking down that street. [*The* GUARDS *go off*.] That's it. You go off that way and I've got the finest chance to escape.

ACT II

A woods and a hermit's cavern. The HERMIT *is at the cavern's entrance.*

HERMIT: For thirty long years I've lived alone and secluded in this wilderness and have seen no human being. But over there I think I see two men coming toward me. I'll go hide.

[*He hides as* DON JUAN *and* HANS WURST *enter.*]

DON JUAN: Well, Hans Wurst, we made it safely out of Barcelona.

HANS WURST: But the guards caught me. Good thing I could lie, and they were so stupid.

DON JUAN: Just keep it up. [*To the Hermit*] My good hermit, if I may trust my servant's word that you dwell in these woods, I'd like to ask you whether you would not like to enter the world again, since you have lived here so long. You could do me a favor by giving me your robe; I'll trade my clothing for it.

HERMIT: Oh no, sir. Heaven itself has given me my robe and I shall keep it until I die.

DON JUAN: I'm also looking for shelter.

HERMIT: If my cell suffices, follow me.

[*Exeunt.*]

HANS WURST: Very slick. There goes my master with that bag of vermin. I only hope he don't catch lice himself. I'll have to wait and see. But look, there comes Sir Vermin again.

[*Enter* HERMIT *wearing Don Juan's clothes.*]

HERMIT: My friend, who is your master?

HANS WURST: A man.

HERMIT: He seems all confused to me. He must have committed a terrible crime.

HANS WURST: Well, he didn't commit a crime exactly, but—

HERMIT: What did he do?

HANS WURST: Well, I'm not supposed to tell; he killed the governor of Barcelona.

[*Enter* DON JUAN *dressed as Hermit.*]

HERMIT: Oh! And, dog that you are, you dare reveal the secret to the first passerby?

DON JUAN [*kills Hermit with his sword*]: Die!

HANS WURST [*punches Hermit in the chest*]: And now I have to bury Sir Vermin.

[*He exits. Enter* DON PHILIPPO. *He sees Don Juan dressed as Hermit.*]

DON PHILIPPO: I cannot find the murderer and seducer, though I was told that he is in these woods. I see a hermit over there; I'll ask him. God be with you, my friend. Have you seen a lost nobleman around here?

DON JUAN: Sir, I notice that you are pursuing a man with vengeful purpose, to kill him perhaps, and that is wrong.

DON PHILIPPO: You are right; but if you knew what heinous crimes that monster has committed, you would not speak as you do. I am not looking for him to murder him but rather to fight him honorably with the sword, and to wash out with his blood the monstrous crimes he has committed.

DON JUAN: How? You would reward evil with evil? Revenge does not belong in human hands. Let heaven forgive all sinners; call on God, ask Him to show you your enemy, but only so that you may lead him back to the path of virtue by means of good precepts. Promise me this; then I myself shall help you look for your enemy. But first put away your weapons and pray to God.

DON PHILIPPO: Godly and righteous man, you are right, I shall ask God to soften and enlighten the recalcitrant heart of Don Juan. [*Kneels.*] Great God in heaven and on earth. [*Prays silently.*]

DON JUAN: Now it's time for my revenge. [*Kills him with his sword*] Traitor, take this thrust from Don Juan!

DON PHILIPPO [*sinking*]: Miserable me, Don Juan is killing me! Marillis, I'm dying for you!

DON JUAN: Worthless rival. Now my desire for vengeance is appeased. [*Enter* HANS WURST.]

HANS WURST: Well, I've buried Sir Louse. [*Trips over the corpse of Don Philippo.*] Oh Christ! Here's another all laid out. What in hell is going on!

DON JUAN: Shut up. That's the one who was going to turn us over to the authorities.

HANS WURST: All right; but whatever did you kill him for?

DON JUAN: You fool, he ran into my blade.

HANS WURST: The whole world seems to run into your blade.

DON JUAN: Don't make a noise; just bury him!

HANS WURST: In your service I do nothing except dig graves and bury the whole world!

DON JUAN: Do as I command. His valuables, if any, are yours. Also, look around for a farm or an inn where we can spend the night.

HANS WURST: Well, go ahead. [*To Corpse*] As for you, I'd better bury you right away, since my master killed you so snugly.

ACT III

An inn in the woods. Enter HANS WURST.

HANS WURST: Damned luck I've got, to keep running around in the woods with nothing to eat and drink anywhere! But look, there's an inn. I'll go and ask whether we can stay there. Hey, you in the inn, open up!

[*The door opens. Enter* FIRST LANDLADY.]

FIRST LANDLADY: Who's out there?

HANS WURST: Tourists!

FIRST LANDLADY: I'm coming. Barbara, my girl, chase them hogs out of the room. We're having guests!

HANS WURST: Anyway, it's a decent place; they send the hogs out of the rooms.

FIRST LANDLADY: At your service, sir; what would you like?

HANS WURST: Beg pardon; are you the inn or its keeper?

FIRST LANDLADY: I am the pretty cowgirl.

HANS WURST: If you're the pretty one, I'd like to see the ugly one!

FIRST LANDLADY: So you want to stay with us. You can have delicious food: buttermilk, sauerkraut, blintzes, dumplings with bacon, whatever you like. S-s-say, are you still unattached?

HANS WURST: I've never been attached.

FIRST LANDLADY: Wouldn't you like to marry me, eh? I like you.

HANS WURST: Is that so? Well, I don't have much stomach for you.

FIRST LANDLADY: Yippee! Today's my wedding day!

HANS WURST: Now wait a minute. I ain't proposed yet.

FIRST LANDLADY: You see there's a wedding on today already, and we could join in the fun like. You and your master will just have to wait a bit.

HANS WURST: All right, we'll do that.

[*Enter* DON JUAN.]

DON JUAN: Well, Hans Wurst, did you find a farmhouse?

HANS WURST: Indeed I did, my lord; I've got an inn, a landlady, and everything together, and there's a wedding thrown in too.

FIRST LANDLADY: Tell me, why is your master so white while you're so black?

HANS WURST: Because he was born by day, and me by night.

FIRST LANDLADY: Oh, that's different. Well, now I'll go. The wedding guests are arriving any minute.

[*She exits.*]

DON JUAN: Hans Wurst, I'll have a little fun; I'm going to steal the bride.

HANS WURST: Master, on my knees, for heaven's sake, don't do it. Those peasants can get very rough.

[*Scene with* HANS WURST. *Wedding guests arrive.* HANS WURST *is to secure the bride, etc. All leave noisily.*]

PART THE THIRD

Act I

A street. Enter DON JUAN *and* HANS WURST.

DON JUAN: We've reached another town, Hans Wurst, where we can spend a few weeks. I do hope that we won't be lacking food and drink.

HANS WURST: I'm with you, master. Devil take it all, we'll drink the stuff till the dust sticks to our throats.

DON JUAN: Well, Hans Wurst, I'm going to the coffeehouse. Go find an inn so we'll have comfortable lodgings; I'll be back here soon.
[*He exits.*]

HANS WURST: Yes sir, go on and have them ladle me out a dish of sausages. I'll be right there, but first I'll find an inn where I can feed my face and drown my sorrows. Well, there's one now; I'll knock at once. Hey, you there in the inn!
[*Enter* SECOND LANDLADY.]

SECOND LANDLADY: Who's out there?

HANS WURST: Come out a little ways!

SECOND LANDLADY: Ah! Your obedient servant! What can I do for you?

HANS WURST: Your most obedient servant. Tell me, my enchanting child, can one find abidements in your abode?

SECOND LANDLADY: Indeed you can, wherever you like: in the back, up on top, down below, on the middle floor, wherever you would like.

HANS WURST: Do you have that many stories?

SECOND LANDLADY: Indeed we do; our house is very large.

HANS WURST: How much is it by the week for a room in the middle?

SECOND LANDLADY: A crown per week.

HANS WURST: No, that's too much for me; I'd like one that costs half a crown.
[*Enter* DON JUAN.]

DON JUAN: Well, well, Hans Wurst. What pleasant entertainment you have found!

HANS WURST: I have, master. This is the landlady.

DON JUAN: Beg pardon, are you Mistress or Miss Landlady? I don't know which is your rightful title.

SECOND LANDLADY: I am still unattached.

HANS WURST: Are you really? Me too.

DON JUAN: Beg pardon, Miss Landlady, but since I am a traveler, forgive my curiosity and tell me what that statue in front of us represents.

HANS WURST: Look, a stone horseman!

SECOND LANDLADY: That's a monument to Don Pietro whom the worthless Don Juan murdered.

DON JUAN: I remember hearing about that.

SECOND LANDLADY: Warrants are out for his arrest. If they're caught, both he and his servant will be turned over to the authorities.

HANS WURST: What's out, master?

DON JUAN: Warrants. This means that they'll be put to the rack if they're caught.

HANS WURST: Put to the rack?

DON JUAN: If they are caught.

HANS WURST: That's all we need! Let's go.

DON JUAN: Shut up, you blasted idiot! Young lady, did you say, that one can find lodging at your house?

HANS WURST: Master, we can't stay. Warrants! Authorities!

DON JUAN: Will you shut up, you idiot! Well then, my dear young miss, prepare a good meal for us.

HANS WURST: Oh no! Don't go to any trouble. Devil take me, I have no appetite for food or drink! Warrants!

DON JUAN: That blasted idiot feels sorry for the two scoundrels.

SECOND LANDLADY: I can believe that; he probably knows them. But you must be hungry; I'll go and prepare you a very good meal.

DON JUAN: You damned fool, how easily you could have given us away with your stupidity!

HANS WURST: Warrants and authorities!

DON JUAN: Well now, to test your courage, I command you to invite that statue to dine with us.

HANS WURST: Now I really see you're a fool. What's that rock pile going to do with a meal? All right, I'll invite him. Look here, you stony stone, you're invited to have some vittles with my master at noon!

[*The* STATUE *makes a sign with a fiery rod.*]

DON JUAN: Well, what did he say? Did he reply?

HANS WURST: Not exactly. But he held a fiery rod to his mug.

DON JUAN: That is not good enough. He has to answer yes or no. So go back there. Go, or else—

HANS WURST: All right, I'm going. You there, my master said if you want to knock down some vittles, to say yes or no!

STATUE: Yes!

DON JUAN: What did he say?

HANS WURST: He said yes.

DON JUAN: If he said yes, he'll come. Let's go eat.

[*He exits.*]

HANS WURST: Well, well, a fine dish of gravy this is going to be! Warrants, authorities, stony rider! It's enough to upset your stomach before you've taken a bite!

ACT II

A room. DON JUAN *and* HANS WURST.

DON JUAN: Well, Hans Wurst, I hope you've had enough to eat and drink.

HANS WURST: Yes, sir, devil take it, I've really stuffed and plastered myself.

DON JUAN: I'm glad to hear it, for you've suffered many hardships with me.

HANS WURST: My lord, there's just one thing: my belly has got so swelled I can hardly drag it around. How's about something to cool us off?

DON JUAN: My thoughts exactly; why don't you ask the landlady to prepare us a salad.

HANS WURST: Yes, master, a salad, I suppose that's it. I'll go see the landlady about it.

[*He wants to leave;* SECOND LANDLADY *enters.*]

LANDLADY: Well sir, may I ask how you enjoyed my cooking?

DON JUAN: Very much, madam. I must admit that you're a first-rate cook.

HANS WURST: We liked it all right; too bad we couldn't make it last a little longer.

DON JUAN: You're a fool; you can't even snort any more. But now, madam, be so kind as to prepare us a salad.

LANDLADY: I'll go right away and prepare a delicious salad for you; just be so kind as to send your servant with me.

[*She exits.*]

HANS WURST: I'm going. If it's a question of stuffing my belly, I don't mind making a little effort!

[*He exits.*]

DON JUAN: How is it, Don Juan, that your hair does not stand on end when you consider the murders you have already committed! The governor, Don Pietro; the hermit; your rival, Don Philippo; you've murdered them all. How shall I stand before the divine judge on the day I must give an accounting for all my actions? Come now, why do I think this nonsense?

[*Enter* HANS WURST.]

HANS WURST: Ha ha, master, look, I've got the salad!

DON JUAN: Put it down over here. But, devil take it, fellow, who is to eat this salad?

HANS WURST: Why, don't you like it?

DON JUAN: It's too crisp. There isn't enough oil in it; take it to the landlady and tell her to mix it better.

HANS WURST: Why take it to the landlady? I don't need her for that!

DON JUAN: Why not?

HANS WURST: I'll mangle it up myself!

[*He sits down.*]

DON JUAN: What are you doing?

HANS WURST: I'm tossing the salad.

DON JUAN: And who in the devil's name will eat that salad? Don't you dare bring that salad to the table!

HANS WURST: Well then, I'll pitch it out!

[*He empties dish. There is a knock.*]

DON JUAN: Hans Wurst, who knocked just now?

HANS WURST: Who knocks?

VOICE: A virgin one hundred eighty years old.

DON JUAN: Let's leave her outside! Who's knocking?

HANS WURST: The door is open. Come on in, whoever is outside! Master, oh damn it all, poor me, poor me!

[*He hides. The* STATUE *enters.*]

STATUE: You see, Don Juan, even as a ghost I am still a gentleman who keeps his word.

DON JUAN: So I see. What can I do for you? Where you come from do you have dancing and carnivals? Hans Wurst, call the landlady; tell her to bring food.

STATUE: Young man, I did not come for mortal food but rather to offer you eternal refreshment. Come to the cemetery tonight at midnight.

DON JUAN: You have my word; I'll come! Hey, Hans Wurst!

HANS WURST: What is it?

DON JUAN: Show the ghost out!

[*Scene between Hans Wurst and Ghost, as desired.*]

ACT III

A churchyard, lights. DON JUAN *and* HANS WURST *enter.*

HANS WURST: How glad I am to get away this time. I think I'll have a glass of *Spiritus Confussionis.* [*He exits.*]

DON JUAN: And now I await the shade of Don Pietro. Let him see that I keep my word too.

[*Enter the* STATUE.]

STATUE: Here I am, Don Juan, ready to receive you, as I promised!

DON JUAN: Well, what do you want? You see that I'm here too. Tell me, Don Pietro, how are things in Elysium? Do they have inns, balls, and other pleasures?

STATUE: Why do you ask about Elysium? You wretch, let me tell you where you are! You are in a place where thousands are buried, all of whom must one day appear before the righteous Judge and await His sentence with fear and trembling, the same Judge before whom I appeared after I died by your accursed hand. Think back on your terrible deeds, the many murders with which you have burdened your soul, the many innocent girls you seduced, the many young men who curse you now because in a small way they emulated your crimes. Wretched youth, repent, for you have very little time left to rue your wicked deeds and to pacify your enraged Judge.

DON JUAN: Tell me, Don Pietro, did you summon me in order to preach repentance and punishment to me? Don't think for a minute that I came to you for that. As it is, I have had to miss the most splendid ball today on your account!

STATUE: Haven't you had enough of your shiftless life? Well then, I shall try to sway you no more, for I see that it is all in vain. Come, touch my hand, that you may experience what I am.

DON JUAN: Very well! I'll do that too, to show you I am not afraid of you—— By heaven and hell, what's the matter with me? Why am I trembling? Why won't my legs support me any longer? I see, you wanted to trick me. But you're wrong; I am Don Juan again. And now adieu; you have nothing new to tell me anyway.

STATUE: No, stay! We're not finished yet: you will never leave for I shall bring you to the place you have tried to forget these many years; but it's too late now to bethink yourself of it. Beg God for mercy!

DON JUAN: I will not! Leave me, or I shall curse the hour of my birth!

STATUE: Then sink into Hell!

[*The Devils violently pull Don Juan into Hell.*]

Mozart, Da Ponte, and *Don Giovanni*
o il dissoluto punito

Puppet plays, vaudevilles, pantomimes, strollers' farces—to such had the ferocious hidalgo descended. "Never," wrote Goldoni, "had so much applause, for so many years, been bestowed as for this play; the very actors marvelled, and some, slyly or innocently, used to say that a pact with the devil kept up the concourse to this foolish comedy."[1] Then, as a century before, true artists apologized when they touched the subject. Only with Mozart (more innocent than the intellectuals of his time) did poetic greatness and popular vigor intersect and flash. After Mozart, the history of Don Juan reverses itself: now he is taken up by the intellectuals, and gradually the masses abandon him, except in the case of Zorrilla's hero. Whether his elevation improved him is, of course, another question.

Not that Mozart's was the first musical setting of Don Juan. Purcell had already composed a few numbers for Shadwell's play. A French vaudeville was heard in 1713; Gluck wrote a Don Juan ballet in 1758. Operatic Don Juans appeared. In 1787 alone, two operas on the subject opened besides Mozart's work. Goethe, who was in Rome at that time, could write that "nobody lives there without seeing once at least Don Giovanni roasting in hell and the commendador flying like a spirit to Heaven."

Zamora and Zorrilla—and Tirso, too, for that matter—are for Spain; Mozart's Da Ponte is for all men. Da Ponte was a coxcomb, yet he wrote three priceless libretti for Mozart: texts without which even Mozart's music would be poorer. We are far from anxious to catch every word of Schikaneder's *Magic Flute,* but who would miss a syllable from even the recitatives of *Così fan tutte,* the jewel of all libretti?

Only a sketch can be given here of the Signore Abbate da Ponte's astonishing career.[2] He was born near Venice in 1749 of Jewish parents but was baptized in 1763. He studied for the priesthood and took major orders to become another one of the elegant abbés who adorned the eighteenth-century church. His professional talents secured him

1. Quoted in A. G. Bragaglia, *Pulcinella* (Rome: G. Cassini, 1953), p. 527.

2. For Da Ponte's life and times, see his *Memoirs,* tr. Elizabeth Abbott (New York: Orion, 1959) and April Fitzlyon, *The Libertine Librettist* (London: John Calder, 1955). The standard account in English of Mozart's texts and music is Edward J. Dent, *Mozart's Operas* (2nd ed.; New York: Oxford University Press, 1947).

various teaching posts; his private ones, a multitude of amorous intrigues. Lover, poet, pamphleteer and priest, the young professor of rhetoric was expelled from his seminary in 1776 for reading his subversive poems at a commencement. His satires having made some noise in Venice, he was conveniently prosecuted for adultery and public concubinage and exiled in 1779.

We pick him up again a few years later in Vienna, where he is "Poet to the Italian Theatre," intimate with Emperor Joseph II, familiar in many great houses, friend to composers and writers—in short, a figure of importance. In 1783 he met Mozart, who had settled in Vienna in 1781 after breaking with the Archbishop of Salzburg. Mozart had as yet composed only two of his major operas, *Idomeneo* and *The Abduction from the Seraglio,* and as always he was somehow impecunious, anxious for a solid appointment, and successful all at the same time. In 1786 Da Ponte took his share of the glory for *The Marriage of Figaro;* in the same year he triumphed with *Una Cosa rara,* written for Martini (and slyly mentioned in *Don Giovanni*), and in 1787 he suggested the subject of Don Juan to Mozart. Gazzaniga's Don Juan opera had been a success in Venice that same year, and Da Ponte helped himself to a few notions from Giovanni Bertati's libretto. No one who has read the latter will dream of accusing Da Ponte of plagiarism, for Bertati's work is the most rudimentary of sketches, as distant from Da Ponte's play (though a source for it) as Dorimon's is from Molière's. It is likely that Mozart worked with Da Ponte on the libretto, both before and after the original performance. In his old age, Da Ponte asserted that while he urged the comic vein, Mozart wished him to write an entirely serious work; and it may be supposed that the well-known emotional oscillations of the opera are the result of this collaboration of opposite, though friendly, purposes.

Da Ponte wrote the original libretto while he was working on two others as well (those were his best years) during a couple of arduous months he spent in his room, equipped with a bottle of Tokay, an inkstand, a box of tobacco, and a pretty girl of sixteen who made herself available whenever he rang the bell—"which, to tell the truth, was rather often." Not all the awkward spots in the libretto, I daresay, can be blamed on the intemperate demands of singers, managers, or the frivolous public.

The première of *Don Giovanni* was held in Prague, with Mozart himself conducting. Da Ponte, who was helping to train the cast, was obliged to return to Vienna at the last moment, and missed the extraordinary ovations which the opera received. But when the news reached Vienna soon after, he had reason to be pleased: "The Emperor sent for me, and overloading me with gracious felicitations, presented me with another hundred sequins." In Vienna the opera was much less successful at first, but it gradually made its way to popularity, although too late for Mozart, who died in 1791, to reap any advantage from it.

Honored and even paid, Da Ponte could look forward to soft and luxurious days in the capital of music. Instead, his protector Joseph II died, and he was exiled once more amidst a welter of quarrels, accusations, scurrilous libels, debts, dangerous amours, and mysterious intrigues. In 1792 we find him a happily married and poverty-stricken resident of London. Though he became poet to the Drury Lane Theatre in 1793, and tried bookselling and publishing in the Haymarket, he was forced to take sudden leave and emigrate to America, a bankrupt with a prodigious record of imprisonments for debt. In New York and for awhile in Sunbury, Pennsylvania, Da Ponte was in turn a grocer, general storekeeper, bookseller once more, impresario (in which role he brought *Don Giovanni* over for its American première in 1826), a bankrupt once again, a professor of Italian Literature at Columbia University (a position whose only drawbacks were that he had neither salary nor students), and most successfully a private tutor in Italian. He is said to have introduced the study of that language in New York, thereby gaining access to several wealthy houses. He died in great poverty and with theatrical bitterness of old age in 1838. That he was indeed the man to write a *Don Giovanni* his career in general proved, and this youthful quatrain in particular:

> La natura dentro il petto
> Una legge sol mi diè,
> Di non far in atto o in detto
> Quel che poi non piace a me.

That is to say, "Nature placed but one law in my bosom, to do and to say nothing but what pleases me."

Although Mozart's work is the supreme expression of the Don Juan matter, Da Ponte deserves more than the bone or two usually tossed him. Out of Molière, Goldoni, Bertati, and who knows what popular farces and puppet plays, he created a fresh and original comedy in the rococo manner, which might amuse an audience even without the music. On the philosophical or moral side, Da Ponte is not likely to give anyone a headache. But his play shows the hand of a refined

Leporello recites the list of Don Juan's conquests (*The Punished Libertine: or Don Giovanni,* Act I, Scene 2). Engraving by Meyer after H. Ramberg.

artist. We owe to him the heroic character of Anna, as well as the immortal one thousand and three.[3] The personages in the play are all alive, light though they may be. If the rhetoric of Anna, Elvira, and Ottavio is fustian, the modern director will turn this to his advantage and allow the three to strut and to orate to their hearts' content.

The action alternates delicately between the comic and the pathetic. Don Juan himself is as unlucky as a novice—he reports only one middling success with Leporello's girl-friend—and yet we are convinced that he is a paragon among lovers. He seems incapable of premeditated murder: he is far too fond of good wines, pretty girls, and fine dinners to be really brutal. At the same time, however, the text does not prepare us for anything like the sublime heroism which Mozart infuses into the routine "Parla! parla! ascoltando ti sto"—the *"Speak, speak! I am listening to you"* which Don Giovanni addresses to the Statue—nor for the shattering power of the whole damnation scene. What had gone in as powdered wig comes out as the locks of Medusa.

Da Ponte's play is most attractive for the elegance which we miscall classical. We can apply to the librettist words which René Dumesnil used for Mozart himself: "he never insists; he never pushes." Nevertheless, Da Ponte has read Rousseau. Already a new amenity and humaneness tinge the atmosphere of this work. The people become more plausible and more touching; the spirit of Elvira sounds the characteristic note. But as yet all things are kept in order. This is still the age of Sheridan and Beaumarchais. The play, for all its exuberance, is deftly disciplined.

3. Dent (p. 139) suggests one of the *Anacreontea* as a source. The little poem is worth quoting. Here is J. M. Edmonds' translation:

> If you can count the leaves of all the trees,
>   The sands of all the seas,
> Then will I have you Lord High Reckoner be
>   Of loves to me.
> First twenty loves, nay, thirty-five set down
>   From Athens town,
> And loves in bunches then from Corinth city
>   (Achaean girls are pretty);
> To Lesbos, Rhodes, Ionia, Caria come
>   And fifty score's the sum.
> What? does your poor head swim? there's Syria yet,
>   And don't forget
> Egypt, nor Crete, where all wares may be had
>   And Love runs mad.
> Shall I add loves beyond Gadire that fall,
>   Ind, Bactria, and all?

(Gadire is Cadiz.) This is No. 14 in the Loeb Classical Library's *Elegy and Iambus with the Anacreontea*, vol. II. The poems were well known in Italy.

Moreover, I would contend that Mozart's music records at the level of the sublime the same order of existence which Da Ponte's libretto expresses upon a humbler terrain. It is the fashion in some quarters to discover in Mozart the torture, the shadows, the agonies, the longings, and the tensions which give art its cachet nowadays. As every epoch has its favorite notions of what makes good art, every epoch tends to bully masterpieces of the past into conforming with these notions. But with the possible exception (perhaps!) of the *Requiem* and certain moments in the chamber music of his last phase, Mozart's music does not transcend its age; it gives that age its final glory. Mozart shows, for example, the ultimate that can be done with clarity. His is a world in which the *questionable*—to use Thomas Mann's perfect word—has as yet no place, even when the mood is somber, melancholy, or satirical; in which it is not only wrong but indeed outlandish to suppose that Anna subconsciously loves her Don Juan. How shall we finally comprehend this world before we leave it for that of Romanticism? By saying, perhaps, that in this world when a matter has been defined, it has also been exhausted: nothing vague, equivocal, alarming, or mysterious is left behind. All is said. And this is the world in which Mozart breathed and was content; or would have been if he had made more money. The point that his music is perfect while Da Ponte's libretti are merely agreeable does not need to be labored; still, the two men, one a king and the other a vassal, were inhabitants of the same moral and intellectual realm.

LORENZO DA PONTE

The Punished Libertine

or

Don Giovanni

A Comic Drama in Two Acts

(1787)

Translated by Adrienne M. Schizzano
and Oscar Mandel

TRANSLATORS' NOTE

This translation attempts in principle to present Da Ponte's work not as the libretto of an opera, but as an actable play with or without incidental musical accompaniment. A few liberties have therefore been taken with the text as it appears in the operatic score. Arias which exist *only* for the sake of the music have been omitted or condensed. Repetitions, effective in music but clearly out of place in spoken drama, are eliminated unless they are dramatically useful. The texts of ensembles are either assigned to the single actors they suit best, or distributed to several. Minor modifications in dialogue and action are made in order to rationalize the work as, for example, in Act II, Scene 4, where Ottavio *tells Anna* that he will follow her to share in her sorrow, rather than soliloquizing to this effect. More important, this version purports to be modern without becoming a twentieth-century streamlined adaptation. Thus, a typical rendering is "I'm dying" where the original has "From my throbbing breast I feel my soul departing." From what we know of Da Ponte's habits, he would have been the last to object to these changes. He was a businesslike stage writer who patched and shuffled and let others patch and shuffle —it is said that Casanova touched up the text at the last moment—as the performance required.

TEXT

Il dissoluto punito ossia il Don Giovanni in *W. A. Mozart; Werke,* Series 5, No. 18. Leipzig: Breitkopf u. Härtel, in the reproduction of J. W. Edwards, Ann Arbor, Michigan: 1955.

Characters

Don Giovanni	Donna Elvira
Donna Anna	Leporello
Ottavio	Masetto
The Commander	Zerlina

Peasants, Servants, Musicians

Synopsis of Scenes

Act I

1. A garden outside the Commander's palace.
2. A street.
3. The countryside near Don Giovanni's palace.
4. Don Giovanni's garden.
5. A ballroom in Don Giovanni's palace.

Act II

1. A street near Donna Elvira's house.
2. A courtyard in Donna Anna's house.
3. A cemetery.
4. A room in Donna Anna's house.
5. A room in Don Giovanni's house.

Place: A Spanish city

ACT I

Scene 1

A garden. On one side the Commander's palace. In front of it, stone benches. Night. LEPORELLO *is on stage.*

LEPORELLO: I must labor day and night, endure the rain and the wind, eat badly and sleep worse, for a man who knows no gratitude. I'd like to act the gentleman myself, and give up the servant's life. My good master is inside with a pretty girl, needless to say, while I play the sentinel. No, no, I've had enough of serving. Look out! I think somebody's coming. I shouldn't like to be overheard.

[*Enter* ANNA *in pursuit of* DON GIOVANNI.]

ANNA: You won't escape without killing me first!

DON GIOVANNI: Fool! It's no use crying. You'll never know who I am.

LEPORELLO: Oh God, such an uproar, such shouting; my master's in trouble again.

ANNA: People! Servants! Kill the traitor!

DON GIOVANNI: Quiet. Don't infuriate me, or you'll regret it.

ANNA: Scoundrel!

DON GIOVANNI: Stupid woman!

ANNA: I'll hunt you down like a fury.

DON GIOVANNI: This raging woman is bent on destroying me.

LEPORELLO: Let's see if the rascal will ruin me too.

[*The* COMMANDER *rushes in.*]

COMMANDER: Let her go, villain, and draw.

[ANNA, *hearing the Commander, enters the house.*]

DON GIOVANNI: Ha, I wouldn't lower myself.

COMMANDER: Is that how you think you'll get away? Fight!

LEPORELLO [*Aside.*]: If I could only escape.

DON GIOVANNI: Imbecile! Wait, if you want to die.

[*They fight.*]

COMMANDER: Help, I'm betrayed! The murderer has struck me down; I'm dying.

LEPORELLO: Another outrage. I'm half dead with fear. I don't know what to do or say.

DON GIOVANNI: The fool is dead. [*Softly*] Leporello, where are you?

LEPORELLO: Here, unfortunately. And you?

DON GIOVANNI: Here.

LEPORELLO: Who is dead? You or the old man?

DON GIOVANNI: Stupid! The old man.

LEPORELLO: Splendid. Two charming adventures—raping the daughter and killing the father.

DON GIOVANNI: He looked for it.

LEPORELLO: What about Donna Anna?

DON GIOVANNI: Shut your mouth. Don't irritate me, and come along unless you want a taste of something too.

LEPORELLO: I don't want a thing, sir, and my mouth is shut.

[*Exeunt. Enter* ANNA, OTTAVIO, *and servants carrying lights.*]

ANNA: My father's in danger; let's rush to his help!

OTTAVIO: I'll pour out all my blood, if necessary. But where is the ruffian?

ANNA: He's here. Oh God, what do I see? Horrible—Father, Father!

OTTAVIO: Sir—

ANNA: The murderer killed him! Blood—this wound—his pale dead face—no more breath—his limbs cold. Father, my father, my dear! I'm dying—

OTTAVIO: Help her, my friends. Hurry. Bring salts. Anna, my love, my friend! Grief is killing the poor girl.

ANNA: Oh!

OTTAVIO: She's reviving. Let her breathe this again.

ANNA: Father—

OTTAVIO: Remove the body from her eyes. Hide the horrible thing. Dear soul, courage, be comforted.

[*The Commander's body is removed.*]

ANNA: Leave me, cruel man! Let me die too now that my father who gave me life is dead.

OTTAVIO: Listen to me, I beg you. Look at me one quick moment. Look at your lover, who lives only for you.

ANNA: You are—forgive me—my dear—the pain—the anguish—oh— Where is my father?

OTTAVIO: Your father — Dearest, don't remind yourself. In me you will have both husband and father.

ANNA: Swear to avenge this blood if you can!

OTTAVIO: I swear it by your eyes. I swear it by our love.

ANNA: A solemn oath! Fearful moment; I feel a hundred storms in my heart.

[*Exeunt.*]

Scene 2

A street in daylight. Enter DON GIOVANNI *and* LEPORELLO.

DON GIOVANNI: Hurry up. What do you want?

LEPORELLO: It's a matter of some importance.

DON GIOVANNI: Undoubtedly.

LEPORELLO: Of extreme importance, in fact.

DON GIOVANNI: Even better. Get it over with.

LEPORELLO: But swear you won't lose your temper.

DON GIOVANNI: I swear on my honor, provided you don't refer to the Commander.

LEPORELLO: Are we alone?

DON GIOVANNI: As you can see.

LEPORELLO: Nobody overhears us?

DON GIOVANNI: On with it!

LEPORELLO: May I speak quite freely?

DON GIOVANNI: Quite.

LEPORELLO: Well, if that's how it is, my dear lord and master, you are leading the life of a ruffian.

DON GIOVANNI: How dare you—

LEPORELLO: And your oath?

DON GIOVANNI: Hang my oath! Shut your mouth, or else—

LEPORELLO: I won't say a word; I won't breathe, dear master.

DON GIOVANNI: Good; now we're friends. Listen to me. Do you know why we're here?

LEPORELLO: I don't know a thing. But since it's almost day, wouldn't it be a new conquest? I have to know in order to enter it in the list.

DON GIOVANNI: You're a statesman. Know then that I am in love with a beauty, and that I'm sure she loves me. I saw her; spoke with her; and tonight she is coming to the Casino with me. [*Suddenly*] Be still. I smell woman.

LEPORELLO: Gad! Quite an olfactory system!

DON GIOVANNI: At first glance she looks beautiful.

LEPORELLO: Good vision too.

DON GIOVANNI: Let's withdraw and plot our course.

LEPORELLO: He's on fire already.

[*Enter* ELVIRA *in traveling clothes.*]

ELVIRA: Oh who will tell me where that monster is, whom I loved to my disgrace and who betrayed me? If I find him, and if he won't return to me, oh, I'll tear out his heart!

DON GIOVANNI [*to Leporello*]: Did you hear that? A charming girl abandoned by her lover. Poor little thing. Let's try to assuage her torment.

LEPORELLO: That's how he has assuaged a thousand eight hundred others.

DON GIOVANNI: Young lady! Young lady!

ELVIRA: Who is it?

DON GIOVANNI: Good heavens, what do I see?

LEPORELLO: Lovely! It's Elvira.

ELVIRA: Don Giovanni, you here! Ogre, blackguard, miscreant!

LEPORELLO: That's what I call literature! Anyway, she knows her man.

DON GIOVANNI: Now now, dear Elvira, calm down a little and let me speak.

ELVIRA: What can you tell me after such an outrage? You gain entrance into my house by stealth, you succeed in ravishing my heart by means of tricks, oaths, and false hopes; I fall in love with you, cruel man! You call me your wife, and then, disobeying the sacred commands of earth and heaven, you depart criminally from Burgos after three days, you abandon me, you fly from me, you leave me a prey to remorse and to tears, the punishment, no doubt, for my excessive love.

LEPORELLO [Aside.]: She talks like a book!

DON GIOVANNI: Oh but I had my reasons. [To LEPORELLO] Isn't it true?

LEPORELLO: It's true, and strong reasons for that matter.

ELVIRA: And what are they, if not your perfidy and your frivolity? But the justice of heaven ordained that I should find you in order to exact its vengeance and mine.

DON GIOVANNI: Come now, be reasonable. [Aside.] She's nothing but trouble. [Aloud.] If you don't believe my own words, you can believe this gentleman.

LEPORELLO [Aside.]: The devil you can!

DON GIOVANNI: Go on—tell her.

LEPORELLO [softly]: What shall I tell her?

DON GIOVANNI [loud]: Yes, of course, tell her everything.
[Exit.]

ELVIRA: Well then, hurry up.

LEPORELLO: Madam—truly—in this world—inasmuch as it might happen sometime—that the square is not a circle—

ELVIRA: Wretch! Are you laughing at my grief? And you— Heavens, the traitor has fled! Miserable me! Where has he gone?

LEPORELLO: Oh, let him go. He isn't worth thinking about.

ELVIRA: The villain deceived and betrayed me—

LEPORELLO: Console yourself! You neither are, nor were, nor will be the first or the last. Look at this rather heavy book; it's crammed with the names of his conquests. Every house, every village, every country has witnessed his amorous ventures. It is a catalogue, dear lady, of the beauties whom my master has loved. I compiled it myself. Look! read it with me. In Italy, six hundred forty; in Germany, two hundred thirty-one. One hundred in France. In Turkey, ninety-one. But in Spain I've entered already a thousand and three! A thousand and three! You'll find, among them, country girls, waitresses, and city girls. We have countesses, duchesses, baronesses, princesses; women of every rank, of every shape, of every age. Blondes he praises for their gentleness; brunettes, for their constancy; grizzled heads, for their sweetness. In winter he likes them chubby; in summer, he likes them skinny. He calls the tall girl majestic and the short girl cuddlesome. He seduces old women for the sheer pleasure of adding them to the list. His greatest appetite is for ripening virgins. But he doesn't care: let her be rich, let her be ugly, let her be beautiful. As long as she wears a skirt, you know what he'll do.
[Exit.]

ELVIRA: Is this how the rascal betrayed me? Is this his inhuman reward for my love? But I'll avenge my wrong. I'll find him before he escapes. Only revenge, spite, and anger speak in my breast.
[Exit.]

Scene 3

Countryside near Don Giovanni's palace. ZERLINA, MASETTO, *and a chorus of peasants are singing and dancing. Enter* DON GIOVANNI *and* LEPORELLO.

DON GIOVANNI: Thank God, she's gone. Oh look, look at these jolly young things! What beautiful girls!

LEPORELLO: There should be something for me too in this plenty.

DON GIOVANNI: Good day, dear friends. Continue your merriment. Continue your music, good people. Is this a wedding feast?

ZERLINA: Yes, sir, and I am the bride.

DON GIOVANNI: This is comforting. And the groom?

MASETTO: Myself, at your service.

DON GIOVANNI: Good fellow: at my service. This is speaking like a gentleman.

LEPORELLO [*Aside.*]: It takes a husband to talk like that.

ZERLINA: My Masetto has a golden heart.

DON GIOVANNI: So have I, as it happens. Well now, I want us to be friends. What is your name?

ZERLINA: Zerlina.

DON GIOVANNI: And yours?

MASETTO: Masetto.

DON GIOVANNI: My dear Masetto! My dear Zerlina! I offer you my protection. Leporello—what are you up to, you monkey?

[LEPORELLO *is flirting with the girls.*]

LEPORELLO: I'm offering my protection too.

DON GIOVANNI: Quick—take these people to my palace at once; let them have chocolate, coffee, wines, and cold cuts; entertain them all; show them the garden, the picture gallery, and the rooms. In short, see that my Masetto is happy. Understood?

LEPORELLO: Understood. [*To the peasants*] Let's go.

MASETTO: Sir!

DON GIOVANNI: What is it?

MASETTO: Zerlina can't stay without me.

LEPORELLO: His Excellency will take your place. He will know how to play your part.

DON GIOVANNI: Oh, Zerlina is in the hands of a man of honour. Don't worry; she'll come along with me presently.

ZERLINA: Go on, don't be afraid. I'm in the hands of a man of honour.

MASETTO: And so—?

ZERLINA: And so there's nothing to fear.

MASETTO: And me? By God—

DON GIOVANNI: Here now, let's stop arguing. If you don't leave without another word, Masetto, watch out, you'll regret it.

MASETTO: I catch on, my lord. I bow my head and I go. Since this is how you want it, I say no more. You're a man of honour indeed; I cannot doubt it. Your kindness to me proves it. [*To Zerlina*] You hussy, you baggage, you always were my undoing. [*To Leporello*] I'm coming, I'm coming! [*To Zerlina*] You can stay; very respectable indeed—let my lord make a lady out of you!

[*Exeunt* MASETTO, LEPORELLO, *and peasants.*]

DON GIOVANNI: At last, sweet Zerlinetta, we're rid of that bumpkin. Did you see me clear the landscape, my love?

ZERLINA: He is my husband, sir.

DON GIOVANNI: Who? That fellow? Do you think that a respectable man, a man of breeding—as I can boast I am—can endure that this sweet, precious face should be pawed by a clodhopper?

ZERLINA: But, sir, I promised to marry him.

DON GIOVANNI: Such promises aren't worth a bean. You're not made to be a farm girl. These roguish eyes, these lovely lips, these white and fragrant little fingers will lead you to a higher station in life. What softness! What perfume!

ZERLINA: I'd rather not.

DON GIOVANNI: What would you rather not?

ZERLINA: Be fooled in the end. I know that you gentlemen are seldom honest and sincere with women.

DON GIOVANNI: This is plebeian propaganda. The honesty of a nobleman is written in his eyes. Well, let's not waste time. I mean to marry you on the spot.

ZERLINA: You?

DON GIOVANNI: Of course. That little house over there is mine: there we'll be alone, my jewel, and there we'll marry; there we'll join hands; there you'll say "I do." Look, it isn't far. Let's leave this place, my love.

ZERLINA [Aside.]: I want to; and then I don't. My heart's in a flutter. It's true I would be happy; but still he might make a fool of me.

DON GIOVANNI: Come, my delight, and soothe the pains of my innocent love.

ZERLINA: I'm sorry for Masetto.

DON GIOVANNI: Your life will begin anew.

ZERLINA: I'm weakening. Let's hurry.

DON GIOVANNI: Come!

ZERLINA: Yes.

[Enter ELVIRA.]

ELVIRA: Stop, scoundrel! Heaven has allowed me to overhear your designs. I've come in time to save this poor, innocent wretch from your barbarous claws.

ZERLINA: Poor me! What do I hear?

DON GIOVANNI [Aside.]: Cupid, inspire me. [To Elvira] My queen, don't you see I was only toying?

ELVIRA: Toying! Is that right? Toying! I know, fiend, how you toy.

ZERLINA: Is what she says true, my lord?

DON GIOVANNI [Aside to Elvira.]: The unhappy girl is in love with me and out of pure pity I'm making believe I love her in return. It is my misfortune to have a kind heart.

ELVIRA: Run from the traitor; don't let him speak; his lips lie and his eyes deceive. Trust a woman who suffers and learn from me to beware of this man.

[*Exeunt* ELVIRA *and* ZERLINA.]

DON GIOVANNI: The devil is enjoying himself at my expense today, spoiling all my delightful schemes. Everything is going wrong.

[*Enter* OTTAVIO *and* ANNA.]

OTTAVIO: Henceforth, my treasure, tears are useless. Our theme is vengeance. Oh, Don Giovanni!

DON GIOVANNI [*Aside.*]: That's all I needed!

ANNA: My friend, we have met you in good time. Are you generous and courageous?

DON GIOVANNI [*Aside.*]: Let's see if the devil has told her something. [*Aloud.*]: What a question. Why do you ask?

ANNA: We need your friendship.

DON GIOVANNI [*Aside.*]: I'm breathing again. [*Aloud.*] Command me! Friends, relations, this hand, this blade, my possessions, my blood— I will spend all to serve you. But my beautiful Anna, why are you crying? Who has dared disturb your peace?

[*Enter* ELVIRA.]

ELVIRA [*to Don Giovanni*]: So I find you again, perfidious monster. [*To Anna*] Wretched woman, don't trust this lecher. He has betrayed me and he'll betray you too.

OTTAVIO [*to Anna*]: Heavens, what nobility in her eyes; what sweet dignity.

ANNA [*to Ottavio*]: Her grief and her tears fill me with pity.

DON GIOVANNI: The poor girl is mad, my friends. Leave me with her. I'll calm her down.

ELVIRA: Don't believe the liar!

DON GIOVANNI: She's mad. Please go away!

ELVIRA: Please stay!

ANNA [*to Ottavio*]: Whom should we believe?

OTTAVIO: I'll not leave without seeing clear in this muddle.

ANNA: She looks quite sane to me.

DON GIOVANNI [*Aside.*]: If I leave they'll suspect something.

ELVIRA: You can read his character in his ugly face!

OTTAVIO [*to Don Giovanni*]: So the girl—

DON GIOVANNI: Is not all there.

ANNA [*to Elvira*]: And so you say—

ELVIRA: He's a fraud!

DON GIOVANNI: Unhappy girl!

ELVIRA: Liar!

ANNA [to Ottavio]: I don't know what to believe.

DON GIOVANNI [to Elvira]: Do lower your voice; you're drawing a crowd and exposing your reputation.

ELVIRA: I don't care. I've thrown caution to the winds. The whole world will ring to your guilt and my misery!

[Exit.]

ANNA [to Ottavio]: This whispering of his, this changing of color— My mind is made up!

DON GIOVANNI: Poor girl! I'd better follow her. Who knows what she might do to herself. Allow me to leave you, beautiful Anna; call on me at home if I can be of any assistance. My friends, good-bye.

[Exit.]

ANNA: Ottavio, I'm dying.

OTTAVIO: What's the matter?

ANNA: Help me.

OTTAVIO: Courage, my love.

ANNA: Oh God! This is the man who murdered my father!

OTTAVIO: What are you saying?

ANNA: No doubt about it! The last words of that scoundrel—his voice recalled the murderer who entered my room—

OTTAVIO: Is it possible that under the sacred cloak of friendship—but tell me again what happened that night.

ANNA: I was alone in my room late at night when I saw a man come in, wrapped in a cloak. At first I mistook him for you, but then I saw my mistake.

OTTAVIO: Heavens! Go on!

ANNA: He came up to me quietly and sought to embrace me. I tried to free myself, but he pressed me close to him. I cried out. Nobody came. With one hand he covered my mouth, and with the other he clutched me so hard that I thought I was lost.

OTTAVIO: The scoundrel! And then?

ANNA: My terror so increased my strength that finally by pulling, bending, and twisting I managed to get free of him.

OTTAVIO: Thank God! I'm breathing again!

ANNA: I redoubled my cries for help until he fled. I ran boldly into the street to stop him. From defense, I leaped to the attack. My poor old father came running and tried to unmask him, but the ruffian was too strong and killed him. Now you know who tried to dishonour me and who deprived me of my father. If your anger needs reviving, remember the wound in his breast and the ground soaked with his blood.

[*Exit.*]

OTTAVIO: Should I believe that a nobleman can commit such a crime? I must use every means to discover the truth. The duty of a husband and a friend speak in my breast. I must undeceive her or avenge her, for my peace depends on hers. Whatever pleases her gives me life, and whatever grieves her, death.

[*Exit.*]

[*Enter* LEPORELLO.]

LEPORELLO: Happen what may, I must break with this madman. Here he comes. Look at his nonchalance.

[*Enter* DON GIOVANNI.]

DON GIOVANNI: My sweet little Leporello, is everything all right?

LEPORELLO: My sweet little Don Giovanni, everything is all wrong.

DON GIOVANNI: What do you mean, all wrong?

LEPORELLO: I obeyed your orders and took all those people into the house.

DON GIOVANNI: Good.

LEPORELLO: I tried to entertain them with the chatter, the jokes, and the lies I've learned from you.

DON GIOVANNI: Good.

LEPORELLO: I told Masetto a thousand stories to take his mind off his jealousy.

DON GIOVANNI: Excellent.

LEPORELLO: I poured the drinks until they were all half drunk. Some were singing, some were joking, and some just drank. In the middle of which, guess who tumbles in?

DON GIOVANNI: Zerlina.

LEPORELLO: Bravo. And who is with her?

DON GIOVANNI: Elvira.

LEPORELLO: Bravo again. And she spoke of you—

DON GIOVANNI: All the evil she could think of.

LEPORELLO: You are a genius.

DON GIOVANNI: And you, what did you do?

LEPORELLO: Nothing.

DON GIOVANNI: And she?

LEPORELLO: Went on shouting.

DON GIOVANNI: And you?

LEPORELLO: When I judged that she had relieved her feelings, I led her gently out of the garden and, locking the door behind her, cunningly left her alone on the road.

DON GIOVANNI: Masterfully done. Things couldn't be better. Well, I'll finish what you started. These little country girls fascinate me. I want to entertain them till nightfall. Keep the feast going. Make their heads swim in wine. If you find a pretty girl in the square, invite her along. There must be disorder in the dancing. Let one do a minuet, another a fandango, another a jig. And I, meantime, will squeeze one here and kiss one there. By tomorrow, I want another dozen on my list.

[*Exeunt.*]

Scene 4

Don Giovanni's garden. The palace in the back, lit up. Peasants asleep or sitting on the grass. Enter ZERLINA *and* MASETTO.

ZERLINA: Masetto, listen to me. Masetto, I say.

MASETTO: Don't touch me.

ZERLINA: Why not?

MASETTO: Why do you ask? Hussy! I won't stand for your tricks.

ZERLINA: Hush. I don't deserve to be treated so cruelly.

MASETTO: What! You have the cheek to excuse yourself? You stay alone with a man; you jilt me on my wedding day; you shame the honour of a peasant! Oh if it weren't for the scandal, I'd like—

ZERLINA: But if I'm innocent, if he lied to me? What are you afraid of? Calm down, my sweet, he didn't even touch my fingertips. Ungrateful boy, don't you believe me? Come here, vent your anger on me, kill me, do with me what you will, but when you're done, dearest Masetto, when you're done, do let's make up. Beat me, my handsome Masetto, beat your poor Zerlina; I'll be here waiting for your blows as meekly as a little lamb. I'll let you pull my hair out and scratch out my eyes too, and I'll kiss your dear hands. But I see you haven't the heart to do it; so let's make peace, and be merry together night and day.

MASETTO: Look how this witch bamboozles me. We men are weak in the head.

DON GIOVANNI [*within*]: Make everything ready for the feast!

ZERLINA: Masetto, do you hear Monsoor Giovanni's voice?

MASETTO: What's that to me?

ZERLINA: He's coming.

MASETTO: Let him come.

ZERLINA: If I could find a hole to hide in—

MASETTO: What are you afraid of? Why is your face white? Oh, I understand, you hussy; you're afraid I might discover what happened between you two. Quick, before he comes I'm going to disappear. Here's a nook from which I can keep an eye on you.

ZERLINA: Where are you going? Don't hide. Poor boy, what will he do if he finds you?

MASETTO: Let him do or say whatever he likes.

ZERLINA: Words won't help you.

MASETTO: Stand here and speak loud enough for me to hear.

ZERLINA: If that isn't silly!

MASETTO [*Aside.*]: I'll know whether she is faithful and what took place between them.

ZERLINA: The ungrateful and cruel man is upsetting everything today.

[*Enter* DON GIOVANNI *and servants.*]

DON GIOVANNI: Wake up, my good people. There will be pleasure and laughter for all. [*To the servants*] Take them to the ballroom, and let there be plenty of refreshments.

[*Peasants and servants leave.*]

ZERLINA: Maybe he won't see me behind this tree.

DON GIOVANNI: Zerlinetta dear, I see you, you can't escape.

ZERLINA: Let me go.

DON GIOVANNI: No, no, stay, delightful girl.

ZERLINA: Is there no pity in your heart?

DON GIOVANNI: Of course there is, I'm all love. Come with me, you'll be glad if you do.

[*He leads* ZERLINA *toward the place where Masetto is concealed.*]

ZERLINA [*Aside.*]: If he sees Masetto, I know what he's capable of.

DON GIOVANNI: Masetto!

MASETTO: Yes, Masetto.

DON GIOVANNI: Why hidden? Your beautiful Zerlina can't bear to be without you.

MASETTO: I understand, sir.

DON GIOVANNI: Come, cheer up; let's go hear the musicians together.

ZERLINA: Yes, let's cheer up, and let's all three go dancing with the others.

[*Exeunt. Enter* ANNA, ELVIRA, *and* OTTAVIO, *masked.*]

ELVIRA: My friends, with a little courage we shall expose his wickedness.

OTTAVIO: Our friend is right. We need courage. My dear, put away your grief and fear.

ANNA: We're taking a dangerous step. Who knows what complications will follow? I fear for all of us.

LEPORELLO [*from the window*]: My lord, come and see the elegant masqueraders.

DON GIOVANNI: Invite them in and tell them that their presence will honor us.

ANNA: His face and his voice give the traitor away.

LEPORELLO: Pst! You—the maskers!

ANNA: Answer him.

OTTAVIO: What do you want?

LEPORELLO: My master invites you to our ball.

OTTAVIO: Thank you for the courtesy. Let's go, dear ladies.

LEPORELLO [*Aside.*]: Here are two more hens for Master Fox.

ELVIRA: God protect us.

Scene 5

An illuminated ballroom in DON GIOVANNI's *palace. Enter* DON GIOVANNI, LEPORELLO, ZERLINA, *and* MASETTO.

DON GIOVANNI: Rest a little, dear girls.

LEPORELLO: Drink, drink, my lads.

DON GIOVANNI: We'll be frolicking again in a moment. Coffee here!

LEPORELLO: Chocolate!

MASETTO: Zerlina, be careful.

DON GIOVANNI: Sherbets!

LEPORELLO: Sweets!

MASETTO: The scene opens too sweetly. It might turn bitter at the end.

DON GIOVANNI: You are lovely, brilliant, Zerlina!

ZERLINA: You're too kind.

MASETTO [*Aside.*]: The hussy is eating it up.

LEPORELLO: Sweet Gianotta, charming Sandrina!

MASETTO [*Aside.*]: Go on—touch her, and the devil take you.

ZERLINA [*Aside.*]: Masetto seems to be in a rage. How very unpleasant.

DON GIOVANNI [*Aside.*]: Masetto seems to be in a rage. This calls for brainwork.

MASETTO [*Aside.*]: Touch her, touch her! The hussy is driving me mad.
[*Enter* ANNA, ELVIRA, *and* OTTAVIO, *masked.*]

LEPORELLO: Come in, pretty maskers!

DON GIOVANNI: It's open house for all. A toast to liberty!

OTTAVIO: We are grateful for so many tokens of your generosity.

ALL FIVE: Liberty!

DON GIOVANNI: Let the players strike up again. [*To* LEPORELLO] Pair
off the dancers. Zerlina, come here, you must dance with me.

LEPORELLO: Everybody dance.

ELVIRA: There's the girl.

ANNA: I can't bear it.

OTTAVIO: Dissemble.

DON GIOVANNI: Everything's running smoothly.

MASETTO [*ironically*]: Everything's running ever so smoothly.

DON GIOVANNI [*to* LEPORELLO]: Keep an eye on Masetto.

LEPORELLO [*to* MASETTO]: Aren't you dancing, poor fellow? Come
along with me, let's join the others.

DON GIOVANNI: I'm your partner, Zerlina. Come with me. [*They
dance.*]

MASETTO: No—I don't want to dance.

LEPORELLO: Yes, you do.

MASETTO: No, I don't.

LEPORELLO: We'll do like everybody else.
[*He dances with* MASETTO.]

ANNA: I can't hold back.

OTTAVIO: I beg you, keep still a little longer.

DON GIOVANNI [*to* ZERLINA]: Follow me, my dearest.

MASETTO [*to* LEPORELLO]: Let me go! [*To Zerlina*] No! Zerlina!

DON GIOVANNI: Come, come.

ZERLINA: Oh Gods, I'm betrayed!
[*Dancing,* DON GIOVANNI *leads* ZERLINA *to a door and forces her to
enter.*]

LEPORELLO: Here comes trouble.
[*He runs to warn Don Giovanni.*]

ANNA: The scoundrel is walking into the trap by himself.

ZERLINA [*within*]: Help! Everybody! Help!

ANNA: Let's help the innocent girl!
[*The musicians, etc., leave in confusion.*]

MASETTO: Zerlina!

ZERLINA [*within*]: Beast!

ANNA: The cries are coming from that side. Tear down the door.

ZERLINA: Help me! I'll die.

OTTAVIO: We're here to defend you.

[*They force the door.* ZERLINA *appears, followed by* DON GIOVANNI, *who, sword in hand, is dragging* LEPORELLO *along, and pretends to threaten him.*]

DON GIOVANNI: Here's the villain who molested you; but I'll punish him. Die, miserable wretch.

LEPORELLO: What are you doing?

DON GIOVANNI: I said, die.

OTTAVIO [*pistol in hand, removes his mask*]: Stop! We've seen through your tricks.

[ANNA *and* ELVIRA *take off their masks.*]

DON GIOVANNI: Elvira!

ELVIRA: Yes, you devil.

DON GIOVANNI: Ottavio!

OTTAVIO: Yes.

DON GIOVANNI [*to Anna*]: Believe me—

OTTAVIO: Everything is known.

ELVIRA: Tremble, rascal. The whole world will know your crimes and your cruelties.

ANNA: Listen to the thunder of vengeance crashing about you. The bolt will fall on your head today.

LEPORELLO: My head's in a whirl; what a horrible storm!

DON GIOVANNI: Do you take me for a coward? I defy you all! If the world itself came down on me, I wouldn't shake.

[*He escapes.*]

ACT II

Scene 1

A street. On one side Donna Elvira's house, with a balcony. Night. Enter DON GIOVANNI *and* LEPORELLO.

DON GIOVANNI: Come on, you clown, don't pester me.

LEPORELLO: Well, I won't stay with you.

DON GIOVANNI: Look here, my friend—

LEPORELLO: I'm leaving, I tell you.

DON GIOVANNI: What have I done to you?

LEPORELLO: Oh nothing at all; just nearly killed me.

DON GIOVANNI: You're a fool. That was only a joke.

LEPORELLO: Well, I'm not joking, and I'm leaving.

DON GIOVANNI: Leporello.

LEPORELLO: Sir?

DON GIOVANNI: Come here. Let's make up. Take this.

LEPORELLO: What is it?

DON GIOVANNI: Four ducats.

LEPORELLO: Well— I'm playing along with this ceremony one more time; but don't get used to it; don't think you can bedevil the likes of me with money, the way you do your women.

DON GIOVANNI: Let's say no more about it. Have you got courage enough to carry out my orders?

LEPORELLO: Provided there are no women in it.

DON GIOVANNI: No women? Idiot! No women! Do you realize that they are more necessary to me than breathing and eating?

LEPORELLO: And in spite of that you keep on cheating them?

DON GIOVANNI: It's all for the sake of love. He who serves one woman only, robs every other. And such is the tenderness of my emotions that I adore them all. Unfortunately women have no common sense and call my good nature treachery.

LEPORELLO: I've never seen a more extensive good nature. Well—what do you want now?

DON GIOVANNI: Listen. Have you seen Elvira's maid?

LEPORELLO: I haven't.

DON GIOVANNI: In that case, my dear Leporello, you have missed a beautiful object. I'm going to try my luck with her. And since it's almost night, I've decided to appear in your clothes in order to sharpen her appetite.

LEPORELLO: Why don't you appear in your own?

DON GIOVANNI: People of her class are suspicious of elegant dress. Well now, hurry up.

LEPORELLO: Sir—I don't feel—

DON GIOVANNI [angry]: Enough. I can't bear objections. [They exchange cloaks. ELVIRA appears at the balcony.]

ELVIRA: Be still, my heart. He is a cruel traitor. To feel for him is a sin.

LEPORELLO: Hush. I hear Donna Elvira's voice.

DON GIOVANNI: I'm going to take advantage of this. Stand here. Elvira, my treasure!

ELVIRA: Isn't that the ingrate speaking?

DON GIOVANNI: Yes, my life, it is I, begging your forgiveness.

ELVIRA [*Aside.*]: Gods, what a strange feeling he wakes in my· breast!

LEPORELLO [*Aside.*]: You'll see how that madwoman will still believe him.

DON GIOVANNI: Come down, joy of my life. You're the one my soul adores. I've already repented.

ELVIRA: No, villain, I don't believe you.

DON GIOVANNI: Believe me, or I will kill myself!

LEPORELLO: If you go on I'm going to laugh.

DON GIOVANNI: Come down, my goddess.

ELVIRA [*Aside.*]: Oh, I'm struggling with myself. Shall I go? Shall I stay? God protect a poor gullible woman!

DON GIOVANNI [*Aside.*]: I hope she falls for this. It's a neat little trick. Was there ever a greater talent than mine?

LEPORELLO [*Aside.*]: The liar is seducing her again. God protect the fool!

[ELVIRA *withdraws from the balcony.*]

DON GIOVANNI: Well, what do you think?

LEPORELLO: I think you have a heart of stone.

DON GIOVANNI: You're a big simpleton. Now listen— When she comes down, take her in your arms, pat her a few times, and imitate my voice. Then use your wits to take her away from here.

LEPORELLO: But—

DON GIOVANNI: Don't answer.

LEPORELLO: And if she recognizes me?

DON GIOVANNI: She won't if you don't want her to. Quiet, she's coming; use your head!

[DON GIOVANNI *conceals himself; enter* ELVIRA.]

ELVIRA: I've come to you.

DON GIOVANNI [*Aside.*]: Let's see what he does.

LEPORELLO [*Aside.*]: What a muddle.

ELVIRA: Can I really believe that my tears have overcome your heart? Is my dear Giovanni returning to his duty and to my love?

LEPORELLO: Yes, my darling.

ELVIRA: Cruel man! If you knew how many tears and sighs I've spent on you!

LEPORELLO: On me?

ELVIRA: Yes, you.

LEPORELLO: Poor dear, I'm so sorry.

ELVIRA: You'll never leave me again?

LEPORELLO: No, sweetie.

ELVIRA: Will you always be mine?

LEPORELLO: Always.

ELVIRA: Dearest.

LEPORELLO: Dearest. [*Aside.*] I'm beginning to enjoy this.

ELVIRA: My treasure!

LEPORELLO: My Venus!

ELVIRA: I'm all fire for you.

LEPORELLO: And I'm burnt to ashes.

DON GIOVANNI [*Aside.*]: The rogue is warming up.

ELVIRA: And you won't betray me?

LEPORELLO: Certainly not.

ELVIRA: Swear it!

LEPORELLO: I swear it to this hand, which I kiss with rapture, and to these two stars—

DON GIOVANNI [*making rough noises*]: You're dead.

ELVIRA and LEPORELLO: Oh! God!

[ELVIRA *and* LEPORELLO *fly.*]

DON GIOVANNI [*laughing*]: Luck is with me. Let's see; these are the windows; now to my song.

[*He sings a serenade.*]

There's someone at the window. Maybe it's she. Pst, pst.

[*Enter* MASETTO, *followed by armed peasants.*]

MASETTO: Let's not give up; I'm sure we'll find him!

DON GIOVANNI [*Aside.*]: Somebody is talking.

MASETTO: Stop! I think somebody's moving there.

DON GIOVANNI [*Aside.*]: If I'm not mistaken it's Masetto.

MASETTO: Who goes there? No answer? Courage; shoulder your muskets. Who goes there?

DON GIOVANNI [*Aside.*]: He's not alone; I've got to be careful. [*Aloud, trying to imitate Leporello's voice*] Friends! [*Aside.*] I don't want to be seen. [*Aloud.*] Is that you, Masetto?

MASETTO: Nobody else, and you?

DON GIOVANNI: Don't you recognize me? Don Giovanni's servant.

MASETTO: Leporello! That scoundrel's servant?

DON GIOVANNI: That's right; the rascal's servant.

MASETTO: Tell me where we can find him. I've a little group here all set to kill him.

DON GIOVANNI [*Aside.*]: A trifle. [*Aloud.*] Excellent. I'm going to join you to get even with that pest of a master. But listen to my sugges-

tion: half of you go one way and half the other. He can't be very far.
If you see a couple walking on the square, or if you hear someone
making declarations under a window, shoot and shoot again; it's
my master. He's wearing a hat with white feathers, a broad cloak,
and a sword at his side. Hurry up men! You alone stay behind with
me. We'll take care of the rest and you'll soon find out what that is.
[*The peasants leave.*]

DON GIOVANNI: All's quiet. Excellent. So we're going to kill him?

MASETTO: That's right.

DON GIOVANNI: You wouldn't be satisfied just to break his bones, or
maybe to knock in a rib or two?

MASETTO: No, I want to kill him and make mincemeat of him.

DON GIOVANNI: Do you have good weapons?

MASETTO: Yes, by thunder. First I've got this musket; then, this pistol.
[*He gives them to Don Giovanni.*]

DON GIOVANNI: Anything else?

MASETTO: Isn't that enough?

DON GIOVANNI: I suppose it is. Now take this for the pistol, and that
for the musket.
[*Beats him.*]

MASETTO: Ouch, ouch, my head!

DON GIOVANNI: Shut up, or I'll butcher you. Take this for killing him;
and that, for the mincemeat. Ruffian! Cutthroat! Dog!
[*Exit* DON GIOVANNI; *enter* ZERLINA *with a lantern.*]

MASETTO: Oh my head! Oh my shoulders! Oh my chest!

ZERLINA: I thought I heard Masetto's voice.

MASETTO: Oh God, Zerlina, help me.

ZERLINA: What happened?

MASETTO: That devil broke all my bones.

ZERLINA: Goodness! Who was it?

MASETTO: Leporello, or some devil that looks like him.

ZERLINA: Fool! Didn't I tell you that your stupid jealousy would bring
you to grief? Where does it hurt?

MASETTO: Here.

ZERLINA: Where else?

MASETTO: Here; and here.

ZERLINA: And nowhere else?

MASETTO: This foot hurts a little; and this arm; and this hand.

ZERLINA: Well, that's no great matter, if the rest of you is sound. Come
home with me. If you promise to be less jealous in the future, I myself

will take care of you, my dear boy. You'll see what a fine remedy I
have for you. It's a natural cure, it has no bad taste, and it's a thing
the druggist doesn't know how to make. I carry it on me all the time,
and I'll give it to you if you want to try it. Would you like to know
where it is? Feel here. Do you hear it beating? Just put your hand
there. There. There.

[*Exeunt.*]

Scene 2

A dark courtyard in Donna Anna's house. Enter LEPORELLO *and*
ELVIRA.

LEPORELLO: I see torches coming near. Let's stay here a little, my
love, until they disappear.

ELVIRA: What are you afraid of, my beloved husband?

LEPORELLO: Nothing. I want to be careful. I'll go see if the lights are
gone. [*Aside.*] How can I get rid of her? [*Aloud.*] Stay here, my jewel.
[*He moves away.*]

ELVIRA: Don't leave me alone in this darkness. My heart is beating so.
I'll die of fear.
[*Groping about.*]

LEPORELLO [*Aside.*]: The more I look for that miserable door, the less
I find it. Softly, I have it! Now's the time to escape. [*He misses the
door. Enter* OTTAVIO *and* ANNA *with torches.*]

OTTAVIO: Dry your tears, dearest, and soothe your grief. Your father's
shade will take pity on your suffering from now on.

ANNA: These tears are my only relief— Don't forbid me to weep. Only
death can dry my eyes.

ELVIRA [*Aside.*]: Where is my husband?

LEPORELLO [*Aside.*]: If she finds me, I'm done for.

ELVIRA: Here's a door. I'll leave quietly.
[*Enter* ZERLINA *and* MASETTO.]

MASETTO: Stop, villain; where are you going?

OTTAVIO: Here's the traitor. What was he doing here?

ANNA: Kill the scoundrel who wronged me.

ELVIRA: He's my husband. Mercy! Forgive him!

ANNA: Donna Elvira! I can hardly believe it.

OTTAVIO: Let him die.
[*He is about to kill* LEPORELLO.]

ELVIRA: Mercy!

LEPORELLO [*on his knees*]: Mercy, mercy, my lords. I'm not him; she's mistaken. Let me live, for pity's sake.

ALL: It's Leporello— What trick is this? I'm dumbfounded— What does this mean?

LEPORELLO: It'll be a miracle if I can save my skin this time.

[ANNA *leaves.*]

ZERLINA: So you're the one who was mauling my Masetto just now.

ELVIRA: So you're the one who duped me playing Don Giovanni with me.

OTTAVIO: So you came disguised to make fools of us.

ELVIRA: His punishment is reserved to me.

ZERLINA: No, to me.

OTTAVIO: No, no, to me.

MASETTO: The three of you join me in beating him up.

LEPORELLO: Mercy, mercy, my lords and ladies. I can explain everything. The crime's not my own. My master robbed me of my innocence. Donna Elvira, pity me—you know what happened. And you can bear witness that I don't know a thing about Masetto. I've been walking about with you for about an hour. [*To* OTTAVIO] To you, dear sir, I don't say anything. I was scared—as luck would have it—light outside—dark here—no way out—the door—the wall—I went to that side—I took cover—I'm sure you understand—but if I'd known—I would have—cleared out!

[*Runs away.*]

ELVIRA: Stop! Stop!

MASETTO: The dog has wings at his feet.

ZERLINA: How cleverly he escaped.

OTTAVIO: Friends: After such egregious crimes, we can no longer hesitate to call Don Giovanni the impious assassin of Donna Anna's father. Remain a few hours in this house. I shall call in the constables, and soon you will all be revenged. So much is required of duty, pity, and love. Meanwhile, go and comfort my bride; wipe her precious tears; tell her I have gone to avenge her wrongs, and that I shall return only with a message of death and destruction.

[*Exeunt all except* ELVIRA.]

ELVIRA: He betrays me, he abandons me, he covers himself with crimes, he calls down on his head the justice of heaven, and yet I pity him. I clamor for vengeance—and then my heart speaks for him. Oh, unhappy girl!

[*Exit* ELVIRA.]

Scene 3

A cemetery surrounded by a wall. Among other statues, that of the COMMANDER *on horseback. Moonlight. Enter* DON GIOVANNI, *climbing down the wall.*

DON GIOVANNI [*laughing*]: That was delicious; now let her find me. What a beautiful night; brighter than the day. It seems made to roam after pretty girls. Is it late? No; not even two. I wonder how the business of Leporello and Elvira ended. I hope he didn't lose his head.

LEPORELLO [*outside the gate*]: He'll be the death of me at last.

DON GIOVANNI: That's him. Hey, Leporello!

LEPORELLO: Who's calling me?

DON GIOVANNI: Don't you know your master?

LEPORELLO: I wish I didn't.

DON GIOVANNI: What's that, you cur?

LEPORELLO: Oh, it's you. Excuse me.

DON GIOVANNI: What happened?

LEPORELLO: I was almost killed on your account.

DON GIOVANNI: Well, wasn't that an honour for you?

LEPORELLO: The honour's all yours.

DON GIOVANNI: Come here; I've a few lovely things to tell you.

LEPORELLO: What are you doing here?

DON GIOVANNI: Come here, and you'll find out. I've had a dozen adventures since I last saw you. But those can wait; just listen to the best one of the lot.

LEPORELLO: Romantic, of course.

DON GIOVANNI: Can you doubt it? I met a beautiful, young, and sprightly girl in the street. I followed her. I took her hand. She tried to run away. I said a few words, and she mistook me for—guess whom?

LEPORELLO: I don't know.

DON GIOVANNI: For Leporello.

LEPORELLO: For me?

DON GIOVANNI: For you.

LEPORELLO: Fine.

DON GIOVANNI: She takes me by the hand.

LEPORELLO: Still better.

DON GIOVANNI: She fondles me, she kisses me. "My dear Leporello. My sweet Leporello." I realized that she was one of your mistresses.

LEPORELLO [*Aside*.]: Damn him.

DON GIOVANNI: I took advantage of her mistake, but finally she recognized me. She began to shout; I heard people and started running. I ran until I came to this wall, jumped over it like a cat, and landed here.

LEPORELLO: And you tell me all this so lightly?

DON GIOVANNI: Why not?

LEPORELLO: Suppose it had been my wife?

DON GIOVANNI [*laughing*]: Better still.

STATUE: Before dawn your laughter will cease.

DON GIOVANNI: Who spoke?

LEPORELLO: It must be a soul from the other world that knows you thoroughly.

DON GIOVANNI: Quiet, fool. Who goes there?

[*He searches the cemetery, striking several statues with his sword.*]

STATUE: Abandoned wretch, leave the dead in peace.

LEPORELLO: I told you so.

DON GIOVANNI [*disdainful*]: It must be somebody over the wall playing a joke on us. Look! Isn't that the Commander's statue? Read the inscription.

LEPORELLO: Excuse me, but I haven't learned to read by moonlight.

DON GIOVANNI: Read, I tell you.

LEPORELLO: "I wait for vengeance against the villain who murdered me." Did you hear that? I'm shaking like a leaf.

DON GIOVANNI: The old clown! Tell him I expect him for dinner tonight.

LEPORELLO: This is insane. But I think— Good God, do you see the terrible looks he's giving us? He seems to be alive; he looks as though he could hear—as though he wanted to speak.

DON GIOVANNI: Proceed, or I'll carve you up and bury you on the spot.

LEPORELLO: Easy, easy. I'm going. Oh distinguished Statue of the great Commander— My heart's beating too fast, I can't finish.

DON GIOVANNI: Finish, or I'll run you through. [*Aside.*] What a lark! I'll make him sweat.

LEPORELLO [*Aside*.]: I'm stuck with it. My blood's curdling. [*Aloud.*] Distinguished Statue, although you're made of marble— Master, look at him stare!

DON GIOVANNI: Die!

LEPORELLO: Wait! [*to the Statue*] Sir—my master—my master desires to dine with you. Oh, oh, what a sight! Oh heavens, he nodded!

Don Giovanni: You're nothing but a clown.

Leporello: Why don't you look?

Don Giovanni: What should I look at?

Leporello: He went [*nods*] with his head.

Don Giovanni [*to the Statue*]: Speak if you can. Will you dine with me?

Statue: Yes.

Leporello: I can't move; I can't breathe. For pity's sake, let's get out of here.

Don Giovanni: It's a strange affair, to be sure. The old man's coming to dinner. Well, a meal has to be prepared, so let's be off.
   [*Exeunt.*]

Scene 4

A room in Donna Anna's house. Lights on the tables. Enter Anna *and* Ottavio.

Ottavio: Calm yourself, my treasure; soon we shall see the excesses of that villain punished.

Anna: But my father—

Ottavio: We must bow to the will of God. Dearest, if tomorrow you should wish to find compensation for your bitter loss—this heart, this hand, which my tender love—

Anna: Oh God, what are you saying, at a time like this?

Ottavio: Will you increase my grief with new delays? Cruel love!

Anna: Not cruel, dearest. It grieves me too to defer what both our souls desire. But what would the world say? Don't tempt me. You know that love pleads for you; you know my constancy. Don't torment yourself, unless you wish me to die. Perhaps some day Heaven will pity me.

Ottavio: Let me go with you and share in your sorrows.
   [*Exeunt.*]

Scene 5

A lighted room in Don Giovanni's house. A table is set for dinner. Enter Don Giovanni, Leporello, *and musicians.*

Don Giovanni: The table is set; play, musicians. I'm spending money and I mean to enjoy myself. Leporello, start serving.

Leporello: I'm ready. Bravo! They're playing "Cosa Rara."

DON GIOVANNI: What do you think of the music?

LEPORELLO: Worthy of you.

DON GIOVANNI: A delicious dish.

LEPORELLO [*Aside.*]: Look at that appetite. Each mouthful would feed a giant. It makes me sick.

DON GIOVANNI [*Aside.*]: Leporello looks hungry. Next course!

LEPORELLO: Coming up.

DON GIOVANNI: Pour the wine.

[*The music changes.*]

LEPORELLO: Ah! They're playing "I Due Litiganti."

DON GIOVANNI: Excellent marzimino!

LEPORELLO [*Aside.*]: I'm going to swallow this chunk of pheasant on the sly.

DON GIOVANNI [*Aside.*]: The scamp is eating my dinner. I'll pretend not to notice.

[*The music changes to "Non più andrai."*]

LEPORELLO: I've heard that one too often.

DON GIOVANNI: Leporello!

LEPORELLO [*with his mouth full*]: Sir.

DON GIOVANNI: Speak clearly, you dog.

LEPORELLO: My cold keeps me from enunciating.

DON GIOVANNI: Whistle a little while I eat.

LEPORELLO: I can't.

DON GIOVANNI: What happened?

LEPORELLO: Forgive me. Your cook is so good that I wanted to sample his skill.

[*Enter* ELVIRA.]

ELVIRA: I want to give you a last proof of my love. I have forgotten your deceptions. I feel only pity for you.

DON GIOVANNI [*Aside.*]: What now?

[*Motions to the musicians to leave.*]

ELVIRA [*kneeling*]: I ask nothing for myself.

DON GIOVANNI: I'm astounded! What do you want? If you don't rise, I'll kneel too.

[*He kneels.*]

ELVIRA: Don't laugh at my sorrow!

LEPORELLO [*Aside.*]: I feel like crying.

DON GIOVANNI [*with feigned tenderness*]: Me? Laugh at you? Why should I? What do you want, my love?

ELVIRA: Mend your life.

DON GIOVANNI: Good girl.

[*He laughs.*]

ELVIRA: Monster!

DON GIOVANNI: Let me continue with my meal; and join me, if you like.

ELVIRA: No—I'll leave you in the stench of your hateful vices, a horrible example to mankind.

LEPORELLO [*Aside.*]: If he's not moved by this, he has a heart of stone, or none at all.

DON GIOVANNI: Long live women! Long live good wine! The comfort and glory of mankind!

[*On her way out,* ELVIRA *shrieks and departs by another door.*]

DON GIOVANNI: What's this scream? Go see what happened.

[LEPORELLO *leaves, shrieks too, and returns.*]

LEPORELLO: Oh!

DON GIOVANNI: What a fiendish scream! Leporello, what is it?

LEPORELLO: Merciful heavens, don't move! It's the man of stone, the white man. Master, I'm going out of my mind! If you'd seen his shape—if you'd heard how he walks—ta, ta, ta, ta.

DON GIOVANNI: I don't understand a word you're saying. You're out of your head.

LEPORELLO: Listen.

DON GIOVANNI: There's a knock. Open!

LEPORELLO: No.

DON GIOVANNI: Open, I say!

LEPORELLO: Aaah!

DON GIOVANNI: Idiot! I'll have to open myself and clear up this mystery.

[*Takes the light and goes to the door.*]

LEPORELLO: I don't want to see the old boy any more. Where can I hide?

[*He hides under the table.*]

[*Enter* DON GIOVANNI *and the* COMMANDER.]

COMMANDER: Don Giovanni, you invited me to dinner, and I have come.

DON GIOVANNI: I would never have believed it. But I'll do what I can. Leporello, another plate!

LEPORELLO: Master—we're dead.

DON GIOVANNI: Go on, I tell you.

COMMANDER: Stop. He who feasts on heavenly fare requires no mortal food. Graver cares brought me back to the world.

LEPORELLO: I've a fever and can't keep my limbs still.

DON GIOVANNI: Well then, speak! What do you want?

COMMANDER: Listen. My time is short.

DON GIOVANNI: Speak. I'm listening.

COMMANDER: You invited me to dinner. Now you know your duty. Answer me: will you dine with me?

LEPORELLO: Hallo! He's engaged; excuse him.

DON GIOVANNI: I'll never be smirched with the name of coward.

COMMANDER: Decide!

DON GIOVANNI: I have decided.

COMMANDER: Will you come?

LEPORELLO: Say no.

DON GIOVANNI: I stand firm and without fear. I'll come!

COMMANDER: Give me your hand as a pledge.

DON GIOVANNI: Here it is. Ay! His grip is like ice.

COMMANDER: Repent! Mend your life. This is your last chance.

DON GIOVANNI [*tries in vain to free himself*]: No, I do not repent. Let me go! Away!

COMMANDER: Repent, scoundrel!

DON GIOVANNI: Never, old fool!

COMMANDER: Repent!

LEPORELLO: Do.

COMMANDER: Repent!

DON GIOVANNI: No.

COMMANDER: Ah! There's no more time.
  [*He vanishes. Fire and thunder.*]

DON GIOVANNI: My mind darkens. The fires of hell surround me. Oh the torment! the delirium! Infernal terror!

INVISIBLE CHORUS: For guilt like yours this is all too little. Come; there's worse below!

DON GIOVANNI: Who is tearing my soul out? Who is burning my flesh?

LEPORELLO: Despair! Terror! Groans! Shouts! Damnation!
  [DON GIOVANNI *disappears. Enter* ANNA, ELVIRA, ZERLINA, OTTAVIO, *and* MASETTO.]

OTTAVIO: Where's the villain?

ELVIRA: Where's the wretch?

ANNA: I must see him in chains.

LEPORELLO: You'll never find him. Stop looking. He's gone forever.

ELVIRA: What happened? Speak!

OTTAVIO: Speak up!

LEPORELLO: A giant came—I can't describe him.

MASETTO: Keep talking!

LEPORELLO: There was fire and smoke—wait a bit—a man of stone—don't come nearer—right here—he took the plunge—right here the devil gulped him down.

ALL: Heavens! Can it be true?

LEPORELLO: Yes, it's true.

ELVIRA: It must have been the ghost I saw.

OTTAVIO: Now, dearest, we are all avenged. Dally no more, and make me the happiest of men.

ANNA: Grant me another year of mourning. Be patient and yield to me, my love.

OTTAVIO: I must yield to the woman who adores me.

ELVIRA: And I will end my life in a convent.

ZERLINA: And Masetto and me are going home for dinner.

LEPORELLO: And I'm off to the nearest inn to find a better master.

ALL: Now let the scoundrel stay with Proserpine and Pluto. And let us all, good people, joyously repeat the old, old song: Such is the end of evildoers! The death of villains is always as evil as their lives!

Part II
THE ROMANTIC
DON JUAN

Der frohe Juan ist aus der Welt entwichen,
Der traurige Juan hat ihn beerbt.

LENAU

The joyous Juan has left the world,
The sad Juan is his heir.

LENAU

Nineteenth-Century Views

(1814-1822)

Don Juan and the Romantic Age   I

The Romantic age is a period marked—if a single phrase can mark it at all—by the *breaking of bounds*. In every phase of human life we are aware of this going beyond, for good or for ill. The most familiar demonstration of this movement is also the most striking; I mean that of listening to a symphony by Haydn and then to the Fifth or Ninth of Beethoven. Striking because the two men are of the same nation, because only a generation separates them, and because they compose so obviously in the same musical idiom. And yet the world of the first man is comparatively small, comfortably settled, precisely bounded, and neatly adorned; that of the second shatters the old, smashes and tramples, aspires and transcends, and if it goes too far now and then, if it loses measure without gaining substance once in a while (and what shall we say of Mahler and Strauss?), it also touches eternities which the Haydns did not so much not care about as not even dream of.

In all else as in music. Benevolence made way for passion, reason for instinct, measure for mystery, greatness for grandeur, the garden for the alp, discomposure for horror, clarity for ambiguity, pleasure for delirium, and the ditch for the abyss. It is not accident that the French Revolution in politics and the Industrial Revolution in economics should have accompanied the more abstract revolutions: they too were a breaking—literal this time—of bounds. The static was giving way to the dynamic. Growth was the order of the day—the breaking of bounds toward higher and better things—"progress"—and while geologists were demonstrating that the earth, no the cosmos! had grown and developed, while historians were demonstrating that history is a vast movement toward a divine event, while biologists were discovering that the creature man had arisen from the slime and might therefore

ascend toward the angel, nations were expanding, developing, growing, and beginning to take for granted that to be healthy is to make,
be, do, have more, more, and more.

The men of the Romantic age were not a new race. Many resisted
the new spirit—even Byron despised, or affected to despise, the new
emotionalism, and in Tennyson's time many a reader of poetry was
still grumbling for the reasonable days of Pope and Johnson. But for
the men who flew with rather than against the "winds of destiny" there
was a sense of release—bounds could be broken and ought to be broken.
A recurrent word, alien to the Classical spirit as it is to the Molecular
temperament, was *rapture*. But the counterbalancing emotions were
magnified in the same proportion, and men abandoned themselves
more willingly to intense melancholy, anguish, and despair. Rapture
made men flock to the standard of the Romantic Napoleon; despair
had made them commit suicide with the Romantic Werther. Both
ecstasies would have been properly ridiculed by Alexander Pope or
Madame de Sévigné.

The spirit of Romanticism declared itself in great and small events
—in the French Revolution or in a lyric by Eichendorff—and we discern
it with perfect clarity in the crook of land we are surveying. When
Lorenzo da Ponte drew Don Juan for Mozart in 1787, he penciled a gay
libertine whom it was prudent to send off to Hell (with a wink) lest
certain Austrian officials be offended—a gay libertine and nothing
more. But when E. T. A. Hoffmann, who had changed one of his three
given names to Amadeus as a token of his Mozart-worship, rediscovered the subject twenty-seven dramatic years later, he could not believe
that Don Juan was a mere philanderer—or rather that a genius like
Mozart could so have understood him—that a genius like Mozart would
have consigned him to Hell for seducing a few women—or that a genius
like Mozart would have accepted Don Juan as *gay*. Did not Don Juan
go from one object to the other and from one place to the other always
looking for the next experience? The Classical mind assumed that Don
Juan was so delighted with the first experience that he must have a
second; the Romantic temperament retorted that he sought the second because of his fatal disappointment over the first. What had been
essentially an unprogressive series of like satisfying events (this is nowhere clearer than in Tirso) became a new thing entirely, namely a
search which, with the easy tumescence of the Romantic vocabulary,
immediately became an aspiration. Aspiration implies present insuffi-
ciency. Don Juan seeks; therefore Don Juan is dissatisfied.

The transformation of Don Juan in the early nineteenth century echoed a transformation in the very lives of his chroniclers, and it would be as instructive to set Hoffmann's diary against Da Ponte's *Memoirs* as it is to place Hoffmann's commentary on Mozart's opera immediately after Da Ponte's text. Hoffmann's interpretation of what Mozart had in mind is absurd—a supreme mind in the Classical mold was not, in fact, capable of the "profound revelations" which were available to every poetaster of the *Sturm und Drang* epoch; but his commentary is of great interest in itself; it has its own intelligence, and it announces the new times for Don Juan. The spirit of this brief essay is to be found again in a hundred plays, poems, and novels of the nineteenth century concerning our lover. Here are the new passionate diction, the easy large adjectives, the reveling in emotions; here is the Rebel, the lonely, unhappy hero; here are the aspirations to the Ideal, cosmic frustrations, spiritual longings, hatred of philistinism; here too is a new appeal to the subconscious and the ambiguous in human nature: and this, at any rate, is unquestionably an intellectual advance over older conceptions of Don Juan.[1] I say an intellectual advance, for Mozart, Molière, and Tirso de Molina, whose versions are greater than those of Grabbe, Zorrilla, Rostand, and Montherlant, worked with limited concepts and naïve interpretations. The paradox is at once mysterious and instructive.

Hoffmann's essay appeared in what was almost his literary debut— the *Fantastic Pieces in the Manner of Callot (Fantasiestücke in Callots Manier)*. Stendhal, too, had a word for Don Juan at the opening of his life as a man of letters. When he wrote the notes, anecdotes, intimate journals, digressions, and analytic essays which were to make up *De l'Amour,* he had behind him only a long and mildly distinguished service under Napoleon and a few happy civilian years in Milan. *De l'Amour* was completed shortly before he departed from that gay city under suspicion of being a French spy. It came out in 1822; and in the next eleven years it found all of seventeen purchasers. The chapter which compares Don Juan with Goethe's Werther rather surprisingly favors the latter, but Stendhal liked to affect the role of sentimental lover as a spice to his hedonism. What is interesting for us here

1. Aspiration is naturally connected with movement, development, and progress. The Romantic Don Juan was to obey the critical dictum that "a character ought to grow." Typically, the Don Juan of Act Five in a Romantic play is a far different creature from what he was in Act One. Growth was not, however, a requirement of the classicists, and the early Don Juan is accordingly the same man from the beginning of an action to the end.

is to see the picture, so alien to the Classical conception, of Don Juan as an old and unhappy man. Stendhal is one of the first to make the mistake of giving Don Juan the living tissue of real manhood, stripping him of his symbolic stature.

But the new spirit manifests itself in the mere fact that Hoffmann's and Stendhal's are dissertations upon the hero. From this point on, side by side with new versions, the presses will deliver scores, perhaps hundreds, of studies: historical, aesthetic, psychological, sociological, medical analyses of Don Juan. The world grows older, and little by little the doing yields to the question why.

From "Don Juan" by E. T. A. Hoffmann

Translated by Christopher Lazare

If the libretto of *Don Juan* is taken by itself and considered only for its literary merit, it is difficult to understand how Mozart could conceive and compose such music to it. A *bon vivant,* excessively fond of wine and women, defiantly invites a man of stone to his rowdy table, the statue representing the old father whom he has struck down in self-defense. There is, truly, nothing very poetical in this, and honestly speaking, such a person is scarcely worth the distinction of being singled out by the infernal powers as a good specimen for their collection; of being exhorted to repentance in his final hour as a sinner by the stone man who, possessed by the spirit of enlightenment, takes the trouble to dismount from his horse to convert him; and of being transported to Hell under escort by the best henchmen the Devil has available for that purpose.

Believe me, Nature equipped Don Juan, as if he were her favorite child, with all that raises man towards divinity, above the common crowd, above the standard product, above the inferior article whose only worth is in number and aggregate; and this destined him to conquer, to dominate. A powerful, handsome body, a personality radiating the spark which kindles the most sublime feelings in the soul; a profound sensibility, a quick, instinctive understanding.

But the terrible consequence of the fall of man is that the Fiend retains the power to beguile man and prepare wicked pitfalls for him, just when he is striving for that perfection which most expresses his godlike nature. This conflict between the divine and demoniac powers begets the notion of life on earth, just as the ensuing victory begets the notion of life above earth. The demands upon life, exacted by his physical and mental qualities, filled Don Juan with unfailing enthusiasm. Insatiable in his desires, fired by a longing which sent the blood boiling through his veins, he was driven to the greedy, restless experience of all the phenomena of this earthly world, hoping in vain to find satisfaction in them.

There is, indeed, nothing here on earth more exalting for the inner nature of man than love. It is love that, so secretly and powerfully effective, disturbs and transfigures the innermost aspects of existence. Small wonder, then, that Don Juan hoped to still, in love, the longing that burned in his heart. And it was here that the Devil slipped the noose around his neck! Through the cunning of man's hereditary enemy, the thought was planted in Don Juan's soul that through love, through the pleasure of the flesh, there could be achieved on earth that which exists in our hearts as a heavenly promise only, and which amounts to just that longing for infinity which weds us to Heaven. Fleeing restlessly from one more beautiful woman to another; drinking his fill of their charms from burning passion to the point of drunken and exhausted satiety; believing himself always deceived in his choice, hoping always to realize the ideal of ultimate satisfaction, the Don was doomed to find all earthly life dull and shallow in the end; more, since he despised humanity anyhow, he revolted against that delusion which at first had spelled the highest of life's ambitions for him, only to betray him so bitterly at last. The enjoyment of woman no longer offered him any satisfaction of his sensuality, but had become an opportunity atrociously to outrage Nature and the Creator.

Don Juan was driven on by deep contempt for the common aspects of life, to which he felt himself superior. He felt bitter mockery for a humanity which hoped to find, in happy love and in the ensuing homely community it created, the merest fulfillment of the higher aspirations that a treacherous nature has inimically planted in our hearts; and he was compelled to revolt primarily against the very thought of such a relationship and to combat boldly, in anticipation of his own ruin, the unknown Being who guides our destiny and who appeared to Don Juan as a monster of malice rejoicing in the unhappiness of others and playing a cruel game with the pitiful creatures created out of his mocking moods. Every betrayal of a loved bride, every joy destroyed by a fierce blow struck at the lovers, every inconsolable grief the Don brings down upon a happy pair, represents an exalted triumph over that hostile monster, and raises the seducer forever above our narrow life, above Nature, above the Creator! He really desires more and more to transcend life, only to sink deeper and more irretrievably into Hell. The seduction of Anna, with the accompanying circumstances, is the very summit of his achievement.

With regard to the highest favors of Nature, Donna Anna is the counterpart of Don Juan. Just as Don Juan was originally a marvelously strong and handsome man, so she is a divine woman, over whose pure spirit the Devil has no power. All the arts of Hell, combined for her undoing, could ruin her only in an earthly fashion. As soon as Satan has accomplished this ruin, according to the dictates of Heaven, the execution of the revenge may no longer be delayed by the powers of Hell.

Don Juan mockingly invites the statue of the murdered old man to his bawdy feast, and the transfigured spirit, seeing Don Juan for the first time as the fallen man (or as Adam expelled from Paradise) and grieving over him, does not disdain to call upon him, in a terrifying guise, in order to bring about his repentance. But the soul of Don Juan is so corrupt, so ridden and anguished, that not even heavenly salvation can throw a ray of hope into his heart and light his way to a better life!

You have surely noticed that I have spoken of Anna's seduction; and I shall do my best, at this hour of the night when thoughts and ideas seem to rise from the depths of my soul and outdistance my words, to tell you briefly how I interpret the conflict of these two natures (Don Juan and Donna Anna) purely in terms of the music and ignoring the text.

I have already mentioned that Anna is the counterpart of the Don. Suppose Anna had been destined by Heaven to let Don Juan recognize, in the love that ruined him through the arts of Satan, the divine nature that dwelled within him, and to tear him away from his own desperate efforts at destruction? But no, it was too late for that! When he first saw her he was already at the height of his crimes, and could only feel the demoniac desire to corrupt her. There was no rescue for her! When he fled the deed was done! The fire of a superhuman sensuality, a glow from Hell, had cast its reflection over her senses and she was powerless to resist. Only he, only Don Juan, could awaken in her the erotic madness which she lavished upon him—he who sinned with the omnipotent rage of Hell.

He wanted to escape, once the deed was done. But for Donna Anna the awareness of her sin was like a dreadful, poisonous, death-spewing monster growing larger and more hideous each moment and coiling itself about her being in racking torture. She thought of her father's death at Don Juan's hand. She remembered her betrothal to frigid, effeminate, prosaic Don Ottavio, whom she had once thought she loved. Even the raging love that consumed her soul with hellish flames, flaring up at the moment of highest gratification, was aglow, now, with annihilating hatred. All this racks her heart now.

She feels that only the destruction of Don Juan can bring peace to her mortally tortured soul; but this peace demands her own earthly downfall. Unceasingly, therefore, she exhorts her indifferent bridegroom to revenge. She pursues the betrayer herself, and she relents only when the powers of the underworld have dragged Don Juan down into the bottomless pit.

But she will not yield to the bridegroom now eager for marriage. *Lascia, o caro, un anno ancora, allo sfogo del mio cor!* She will not outlive that year; Don Ottavio will never embrace the woman whose devotion has saved her from becoming Satan's chosen bride.

How vividly I felt all this in the tragic chords of the first recitative and of the account of the night attack! Even Donna Anna's scene in the second act: *Crudele* (which, considered superficially, refers only to Don Ottavio), expresses in secret harmonies, in the most wonderful inferences, that inner state of the soul that consumes all earthly happiness. What other meaning can we find in the passage added and altered by the poet: *forse un giorno il cielo ancora sentirà pieta di me!*

Two o'clock strikes! A warm, electric breath floats over me. I recognize the caressing scent of fine Italian perfume that I first noticed yesterday in the presence of my beautiful neighbor; I am seized by an ecstatic feeling that can be expressed only in music. The air billows more violently through the house, the strings of the piano in the pit vibrate like a harp. Heaven! As from a great distance, accompanied by the harmonica of an aerial orchestra, I seem to hear Anna's voice: *Non mi dir bell'idol mio!*

Open out before me, oh distant, unknown realm of spirits! Open out, oh land of genii and jinn! Open out, realm of all splendor whence mystic and celestial pain falls on me like a joy unutterable, fulfilling everything that was ever promised to the enraptured soul here below! Let me enter the circle of most loved apparitions! Let the dreams sent to me from this enchanted kingdom now terrify me as I shudder, now calm me as a benign messenger to earthly men! And in the hour when sleep holds the body captive in its leaden bonds, let those dreams carry my spirit gently into ethereal fields!   (1814)

Extracted from "Don Juan or A Fabulous Adventure that Befell a Music Enthusiast on his Travels" in *Tales from Hoffmann*. Edited by Christopher Lazare. New York: A. A. Wyn, 1946.

From *On Love* by Stendhal

Translated by Philip Sidney Woolf and Cecil N. Sidney Woolf

I beg to be allowed to draw a picture of my most intimate friend. Don Juan renounces all the duties which bind him to the rest of men. In the great market of life he is a dishonest merchant, who is always buying and never paying. The idea of equality inspires the same rage in him as water in a man with hydrophobia; it is for this reason that pride of birth goes so well with the character of Don Juan. With the idea of the equality of rights disappears that of justice, or, rather, if Don Juan is sprung from an illustrious family, such common ideas have never come to him. I could easily believe that a man with an historic name is sooner disposed than another to set fire to the town in order to get his egg cooked. We must excuse him; he is so possessed with self-love that he comes to the point of losing all idea of the evil he causes, and of seeing no longer anything in the universe capable of joy or sorrow except himself. In the fire of youth, when passion fills our own hearts with the pulse of life and keeps us from mistrust of others, Don Juan, all senses and apparent happiness, applauds himself for thinking only of himself, while he sees other men pay their sacrifices to duty. He imagines that he has found out the great art of living. But, in the midst of his triumph, while still scarcely thirty years of age, he perceives to his astonishment that life is wanting, and feels a growing disgust for what were all his pleasures. Don Juan told me at Thorn, in an access of melancholy: "There are not twenty different sorts of women, and once you have had two or three of each sort, satiety sets in." I answered: "It is only imagination that can for ever escape satiety. Each woman inspires a different interest, and, what is more, if chance throws the same woman in your way two or three years earlier or later in the course of life, and if chance means you to love, you can love the same woman in different manners. But a woman of gentle heart, even when she loved you, would produce in you, because of her pretensions to equality, only irritation to your pride. Your way of having women kills all the other pleasures of life; Werther's increases them a hundredfold."

This sad tragedy reaches the last act. You see Don Juan in old age, turning on this and that, never on himself, as the cause of his own satiety. You see him, tormented by a consuming poison, flying from this to that in a continual change of purpose. But, however brilliant the appearances may be, in the end he only changes one misery for another. He tries the boredom of inaction, he tries the boredom of excitement—there is nothing else for him to choose.

At last he discovers the fatal truth and confesses it to himself; henceforward he is reduced for all his enjoyment to making display of his power, and openly doing evil for evil's sake. In short, 'tis the last degree of settled gloom; no poet has dared give us a faithful picture of it—the picture, if true, would strike horror. But one may hope that a man, above the ordinary, will retrace his steps along this fatal path; for at the bottom of Don Juan's character there is a contradiction. I have supposed him a man of great intellect, and great intellect leads us to the discovery of virtue by the road that runs to the temple of glory.

La Rochefoucauld, who, however, was a master of self-love, and who in real life was nothing but a silly man of letters, says (267): "The pleasure of love consists in loving, and a man gets more happiness from the passion he feels than from the passion he inspires."

Don Juan's happiness consists in vanity, based, it is true, on circumstances brought about by great intelligence and activity; but he must feel that the most inconsiderable general who wins a battle, the most inconsiderable prefect who keeps his department in order, realizes a more signal enjoyment than his own. . . .   (1822)

Extracted from Stendhal, *On Love*, Chapter 59. Translated by Philip Sidney Woolf and Cecil N. Sidney Woolf. New York: Brentano, 1916.

Don Juan as Titan (1829)

Christian Dietrich Grabbe and *Don Juan und Faust*

The figure of Faust had assumed titanic proportions at the same time as that of Don Juan, and in the nineteenth century the two were often juxtaposed, fused, or compared. Both were seen as great rebels and aspirers to that convenient realm known as the Infinite. Faust represented Intellect, and Don Juan the Flesh. Or again, the first was the northern Protestant, and the second the southern Catholic spirit. In a very curious piece of claptrap by one Nicolas Vogt, *Der Farberhof oder die Buchdrückerei in Mainz* (1809), the characters of Faust and Don Juan are fused. Faust the intellectual seeker reappears as Don Juan when his mind turns to the flesh. Characteristically, Vogt's purpose, announced in his preface, was to symbolize nothing less than the struggle between Good and Evil, Heaven and Hell, and Christianity and Paganism.

One of the more interesting pieces of grandiose pessimism of that time is undoubtedly Grabbe's *Don Juan und Faust,* given here in its first English translation. Grabbe was another of the many troubled, unbalanced and short-lived wits of the epoch, an angular personage with a genius for quarreling with everybody and an approach to reality as bizarre and tormented as that of Emily Brontë. This lonely offspring of kindly burghers saw the light in Detmold (Westphalia) in 1801. Like so many other writers, he studied and practiced law, and had something of a mediocre career in the civil service. Heine, Tieck, and Immermann were among his admirers and supporters, but he managed to quarrel with all three, and with his wife besides. When, in 1836, he returned to Detmold to die—after unhappy residences in several cities —he had to call on the authorities to gain admittance to his own house. His plays had found publishers, however, and the reviewers had praised them, though they recognized his "baroque" manner and expressed their wonder at it. He remains as one of the important German play-wrights of his time, alongside Büchner, Kleist, and Hebbel.

Grabbe's play falls on the reader like an avalanche. A kind of over-loaded rage pervades it. Farce, philosophy, Gothic romance, heroic drama, comic intrigue, melodrama—nothing is missing except meas-ure. No work better exemplifies the Romantic need to break through limits, and the Romantic disdain for regular form. The passions are titanic—and the lapses funny. "Sublime and trivial," Farinelli calls the play; and Grillparzer remarked that Grabbe had sovereign genius, but small talent. There is, in fact, a real impatience with mere talent in this play. Grabbe must push to the extreme of every situation, not minding the sense and the decencies and the harmonies which he topples on the way.

His pessimism is dynamic, unlike that of twentieth-century writers. Faust and Don Juan are both cold scoundrels—the whole play is as cold as it is magniloquent—but even though Anna, Octavio, and the Governor presumably ascend to Heaven, this is patently no assurance that they are right and the scoundrels wrong. Heaven is for philistines, and Hell is the site for a Byronic Satan, still challenging the dull forces of Jehovah. But Grabbe is not so simple. With him we feel there is no affirmation of any kind, unless it be the affirmation of license. He is, in a sense, the Shadwell of Romanticism, although his Don Juan differs from the Romantic type in that he thoroughly enjoys himself. He enjoys his murders and his seductions; he enjoys bad weather and defeat; and when he hears that Anna is dead, he enjoys the prospect of new adventures. Grabbe has bestowed the temper of Romantic dissatisfaction on Don Juan's alter ego, Faust. Faust is the aspirer; Don Juan is the enjoyer. The first strives and is miserable; the latter accepts whatever happens and is happy. Why then does the Devil assert at the end that the two strove for the same goal? He can mean only that they both sought their own pleasure; for Grabbe has made it plain that the Commander's honor, Anna's love, Faust's knowledge, and Don Juan's sensuality are all modes—and ethi-cally equivalent modes—of pleasure.

For all its magical hocus-pocus, its facile imagery of lightning, fire, eagles, and ice, its curses, its castles on Mont Blanc, and its unbridled passions, the play is oddly modern, chiefly because of its nihilism. There is no moral anchorage here for the "decent reader." Anna's love, hatred and virtue (Grabbe used Hoffmann's suggestion that Anna has been bewitched by Don Juan) are as unappealing as Faust's barren rage against everything or Don Juan's impudent criminality. The play is, therefore, utterly unsentimental. It blames no one, accuses no one, and likes no one. No one is converted to another viewpoint. "Mit Donnerstimme geb' ich die Antwort: Nein!"—*"I give the answer with a voice of thunder: No!"*—seems to be Grabbe's own final answer to the universe.

CHRISTIAN DIETRICH GRABBE

Don Juan and Faust

A Tragedy in Four Acts

(1829)

Translated by Maurice Edwards

TEXT

Christian Dietrich Grabbe: Werke, vol. I. Edited by A. Bergmann.
Göttinger Akademie Ausgabe. Emsdetten: Verlag Lechte, 1960.

Dramatis Personae

The Governor, *Don Gusman*
Donna Anna, *his daughter*
Don Octavio
Don Juan, *a Spanish grandee*
Doctor Faust
A Knight
Signor Rubio, *Chief of Police*

Signor Negro
Leporello, *Don Juan's servant*
Lisette, *Donna Anna's maid*
Gasparo, *the Governor's aide*
A Priest
First Gnome
Second Gnome

Guests, servants, policemen, gnomes, and devils

Synopsis of Scenes

Act I

1. Vicinity of the Piazza di Spagna, Rome.
2. Dr. Faust's study on the Aventine Hill, Rome.

Act II

1. The garden of the Governor's residence, Rome.
2. Salon in the Governor's residence.

Act III

1. Square before one of Rome's northern gates.
2. A chamber in Faust's Magic Castle on the peak of Mont Blanc.
3. A wild region on Mont Blanc.

Act IV

1. A graveyard near Rome.
2. Mine shafts under Mont Blanc.
3. A room in Faust's Magic Castle.
4. A hall in Don Juan's residence, Rome.

333

ACT I

Scene 1

Rome. Vicinity of the Piazza di Spagna. DON JUAN *enters with* LEPORELLO *right on his heels.*

DON JUAN: The plazas and the streets are still; only the fountains splash and dawdle in the dark. Rome, eternal Rome, sleeps, worn out by a thousand years of strife. Or is it perhaps from the burden of her fame? Poor Empress of the World! She has never known love. [*Stepping out further*] Oh, what a breeze! How fresh it blows from Alba's hills: the very air that Caesar breathed; the air, the very atmosphere my beloved breathes today!

LEPORELLO: Correction, sir, if you please: it's the reek from the nearby chophouse, where a gang of lusty fellows are making merry. That's what tickles our nose.

DON JUAN: Oh, it's you, Leporello! Well, what did you find out?

LEPORELLO: The girl is the genuine article, all right. Good enough to add to your collection.

DON JUAN: She is dazzling—a magnificent specimen!

LEPORELLO: Don, I'm spellbound; I saw her in the flesh!

DON JUAN: Quick, then, tell me, how does she move? And what about her figure?

LEPORELLO: What do you mean? Haven't you seen her yourself?

DON JUAN: I have spoken with her—yes. Of course I've seen her. But I was blinded by her eyes.

LEPORELLO: Yes, by heaven, they *are* beautiful; but so is everything else about her.

DON JUAN: She's the brightest star in the sky—by Jove, the steady North Star. From this moment on, she—and she alone—will light my life.

LEPORELLO: You mean she alone and about two thousand others, don't you?

DON JUAN: This love is different, entirely different.

LEPORELLO: To how many hundred have you said that already?

DON JUAN: What did you find out about her father?

LEPORELLO: He's the Governor of Seville, the conqueror of Granada's

Moorish hordes, now assigned to Rome as Spanish ambassador to the Vatican.

DON JUAN: A Spaniard! Then we're compatriots, she and I.

LEPORELLO: The father, sir, is old and very strict.

DON JUAN: So—my golden fruit has ripened on an old stem.

LEPORELLO: The stem is indeed remarkable: the fruit hangs high.

DON JUAN: The nearer the sun, the riper the fruit; and what is ripe, falls. I'll have her no later than tomorrow night!

LEPORELLO: What about her fiancé?

DON JUAN: Her fiancé? Nonsense! I've no use for that word. A booby who amuses himself with courtship and marriage, not knowing he'll be cuckolded by the first gallant who comes along. Who is he?

LEPORELLO: The Governor's nephew. His name is Don Octavio. A handsome gentleman and well turned out; his heart's in the right place, too. He wears kid gloves—

DON JUAN: —leads a moderate life, gives no offense, dances well, rides passably, speaks French, moves in the best circles, and may even spell correctly. I like nothing better than to lock horns with such rogues.

LEPORELLO: Me, too. A scoundrel of a correct speller who insists on kissing my girl correctly, deceives himself, the girl, and me as well. Only crooked paths make the goal worthwhile.

DON JUAN: Hush—the goal! Don't spell it out for me, even though I strive for it. Curse the very thought. To reach the goal is the death of desire. Happy he who strives forever; yes, hail to him who hungers eternally!

LEPORELLO: Thanks. I realize you starve me on principle. If only my stomach could stand it! But no, it continues to cry out: "Hail to him who's forever gobbling something down!"

DON JUAN: I burn with impatience. Here we are at the Governor's residence—where she must live. Let's make a disturbance. The din and clamor will lure her to the window.

[He draws his sword.]

LEPORELLO: Holy Jacob, his sword! I'm clearing out.

DON JUAN: Coward, it's only make-believe! I won't harm you. . . . Draw! . . . Draw, I say, or I'll pin you to the ground like a worm.

LEPORELLO: Christ! Help! I'm lost! He doesn't joke with the sword. The clang of steel makes him rage like a wolf at the scent of blood. I have no choice but to defend myself.

DON JUAN: Excellent! Bravo, friend Leporello! . . . Oh, how bold! It must be the effect of Roman soil. True mother of heroes, she makes a new man of you; she bears you for the second time. . . . Now off with you! Call out: *Guards, Murderers, Assault, Treason!* And to make it sound more natural, take this slight wound on your arm. . . . But don't run too far, or you won't hear when I call you later.

LEPORELLO: The deuce! My arm—I'm dying! Guards! Guards! Help!

DON JUAN: Ho! Help! Save me! Catch the bandit!

[LEPORELLO *exits. Tumult in the Governor's palace.*]

GOVERNOR [*from within*]: Lights! To arms! Follow me, Don Octavio!

DON OCTAVIO [*within*]: I'm at your service, with my life and all I own!

DON JUAN [*to himself*]: If that were so, you wouldn't say it. Such braggadocio! . . . The time draws near when War and Peace, Love and Luck, God and Faith will all be empty words, mere shells of what they were. Then, most respectfully, we'll give the beggar a kick in the pants, and most humbly demand a glass of water for the servant.

[*In the window of the Governor's palace a maid appears with lights; then* DONNA ANNA, *who peers out searchingly for a moment.*]

DON JUAN [*seeing Donna Anna*]: Ha, like a golden eagle a flash of lightning bolts free from the summit of the nocturnal heavens; before it, a forest of oak crumbles to dust, flaming up in blissful annihilation. So, too, woman, do I sink at your feet, yet exult aloud in my love for you! [DONNA ANNA *angrily motions him away and disappears.*] Pshaw! You dismiss me in vain. I will reach you even if I have to step over corpses and wade through your father's blood. [*The* GOVERNOR, DON OCTAVIO, *and a valet carrying lights emerge from the palace.*]

GOVERNOR: Uproar and commotion under my daughter's window! Death to the man who dares! Find him!

DON OCTAVIO: I beg you to be calm, Governor; we're in a foreign land.

GOVERNOR: I'm the ambassador here and exercise my own jurisdiction. Wherever I step is Spanish ground; wherever I breathe, Spanish air. And now that my honor has been wantonly injured, should I stand calmly by without punishing the culprit?

DON OCTAVIO: Just a little noise—God knows where it came from— does not compromise the honor of my bride.

GOVERNOR: What are you saying, my boy? Honor is my eye: the most minute speck of dust that invades it blinds me with rage and pain.

DON OCTAVIO: But the culprit has escaped already.

GOVERNOR: Then let's look for him!

DON JUAN [*stepping out*]: That won't be necessary. I know where he lodges.

GOVERNOR: Who are you? Speak.

DON JUAN: I am a Spanish grandee. My name is Don Juan.

GOVERNOR: The Don Juan who fought and won for the King on the Guadiana?

DON JUAN: He stands before you.

GOVERNOR: Give me your hand! Whoever fights for the King is my brother.

DON JUAN: Sir, I understand: you are a true compatriot. [*Aside.*] I'll win him over with patriotic phrases—the more so since I mean them in all sincerity. [*Aloud.*] Greetings in this foreign land. I breathe easier wherever Spain is mentioned. No thunder in heaven, no sound on earth, even from the sweetest, most beautiful lips, can equal the power of the word *Fatherland!* It has stirred my heart in battle far more than the boldest trumpet blast. At its ringing tone, Hispania, with her high mountains and streams, her heroes and heroes' graves, rises in the morning light out of the dark sea. Contemptible is individual pride, but glorious as only the Fatherland itself can be is pride in the Fatherland.

DON OCTAVIO: Your words don't quite match your actions. I've already heard much about you. You are more often crowned with the roses of love than with oak leaves.

DON JUAN [*to himself*]: Has he noticed anything? Is he jealous? A jealous man neither loves nor is loved. My hopes rise! [*Aloud.*] Friend, first learn the old motto: *King and Glory, Fatherland and Love!* Love and desire budding in the heart are like a stale, flat drink if these four words do not blaze together in one crown of flame.

DON OCTAVIO: You forgot one word: *Fidelity!*

DON JUAN: I am no slave. Who wants to wear chains?

GOVERNOR: Enough. The man who loves King and Glory cannot abandon them, for there is nothing higher in the world. Now tell me: what villain raised such a commotion here—and, if I'm not mistaken, called out for my daughter?

DON JUAN: Are you not aware that a great wizard from the icy wastes of northern Germany now lives in Rome and poisons the very air? He skulks about the Aventine in a black cloak, his white face never reddened by the sun. The guards try to capture him—but in vain. Helped by spirits, he always manages to slip away.

GOVERNOR: You mean Dr. Faust?

DON JUAN: Like a hawk he draws magic circles around your daughter. It was he who tried to lure her with exorcisms and entreaties to the balcony today. Yet steel and manly courage are stronger than magic. My sword showed him the way!

GOVERNOR: I thank you. But know this: neither sorcery nor steel endangers or protects Donna Anna's honor. Honor treads its own path in spite of all the whirling of magic circles and brandishing of swords. Death means less to her than Honor. Honor only knows how to conquer or die; so, too, my daughter! Poor fellow, this Faust, who strives with the impotent arts of Hell to win the pure heart of Donna Anna. Not all the magic of Heaven would bedazzle it; for Heaven knows no spot more beautiful than her childlike heart.

DON JUAN [to himself]: Unwittingly, the father fans my passion to a white heat. How divine to triumph over such a woman! Worlds may spin, abandoned and soulless, through empty space, yet where beats a feeling heart, worlds stir, and stars, the sun and moon, the red of the morning dawn, the fading glow of evening, embrace one another in the tightest of circles with all the pain and joy of love. He who conquers a heart is greater than any world conqueror!

GOVERNOR: Octavio, the sorcerer must be caught and burned at the stake. [To Don Juan] Will you accompany us, sir?

DON JUAN: Impossible, sir; my house is empty and unguarded. I must go there first. But do you want me to call out the guard for you on my way?

GOVERNOR: Yes, thank you; and perhaps you will honor me by accepting an invitation to my daughter's marriage to Don Octavio tomorrow?

DON JUAN: You can count on me.

DON OCTAVIO: We shall be greatly honored.

DON JUAN: Sir—the honor is all mine.

GOVERNOR: Farewell until then.

DON JUAN [to himself]: Go to the Devil, you fools! [GOVERNOR and DON OCTAVIO exit.] Talk and more talk—idle as empty air. When I kiss my lady, I'll know silent bliss. And yet, I too exclaim and lament like a wind-tossed tree! But I'm glad I managed to bait those two fools into hounding Faust—Faust, that prince of melancholy who would go to Hell rather than know the heaven of Donna Anna's beauty!

Now let Faust prove whether he can conjure or not! As for myself, I favor reality. The Governor and Octavio are gone. The house is open. And victory is mine. [*He tries to open the door to the house, but finds it locked.*] Damn it! Those sly dogs were on the alert: the door is locked tight. . . . Never mind, I stick to my goal: as long as there is one goal, a thousand paths lead to it. . . . Hey, Leporello! Leporello!

[LEPORELLO *enters.*]

LEPORELLO: My arm! Oh, my arm! The surgeon's head drooped like a weeping willow when he saw it. He put his finger to his nose and rattled off something about scruples, scrofula and cachexia. In short, you've made me a cripple for life. A nice reward for my faithful services. Oh, the way of the world!

DON JUAN: Quiet, I warn you. Or else a second wound will help you forget the first. Do you know Donna Anna's maid?

LEPORELLO: Sir, whom do you take me for? I should know a servant? And this one in particular?

DON JUAN: Don't be ridiculous! You've been sneaking about this house on my orders for the last three days. How could you have overlooked the maid—the one who lit Anna's way to the window? She has black eyes, dimpled cheeks, a white complexion, full, tender, round arms, and a narrow waistline. Nobody can deny her that.

LEPORELLO: And you saw all that while Anna's lightning beauty bolted down upon you like an eagle from the sky—as you have just re- ported?

DON JUAN: Why not? After all, the maid stood right next to her.

LEPORELLO: You are a universal genius! To love the mistress and be charmed by the maid—and all that, helter-skelter, in one and the same moment. My head swims.

DON JUAN: Do you take me for a silly pedant fettered by systems? I value beauty wherever I find it and whatever its brand. The maid makes love one way, her mistress another. Only variety lends spice to life and helps us forget how unbearable it is. Tell me, where is the girl's room?

LEPORELLO: It would be a sin for me to let you in on that! The angel lives on the ground floor. Oh, may all the devils guard her; for you have no fear of angels whatsoever!

DON JUAN: Hurry to the chamber window. Try to finagle from her where we could meet Donna Anna outside the palace tomorrow.

LEPORELLO: You expect me to do that in the middle of the night?

DON JUAN: Yes, that's what I want; it's so romantic. What's more, I don't like waiting. Wake her up like a fondly caressing lover. What could be sweeter for a girl than to be awakened by flattery? Like spring, it makes even old women bloom again.

LEPORELLO: Well, I'll try. I'll sing her a song—something that would melt the heart of a bear and make hibernating badgers' ears point heavenward like village spires.

DON JUAN: Warble as softly as you can.

LEPORELLO: Don't worry. Just listen. It's an old song, a rare song, which a rejected lover after many a long sigh finally poured forth on a summer's night.

[Sings]

> A bug sat on a fence—zum, zum
> A fly sat snug below—buzz, buzz
> "Fly, if you'll marry me—zum, zum
> "I'll give you a guinea, oh!"—buzz, buzz.

DON JUAN: Hush. Be reasonable!

LEPORELLO: Reasonable? Then I'll have to resort to talk, because singsong always winds up unreasonably! [Whispering into the window] Sleeping already, little Lisette? . . . Not a word? . . . Oh, so you're not asleep yet? Just peeved? My little ermine, my little doll, how can you be peeved with me? [To Don Juan] The cussed little rat's not asleep or she'd have woken up long ago and answered me. She's awake; she's teasing me with her silence.

DON JUAN: How do you know her name?

LEPORELLO: Her name? Why, I read it from her figure and her physiognomy. Sir, a person looks just like his name. You can't imagine what the sound of a name does to me— Amelias are tall and full of ardor; Carolines robust and cunning, Julias snug and lively; Wilhelminas and Christinas have the feel of used coins, and look shabby, thin, and pale; the Augustas generally turn out to be brunettes— Oh, sir, if I'm a child of misfortune, it's because my parents baptised me Leporello. [At the window, again] Lisette! Most beautiful of maidens! Most beloved! Just one syllable, please. I can't sleep, I can't eat. Your beauty, your virtue, move me to tears.

DON JUAN: Like onions!

LEPORELLO: What is your mistress compared to you? A paltry, wretched thing, a mere worm.

DON JUAN: Scoundrel!

LEPORELLO: Hush, watch now! This will do the trick; this is something she'll believe.

DON JUAN: You're right--girls treat belief as the rich do food. They eat only what they like.

LISETTE [inside]: Fie! Shame on you! Who's that rowdy brawler out there? Will the scoundrel never stop?

LEPORELLO: Do you hear that? "Will the scoundrel never stop!" She's been listening for some time now!

DON JUAN: She scolds! And scolding is the siren of courtesans.

LEPORELLO: You know the routine; so do I, to some extent. [Pulling a ring from his finger] See! In a girl's eyes, such a ring is as good as squaring a circle; the true magic ring. Good girls give up their innocence three times just to gain one husband.

DON JUAN: Let noblemen henceforth be advised to wear the wedding ring in their nose instead of on their finger.

LEPORELLO [at the window]: Dearest Lisette, don't you know me. I've brought your wedding ring; and tomorrow I shall lead you to the altar.

DON JUAN: They used to lead calves and sheep to the altar for slaughter; now they lead girls to the altar for marriage. Nothing new under the sun!

LISETTE: Count Leporello—

DON JUAN: What's that, scoundrel? You're passing yourself off as a count?

LEPORELLO: Si, Signore—I always make love as a count.

LISETTE: Count Leporello, don't deceive a poor girl. Mind you, be on your guard; poor as I am, I'm still a woman of Rome. By the Holy Virgin, I'll kill you if you betray me! Wait! I'm coming. Where's the ring?

LEPORELLO: Here, my sweetheart! Take it. My love is as true and genuine as its gold! [To Don Juan] Never fear, sir, it's only copper and worth six pennies. However, I'll ask you to repay me that tomorrow.

LISETTE [taking the ring]: Yes, Count, I have put on this pledge of your faithfulness—and with it, I follow you to the grave!

LEPORELLO: Now you're mine. O happy Fate! Oh, mother! I see her frowning down on this misalliance; poor woman, the pain will kill her. But let the whole world collapse—though I'm sure it won't—what do I care if only I possess you! . . . By the way, where would I have the best chance of running into Donna Anna tomorrow? I have to speak with her on your behalf.

LISETTE: Donna Anna will be taking a walk tomorrow in her father's garden.

LEPORELLO: And where is that?

LISETTE: To the east, by the Tiber Gate.

LEPORELLO: Enough. Just one farewell kiss, most gracious one.

LISETTE: You're leaving me already, unfaithful man?

LEPORELLO: Only until tomorrow, my sweet idol. Then I'll come with horses and carriage and lead you to the Ebro, where my castle towers high into the azure sky.

LISETTE: Come, take this kiss, and forget me not.

DON JUAN: Step back! Who dares kiss in my presence?

LEPORELLO: Oh, sir—

DON JUAN: By your life, be still. The kiss is the one dish I can never have too much of; taken in my presence, it's like snatching food right out of my mouth.

LISETTE: Count, oh my Count, where are you? Oh, heavens! He's leaving me, disdaining the kiss I offer him. May he be struck down by a thunderbolt! I'll slam my window tight.

DON JUAN [to Leporello]: You know how to take the thunderclap of that slammed window, I'm sure. And now, Night before us—until Aurora blushes with shame that Donna Anna is so much more beautiful than she! . . . Leporello, ask Count Lucar and Count Sanvitale to come and see me.

LEPORELLO: For a little game, you mean?

DON JUAN: Yes, my good fellow, and for wine. To gamble all on just one card, one little scrap of paper—your money, your life poised in mid-air, exposed to the storm of fate—that's what I call a lovely pastime! Even if everything blows up, the stake was worth just this venture. *Va banque** with tomfoolery!

LEPORELLO: You haven't slept for two nights.

DON JUAN: Fie, fie on sleep; time unslept, I call time won back from death. Eyes ever open, like never-tiring suns!
[He exits.]

LEPORELLO: This man is insatiable in pleasure. And, to tell the truth, if I had his rank and his riches, I'd be twice as bad as he—or worse! Now, to Sanvitale!
[He exits.]

*Gambling expression: *to stake everything on.* [Translator's note.]

Scene 2

Rome. Dr. Faust's study on the Aventine. A burning light. FAUST *is seated at his writing desk.*

FAUST [*getting up from his desk*]: Ominous night, will you never end? . . . Alas, night has just begun. Not quite eleven. So back to work.

To work! To study! Misery and shame!

Deadly thirst, never quenched! Piling grains of sand, one upon another, surrounding oneself with boundless wastes and deserts; and then to lie in wait, parched, hungering, and doubting! . . . Ha, man turns into a beast of prey simply to sustain himself. He seizes upon feelings, thoughts . . . hearts, souls . . . people and life . . . worlds and gods . . . strangling his prey, yelling in hunger and rage when there are scarcely ten drops of blood left in their veins.

Who has ever labored like me? Where is the path of art and science I have not trodden? But I push on further than all the others; more boldly, I dare say, than those who turn back at the first milestone, filled with the wonders of their journey, and pass themselves off boastfully as learned savants—self-satisfied fools preening before the still greater fools who stare at them in astonishment.

But *I* have wandered on, leaving the sun behind; and only at times have I felt its clouded gaze trailing me through the mist, like a mother's eyes reddened with weeping. Out with the sun! I sought a more beautiful light! And look, there is the goal: the abyss into which streams of thought and feeling foam and roar without return, and in whose fumes and vapors the Hydra of Doubt, flaming with scarlet, venomous tongue, twists and turns and feeds!

Golgotha,

you mound of skulls where the Light of the World gave itself up to the night of Death that it might be transfigured! Not even *your* light reaches anything here!

You great book, you Bible—Rock of Faith, they say—burdened with variants and double meanings, full of wisdom and strange aphorisms: your leaves offer no refuge in this raging storm; parched and withered, they fall like foliage in autumn; for, if I do not feel it within myself, not a thousand Bibles, not a thousand Paradises, not all the Eternities can lead me to salvation!

Oh, what a script of flame burns in my head:

You can believe nothing until you *know* it;
you can know nothing until you *believe* it!

There's no earthly spirit who divines this riddle and does not sigh
for its solution—and none who has found it. Blessed be those who,
blinded by the sheen of appearance, are weak enough to mistake
that sheen for light—who blindly believe because blindly they hope.
The sleep-drugged souls! . . . Yet I would rather bleed under torture
than rejoice in stupidity. This planet earth, this soil which bore
me and in which I must take root—I am a ripped-out, withered tree,
if in your very marrow I cannot sink my being and draw power and
joy from you—and if, uprooted, I throw myself into that blue abyss
which yawns over our heads, driven by the bigoted hope of finding
something in that barren waste, distant and infinite, which I do
not find in this close, finite spot of earth!

 Close!

What is closer to me than my native land? Only the Fatherland can
make us happy: treason to prefer the foreign! I would not be Faust
were I not a German! O Germany! Land of my fathers! I weep to
think of you. No country is more magnificent; no people mightier,
nobler. Proud and strong, crowned with green grapes, the Rhine
makes a resolute stand against its undeserved dissolution in the sands
of the Netherlands. Bold and jubilant, the Danube plunges into
being at its very source. Innumerable German veins throb and flow,
proud and bold as German streams! . . . Look: high over Tyrol's
ice-capped mountains, the eagle rises sunward as if his native eyrie
were there. Under his glance the mountains shrink to dots of dust;
and still lower, in Tyrol's cramped, narrow valleys, many a heart
soars far higher for Emperor and for Honor than the eagle dares
ascend.

 Even this Rome:

who broke this cage in which the nations learned to conquer first
the Roman, then the popish way? Ah, here the victorious banners of
Alaric the Goth, Charlemagne the Frank, and the Hohenstaufens
rustled in the wind, caressed by the hot wind which slew kings in
bygone days. Here the dome of St. Peter's vaults heavenward to
capture man's glimpse into Eternity—yet disgracefully cracked now
by the thunderous voice resounding over the Alps from Wittenberg,
my native city, from the mouth of Luther, the greatest of my contemporaries.

 And yet—oh, yet—Luther! You, too! You banished an illusion, you
pulverized it like lightning; only you failed to give us something in
its place, something lasting, reassuring—Truth. The gulf gapes wider
than ever before the disappointed eye. To wreck and then to build

another heap of ruins upon these ruins—*that* man is able to do, that he can do, indefatigably carrying baskets and pails, setting stone upon stone, pouring drop upon drop. That he calls Art and Science! God creates out of nothing, man out of ruins. We must break our-ourselves to pieces before we know what we are, what we can be and do! Horrible Fate!

Yet, so it is!

It is my lot, too, and I follow my stars.

Germany! Fatherland!

You are the heart of Europe, torn asunder as only a heart can be—and I couldn't even die fighting for you on the battlefield.

Oh, Rome! I fled to you in order to embrace within myself all the joys and woes of mankind, and to satisfy my thirst in this fulfillment. For you, Rome, are the broken mirror of the all-encompassing past; and the deeper one peers within, the more fragmented heroic images, sparkling in the gloss of the blood of nations and their peoples, emerge as stars do out of the deep night. You are the city where millennia fuse into one moment: the Pope on the Capitol; and yesteryear's ivy on the Pantheon!

Rome, Empress of the World! Woe, thrice woe to him who comes to you like myself to be exalted! All empires sank to dust before you. Why? Nobody knows. You were not better than they. And after your sword had won the world, you fell too, taking all with you into the dark night of barbarity. Out of this issued a *new* blood, a *new* light; you have battled and killed in vain. Only the clatter of the mind's burst fetters—fetters which had wound round half of Europe—still lingers on in the tongues of France, Spain, and Italy!

Had all this slaughter and destruction of peoples no other purpose than to serve as a didactic fairy tale? Does the individual *historical event* signify less than the idea of *world history*? Then woe to us! History has never improved mankind. In the midst of the lava of destruction, only a Don Juan can revel in a million flowers without reflecting that though they are a multitude all are fleeting—that only distraction, rather than security and peace, may be found where the One, the Everlasting, does not bloom!

Then, let it be! I can bear it no longer! I sought God, but find myself at the Gate of Hell. Yet I can still go on, plunge deeper, even be engulfed in flames—but I must have an aim, an ultimate goal. If there is a road to Heaven, it must lead through Hell—at least for me!

Well, then—I dare risk it!

I did not master the magic for uprooting this globe and extinguishing the stars—though not my doubts—that it should grow stale as unused theory. . . . Aha, there lies my Master of Hell conjuring book—no Master of Hearts, alas!

[*Roaring wind behind the scene.* FAUST *steps toward the window.*]

Do you feel what I am about to undertake, you elements? Pale shines the moon, and the clouds flee fearfully beneath it. [*He steps back again and takes the Master of Hell folio bound with chains out of the locked chest and places it on the table.*] Let them flee! I open the Book of the Deep. . . . [*The instant he opens the folio, the candle on his table is extinguished.*]

What's that? The earthly light snuffed out? Much I care. Countless nights of standing over the lectern did nothing to enlighten me. I summon to my service another eternal light out of this Pit, which even the midday sun never penetrates. Emerge and light my way!

[*A red-glowing flame rises on the spot where Faust's light was put out and illuminates him during the entire scene that follows.* FAUST *grasps his forehead as if faint.*]

Oh, sparks of hell! Am I lost?

Courage! Courage! Forward! [*Looking into the Master of Hell folio*] What strange symbols. I myself traced those characters—and now . . . Curses! Only after having done the deed does the man know what he's done, and the Devil's hands more often than not invisibly played their part in it! [*Again lost in perusal of the book*] Here it twists, writhing like fabled dragons—sulphurous glow flicking in between.

Oh, disaster and despair! What are tigers?

What are crocodiles? Nothing! Nothing! A farce compared to this! . . . I'm enveloped by vapors—vapors no mortal soul can bear.

[*Turning vehemently from the book and staring into the void*]

I see them: the Gates of Hell!

Burnished brass, burning hot

from the fire that glows behind them,

red as the glowing overpainted cheeks of virgins and whores!

All the same!

Woe to him who looks back!

I knock though the earth should yawn and swallow me.

Adieu, you angels, dear children, good night!

Away with the hopeful dreams with which you deceived me so bitterly.

Oh, to awaken and *know* that I am awake: that is what I want
though it take the sting of Hell to do it. [*Solemnly, hand laid on
the Master of Hell folio*]

   Satan! By that name which belongs to you alone,
which makes even you blanch,
which roars eternally in your heart,
which no man has ever heard,
which is greater than you who bear it,
which stands here inscribed—
I invoke you: appear, appear, and serve me!
[*Staring again into the void*]
Aha! The Gates of Horror cleave and open:
the clatter, the clanking!
A river of flame spurts down my chest . . .
wretched flames: are you God's punishment?
Oh, my own breast burns hotter than you!

   Yet look: Here it comes!
A yellow-eyed snake moving toward me . . . scaly . . . lashing Tartarus
and the stars with its tail . . . the air is stifling me. . . . I can't breathe
. . . already the monster clutches my house, separating me from the
world like the arm of the sea severing the distant outlying island
from the mainland.
[*The bell tolls midnight.* FAUST *listens.*]
Woe is me: that was the last bell from the high tower, calling out
to me from the circle of mankind! It has struck: the last hour I lived
as a man among men!
[*Three strong knocks on the door, each accompanied by a violent
clap of thunder.*]
Listen! Those are the strokes of the bell I shall hear henceforth.
. . . The fiend nears! And I do not call for help. Rather unconscious-
ness and death than fear! . . . Come in!
[FAUST *drops unconscious into a chair. A* KNIGHT *enters. Middle-
aged, of pale countenance, he is dressed in a sixteenth-century cos-
tume—all in black, however.*]
KNIGHT: What is this? The proud summoner falls unconscious when
   we approach? So much hullabaloo and so little boldness. [*Shaking*
   FAUST] Wake up, dog!
FAUST [*lifting himself out of the stupor*]: Who—who calls me dog? . . .
   You? Viper! Tremble at the feet of your lord and master.

KNIGHT: Lord? Lord, just now you lay before your slave in a deep faint.

FAUST: Once; but never again. Only the body was weak, not the spirit. The shape you took was too horrible to bear.

KNIGHT: Nonsense! What sees is not the eye but the spirit behind it. Don't use your pure, spiritual inner vision as an excuse for your frailty.

FAUST: Then where is the dichotomy of body and spirit?

KNIGHT: Before answering, I must know why you summoned me. And under what conditions.

FAUST: The man who bargains with the Devil will be cheated.

KNIGHT: Even the wise Faust?

FAUST: He'll take the risk.

KNIGHT: Good. By grasping the near you reach the distant. Here, take my hand. . . . Don't shrink back; you've nothing to be afraid of. You're not His creature. This hand fought Him once, and will continue to spar with Him until He masters me or I master Him!

FAUST: You braggart! You were beaten long ago.

KNIGHT: Beaten? Aha, blasphemer—[*Again, cold and calm*] Yes, we fell; chance often decides the outcome of battles. Cunning overcame us, too. *He* wanted to rule; I, his equal, also wanted to rule. But I was candid about it and he hypocritical. *He* called the chains "Love"; and lo and behold, fools everywhere heard the sound of the word and not the rattle of chains.

Yet Night is inexhaustible, while Light needs nourishment and is easily extinguished for lack of it. Stars and suns burn out, love satiates itself, while the old darkness in which we envelop the world as far as it extends breaks through wherever a crack appears. Even now we attack and *He* must defend himself again! Our throne stands close to Heaven—not a hand's breadth away. . . . Show me the heart, no matter how stuffed with edifying catechisms, that deep down doesn't reserve just a little corner for us.

FAUST: You talk of Darkness but I want Light!

KNIGHT: Now, Doctor, doesn't Night give birth to Light? Don't you see me standing here because the glow which colors your horizon is merely illusion on a black foil? Don't you want to find those veins of lava which run in the deepest of Nights, inflaming and also enchanting All?

FAUST: Oh, what ecstasy, what delight! If I could feel you, deepest pulse of Nature!

KNIGHT: You *shall* feel it, Doctor . . . [*To himself*] if you don't scorch your finger in the act.

FAUST: Chanced and won! Eternities gambled away for moments! Better ready cash than dubious mortgages on the future! You are *mine* in this life; I am *yours* in death. But in exchange I demand the total power that dwells within you as a Seraph. I demand that you bear me on your mighty wings from the Borders of Knowledge to the Kingdom of Belief; that you help me to understand the World and Mankind, to decipher the essence of their Being and their Purpose; that you try to show me—though only for the sake of theory, and though by the light of Hell's flames—the path by which I might have found Peace and Happiness!

KNIGHT: A bagatelle! A great big bagatelle!

FAUST [*to himself*]: Equivocator! [*Aloud.*] A bagatelle—but why a big one?

KNIGHT: I must first ask for a few drops of blood—we are, after all, on intimate enough terms for that—to sign the pact. Here is pen and paper.

FAUST: Everything ready? So much caution and foresight.

KNIGHT [*to himself*]: So much the less hindsight.

[FAUST *cuts his hand and signs the paper with his blood. Then he returns the pact to the Knight.*]

FAUST: Here—take the ridiculous formality away.

KNIGHT [*to himself*]: He is mine! [*Aloud.*] Now you must—

FAUST: *Must?* Slave, why so impudent with me? What *must* I? Who gives *me* orders?

KNIGHT: Doctor . . . Master . . . I grovel before you in the dust.

FAUST: Lie there and tremble. [*To himself*] Aha, the Snake! He coils as if to strike. How terrifying when his time will come.

KNIGHT: My dear Doctor, do you wish to know what happiness is? Happiness is the modesty of the worm which crawls no further than its power permits. It is happiness always to gratify the appetite—like Don Juan, from whom you may learn much—and still not upset the stomach. But it's your misfortune that your spirit is too weak to digest good, solid earthly food and begins to snap up airy visions.

FAUST: It's lucky for you, Sir Knight, that you lie there so miserable on the floor before me, otherwise I'd whip you for this drivel. Wretched fool, I've tested long ago what you've just described. What do you take me for? Oh, well I know: Hell is the best preacher of Christianity: people fear it! Yet only the proud Devil himself could expect to terrify Faust before whom he now whimpers.

KNIGHT: Whimpers! One also whimpers for revenge! Oh, you hands: stretch out and seize him! Claw his breast!

FAUST: Silence! Don't threaten me with your paws; I might slap them. I'm still master here. Fulfill the pact!

KNIGHT [*raising himself*]: Easily done. You haven't far to fly. You want to believe? You wish to love? Well, then, fall in love with Donna Anna, the most beautiful woman ever to walk in Rome! Then you'll experience all you want together, for he who falls in love, sighs and hopes, believes and exults!

FAUST: Did I snatch you away from the sulphurous pool just to conjure myself into the magic circle of a girl? To loosen pins instead of the bolts which lock away the secrets of the universe?

KNIGHT: The hour will come when the brooch on Donna Anna's bosom will hold far more for you than all the world can offer.

FAUST: Let's away now! The world thoroughly explored from start to finish! High above the mountain peak, strewn with dust from suns as from flakes of snow, rises the sky. Dark and ever darker, the gulf opens up below: a black, dank eye spies and threatens with hidden malice—

KNIGHT: So it does—and you tremble?

FAUST: Why tremble? Joy beats in my heart. Take me down to Hell, then back to the heights of the constellations. If depth has a firm base, my foot shall tread it; if height offers an open view, my eye shall revel in it!

KNIGHT: Right! I only fear your foot may falter on the bottom of the deep and your eye may grow giddy from the view on high.

FAUST: Who wanted to show me the pulse of Nature just now?

KNIGHT: Doctor, it was I! But remember, little man, only in passing can you bear the view of Nature unveiled. If suddenly you should wander out alone where suns fly, comets blaze, and the Milky Way flares up to the throne of the Sovereign of Spirits, you'll behave exactly—if I may be allowed to say so—like a cat in the rain. You'll scurry frantically for shelter! And I will pity you.

FAUST: I've crept through the dust of books without being stifled: I breathe freely in the glow of the firmament! So spare me your sympathy. I don't want it. If I feel any pain, let it be my own pain; another's would only double it, Sir Knight!

KNIGHT: Powerfully stated! Then hold on to me! Look: my cloak floats about you like a raven's wing—depend upon it: it will keep us aloft. Earth to one side! . . . Listen: footsteps approaching! . . . First, down under; then, up on High, as you commanded!

[*He sinks down with Faust. The* GOVERNOR, DON OCTAVIO, *and servants enter.*]

GOVERNOR: This is the Sorcerer's room. What a thick vapor! A demon must have breathed here!

DON OCTAVIO: It steams like the breath of pestilence!

GOVERNOR: Faust has vanished. Is there another way out of this room?

DON OCTAVIO: I see only the door through which we came.

GOVERNOR: Then he must have gone to Hell.

DON OCTAVIO: Father, you're growing pale.

GOVERNOR: You, too.

DON OCTAVIO: We'd better leave—quick, away! [*While leading the* GOVERNOR *out, he turns once again to the servants.*] Open the windows. . . . I'm beginning to believe in sorcery myself.

[*Exeunt all.*]

ACT II

Scene 1

Rome. The Governor's garden. DON JUAN *and* LEPORELLO *enter.*

LEPORELLO: Ah, sir, it's four in the afternoon, and she hasn't come yet. Let's go home and sleep off last night's feasting and carousing.

DON JUAN: Go home and sleep? Don't you see this garden, this heaven? How blue the sky is, and how bright the sun, like a diamond in the dark. Not the smallest cloud in view. Magnificent! It's a poor eye that can slumber here. Heaven arches overhead, an open chalice filled with lust and power. Nature and man drink of it and are made drunk. The dark red grapes sparkle on the hills!

LEPORELLO: And the fresh faces of blooming girls sparkle between the grapes. Those enchanting little grape-pickers with their tucked-up skirts and well-rounded calves, their feet so nimble and slender—my mouth waters!

DON JUAN: A wondrous day; even the ruins, like transfigured ghosts, glow in its shimmer. Such an autumn falls only in Rome. Like its Roman ancestors, the countryside wraps itself in garbs of victory before dying out. Nature, a golden frame, lies ready to receive the most beautiful of portraits—Donna Anna!

LEPORELLO: Here she comes. A lady's white dress flickers through the greenery. Oh, Lisette! Lisette isn't with her! Then I'm sure to find her in her room; and cautious love favors locked doors.

DON JUAN: She is coming! Tell me, what rustles most beautifully?

LEPORELLO: Gold in the purse.

DON JUAN: The gown of a mistress.

LEPORELLO: True, as long as you've not yet—Don, you never did read any book twice.

DON JUAN: Off with you. Here she is.

LEPORELLO: Poor thing, if she lets herself be deceived.

DON JUAN: I love her!

LEPORELLO: You love? Now, tell me: who loves roast veal, girls, wine, and dancing—everything that tastes good and looks good? So much so that when he enjoys one, he immediately forgets the other? Who, at the whiff of a good roast, for example, hardly thinks of his mistress? Ask a university student whether a man in love behaves like that! Your young cousin, Señor Pedro, once told me you never really loved; all you know is pleasure and the anticipation of pleasure.

DON JUAN: What? Could my love be nothing but fantasy?

LEPORELLO: Thus speaketh your cousin!

DON JUAN: In that case, fantasy's a thousand times better than reality! Go now.

[LEPORELLO leaves. DONNA ANNA enters without noticing Don Juan. He steps aside.]

DONNA ANNA: A shining day, blinding the eyes—my heart so troubled —my wedding so near, happiness so far away. I grow dizzy when I see my image reflected in the crystal brook, and the gay bridal wreath in my hair: the wreath stays green for a while; my tears keep it fresh! . . . Alas, I know what clouds my soul! Last night I heard the clang of his sword and his voice ringing out. Oh, let him be the God of Hell; to you, Octavio, I remain faithful! You have my word! I will, I must love you, though it break my heart. Love means less than honor. Oh, how tired I am! The bustle and hum of the wedding and the white robes' swirl of splendor float before me like white storm clouds. I am exhausted, as before a storm. If only I could close my eyes and go to sleep. . . . Oh, I will not smile again!

[She reclines on a lawn bench, as though about to fall asleep.]

DON JUAN: What did I hear? Love engenders love! And if it didn't, I'd find another sure means: contempt. A woman is too vain to suffer that. . . . Ha, she loves me! Only virtue and loyalty protect her.

What is iron in a smelting furnace, and what is virtue in the enamored? If a man's bold enough, he can knock virtue off its pedestal. For with women it's only a kind of coquetry to sweeten our victory. The best of innocence is to lose it: instinct teaches that to women. Even Donna Anna has an inkling of it. [*He approaches Donna Anna.*] Awaken, my dearest!

DONNA ANNA [*looking up from her doze*]: Madonna! It's he—himself! Away, villain! Why do you want to ensnare me? Help, servants! Servants!

DON JUAN: Your servants are nowhere to be seen. Forgive me: your eyelids had dropped in slumber. I could not bear it; for when you close your eyes, it is night about me.

DONNA ANNA: Go away! You frighten me!

DON JUAN: Only where you breathe can I live. You drive me into the wasteland if you reject me.

DONNA ANNA: Impostor!

DON JUAN: Neither God nor all Hell could force me from this blessed spot.

DONNA ANNA: Octavio! Octavio!

DON JUAN: That dandy! I swear by this sword I'll do away with him because you gave him a thought!

DONNA ANNA: Detestable, impudent creature!

DON JUAN: He should deem himself lucky: your lips named him; the most beautiful epitaph a man ever deserved.

DONNA ANNA: Angels of light, are you unfaithful, too? Does the roaring storm blow you away like shifting clouds? [*Aside.*] I weep, I smile—and hate him; yes, I hate you, and with good reason!

DON JUAN: You hate me? Me? Whose only sin is to be an eagle soaring through the sky who, blinded by a ray of your beauty, now plunges at your feet? Well, then, do hate, for even hate becomes you.

DONNA ANNA: Leave me alone. You don't impose on me. It's not love, but the flame of the abyss which glows in your eye. It singes my heart. Yet if my heart burns to ashes, it will be my sacrifice to love and faithfulness. Accept it graciously, you good spirits!

DON JUAN: Could you have loved Octavio?

DONNA ANNA: What right have you to question me?

DON JUAN: Unhappy soul, you want to destroy both of us by keeping up appearances and resisting the truth; it would be my death and yours. You gave Octavio your word. Should that word— that ice in which you sealed your freedom before the fire of love had even touched you—should that word continue to bind you now when the spring of life rises magically high above us? When a new life, a new being, pulsates in our veins? I implore you, I take your hand, your verdict will mean life or death to me: tell me in one word, in one syllable, do you wish to see me die or wish to love me?

DONNA ANNA: I love you—and now, farewell! Never, terrible man, will I be yours!

DON JUAN: You love me? Look: the night of my life flares up, touched by the first ray of morning. The stars which formerly lit my path, one by one, vanish in this splendor!

DONNA ANNA: Ah, not the friendly light of morning. No—but the lightning that shatters this heavy hour with wings of fire.

DON JUAN: Do not drop your head, and have no fear of lightning. Love makes you glorious, not guilty! It wraps you in imperial robes; your cheeks glow!

DONNA ANNA: Don Juan, would that I could rest deep in the grave!

DON JUAN: Darling, do not weep, or else I would kiss away your jeweled tears, and let them cut my heart like diamonds.

[*He tries to embrace her.*]

DONNA ANNA: Don't touch me—by God, you'd die, or I would.
I can't escape love, but I can save honor!

DON JUAN: Don't run away. Conquered, I'll follow you wherever you go.

DONNA ANNA: No ship speeds with more fear before the storm than I from you.

DON JUAN: Am I a storm? Oh smile, do smile but once, and as you do so, the stormy sea which rages within me will smooth to mirror that smile, and the cloud that shadows my forehead will dissipate like a bad dream.

DONNA ANNA: Oh, if I could smile away that dream.

DON JUAN: Only now do I understand what Death is: it shuts off life and opens up Olympus! Under your joyous glance, the past is shamed into death; and a new Eden arises and takes its place. Whoever looks into your eye, drinks from Lethe.

DONNA ANNA: Seducer! Greatest pain and highest happiness embrace when I see you, when I hear you!

DON JUAN: Since the beginning of the world, suffering and joy—coupled in word and deed—make for the truest wedlock. Oh, do not hesitate!

DONNA ANNA: Heaven be thanked! Here comes Octavio.

DON JUAN [*to himself*]: Damn it, I was in the best of form. The images poured forth by the dozen. [*Aloud.*] Señorita, God be with you. That Don turns my stomach. We'll meet again.

DONNA ANNA: Never!

DON JUAN: Oh yes, we will. [*To himself*] Octavio didn't see me. . . . Note the slow bourgeois approach. I'll step into this thicket and eavesdrop on his nice way of talking, those pretty commonplaces of his. One can learn a lot from such rogues; they are full of feeling. That is, instead of having enough fantasy and spirit to play with passion and let it crown the horizon of life, they are tortured by it, yell with pain, and auction these wares off as free and independent sensations. And yet—women are so stupid, only stupidity can conquer them. Ah, to do as the Romans do, and affect piety with women, dance, and lie!

[*He steps aside into the bushes, remaining visible, however, to the audience.*]

DONNA ANNA: Octavio draws near! The man to whom I am pledged. Shall I tell him that Don Juan loves me? No, no—the sleeper shall not learn what cloud passed over him. Courage, poor Anna! Courage! The daughter of Don Gusman must not fear death, much less her heart. Fidelity is eternal; love is mortal. May eternity win!

DON OCTAVIO [*enters; to Donna Anna*]: The day has come—the day which will fulfill our childhood dream.

DONNA ANNA: Our childhood dream!

DON OCTAVIO: Adorned for the wedding dance, you stand adorned for me.

DONNA ANNA: Adorned for you!

DON JUAN [*to himself*]: The echo sounds suspicious: it changes the meaning.

DON OCTAVIO: The wreath glows green as the glimmer of hope through your dark curls. Enraptured is he who perceives such a glimmer in such darkness!

DON JUAN: How long will it go on? How long until the señor speaks of cloak and beret, of money and dowry, of procreation, child-rearing, and education? He will gently rock the little dolls in his arms: the little 'Tavies, bawling witnesses to his chaste glow. What puking rot!

DON OCTAVIO: Even as a boy I venerated your divine image, and stole away to be near you. But near as I came, you remained—or so it seemed to me, even when you greeted me amicably—a beautiful but distant, far distant star! I dared not dream that the divine happiness promised by your voice and by your gaze could ever come so near!

DON JUAN [*to himself*]: Spell of the wedding! Potency of the wine! I'll swear the impending marriage has made the dry Mr. Bridegroom bold enough to drink three glasses of wine. Look, he waxes poetic before the ceremony!

DON OCTAVIO: My every longing and hope is consummated. I am imbued with the fullness of being—

DON JUAN [*to himself*]: Me! I! Himself! The Self-ist!*

DON OCTAVIO: I can never be more divinely happy than I am now.

DON JUAN [*to himself*]: Then it's time you died, tonight!

DONNA ANNA: Octavio, I am yours: take my hand and lead me to the altar.

DON OCTAVIO: I'll take you there, but first let us obtain your father's blessing.

DON JUAN [*to himself*]: Bravo! Nothing omitted from the old rigmarole; the father's blessing promotes love as much as cats help at catching fish.

DON OCTAVIO: After the wedding, dearest—

DON JUAN [*to himself*]: How adorable.

DON OCTAVIO: —we'll return, I think, to our own country. I'm sure your father will be happy to accompany us.

DONNA ANNA: No: he serves the King as long as he lives!

DON OCTAVIO: But perhaps our entreaties would move him; rest and quiet, children's love, and liberal income beckon him to our estates.

DONNA ANNA: Income—he doesn't give it a thought. He has more than enough.

DON OCTAVIO: Oh, don't be angry, my dear—I meant well.

DONNA ANNA: Can I be angry with you? Must I not love you forever?

DON OCTAVIO: Come; I want to deserve your love!

[DONNA ANNA *and* DON OCTAVIO *leave.*]

DON JUAN [*stepping out again*]: The poor thing! Money, marriage, and income: the pillars of his existence! What a shame there aren't machines to replace such people in the marriage bed, in church, in the fields, and in the kitchen. Señor Octavio is much mistaken, however, if he expects to climb into the bridal bed tonight. No, he's going to drop into a pool of his own blood in the middle of the marriage ceremony—or Don Juan's not my name.

*For *Selbst-ling*—also a manufactured word. [*Translator's note.*]

LEPORELLO [*enters*]: Sir, are you ready?

DON JUAN: Not yet. How are you doing with Lisette?

LEPORELLO: Sir, just as you would be doing with Donna Anna after you were fed up with her. Let's get out of Rome. In nine months she'll be suing me for marriage!

DON JUAN: Marriage? Does she know you're not a count?

LEPORELLO: Pshaw! Count or no count, I'm a dapper fellow, and that's worth a kingdom to a girl.

DON JUAN: But tonight is Donna Anna's wedding.

LEPORELLO: Damn it!

DON JUAN: Soon they'll be lighting the candles in the wedding hall, and every candle will flick me in the eye like a flash of lightning. Octavio must fall!

LEPORELLO: Donna Anna must be won!

DON JUAN: And you must help.

LEPORELLO: Gladly—if you'll protect me as on similar occasions.

DON JUAN: Depend on it. Here is money: dispense it as cleverly as you can. The wedding—to which I've been invited—is about to begin. Provoke Octavio to the brink of anger—make him insult you—so that they think I'm justified in entering the fight on your behalf.

LEPORELLO: Easily said, easily done. But what if he hits me?

DON JUAN: I'll give you four scudi for every blow.

LEPORELLO: So one hundred thousand hits will net me 400,000 scudi!

DON JUAN: Go to it now!

[*He exits.*]

LEPORELLO: This purse isn't light. Now, first things first: half for me —as for the rest, I'll manage. I know how to sharpen the master's dagger myself, the one that'll stab the bridegroom. And in any old corner I can pick up the five devil's henchmen who'll do the dirty work—and pay them off in pennies. Finally, I won't buy, I'll simply hire six horses to carry the bride off with us. Which will leave the stableman empty-handed. But let him worry about that!

[*He exits.* FAUST *and the* KNIGHT *enter.*]

KNIGHT: Whoa, Master! Shall we rest on this pretty spot?

FAUST: Rest from what, slave?

KNIGHT [*to himself*]: He calls me slave! He'll atone that for centuries! [*Aloud.*] Why, rest from the glare of the comets and planets which blinded you, and from the darkness of the abyss which turned you pale. Are you satisfied now? Do you comprehend now what I, what World, and what God—as you call Him—are?

FAUST: Weakling, do you think I can be satisfied by mere acquisition like a miser, or by piling greatness upon greatness like some silly conqueror, eternally striving, never ceasing? Oh, yes, the wanderer may lose his breath watching the wild play of the stars as they chase each other through the galaxies, hot and yellow, like a sandstorm in the desert. But you don't need the firmanent for that since you can lose your breath in the Sahara as well. Show me the abyss I could not imagine more bottomless; the mountain peak, more vertiginous; the universe, more boundless. What I have apprehended from the world so far only proves there is neither greatness nor smallness in it, and that the mite is as strange a creation as the elephant. I have sought the purpose and essence of power, not its outer shell!

KNIGHT: But you don't understand power and its purpose, even when I decipher it for you.

FAUST: Why not?

KNIGHT: Because its meaning lies on the other side of language. And you can conceive only what can be put into words.

FAUST: What do you mean? Language is greater than man?

KNIGHT: So it is!

FAUST: Then what are longing and feeling—all those wordless sensations which palpitate through us like thunderstorms? What are they?

KNIGHT: Mere mist and fog. What is wordless is without sense or clarity.

FAUST: So mankind is nothing but babble! Then why do I feel this thirst to explore beyond language?

KNIGHT: Because you work it up artifically in yourself. Do rather like millions of your fellow men: eat, sleep, drink, and be merry.

FAUST: Aha! What Shadow suddenly convulsed Heaven and Hell when you showed them in full splendor? When the Shadow broke in, there you stood—angels, devils, God and yourself—frozen like wax figures.

KNIGHT [trembling and confused]: What Shadow are you talking about? Why, I believe this Shadow—though perhaps it was only an all-too-bright Light?—often terrifies many a spirit. But I don't know . . . it may have fallen into the world from outside—

FAUST: What?

KNIGHT: Yes: for you see and understand only the world, the Devil, and the God you fathom.

FAUST: Liar and traitor! You promised to show me the deepest pulse of Nature. Where is it?

KNIGHT: It beats in every blade of grass under your feet.

FAUST: You pitiful shadow!

KNIGHT [*to himself*]: He scolds! The worm scolds! What a sea of poison seethes up in me!

FAUST: I feel it: a devil knows no more than a man.   -

KNIGHT: Whoever takes refuge with Satan hoping to find peace—or whatever you call it—is a fool! All Hell rejoiced when it heard your call. But if you expect to find happiness and bliss, you'll first have to rise to the greatness of the Giant Spirit who plunged from the heights of Heaven, unterrified and self-sufficient, blunting the tongues of millennial flames, and despite doubts which rip out feeling and thought by the roots, eternally hating and fighting in hopes of victory.

FAUST: That Spirit who resigns himself to doubt instead of resolving it, and contents himself with hate instead of exploring the basic fact of love, is for bears, not men or angels. Friend, you have sorely disappointed me.

KNIGHT [*to himself*]: That I know.

FAUST: I cannot use you to any great purpose. Yet we are still pledged to one another. Therefore, as long as you are mine, I will employ you as a slave and make some use of your tricks.

KNIGHT: Sir, I am entirely at your service—but what a shame you're only human! For a true God dwells within you. It saddens me to learn I'm too small to satisfy your longings. Yet like attracts like. He who is dazzled by suns is all the more easily bedazzled by the eyes of young girls. Look into this mirror! What do you think of the woman's face reflected there?

FAUST: That woman's face—but I have a wife.

KNIGHT: She doesn't count.

FAUST: I've had my fill of women.

KNIGHT: Aha! What do you mean by that? Have you never loved?

FAUST: I have kissed, hoped, longed for—but the world is little and longing is great. How could I love women before God was clear to me?

KNIGHT: Quite easily! One often forgets the ugliness of a master in the presence of his beautiful creation; with women, men forget God and the Devil. Don't expect on your life's journey to traverse the torrid zones where the heavens burn with love and not get involved yourself. Your soul may want to feast or fast; you may wish to steer to the fruitful valley of autumn or to the mountain glacier of winter; but first you must live through the first love of summer. And I'd say you need a new crutch now that you're nearing the point where every support fails you! [*Holding the portrait up to Faust*] Look, Faust, the woman! [*To himself*] Now, all you hell-fires, gather within the confines of this painting, bespangle the portrait of Donna Anna, and bedazzle the high and mighty Doctor!

FAUST [*contemplating the portrait*]: Beautiful . . . most beautiful. Never did I see anything so magnificent. . . . How the forehead emerges from the darkness of these curls. So breaks the god of the sun from the rim of night! I know. All this is a deception of Hell! I see the sparkle about the countenance. Yet deception or not, it's worth more than the truth; more than to know that man knows nothing!

KNIGHT: This is the true portrait of Donna Anna.

FAUST: I look and look . . . I become a child again . . . a home I never knew smiles on me. But is there another home than the land of one's birth? Ah, the brown of these eyes steals over me like the dusk of evening: the day grows pale. Yet countless stars emerge from the abyss transfiguring the darkness. The depths of heaven are sand bars compared to the depths of these eyes!

KNIGHT [*to himself*]: Now the drake caresses his duck and forgets philosophy, mathematics, and astronomy.

FAUST: It's nonsense that a mere portrait should so entrance me. I see no grounds for it, and yet I am enchanted.

KNIGHT: The fool! Even in love he seeks the grounds. The less ground, the deeper he seeks.

FAUST: Did you say this is the portrait of Donna Anna?

KNIGHT: Yes, it is.

FAUST: Then lead me to her: I want to see her and speak to her.

KNIGHT: But her father is looking for you!

FAUST: Call me Count Mezzocampi, and rejuvenate me through your magic art.

KNIGHT: I am your slave. But are you aware that the lady Anna is to marry Don Octavio this evening?

FAUST: She's marrying?

KNIGHT: Yes, indeed! Listen: already the music swells for the wedding dance.

FAUST: Music! Music! They rejoice while pain grips me! I shall drop in on this fête like a clap of thunder on a summer's day. Hell serves me, and with its help I'll storm my way to Heaven.

KNIGHT: Don Juan will block your scheme: he plans on doing away with Sir Octavio and winning Donna Anna over to himself.

FAUST: Let him kill Octavio and play right into my hands. After he's done away with the bridegroom and started to abduct the bride, I'll tap him on the shoulder, strike him down, and carry her off myself!

KNIGHT: You can do it all through my power.

FAUST: Through your power? What do you mean? The sword would be more than he who holds it?

KNIGHT [to himself]: What vanity!

FAUST: Show me Anna this very moment, for the seconds drop on my head like molten lead. Let me see her!

KNIGHT: And smell and feel her! Come!

[He exits with Faust.]

Scene 2

Rome. Salon in the Governor's residence, with the perspective giving out on several other festively lit drawing rooms, all filled with guests. Music. Dance. SIGNOR RUBIO *and* SIGNOR NEGRO *enter.*

SIGNOR RUBIO: The Governor spared no pains, you might say, to make a brilliant affair of his daughter's marriage.

SIGNOR NEGRO: Like all Spaniards, he's a fool. There's nothing, absolutely nothing to be done with him. If you shake his hand, you shake his honor. Honor! Honor! It's the first, second, third, and last word with him. He feeds on it; but we Romans have inherited more than enough to hold in reserve.

SIGNOR RUBIO: Yes, we are Romans—and Christians, to boot—you might say.

SIGNOR NEGRO: Listen to the music they're playing at the ball. How coarse, how very Spanish! So tiresome, so dull; no life, no fire, no divine inspiration; no form, no melody— Two glasses of punch, please.

SIGNOR RUBIO: No more for me, Signore. I am, you might say, a little tipsy.

SIGNOR NEGRO: You, tipsy? Heaven help us! Aren't you the Commissioner of Police? Who'll keep order here if you get drunk?

SIGNOR RUBIO: Ah, order! Once order is established, it will keep itself. Otherwise it's a poor order. You don't know my police force. Even when drunk, they stay as sober as possible. Look, I can't stand on one leg anymore.

SIGNOR NEGRO: For Christ's sake, Commissioner, be reasonable. Don't try any of your fancy tricks. Be happy if you can stay up on both legs.

SIGNOR RUBIO: What? And take a double spill? Now each foot is drunk, and if I stand on two feet, I'll fall down twice. You have to be mighty careful around here.

SIGNOR NEGRO: Drink tea—take ice—

SIGNOR RUBIO: The bride's not here yet. The ball has only just begun. Sir, what'll become of us after the ball is over? Oh, look how they dance: tum, tum—rum, dum—didel-dee-dum—stretching their legs simultaneously east and west—it makes me dizzy! And how they whirl—whirl to the devil. Why, they're going too far.

[*He flings himself into a chair.*]

SIGNOR NEGRO: The souse! A commissioner of police and asleep! Oh, if only I were in his boots. Hey, doorman, cart him off to bed.

SIGNOR RUBIO: To bed? Why? I'm still quite sober—you might say.

[*He is carried off.*]

SIGNOR NEGRO [*after looking into the ballroom*]: Where's the bride? Something's out of joint. [DON JUAN *and* LEPORELLO *enter.*] Who are they? The tall one must be the master; the dry, skinny one, the lackey. And Spaniards, too! [*Looking Don Juan over*] I smell a Don in that wild gaze and in that nose hooked like an eagle's beak.

DON JUAN [*to Leporello*]: First wine, then dance, then murder.

LEPORELLO: So be it. That'll make for a wild night!

DON JUAN: Are Octavio and his bride here already?

LEPORELLO: Not yet.

DON JUAN: Then bring the wine.

LEPORELLO [*bringing several bottles from the adjacent buffet*]: Rhine wine, burgundy, and champagne!

DON JUAN: Put them back: here comes the Donna.

[*The* GOVERNOR, DONNA ANNA *and* DON OCTAVIO *enter.*]

GOVERNOR: Joined at the altar by the hand of the priest, may you be true to each other until death do you part!

DON JUAN [*to himself*]: A short troth! I plan an early death.

GOVERNOR: Farewell, daughter: be happy. You are no longer mine.

DONNA ANNA: Father, father, are you weeping?

GOVERNOR: Who doesn't weep on seeing his daughter happy? Yet you are somber, too.

DONNA ANNA: Doesn't the greatest joy always make one somber? [*to herself*] Ah, what a hypocrite I am!

DON OCTAVIO: Silent joy is too much to bear. Let us muffle it with music and dance!

DONNA ANNA [*seeing Don Juan, with a start*]: Yes; music, dance! I'll have the next dance with you, my lord and husband.

DON OCTAVIO: Dearest, come.

DON JUAN [*to himself*]: He dances like a dancing master, not like the husband of the most beautiful girl in the world!

SIGNOR NEGRO [*to the Governor*]: Congratulations, my lord. Your daughter is a goddess; Don Octavio, a god!

GOVERNOR: I thank you—in both their names.

SIGNOR NEGRO: The sun never looked down on the like.

GOVERNOR: You flatter.

SIGNOR NEGRO: Who can flatter seeing the pair dancing there? However extravagant the praise, it still falls short of the truth.

GOVERNOR: Will you accompany me into the ballroom?

[*The* GOVERNOR *and* SIGNOR NEGRO *go into the next salon.*]

DON JUAN: She noticed me: trembling, she dances out of terror. And where I terrify, I win. She glides like an angel on the wave of the music, a bolt of beauty flashing through the rows of dancers; now emerging, now disappearing. And my heartbeat is the thunder which accompanies her.

LEPORELLO: Is this the moment to start the fracas with Don Octavio?

DON JUAN: Not quite. First, let me dance a little . . . but right after that!

LEPORELLO: As you wish. We can break away whenever you want; horse, carriage, and accomplices are standing by.

DON JUAN: Good!

[*He goes and mixes with the dancers.* LEPORELLO *steps aside. The* KNIGHT *and* FAUST *enter, the latter with rejuvenated face and in magnificent dress.*]

KNIGHT: Not a soul will recognize you as Faust. You were a powerful man before, but now you are incomparable. An infernal melancholy quivers about your face and figure. There you stand, like the spruce which glows inwardly and round which all burns. You can rest assured that with such fires of sensitivity and knowledge, summer's heat and winter's oven-glow, you'll soon see every woman at your feet. Especially now with your body in its prime, shining like Apollo. . . . Look, they're ogling you already, all except Donna Anna. She will be more difficult; she is the true daughter of Don Gusman.

FAUST [*watching the dance, and hardly hearing the Knight*]: A marriage ball! How festive the gleaming hall. The ladies fill it as flowers fill the spring.

KNIGHT: Yes, Doctor, mankind shines by night at promenades, at marriages, and at victory feasts—by the light of lamps or the blaze of rockets.

FAUST: Joy dwells in their cheeks, and tender roses spring up in their glow.

KNIGHT: The hot roses in the women's cheeks belong to me. They are the worst and finest flames of Hell. No breast is too deep for them.

FAUST: Look: there she is. Introduce us!

KNIGHT: Just the right moment for it; there is a pause in the dancing. [*He enters the ballroom with Faust. The* GOVERNOR, SIGNOR NEGRO, *and others break into the foreground.*]

GOVERNOR: What's happened?

FIRST GENTLEMAN: Panic seizes the crowd.

SECOND GENTLEMAN: Everyone's petrified.

GOVERNOR [*to an Aide*]: Anything wrong in the city? Fire? A revolt?

AIDE: Sir, the town is calmer than ever: nothing new in the air.

GOVERNOR: Then it's blind terror spreading among us.

SIGNOR NEGRO: Hardly that, Sir Governor. I swear it's that man with the corpselike face who just stepped into the ballroom. He must be provoking this panic.

GOVERNOR: You mean that knight introducing Count Mezzocampi to my daughter?

SIGNOR NEGRO: That monster, I would say. And that wild count at his side; something burns and flashes about his countenance as if all his features were aflame. Indeed, the beauty of Hell seems stamped on his forehead.

GOVERNOR: Oh, it's nothing, then; only a silly, childish scare! Look, my daughter is talking with them both, and she's much calmer than we are. What does a bad face or even a fearfully wild face mean, after all? At least, it does not feign to be anything else, as does many a tender face. . . . Gentlemen, let us begin the fête anew.

SIGNOR NEGRO [*half to himself*]: Hmn, yet that is not quite correct! It wasn't just dread of "fearfully wild faces." God alone knows what came over me at the sight of that unearthly cavalier and his fire-breathing companion.

[*They all return to the ballroom.* FAUST *and the* KNIGHT *re-enter.*]

FAUST: No: it's impossible that in a single moment I, Faust, for whom the universe has become too narrow, should lose myself to a girl's face, to the mere whisper of a girl's lips. But so it is!

KNIGHT: Did I not prophesy it? The soil out of which plants rise must be manured before they can take root freely and shoot up. The manure—whether avarice or fame, superstition or love—you call passion.

At last you stand at the zenith of life, where the giant trees of hope and longing, their roots reaching down to Tartarus, raise themselves, swift and fearsome, to the highest stretches of the sky, and the stars glimmer like golden fruit on their lofty boughs—where the Word, through which the world was once created in madness, half whispered as in a dream on the day of creation, rings out near and far, euphonious as a silver bell suspended in the dome of Heaven. First love? Oh, even I—myriads of years have since flown by—was full of the Word!

FAUST: What? Does Satan wax sentimental?

KNIGHT: Quite possibly he was—long ago. Now he laughs it off as a joke. How could he hate so unspeakably if he had not loved so mightily before? Red-hot iron is soft before it is forged into a sword. Bad luck crosses only the lucky. The Devil is nearer to God than the mite.

FAUST: Don Juan steps out of the row of dancers and approaches with his lackey. Soon he will begin his bloody work. High time we get ready to snatch his prey from him.

KNIGHT: You are the more powerful! What does the sparrow hawk want? You hover over him like an eagle, ensnaring him in ever-narrowing circles.

FAUST: Quick! With your magic power, build me a castle of ice and snow more glittering than the world has ever seen, a palace high up on Mont Blanc. Let it be enveloped by the golden breath of spring and lovingly embraced by rainbows. Let the windows light up like Donna Anna's beauty. Crimson more fiery than the innocent red of young girls' cheeks shall adorn all the walls—with rugs swelling voluptuously under Anna's step as it kisses the floor. All that the womb of the sea and the bowels of the earth yield in pearls and jewels shall sparkle there.

KNIGHT: It was done as you spoke: the castle stands high up on Mont Blanc!

FAUST: I rip fixed stars loose from their sites just to irradiate the hem of the beloved's gown—bringing them down to be servants to women!

DON JUAN [stepping into the foreground with Leporello]: The hour has come. The ball is over . . . they are entering the antechamber here . . . they're ready for bed. Leporello, step on his feet.

[*During this time,* DONNA ANNA, DON OCTAVIO, *ladies and gentlemen have entered the antechamber.*]

LEPORELLO [*to Don Juan*]: Easily done. [*To Don Octavio*] Pardon me, sir; I just stepped on your foot.

DON OCTAVIO: Forgiven already.

LEPORELLO: Oh my, there I've done it again; please excuse me.

DON OCTAVIO [*to his servants, pointing at Leporello*]: Throw him out, the drunken oaf.

LEPORELLO: So you're throwing me out, are you? Sir, do you know whom you're addressing? A nobleman. I come from Biscay where a peasant is as noble as a grandee in Seville.

DON OCTAVIO: Men, do as I order!

LEPORELLO: Halloo! Where's my lord? Oh, Don Juan, help! Stand by me!

DON JUAN [*stepping forward*]: Whoever molests my servant here is a scoundrel!

DONNA ANNA: Alas, this lightning flashes down on my head! Where is my father? Call the Governor!

A SERVANT: The Governor is at the banquet with Signor Negro.

DONNA ANNA: Call him! Call, call, call him!

[*Exit servant.*]

DON OCTAVIO [*to Don Juan*]: Whoever calls me a scoundrel without cause, is himself a scoundrel!

LEPORELLO [*to Don Juan*]: He treats me like a drunkard. Now, you know me, sir; speak the truth, I beg you. Is it possible for me ever to get drunk? The grapes have yet to be grown which can intoxicate me.

DON JUAN: Whoever hurts a servant of mine, hurts me. Draw your sword!

DONNA ANNA AND SEVERAL OTHERS: Stop!

DON OCTAVIO [*to Don Juan*]: You're asking for this.

DON JUAN: Blood for that insult! [*Sword play between him and Don Octavio.*] Splendid! That hit the mark.

DON OCTAVIO [*falling to the ground*]: Alas, I'm done for . . . I'm hit . . . blood! I'm dying. . . . Anna, remember me, slain criminally at your feet.

[*He expires.*]

VOICES OF THE GOVERNOR AND SIGNOR NEGRO [*from the rear banquet room*]: May Donna Anna and Don Octavio live a thousand years!

[*Clinking of glasses and fanfare.*]

DON JUAN: *Vivant!* But, alas, the bridegroom is already dead, and his bride is mine!

LEPORELLO: Come, young lady.

FAUST [*stepping behind* DON JUAN *and tapping him on the shoulder*]: You are mistaken, friend: she is mine!

DONNA ANNA: Neither yours, nor his. [*Pointing to Don Octavio's corpse*] He remains my master!

MANY OF THOSE PRESENT [*converging upon Don Juan and Faust*]: Seize the murderer! Seize the abductor!

FAUST: Gentlemen, don't move! I am Faust. Hell is my servant; I can destroy you. And what I can do, I shall also want to do from time to time. Away with the bride!

DONNA ANNA: Help! Help! Save me!

KNIGHT [*quickly, into Don Juan's ear*]: I see you are benumbed by sorcery. Yet remember these words; do not forget them: *he is taking Donna Anna up to Mont Blanc!* [*To himself*] The Devil may have to serve him, but he can still betray him behind his back!

[FAUST *and the* KNIGHT *exit with* DONNA ANNA. *The* GOVERNOR, SIGNOR NEGRO *and other gentlemen burst in.*]

GOVERNOR: I heard my child's voice. Speak: where is my daughter?

DON JUAN: Now my lie becomes the truth. Faust has really abducted her.

GOVERNOR: My child gone? What do I see ahead of me? A gaping emptiness in the world! . . . After the sorcerer!

LEPORELLO: Can you fly through the air, you ancient mariner?

SIGNOR NEGRO: And Don Octavio lies bleeding on the floor!

GOVERNOR: Have I lived eighty years to witness this?

DON JUAN: Quite possibly.

GOVERNOR: My own child in a magician's arms!

DON JUAN: Don't worry: I shall free her.

GOVERNOR: Who slew this man?

DON JUAN: I. In duel.

GOVERNOR: You?

DON JUAN: He wounded my man; so I punished him, and now I boast of the deed.

SEVERAL GUESTS: Governor, sir, don't believe him. The villain wanted to drag off your daughter, too; that's why he staged this scuffle with his lackey.

SIGNOR NEGRO: I'll be damned if I didn't suspect it, too. Guards! Oh, if only I were sober now. Signor Rubio!

MANY GUESTS: Draw your daggers! Out with your stilettos! Avenge Octavio and kill Juan!

LEPORELLO: Sir, sir, let's run!

DON JUAN: Run away? Because I won a duel according to the book? I know the Governor and his honor. To protect him, I stepped before this mob. I shall give revenge to anyone who asks for it. The nobleman avenges in person. Not with the help of guards, bloodhounds, and stilettos, but with his sword.

GOVERNOR: Truly spoken—and like a Spaniard. [*To the pressing crowd*] Stand back: I take him under my protection. Oh God, I'd give him all of Spain, if I could see my daughter's hand again! How low have I fallen! Even the King's image, which shone so long and proudly as my polar star, now dims at the thought of Anna's sorrow. Yet I do recommend Faust to God; Anna to her virtue; and you, Don Juan, to my sword!

LEPORELLO [*to himself*]: The Governor has heard his last bell toll.

DON JUAN: At your service, sir. Leporello, see to the requirements for fight and flight. [*To himself*] Two palms in the desert stood protecting the source: Don Octavio and the Governor. There lies one of them; the other will be felled in an instant. Then I shall pounce on her. Faust, the conjuror, will not stop me; for even if the throne of Hell were his, she would spurn him. I'll bring her down from Mont Blanc, make love to her, and—

LEPORELLO: And?

DON JUAN: Governor, I am ready!

GOVERNOR: Then come! Who are your seconds?

DON JUAN: This man only.

GOVERNOR: Then I, too, shall have only one. [*He nods to an aide*] Gasparo, follow me!

GASPARO: In life and death, sir!

GOVERNOR [*pointing to Don Octavio's corpse*]: Dispose of the body. [*To* DON JUAN] And now to the duel!

[*The* GOVERNOR *goes off with* DON JUAN, GASPARO, *and* LEPORELLO.]

SIGNOR NEGRO: True Spanish manners! Instead of calling down the law upon the murderer or stabbing him in the back, an eye for an eye, a tooth for a tooth! If only I could wake Rubio. This is a blood wedding.

THOSE PRESENT: Ghastly! Horrible!

[*All leave.*]

ACT III

Scene 1

Square before one of the northern gates of Rome. Night; not very dark, however. The GOVERNOR, *his aide* GASPARO, DON JUAN, *and* LEPORELLO *enter.*

GOVERNOR: Shall we be undisturbed here, Gasparo?

GASPARO: Yes, sir.

GOVERNOR: Then draw your sword, Don Juan.

DON JUAN: Easily done. My sword is not ashamed of nakedness.

LEPORELLO [*to himself*]: Only blood makes it blush.

GOVERNOR: The memory of both Donna Anna and Octavio hangs over this blade.

DON JUAN: Amen. Words sound pointless next to the true ring of steel. To the point, then, sir. Defend yourself, now. I attack!

[*Sword play.*]

LEPORELLO: Ha, the first pass! The old man holds his own bravely. The second pass . . . and still not finished? Sir, sir, get it over fast . . . before the police show up, slow as they may be! The third pass. . . .

DON JUAN: There—thrust home!

LEPORELLO: All good things come in threes!

GOVERNOR: This is the end . . . get a priest.

[*Exit* GASPARO.]

DON JUAN: They call the clergy when nothing else avails. And that's quite logical; no one helps as little as a priest.

GOVERNOR: Honorably I fall . . . true to my tradition. . . . Yet now any fight for life seems a sin, be it duel or murder. . . . Oh, Christ, Saviour, be gracious and open the Gates of Heaven to me. Forgive this old man who fell in pursuing the prejudices of his youth! Jesus, sweet Comforter, your name alone stills my fear. With shame and joy I feel how minute are our shortcomings when compared to the Divine Grace—mere drops in the ocean!

LEPORELLO: Sir, let's get away. Listen how the horses stamp and snort. They smell blood and the blood-ban!

DON JUAN: I'm coming—but look: the old man wants another word with me.

GOVERNOR: Don Juan, do you see this stream of blood? Let it force its way into you like lava and light up your darkness with its red flame, just as your blood too might horrify me had I been the winner. Then think on God and your transgression. Think of my poor daughter. Do not pursue her; but save her from Faust, and lead her into the refuge of a convent.

DON JUAN: I will not lie to you in death. Therefore, hear me: it would be a pity if your daughter became a nun; she is too beautiful to whither away unused. I can smell old courtesans among the devotees just as certainly as I can distinguish an old flower pot by its broken pieces. Donna Anna is still pure and noble. As for my transgression, what do you mean by that? You don't know what I have done in the past; and what I did today was all very natural. The natural thing, my good man, is certainly the right thing. I was in love with Anna —is she not lovely? By marrying her, Octavio wished to rob me of her—was I not clever to prevent that? You forced me into a duel—I had to defend myself, even if that meant killing you. True, you believe right was on your side. But I believe it was on mine. Right is hundredfold, and everyone is entitled to his own version. I was led on by what you, what I, what every inhabitant on this earth is moved by. Only we give it a different name. Why does the priest pray? Why does the business man worry? Why do kings wage battles which outdo thunder and lightning in their tumult and destruction? Because, in the final analysis they want to enjoy life—to be satisfied, to please themselves. I always repeat the old motto: *King and Glory, Fatherland and Love.* But I do so only because it pleases me to sacrifice myself for them.

GOVERNOR: Oh, my daughter!— Don Juan, won't you grant me one last consolation and give her up?

DON JUAN: Never!

GOVERNOR: Then listen to what a dying man tells you; let my words flash through the night of death like lightning. There is a God.

DON JUAN: I can't care less! The earth is so delightful, I haven't time to meditate on Him who created it. If it is God, so much the greater be His glory. The best compliment you can pay a cook is to enjoy his cooking.

GOVERNOR: Don Juan, crime is nothing but a joke to you! You mock the death of my son-in-law and me, the father, while still hoping to abduct an innocent girl. Yet know this—in dying, I sense it all too clearly—there is a seriousness infinitely greater than mere pleasure. Only virtue is immortal, not lust; death is more than life; and the reprisal longer lasting and more horrible than the offense.

DON JUAN: Hey, Leporello! Can we spare any more time for this moralist?

LEPORELLO: People are coming!

DON JUAN: Don, die now, die well!* Look, there is the Pantheon; and remember, in Rome one death doesn't amount to much! Thanks for the sermon. I shall seek out Donna Anna; I hope to rest more blissfully in her embrace than you do on beholding God in Paradise.

[*Exeunt* DON JUAN *and* LEPORELLO,]

GOVERNOR: Still defiant! Very soon I'll stand before the throne from which His Grace will flame down—and revenge. I'll think of you there, Juan! . . . Alas, my senses falter. Where am I? Tongues of lions glitter and lick . . . hideous vermin crawl over my chest. Ha . . . yes! My country and Donna Anna: were those not words I once heard or spoke?

[*He dies.* GASPARO *returns with a priest.*]

GASPARO: He is dead.

THE PRIEST: We are too late. Oh, Almighty God, forgive his sins!

GASPARO: The plea is superfluous; I served him a long time and know of no sin he has committed.

PRIEST: What? But he just fell in duel.

GASPARO: Sir, he fell in battle over Don Octavio's blood and Donna Anna's honor.

PRIEST: Only God—not man—can mete out punishment and revenge.

GASPARO: The Governor thought otherwise. God punishes so seldom, he probably thought it might be good if man would lend Him a helping hand.

[GASPARO *and the* PRIEST *carry off the body.*]

Scene 2

Peak of Mont Blanc. A magnificent chamber in Faust's Magic Castle. View of the Alps and surrounding countryside. FAUST *and the* KNIGHT *enter.*

FAUST [*angry*]: The art you display here is deplorable. This castle and this hall are not worthy of her view. I'm ashamed of what you've done: a would-be devil, and you can't even dazzle with brilliance, counterfeit as it may be!

KNIGHT: Your eye may be too weak, the brilliance too blinding. Tell

---

*In the original, meant as a parody on "farewell"—the German "sterbt wohl" echoing the casual "lebe wohl." [*Translator's note.*]

me, what's wrong with this castle? Here rays of pearl and diamond gouged out of the deepest ocean beds and rock-grounded mountains compete with one another from wall to wall. A deep reddish purple, more blazing than the scorching glow of the African sun, inflames you everywhere. Here the most beautiful fruit and flowers from all the realms of the earth trickle down from the roof and patios like the rain of the sun. The greatest emperor cannot boast such a brilliant palace.

FAUST: Did you say emperor? What should that mean to me? I have more power than any living being. Yet this castle fails to satisfy me; it does not do justice to my feeling for Donna Anna.

KNIGHT: Everything possible has been done. But you love the impossible—the infinite!

FAUST: Art, science, mind, and heart are endless and limitless; so is my love!

KNIGHT: Power and endurance live only in limitations.

FAUST: Poor aphorism; it smacks of the one-sided hate of Hell. What I feel as unbounded, I must be able boundlessly to achieve. Why else would I feel it?

KNIGHT: I would answer that if the lady were not approaching.

FAUST: So get out of this room, and fast!

[*The* KNIGHT *exits.*]

All you spirits who are my servants:
greet her with peals of thunder and soft waves of music!
Descend, you spheres, and dance about her,
ecstatic with your harmonies!
Let the light of spring shine upon all
earths, seas, and islands now that I see her—
for it is she, it is she: my Queen!

[*Music and brilliant sunshine.* DONNA ANNA *appears.*]

DONNA ANNA: Alas!

FAUST: Trembling—and it is the first time I tremble—I approach you, my beloved!

DONNA ANNA: You tremble? [*To herself*] I tremble myself at his trembling. [*Aloud again, summoning up her courage*] The thought of your guilt makes you tremble!

FAUST: No, the sight of your beauty.

DONNA ANNA: Then would my beauty were a fire to consume you, destroyer of my father and Don Octavio!

FAUST: Aha! Do you know who I am?

DONNA ANNA: I know only what you did.

FAUST: Maiden, take care. The man who conquered the realm of the spirits because the earth was too confining, the man for whom that realm still does not suffice—this Faust—stands before you!

DONNA ANNA: Be Faust, be God! Do you fancy you can force love?

FAUST: Oh, Anna! Meteor of love! Do not look down on me with anger. When you rose blinding on the horizon of my life—oh, jewel of the firmament, heart's delight—I reached out drunkenly for the light that enraptured me. I became, I remained a child; I wanted to possess what pleased me so.

DONNA ANNA: Must you possess what pleases you? The stars following the paths of their orbits are unreachable, yet we take delight in them.

FAUST: The stars are tinsel and trifle. Life for me lies only in your eye; I die if you close it to me. Oh, heaven, what are hate and scorn? Transient emotions, creating nothing, self-created. Love is the only creative omnipotence! Oh, my breast, how it swells; and how my head reels! All my old worlds crumble; new seas boil up and spit forth new continents like shells! Everything but you shrivels for me. I'd throw over the entire world for the little spot your foot treads on. I should be ashamed of myself! And you, heartless, unmoved, do you want to damn me to the torture of tortures, unrequited love? Now, answer me.

DONNA ANNA [*very serious*]: Where is my father? Did Don Octavio fall?

FAUST: Oh, snake goddess—as beautifully adorned as you are cruel and ferocious!

DONNA ANNA: Monster! Oh, God, save me, he lusts for love as the tiger for blood!

FAUST: Look! There lie the Alps, grey, and high as heaven, like a senate of primeval Earth Titans looking with silent, icy scorn toward the sun, their feet chained, though unconquered. At the softest noise that dares disturb their dream, they punish with the devastation of plunging avalanches. Look further: my art draws the uttermost distance into your circle of vision: there flows the Rhone, proud of Lyons reflected in the mirror of its waves; next, the green fields of Provence open out, full of love and song. And now—as I burst asunder the chain of the Pyrenees to give you a clear line of vision—Hispania appears, bathing her hot breasts voluptuously in two seas. And there, their spires quivering like lightning flashes toward the clouds, are the towers of your native city, Seville—

DONNA ANNA: Ah, Seville! Magnificent, never-forgotten image from my childhood, I see you again. Yes, it is you! The white marble there between the cypresses covers my mother's grave. Oh, my mother!

FAUST: And all this—mountains and lands, rivers and oceans—I pour at your feet, yes, even my tears!

DONNA ANNA: You show me my mother's grave, and think your tears might move me!

FAUST: Beware my tears; they are soft rocks crumbling down the mountainside.

DONNA ANNA: He is like a god of the deep. Yet what if I call him by the name he was born with? It will strengthen me against him. Man, remember your wife and let me go free.

FAUST: My wife? Who betrayed that to you?

DONNA ANNA: If I had not already known it, your blush would have betrayed it.

FAUST: My blush! Yes, the evening sky reddens when night tempests threaten. Sir Knight! Sir Knight!

KNIGHT [entering]: My dear Doctor—

FAUST: Dog! Traitor!

KNIGHT: Mere words.

FAUST: Then here is action: you spirits of the deep whom he has tyrannized, gorged with the accumulated gall and rancour of millions of centuries, take him away! Unloose that rancour; torment and martyr him until his screaming moves and terrifies even his enemies.

KNIGHT: Friend, sow—just sow the seed you'll one day harvest howling; it falls upon a ground soil of fire, hot enough to drive thousandfold fruit from every kernel. Every torment will teach me how I can double back the same on you in the future.

FAUST: The future no longer threatens me. I feel it already: the year is short, the hour long. If there is a future, if there are eternities—they are to be found in the present. I know it from one look in Donna Anna's face. If I were happy once, I would remain so forever, in spite of hell and torture. Only a devil thinks he can drive out inner happiness with outer abuse.

KNIGHT: What insolence! You're much less than a devil: you are only a man!

FAUST: My dear Knight, you have shown me the universe, high and low—yet, believe me, small as man may be, he is far greater than the world. He is infinite; strong enough not to bother with taming the devil, but also strong enough to hope that he may one day share God's throne, even if he has to fight for it.

DONNA ANNA: Monster!

FAUST [to Donna Anna]: Do not say that; though my spirit, even as the worm turns, was once contorted down to Hell, toward that devil there, it has now raised itself through the greatness of love. I feel now that all spirits are equal, from the highest to the lowest; no matter how great the one is, the other can and well may become as great.

KNIGHT: Become! Those who wanted to become archangels became dragons!

FAUST [still to Donna Anna]: My precious girl, don't be afraid! I know what love is. I know that it arises out of little nothings—the blink of an eye, the play with white hands, delight in a fine, beautifully groomed figure—out of the dark drive of the senses; I know that a man haunts his beloved with bad, sugar-coated sonnets, sweet looks, the clandestine attack— I know all this and know that it is only a bauble; yet this bauble affects me like a tiny spark dropped on the powder mine of a fortress. It stirs in me, not tender glances, no, it stirs an old, inborn power, a glow up to the firmament. With it, I defy God, Satan, and myself! Therefore, if I humiliate this fellow here, storm Heaven, convulse earth and ocean, all this is only an expression of my love for you—even though it manifests itself in an uncommon way! . . . Away with him, and torture him as I commanded!

KNIGHT: Oh, ohah, oahah!

[He is torn away.]

DONNA ANNA: God protect me! What a shriek! That was no earthly sound: my heart broke hearing it.

FAUST: Such is the sound when anger and sorrow, revenge, terror and contrition crush indestructible Princes of the Spirit!

DONNA ANNA: My head! Oh, the hammering pain!

FAUST: I have medicine for that.

DONNA ANNA: I beg you with tears to give me poison instead.

FAUST: No, you shall remain mine against your will. You spoke of my wife. You were right: I have a wife. Look toward the north; there is the river, the grey city—

DONNA ANNA: Horrible and gloomy like yourself!

FAUST: Respect it! There on the Elbe River wanders the Destroyer;

whose pen, as he wrote the truth on the church door of Wittenberg that all earthly laws and precepts are subordinate to the Word and Reason, grew and grew like a comet's tail; until it spread all over Germany and Switzerland and swept down your Pope's three-towered crown!

DONNA ANNA: Oh, Luther, the heretic. And this, his admirer! My Christ, in whose hands have I fallen?

FAUST: How popish that sounds and consistent with a Spanish up-bringing—yet it rings sweetly from your lips. The pious error even makes you charming, more than charming: it makes you more human. Often the loveliest face needs only a little scar to give it supreme beauty.

DONNA ANNA: You make me smile. You burn with love and philosophize at the same time?

FAUST: I am a German and a scholar; and Germans analyze in Hell, in the lap of God's magnificence, or even when mad with desire. . . . The woman sighing and wringing her hands in the little room in that city is—my wife. She's weeping over me. Now, you throw in my face that I'm married to her. But with a wave of my hand, the plague kills her. . . . She sinks down! Speak no more of my wife: I have none!

DONNA ANNA [crying out]: Aie! He killed his wife!

FAUST: Yes, and I will kill king and people, I will sink ships and devastate the earth, anything and everything for you!

DONNA ANNA: Father, oh father! In Jesus' name, raise the crosspiece of your sword and save your child from this demon!

FAUST: Fool! Your father outlived Don Octavio by less than an hour. He is dead.

DONNA ANNA: Dead!

FAUST: Don Juan killed him.

DONNA ANNA [going pale]: Don Juan!

FAUST: You love him?

DONNA ANNA: Love? Him? Even if it were so— I beseech you: avenge my father on him! You have the power. I know it only too well.

FAUST: And even if you did not love him, I know he loves you—though he shouldn't dare. Let him strive, but despair of ever reaching you!

DONNA ANNA: My head! I thank you for burning with such compassionate pain that I almost forget the greater pain! Think of me, Father, before God's throne. His is the revenge, but ours is the sorrow!

[She sinks into an armchair.]

FAUST: And if she lay there in blood, I would not waver in my resolution to conquer her. . . . Spirits, up! Heal her with magic balsam.
. . . I notice that Don Juan approaches; he is not entirely a stranger
to her heart; let us encounter him!
[*He exits.*]

Scene 3

A wild region on Mont Blanc. DON JUAN *and* LEPORELLO *enter.*

LEPORELLO: You'll never reach Faust's magic castle. We're already so
high up we're running out of breath—like kings on thrones! But for
all that, there's nothing in sight. Let's go back; this is no place to
settle down.

DON JUAN: I like it very much here. One false step could cancel life.
Mountain-deep chasms gape under the thin snow. Friend, only in
danger does life take on any meaning.

LEPORELLO: Yes, indeed; only when your money runs out do you need
it most. Let's turn back, sir!

DON JUAN: I can still go on.

LEPORELLO: My God, look ahead! We've left the last clouds behind us,
and the mountain peaks still rise higher and higher! When you look
up, it's as though the world had turned itself upside down like a
bucket—as if height were depth—and one could fall into Heaven!

DON JUAN: No danger of that. The expression, however, was original;
here's a gold piece for it.

LEPORELLO: A gold piece? If only I were sitting behind the oven at
the inn! But here nothing but frost and snow, nothing living, the
ridges of the Alps all about, like frozen backs of whales in the Arctic
Sea, and us in between, lonesome and innocent as flies in milk.
Ah, when Mama bore me in suffering, she never dreamed her unfortunate son would end up in such a desolate situation. Oh, my good
mother—sir, I weep!

DON JUAN: You make me laugh! Show me the tears, the genuine fruit
of the Alps, and I'll give them to the museum of natural history.

LEPORELLO: Take pity, sir! Turn back! I'll pray to all the saints if I'm
saved from this situation, I will—even—marry—Lisette!

DON JUAN [*becoming serious for the moment*]: On my honor, that's a
lot! Killing robbers is a trifle, but marriage! Marriage! Ha, that's the
winter which freezes the wave of the brook, the artificial, mischievous attempt to lure the freest godlike sensation—have I not experi-

enced it already?—out of the freedom of the open woods into the confines of family life—that is, to cage the nightingale, an ardor that neither can, nor ever should, become a habit. A deathly frost envelops us here, but it is a flame compared to the idea of marriage. Ha! I embrace the girl I love; I marry the one I hate or the one who has money.

LEPORELLO: Sir, it's much the same with my marriage to Lisette. I hate her like a toad. You'll understand when I explain. The little I loved in her has been enjoyed already, and, as you well know, one never eats the same meal twice. [DON JUAN *starts to climb higher*. LEPORELLO *holds him back.*] Stop, sir! Look at the abyss under our feet!

DON JUAN: We can bypass it.

LEPORELLO: Look, someone's plowing through the rocks beyond it as though through brushwood.

DON JUAN: No doubt it's the Devil's Knight who told us the secret whereabouts of Donna Anna and offered us his help.

FAUST [*appearing*]: No, my dear fellow, it is not he; he's already suffering the punishment he deserves. No, it's Faust himself.

DON JUAN: The heroic Faust himself! And I am Don Juan—Don Juan himself!

LEPORELLO: Don, let's get out of here. He's a sorcerer. He can kill us, destroy us, turn you into a hare and me into a lion.

DON JUAN: I scorn all sorcery! It may be fine for tricks and sleight-of-hand, for changing face and other fun; but it can never transform the spirit. Never. That either turns to dust or stays the same as ever. Were I turned into a hare and you into a lion, I'd still remain Don Juan and you, Leporello, my servant and lackey.

FAUST: Juan, go back. You'll never reach the one you seek!

DON JUAN: As long as I breathe, I shall hope to find her.

FAUST: Retreat, I say, before the explosion of my power.

DON JUAN: Your power? A power which is not even strong enough to satisfy yourself, you narrow-chested weakling! You, who longed for the passions of Hell while still in the prime of life!

FAUST: Happy the slave in chains—so long as he has not tasted freedom!

DON JUAN: Who lies in chains? Who storms the heart of Anna with superhuman might and fails to conquer that tiny place? Why superhuman if you remain just human?

FAUST: Why human if you don't reach for the superhuman?

DON JUAN: The love of woman is as foreign to a superman, be he devil or angel, as to any kind of subhuman creature, be it frog, baboon or ape. And it is I, my friend, who live in the heart of Donna Anna!

LEPORELLO: Sir, we are lost—you go too far! Let me hang on to your coattails. Hurricane and tempest fulminate from his eyes!

FAUST: Ha, if that is so, as I have feared all along, then I'll tear out Anna's heart, roots and all, along with your image! But first I'll toss you down to the Governor's grave—the only place on earth, perhaps, where you'll quake before ghosts.

DON JUAN: You're mistaken! I quake neither before you nor ghosts.

FAUST: Spirits, whisk him away!

LEPORELLO: Take me along, sir! Look—clouds! winds! . . . Ah, there goes my pretty cap into the bargain.

[Upon a sign from Faust, DON JUAN and LEPORELLO are carried off by the storm.]

FAUST: She loves him! Shall I tear her to pieces? The Devil was right; he did not lie when he said he once loved ineffably!

Only he who has loved, knows hate, knows rage.

Only he who was pious, can grow Satanic.

Only he who has once been Satanic, can become truly pious.

Donna Anna who rejects me—who knows what is more passionate, my love for her or my hate?

[He exits.]

ACT IV

Scene 1

A graveyard near Rome, with the STATUE OF THE GOVERNOR. *Dusk.* DON JUAN *and* LEPORELLO *are on stage.*

DON JUAN: Hey! Leporello!

LEPORELLO: Sir, I've still not recovered my senses.

DON JUAN: Faust is a conjuror; yet all my life I'll be grateful to him for giving us this ride through the sky. How the clear, calm lakes and silvery-ribboned streams, the mountains and valleys, the tilled fields and lively cities flew by. Before we had a chance to be spoiled by one view, another was already in sight. The ecstasy that flashes through the eagle flying proudly over white glaciers still holds me in thrall. . . . Where are we?

LEPORELLO: In the Devil's kitchen. Either I must have a poor sense of smell, or it reeks here of the Devil's roast—if not of corpses.

DON JUAN: The region is not unknown to me. I recognize the heights in the west, drenched in the blood-red glow of the evening sun. Ho, Leporello! Rascal, do you see that double-domed heaven over there —St. Peter's cupola and the sky? We're outside Rome.

LEPORELLO: Better we were sitting inside Vesuvius.

DON JUAN: Why? The tenderest grass sprouts on ruins; there the cicada sings most brilliantly; the cry of joy sounds boldest in the midst of destruction; and wine tastes most delicious on the graves of the Scipios!

LEPORELLO: What about the murder of Octavio and the Governor? What about the police?

DON JUAN: Murder? Police? Tonight, dinner in Rome; tomorrow, another assault on Donna Anna. The police? Just let them come; if insolence won't hold them off, connections will. I'm on good terms with all the Spanish cardinals.

LEPORELLO: Connections! Yes, not bad if they work. Connections are much; brains, crime, and law, nothing. Better to lose one's brains than one's connections. I had an uncle who had an aunt; she had a niece who was the mistress of a bishop, and—

DON JUAN: Never mind your friendships! What are those figures glimmering so white and silent?

LEPORELLO: That Faust! Oh, that Faust! He's kept his promise. We're in the cemetery, and that marble knight with staff in hand—why, it's the monument on the Governor's grave.

DON JUAN: They've built him a monument already? He needed it. Otherwise they would have forgotten him all too easily.

LEPORELLO: I beg you, don't mock here where the dead sleep at our feet.

DON JUAN: You're worried about being food for worms? That's what the dead are.

LEPORELLO: If worms were reasonable, they wouldn't take chances on corpses.

DON JUAN: So reason makes cowards of us? And being unreasonable makes us brave?

LEPORELLO: What you don't know, doesn't hurt you. That's the way the ox feels when he's got the blinders before his eyes.

DON JUAN: And when the blinders are removed, the steer runs away. Yet I maintain there's nothing to worry about even in what you do see. . . . Read me the inscription on the base of the monument.

LEPORELLO: If only I could read!

DON JUAN: Must I teach you, scoundrel?

LEPORELLO: But I can't tell one letter from another. [*To himself*] If I could get out of here, I'd never go near this tomb again.

DON JUAN: Dog! I'll beat you to a pulp if you hesitate another instant. Fear the living, not the dead.

LEPORELLO: So I'll have to read. Well, let's try it—necessity is the mother of invention.

DON JUAN: Right. If one's cowardly enough to let invention mother necessity. Well, come on!

LEPORELLO: Oh, God! Oh, God!

DON JUAN: Well?

LEPORELLO: Yes, by God, I feel strange—I'm learning already. I'm learning; knowledge dawns on me. I can read letters I never knew or saw before, even Chinese. . . . It says: *Here rests Governor Don Gusman.*

DON JUAN: Here he rests and rots. Read the rest!

LEPORELLO: Oh! *And revenge awaits his murderer.*

DON JUAN: Whoever concocted this inscription is a dolt; it's neither Christian nor heathen. [*To the Statue*] Governor, you stand there like a Christian and threaten me with revenge? Is that godly? Did I not love you unto the second generation, even unto your daughter? And did I not slay you and the soft-spoken Octavio out of love? How could I more powerfully prove my love than by *not* shrinking from murdering my future father-in-law and the former bridegroom?

LEPORELLO: Don, oh, Don! Oh, Christ! Look, the statue moved!

DON JUAN: Are you moon-sick? The moon is rising.

LEPORELLO: No, the statue is moving!

DON JUAN: That's only because they set it carelessly on the pedestal.

LEPORELLO: No, there's life in it: its face moved. It was outraged by what you said.

DON JUAN: I thought only Doctor Faust played hocus-pocus. Now the dead do, too? Does stone begin to rave? If so, it would be a shame indeed if we didn't try our hand. Get up, Leporello, and prepare a feast tonight in our old home, so exquisite that the aroma alone will make us dizzy. Bring wine that burns with the glow of a hundred summers. Invite scarlet-mouthed maidens who consume kisses like sparks of fire with lips eternally burning, never extinguished, never satisfied—and with bosoms white and firm as frozen snow, yet burning, too. Then we'll see who's mightier, the spirit of the grave or that of the wine; whether shadows dare to fight flesh and blood in the light of day! All right, lackey, invite the Stone Governor at once to this banquet!

LEPORELLO: Have pity! What! Invite stones to a feast? Do stones eat? Do they drink?

DON JUAN: If they can make faces, perhaps they can eat too!

LEPORELLO: I beg you—

DON JUAN: I command you! Speak to him!

LEPORELLO: First let me make the sign of the cross.

DON JUAN: I'll cross you—

[He threatens him.]

LEPORELLO: Spare me! Listen, I'm talking already! Listen! Most esteemed, departed Governor of Marble—oh, Don, my tongue is paralyzed, and my knees—my master over there—not I—asks your Grace, with all due esteem and respect—

DON JUAN: Cut the respect!

LEPORELLO: —whether you will dine with him tonight.

DON JUAN: Don't whisper, speak up! Statues are hard of hearing.

LEPORELLO: Oh, angels of God, we're lost! He's nodding his head!

DON JUAN: Is he drunk?

LEPORELLO: Good spirits: praise the Lord, our God!

DON JUAN: Is this delusion or truth? [With sure, proud step, he walks around the monument, examining it. Then he speaks.] No: no impostor lies hidden here. So I myself must try and question clearly! My dear Governor—you are a rogue and a coward if you don't answer me—I ask you in good Spanish, and with clear brow [in a powerful voice]: Will you be my guest tonight?

GOVERNOR'S STATUE [with an affirmative nod]: Yes!

[Thunder and lightning.]

LEPORELLO: That was short, bright and clear!

DON JUAN: Strange! [To the Statue again] Then come; I'll roll out the red carpet for you. [To Leporello] Make arrangements for him, too.

LEPORELLO: Oh, if he should come, he'd make two mouthfuls of us!

DON JUAN: Where am I? Oh, yes! He answered. That's natural; because whatever happens is natural. So let him come: I await him without fear or trembling. Let's go!

LEPORELLO: Gladly! [Both leave; when they are about to walk off stage, LEPORELLO picks up a stone.] Sir, this pebble burns my palm. May I toss it at the Governor's head?

DON JUAN: Now you're brave?

LEPORELLO: Sixty feet away, I'm always brave. I just can't stand proximity. I can bear danger, but I can't bear to see it.

DON JUAN: Throw it.

LEPORELLO [*throwing it*]: Listen: a hit! I must have chipped his nose! Let's run!

DON JUAN: Yes, run and prepare the dinner. Neither Hell nor death shall spoil my appetite! [*Pointing to the Statue*] He wants to come! Droll! Unique!

[*Exeunt.*]

Scene 2

Mine shafts under Mont Blanc.

FAUST [*appearing*]: Diversion in the depths of the earth! [*Pounding the rocks with a hammer*] Slag and gold—and tin, lead, and copper. Fine for a rock collector. . . . Rise up, gnomes and demons!

FIRST GNOME: Come, here beats a heart!

SECOND GNOME: Come, here trouble dwells!

FIRST GNOME: Ah, yes: the gnomes' sport!

SECOND GNOME: Huddle close and mark
How it thumps and swells!

FIRST GNOME: Could that be the hero who for a prank
Had our master dragged round Mont Blanc?

FAUST: What's that mumbling? You little spirits? Go on; I won't harm you. Mock and rave on. Even if I dug down to the innermost core of this globe, I'd only bury myself.

FIRST GNOME: Scorn the fool who seeks by night
What he's lost in broad daylight!

MANY GNOMES [*singing*]: What's the heart to beat like that?
Do you know the little beast?
It's a vampire, round and fat,
That hourly on Faust's blood does feast!

FAUST: You call that sarcasm? It's nothing but the truth. And truth never offends Faust; it only hurts.

FIRST GNOME: Envelop him with deathlike cold,
Mile-long earthworm, black and bold,
Entwine him, hook him, fill him with fear!

FAUST: What pandemonium! Could I live here?

THE GNOMES: Oh, little doctor, you are enclosed:
it draws nearer and nearer

ringing you in from everywhere
tighter than you supposed!

FAUST: Nothing can tie me down!

FIRST GNOME: Nothing could harm you if you were tied down!

FAUST: A wild horse is a skeleton: it grows fat in town!

THE GNOMES [sing]: Blessed he, who, in narrow band,
  Hedged in by his house and land,
  Does not look to greener fields,
  But enjoys what life yields.
  Playing hide-and-seek with sorrow,
  He does not yearn for the morrow.
  All heaven closes in on him—
  Even the horizon, stars on its rim.

FAUST: They're trying to irritate me, to stir me up; so they resort to ridicule!

    Now tremble, you dumb dogs, and listen in all seriousness to what I have to say: I know how you gathered in a diamond bowl those tears which my abandoned Amalia shed over me at her death; and how you collected the tears of dethroned usurpers as they rolled down like ripe fruit after long battle-glow; I know, too, how the hot flame of eternal revenge hisses in your own hollow breasts. Mix all that here before me, and hand over the refreshing drink, so full of pain that it makes me forget all other pain!

GNOME: The cauldron gushes: we brew, Faust, we brew!
  It foams! Here, empty it: the drink of horror and rue!

FAUST: All Hells bless this drink; and may it destroy me!

GNOMES: Cheers! Cheers to you!

FAUST [after emptying the goblet, throws it to the ground]: Aha, child's play of the spooks! No use to me: it's harmless! The giant I fear lives only in myself. I scorn you! One sound, one name, is mightier than all of you: *Donna Anna!* Oh, Donna Anna!
  [*He exits.*]

FIRST GNOME: Heh, heh! Donna Anna! Torture and woe:
  Our Faust falls in love with a face!
  A man who would fathom the world below
  And can't even find his own place!

GNOMES: So let us rejoice and make noise:
  In man's suffering, we find voice!
  [*They disappear.*]

Scene 3

Mont Blanc. A room in Faust's Magic Castle. FAUST *enters.*

FAUST: What I want, I must get or I destroy it! Yearning, whether for Heaven or for Love, does not satisfy me as it does some lovesick fools; nor do I indulge in sweet melancholy and smug self-satisfaction. No, no: I prefer to imitate the tiger who hungers until he's had enough to eat, and has torn to pieces the prey over which he lurks. But must a man tear to pieces in order to enjoy? Digestion almost makes me believe it. Uncut pieces taste bad: my stomach and soul tell me so.

Well, then? She—oh, what beauty and grace are summed up in that *she!* How much this little word can mean! She—Don Juan in her heart; she—my one love, somebody else's? When her dark curls first caught my eye like an electric storm cloud—was that a sign the sultry heaviness of day would follow? When, as I was wandering between Heaven and Hell, the gulf stream of her glance, lifted me out of the cold muddy sea of despair and tossed me purged and cleansed on the surface of the ocean, was it that I might fall crushed here, entranced at a maiden's feet, instead of being lost out there in the vast wastes of Creation?

She does not love me: that in itself is Death!

But that she loves another: that is Hell!

Is that why I flew to Satan—that I might glimpse happiness but not achieve it? And who is this little fool? Her intellect is limited. If virtue can pass for intelligence, she may be clever enough. As for her body—true, she has an excellent figure, her skin is smooth and white, her hair just the right shade of brown—but what does all that mean? A thousand women are more beautiful than she. . . . And who am I? I am Faust; I am the heaven-storming giant engulfed by the horrors of the underworld. And she . . . she . . . Ah, she is the girl I tenderly love!

The heart! Oh, the heart! Reason is clear and pure, but out of the heart wells the storm that darkens it. He who has loved, hated, hoped and feared—who, deserted by God, sold himself to the Devil—something beat in his heart; there fell the hammer-stroke that forged the sword of his madness, and sprayed the sparks of his infatuation! . . . And it may well be that she had a reason for preferring him. . . . I will no longer endure her coldness. I will not flatter like a dog only to be kicked in return. I threw art and science aside with mockery and laughter when I beheld her; I killed my wife. And she spurns me.

DONNA ANNA [*entering, she notices Faust*]: Ha, there he is! If Don Juan was the lightning bolt, swift and fiery as he is charming—to my shame, I must confess it!—then *he* is the storm cloud—without lightning, but full of flashes. One can only shy away from such weather, not love it! I see that he's about to explode; yet what would virtue be if it ever trembled? I face him with steady pride!

FAUST [*to Donna Anna*]: Will your mourning never cease? It's high time it did!

DONNA ANNA: If you are a man of honor, you will let me go.

FAUST: I am a man of power, and power creates its own honor.

DONNA ANNA: Honor is not created; true power is created by honor.

FAUST: As you please. Honor, power—they create, they do not create—phrases can be turned inside out like a glove and worn on both sides. You speak like your father.

DONNA ANNA: How glorious to think and act like him!

FAUST: No glory! Why should there be time, years, hours? The young ought to grow wiser than their elders, children cleverer than their parents. . . . It makes no difference. Why do you love Don Juan?

DONNA ANNA: You ask? And if I did, is there any *why* to love? The sun shines, and pearly-dewed meadows sparkle in their lustre; lightning strikes wild and free out of the night, killing horse and rider; and who asks *why?*

FAUST: I do!

DONNA ANNA: Love is free, hate is slavery.

FAUST: And do you hate Don Juan?

DONNA ANNA: The more fiery my love for him, the stronger my hate!

FAUST: What? Do love and hate sleep in one bosom?

DONNA ANNA: Doesn't the lion sleep in the sun?

FAUST: Yes, he does, and he's aroused in me! Are you a rock? So am I. Let's see how we face each other! Do you reject me? Even if you were the first of the angels, I'd reject you in turn! The world-conqueror Attila storms through one country after another. They are his sole joy; he extends his hands yearningly toward them; they refuse him. He tramples them under his horses, plants a column of fire for his flag, and lets it spread from horizon to horizon. He does not conquer, he destroys. And do you expect me, globe-conqueror that I am, to be milder? I have but to utter one syllable and you will sink dead at my feet! . . . You keep silent?

DONNA ANNA: I am thinking of my father and Don Octavio.

FAUST: I shall disturb them in Heaven itself. . . . Still silent?

DONNA ANNA: You don't deserve an answer. If you weren't a thief and an abductor, I'd advise you to approach a girl with charm, not with scorn.

FAUST: Tell that to anyone but Faust. Charm and graciousness are mere shells; truth is the kernel. I cannot flatter or bow down before anyone, not even God. Yet I am capable of proving whom I am and have done so already—through power and death. . . . Will you be mine? I warn you! Death has flickered on my lips for some time now; and evil, you know, slips easily from the tongue.

DONNA ANNA [*turned away from Faust, and looking up*]: Oh, golden flower of virtue, come wind about me, and let me be a sacrifice to you.

FAUST: What I said, I say again and will do because I said it! Beware, my lips are quivering. I shall not sigh one minute longer for you— you whom I can destroy with one word. I never sigh without avenging myself. Do you hate me?

DONNA ANNA: Yes!

FAUST: Then die.

DONNA ANNA: Alas, I die!

[*She dies.*]

FAUST [*frozen*]: My power is almost quicker than my tongue. Dead. Gone. What is the world? It is—it was worth much; there one can love! But what is love without an object? Nothing, nothing. The woman I love is everything; I feel it now near Donna Anna's body. Man is pitiful! Nothing great, neither religion nor love, comes to him directly; he needs a conductor. If only I hadn't sold myself to Hell the moment I looked on this woman! . . . Anna, awake! . . . [*Calling loud*] Knight!

KNIGHT [*entering*]: Thanks for all the tortures to which you sentenced me: they teach me how to torture you in return.

FAUST: Raise the dead!

KNIGHT: Ay, ay, Donna Anna. That's settled. I cannot resurrect her; the dead are mine only when they go to Hell.

FAUST: Anna, how nobly beautiful! Even in death! I sense it through these tears I shed. There was once a God and he was smashed to pieces. We are his pieces; speech and melancholy, love and religion and pain are only dreams of his.

KNIGHT: You God dreamer!

FAUST: That I am!

KNIGHT: What a shame the girl died too soon for you to corrupt her!

FAUST: Corrupt *her*?

KNIGHT: Of course! Does the tree fall at one blow? And trees offer the axe only wood, bark, and leaves. A woman has hands, cheeks, breast, and reason; a man can assault her in a hundred spots.

FAUST: Anna, forgive me! I did not treat you as I should have. Hear my remorse; it says far more than tears. *Devil, in one hour I am yours!*

KNIGHT: In one hour, Doctor?

FAUST: Absolutely.

KNIGHT: Sir, that's much: it's self-conquest. I'll reward you generously—

FAUST: Hypocrite!

KNIGHT: Let me kiss your feet [*to himself*] for the last time.

FAUST: Another man who loved her is still alive. I'll let Don Juan know that she is dead. Then all my earthly business is finished.

KNIGHT: The Don will be shocked!

FAUST: Only shocked? Shock is nothing. He will groan like me!

KNIGHT [*to himself*]: When he does that, I'll join the party!

[*Exeunt.*]

Scene 4

Rome. A magnificent hall in Don Juan's residence. Moonlight and starlight stream in through the window. The KNIGHT *appears.*

KNIGHT. Here in Don Juan's magnificent hall I establish the seat of Hell; it is enthroned wherever I am. Now both are mine; Faust by his own will and Don Juan through pious spirits! Ha! Finally I triumph. But how I have cowered and cringed for this, and groveled, always groveling, only to rise again that much more terrifying from the mire.

   Now I rise—

And look, the stars grow pale, and night breaks through like dark waves of the sea! [*It becomes dark and clouds gather.*] Off with the disguise! [*He rips off the black cloak and mask, and stands clothed in red, face flaming with fury.*] I wear the colors of my element again! [*Dreadful lightning and thunder.*] Ah, you recognize me? Greeting me with jubilation, the lightning crashes down at my feet. My thanks to you! Justice means nothing . . . and Hell is joy . . . only if you win out in the end. Might makes right!

Must I think of it now, the hour for which I strive, the hour when I shall bury Him in the rubble of His magnificence? Him, whose presumptuous name I do not pronounce—and, instead of His own light, let the flaming tongue of Hell burn and devour it? And yet, O hour, you approach. I feel it. I shall look upon you yet, for I am immortal and untiring! . . . Don Juan and his lackey are coming in. I'll mark time, invisible here, until the hour tolls for Faust, and then for him!

[*He steps into the background and paces back and forth.* DON JUAN *and* LEPORELLO *enter.*]

DON JUAN: A little ditty hums in my ear like water running over a millwheel:

> With fresh spirits through life,
> Proud, never stooping to wive,
> Every maid kissed with pleasure,
> Every fool snubbed at leisure,
> So will you be lucky and great,
> So will you make your own fate!

LEPORELLO: Didn't you notice a storm brewing?

DON JUAN: What does a storm mean to me?

LEPORELLO: How sultry and sinister it is, as though a thunder cloud were bottled up in here.

DON JUAN: Fetch candles and open the windows.

LEPORELLO [*pointing to the background where the invisible Knight is pacing up and down*]: Don't you see those red sparks flashing there?

DON JUAN: Light, I say, light!

LEPORELLO: Right away, sir, right away.

[*He exits.*]

DON JUAN: It's true, it is sultry in this room! It's unnaturally dense! But the odor of the roast will cut through that. Nothing more dependable in the world than the sense of smell; in no time at all it enchants us into the realm of reality. So much so, that if, in Eden, you were to smell the aroma of cooking or feel the aura of the tomb, you'd think yourself transported out of Eden and set down at a feast or in a vault on earth.

[LEPORELLO *returns with lit candelabra.*]

LEPORELLO: Sir, there's noise on the steps.

DON JUAN: It must be the guests I've invited.

LEPORELLO: No, no, not civilian footsteps; they're police steps!

DON JUAN: How can you tell?

LEPORELLO: By their dignified coarseness.

DON JUAN: Dignity with coarseness is absurd. Let the police in.

LEPORELLO: Sir, do you know what you're doing?

DON JUAN: Let them in!

[SIGNOR RUBIO *and* SIGNOR NEGRO *enter with policemen.*]

SIGNOR NEGRO: What's wrong with me? It's just as stuffy in here, with the air pressing down on the heart, as at the Governor's Dance of Death. Are these fumes of blood or fumes of fire?

DON JUAN: What do you people want?

SIGNOR NEGRO: We're not "people," Sir! This man here is Rubio, Chief of Police, and I am Signor Negro.

DON JUAN: And so, not "people" or "men": you, a signor; that one, a chief. My dear chief, what do you wish?

SIGNOR RUBIO: I arrest you, sir, as you might say, because you murdered the Governor and Octavio, as you might say.

DON JUAN: Thanks to you, Signor Negro! What a droll fellow you are, proud, but without strength or courage. Instead of executing the worst criminal yourself, you just greedily track him down; instead of wielding the dagger, you turn informer, and seek to torture and strangle by law and the scaffold. . . . Up with you, Leporello, and throw the signor out of here—boldly, now—you can force him out—

LEPORELLO: I've got my heart set on it.

SIGNOR NEGRO: Oh, chief! Signor Rubio!

SIGNOR RUBIO: Help him, men!

[LEPORELLO *throws* SIGNOR NEGRO *out and follows after him.*]

DON JUAN [*holding back* SIGNOR RUBIO *and his men*]: My dear chief, I am exercising my house rights on Negro. He is not authorized to break in here on suspicion of murder. All respect to you, however, as an officer. Only, I beg you, tell your men to be quiet.

SIGNOR RUBIO: Sir, you dare—

DON JUAN: All that I can.

SIGNOR RUBIO: You are—

DON JUAN: What I am!

SIGNOR RUBIO: You have—

DON JUAN: Done what I've liked!

SIGNOR RUBIO: Eh! First let me finish what I'm saying, man!

DON JUAN: In a minute! But first tell me who you are.

SIGNOR RUBIO: You've known for some time! I am, as you might say, the police.

DON JUAN: Do you have a pass? A warrant?

SIGNOR RUBIO: What? Are you mad? The police need warrants?

DON JUAN: Yes, they need them; even you can't be trusted without a pass.

SIGNOR RUBIO: Are you serious?

DON JUAN: I wouldn't bet a farthing on you. How old are you?

SIGNOR RUBIO: About fifty-six.

DON JUAN: What's your name?

SIGNOR RUBIO: Signor Rubio, as you might say.

DON JUAN: That same Rubio who was drunk at Octavio's wedding feast?

SIGNOR RUBIO: Why are you questioning me?

DON JUAN: Why did you answer me?

SIGNOR RUBIO: It just happened that way!

DON JUAN: You see—it happened! The unforeseen happens easily. Now pay attention: there is an upper-echelon police and a lower echelon. The upper is the smarter, it is concerned only with what's expedient, while the lower just notices what goes wrong. It's true that I tried to snare Donna Anna, as well as other girls, and still try. And that's why I killed the Governor and Don Octavio. But it's also true that I am a Spanish grandee, Cardinal Gonzalo's nephew, and the Pope's favorite. Speak, sir: what have you to say now?

SIGNOR RUBIO: Good Lord, a grandee! Nephew to the all-powerful Gonzalo! Don, forgive me. I was mistaken in your person! That cursed Negro, as you might say! Well, now, it's not a question of the police, it's a question of politics! Did I speak of murder, sir? What does that amount to, as you might say? Such a little murder, and among good friends, can happen all too easily. And the consequence? One is dead, and the other still living! All quite natural. With the common run of people, of course, one has to punish the ordinary. Otherwise it will occur too often, and become the rule. Commoners don't murder for honor or fame, but out of hate.

DON JUAN: Which brings matters to a close with us. Therefore get out of this room! Pardon me, quite ordinary and natural. . . . There, take that! [He punches him in the back.] Oh, all quite natural. Don't you dare come back with your hoodlums and henchmen! Quite ordinary, as you might say.

SIGNOR RUBIO: I take my leave of you!

DON JUAN: It's high time you did. [SIGNOR RUBIO and his following are driven out by DON JUAN. LEPORELLO returns.] Is Signor Negro thoroughly despatched?

LEPORELLO: Head over heels.

DON JUAN: Good. Now bring the food.

LEPORELLO: Sir, sir, black thunderclouds, pitch-black as a Moor's fist, are converging toward the sun; they're threatening the world!

DON JUAN: Let them rise, and let lightning hiss and flash with pleasure. I'm for drinking and dining now!

LEPORELLO: Listen to the roaring of the wind.

DON JUAN: It sounds dreadful, but beautiful.

LEPORELLO: Someone's knocking! Could it be—? Approach! Who's out there?

[FAUST *enters, face distorted and pale: the lingering* KNIGHT *in the background is about to pounce upon him.*]

FAUST [*to the Knight*]: Back with you! Wait your turn! First I must speak with him.

DON JUAN: With whom does anyone speak here but with me? . . . Faust! Oh, he makes me shudder. He looks like the crushed ruins of the world glimmering in the evening dusk.

FAUST: Alas, by the hour grows my love, grows my pain! [*To Don Juan*] Did you love her, too?

DON JUAN: Anna, you mean?

FAUST: Yes, Anna!

DON JUAN: How can you ask? Is she not beautiful?

FAUST: Dead! She is dead! Hear and despair with me!

DON JUAN: Despair? When the high waves of misfortune and sorrow crash down, a man must raise the flag on the mast of life, and battle for that flag's honor and renown to the very pit of ruin! . . . Yes, I am shaken by Donna Anna's death. It moves my innermost heart! Yet, I set sail again, and with a fresh wind. Are there not a thousand other beautiful girls? Why should I grieve over one? By not shying away from death to avenge her, I'll show that I loved her! I'm sure you're the one who killed her. It's like you to wreck your own heaven —Draw your sword! Try a few passes!

FAUST: "To wreck my own heaven!" He dares to reproach me. And he is right. I crushed the most magnificent thing because I did not understand it! . . . You are lost to me, oh Donna Anna! Never will I see the lustre of your eye or bathe in the brilliance of your beauty again; never will a little word, rendered beautiful through the magic of your voice, sound out for me. Yet I shall think of you forever, and this thought will defeat the reality of Hell! [*To the Knight, who has neared Faust again*] With defiance I fall into your arms. Know this, however: if I am an eternal being, I shall struggle with you through all eternities; and I may win, trampling you underfoot once again, as before!

KNIGHT [*seizing* FAUST *and immediately choking him to death*]: We'll be waiting! Down to the deepest pit with him! Heap mountains of burning oil on him, the Mount of Olives* from the City of Zion among them; heap mountains of fire on his soul. Never mind the body. Do it well, you spirits; I'll return soon with Don Juan!

[*He steps into the background again, and remains there during the entire scene, eyes fixed on Don Juan.*]

DON JUAN: Is the witch doctor bewitched? Is he talking to thin air?

LEPORELLO: He falls from the chair. He dies, you saints—and his face is coal-black, turned backwards on his twisted neck!† This room is haunted by a devil!

DON JUAN: Fool! Cut the grimaces! He had a stroke. Take him away from there.

LEPORELLO: Take him away? Him? Touch a man marked by God?

DON JUAN: You just spoke of the Devil.

LEPORELLO: It's all the same. God marks with the Devil as children draw with charcoal.

DON JUAN [*threatening*]: Remove the body!

LEPORELLO [*shivering, he removes Faust's corpse and returns*]: I can breathe again. The monster is cleared off!

DON JUAN: Friend, what did you promise up on Mont Blanc? Didn't you say you wanted to improve yourself—to marry Lisette?

LEPORELLO: Remember, Don, it's easier to make a promise than to keep it. What I promise, I promise; and what I keep, I keep. Besides, I've had no word my offer was accepted.

DON JUAN: Set the table. Where are our guests?

LEPORELLO: Guests? Don't you hear the gusts of wind whisk ahead of the thunder, sweeping the streets clean of dust and people? Can guests still come?

DON JUAN: Set the table.

---

*There is a pun here in the German—"Oelberg" meaning both mountain of oil and Mount of Olives. [*Translator's note.*]

†According to some medieval traditions, signs of the Devil's hand in murder or death. See *The Second Report of Doctor John Faustus* (London: 1894): "At length hee was found . . . by his bed starke dead, and his face turned backwards. . . !" See also *Dr. Johannes Faustus Puppet Play done into English*, 1893: "Good sirs, don't enter into evil/Communication with the Devil;/For in the end he's sure to cheat you,/And to a twisted neck to treat you." [*Translator's note.*]

LEPORELLO: Yes, sir.

[*He sets the table and brings in food and wine.*]

DON JUAN [*pouring wine*]: Oh, Donna Anna! Wine, overflow! Drown her out! Oh, this French champagne! Like an untamed falcon, you bubble up to the ceiling; but my jubilation—in spite of Anna, in spite of sorrow—shall reach the stars! . . . Rogue, what are you doing?

LEPORELLO: I was just drinking to your health. The good wishes of your faithful knave.

DON JUAN: Pastry—roasts—salads! [*He eats.*] All passably prepared. Have you ordered the musicians?

LEPORELLO: Sir, they are outside. May they come in?

DON JUAN: Why should I see them blowing and scratching away? Let them play, but out of sight. [LEPORELLO *goes off and comes right back. Then music.*] Music is a good test at meals; if the food is good, one doesn't hear it! [*Eating*] Excellent! I don't hear it. [*To Leporello*] Man—what are you eating?

LEPORELLO: What am I eating? I'm sampling the pheasant to see if it's well roasted. Eating and sampling: a great difference. Oh, if only the world were a roast capon, and I the one to gnaw at it. Horrible, how you let me starve.

DON JUAN: Scoundrel, I give you nothing because I know you steal it anyway. . . . Wine, wine! The bottles are empty! [LEPORELLO *gets new bottles.*] Long live Mohammed! He forbade wine because he loved it so much. For the prohibition, as he correctly concluded, doubles the pleasure!

[*Thunder and lightning.*]

LEPORELLO [*at the window*]: Sir, be Christian, be Christian! Look, look at the clouds! Rain—lightning—and—thunder! No end to it. Heaven hangs over us like a fire-spewing volcano. . . . There, a bolt just struck the archbishop's palace!

DON JUAN: *Da capo!* Let lightning bolts start eternal fires, especially when they strike!

LEPORELLO: Mercy! Mercy! Lightning and thunder again! How the storm rages!

DON JUAN [*downing a glass of wine*]: Cheers to thunder: may it rumble on for a thousand years like today!

LEPORELLO: Sir, the storm—it's closing in on us—I can hardly breathe. Sir, it's meant for us!

DON JUAN: The juice of the vine makes me hot; thunder and lightning are cold as snow in comparison!

LEPORELLO: Do I have any iron on me? They say that lightning is drawn to it [*throwing away keys, shoes, etc.*] There! Keys!—hobnailed shoes—away with them all! Oh, God, do you hear that heavy tread? Someone's coming: listen to him stamping his way through the thunderstorm!

DON JUAN: One of our guests.

LEPORELLO: I hope it's not the statue you invited. Those aren't human footsteps, no: those are earthquakes approaching!

DON JUAN: A sword! My sword!

LEPORELLO: Here it is!

DON JUAN [*unsheathing his sword*]: Welcome, most trusted friend! You kill the enemy, and will never leave me until my hand falls off! Now be my prober: let me test the marble guest with your tip. [*To Leporello*] Open the door.

LEPORELLO: Unnecessary! He knocked so hard the door broke open by itself.

DON JUAN: Who dares step so brazenly into my room? [*The* GOVERNOR'S STATUE *enters.*] Ha!

LEPORELLO: Oh, Jesus, Mary, and Joseph! The statue from the cemetery—I'm dead!

DON JUAN: Terrifying, but also idiotic! Quiet, Leporello!

LEPORELLO: If only I could hear a hen cackle—or a dumb duck quack —I'd feel the earth again. But this is the realm of the spirits.

STATUE: Don Juan—

LEPORELLO: Oh, what a voice! It freezes my marrow.

STATUE: You have commanded, and I have appeared!

DON JUAN: Is it a statue or is it not? Its eye is white, but there's no life in it. I fall to the ground! And yet I call out my name; though bloodstained, it is honorable! And just as a gong arouses city and country, so do I, with the full ring of that name, summon up all my power and all my courage. *My name is Don Juan and I defy you!*

STATUE: Weakling, no living man can defy me.

DON JUAN [*grasping his forehead*]: What a voice! . . . Still, it may be a fraud. Let's see whether this is genuine stone quarried in Bohemia; can it take the slash of steel? [*He hacks at the Governor's Statue and splinters his sword.*] Genuine! I still have a dagger—shorter than the sword, of course, but surer, closer! [*He pulls the dagger and swings it wildly over his head.*] I'm still armed, so why be afraid? [*To Leporello*] Where are the musicians? Why do they interrupt their playing? [*Thunder and lightning.*]

LEPORELLO: Don't you hear, sir? There's the music that broke the strings!

DON JUAN: My dear Governor, is it your pleasure to be seated? Here is a chair—

LEPORELLO: The chair will be crushed under his weight like grain under a millstone!

DON JUAN: Here is turtle soup—here, roast venison—also beefsteak—roast beef—fricassee—endive salad—there, wine—tokay—champagne and burgundy—help yourself, sir!

STATUE: I come from the stars. I have no need of earthly food.

DON JUAN: Since I cannot serve star food, I invite you to this earthly meal. You're a fool if you came in hope of other pleasures.

STATUE: Donna Anna and Don Octavio, reunited in Heaven, their earthly pain changed to bliss, their tears transformed to pearls, remembered you in their holy felicity, and sent me down here that I might admonish you to repent and reform.

DON JUAN: Thanks for the greeting! But I have nothing to repent; I feel no remorse; everything I've ever done pleases me. Why should I reform when I'm only too happy with myself?

LEPORELLO: Pretend, sir, pretend—and give in a little. Lie to him. We can worry about it afterwards. Remember, you get poor guiltless me out of this scrape along with you! . . . Oh, oh, the marble creaks again!

STATUE: Have you the courage to give me your hand and swear you will not reform?

DON JUAN: My hand! My hand! . . . Yet am I not in Rome? Here Scaevola plunged his right hand in the fire. I do more. I extend mine boldly into the realm of the underworld, and speak: life is nothing if it does not face all that it meets! Here! [*He gives his hand to the Governor's Statue, which holds it fast for a few moments and then lets it go.*] Oh, despicable rogue! Deathly cold flows from your hand into my veins! Is that how you reward the handshake of a Spaniard? Scoundrel, you should live again for me to kill again! [*He attacks the Governor's Statue with his dagger.*]

STATUE: Get back! [DON JUAN *tumbles back.*] Look, the dark flame behind you is coming toward you! It is Satan dressed for a feast!

LEPORELLO: Oh, oh, my foreboding. That's why it was so suffocating in this room. . . . Satan, sir! I'm not worth your trouble. [*Pointing to Don Juan*] Take *him,* he's worth your while!

STATUE: He lies in wait to join you with Faust. Yet I can save you if only you will repent. For the last time, I ask you in the thunderous voice of God: will you repent and reform?

DON JUAN: What I am, I will remain. I am Don Juan; if I become somebody else, I shall be nobody! Rather Don Juan in the brimstone of the Abyss than a saint in the light of Paradise! You asked me with a voice of thunder. With a voice of thunder, I answer: No!

STATUE: We shall not meet again.

[*It disappears.*]

KNIGHT [*throwing his red cloak into the air*]: Cloak, spread out, unfold your fabric, set this house aflame and consume its denizens one and all! [*Conflagration and rain of fire.*] But you, Juan, I take with me —and chain you to Faust. I know you will roll in the same direction, though in two different coaches!

DON JUAN: Now I call out my last utterance on earth: *King and Glory, Fatherland and Love!*

[*The* KNIGHT *disappears, pulling* DON JUAN *down with him.*]

LEPORELLO: Fire in every corner; I'll burn to death. Is there no help anywhere? Help, the flames are upon me! They're here! No escape! I'll burn to death!

[*The curtain falls amidst fire, thunder, and lightning.*]

Don Juan on the Musical Stage (1817-1820)

Moncrieff and the London Theatre

In England the subject of Don Juan, though never forgotten, came into its own only after Mozart. Don Juan plays began to abound at the two royal theatres (Drury Lane and Covent Garden) and at many of the competing "minors." These plays must be considered as disreputable offsprings of Mozart's masterpiece—

> each one
> Of sundrie shapes, yet all ill-favored;

and most were, in fact, musicals using popular tunes or snatches of Mozart and any other handy composer. Since straight drama was forbidden at the minors until 1843, Londoners were treated to melodramas, operettas, burlesques, farces, extravaganzas, burlettas and pantomimes (not to mention animal shows and water spectacles)—the equivalents, more or less, of our own musical comedies, vaudeville, and film spectaculars. These were so successful that the legitimate theatres were compelled to imitate them in order to survive. It was not, as everybody knows, a great age for the British theatre.

In 1820 it was difficult for a self-respecting, moral, London middle-class citizen to take his family to the theatre. Quite apart from the physical inconveniences attendant on the unruly manners of the crowd, he would find the playhouse filled almost entirely by the young bloods and the riff-raff of lower-class society. Prostitutes walked the lobbies and spectators were liable to insult or abuse from uncontrolled drunkards.[1]

To the low estate of this theatre, William Thomas Moncrieff (1794–1857) was a diligent contributor. He wrote some 170 dramatic pieces

1. Allardyce Nicoll, "The Theatre," in G. M. Young (ed.), *Early Victorian England* (London: Oxford University Press, 1934), II, 279.

for a number of playhouses which he also managed. Even failing sight could not stop him. (It is sometimes forgotten that mediocrity has its heroes too.) "The author," an anonymous writer says of him, "knew his audience, and catered for them to a nicety." At Astley's Royal Amphitheatre, where the common people and the elite met to watch horse shows, his "equestrian drama," *The Dandy Family*, ran for almost one hundred nights. Even more successful was his adaptation of Egan's *Life in London,* at the Adelphi in 1821. For his *Cataract of the Ganges! or, The Rajah's Daughter*, played at Drury Lane, he created a real waterfall. His subjects, like those of his contemporaries, were touching or picturesque, and always "romantic." I mention only *The Diamond Arrow; or, The Postmaster's Wife and the Mayor's Daughter. Gipsy Jack; or, The Napoleon of Humble Life. The Lear of Private Life!* (popular taste ran to the exclamative). *The Pestilence of Marseilles; or, the Four Thieves. Shipwreck of the Medusa; or, the Fatal Raft!* And the like.

In 1817 at least two plays about Don Juan appeared in London. One was Thomas J. Dibdin's *Don Giovanni; or, A Spectre on Horseback! a Comic, Heroic, Operatic, Tragic, Pantomimic, Burletta-Spectacular Extravaganza*, the best line of which is its title; and the other was Moncrieff's "operatic extravaganza" reprinted here. It provides us with a vaudeville interlude, a glimpse at average entertainment in one of the world's capitals in the early nineteenth century, and proof that despite Mozart, the *buffo* tradition of Don Juan was still alive while Keats and Shelley flourished. Only gradually did the serious Don Juan dislodge the clown.

Moncrieff's work, written for the Olympic Theatre, was a decided success. Its songs were printed separately, and the play itself was reprinted a number of times for a quarter of a century. It accompanied Moncrieff to Drury Lane in 1820, where it was acted twenty-nine times in that season, and where it still held the stage in 1827.[2] Indeed, in that year it ran in both legitimate houses, and in each case the part of Don Giovanni was played by a woman—at Covent Garden by Madame Vestris, one of the most notable and notorious theatrical ladies of the day.

In 1820, probably encouraged by the applause, Moncrieff produced a sequel to his play, *Giovanni in the Country*, copiously advertised as

2. See, for example, John Genest, *Some Account of the English Stage from the Restoration in 1660 to 1820* (Bath: 1832), IX, 36, 38; and playbills in *The Theatrical Observer* for 1827, passim.

The duel between Giovanni and Finikin (*Giovanni in London,* Act II, Scene 1). Engraving by Bonner from a Cruikshank drawing in *Cumberland's British Theatre* (1828). Reproduced by permission of The Huntington Library, San Marino, California.

"The New Comic Operatic Melo-Dramatic Pantomimic Moral Satirical Gallymaufrical Parodiacal Salmagundical Olla Podriacal Extravaganza Bizarro Entertainment," wherein only the last word is a certain lie. But others were no less prompt than Moncrieff himself. A *Giovanni in Paris,* another *Giovanni in the Country* (this one a "hippodrame") and a *Giovanni the Vampire* appeared successively at the East London, Astley's, and the Adelphi; and I daresay that others could be uncovered. For the rest, the list of English plays about, or more or less about, Don Juan in the nineteenth century is as long as it is invidious. They remain unread even by the most meticulous specialists in minor drama.[3] As usual, the best of such plays are the least serious, and Moncrieff cannot be denied something which almost resembles talent. What is regrettable is not that plays like Moncrieff's should have existed, and even prospered, but that nothing much better was born.

Moncrieff's musical comedy has one good idea, which was to occur to Rostand as well: that of sending Don Juan back to earth after his little misadventure with the Statue. In Moncrieff's version he is ejected from Hell by a jealous Pluto who has caught him kissing Proserpine. Another idea, that of marrying Anna to Leporello, is far from inspired, but it is at least an idea. Moncrieff makes not so much as a gesture toward coherence or even the logic of farce in his plot, but one or two of his quips are passable, the song "We are three jolly widowers" is well turned, and the rest is cocky and unsentimental. The serious student can demonstrate with this play that "in the period of the Industrial Revolution the bourgeois Don Juan triumphs over the aristocratic concept." What is more, Don Juan's redemption by true love and marriage marks the work as a post-classical farce, since even the most trifling scribble participates in "cultural trends." But does Moncrieff really mean Don Juan to be redeemed by marriage? In view of his jests about husbands and wives, we might speak of a certain ambiguity in the finale, or perhaps of a tension between two literary eras.

3. For an account of the equally inglorious career of Don Juan in the United States, see Armand E. Singer, "Don Juan in America," *Kentucky Foreign Language Quarterly,* VII (1960), 226–232.

WILLIAM T. MONCRIEFF

Giovanni in London

or

The Libertine Reclaimed

An Operatic Extravaganza
in Two Acts

(1817)

EDITOR'S NOTE

Directions pertaining to the relative positions of the performers on the stage have been omitted, obvious typographical errors corrected, and the format made consistent with that of other plays in this volume; otherwise the text follows that of the acting copy published in 1828. Since an "operatic extravaganza" was primarily a spectacle, the descriptions of costumes and "fanciful lights" have been retained and appear following the scene synopsis. The "fine wood engraving, By Mr. BONNER, from a Drawing taken in the Theatre, by Mr. R. CRUIKSHANK," from the original edition is reproduced on page 400, courtesy of the Henry E. Huntington Library, San Marino, California.

TEXT

Giovanni in London by W. T. Moncrieff in *Cumberland's British Theatre*, vol. XVII, n.p. London: John Cumberland, 1828. Reprinted by permission of the Henry E. Huntington Library, San Marino, California.

Cast of Characters

Don Giovanni, *the Libertine reclaimed*
Leporello, *his Valet of all work*
Finikin, *an amorous Haberdasher*
Deputy English, *an eminent Common Councilman*
Pluto, *King of the Infernal Regions*
Mercury, *Turnkey and Messenger of Pluto*
Charon, *the Ferryman of Styx*
Firedrake, *a singing Demon*
Drainemdry, *Landlord of the Punch Bowl and Magpie*
Porous, *a flourishing coachmaker*
Simpkins, *an eminent tailor*
Popinjay, *Foreman to Finikin*
Shirk, ⎫
Spunge, ⎭ *Debtors*

Nokes, ⎫
Styles, ⎭ *Bailiffs*
Counsellor
A Lawyer
A Turnkey
A Watchman
A Cobbler
Proserpine, *Queen of the Infernal Regions*
Mrs. Leporello, *wife to Leporello, late Donna Anna*
Miss Constantia Quixote, *a young lady of fortune*
Mrs. English, *the Deputy's wife*
Mrs. Drainemdry, ⎫
Mrs. Porous,   ⎬ *Rescued souls*
Mrs. Simpkins,   ⎭
Squalling Fanny, *ci-devant Bride*
Succubus, ⎫
Tartarus, ⎭ *Amorous Furies*

Demons, Furies, Neighbours, Masquerade Characters, Debtors and Creditors.

Synopsis of Scenes

Act I

1. The Infernal Regions.
2. The River Styx.
3. A Street in London: Exterior of the Magpie and Punch Bowl.
4. St. Giles's, London:
5. Grand Saloon at Deputy English's.

Act II

1. Chalk Farm, Primrose Hill.
2. Outside of Deputy English's house.
3. Outside of Westminster Hall.
4. Interior of the King's Bench, gaol for debtors.
5. Exterior of the Insolvent Court.
6. Charing Cross.
7. Grand Saloon at Deputy English's.

Costume

DON GIOVANNI.—*First dress:* White cloth tunic, trimmed with crimson and gold—white silk pantaloons—red or yellow morocco half-boots—sash—white Spanish hat and feathers. *Second dress:* Fashionable brown coat—white pantaloons—hat—boots—hand whip.

LEPORELLO.—*First dress:* A brown Spanish dress, trimmed with red worsted binding—small cloak—hat, with a cock's feather in front —red stockings with white clocks—russet shoes—comic ruff. *Second dress:* Brown livery coat—livery hat—white pantaloons and shoes.

DEPUTY ENGLISH.—Old-fashioned brown coat and vest—black velveteen breeches—brown george wig—cocked hat—white worsted stockings—shoes and buckles.

FINIKIN.—Coat in the extreme of fashion—white waistcoat—light blue pantaloons, *à la militaire*—fashionable hat—enormous whiskers—eyeglass, suspended with a broad black ribbon.

POPINJAY.—Green coat in the extreme of fashion—white waistcoat and pantaloons—fashionable hat—enormous whiskers—eyeglass.

DRAINEMDRY.—Brown coat—red waistcoat—black velvet breeches —black and white worsted stockings—shoes and buckles—green apron—bush wig—cocked hat.

POROUS.—Drab coat and waistcoat—black velvet breeches—worsted stockings—shoes and buckles—bush wig—cocked hat.

SIMPKINS.—Claret-coloured coat and waistcoat—blue stockings, and little hat.

NOKES.—Blue coat—red waistcoat—blue pantaloons, shoes, and hat.

PLUTO.—Flesh-coloured body and pantaloons—crimson tunic, interlaced with gold trimming—crimson cloak—embroidered crown—long hair—belt—sandals.

CHARON.—Flesh coloured body—tunic, with red worsted binding —half the body and arms naked.

MERCURY.—White spangled shirt—flesh arms and legs—sandals—wings to his heels—cap with wings—caduceus.

LAWYER.—Black dress—green bag.

COUNSELLOR.—Black dress—gown—wig.

SHIRK.—Shabby nankeen pantaloons—little light blue coat, buttoned up—little hat.

FIREDRAKE.—Tight black dress—black petticoat shirt—long hair, and a snake twisted round his head.

DEMONS.—The same as Firedrake.

MRS. ENGLISH.—White fashionable walking dress—white hat with ostrich feathers—scarf.

CONSTANTINE.—White muslin dress.

MRS. LEPORELLO.—*First dress:* Gray Spanish dress, trimmed with points and white tape. *Second dress:* As an old woman—antique gown —high cap, &c.

SQUALLING FAN.—Red striped gown—red petticoat—mob cap— handkerchief—cottage-hat—blue stockings—shoes and buckles.

PROSERPINE.—Crimson dress—richly embroidered crown—train cloak—flesh stockings—sandals.

SUCCUBUS AND TARTARUS.—Black dress—black arms, stockings, and sandals—long black hair.

FEMALE FURIES.—The same as above.

MRS. SIMPKINS.—White gown and bonnet, with flowers—red spencer.

MRS. DRAINEMDRY.—White gown and bonnet, with flowers— blue spencer.

MRS. POROUS.—White gown and bonnet, with flowers—black spencer.

THE SCENERY IS DISPLAYED IN THE FOLLOWING FANCIFUL LIGHTS:

The Infernal Regions, by fire and torchlight.—The River Styx, by twilight.—The Magpie and Punch Bowl Public House, by lamplight.— St. Giles's, by gaslight.—Masquerade al Fresco, by a variegated light. —Chalk Farm, by daylight.—A Street, by starlight.—Westminster Hall, in a new light.—Interior of the King's Bench, in its true light.—Charing Cross, by a blue light.—Grand Saloon, by a fanlight.

ACT I

Scene 1

Infernal Regions by fire and torchlight. DON GIOVANNI *comes up through the floor, and lays on the ground, in the centre of the stage.* FIREDRAKE *standing over him, flashing his torch.*

DUET *and* CHORUS—FIREDRAKE, GIOVANNI, *and Demons.*
AIR—*"Fly not yet."*

FIREDRAKE: Come along, 'tis just the hour,
When Demons have the greatest power
To feed the libertine's desires,
And make him burn with real fires,
    So bring your flambeaux near.

[*Enter* DEMONS *with torches; forming a circle—*FIREDRAKE *standing at the front.*]

GIOVANNI: Oh pray! oh stay!
No log am I, your flames restrain;
Burn not yet, for oh! 'tis pain;
    Then take your links away.

[*Enter* FEMALE FURIES *with wands twined with Serpents.*]

DEMONS: Nay! nay! Nay! nay!
We are like earth's gaslights here,
We always burn when night is near,
    Make light of it, we pray.

CHORUS—*Firedrake and Demons.*
[*During this Chorus the female Furies dance round Giovanni. Demons flash their torches.*]
AIR—*"Round about the Maypole."*

Round about the sinner, let us trot,
    Scot,
    Lot,
    Hissing hot!
    Turning,
    Burning

Torching,

Scorching,

Perplexing, vexing, and what not.

Round about the sinner, &c.

SONG—*Giovanni.* [*Kneeling.*]

AIR—*"Pray Goody."*

Pray, Demons, please to moderate the fury of your fire,

Nor flash those sparks of sulphur from each link;

Remember, I'm but flesh and blood, so kindly check your ire,

And, 'pon my soul, I'll treat you all to drink.

Ply me,

Try me,

Prove me, ere you fry me,

Do not roast me

Pray, but toast me,

I'll soon find the chink!

Pray, Demons, please, &c.

FIREDRAKE: Don Giovanni, the attempt is vain—that oil of flattery on thy tongue, that wheedled woman's innocence away in the other world, will increase the fires that torture you in this. The world's wickedness gives no lack of employment here! We leave you, Don Giovanni, and let this interval of ease be cursed by the anticipation of our return.

[*Exeunt* FIREDRAKE, *Demons and Furies.*]

GIOVANNI: And was it for this I sighed at woman's feet? Can I, for having spent my life with angels, be sent to spend eternity with devils? Were they but she-devils, I might yet be content. By all my hopes, a female fury comes this way!—A fury!—well, no matter—many an angel in the other world has proved a fury in the end;—so I'll try in this if I cannot prove it "vice versa."

[*Enter* SUCCUBUS; *she advances towards Giovanni, who makes love to her.*]

SONG—*Giovanni.*

AIR—*German Melody, by Kunzen, from "Die Weinlese."*

Gentle fury, see me languish,

And in pity quench my flame;

Lovely Brimstone, ease my anguish;

No tongue my warmth can name.

I burn, I burn,
Gentle fury—yes!
Burn with a flame, I must not express.
Pretty devil,
Oh be civil!
I am scorching with love!
I'm on fire,
With desire,
Then a match let it prove.

Oh she's won! the Fury's won! [*Aside.*] Oh, Giovanni, thy power still avails thee here! [*Attempts to kiss her*] My gentle fury, one burning kiss I must impart upon thy brimstone lips, to seal our contract. Ah! whom have we here? By all the shades of my departed bliss, 'tis Tartarus—come to torment me for the pleasures she formerly bestowed. I must dissemble, and woo them both; it is a custom that has not yet forsaken me.

[*Enter* TARTARUS, *sees Succubus and becomes jealous; advances toward Giovanni, and reproaches him.* SUCCUBUS *becoming jealous in turn, does the same; they alternately pull him towards each other.*] Sweet Flour of Brimstone! [*To Succubus, aside.*] Charming Cream of Tartar! [*To Tartarus, aside.*] Flour of the one, and, oh! cream of the other! [*They turn away angrily.*] Out of the frying pan into the fire, faith! [*Aside.*] What shall I do to quell their ire.

SONG—*Giovanni.*
AIR—*"I've kiss'd and I've prattled."*

I've kissed and I've prattled with fifty she-devils,
    And changed them sans ceremonie;
But of all the sweet Furies that e'er drove man mad,
    Flour of Brimstone's the fury for me.
[*Aside to Succubus.*]
    Of all the sweet Furies that e'er drove man mad,
        Cream of Tartar's the Fury for me.
[*Aside to Tartarus. Furies appear inclined to mollify. Gong sounds. Enter* PROSERPINE, *enraged.*]

PROSERPINE: And can Giovanni be so base, so mean spirited, as to leave the infernal queen, the too-susceptible, too-trusting Proserpine, for such petty furies as these? I'll be revenged! What ho! My faithful slaves, appear! [*Calling*] Tear these vile furies in ten thousand pieces!

[*Gong sounds. Enter all the Fiends, flashing torches at each other.* PLUTO *descends on a fiery Dragon, and comes forward. Dragon ascends. Infernal uproar.*]

PLUTO: Who dares disturb this peaceful realm, where Pluto reigns?

ALL THE FIENDS: 'Twas that base, perjured villain, Don Giovanni!

PLUTO: Ah Giovanni! I remember, when he first came amongst us, we were warned that he would soon make the place too hot to hold us. He has seduced my furies, enticed my queen from a loved husband's arms; but to be revenged on the world which sent him here, I'll send him back again—Nay, nay! No pleading—away!

Devils, to the right about,
And with your pitchforks drive the villain out.

CHORUS—*Demons.*
AIR—*"Turn Out."*

From our regions infernal turn out, turn out;
From our regions infernal turn out!
Since first here you came,
You've set hell in a flame,
So now, Don Giovanni, turn out, turn out!
So now, Don Giovanni, turn out!

A match for the Devil, turn out, turn out!
A match for the Devil, turn out!
For us, Don Giovanni,
You've prov'd one too many;
So, as quick as you can, Don, turn out, turn out!
As quick as you can, Don, turn out!

[*Pluto, Demons, Furies, &c. turn Giovanni out amidst a variety of combustible matter. They return. Exeunt* PROSERPINE, PLUTO, *Demons, Furies.*]

Scene 2

The river Styx, by twilight. Entrance to the Infernal Regions, emitting flames, on one side. River Styx in the background. MERCURY *enters, calls* CHARON, *signs him to ferry over condemned souls; exit Charon, in his boat.* MERCURY *watches till the boat reappears.* CHARON *re-enters in his boat, with a well-known* LAWYER *and a* COUNSELLOR.

GLEE—*Condemned Souls.*
AIR—*"Canadian Boat-Song."* [*Sung behind the scenes.*]

Ply the oar, Charon, and speed the boat,
While o'er Styx' dusky waves we float—
Erebus' tide! the trembling moon
Will see us in purgatory soon.

CHARON: Before you land, my souls, tip me my fare, and then I'll commit you both to Mercury, who is such an obliging gentleman he'll hand you in a twinkling to the Devil. [*Lawyer and Counsellor give Charon money, and land.*] Here, my quicksilver, Mercury, here's another cargo.

MERCURY: The more the merrier! Stop, sir, [*To Lawyer*] be good enough to tell me what your honest soul was sent below for? [*Crosses to Lawyer.*]

LAWYER: I am a lawyer.

CHARON [*Aside.*]: That's the ninth I've ferried over today.

MERCURY: A lawyer! I am answered! Here, sir, you shall never want a fieri facias. [*Crosses to Counsellor.*] And you, sir?

COUNSELLOR: I, sir, am a counsellor.

MERCURY: And for following your own councils are condemned at last. It is but just, since so many have suffered by them in the other world, that you should feel their effects in this. But, gentlemen, your pardon for detaining you; walk in, walk in.

[MERCURY *and* CHARON *drive* LAWYER *and* COUNSELLOR *into the cave.* —Exit MERCURY *with them.*]

CHARON: A good day's work; I've made a pretty penny this morning. Lawyers are used to feeing.

[*Voices of all the Demons heard without.*]

From our regions infernal, turn out, turn out,
From our regions infernal, turn out.

CHARON [*To Mercury, who re-enters.*]: Hey! Merky! what means that infernal shout? [*Gong sounds. Enter* GIOVANNI *in double-quick time, as if driven out by Furies.*] Giovanni! yes, 'tis he, sure enough! Pray, my good friend, what's all this row about!

GIOVANNI: They've turned me out, and here I am, and my heart is so elated with joy!

MERCURY: And why are you so rejoiced?

GIOVANNI: Can you ask me why? Shall I not change the swarthy beauties of these nether regions for the bright blue eyes of English maids. Pray which is the nearest way to London, for I sleep there tonight; therefore I must wish you a good day. Old Chary, turn your boat and ply your oar, and wisk me over to the other side, my lad.

CHARON: With all my heart; but pay me my fare first, if you please— your money, sir!

GIOVANNI: Money! pshaw! nonsense! every philosopher, from Pythagoras to Sir Isaac Newton, has taught us that money was made alone for the other world, and was of no use in this—come, come.

CHARON: As to Isaac Newton I have never had to do with him—however, no money, no passage.

GIOVANNI: Oh, that I should be placed in such a dilemma as this, merely from not having a penny in my pocket, and from too firm a credence in philosophers. Ah! Mercury's wings, [*Retires to back.*] egad, they perhaps may serve to bear me o'er this barrier between me and pleasure. [*Takes up the wings. Mesdames Drainemdry, Porous, and Simpkins, three condemned souls, call without.*] Cary! Cary! Cary!

CHARON: Heyday! another fare, three females!

[CHARON *gets into the boat, and exit at the back of the stage.* MERCURY *looks out.*]

GIOVANNI: Yes, females, and coming here!

[*Enter* CHARON *and the* LADIES *in a boat.* CHARON *gets out.*]

CHARON: My fare before you land.

[*They give a one-pound note;* CHARON *and* MERCURY *come forward. The* LADIES *beckon Giovanni to take boat with them.*]

CHARON [*looks at the note*]: A piece of paper! Mercury, what's this!

MERCURY: A one-pound note, by mortals called a flimsey—a thing, good Charon, that has supplied your boat with many a fare.

CHARON: Will you change it?

MERCURY: Provided it be a good one.

GIOVANNI: Ah! this one-pound note gives me a golden opportunity; I'll seize on Charon's boat and bear these lovely females back again.

MERCURY [*Examines the note.*]: Yes, it will do.

GIOVANNI [*After taking Mercury's wings, jumps into the boat and pushes it off.*]: Farewell, Cary! we're off!

CHARON: Heyday! that fellow's got into my boat. Stop, stop!

[CHARON *and* MERCURY *run up the stage. Scene closes on the confusion.*]

Scene 3

*A Street in the Borough: exterior of the Magpie and Punch Bowl
public house, by daylight. Enter* MESDAMES DRAINEMDRY, POROUS, *and*
SIMPKINS, *with* GIOVANNI.

GIOVANNI: So, here, my lovely souls, we are at last. Thanks to Merky's
wings, we've travelled briskly enough: we've left the mail and steam-
boat far behind us:—and this is London, dear emporium of pleasure.
[*Looks about.*]

MRS. DRAINEMDRY: Yes, dear Don; and this is my house, the Magpie
and Punch Bowl—you see the sign—my husband's face and mine are
painted on it; he's famed for drinking punch, and I for chattering;
so they call him the punch bowl, and me the magpie. Order the best,
you may command everything here.

GIOVANNI: Thanks. [*Kisses her.*] I'll repay you, love: you understand.

MRS. DRAINEMDRY: Fie!

GIOVANNI: I'faith! you've had a rare escape, you rogues! What were
you condemned for? Come, confess the caper.

MRS. DRAINEMDRY: Why, dearest Don, between you and me, I was sent
down because I was a shrew.

GIOVANNI [*to Mrs. Porous*]: And you?

MRS. POROUS: 'Faith, I was sent for scolding, as well as she.

GIOVANNI [*to Mrs. Simpkins*]: And, pray, what was you sent to old
Nick for, my love?

MRS. SIMPKINS: If I must tell you—though, really, it makes me blush—
I was sent below for a slight faux paux, Don.

GIOVANNI: A slight faux paux!

MRS. SIMPKINS: And for that they were old-fashioned enough to send
me to—

GIOVANNI: Where I brought you from. [*Laughing heard, inside the
public house.*] Eh! some one comes!

MRS. DRAINEMDRY [*Peeping in at the door.*]: My spouse, as I live.

MRS. POROUS [*peeping*]: And mine.

MRS. SIMPKINS [*peeping*]: Mine, too.

MRS. DRAINEMDRY: Let's stand aside, and watch them; they'll finely
stare to see us here again; and will be rarely rejoiced, no doubt.

GIOVANNI: Don't be too sure of that.

[GIOVANNI, MESDAMES DRAINEMDRY, POROUS, *and* SIMPKINS, *stand
aside, the wives occasionally peeping at the proceedings of their
husbands.*]

[*Enter* DRAINEMDRY, POROUS, *and* SIMPKINS, *with a jug, from the public house.*]

GLEE—*Drainemdry, Porous, and Simpkins.*
AIR—*"Deadly Lively."*

We are three jolly widowers,
    That have just lost our wives;
And ne'er, since we were bachelors,
    So blest have been our lives.
They lie in yonder churchyard,
    And there we'll let them be;
Peace to their souls! they're now at rest,
    And so, for once, are we.

Fol, dol, lol, &c.

MESDAMES DRAINEMDRY, POROUS, *and* SIMPKINS [*Peeping from behind*]:
Oh! the vile fellows! but they shall dearly pay for this.
[*Leporello sings within.*]
GIOVANNI [*peeping*]: Here comes another! Who's this fellow, eh?
[*Enter* LEPORELLO, *from public house.*]

STAVE—*Leporello.*
AIR—*"Galloping Dreary Dun."*

A master I had, a wicked and sly,
    Amorous, fighting Don;
He's gone to the devil, and so won't I;
    No, I'll take care of number one.

GIOVANNI [*peeping*]: Eh! do I dream? Surely I know that face—why, zounds! it is my rascal, Leporello!
LEPORELLO [*to Drainemdry, &c.*]: I must be off—
SIMPKINS: Don't leave us; give us your company, such as it is.
LEPORELLO: I must go; my wife is sitting up for me; besides, she'll read me a curtain-lecture, if I don't.
SIMPKINS: Vell, and that's nat'ral, if you neglects her.
LEPORELLO: Hum! You've no wife at home?
POROUS: No, thank heaven! mine died last week: rest her soul!
DRAINEMDRY: So did mine.
SIMPKINS: And mine.
POROUS: Well, then, let's have another pot of good brown stout to keep our spirits up. Come, here's old England and liberty!
[*Drinks.*]

DRAINEMDRY: Old England and liberty!

[*Drinks.*]

SIMPKINS: Old England and liberty!

[*Drinks.*]

LEPORELLO: Old England! you'll excuse the liberty; my wife's not dead, you know.

POROUS: Leporello, you have often, my prince of fellows, promised to tell us all about your master, Don Giovanni: give us his character.

LEPORELLO: Have I? Well, then, as I'm in a merry humour, I'll be as good as my word for once. I'll give him a character, though he refused to give me one.

SONG—*Leporello.*

AIR—*"Heigho! says Rowley."*

There liv'd in Spain, as stories tell, oh!
  One Don Giovanni,
Among the girls a deuce of a fellow;
And he had a servant they call'd Leporello,
With his primo, buffo, canto, basso:
  Heigho! said Don Giovanni.

He serenaded Donna Anna,
  Did Don Giovanni;
He swore she was more sweet than manna;
Then into her window he stole to trepan her,
With his wheedle, tweedle, lango, dillo;
  Oh! wicked Don Giovanni.

The commandant, her guardian true,
  Caught Don Giovanni;
Says he, "You're a blackguard—run, sir, do;"
"I will," says Giovey, and run him through,
With his carte-o, tierce-o, thrust-o, pierce-o;
When away ran Don Giovanni.

A wedding he met, and the bride 'gan to woo:
  Fie! Don Giovanni!
"I am running away, will you run away, too?"
Said he—"Yes," says she, "I don't care if I do,
With my helter, skelter, questo, presto;"
  What a devil was Don Giovanni!

To a churchyard he came, being once at a loss;
  Lost Don Giovanni!

Where the commandant's statue sat on a stone horse,
Like King Charles's statue that's at Charing Cross,
With his saddle, bridle, falchion, truncheon.
"Will you give me a call?" said Giovanni.

To call on Giovanni, the statue wasn't slow:
  Bold Don Giovanni!
"Will you sup, Mr. Statue?" said he:—it cry'd, "No;
For you must sup with me in the regions below,
Off my brimstone, sulphur, coke-oh, and smoke-oh!"
"I'll be d—d if I do!" cry'd Giovanni.

Yet he was condemned, in spite of all he could say; for
there is no denying the devil when he claims his due.

GIOVANNI [comes forward]: Say you so, ungrateful rascal!
  [DRAINEMDRY, &c. retreat alarmed, holding by each other's coat.]
DRAINEMDRY: Giovanni! talk of the devil you see—
LEPORELLO: Eh! what! it cannot be, you are not my master!
GIOVANNI: You are drunk, rogue.
LEPORELLO: Oh! no, sir; don't say so, you hurt my tender feelings.
GIOVANNI: Then, sir, acknowledge me this instant.
LEPORELLO [Aside.]: To be sure it is he! no place can hold him, that's
  clear; but I'll not know him, or I shall pay dearly for it. [Advancing
  to Giovanni] Acknowledge you, sir! I know you not; never saw you,
  sir.—
GIOVANNI: Not know me, rascal? [Caning him.] Do you know me now?
LEPORELLO: Oh! yes, sir; these are striking proofs. Get him away; [To
  Drainemdry, Porous, and Simpkins] he intends some mischief, dear
  friends, to a certainty. [To Giovanni.] But can you really be my
  worthy master?
GIOVANNI: I am; acknowledge it.
LEPORELLO: Why, sir, he went to—yes, sir—legions of fiends took him
  posthaste to the infernal regions, with fifty little devils for outriders
  and postillions.
GIOVANNI: Well, what of that, scoundrel? And I'm come post from the
  infernal regions back again.
DRAINEMDRY: Come from the infernal regions! Oh! it's very clear he's
  an impostor; but we'll soon expose him. [Calling.] Here, neighbours!
  watch!
GIOVANNI: Stay, sir. [To Drainemdry] You had a wife?

DRAINEMDRY: Yes, sir, I had; but, (rest her!) she's departed this life, sir.
GIOVANNI: Is she?

TRIO—*Drainemdry, Porous, and Simpkins.*

AIR—*From "Midas."*

Oh! what pleasure does abound
Now my wife is under ground!
Green turfs cover her, I'll dance over her.
Tol, lol, lol.

[*They dance round while singing.*]

GIOVANNI: I am sorry, messieurs, to disturb your mirth; but know, your darlings are not in the world below; as witnesses that I was really there, I've brought them with me here; and there they are, gentlemen.

[THE WIVES *rush forward; each seizes her respective husband by the hair.*]

SESTETTO—*Messieurs and Mesdames Drainemdry, Porous, and Simpkins.*

AIR—*"Deadly Lively."*

MESDAMES DRAINEMDRY, POROUS *and* SIMPKINS: You cruel perjured villains!

MESSIEURS DRAINEMDRY, POROUS, *and* SIMPKINS: Oh, zounds, let go our hair!

MESDAMES DRAINEMDRY, POROUS, *and* SIMPKINS: Disown your lawful wives, now, you scoundrels, if you dare!

MESSIEURS DRAINEMDRY, POROUS, *and* SIMPKINS: Our wives! a pretty joke—it is some hoax, that's clear,
Their bodies in the churchyard lie—

MESDAMES DRAINEMDRY, POROUS, *and* SIMPKINS: Yes, but our souls are here.

ALL: Tol, lol, lol, de rol, &c.

[*The Men dolefully, the Women with great glee.*]

DRAINEMDRY: Brought back our wives! he must be the devil himself, then. [*Calling*] Neighbours, neighbours! Watch! Watch!

[*Enter Neighbours.*]

CHORUS OF NEIGHBOURS.

AIR—*"Oh! dear, what can the Matter be."*

Here, here, what can the matter be?

> Dear, dear, what can the matter be?
> Oh dear, what can the matter be?
> What's all this hubbub, we pray?

TRIO—*Messieurs Drainemdry, Porous, and Simpkins.*

SAME AIR

> This fellow has come from the regions infernal,
> And brought back our wives who were dead as a doornail:
> Disturbing our quiet with click-clack eternal;
> To the roundhouse pray bear him away!

Chorus of Neighbours.

SAME AIR

> Eh! what! brought back your wives to you!
> Why not, may'nt he bring ours back too?
> We'll not have with him aught to do;
> Let those meddle with him that may.

[*Exeunt Neighbours, hastily.*]

MRS. DRAINEMDRY [*to Mr. Drainemdry and others*]: Now, sirs, I hope you'll own we are your wives; the rulers of the roost, yourselves, and houses; you all acknowledge us to be your better halves.

DRAINEMDRY: Oh! yes, ducky—[*Embrace, and aside.*] needs must when the devil drives.

GIOVANNI [*to Leporello, who implores pardon*]: I pardon you, sir; and as a proof of it, take you into my service once more.

MRS. DRAINEMDRY: To drink our hero's health, we'll tap a barrel, and have a jig and stave—hang fighting and quarrelling.

GLEE—*All.*

AIR—"*Away with Melancholy.*"

> Away with fight and quarrel,
>   Black eyes, crack'd heads that bring;
> Let us attack the barrel,
>   And jollily, jollily sing.—Tol, lol.
> Let's drink like hearty fellows,
>   Our country and our king;
> Burn old King Rose's bellows,
>   And jollily dance and sing.—Tol, lol.

[*Exeunt. The* LADIES *marching* GIOVANNI *off in triumph.*]

Scene 4

St. Giles's, by gaslight. Watchman crosses stage, crying "Past ten o'clock and a cloudy morning." *Enter* MRS. LEPORELLO, *with infant, from a house.*

MRS. LEPORELLO: Past ten! In vain the sleepy watchman snores the hour—no—Leporello comes not to ease my pain! immured in beer, the sot is getting drunk. Oh, false Giovanni, to desert me thus, and leave none but Leporello as the husband of your Anna, and the father of your baby.

SONG—*Mrs. Leporello.*
AIR—*"O rest thee, Babe."*

Oh! hush thee, my darling, the hour will soon come,
When thy sire from the ale-house, half drunk, will reel home.
Oh! rest thee, babe, rest thee, babe, sleep while you may,
For, when he comes, there'll be the devil to pay.

[*Goes into the house. Enter* GIOVANNI *and* LEPORELLO.]

GIOVANNI: Now that you're sober, tell me, Leporello, when last I disappeared, what became of all my wives and ladies? Did they die in despair?

LEPORELLO: Why, when you went, sir, to—I beg pardon—Well, sir; when you went—downstairs, their pretty eyes, of course, were filled with tears: and so I brought them all to England with me.

GIOVANNI: To England! Ah! then perhaps the charming bride I snatched from her husband's arms and made mine, the very moment he had the right to call her his, is in England! Tell me, where is my love?

LEPORELLO: Where is your Love? Why, your love is—but stop: whenever you mention love, poetry always comes into my head, because rhyme is of more use than reason; so allow me to tell you poor Fanny's fate.

TRIO—*Leporello, Giovanni, and Squalling Fanny.*
AIR—*"Young Love."*

LEPORELLO: Your love she lives in yon humble shed,
           Where turnips selling,
           And "greens, oh!" yelling,
       She gets a daily bit of bread,
       And wild and sweet is the life she has led;

Her stall has flourish'd,
Her barrow's nourished
The natives with savoys and beans:
For working folks must still be fed;
And pickled pork eats best with greens.

[*Fetches* SQUALLING FANNY *from her stall, in the centre of flat.*]

GIOVANNI: Zounds! what poor wretch is this I spy,
Who has come hither
Her sweets to wither;
Her beauty now is all my eye;
Plague on't! don't let the witch come nigh.

FANNY: Dear Don Giovanni,
Don't scorn poor Fanny:
All day my greens for you I'll cry.

GIOVANNI: My once-lov'd Fanny, cry away,
But not for me—no, faith—good b'ye!

FANNY [*to Giovanni*]: And do you leave me, after all my truth?

DUETTO—*Squalling Fanny and Leporello.*
AIR—*"Wapping Old Stairs."*

FANNY: Your Fanny has never been false, she declares,
Since the man on the horse came and took you—

LEPORELLO [*Stopping her.*]: Down stairs.

FANNY: When you vow'd that you still would continue
the same,
And gave me the reticule work'd with your name.
Then be constant and true, nor your Fanny forsake;
Still your cossacks I'll wash, and your negus I'll make.

Nay, though I do cry my greens through Covent Garden, don't steel
your heart against poor Squalling Fanny; but let's live o'er those
charming days, my love, that once I passed with you in native Spain.

DUETTO—*Squalling Fanny and Giovanni.*
AIR—*"Guaracha."*

FANNY: Oh! Remember the time in La Mancha's plains,
I had just been to church to be wed,
When you swore that my bridegroom wasn't burden'd with brains;
And clapp'd two huge horns on his head.

GIOVANNI: O! yes, then you were sweet as the breath of the south,
And I thought you were truly a prize:
But now, crying greens, Fan, has widen'd your mouth,

Crack'd your voice—aye, and dimm'd your bright eyes.

LEPORELLO [*Waltzes Squalling Fanny off, and returns*]: I have waltzed her off, sir!

GIOVANNI: But where are the wives of the fishermen I shot?

LEPORELLO: They're here, and still in the fish line, sir; one lives at Billingsgate, and t'other in Lumber Court.

[GIOVANNI *and* LEPORELLO *listen.* MRS. LEPORELLO *sings within.*]

MRS. LEPORELLO: Oh! rest thee, my baby, the hour will soon come,
When thy sire from the ale-house, blind drunk, will reel home.

LEPORELLO: That's Mrs. L's voice; she's nursing my little one; instilling into his infant mind the virtues of his father.

GIOVANNI: Well, well, to leave your virtues out of the question—

LEPORELLO: Oh! my virtues are not to be questioned.

GIOVANNI: But what place is there in the city, where we can amuse ourselves an hour or two?

LEPORELLO: What place? Why, plenty. Since business has been stopped, amusement has been the order of the day: tonight, for instance, Sir John English gives a grand masquerade.

GIOVANNI: A masquerade! I'll go, but then what character must I assume?

LEPORELLO: Any but your own, and you will be admitted, but if you would be a beau, take a lesson from me.

SONG—*Leporello.*
AIR—*"Quite Politely."*

If in London town you'd live,
    Quite politely, quite politely,
Let me, sir, this lesson give,
    And be, complete, a beau, sir.
Cossacks you like sacks must wear,
In a brutus cock your hair,
And wear of wellingtons a pair,
    To shine from top to toe, sir!
                    Tol de rol, &c.
You must get a pair of stays,
    Like the ladies, like the ladies;
Through an eyeglass still must gaze,
    And stare at all you meet, sir!
With sham collar hide your nose,
Wear false calves like other beaux,

And still a brazen front disclose,
  With brass heels on your feet, sir.
                    Tol de rol, &c.
To the Opera you must go,
  Don Giovanni, Don Giovanni,
And talk as fashionables do,
  Most loudly while they're singing;
You must go to ball and play,
Drink, game, swear, and lie all day,
Protect some graceless chère amie,
  Yourself to ruin bringing.
                    Tol de rol, &c.
You must visit, race, and fight,
  Betting on, two to one, sir;
Four-in-hand to drive delight,
  Like groom and jockey clever.
With your tailor debts contract,
In the Bench for three months pack'd,
Get out by the white-washing act,
  And be as clean as ever.
                    Tol de rol, &c.

[*Exeunt* GIOVANNI *and* LEPORELLO, *dancing.*]

Scene 5

Grand Saloon at Sir John English's. Enter Masquerade Characters.
CONSTANTIA *and* FINIKIN *come forward.*

CONSTANTIA: 'Tis no use teasing, Mr. Finikin.
FINIKIN: Why, miss, are you not shortly to be mine?
CONSTANTIA: Never.
FINIKIN: Your pa, miss, vows and swears you shall.
CONSTANTIA: I vow and swear I won't—Pa's own girl, to a T.
FINIKIN: But, my dear creature, I love—
CONSTANTIA: I know—my thirty thousand pounds you love; but neither
  I nor my thirty thousand pounds love you.

DUET—*Constantia and Finikin.*
AIR, *"Oh! thou wert born to please me."*

CONSTANTIA: Oh, thou wert born to tease me!
FINIKIN: Nay, don't say so, my love.
CONSTANTIA: I'm sure you'll never please me.

FINIKIN: I'll sure your pleasure prove.

CONSTANTIA: Oh! never, never!

FINIKIN: Fie, miss.

CONSTANTIA: You cannot!

FINIKIN: Pr'ythee, try, miss!

CONSTANTIA: 'Twould be to little purpose, you namby, pamby, thing!

FINIKIN: Oh, cruel! From my tester I very soon shall swing.

[CONSTANTIA *and* FINIKIN *retire up the stage. Pantomime business— at end of which,* LEPORELLO *comes forward. Enter* GIOVANNI.]

LEPORELLO [*brings forward Giovanni, and points to Constantia*]: Thirty thousand pounds! I never heard of such a sum! She's an heiress! I wonder who she is, but that's no matter, since she's rich; cash is a plaster for every evil. I'll patch up a reputation for her; it can give a woman a thousand charms! Oh! I must introduce my master to her.

SONG—*Leporello to Giovanni.*
AIR—*"See that pretty Creature there."*

> See that pretty creature there,
> Oh, how charming! oh how fair!
> Hug her, kiss her, sir, for zounds,
> She's got thirty thousand pounds.

[LEPORELLO, *as by accident, treads on* DEPUTY ENGLISH's *gouty toes, who, just at that moment, enters with* MRS. ENGLISH *in search of his ward* CONSTANTIA; LEPORELLO *is beaten off by* DEPUTY ENGLISH, *followed by* FINIKIN *and* MRS. ENGLISH; GIOVANNI *advances towards* CONSTANTIA, *makes love to her, and takes her up the stage.* GIOVANNI *and* CONSTANTIA *come forward.*]

DUET—*Giovanni and Constantia.*
AIR—*"Voulez-vous danser."*

GIOVANNI: Will you dance with me, dear ma'am'selle,
> Cheer my heart, nor
> Slight your partner?
> I can quadrille and waltz as well,
> La poule et la finale.
> In the waltz our forms we'll twine,
> Thine to mine, and mine to thine;
> And all as sweet
> Our hearts shall meet,
> Should we in love's circle join.

CONSTANTIA: Willingly, sir, with you I'll dance,

> Cheer your heart, nor
> Slight my partner,
> For, ah! who could refuse to prance,
> Requested so genteelly?

[FINIKIN *advances to interrupt Giovanni, and begins setting to Constantia;* LEPORELLO *seizes the tail of his coat, and dances him off.*]

CONSTANTIA: But may I believe you, sir?

GIOVANNI: Believe me!

AIR—*Giovanni.*
AIR—"*Grammachree Molly.*"

> Had I a heart for falsehood giv'n,
> To you I should be true;
> I sooner could be false to heav'n
> Than to those eyes of blue.

[GIOVANNI *and* CONSTANTIA *going,* LEPORELLO *calls him aside.*]

LEPORELLO [*coming from the crowd*]: Oh! master, I beg your pardon, but—

GIOVANNI: But what?

LEPORELLO: The lady, sir.

GIOVANNI: Is pretty?

LEPORELLO: Yes, sir; that is true enough, but sir, she is a ward in chancery, and if you run away with her, it will be a contempt of court and the law.

GIOVANNI: Where love is paramount, away with law. Constantia shall be mine, were she a ward of a thousand chanceries.

LEPORELLO: Well, sir, follow your own courses, [*Sees Mrs. Leporello*] while I follow that little Spanish girl, and see if she will follow me.

[*Enter* MRS. LEPORELLO, *in a Spanish dress, from amongst the Dancers.*]

MRS. LEPORELLO: There is my husband at his tricks, as usual. Now to entrap the rogue.

[*Follows him, and mixes with crowd.* LEPORELLO *brings her from the crowd, makes love, falls on his knees; she takes off her mask, slaps his face; all the characters laugh.*]

[*Enter* FINIKIN.]

DUET—*Leporello and Finikin.*
AIR—"*Blue Bells of Scotland.*"

FINIKIN: Oh! where, and oh! where, is my own dear maiden gone?

LEPORELLO: She's gone with Don Giovanni, and won't a maid return.

FINIKIN: Then it's heigho! my heart for she's left me all forlorn.
Torn from me! Torn from me! Which way did they take her?

LEPORELLO: They've gone to Long Acre, along with a baker.

[*Exit with* FINIKIN. GIOVANNI *and* CONSTANTIA *advance from crowd, and are going off, but are met by* DEPUTY *and* MRS. ENGLISH, *with* WATCHMAN. GIOVANNI *and* CONSTANTIA *try to escape on opposite side, but are met by* FINIKIN *and* WATCHMAN; GIOVANNI *and* CONSTANTIA *are parted; great bustle, and great noise; all the Masks in motion. Curtain falls on the confusion.*]

ACT II

Scene 1

Chalk Farm, Primrose Hill, by daylight; a clump of trees at the back of the stage.

Enter GIOVANNI *and* LEPORELLO *in modern dresses, the one as a dashing young Man of Fashion, of the present day; the other, a genteel Servant. Leporello carries a pair of pistols with him.*

GIOVANNI: First on the ground, however! Egad, a pretty scrape I have involved myself in, for though I have lost the lady, I must fight for her.

LEPORELLO: True! having affronted the gentleman you can do no less than blow out his brains to give him satisfaction: but will you not leave poor Leporello a legacy?

GIOVANNI: I have nothing left to leave but the body of Giovanni.

[*Enter* FINIKIN *and* POPINJAY.]

FINIKIN [*Aside to Popinjay.*]: You're sure that you sent for the officers?

POPINJAY: Oh, yes! I went to Bow Street myself after them.

GIOVANNI [*to Finikin*]: Your servant, sir; you're late!

FINIKIN [*Aside.*]: Late! I think, too soon. Dear, dear! I wish I were in Pimlico; anywhere but here.

GIOVANNI: I've waited, sir—but we'll to business at once, and make up for lost time.

FINIKIN: Oh, sir! I can wait; I'm in no sort of hurry, I can assure you. [*Aside.*] Where are these officers?

GIOVANNI: Here, Leporello, measure the ground, eight paces. D'ye hear, sir?

LEPORELLO: Only eight paces?

GIOVANNI: Yes, sir; they're plenty.

LEPORELLO: If I was going to fight, I'd have eleven-and-forty. [*Aside.*] Then, sir, you've quite made up your mind to have a pop at him?

GIOVANNI: Ay, sir; and at you, too, if you don't bestir yourself.

LEPORELLO: Oh, Lord!

GIOVANNI [*to Finikin*]: Your second, sir, will help to measure the ground.

FINIKIN: Oh! sir, assuredly; with a deal of pleasure. [*Aside.*] Where are these runners? Are there no means of escaping?

POPINJAY: Measure the ground! I'd rather be measuring tape, a good deal. [*Aside, to Leporello*] Young man, as you appear to have a good understanding, pray step out as much as you possibly can.

LEPORELLO: Don't young man me. [*Measuring ground.*] One, two, three, four—jump; [*Jumps.*] five, six, seven, eight—jump.

POPINJAY [*to Leporello*]: I beg your pardon, but really you've mis-counted!

LEPORELLO: Upon my honour, no; I've given full measure, you may depend on't.

POPINJAY: Eh, your honour, I'm satisfied.

GIOVANNI [*to Finikin*]: Now, sir, we wait for you.

FINIKIN: You sha'n't wait long, sir; I'll attend you instantly.

POPINJAY: This is a very awful moment!

GIOVANNI [*to Finikin*]: Take your ground, sir.

POPINJAY: Dear me! I'm terribly afraid that I'm about to swound! Sir Fin, have you any hartshorn about you?

FINIKIN: I have no hartshorn, [*Giving him a large bottle out of his pocket*] but here's a little rose water.

POPINJAY: That will do quite as well. You like perfumes; which are you most partial to?

FINIKIN: Just now, I think I should prefer—[*Calling aloud*] Lavender.

GIOVANNI [*to Finikin*]: Here are pistols, sir.

FINIKIN: I'm extremely obliged to you; but if it makes no difference, we'll use mine. [*Aside.*] They're loaded with blank cartridge.

GIOVANNI: As you please, sir.

POPINJAY [*to Giovanni*]: You couldn't allow me to go home for a few minutes, or so, could you, sir?

GIOVANNI: Go home! when you're a second!

POPINJAY: Oh, true! I'd forgot that.

GIOVANNI [*to Finikin, who has got behind a tree*]: You have taken the wrong ground, sir.

FINIKIN: Have I?

LEPORELLO: This is your place. You can hit him here, sir, can't you?

GIOVANNI: To a nicety. Throw the dead body into the Regent's Canal. I have ordered coffee for the survivor!

POPINJAY [*Goes up to Giovanni.*]: I beg your pardon, sir; but will you have the goodness to wait till I get behind this bush: balls are apt to fly, you know.

[*Crosses to the back of the stage, and hides behind a bush.*]

GIOVANNI [*to Finikin*]: Now, sir, it seems we're all prepared; therefore, I'll just try if I can give you satisfaction.

SONG—*Giovanni.*

AIR—*"The Black Joke."*

Our ground we have taken, our pistols we have;
We have nothing to do but the signal to give
Of one, two, three—fire away!
So, dear sir, your best I'd advise you to do,
For if you don't wing me, faith, I shall wing you.
Now ready, sir, stand, take your pistol in hand,
For I'm going to sing out the word of command—
Hip—one, two, three—fire away!

[GIOVANNI *and* FINIKIN *exchange shots.* FINIKIN, LEPORELLO, *and* POPINJAY, *all fall as if wounded.*]

GIOVANNI: I'm safe! my rival has it, though, I think. Three at one shot! Eh! what the plague in this? Zounds! what has killed you, sir—a ball, or fear?

LEPORELLO: A ball, I fear, sir; it passed through you, and, as I stood behind you, entered me. You're winged, sir, a'n't you?

GIOVANNI: Winged! Not I, faith.

FINIKIN: I wish that I were winged, that I might fly! [*Aside.*] You're not hurt, Poppy!

POPINJAY: No, but I'm excruciatingly alarmed!

FINIKIN: Then help me up.

POPINJAY [*helping Finikin up*]: Why, you're as heavy as if you had a bullet in you.

GIOVANNI: Now, sir, we'll try with my pops.

FINIKIN: With a deal of pleasure, sir; but I—

POPINJAY: And I—

LEPORELLO: And I—

FINIKIN: We're satisfied!

GIOVANNI: If you are satisfied, sir, I can't say I am; but challenge you to have another shot.

FINIKIN: Won't an apology do, instead?

GIOVANNI: No, sir; apologies won't do, sir; you, in writing, must give miss up.

FINIKIN: With pleasure.

POPINJAY [to Finikin]: Can you write, sir?

FINIKIN: A running hand.

GIOVANNI: Then it will be all right. Here, Leporello, bring the pen and ink.

LEPORELLO [Aside.]: Yes, and I'll get a drop of something to drink, at the same time.

GIOVANNI: Stay: now I think of it, our coffee must be ready by this time; so you can give up the lady over that. This way—

FINIKIN: Sir, I attend you. After you, sir.

[Exeunt GIOVANNI and FINIKIN into Chalk Farm.]

LEPORELLO [to Popinjay]: This way—

POPINJAY [Running off the opposite side.]: No, this is mine.

LEPORELLO: Stop, that won't do, my fine fellow.

[Runs after him, pulls him back by the tail of his coat; POPINJAY falls; LEPORELLO cocks a pistol at him; he hides his face under his neckcloth, and is led into the house. Enter DEPUTY ENGLISH and MRS. ENGLISH.]

DEPUTY: Ah! here, indeed, we breathe the country air; a very rural spot, upon my life! Here's every thing one can desire. So, here I'll enjoy myself.

SONG—*Deputy English.*

AIR—"*Oh! the Roast Beef of Old England.*"

I'll get me a pipe, and I'll get me a pot,
And in that rural box there, I'll sit and I'll sot,
And I'll not budge a foot till my dinner I've got
    Off the roast beef of Old England,
    Off the Old English Roast beef.

[He exits. Enter GIOVANNI, from the house.]

GIOVANNI: Charming woman!

MRS. ENGLISH: Sir!

GIOVANNI: Nay, you must not be offended; your husband's old—I am young—Love and pleasure were made for youth; let us enjoy it.

MRS. ENGLISH: Ah, Giovanni! your inconstancy is too well known, to permit me to trust you.

GIOVANNI: You shall teach me to be constant, and by this kiss I swear— [*Attempts to kiss her.*]

MRS. ENGLISH: Hold, sir!

[*Enter the* DEPUTY, *who perceives Giovanni.*]

GIOVANNI [*Aside.*]: Her husband here! the devil! [*To the* DEPUTY] I beg your pardon, sir, I was only pointing out the pleasant prospects to Mrs. English.

DEPUTY: Why, wife! Do you know this is the famous Giovanni? And, from what I have heard, a foreigner and a singer. So sir, like a true John Bull, I am glad to see you; and, though I may not understand you, sir, I like you; and any service I can render you, you may freely command.

DUETTO *and* CHORUS—*Giovanni and Mrs. English.*

AIR—*"The Tyrolese to Liberty."*

GIOVANNI: Merrily every bosom boundeth,
      Merrily oh! merrily oh!
  Now Giovanni's freedom soundeth,
      Merrily oh! merrily oh!
  Here the pistol's balls fly more fleetly,
  Here the syllabubs eat more sweetly,
  Every joy Chalk Farm surroundeth,
      Merrily oh! merrily oh!

CHORUS: Merrily, merrily, oh! &c.

MRS. ENGLISH: Cheerily now from Hampstead's valley,
      Cheerily oh! cheerily oh!
  Over Primrose Hill we'll sally,
      Cheerily oh! cheerily oh!
  If a charming girl, won by bravery,
  Sweeter be than one kept by knavery,
  Round Giovanni's pistol rally,
      Cheerily oh! cheerily oh!

CHORUS: Cheerily, cheerily oh! &c.

[*Exeunt* DEPUTY ENGLISH, MRS. ENGLISH, *and* GIOVANNI.]

Scene 2

Outside of Deputy English's House. It is getting dark. Enter Constantia.

Constantia: So, Don Giovanni's fought for me, I hear; that is a sign he bears me still in mind; and though he is flirting with Mrs. English, that he is fond of me, I think I'm sure. I've heard an old proverb, which says, a reformed rake always makes a good husband; and to reform him, I've a scheme with Mrs. E. of which he'll little dream. But he is here; I'll stand aside and watch him. We've laid our snares so well, we must succeed.

[*She exits. Enter* Giovanni.]

Giovanni: Yes, here's the house; I've found it, though it is in the dark. He certainly may be called a spark who lights himself. Old English has gone out to spend the evening, left his wife for his club, so that's all right. [*Calling at the Deputy's door.*] Hist, hist! But then, Constantia, what a pang thrills through my heart. Could I but gain her hand! She's young and rich! She shall, she must be mine! But what am I about? I'll think of lovely Con some other time. Now for the signal.

[*He knocks.* Mrs. English *appears at the door of the house.*]

Mrs. English: Giovanni!

Giovanni: Yes.

Mrs. English: Come in, and make no noise.

Giovanni: I will, my love! Now, for ten thousand raptures.

[*He enters the house with Mrs. English. Enter* Leporello, *with lanthorn and ladder.*]

SONG—*Leporello.*
Air—*"Hey randy dandy, O!"*

Giovanni is leading his usual life;
　　Hey randy dandy, O!
He's come here to make love to another man's wife,
　　With his galloping randy dandy, O!
Three bottles he drank at a tavern today,
　　Hey randy dandy, O!
So it's odds, but there'll soon be the devil to pay,
　　With his galloping randy dandy, O!
I've brought him a ladder, and brought him a lamp,
　　Hey randy dandy, O!

For a notion I have, when he means to decamp,
   That he'll find them devilish handy, O!
I don't know how it is, but I feel tonight
   Hey randy dandy, O!
So I'll go to the whiskey shop down by the right,
   And get a few quarterns of brandy, O!

[*Knocks loudly at* Mrs. *English's door, and calls "Giovanni, Giovanni!" then exits hastily.* GIOVANNI *opens the door and comes forward.* MRS. ENGLISH *shuts the door on him unperceived.*]

GIOVANNI: Who's there? no one: it was Con's voice, I'm sure. It came, 'faith! devilish mal-a-propos. Well, I'll go back. [*Finds the door shut.*] Zounds! why the door is fast. Holloa! hist, hist! plague on't, shut out at such a moment! Eh! where's the lanthorn! Where's Leporello? And where's the ladder? Devil take the scoundrel! I've drank too much; but, 'faith! could not refuse the glass offered by such a hand. The charming wench! she'll bless my love, no question. 'Twas cruel of her, though, to shut me out. Oh! here my rascal comes without his light. [*Enter* DEPUTY ENGLISH. *Mistaking him for* Leporello] Come here, you dog! I've had such luck this evening!

DEPUTY [*Aside.*]: Eh! who's this, the Don? The funny rogue! He takes me for his servant, Leporello. I'll listen to him; he seems very fresh.

GIOVANNI: I've been with such a charmer, and so kind.

DEPUTY: Who?

GIOVANNI: English's wife.

DEPUTY: My wife! Death and the devil!

DUET—*Giovanni and Deputy English.*
AIR—*"Chanson d'Amour."*

GIOVANNI: I gave her kisses one,
              Half afraid;
              I gave her kisses one,
              She frown'd, and cried, "Have done!"
              But, "Go on," her pretty blue eyes plainly said.
              I gave her kisses two,
              Bolder grown;
              I gave her kisses four—

[DEPUTY *throws off his cloak.*]

DEPUTY: Oh, zounds? I'll hear no more;
              I've heard too much already, Mr. Don.

[*Exeunt* DEPUTY *into the house, greatly enraged,* GIOVANNI *laughing.*]

Scene 3

Outside of Westminster Hall, in a new light. Enter LEPORELLO *and* CONSTANTIA, *in counsellors' gowns and bands: Leporello with a wig and green bag.*

LEPORELLO: But tell me, miss, why are we disguised thus?

CONSTANTIA: Oh! 'tis a little bit of roguery.

LEPORELLO: Of course; or else we need not be lawyers.

CONSTANTIA: This cause, English *versus* Giovanni, we have told him, stands for today; we are his counsel. We meet him here to consult him for the defendant—but our consultation must be how much we can make him pay, that his creditors may bring him to his senses.

LEPORELLO: Ay, like true lawyers; I'm quite of your opinion. But stop, my learned sister, where's my fee?

CONSTANTIA: That we must get from him—he comes.

[*Enter* GIOVANNI.]

GIOVANNI: In love, in law, I'm in a pretty hobble! My awkward trial, too, comes on today: there'll be the devil to pay! [*Sees* LEPORELLO *and* CONSTANTIA.] My lawyers!

LEPORELLO [*Aside to Constantia.*]: He means us! [*Coming forward*] Your servant, Don! With your leave, as cause comes on today, we've come for fees.

TRIO—*Constantia, Leporello, and Giovanni.*
AIR—*"Soldier gave me one Pound."*

LEPORELLO:	Giovanni, give me one pound,
CONSTANTIA:	Giovanni, give me two.
LEPORELLO:	Trial it comes on to-day;
CONSTANTIA:	And nothing we can do—
LEPORELLO:	Unless you give a fee
	Both to me—
CONSTANTIA:	And me.
BOTH:	For, oh! the law's a mill that without grist will never go.
LEPORELLO:	Giovanni, give me one pound,
CONSTANTIA:	Giovanni, give me two.
BOTH:	For, oh! a brief without a fee will never, never do.
CONSTANTIA:	Don't you know, the law—
LEPORELLO:	Has clapp'd on you its claw?
BOTH:	And, oh! the law's a mill that without grist will never go.

GIOVANNI [*Gives Leporello money.*]:

Lawyer, there is one pound,
[*Gives Constantia money.*]
   Lawyer, there are two,
And now I am without a pound,
   Thanks to the law and you!
      For, oh! I feel the law
      Has clapp'd on me its claw;
   And, oh! the law's a mill that
      without grist will never go.

LEPORELLO: Now, then, my learned brother, to the hall. English against Giovanni; it comes on first. I a rare philippic shall speak, sir. We lawyers like to talk about crim con. We've bled him nicely! [*Aside.*] Come, my learned brother, Coke upon Littleton—Budge *versus* Fudge.
[*Exit, with* CONSTANTIA, *as if going to the court.*]

   SONG—*Giovanni.*
   AIR—"*The Woodpecker.*"

I knew by the wigs, that so greasefully curl'd,
   Adown their lank chops, that they wanted a fee;
And I said, if I had but a pound in the world,
   These devils of lawyers would take it from me.
All was still in the court, not a sound did I fear,
   But the bailiff quick tapping my shoulder, oh, dear!

[*Enter* LEPORELLO *and* CONSTANTIA, *as from court.*]
GIOVANNI: Have you a verdict?
LEPORELLO: Yes, sir.
GIOVANNI: Name it; quick.
LEPORELLO: Guilty: the damages, ten thousand pounds.
GIOVANNI: Ten thousand pounds for nothing but a kiss!
LEPORELLO: 'Twould have been twice as much but for my skill. It was in vain, their counsel I overhauled—they went so far, Don, as to prove the fact.
GIOVANNI: 'Tis false!
LEPORELLO: We'll leave our bill of costs for the defence, and call for the amount when next we're at the hall. Good day! My learned brother, shall we trudge it? As I said in that cause of Fudge and Budge: "Botherum, gatherem, client Simpletoni, distressem pluckem ex-contini, &c."

[*Exit with* CONSTANTIA.]

GIOVANNI: Ten thousand pounds, and I'm not worth a shilling! In debt, in love, in law! Undone Giovanni! I've only now to get in wine to be completely ruined.

[*Enter* NOKES *and* STYLES, *watching Giovanni.*]

NOKES: This is our man, let me make the caption.

STYLES: I will; but mind you take care of the fee.

GIOVANNI: A ruin'd wretch! ah! whither shall I wander? Who will provide Giovanni now with a home?

NOKES: I will.

GIOVANNI: Kind friend!

NOKES: A snug one, in the Bench; where you may still enjoy your glass and girl. I'm glad I've found you.

GIOVANNI: So am I.

NOKES: You know, of course, that you're my prisoner; so hand us out our fee.

GIOVANNI: Your prisoner, fellow!

NOKES: Ay, Don, unless you pay ten thousand pounds.

GIOVANNI: Ten thousand pounds, dog! I can't pay one farthing.

NOKES: Oh! oh! then you must go over the water, Mr. Giovanni.

DUET—*Nokes and Styles.*
AIR—*"Over the Water to Charley."*

NOKES: Over the water and over the bridge,
               And into the King's Bench, Giovanni;
               And over the water we now must trudge,
               Or get in a coach, Giovanni.

               Giovanni, you love ale and wine;
               Giovanni, you love brandy;
               Giovanni, you love a pretty girl,
GIOVANNI: As sweet as sugar-candy.
STYLES: Then sure, to pay you will not grudge:
               You kiss'd the wench, Giovanni;
               So over the water and over the bridge,
               And into the Bench, Giovanni.

[*Exit* GIOVANNI, *with* NOKES *and* STYLES.]

Scene 4

Interior of the King's Bench, in its true light. SHIRK, SPUNGE, *and other Debtors discovered; some walking about, others playing at rackets, &c.*

CHORUS OF DEBTORS
AIR--*"Peggy of Derby, oh!"*

Oh! laugh at the hour,
When, in John Doe's power,
We debtors to the Surrey College came.
Let's hasten to our play;
Three months soon will pass away.
What is life, after all, but a racket-game?

Then, debtors, get your jackets,
And let us go to rackets:
Like a ball, we're up and down at fortune's smile—the
wench!
Like our balls, we here remain,
But, one day, to ease our pain,
Like a bat, the Act will soundly knock us out of the
Bench.

SHIRK: Ay, ay, my boys; let's hasten to our play, and leave work to our creditors.

ALL: Bravo!

[*Loud cries outside,* Giovanni, Giovanni! *Enter* GIOVANNI, *conducted in by* NOKES *and* STYLES.]

SPUNGE: Giovanni, welcome to this sacred spot, where lawyers, bailiffs, duns, daren't show their faces! What, downcast! psha! my dear Don, pour a glass of spirits down to keep your spirits up.

GIOVANNI: Spirits! why they're forbidden.

SPUNGE: Well, then, tape. We find a way to evade the law, Don: rum Charley helps us: every morning a gallon of rum walks in within his wooden leg. You'll pay your entrance, of course; 'tis usual, sir.

GIOVANNI: This place is well called college, since it supplies so much and various learning. But, zounds! I've not a note to treat these brothers.

[*Enter* TURNKEY, *with a Letter.*]

TURNKEY: Here's a note for you, sir.

[*Exit.*]

GIOVANNI: Psha! I want some of Henry Hase. What's this? Constantia's hand! [*Reads*] "Though you forsook me, I can't forsake you in the hour of want." Ah! a friend, indeed! "I have enclosed you a retaining fee; with this brief counsel, remember me." Dear girl! ten pounds! this I never can forget: now, now I feel I am indeed a debtor. Here, you rogues! here, here is my entrance-money.

[*He gives money to debtors, who shout.*]

SPUNGE: You'll find here, Don, the best of company: all the great wits and authors are here. We have some players, too, of no mean note; and as for gentlemen, we're full of them. We're not confined in living, neither; though prisoners, we feed like princes here.

GIOVANNI: Well, for poor debtors that is very odd.

SPUNGE: But I say, Don, as you're a stranger, I must talk to you about your chum.

GIOVANNI: My chum!

SPUNGE: Your bedfellow, that is to be: but stop, you'd better leave it to my care.

GIOVANNI: Nay, if you please, I'll see to that myself. I have a little damsel in my eye, will come and--

SPUNGE: Oh! my dear Don, for shame! [*Aside.*] An easy blade this, I must try and bubble him: he's got some money, 'twill be little trouble. My dear Don, let me put you on your guard while you are here; I speak quite disinterestedly: some of our brothers, I am sorry to say, are very apt to borrow and not return. I give you just a hint: it's not my way; I like to do as I'd be done by. You couldn't lend me a pound note, could you?

GIOVANNI: With pleasure.

[*He gives money.*]

SPUNGE [*Aside.*]: Zounds! I wish I'd asked for two. Depend on't, it shall be punctually repaid. Some day or other I may assist you: just now I happen to be rather short. You couldn't lend me a few shillings more?

GIOVANNI [*He gives money.*]: Oh! yes.

SPUNGE: I'm very much obliged; I am, indeed. Perhaps you'd like to read the newspaper? I'll go and fetch it. [*Aside.*] I must bleed him again. It must have come down from the upper rooms by this time; so you can see what's going on in town.

[*Exeunt* SHIRK, SPUNGE, *and other debtors.*]

GIOVANNI: Alas! what is the town or world to me? In love, in limbo!

when shall I get released? Constantia, love, now do I think upon thy charms!

AIR—*Giovanni*
AIR—*"Robin Adair"*

> What's the gay town to me,
>   In the King's Bench?
> Oh! when shall I get free
>   From the King's Bench?
> Ah! still to joy and mirth,
> Freedom it is gives birth:
> Confinement's hell on earth,
>   In the King's Bench.

[*Exit. Enter* SHIRK, SPUNGE, *and Debtors.*]

SHIRK: Pull up, pull up! a lawyer's at the gate: the fool's not aware, I dare say, how we serve gentlemen of his calling. We'll give it to the dog: but mind, be steady, lads; go some of you and get the pump and blanket ready.

[*Exeunt Debtors. Enter* LEPORELLO, *in a counsellor's dress, with a blue bag.*]

LEPORELLO: I come from twelve and thirteen, Clement's Inn: I'm a lawyer! Is Giovanni, pray, within? But there's no fear of his being at home here; you gentlemen are not much given to ramble.

SHIRK: Yes, he's at home; but before you can see him, we must bestow the lawyer's fee on you.

LEPORELLO: Oh, certainly! give me my fee; I'll take anything.

SHIRK: By rights, you should have six and eightpence; but two half-crowns are all the fee we give.

LEPORELLO: Well, two half-crowns. What a pack of fools!

SHIRK: Now your crown must be crack'd, ere you've two halves! So, ere we cool your courage with the pump, we'll try how high your ambition will carry you; send you on a visit to the man in the moon. Bring the blanket, boys!

LEPORELLO: A blanket! zounds! they mean to murder me! Help! help here! [*Running away*] I'll indict you all for assault and battery!

[SHIRK, SPUNGE, *and Debtors, bring back* LEPORELLO, *and toss him in a blanket, he exclaiming all the time "I'm no lawyer!" &c. They then hurry him off, crying "To the pump!"*]

[*Enter* GIOVANNI.]

GIOVANNI: No one arrived; not even Leporello to get me bail! ungrateful villain! If my dear Constantia would but visit me—but can I hope it—

[*Enter* POROUS, DRAINEMDRY, SIMPKINS, *and other Creditors of Giovanni.*]

Bless me! who are these? Zounds, all my creditors. Whither shall I fly?

DRAINEMDRY: We've called to know, Don, what you mean to propose, and when you think it's likely you can pay?

GIOVANNI: Pay!

SIMPKINS: Yes, you've surely something to say.

POROUS: Let us have a part, Don, if you can't pay us all, and give us security for the remainder.

GIOVANNI: Zounds, how shall I get rid of these fiends? Ah, my Constantia!

[*Enter* CONSTANTIA, *who crosses to Giovanni.*]

This makes amends for everything.

> BRAVURA—*Constantia to Creditors.*
> AIR—"*Cease your Funning.*"

> Cease your dunning,
> Serjeant Running-
> —ton shall set Giovanni free!
> Then how soothing,
> Owing nothing,
> What a happy man he'll be!
> Leaving roving,
> True to loving,
> True he'll to Constantia be.

[SHIRK, SPUNGE, *and Debtors, rush in, and hustle off* DRAINEMDRY, POROUS, SIMPKINS, *and Creditors.*]

Scene 5

Exterior of the Insolvent Court. Enter DRAINEMDRY, POROUS, SIMPKINS, COBBLER, *and other Creditors of Giovanni.*

DRAINEMDRY: What, take the act, and cheat me of my money! a pretty swindler this Don Giovanni, upon my word!

COBBLER: He'll be my ruin! nothing can redeem me, upon my soul, unless he pays my bill.

POROUS: Why, how much is it?

COBBLER: Fourteen and sevenpence, welting boots and mending—

SIMPKINS: Psha! that's a trifle! he owes me fifty pounds.

DRAINEMDRY: Pooh! he owes me fourscore—Oh! here he is.

    [*Enter* GIOVANNI, CONSTANTIA, *and Bailiffs.*] You rogue!

POROUS: You swindler!

SIMPKINS: You cheat!

DRAINEMDRY: But you shan't escape us,—we will all oppose you.

GIOVANNI: Be patient, I am willing to pay you all, but I am now
reduced to my last shilling.

GIOVANNI'S ADDRESS TO HIS OPPOSING CREDITORS
AIR—*"Scots wha ha'e wi' Wallace Bled."*

> Duns that give Giovanni trust,
> Duns, doubt not I shall be just,
> But take the benefit I must,
> For 'tis for liberty!
> Now's the day, and now's the hour,
>   See the bailiff grimly lour,
> See approach the sheriff's power,
>   Writs and slavery.
> Who would be a debtor, eh?
> Who in the King's Bench would stay?
> Who would be confin'd all day?
>   Let him prisoner be!
> Who for the Insolvent Laws,
> Freedom's schedule freely draws,
> Freeman stand in freedom's cause,
>   On to court with me.

    [*Exit with Bailiffs into court.*]

DRAINEMDRY: Come, friends, we'll all oppose him.

SIMPKINS: Ay, every man of us.

COBBLER: Oh, my poor bill!

    [*Exeunt* DRAINEMDRY, POROUS, SIMPKINS, *and Creditors, into court.
Enter* LEPORELLO.]

LEPORELLO: I'll not oppose him, though he is in my debt; no doubt I
shall get my wages some time or another; that's if the plot don't fail,
which now we're trying. His long confinement must have tamed his
roving by this time, and made him steady, or the devil's in it! If so,
all will be well; if not, poor Miss Constantia! I wonder if they'll

grant him his discharge—[*Noise without, and cries of* "Giovanni's free! huzza!" *and* "shame, shame!"] Odsflesh! what means that clamour? Zounds, they've cleared him! Oh, my dear master!

[*Enter* GIOVANNI, CONSTANTIA, *and Creditors.* GIOVANNI *crosses to back of stage.*]

DRAINEMDRY [*to Giovanni as he passes him*]: Shame, shame! you swin-dler! You think you've cheated me, but you ar'n't, for I always charged double!

[*Exit.*]

POROUS [*to Giovanni as he passes him*]: You are a nice young fellow, I don't think!

[*Exit.*]

SIMPKINS [*goes up to Giovanni*]: Ar'n't you a pretty fellow, you have swindled me nicely, and—[*Leporello pushes him off. The Cobbler, overcome by the immensity and utter hopelessness of his loss, makes several ineffectual attempts to express his feelings; but finding himself unequal to the task, retires, plunged in grief.*]

GIOVANNI [*Comes forward*]: I'll now make up for my temperance in the Bench; I'll revel, dance, sing, drink, game, swear, everything—

[*He exits, laughing.*]

Scene 6

Charing Cross by a blue light. Equestrian statue of King Charles. Enter LEPORELLO.

LEPORELLO: Giovanni free, proves he is still Giovanni: he's ranging everywhere in search of petticoats. Oh! if we could but reclaim this libertine, it would immortalize us—but how? Ah! there's the rub. He is to meet me in Cockspur Street soon, by appointment; he must pass by this statue, so, like the commandant upon his horse—I have it—in this blue light 'twill answer certainly: just so he looked who asked the Don to sup where he was supped on. I'll try it—there can be no harm in trying—the coast is clear—no one has observed me, so up I go. A footstep—some one comes—it is Giovanni, mum! [*He climbs up the Statue. A Female crosses the stage hastily. Enter* GIOVANNI *in pursuit.*]

GIOVANNI: That was a lovely girl I met just now; she's set me all on fire. Confound the wench! she went this way! I'll after her at once. [*Starting to go.*]

BALLAD—*Leporello.* [*Very ghostily.*]
AIR—*"Barney, leave the girls alone."*

Giovanni, leave the girls alone;
Giovanni, leave the girls alone;
For oh! your tricks move stock and stone;
    Then quiet let them be.

Pluto put the kettle on;
Pluto put the kettle on;
To supper once I asked the Don,
    I ask him now to tea.

GIOVANNI: Odsblood! what's this? The commandant here! How the devil has the fellow found his way from Spain? Instead of raking, I'd best go to praying, or he may alight and take me—

LEPORELLO [*in a hollow voice*]: From whence you came!

GIOVANNI: Who has spoken? Oh, lord! good Mr. Statue, I'll amend. Thoughts of old times have made me devilish warm. Should I go down below again, I fear it would be long enough ere I got back again. Yes, I'll reform, for dear Constantia's sake. Good bye, old Stoney! Morning will soon beam, so you had better take yourself and your horse off.

[*He exits.*]

LEPORELLO [*descends from the statue*]: Ha, ha, ha!
    Pluto put the kettle on, Pluto put the kettle on;
    Prossy, take it off again, Giovanni's run away.
I've frightened him a bit, I think. Why, hang it! he must have been in liquor: yet this blue moonlight, shining on the horse, I must say, is monstrous striking. Eh! here again!

[*Re-enter GIOVANNI.*]

GIOVANNI: It must have been delusion, but that I'll soon find out: no, here's the man and horse. [*Sees Leporello.*] Ah! Leporello, speak, what are you alarmed at, sirrah!

LEPORELLO [*pretending to be dreadfully frightened.*]: Oh, sir! he has spoken.

GIOVANNI: Who has spoken?

LEPORELLO: Oh, sir! the man from that stone horse has spoken. It has, upon my word, spoken to me, and said that he was sent up stairs to fetch you—down again, if you didn't immediately reform. Look, sir, how firm he sits: be warned in time, sir, and list to reason.

GIOVANNI: I will, I will.

LEPORELLO: You know you're very poor; now, sir, hard by lives an old maid who rolls in riches, and who wants a husband; what do you say, sir, to a good estate? you will not have a chicken for your bride, but what of that, sir, you'll be rich for life.

GIOVANNI: It shall be so—lead on—my mind's made up. I'll marry the rich old maid and repent at once.

[*Exeunt.*]

Scene 7

Grand Saloon at Deputy English's by a fanlight. Enter MRS. LEPO-RELLO, disguised as an old maid.

MRS. LEPORELLO: I think this dress will do; this air and manner will serve, at least, somebody to entrap. Should the Don come, I'll try if I can't win him; if he resists me now, the deuce is in it.

SONG—*Mrs. Leporello.*
AIR—*"Nobody coming to marry me."*

A maid at sixty-six,
    Must not refuse a man;
But ah! not a soul can I fix,
    Though, I'm sure, I do all that I can.
    Oh, dear! what will become of me?
        Dear, dear! what shall I do?
    Nobody coming to marry me,
        Nobody coming to woo.

[*Enter* LEPORELLO *conducting* GIOVANNI.]

LEPORELLO: There she is, sir; see what a valuable concern! Why, there's a thousand pound in every feature. Her nose is worth five hundred, and her eyes--why, they are Jew's eyes, sir. Attack her, then, at once.

GIOVANNI: I will. Charming woman!

[*Music.* GIOVANNI *makes love to* MRS. LEPORELLO *in dumb show; she coyly yields to him; he falls on one knee, She sits upon it.*]

MRS. LEPORELLO: Oh, Don! you're too polite, you are, indeed: and then you plead in such a tender way, I can't refuse you! no, dear Don, I can't. There is my hand; make me at once your wife.

LEPORELLO: Take her at once: our fortune's made. Why, zounds! sir, how you stand!

[*Aside to Giovanni.*]

GIOVANNI: Shall I, then, for the withered arms of age, leave the blooming charms of my young, my kind Constantia, because at fortune's frown, like me, she's poor? Perish the thought! No; if Giovanni must a husband be, still, as of old, it shall be "All for love." [*Enter* CONSTANTIA, DEPUTY ENGLISH, *and* MRS. ENGLISH, *who stand in the background, watching.*] I'll seek Constantia out; reform, repent; and make that charming, faithful girl, my wife.

CONSTANTIA [*coming forward*]: My own, my tried Giovanni! Know, to reward your love and constancy, Constantia still is rich and worthy of you. This lady, with her formal dress and air, was once your favourite.

GIOVANNI: Eh! Donna Anna?

[MRS. LEPORELLO *throws off her old maid's dress and appears as herself;* GIOVANNI *salutes her.*]

LEPORELLO: She's not Donna Anna now, but Mrs. Leporello.

DEPUTY: Welcome, Giovanni!

GIOVANNI: The deputy!

DEPUTY: Yes.

GIOVANNI: The trial—

DEPUTY: Was a hoax, played to try you; you must pardon all our tricks, now that they're over. Constantia was my ward; so take her hand, with my consent; and may you try to deserve her.

GIOVANNI: Then here I swear eternal constancy and love.

A milder path to find reform you've given

Than others did, since yours will lead to heaven.

[*Scene draws off at the back, and exhibits a splendid fancy pavilion. Ladies and gentlemen enter from all sides, in rich dresses. A grand display of fireworks takes place. During the singing of the finale, Giovanni's name appears in illuminated characters.*]

FINALE

AIR—"*Here's a Health to all good Lasses.*"

DEPUTY:	Here's success to Don Giovanni!
FINIKIN *and* CONSTANTIA:	Here's success to Don Giovanni!
ALL:	All success to Don Giovanni!
	Though his follies have been many,
	Here he makes amends at last.
LADIES:	Worthy patrons,
GENTLEMEN:	Kindly shield him;

LADIES:	Do not blame him.
GENTLEMEN:	Pardon yield him.
ALL:	Here's success to Don Giovanni!
	Though his follies have been many,
	Overlook his errors past.

Nineteenth-Century Views
(1832-1843)

Don Juan and the Romantic Age   II

No attempt is made in these pages to survey the enormous Don Juan literature of the nineteenth century.[1] Even the temptation to discuss at length Byron's *Don Juan* (1818–1823) or to reprint portions of his masterpiece must be resisted. I have defined the subject of this volume as the legend created by Tirso de Molina, taking in at the farthest extreme the legends surrounding Don Miguel Mañara. But Byron used nothing from this storehouse except the name of the popular hero. He had learned to keep a sharp eye on the marketplace, and obviously knew that a lover named Don Juan would command a price on it sight unseen. Why not call *his* hero and alter ego Don Juan?[2]

Byron was of course familiar with a number of Don Juan versions, for example (to go no farther than his own poem) with a London pantomime, *Don Juan; or the Libertine Destroyed,* in which the famous Grimaldi played Scaramouch, and to which Byron alludes in his first stanza:

> We all have seen him, in the pantomime,
> Sent to the devil somewhat ere his time.

But never does he seem to have even entertained a thought of using the traditional materials. "No man ever borrowed less, or made his materials more his own," he wrote to his publisher in 1821. In another letter, written in the same month, he had already made plain what he meant by making the materials his own: "Almost all *Don Juan* is *real*

---

1. The reader is referred to the histories and bibliographies listed on p. 725.
2. His letters concerning *Don Juan* are full of facetious yet at bottom serious references to financial matters. See *Lord Byron's Correspondence*, (London: John Murray, 1922), II, 89 ff.

life, either my own, or from people I knew."[3] Indeed, Peter Quennell suggests in his *Byron in Italy* that the poem is "an essential residue" of Byron's Memoirs, composed from 1818 to 1821 and later burned. Professor Weinstein recently has summarized the case:

Byron's Don Juan has so little in common with any of his predecessors that, were it not for his name, he would probably not be thought of as belonging to the Don Juan legend. The same can be said for the plot. Gone are all the traditional events except the shipwreck and, if we want to stretch a point, the encounter between lover and husband (I, 183–186). Gone, likewise, are the traditional characters: the servant, Anna, Elvira, the Commander, etc.[4]

Of course, Byron's hero is *a* Don Juan—that is to say, he has many love affairs. In this connection it is worth observing that a typical shift from the original is fully accomplished in Byron: Don Juan is no longer a man who wants many women, whether or not he wins them, but a man who wins many women, whether or not he wants them. Needless to say, this was a theme for which Byron did not need literary sources. Fortunately, he saw its humorous and satirical possibilities. His secret was the teasing of his own Romantic fervors by his Restoration wit, a conjunction from which leaped a young hero as fresh and vigorous as Tirso's own, usurper of the name though he might be.

In 1839 appeared Pushkin's posthumous *The Stone Guest*, actually written in 1830. A translation of this work can be found in the Modern Library edition of Pushkin's works, but it will not suggest to the reader that this is, in Belinsky's words, "the pearl of the creations of Pushkin, the richest and most splendid diamond in his poetic career."[5] We must take on faith that its poetry elevates the very slight merit of its bare episodes. It is a brief play, almost a sketch. Its Don Juan is a superficial but rather amiable blade converted to true love by Anna, who is here the widow of a man whom Don Juan killed for a reason Pushkin does not choose to divulge to the reader. The Statue still

---

3. Both are quoted in T. Guy Steffan, *Byron's Don Juan, the Making of a Masterpiece* (Dallas: University of Texas Press, 1957), I, 36.

4. *The Metamorphoses of Don Juan* (Stanford: Stanford University Press, 1959), p. 79. As for the encounter between lover and husband, it must be pointed out that the real Don Juan encounters a father, not a husband; that unlike Byron's hero, he kills his pursuer; that this kind of episode is more than common; and that Byron drew the entire "Julian" story from an account he heard.

5. Quoted by C. A. Manning, "Russian Versions of Don Juan," *PMLA*, XXXVIII (1923), 479. For an excellent account, see André Meynieux, "Pouchkine et Don Juan," in the Don Juan issue of *La Table Ronde*, No. 119 (November 1957), pp. 90–107. Maynieux points out that the frivolous and cynical heartbreaker is a typical figure in Pushkin's works, modeled on the poet himself.

comes to carry Don Juan away, but it has lost every meaning which it once had, since now Don Juan is really saved—saved by a woman. It remained for Zorrilla to carry this theme to its logical conclusion by having the woman open Heaven's gates to the redeemed ruffian.

Don Juan in love is the first great discovery of Romanticism (although Zamora had anticipated the event); the second is Don Juan the irresistible charmer, the man who brings to women a moment—and a moment is enough—of the sublime in their lives of sodden middle-class domesticity. Now a man well qualified to project this magnetic power was Alfred de Musset, and in his rambling, desultory *Namouna* (1832),[6] a narrative with nothing to narrate, he gave Don Juan his final stamp as the Romantic hero. Musset's Don Juan, mysterious and fascinating, loathes "truth" and goes looking for ideal beauty. He never finds it and never can find it, for it does not exist, but the search gives him his superiority over the bourgeoisie. Unlike Madame Bovary, in whom this type of idealism is satirized, such a hero dies with bitter and theatrical satisfaction.

Musset was a rhymester, not a poet. *Namouna* is slack, pleonastic, facile, and bombastic as verse, and worse than childish in concept, but it is a pure draught from the fountain of popular Romanticism—the kind of Romanticism which was accessible to any young person of good family and sensitive temperament. To us it is of interest simply as a characteristic critical piece—a critical piece which in this case happens to scan and, in French, to rhyme.

From *Namouna:* Canto II by Alfred de Musset

Translated by Oscar Mandel

38

Yes, Don Juan. Here is the name all men repeat,
The mysterious name the world pronounces,
Each man would talk about, and no man understands;
A name so vast and mighty, each poet
Who lifted it into his mind or heart
Became the greater for the attempt he made.

6. This appeared in a collection entitled *Un Spectacle dans un fauteuil.*

39

Madman that I am! What am I doing now?
Was it then my turn to speak of you,
Great shade? Why—whence do you come to me?
You come because the others, those who doubted
And blasphemed and loathed, did not love you;
But I do, as an old minstrel loves his king.

40

Who will fling me on your swift courser
And who will lend me the flying cloak
To follow you weeping, guileless corrupter?
Who will unroll the homicidal list,
That list of loves, so full and yet so empty,
Which your hand peopled with those your heart forgot?

41

Three thousand lovely names! Three thousand women's names!
Not one you did not stammer tearfully!
And not one of these three thousand loves
Drowned the fire of love that ate your soul,
The fire which rose, the day you died, out of your blood
Into the sky, like a forgotten angel!

42

And yet they loved you, the frenzied girls
You pressed against your iron bosom;
One same wind carried you and them away;
They loved you, Don Juan, the poor girls you left,
Who covered with kisses the shadow of your love,
Who gave you their lives and enjoyed but a day!

43

And you, weak spectre, what did you do with them?
Oh, massacre and misery! you loved them too,
Yes! believing each time that the sun was rising
From your eternal nights over your new loves,
And saying each night: "Here is the sun, perhaps,"
And waiting still for it and growing old.

44

Demanding of the forests, the sea, the plain,
The morning breezes, every hour, every place,
The woman of your soul and your first hope!
Taking for your betrothed a dream, a shade,
And ransacking a human hecatomb
To find in it, oh desperate priest, your god.

45

And what did you want? Still after three hundred years
The world speaks low and asks the question.
The sphinx with piercing eyes awaits the answer.
They know how to count the hours, they know
Their earth is round, and they walk the sky by compass,
But that which you wanted, they do not know.

46

"Who," they ask, "who is the unknown woman
Would have broken the gallop of his steed,
Whom he called always and who did not come?
Where had he found her? Where had he lost her?
What was the knot which so held them together
That, if she could not come, neither could he forget?

47

"Was there not one, nobler, more beautiful,
Among so many beauties, who resembled
Somewhat or much the vague ideal he cherished?
Why did he not keep her? Tell us, which one it was!"
They all resembled her; but they were not she;
They all resembled her; but you, Don Juan, walked on!

51

You were in Madrid, Paris, Naples and Florence;
Great lord in the palace, thief at the crossroads;
Not counting money, or the days and the nights;
Learning the ballads of any passer-by;
Asking of God, so you might treasure life,
Only your wide horizons and your many loves.

52

Wherever you went you found truth hideous,
Never what your ardent desire sought.
Everywhere the eternal hydra bared its teeth;
And still pursuing your life of adventure,
Looking beneath you at the tempestuous sea,
Softly you spoke to yourself: "Within lies my pearl."

53

You died full of hope on your infinite road
And caring little if here below you had left
Traces behind you of blood and tears.
Vaster than the sky and greater than life
You lost your beauty, glory and genius
For an impossible being who did not exist.

54

And on the day the Stony Guest appeared,
You met him halfway and reached him your hand
And fell struck down over your last banquet:
Magnificent symbol of man on earth,
With your left hand trying to lift your glass,
And the right surrendered to the hand of fate!

(1832)

Don Juan de Mañara

The humane nineteenth century had already converted Don Juan into an idealist, a true lover, and a fatal charmer. He was holding these virtues in precarious balance with his crimes, when the simpler expedient was found of assigning his crimes to his youth and his virtues to his maturity. In short, Don Juan was saved. At this point, a legend which had nothing to do with Tirso's Juan Tenorio entered into his history to function as the vehicle of his salvation. This was the story, part truth and part fiction, of the very real Don Miguel Mañara Vincentelo de Leca, born in Seville in 1626, that is to say near the time Tirso was probably creating the Sevillan Burlador. Of Mañara we

know, through biographies and testimonials, that he led a vaguely
wild youth (like most aspirants to beatification) in which he sought to
emulate the fictive but notorious Tenorio. I will mention here only
the episodes in the biography and legend which playwrights and novelists were to use. He had a strict and religious upbringing (indeed, his
mother reminds one of the mother of Byron's Don Juan); he enjoyed a
few brief years of happy marriage; after a certain bloody affair he
enlisted in the Spanish army and saw service abroad; once he asked a
man across a river for a light, and the latter, who turned out to be the
devil, stretched out his arm and lit Don Miguel's cigar; when a companion, seeing the list of his conquests, mentioned that only God was
missing from the cuckolds, Miguel proceeded to seduce a nun; on his
way to the elopement he came across a funeral procession and was so
horrified to discover that it was his own that he fainted, repented, and
took up a holy life, whereupon the nun died of grief, saying "he never
loved me"; thereafter he led a life of strenuous sanctity, devoting himself to the sick and the poor, humiliating himself, performing several
miracles, and (this beyond doubt) erecting a church and a hospital
which can be visited to this day. His epitaph informs the passer-by that
he was the worst of mortals, but this piece of vanity did not prevent
him from being elevated to the rank of Venerable by the Vatican in
1778.[1]

It seems that the legends concerning Don Miguel were circulating
freely in Seville and were themselves influenced by the fables which
had accrued to Don Juan Tenorio over the years. But it was Prosper
Mérimée, a man well acquainted with the Spanish scene, who in 1834
fused the two stories in a fine novella, *Les Ames du purgatoire*. This
cool and rapid tale is still worth reading, though it does not come near
his masterful *Colomba*. Mérimée calls his hero Don Juan Maraña, a
metathesis of the true name. Under this name, equipped with two sets
of adventures and available for salvation, Don Juan prospered mightily,
if we can call mere abundance of versions prosperity: for the truth is
that the meeting with Mañara did not improve the hero's aesthetic
health. The once so solid and powerful rascal now had anxieties,
visions, a change of heart, a Pure Woman to guide him, and lachrymose
angels to conduct him to paradise with all too few questions asked.
Don Juan became the subject of rather vulgar edifying tales for Cath-

1. The best account is that of Esther van Loo, *Le Vrai Don Juan: Don Miguel de
Mañara* (Paris: SFELT, 1950). Professor Weinstein gives a satisfactory compendium in
his volume, as well as further references.

olic audiences, smothered in a sentimentality which that vigorous monk, Gabriel Téllez, would never have tolerated.

Two years after the appearance of Mérimée's tale, Alexandre Dumas père sent to the stage his own *Don Juan de Maraña, ou la chute d'un Ange,* a play so trashy as to be magnificent. It would be hard to make a complete list of the props Dumas managed to use for his play. Among them are a good and a bad angel struggling for Don Juan's soul; a rivalry of brothers over an inheritance and a woman; the usual castle with gloomy chambers and deep dungeons; the murder of a priest; a visit to the realm of the dead to obtain a father's signature on a legal document (the Gothic romance had been complicated with business matters in the reign of Louis-Philippe); a card game with a beautiful woman at stake, who later poisons herself; the conversion of Don Juan, who becomes a Trappist monk; a pact between a nun and the devil; a resurrection of the dead; and an appearance of the Virgin Mary. All the women Don Juan meets he devours, and in the end, in a sense, he seduces his way into heaven.[2]

Meanwhile, the first reactions against the ideal Don Juan were making themselves heard. Notable among these is Théophile Gautier's long and diffuse poem, *La Comédie de la Mort* (1838), in which Faust and Don Juan appear side by side once more, but this time in interviews with Gautier himself. Faust has already recommended that the young man drop science in favor of love. Then Don Juan arrives. He looks like a dashing young gentleman of the era of Louis XIII, but on closer inspection he turns out to be old and white-haired; his forehead is furrowed; his cheeks are so hollow "that you could count his teeth"; his pallor shows through his mascara; under his laugh "you saw that fever kissed him every night"; his back is bent; his feet are swollen; his hands tremble; his fingers are so thin that they let his rings escape. We gather, in short, that he has not had a happy time of it. He never found love. Perhaps he should have tried virtue. He concludes that science is a better occupation than love.

Clearly the Maytime of Romanticism is over, and we are well on our way to the old wreck recently depicted by Montherlant. The Romantic and the Molecular Don Juan were to travel together for a number of years. But indeed, the first has not died to this day, for he keeps reap-

2. Arnold Bennett reworked and took the life out of Dumas' play in his own *Don Juan de Maraña* (1913). Thackeray has a rollicking but finally indignant account of Dumas' work in the chapter on "French Drama and Melodrama" in *The Paris Sketch-Book* (1841).

pearing in Spanish and Spanish-American versions (worlds in which our own cynicism has not yet dissolved the old Catholic *caballería*), usually under the tutelage of Mañara. And so he showed up in 1840, two years after Gautier's disillusioned statement, in José de Espronceda's *El Estudiante de Salamanca*. Espronceda, the Spanish Byron—lover, conspirator, anarchist, idealist—was coming to the end of his brief but crowded life, and he endowed his Don Juan (who goes here under the name of Don Félix de Montemar) with his own indomitably rebellious instincts. *El Estudiante* is part lyric poem, part poetic drama; it is Gothic but also light; and it abounds in priceless lyrical passages, unfortunately defying translation. In the final part, taken from one of the Mañara legends, Don Félix meets with a mysterious shape, which he follows through a long, wild, and labyrinthine danse macabre. There are mausoleums, vast and gloomy halls, tortuous stairs, spectres, tombs, winds, thunder, howling, and of course Félix sees his own funeral. The shade turns out to be Elvira's cadaver. The skeleton kisses and caresses the intrepid and defiant rebel, who dies unrepentant:

> Alma rebelde que el temor no espanta,
> Hollada sí, pero jamás vencida.[3]

Don Juan and the Romantic Age   III

The mark of Mozart's *Don Giovanni* is on many versions and many interpretations of the Tenorio matter. Its touch was not so decisive in the Spanish world, where the legend of Miguel Mañara made a deep and lasting impression on those who set about rehandling the ancient stories; but elsewhere Mozart's work became the chief, and sometimes the only, point of reference for a great number of writers, down, in fact, to the puppet-play makers.

Hoffmann's comments on *Don Giovanni* are worthy of attention; but the greater genius of Kierkegaard commands it. His remarks, like those of Nietzsche, bring a glow to every subject. The brilliance is sometimes deceptive; we ordinary men, afflicted with common sense, must occasionally refuse to be carried away; and yet such is the thrust of true genius that even its errors compel admiration.

For Kierkegaard, if I understand him, the sensuality of Don Juan as

3. Rebellious soul unterrified by fears,/Trampled, yes, but never vanquished.

expressed in music is the ideal example of the so-called aesthetic stage of mankind, the stage which precedes the ethical and the religious. Hence it would be idle to apply moral or theological criteria to Don Juan. Furthermore, the sensual is daemonic, and the daemonic is best expressed through music. Words introduce reflection and analysis, hence ethical judgment: this then is the end of the sheerly aesthetic stage.

Kierkegaard's interpretation of the one thousand and three is masterful. This number, ludicrous when subjected to verbal scrutiny, appears utterly normal in its musical setting, symbolizing "the power of nature, which never tires of seduction, which is never done with seduction, as the wind never tires of storming, the sea of heaving, or the waterfall of rushing into the deep." The number also suggests that the list is not closed, that Don Juan is still on the march. It is a daemonic number.

This march, for Kierkegaard, is very different indeed from the march envisaged by Musset. For Musset it is the weary search for the unattainable from the starting point of the unattained. Here it is the ever victorious sweep from enjoyment to enjoyment. Don Juan, as the symbol of sensuality, seduces and delights in *every* woman. Music expresses him as infinite passion, infinite power, and infinite victory. Kierkegaard does not show him as seeking the ideal woman; quite on the contrary: woman, as such, any and every woman, is his ideal— though this ethical word is in any case misapplied here. Don Juan is always satisfied, and untouched by the world of ethics.

From *Either/Or* by Søren Kierkegaard

Translated by David F. Swenson
and Lillian Marvin Swenson

Chivalrous love is also psychical and, therefore, in accordance with its concept, is essentially faithful; only sensuous love, in terms of its very concept, is essentially faithless. But this, its faithlessness, appears also in another way; it becomes in fact only a constant repetition. Psychical love has the dialectic in it in a double sense. For partly it has the doubt and unrest in it, as to whether it will also be happy, see its desire fulfilled, and be requited. This anxiety sensuous love does not have. Even a Jupiter is doubtful about his victory, and this cannot be otherwise;

moreover, he himself cannot desire it otherwise. With Don Juan this is not the case; he makes short work of it and must always be regarded as absolutely victorious. This might seem an advantage to him, but it is precisely poverty. On the other hand, psychical love has also another dialectic, it is in fact different in its relation to every single individual who is the object of love. Therein lies its wealth, its rich content. But such is not the case with Don Juan. For this, indeed, he has not time; everything for him is a matter of the moment only. To see her and to love her, that was one and the same. One may say this in a certain sense about psychical love, but in that there is only suggested a beginning. With regard to Don Juan it is valid in another way. To see her and to love her is the same thing; it is in the moment, in the same moment everything is over, and the same thing repeats itself endlessly. If one imagines a psychical love in Don Juan, it becomes at once ridiculous and a self-contradiction, which is not even in accord with the idea of positing 1,003 in Spain. It becomes an over-emphasis which acts disturbingly, even if one imagined oneself considering him ideally. Now if we had no other medium for describing this love than language, we should be up against it, for as soon as we have abandoned the naïveté which in all simplicity can insist that there were 1,003 in Spain, then we require something more, namely, the psychical individualization. The aesthetic is by no means satisfied that everything should thus be lumped together, and is astonished at the number. Psychical love does not exactly move in the rich manifold of the individual life, where the nuances are really significant. Sensuous love, on the other hand, can lump everything together. The essential for it is woman in the abstract, and at most is a more sensuous difference. Psychical love is a continuance in time, sensuous love a disappearance in time, but the medium which exactly expresses this is music. Music is excellently fitted to accomplish this, since it is far more abstract than language, and therefore does not express the individual but the general in all its generality, and yet it expresses the general not in reflective abstraction, but in the immediate concrete.

As an example of what I mean, I shall discuss a little more carefully the servant's second aria: the List of the Seduced. This number may be regarded as the real epic of Don Juan. Consequently, make this experiment, if you are sceptical about the truth of my assertion! Imagine a poet more happily endowed by nature than anyone before him; give him vigor of expression, give him mastery and authority over the power of language, let everything wherein there is the breath of life be obedient unto him, let his slightest suggestion be deferred to, let everything wait, ready and prepared for his word of command; let him be surrounded by a numerous band of light skirmishers, swift-footed messengers who overtake thought in its most hurried flight; let nothing escape him, not the least movement; let nothing secret, nothing unutterable be left behind in the whole world—give him, after all this, the task of singing Don Juan as an epic, of unrolling the list of the seduced. What will the result be? He will never finish! The epic has the fault, if one wishes to call it that, of being able to go on as long as you will. His hero, the improviser, Don Juan, can go on indefinitely. The poet may now enter into the manifold, there will always be enough there which will give pleasure, but he will never achieve the effect which Mozart has obtained. For even if he finally finishes, he will still not have said half of what Mozart has expressed in this one number. Mozart has not even attempted the manifold; he deals only with certain great formations which are set in motion. This finds its sufficient explanation in the medium itself, in the music which is too abstract to express the differences. The musical epic thus becomes something comparatively short, and yet it has in an inimitable manner the epic quality that it can go on as long as it will, since one can constantly let it begin again from the beginning, and hear it over and over again, just because it expresses the general in the concreteness of immediacy. Here we do not hear Don Juan as a particular individual, nor his speech, but we hear a voice, the voice of sensuousness, and we hear it through the longing of womanhood. Only in this manner can Don Juan become epic, in that he constantly finishes, and constantly begins again from the beginning, for his life is the sum of repellent moments which have no coherence, his life as moment is the sum of the moments, as the sum of the moments is the moment.

In this generality, in this floating between being an individual and being a force of nature, lies Don Juan; as soon as he becomes individual the aesthetic acquires quite other categories. Therefore it is entirely proper, and it has a profound inner significance, that in the seduction which takes place in the play, Zerlina, the girl, should be a common peasant girl. Hypocritical aestheticists who, under the show of understanding poets and composers, contribute everything to their being misunderstood, will perhaps instruct us that Zerlina is an unusual girl. Anyone who believes this shows that he has totally misunderstood Mozart, and that he is using wrong categories. That he misunderstands Mozart is evident enough; for Mozart has purposely made Zerlina as insignificant as possible, something Hotho has also called attention to, yet without seeing the real reason for it. If, for instance, Don Juan's love were qualified as other than sensuous, if he were a seducer in an intellectual sense (a type which we shall consider presently), then it would have been a radical fault in the play for the heroine in the seduction which dramatically engages our attention to be only a little peasant girl. Then the aesthetic would require that Don Juan should have been set a more difficult task. To Don Juan, however, these differences mean nothing. If I could imagine him making such a speech about himself, he might perhaps say: "You are wrong. I am no husband who requires an unusual girl to make me happy; every girl has that which makes me happy, and therefore I take them all." In some such way we have to understand the saying I earlier referred to: "even sixty-year coquettes"—or in another place: *pur chè porti la gonella, voi sapete quel chè fà.*[1] To Don Juan every girl is an ordinary girl, every love affair an everyday story. Zerlina is young and pretty, and she is a woman; this is the uncommon which she has in common with hundreds of others; but it is not the uncommon that Don Juan desires, but the common, and this she has in common with every woman. If this is not the case, then Don Juan ceases to be absolutely musical, and aesthetics requires speech, dialogue, while now, since it *is* the case, Don Juan is absolutely musical.

From another point of view I may throw some additional light upon this by analyzing the inner structure of the play. Elvira is Don Juan's mortal enemy; in the dialogue for which the Danish translator is responsible, this is frequently emphasized.[2] That it is an error for Don Juan to make a speech is certain enough, but because of this it does not follow that the speech might not contain an occasional good observation. Well then, Don Juan fears Elvira. Now probably some aestheticist or other believes that he can profoundly explain this by coming forward with a long disquisition about Elvira's being a very unusual girl and so on. This altogether misses the mark. She is dangerous to him because she has been seduced. In the same sense, exactly in the same sense, Zerlina becomes dangerous to him when she is seduced. As soon as she is seduced, she is elevated to a higher sphere, to a consciousness which Don Juan does not have. Therefore, she is dangerous to him. Hence, it is not by means of the accidental but by means of the general that she is dangerous to him.

Don Juan, then, is a seducer; in him the erotic takes the form of

1. "If she only wears a petticoat, you know well what he does." See "The List," *Don Juan.*
2. An arrangement of *Don Juan,* adapted to Mozart's music by L. Kruse.

seduction. Here much is well said when it is rightly understood, little when it is understood with a general lack of clarity. We have already noted that the concept, a seducer, is essentially modified with respect to Don Juan, as the object of his desire is the sensuous, and that alone. This is of importance in order to show the musical in Don Juan. In ancient times the sensuous found its expression in the silent stillness of plastic art; in the Christian world the sensuous must burst forth in all its impatient passion. Although one may say with truth that Don Juan is a seducer, this expression, which can work so disturbingly upon the weak brains of certain aestheticians, has often given rise to misunderstandings, as they have scraped this and that together that could be said about such a one, and have at once applied it to Don Juan. At times they have exposed their own cunning in tracking down Don Juan's, at times they talk themselves hoarse in explaining his intrigues and his subtlety; in short, the word *seducer* has given rise to the situation that everybody has been against him to the limit of his power, has contributed his mite to the total misunderstanding. Of Don Juan we must use the word *seducer* with great caution—assuming, that is, that it is more important to say something right than simply to say something. This is not because Don Juan is too good, but because he simply does not fall under ethical categories. Hence I should rather not call him a deceiver, since there is always something more ambiguous in that word. To be a seducer requires a certain amount of reflection and consciousness, and as soon as this is present, then it is proper to speak of cunning and intrigues and crafty plans. This consciousness is lacking in Don Juan. Therefore, he does not seduce. He desires, and this desire acts seductively. To that extent he seduces. He enjoys the satisfaction of desire; as soon as he has enjoyed it, he seeks a new object, and so on endlessly. Therefore, I suppose he is a deceiver, but yet not so that he plans his deceptions in advance; it is the inherent power of sensuousness which deceives the seduced, and it is rather a kind of Nemesis. He desires, and is constantly desiring, and constantly enjoys the satisfaction of the desire. To be a seducer, he lacks time in advance in which to lay his plans, and time afterward in which to become conscious of his act. A seducer, therefore, ought to be in possession of a power Don Juan does not have, however well equipped he may otherwise be—the power of eloquence. As soon as we grant him eloquence he ceases to be musical, and the aesthetic interest becomes an entirely different matter.

Achim v. Arnim tells somewhere of a seducer of a very different style, a seducer who falls under ethical categories. About him he uses an expression which in truth, boldness, and conciseness is almost equal to Mozart's stroke of the bow. He says he could so talk with a woman that, if the devil caught him, he could wheedle himself out of it if he had a chance to talk with the devil's grandmother.[3] This is the real seducer; the aesthetic interest here is also different, namely: how, the method. There is evidently something very profound here, which has perhaps escaped the attention of most people, in that Faust, who reproduces Don Juan, seduces only one girl, while Don Juan seduces hundreds; but this one girl is also, in an intensive sense, seduced and crushed quite differently from all those Don Juan has deceived, simply because Faust, as reproduction, falls under the category of the intellectual. The power of such a seducer is speech, i.e., the lie. A few days ago I heard one soldier talking to another about a third who had betrayed a girl; he did not give a long-winded description, and yet his expression was very pithy: "He gets away with things like that by lies and things like that." Such a seducer is of quite a different sort from Don Juan, is essentially different from him, as one can see from the fact that he and his activities are extremely unmusical, and from the aesthetic stand-point come within the category of the interesting. The object of his desire is accordingly, when one rightly considers him aesthetically, something more than the merely sensuous.

But what is this force, then, by which Don Juan seduces? It is desire, the energy of sensuous desire. He desires in every woman the whole of womanhood, and therein lies the sensuously idealizing power with which he at once embellishes and overcomes his prey. The reaction to this gigantic passion beautifies and develops the one desired, who flushes in enhanced beauty by its reflection. As the enthusiast's fire with seductive splendor illumines even those who stand in a casual relation to him, so Don Juan transfigures in a far deeper sense every girl, since his relation to her is an essential one. Therefore all finite differences fade away before him in comparison with the main thing: being a woman. He rejuvenates the older woman into the beautiful middle age of womanhood; he matures the child almost instantly; everything which is woman is his prey *(pur chè porti la gonella, voi sapete quel chè fà)*. On the other hand, we must by no means understand this as if his sensuousness were blind; instinctively he knows very well how to dis-criminate and, above all, he idealizes. If for a moment I here think

3. *Armuth, Reichtum, Schuld und Busse der Gräfin Dolores (Werke,* **VIII,** 25).

back to the Page in a preceding stage, the reader will perhaps remember that once when we spoke of the Page, I compared a speech of his with one of Don Juan's. The mythical Page I felt standing, the real one I sent away to the army. If I now imagined that the mythical Page had liberated himself, was free to move about, then I would recall here a speech of the Page which is appropriate to Don Juan. As Cherubino, light as a bird and daring, springs out of the window, it makes so strong an impression upon Susanne that she almost swoons, and when she recovers, she exclaims: "See how he runs! My, won't he make conquests among the girls!" This is quite correctly said by Susanne, and the reason for her swoon is not only the idea of the daring leap, but rather that he had already "got around her." The Page is really the future Don Juan, though without this being understood in a ridiculous way, as if the Page by becoming older became Don Juan. Now Don Juan cannot only have his way with the girls, but he makes them happy and—unhappy, but, curiously enough, in such wise that that's the way they want it, and a foolish girl it would be who would not choose to be unhappy for the sake of having once been happy with Don Juan. If I still continue, therefore, to call him a seducer, I by no means imagine him slyly formulating his plans, craftily calculating the effect of his intrigues. His power to deceive lies in the essential genius of sensuousness, whose incarnation he really is. Shrewd sober-mindedness is lacking in him; his life is as effervescent as the wine with which he stimulates himself; his life is dramatic like the strains which accompany his joyous feast; always he is triumphant. He requires no preparation, no plan, no time; for he is always prepared. Energy is always in him and also desire, and only when he desires is he rightly in his element. He sits feasting, joyous as a god he swings his cup—he rises with his napkin in his hand, ready for attack. If Leporello rouses him in the middle of the night, he awakens, always certain of his victory. But this energy, this power, cannot be expressed in words, only music can give us a conception of it. It is inexpressible for reflection and thought. The cunning of an ethically determined seducer I can clearly set forth in words, and music will try in vain to solve this problem. With Don Juan, the converse holds true. What is this power?—No one can say. Even if I questioned Zerlina about it before she goes to the dance: "What is this power by which he captivates you?"—she would answer: "No one knows," and I would say: "Well said, my child! You speak more wisely than the sages of India; *richtig, das weiss man nicht;* and the unfortunate thing is that I can't tell you either."

This force in Don Juan, this omnipotence, this animation, only music can express, and I know no other predicate to describe it than this: it is exuberant joy of life. When, therefore, Kruse lets his Don Juan say, as he comes upon the scene at Zerlina's wedding: "Cheer up, children, you are all of you dressed as for a wedding," he says something that is quite proper and also perhaps something more than he is aware of. He himself brings the gaiety with him, and no matter whose wedding it is, it is not unimportant that everyone be dressed as for a wedding; for Don Juan is not only husband to Zerlina, but he celebrates with sport and song the wedding of all the young girls in the parish. What wonder, then, that they crowd about him, the happy maidens! Nor are they disappointed, for he has enough for them all. Flattery, sighs, daring glances, soft handclasps, secret whispers, dangerous proximity, alluring withdrawal—and yet these are only the lesser mysteries, the gifts before the wedding.[4] It is a pleasure to Don Juan to look out over so rich a harvest; he takes charge of the whole parish, and yet perhaps it does not cost him as much time as Leporello spends in his office.

By these considerations we are again brought to the main subject of this inquiry, that Don Juan is absolutely musical. He desires sensuously, he seduces with the daemonic power of sensuousness, he seduces everyone. Speech, dialogue, are not for him, for then he would be at once a reflective individual. Thus he does not have stable existence at all, but he hurries in a perpetual vanishing, precisely like music, about which it is true that it is over as soon as it has ceased to sound, and only comes into being again, when it again sounds.   (1843)

Extracted from *Either/Or,* "The Immediate Stages of the Erotic," I, 93–101. Anchor edition. New York: Doubleday, 1959.

4. The lesser mysteries were a preparatory celebration in Athens, before the celebration of the great festival of the mysteries at Eleusis.

The Apotheosis of Don Juan (1844)

José Zorrilla and *Don Juan Tenorio*

José Zorrilla y Moral was born in Valladolid in 1817. His father was a stern, virtuous, and dangerous man who served in a high post in Ferdinand VII's police. At the age of nine, the boy entered a Jesuit academy in Madrid to which the best families of the time sent their sons. There, while ostensibly studying philosophy and science (neither of which appear to have made much of an impression on him), he fed sub rosa on the most fervid Romantic literature. Fortunately, the Jesuits encouraged his poetic talent and his taste for the theatre.

In 1833 Zorrilla entered the University of Toledo to study law. He scandalized his family by his bohemian inattention to serious matters and was sent on to the University of Valladolid, where an uncle could supervise him. But he continued to frequent cemeteries at night, as was expected of a young poet, and to study old churches, ruins, and local traditions. He was also often seen at sociable reunions and in the theatres. When his father threatened to confine him to the family estate, Zorrilla made a romantic escape by leaping from a carriage to a mule and vanishing into Madrid. Here his ardent temperament found expression in revolutionary café-speeches and articles for a subversive periodical. Once, to avoid arrest and exile to the Philippines, he leaped off a balcony—as the Burlador himself had done—and fled the city under heavy disguise.

But, like Tennyson, whose person, career, talent, and national prestige offer many parallels with his own, Zorrilla was destined to become famous and respectable. In 1837, some mediocre verses which he read over Larra's grave brought him instant fame. The next twelve years were his best. He turned out poems, legends, and plays with prodigious facility and triumphed in every quarter except the financial one. He sought consciously to become, and did become, the national poet of Spain. His poetry was easy and sonorous, colorful and eloquent; his themes thoroughly Spanish; and his religion and patriotism impeccable. The best wits eventually left him behind, but he never lost the loyalty of the general public.

After 1850 Zorrilla's work declined. He spent several years in Paris, partly for affairs of the heart, and frequented its literary circles. Then he proceeded to Mexico, where he became the favorite of Maximilian, and lectured in Cuba to great applause. His return to Spain in 1866 occasioned enthusiastic celebrations. Though poor and indebted, Zorrilla was known to every Spaniard and South American. In 1889 occurred his apotheosis, when he was crowned in Granada in an impressive ceremony, patronized by royalty and witnessed by 14,000 persons. His death in 1893 was a day of national mourning.

In 1844, at the height of his powers, Zorrilla hurriedly wrote his *Don Juan Tenorio* for the Teatro de la Cruz, which was having difficulties. As was not unusual, he sold all the rights of the play to his publisher before opening night. The play was received at first with moderate applause. But it triumphed that same November and thereafter became the national institution which it is to this very day. Every year it is performed around All Souls' Day, the second of November, in the entire Spanish-speaking world. "This play," writes Unamuno, "so deeply felt by Zorrilla as a religious mystery, is still today, in Spain, a national Catholic cult. And popular and secular, too. Every year, during the days of the commemoration of the dead, the blessed souls in Purgatory, the people come as to a mass, a procession, a funeral, to hear and see, to admire, to fear, and to pity Don Juan, and to adore Doña Inés—'doña Inés of my soul'—maternal and virginal at the same time."

Here is an account in somewhat different terms of the play's fortunes in Mexico, taken from an article in the *New York Times*, November 25, 1962:

To attend one of the various productions of Don Juan each November is as traditional in Mexico as participation in the posada at Christmas time. . . . In a single city, such as the Mexican capital during All Souls Week, there may be as many as 10 "Don Juans" running simultaneously, and each of them, while alike in basic plot, is completely different in superstructure.

This is at the bottom of the present official complaint. The leading comedians produce their own versions of "Don Juan" in the various burlesque houses here. They not only supply some purple ad-libs to the venerable old play but even manage, night after night, to throw in some caustic comments on the national political scene.

All of this is done in the rotund verse structure of Zorrilla. It is not uncommon

A Spanish conception of Don Juan and the Commander: "The Stone Guest" by Francisco Goya (1746-1828).

for the solemn drama to stop while a chorus goes through a can-can or Mexican version of the twist while at the same time the comic declaims sonorously in verse on the eccentricities of political life. . . . The authorities have been left gasping in some instances to see Doña Inez rock'n'rolling across the stage in a short skirt and a tight sweater.[1]

And the authorities to fulminate—in vain, of course. But already in his own lifetime Zorrilla had much cause to repent his hasty sale. "Don Juan Tenorio," he wrote, "which brings thousands of *duros* and six days of entertainment every year in Spain and Spanish America, brings me not a single *real;* but it brings me more than to any actor, manager, bookseller or spectator, because the appearance of my Don Juan on the stage is for the author a phoenix who is born again every year. Because of Don Juan I cannot grow old or die. Don Juan increases a hundred-fold every year my popularity and the affection which the Spanish people feel for me. . . . When I am absolutely incapable of working more and must go begging, . . . I shall be able to say without shame at the doors of theatres: give your mite to the author of Don Juan; for there will not pass by me a single Spaniard who does not know him or me."[2] Nevertheless, in his later years Zorrilla denigrated the play; and since then his judgment has been seconded by most of the best critics of Spain. But the play lives on. Like *Cyrano de Bergerac*, it has the magic theatrical touch and a way of irritating the more formidable critics.

The fact is that Zorrilla's work is full of the melodrama, the cheap spiritual flights, the sentimentalities, and the scenic crowding that all but killed the theatre in the nineteenth century. It is opera more than play. The conclusion would be offensive if it could be taken seriously. Perhaps the final stage direction catches the spirit of the entire play: "Out of their mouths rise their souls, represented by two brilliant flames, which lose themselves in space to the sound of music." This is the finale of Goethe's *Faust* reduced to puerility. *Das ewige Weibliche* is now embodied in a Victorian Pure Maiden for whom Don Juan melts into adolescent worship. This Don Juan is actually caught kneeling before the Comendador and asking for his daughter's hand!

1. Actually, parodies and burlesques began to appear soon after the play's initial production. There was a *Tenorio, Juan el Perdío* in 1848, a *Don Juan Trapisonda o el demonio en una casa* in 1850, Zorrilla's own zarzuela based on his play in 1877, a *Juanito Tenorio* in 1886, and a *Tenorio modernista* in 1906.

2. Guillermo Díaz-Plaja, *Nuevo asedio a Don Juan* (Buenos Aires: Editorial Sudamerica, 1947), p. 112.

For all that, the play disarms one. Here is the perfect Spanish hidalgo, proud, impetuous, sensual, generous, capable of the best and the worst when but tickled, elegant, refined, and young. What play more lively, more colorful? Granted, it is naïve. But it is also refreshing. Its first act, at once headlong and symmetrical, has a candid enthusiasm which only a sour disposition will question or submit to exacting intellectual tests. For the rest, Zorrilla avoids the excesses of Dumas. There are depths to which he refuses to sink.

Finally the poetry itself, which is hard to capture in English, has been enough to keep this play alive. Zorrilla has the inevitable phrase, the memorable cadence, the easy thought launched out and traveling in a perfect curve:

> Yo a los palacios subí
> y a las cabañas bajé
> y en todas partes dejé
> memoria triste de mí.

Every Spanish schoolboy can recite Zorrilla, and I think few Spanish poets would even today scorn to swing with something of his stride.

JOSÉ ZORRILLA Y MORAL

Don Juan Tenorio

(1844)

Translated by William I. Oliver

EDITOR'S NOTE

Scene divisions which denote only the entrance or exit of a character have been omitted. The entrances and exits are indicated by the appropriate stage direction, according to American and British usage.

TEXT

Obras, vol. II. Paris: Garnier, n.d.

Cast of Characters
(in the order of their appearance)

Cristafano Buttarelli, *an innkeeper*

Don Juan Tenorio

Ciutti, *Servant of Don Juan*

Miguel, *a servant at the inn*

Don Gonzalo Ulloa, *Commander of the Order of Calatrava*

Don Diego Tenorio, *Father of Don Juan*

Captain Centellas, ⎫ *Friends of*
Avellaneda, ⎭ *Don Juan*

Two Gentlemen, *Friends of Centellas and Avellaneda*

Don Luis Mejia

Gaston, *his servant*

First Officer of the Watch

Second Officer of the Watch

Pascual, *Servant of Doña Ana de Pantoja*

Doña Ana de Pantoja, *affianced to Don Luis Mejia*

Brigida, *Duenna of Doña Ines*

Lucie, *Doña Ana's maid*

The Abbess

Doña Ines, *Daughter of Don Gonzalo Ulloa*

Doorkeeper at the Convent

First Constable

Second Constable

Sculptor

Page

Carnival revelers, Onlookers, Officers of the Watch, Constables and Soldiers, Ghosts, Skeletons, Spirits, Angels, and Cherubim

Scenes

Part One

Act I. *Uproar and Licentiousness.* Buttarelli's inn, Seville.

Act II. *Skill.* The street outside Doña Ana's house.

Act III. *Profanation.* Doña Ines' convent cell.

Act IV. *The Devil at the Gates of Heaven.* Don Juan's country house near Seville.

Part Two

Act I. *The Ghost of Doña Ines.* The burial grounds of the Tenorio family, Seville.

Act II. *The Statue of Don Gonzalo.* Don Juan's room.

Act III. *The Mercy of God and the Apotheosis of Love.* The burial grounds of the Tenorio family.

471

PART ONE

ACT I

Uproar and Licentiousness

Cristafano Buttarelli's inn. The door to the street is upstage. The place is furnished with tables, wine jars, and other objects.

DON JUAN, *in a mask, is seated at one of the tables writing a letter.* CIUTTI *and* BUTTARELLI *are off to one side waiting. As the curtain rises, we see through the door that opens onto the street costumed revelers, students—in short, the carnival crowd as it passes by carrying torches, playing music, singing and dancing.*

DON JUAN: Damn their noise! May I be struck by lightning if I don't shut their mouths for them as soon as I've finished this letter.

BUTTARELLI [*to Ciutti*]: It's a good Carnival.

CIUTTI: You mean a good harvest for your till.

BUTTARELLI: Ha! The only things you'll find in Seville at times like these are bad taste and green wine. What's more, the big fish don't swim into nets like mine. Inns like these are avoided by the gentry. Sometimes even by the rabble!

CIUTTI: But today—

BUTTARELLI: Today's another matter, Ciutti. I've done very good business.

CIUTTI: Sh! Not so loud! My master's temper is very short.

BUTTARELLI: How long have you served him?

CIUTTI: A year now.

BUTTARELLI: How do you like it?

CIUTTI: I'm better off than a prior. I've got all that I could want and then some! Time to myself, full purse, fine women, good wine.

BUTTARELLI: My God! What luck!

CIUTTI [*pointing at Don Juan*]: And all at his expense.

BUTTARELLI: Rich, eh?

CIUTTI: Spends money like confetti.

BUTTARELLI: Straightforward?

CIUTTI: Like a student.

BUTTARELLI: Noble, I suppose?

CIUTTI: Like a prince.

BUTTARELLI: Brave?

CIUTTI: A pirate.

BUTTARELLI: A Spaniard?

CIUTTI: I think so.

BUTTARELLI: His name?

CIUTTI: It slips my mind.

BUTTARELLI: You dog! And he's going to . . .?

CIUTTI: Stay here.

BUTTARELLI: Look at him scribble.

CIUTTI: He wields a mighty quill.

BUTTARELLI: And who the devil is he writing to so long and carefully?

CIUTTI: His father.

BUTTARELLI: Now there's a son for you!

CIUTTI: In times like these—extraordinary. But—sh!

DON JUAN [*folding the letter*]: Signed and folded. Ciutti!

CIUTTI: Sir?

DON JUAN: I want this letter in Doña Ines' hands. Slip it between the pages of her breviary.

CIUTTI: Shall I wait for an answer?

DON JUAN: Yes; from that devil in petticoats, her duenna, who knows my plans. She'll give you a key, a time, and a sign. And then race the wind back—and see that you get here first!

CIUTTI: Very good, sir.

[*He exits.*]

DON JUAN: Cristofano, *vieni qua.*

BUTTARELLI: *Eccellenza!*

DON JUAN: *Senti.*

BUTTARELLI: *Sento.* [*He sits down*] *Ma ho imparatto il castigliano, se è più facile al signor la sua lingua.*

DON JUAN: Yes, that's easier. *Lascia dunque il tuo toscano.* Tell me, has Don Luis Mejia been here today?

BUTTARELLI: He's not even in Seville, your excellency.

DON JUAN: He's still away?

BUTTARELLI: I think so.

DON JUAN: Have you no word of him?

BUTTARELLI: I remember a story now that might perhaps—

DON JUAN: Shed some light on the subject?

BUTTARELLI: Perhaps.

DON JUAN: Well, then, speak up.

BUTTARELLI [*to himself*]: No—no mistake! The year is up tonight. I'd forgotten.

DON JUAN: God, man! Finish your story.

BUTTARELLI: Forgive me. I was recalling how it went.

DON JUAN: Well, out with it before I lose my temper.

BUTTARELLI: Well, sir, it's this: One fine day our gentleman, Señor Mejia, hit upon the wildest escapade that could ever enter a man's head.

DON JUAN: Skip the escapade. I know all about their wager—to see who could do more harm with more luck in the course of one year, Luis Mejia or Don Juan Tenorio.

BUTTARELLI: Oh, then you know the story?

DON JUAN: From beginning to end. Which is why I asked you if you'd seen Mejia.

BUTTARELLI: I wish they'd settle their bet. They certainly know to settle their bills!

DON JUAN: And you have reason to think Don Luis will not keep his appointment?

BUTTARELLI: Ho! Not a chance. The year's almost up and I'll be damned if either of them so much as remembers it.

DON JUAN: That's enough. Here.

[*He gives him a coin.*]

BUTTARELLI: Your Excellency! And have you had word of either of them?

DON JUAN: Perhaps.

BUTTARELLI: Will they come?

DON JUAN: One of them at least. But if the other one should make his way back, two of your best bottles! Go fetch them now.

BUTTARELLI: But—

DON JUAN: Mum! Goodbye.

[*He exits.*]

BUTTARELLI: Santa Madonna! Tenorio and Mejia are back to pick up where they left off. Oh, it must be! That man knew what he was talking about. [*A noise off stage.*] Now what? [*He goes to the door.*] Well! It's the stranger fighting in the square. God almighty, what a racket! Ha! Look at that rabble go for him—and look how he beats them off. Alone! Puff!—a massacre. Oh ho, look at them run. Oh, there's no doubt about it, the two of them are back and the whole city will be turned upside down. Miguel!

[MIGUEL *enters.*]

MIGUEL: *Che commanda?*

BUTTARELLI: *Presto, qui servi una tavola, amico, e del Lacryma più antico, porta due bottiglie.*

MIGUEL: *Gia mi affretto, signor padrone.*

[*He exits.* DON GONZALO *enters from the street.*]

DON GONZALO: This is it. Service.

BUTTARELLI: Sir?

DON GONZALO: Are you the innkeeper?

BUTTARELLI: Yes. I'm in a hurry, so please be quick.

DON GONZALO: Look at this coin. If you think it's good money, perhaps you'll answer my questions.

BUTTARELLI: Oh, your Excellency?

DON GONZALO: Do you know Don Juan Tenorio?

BUTTARELLI: I do.

DON GONZALO: And is he keeping an engagement here today?

BUTTARELLI: Then you must be the other one!

DON GONZALO: What other one?

BUTTARELLI: Don Luis.

DON GONZALO: No. But I want to be here when they meet.

BUTTARELLI: I'm setting this table for them. But if you'll be so kind as to sit at this one, you'll be able to watch them eat. It'll be a scene to remember.

DON GONZALO: I suppose so.

BUTTARELLI: There's no doubt about it. They're the finest men in Spain.

DON GONZALO: And the worst.

BUTTARELLI: Bah! Nothing but gossip! Whatever evil happens in Spain, presto, it's laid at their door. Nothing but gossip! The fact is, no one pays bills like Tenorio and Mejia.

DON GONZALO: Enough!

BUTTARELLI: It's nothing but gossip. Because as far as I'm concerned, absolutely no one pays the way they do. I give you my word.

DON GONZALO: There's no need. But . . .

BUTTARELLI: Yes?

DON GONZALO: I would like to see without being seen; do you follow? I don't want to be recognized.

BUTTARELLI: There's nothing simpler. During Carnival the noblest of men can wear a mask without dishonor. And in disguise—well! Who knows what kind of meat is in a pie when it's hidden under the crust?

DON GONZALO: I'd prefer to watch from another room.

BUTTARELLI: There is none.

DON GONZALO: Well, fetch me the mask, then.

BUTTARELLI: Right away, sir.

[*He exits.*]

DON GONZALO: I can't bring myself to believe that such villainy exists, and I don't want to judge him unfairly. I'll unearth the truth myself. And if I find this wager to be a fact, I'll see her dead before she marries him. If he soils her, what's life to me? I'll be a father first— the man of the world can wait. It's a good and profitable match, but I won't have Tenorio cut her bridal veil into a shroud.

[BUTTARELLI *returns bringing mask.*]

BUTTARELLI: Here you are.

DON GONZALO: Thank you. Will they be long in coming?

BUTTARELLI: If they come at all, they won't be long. It's almost eight.

DON GONZALO: Is that the hour?

BUTTARELLI: The year falls due at eight. The one that isn't here on the first stroke of the hour—loses.

DON GONZALO: Pray God it's just a joke, and not what people say.

BUTTARELLI: For all I know, they may disappoint us yet. But if it is so important to you, the time is almost up and you'll know before long.

DON GONZALO: Then I'll put on my mask and sit down.

[*He sits at a table to the right and puts on the mask.*]

BUTTARELLI [*to himself*]: This old man's so mysterious he's made me curious. I won't be satisfied until I know who he is.

DON GONZALO [*to himself*]: That a man like myself should have to wait in a place like this and disguise himself in this fashion! But my family means much to me, and the happiness of my daughter, so simple and so pure, is not a thing to gamble away.

[DON DIEGO, *masked, comes to the door.*]

DON DIEGO: The sign is very clear; this is it. My directions were good. Well, I'm here.

BUTTARELLI: Another mask!

DON DIEGO: Service!

BUTTARELLI: Come in.

DON DIEGO: The Inn of the Laurel?

BUTTARELLI: It's all around you, sir.

DON DIEGO: The innkeeper?

BUTTARELLI: Speaking.

DON DIEGO: Are you Buttarelli?

BUTTARELLI: None other.

DON DIEGO: Does Tenorio have an appointment here today?

BUTTARELLI: Yes.

DON DIEGO: Has he kept it?

BUTTARELLI: No.

DON DIEGO: But he will keep it?

BUTTARELLI: I don't know.

DON DIEGO: You expect him?

BUTTARELLI: If he decides to come.

DON DIEGO: In that case, I too will wait.

[*He sits at a table Left, opposite Don Gonzalo.*]

BUTTARELLI: Would you care for something while you wait?

DON DIEGO: No. Here, take this.

BUTTARELLI: Excellency!

DON DIEGO: And spare me your talk.

BUTTARELLI: Forgive me.

DON DIEGO: I do. Now leave me alone.

BUTTARELLI [*Aside.*]: Dear God! I've never seen such a foul-tempered man in my life.

DON DIEGO [*to himself*]: That a man of my rank should have to descend into a hole like this! But there is no humiliation a father won't endure for his son. I must see the proof with my own eyes: this monster of vice that I've sired!

[BUTTARELLI *eyes Don Diego and Don Gonzalo as he goes about setting his table. They in turn sit silent and masked.*]

BUTTARELLI: What a pair! They might as well be made of stone. I can certainly fill their order—and then some. Ha, they pay and order nothing. Good business!

[CAPTAIN CENTELLAS, AVELLANEDA, *and two* GENTLEMEN *enter.*]

AVELLANEDA: They've come back. And I promise you they'll settle their wager.

CENTELLAS: Let's go in. Buttarelli!

BUTTARELLI: Oh, Captain Centellas! You here?

CENTELLAS: Certainly, Cristofano. Was there ever an orgy that left its mark on the times without me?

BUTTARELLI: Since I haven't seen you for so long—

CENTELLAS: The wars of the Emperor led me to Tunis. But I've come back to Seville to manage my estate. And just in time, so I'm told, to renew old acquaintances. Hurry now and fetch us a bottle or two.

And while we wet our throats, tell us the real story of the wager that's causing so much talk.

BUTTARELLI: One thing at a time. First, let me go to the cellar.

SEVERAL: Yes, yes. Go on.

[*He exits.*]

CENTELLAS: Sit down, gentlemen, and let Avellaneda tell us the rest of the story of Don Luis.

AVELLANEDA: There's nothing more to say—except that I think it's impossible for Tenorio's story to be wilder than this. I bet on Don Luis!

CENTELLAS: You may lose. It's well known that Tenorio is the devil himself. He can beat anyone without even trying. Just think what he can do once he sets his mind to something.

AVELLANEDA: I know that Mejia has done such things that it's a sure bet.

CENTELLAS: Well! Captain Centellas stakes all he owns on Tenorio.

AVELLANEDA: Well! I accept; and bet on Don Luis who happens to be my friend.

CENTELLAS: The odds are all on my side. There's not another man like Tenorio on the face of this earth. His good luck is as proverbial as his deeds are reckless.

[BUTTARELLI *enters with bottles.*]

BUTTARELLI: Here we are—Falernian, Burgundy, and Sorrento.

CENTELLAS: Anything you like, Cristofano. And now, tell us, just what is there to the bet that Don Juan Tenorio made with Don Luis Mejia last year?

BUTTARELLI: Well, Captain—I don't know enough about the matter to answer all your questions, but I'll tell you what I do know.

SEVERAL: Out with it. Speak.

BUTTARELLI: To tell the truth, even though the whole affair took place here in this very inn, they set such a long term to their wager I never believed they'd settle it. I'd forgotten all about it until just about an hour ago. You see, this very evening, just about nightfall, a gentleman comes in and asks me for pen and paper. Now, while he was busy writing, I was able to talk to his page, a countryman of mine— from Genoa. I didn't get a thing out of him, because, by God, he's as slippery as an eel. But when his master finished his letter he sent the page to deliver it. Then the gentleman turned to me and asked me, in my native tongue, for news of Don Luis. He said he knew all about the wager and that one of them, at least, would be on time. I tried to learn more about him but he put two gold coins in my hand and said, "Just in case the two of them arrive on time be sure to make ready the two best bottles in the house." And off he went without a word. So, prompted by his gold, I've set them the very same place where they made their wager—this table. You see—two chairs, two cups, and two bottles.

AVELLANEDA: There's no doubt about it, Gentlemen, it was Don Luis.

CENTELLAS: It was Don Juan.

AVELLENEDA: Didn't you see his face?

BUTTARELLI: He was wearing a mask.

CENTELLAS: But, man, have you forgotten what he looked like? Can't you tell people by their manner and their bearing as easily as by their face?

BUTTARELLI: I admit I was stupid. I honestly tried to recognize him but I couldn't. Wait. Quiet.

AVELLANEDA: What's wrong?

BUTTARELLI: The clock! It's striking a quarter before the hour.

CENTELLAS: Look! Look at the people coming in.

AVELLANEDA: It seems the whole city is curious about this bet.

[*As the bells strike several persons enter silently and find places to stand or sit. On the last stroke of the bell,* DON JUAN, *still masked, enters, crosses to the table prepared by Buttarelli and begins to sit down. Immediately after,* DON LUIS, *also in a mask, enters and crosses to the other chair. He is accompanied by his servant,* GASTON. *Everyone stares.*]

AVELLANEDA [*to Centellas, indicating Don Juan as he enters*]: If our party shows up, he's in for a terrible surprise.

CENTELLAS [*to Avellaneda, indicating Don Luis as he enters*]: And there's another. Ho! Are they in for it!

DON JUAN [*to Don Luis*]: That chair is paid for, sir.

DON LUIS [*to Don Juan*]: I can say the same for that chair, sir. I've reserved it for a friend.

DON JUAN: Let me be plain. This is my chair.

DON LUIS: Let me be just as plain about this one!

DON JUAN: Then you must be Don Luis Mejia.

DON LUIS: And you, then, are Don Juan Tenorio.

DON JUAN: That may be.

DON LUIS: So you say.

DON JUAN: My word won't do?

DON LUIS: No.

DON JUAN: Nor will yours.

DON LUIS: Enough play acting!

DON JUAN: I am Don Juan.

[*He removes his mask.*]

DON LUIS [*doing the same*]: And I, Don Luis.

[*They remove their hats and sit down.* CAPTAIN CENTELLAS, AVEL-
LANEDA, BUTTARELLI, *and several others go to them and greet them,
shaking hands, embracing, and so forth.* DON JUAN *and* DON LUIS
accept these greetings cordially.]

CENTELLAS: Don Juan!

AVELLANEDA: Don Luis!

DON JUAN: Gentlemen!

DON LUIS: Well, Gentlemen. Welcome.

AVELLANEDA: We heard of your wager and had to come and see.

DON LUIS: Don Juan and I thank you for your interest.

DON JUAN: Let's not waste time, Don Luis. [*To the others.*] Draw your
chairs up closer. [*To those farther off*] Gentlemen, if I'm not mistaken, you too were drawn here by our wager. I, for one, have no
objection to your presence.

DON LUIS: Nor I. For though the matter lies between the two of us,
by God, let no one say that I am ashamed of it!

DON JUAN: And I most certainly am not. The whole world bears witness that I'm no hypocrite. Where I go, scandal goes!

DON LUIS: Ah! [*to Don Diego and Don Gonzalo*] And you two—don't
you want to come closer? You, gentlemen?

DON DIEGO: I'm comfortable, thank you.

DON LUIS: And you, sir.

DON GONZALO: I can hear very well from here.

DON LUIS: They must have their reasons.

[*They all take their places around the table with Don Juan Tenorio
and Don Luis Mejia at either end.*]

DON JUAN: Are we ready?

DON LUIS: Ready.

DON JUAN: And so—we kept our pledge.

DON LUIS: Let's see, now, what we did.

DON JUAN: A drink first.

DON LUIS: Agreed.

[*They drink.*]

DON JUAN: The wager took place—

DON LUIS: Because one day I happened to say that no man in all of
Spain could do what I can do.

DON JUAN: And being of a somewhat different opinion, I answered that no man would do what Juan Tenorio would! Am I right?

DON LUIS: Exactly. And so we bet on who could do more harm with more luck in the course of one year—promising to meet here now to prove our claims.

DON JUAN: And here I am.

DON LUIS: And I.

CENTELLAS: Now there's a wild venture for you!

DON JUAN: Speak up, then.

DON LUIS: No, you started it.

DON JUAN: Very well; it's all one to me. I've never kept anyone waiting. Well, sir, finding this city a little cramped for adventure, I hit upon going to Italy. That country is a true palace of pleasure. It's the ancient and classical residence of war and love. And what with the Emperor there fighting both France and Italy, I said to myself, "What could be better? Where there are soldiers, there's bound to be gambling, brawling, and love!" So I flung myself on Italy in search of blood, fire, love, and duels. In Rome I hung a sign above my door that read as follows: *"Here lives Don Juan ready for anything and everything!"* I won't go into detail about those days. You can guess what I did and the scandal I caused from the wording of my sign! Those spry little Roman girls, their free and easy ways, and I, good-looking and hot-blooded—there was no holding me back! In the long run, I had to skip out, as you can imagine. I dressed up as a tramp and rode off on a flea-bitten nag. They wanted to hang me! Then I joined the Spanish. All countrymen, you know: soldiers and abroad. Five or six duels and I left them behind. Naples was next. A bower of love! An emporium of pleasure! There, I hung a second sign. *"Here lives Don Juan Tenorio. There's not a man that can touch him! From fishmonger to princess there's not a woman he won't love. There's not a scheme that he won't tackle if there's money in the plot. If you're a fighter, seek me out. If you're a gambler, fence me in. And if you've got an itchy sword, try and scratch me out. Come one, come all, you stupid fishes, and see if you can beat me at cards, or swords, or kisses."* That's what I wrote. And during the six months that Naples enjoyed my presence, there wasn't a scandal or outrage in which I didn't figure prominently. Wherever I went, I trod upon reason, scoffed at virtue, laughed at the law, and seduced the women. I descended upon cottages, scaled palace walls, and took the convents by storm! I left a bitter memory wherever I went. I held nothing sacred, nor was there a cause or place that I respected. Clergyman or layman was all the same to me. I challenged anyone I wished, I fought anyone who wished, and I never, for a moment, thought that the man that I was killing could possibly kill me. That's what I accomplished! And what I've done I've written here—and what I've written, I'll maintain.

DON LUIS: Read it, then.

DON JUAN: No. First let's have the story of your wild escapades. For if you've brought a list we'll compare them at our leisure.

DON LUIS: Very well, Don Juan, that seems fair to me—though in my opinion there's very little difference between my tale and yours.

DON JUAN: Begin.

DON LUIS: Here it is! Like you, in search of a setting for adventure, I asked myself, "Good God, if love and quarrels are my aim, what better goal than Flanders? In the midst of war, loving, fighting, and adventure will be multiplied a hundredfold!" So, off to Flanders I went, but with the blackest luck that ever a man did have! Within the month I'd lost everything I had—one by one, doubloon by doubloon! Seeing me in such financial straits, men avoided me like a leper. And since I'm fond of company, I joined a gang of bandits. We did very well, if I say so myself! We did so well, in fact, that we sacked the palace of the bishop at Ghent. What a night that was! The bishop, observing the Christmas services, had gone down to conduct the choir. My hair still stands on end when I remember the treasure that we took! Our captain, however, a greedy man, tried to make off with my share. We fought, of course—I was quick and he was slow. I riddled him beyond repair! The men then made me their captain, as the bravest of their lot. I swore them my good will, but on the following night I made off with the loot and left them flat. I remembered the saying, you see, "If you rob a thief, from Hell a century's relief!" So, with one eye peeled for my salvation, I relieved them of their money and slipped into Germany with a full purse. But a little priest who'd fled from Ghent, a clever little beast, spotted and denounced me to the courts with an anonymous note. Well, by means of my money I earned back my freedom and that note. Then, coming across him, just by chance, on one fine Sunday afternoon, I returned the note to the little friar neatly wrapped up in a bullet. Then I skipped over into France. What a country! As you did in Naples, so did I in Paris. I hung a sign above my door: *"Here lives a certain Don Luis who's worth two of any of you! And here he'll* live a month or more with nothing else to do than to love the little Parisienne and drown all Frenchmen in the Seine." That was my sign. And during the six months that Paris enjoyed my presence there wasn't a scandal or outrage in which I didn't figure prominently. But like you, Don Juan, I too decline to draw my story out. It's enough for me to cite the memory—the magnificent memory that my sign and I have left behind. Like you, my friend, wherever I went I trod upon reason, scoffed at virtue, laughed at the law, and seduced the women. I've squandered my fortune three times over!— and now it's time for repairs. My engagement with Doña Ana de Pantoja is the very thing I need. They've given me a very, very wealthy bride, and tomorrow I'll bring it off. I mention this, Don Juan, in case you wish to come. That's what I accomplished! And what I've done I've written here—and what I've written, I'll maintain.

DON JUAN: Your story is so like mine our scale stands even. But now let's get the true weight of the matter: the value of our lists. On with it.

DON LUIS: You're right. Here's mine! For the sake of clarity, I placed all names on this side of the line.

DON JUAN: I kept my accounts by the very same method. One column for the dead and another for the women.

DON LUIS: Count off.

DON JUAN: Twenty-three.

DON LUIS: Dead, that is. And now for yours. By Saint Andrew's Cross! You've got thirty-two!

DON JUAN: Dead, that is.

DON LUIS: Slaughtered, you mean.

DON JUAN: I'm nine ahead.

DON LUIS: You've beaten me there. But now let's move on to the women.

DON JUAN: By my count—fifty-six.

DON LUIS: And your tally adds up to—seventy-two!

DON JUAN: You've lost.

DON LUIS: It's unbelievable.

DON JUAN: If you have your doubts, question the witnesses listed there and they'll confirm my tally.

DON LUIS: A thorough list, by God!

DON JUAN: From a princess to a fisherman's daughter. I've loved my way up and down the social ladder! Do you find fault with any of it?

DON LUIS: It lacks one thing.

DON JUAN: What's that?

DON LUIS: Why, a novice on the eve of taking her vows.

DON JUAN: Bah! I'll be glad to oblige you—and with a vengeance! For along with the novice, I'll throw in—the bride of a friend who's about to marry.

DON LUIS: By God, you go too far!

DON JUAN: Then take up my bet.

DON LUIS: Taken! And as good as won. Will twenty days be enough?

DON JUAN: Six.

DON LUIS: Good God, man, you're a monster! How many days do you spend per seduction?

DON JUAN: Divide the days you'll find in a year by the number of names you'll find on my list. One day to court 'em, one day to trap 'em, one day to jilt 'em, two to replace 'em, and an hour, more or less, to forget 'em. But—to the point—I wouldn't think of asking more time of you, because by tomorrow I will have robbed you of Doña Ana de Pantoja.

DON LUIS: What are you saying, Don Juan?

DON JUAN: What you hear, Don Luis.

DON LUIS: Consider, Don Juan, what you are undertaking.

DON JUAN: Nothing I can't achieve, Don Luis.

DON LUIS: Gaston!

GASTON: Sir.

DON LUIS: Come here.

[DON LUIS *whispers to him and* GASTON *hurries off.*]

DON JUAN: Ciutti!

CIUTTI: Sir.

DON JUAN: Come here.

[DON JUAN *whispers to Ciutti, who hurries off.*]

DON LUIS: You stand by your wager?

DON JUAN: I do.

DON LUIS: You've staked your life.

DON JUAN: So be it.

[DON GONZALO *rises from his seat where he has remained motionless during the preceding scene, and now confronts Don Juan and Don Luis.*]

DON GONZALO: You scum! As God is my witness, if my hands were steady I'd club you to death like the dogs you are!

DON JUAN *and* DON LUIS [*laying their hands to their swords*]: All right! Let's see.

DON GONZALO: Where my strength cannot second it, I swallow my pride. I'm old enough to know that.

DON JUAN: Then get out!

DON GONZALO: You'll hear me out, Don Juan, before I go. Your good father, Don Diego, arranged a match for you as a means of settling some legal suit. Your wedding was all planned. But I wanted to see for myself what sort of man you were, and the sight of you disgusts me.

DON JUAN: By the devil, you old bag of bones, I don't know what's kept me from slapping your head off your shoulders. But tell me, who are you? For I'd as soon rip off your mask as rip out your soul.

DON GONZALO: Don Juan!

DON JUAN: Out with it!

DON GONZALO: Look then.

[*He removes his mask.*]

DON JUAN: Don Gonzalo!

DON GONZALO: The same. And now, Don Juan, farewell. From this instant on, give up all hope of Doña Ines. Because I swear before God, sooner than give her up to you I'll fling her into the grave!

DON JUAN: Don Gonzalo, you make me laugh. You're like the man who threatens a lion with a twig. Since there's still time to change your mind, I warn you now—either you give your daughter to me, or, by God I'll come and take her.

DON GONZALO: Wretch!

DON JUAN: You heard, and so you know my list is complete except for a girl like her. Now go away, she's already taken her place in my wager.

[*DON DIEGO, rising from the table where he has remained masked through the whole of the preceding scene, crosses and faces Don Juan.*]

DON DIEGO: Don Juan, I'll listen to you no longer! I'm sure that Heaven is saving a bolt of lightning especially for you. I couldn't believe what they said of you; I had to come and see for myself. But I'm sorry that I came, you cur; for I leave convinced of what I should have left unknown! Go your beastly way. I no longer know you.

DON JUAN: Since I've never asked your help, and you have no cause to talk to me like this, why should I care if you've forgotten me? I couldn't care less!

DON DIEGO: Goodbye, then. But remember—God is just!

DON JUAN: Wait.

[*He detains DON DIEGO.*]

DON DIEGO: What do you want?

DON JUAN: Your face.

DON DIEGO: Never.

DON JUAN: Never?

DON DIEGO: No.

DON JUAN: Whenever I please!

DON DIEGO: How?

DON JUAN: Like this!

[*He rips off the mask.*]

DON DIEGO: You villain! You laid your hand on my face!

DON JUAN: By God, it's my father!

DON DIEGO: You lie. I never was your father.

DON JUAN: Go to the devil!

DON DIEGO: Go yourself. He's your father, not I. Commander, what's passed tonight must be forgotten.

DON GONZALO: I've forgotten already. Let's be off.

DON DIEGO: Yes; away from the sight of this monster. Don Juan, I leave you to your vice. You are killing me—but I forgive you. The judgment is God's.

DON JUAN: My judgment's a long way off! You have given me good terms. But take notice, I've never asked your pardon. Forget me. I have lived as I have lived, and I don't mean to change.

[*They leave.*]

DON JUAN: Well, that's over, thank God. And forgive the little sermon —a family spat. Pay no attention to it. So, Don Luis, as we agreed, we play for Doña Ana and Doña Ines.

DON LUIS: And the forfeit is our life.

DON JUAN: As you say. Agreed?

DON LUIS: Agreed.

[*As they start out, a* WATCH *stops them at the door.*]

OFFICER: Halt. Don Juan Tenorio.

DON JUAN: Here.

OFFICER: You're under arrest.

DON JUAN: I must be dreaming! Why?

OFFICER: You'll know soon enough.

DON LUIS [*crossing to Don Juan and laughing*]: Don't look so surprised! In view of our wager I had my man press charges to make sure you'd lose.

DON JUAN: Well! I never gave you credit for such a ready wit.

DON LUIS: Off with you! For once, Don Juan, the game is mine.

DON JUAN: Well, then, let's go.

[*As they start to leave, another* WATCH *enters and detains them.*]

SECOND OFFICER: Halt! Don Luis Mejia?

DON LUIS: Here.

SECOND OFFICER: You're under arrest.

DON LUIS: I must be dreaming! Prisoner?

DON JUAN [*bursting into laughter*]: Mejia, don't be too surprised! In view of our wager I had *my* man press charges to get you out of the way.

DON LUIS: All right, all right, I don't care. Even if the *two* of us should die.

DON JUAN: We're off! And so, my friends, the wager's under way.

[*The* WATCH *take* DON LUIS *and* DON JUAN *away. The crowd follows them. Centellas, Avellaneda, and their friends stay behind.*]

AVELLANEDA: It seems incredible.

CENTELLAS: If I hadn't seen it, I wouldn't believe it.

AVELLANEDA: I still bet on Mejia.

CENTELLAS: Tenorio is the man for me.

ACT II

Skill

Exterior of Doña Ana's house seen from the corner. The two walls that form the angle of the house extend far enough to reveal a window covered with an iron grille in one wall. In the other wall, there is a door and a grille-covered window.

DON LUIS MEJIA *enters. His face is muffled by a cloak.*

DON LUIS: Well, here I am at Doña Ana's house—she must be warned of what's afoot in this city tonight. Thank God I met no one on the way! What confusion! Well, Don Juan, for the time being it's every man for himself. When honor and life are at stake I'll surely match mine against yours. . . . Someone's coming.

[*Enter* PASCUAL.]

PASCUAL: My God! Who'd believe it? Both of them in jail! What a scandal.

DON LUIS: Who's this? Pascual?

PASCUAL: I still can't get it through my head.

DON LUIS: Pascual!

PASCUAL: Who calls?

DON LUIS: I do. Don Luis.

PASCUAL: God in heaven!

DON LUIS: Why so shocked?

PASCUAL: It's you! You!

DON LUIS: That's my luck. In fact, if I hadn't met you now, the honor of my bride, Doña Ana, would be destroyed tonight.

PASCUAL: What are you saying?

DON LUIS: Do you know Don Juan Tenorio?

PASCUAL: Of course. Who doesn't? But rumor had it that you were both in jail. Oh, the stories people tell!

DON LUIS: They spoke true for once. And, by God, if my cousin, the royal treasurer, hadn't bailed me out, Pascual, I would have lost tonight what I hold most dear.

PASCUAL: How so?

DON LUIS: Can I count on you?

PASCUAL: With my life!

DON LUIS: Then listen to me. Don Juan and I are engaged in a terrible struggle, but if you'll help me you can save more than my life!

PASCUAL: What's to be done?

DON LUIS: Sometime ago, in a fit of madness, it occurred to us to bet on which could do more harm with more luck. We've both behaved like wild men—worse! But he's the devil himself! He won out. Then —don't ask me why—I hedged somehow—I said some things—I don't know what—and the upshot of it was that he became insulting and taunted me. "If my record doesn't satisfy you and you have the guts for more, I'll bet I'll snatch your bride from your arms by tomorrow."

PASCUAL: Now there's a boast for you! I wonder he dared to utter it.

DON LUIS: Let him say what he will, so long as he doesn't do what he says.

PASCUAL: Do? He won't do a thing! Not as long as I'm about. Rest assured of that, Don Luis.

DON LUIS: Pascual, I swear to you, if I don't prevent him, it'll be the end of me!

PASCUAL: Dear God in heaven! You seem afraid of him.

DON LUIS: No! As God's my witness I'm not! But that man has the devil on his side!

PASCUAL: You've no need to worry.

DON LUIS: Oh! I tell you I'm so anxious—and against a man like that, I wouldn't even trust myself.

PASCUAL: Well, I swear to you by all that's holy that with all his daring, all it takes to settle his business is one Aragonese like myself. We'll see each other later.

DON LUIS: You don't know what you're taking on.

PASCUAL: I've been in far worse scrapes and come out without a scratch.

DON LUIS: It all hinges on time and the fact that he's the kind of man he is!

PASCUAL: No Tenorio is a match for a good Aragonese. All those tongue-flapping, sword-slapping braggarts put up a good front but are hollow inside. When it comes to maligning women their tongue is long enough. When it comes to insulting old men and tradesmen their arm is strong enough. But when they face a good long sword in the hand of a good strong man all their courage melts away, and what remains of all their noisy adventures is smutty slander of women and playing hide-and-seek with the law.

DON LUIS: Pascual!

PASCUAL: I don't mean you. Even though you have the reputation of a madcap, you've got a good stout heart and can handle a sword, by God!

DON LUIS: Well, if my courage is so well known, Pascual, let me say that courage is Tenorio's second name. I respect his courage, and fear lest his cunning tumble my honor into mud.

PASCUAL: Since your jealousy goads you—now that you're out of jail all you have to do is counter cunning with cunning. What can he possibly do?

DON LUIS: I don't know. But I'm afraid tonight's the night he'll carry out his plan.

PASCUAL: You're dreaming.

DON LUIS: Why?

PASCUAL: Isn't he in prison?

DON LUIS: Of course! But so was I until someone bailed me out.

PASCUAL: Who would rescue him?

DON LUIS: I don't know. But what I do know is that there's only one way to put my mind at rest.

PASCUAL: Which is?

DON LUIS: To spend the night in Doña Ana's house!

PASCUAL: Consider, consider! Doña Ana's honor would be as good as lost.

DON LUIS: Damnation! Am I or am I not to be her husband tomorrow?

PASCUAL: But have I or have I not sworn to put my life at your disposal?

DON LUIS: You have—and you can help me in a quarrel but never in a trick. And so either I spend the night in this house or I'll take this street and hold it against all who come—the Watch itself.

PASCUAL: My dear Don Luis, don't be stubborn. Leave this whim, I beg you. All will be well.

DON LUIS: I won't leave it, Pascual.

PASCUAL: Don Luis!

DON LUIS: That's all!

PASCUAL: Dear God! Why so stubborn?

DON LUIS: Say what you want. In fact, I trust women even less than I trust Don Juan. This is a fight between madmen—and if one of them has no scruples, the other must have daring.

PASCUAL: Choose your words with care, because I've served Doña Ana from the day she was born! And don't forget, Don Luis, you're going to marry the lady tomorrow.

DON LUIS: When that time's past, when she's my wife at last, I'll make her a good husband and keep her a good wife. But until then—

PASCUAL: Not another word! I've known you both since you were this high, and by the life of Barabbas, I know how much you care for each other. Listen— my room is large enough. You can stay the night with me. But give me your word to be absolutely silent.

DON LUIS: You have it.

PASCUAL: Together we'll keep a double watch the whole night through.

DON LUIS: And Doña Ana will be saved.

PASCUAL: God willing.

DON LUIS: Let's go then.

PASCUAL: Wait. What are you going to do?

DON LUIS: Go in.

PASCUAL: So soon?

DON LUIS: Who knows what he'll do?

PASCUAL: Check that jealousy of yours. As long as my master, Don Gil de Pantoja, isn't up and about and the house is quiet you can assume that everything is all right.

DON LUIS: By God—

PASCUAL: Come. Once and for all, make a truce with your lover's frenzy.

DON LUIS: At what time does he go to bed?

PASCUAL: At ten. In that alley is a window. Call me there at ten and leave the rest to me.

DON LUIS: Count on me.

PASCUAL: Well, Don Luis, until later.

DON LUIS: Goodbye, Pascual—I'll see you soon.

[*Exit* PASCUAL.]

DON LUIS: I've never suffered like this before. My very life seems in the balance tonight; I can't rid my soul of fears, of dim forebodings, a sense of onrushing ruin. By God, I never knew I loved her so. I've never felt for others what I feel for her. What frightens me about Don Juan is not his courage; Satan himself assures him of luck in everything he does! No, no—he's the Devil's own man and as sure as I am standing here if I were to move away, that man would certainly undo me. Pascual be hanged! Let him think what he wants, I want to get in. Where Don Juan's concerned no precaution is foolish.

[*He knocks at the window.*]

DOÑA ANA [*from within*]: Who's there?

DON LUIS: Pascual?

DOÑA ANA: Don Luis!

[*She opens the window.*]

DON LUIS: Doña Ana!

DOÑA ANA: Have you taken to calling at windows?

DON LUIS: Oh, Doña Ana, you couldn't have come at a better time.

DOÑA ANA: What seems to be the trouble?

DON LUIS: Trouble prompted by your beauty between myself and a man I fear.

DOÑA ANA: Why so anxious, Don Luis? You are the master of my soul.

DON LUIS: Doña Ana, until you know his name, until you know his luck, you know nothing of this man.

DOÑA ANA: His luck won't hold where I'm concerned. There! In a few hours we'll be man and wife. Why do you worry so?

DON LUIS: As God is my witness, he would never frighten me so long as I held a sword in my hand and he met you face to face. But when the lion turns cunning, wise, and cautious, and develops the tricks of a snake—

DOÑA ANA: Bah, go to bed, Don Luis, and sleep in peace. His cunning and his tricks will never catch me . . . for you are my future, my life!

DON LUIS: Very well, Doña Ana, in order to stay my fears of that man, and in the name of that love you profess, I'm going to beg a favor of you.

DOÑA ANA: Speak softly, there may be someone near.

DON LUIS: Listen.

[DOÑA ANA, and DON LUIS *remain at the window, right;* DON JUAN *and* CIUTTI *enter down the street, left.*]

CIUTTI: By my life, your luck is as good as it is endless.

DON JUAN: Ciutti, there's no one to touch me! You saw how easily the wise jailer came round and let me loose. But enough of that. Have you carried out my orders?

CIUTTI: Every one of them—and better than you anticipated.

DON JUAN: The duenna?

CIUTTI: Here's the key to the garden, but you'll have climbing to do just the same. As you know, the outer walls of the convent have no doors at all.

DON JUAN: Did she give you a letter?

CIUTTI: No, but she did say she'd be coming by here at any moment now, on her way back to the convent, and that she would talk to you then.

DON JUAN: That's better.

CIUTTI: I agree.

DON JUAN: And the horses?

CIUTTI: Saddled and ready.

DON JUAN: And the men?

CIUTTI: Close by.

DON JUAN: Good work, Ciutti. And now—while Seville sleeps soundly thinking I'm in jail, I add two more names to my wonderful list. [*He laughs.*]

CIUTTI: Sir.

DON JUAN: What?

CIUTTI: Quiet.

DON JUAN: What is it?

CIUTTI: As we passed the corner I saw a man standing at that window.

DON JUAN: You're right. Well now, that adds spice to the adventure! And if it happens to be he!

CIUTTI: Who?

DON JUAN: Don Luis.

CIUTTI: Impossible.

DON JUAN: Idiot. Didn't I get out?

CIUTTI: That's what makes the difference between you and Don Luis.

DON JUAN: I need evidence, Ciutti, before I'll believe that. There's a woman on the other side of that window.

CIUTTI: A maid-servant, perhaps.

DON JUAN: I must make sure, by God. I stand a chance of losing both wager and reputation. Ciutti, take several of the men you hired, circle the house, and come down that street pretending you're the Watch.

CIUTTI: That's sure to make her close the window.

DON JUAN: That's the point. He'll be arrested, she won't know it, and the way is clear for me.

CIUTTI: Good idea.

DON JUAN: Now hurry and take him. My success depends on it.

CIUTTI: And if the dog resists us?

DON JUAN: Cut him in two.

[*Exit* CIUTTI.]

DON LUIS: You agree then?

DOÑA ANA: I do.

DON LUIS: You'll do this for me? To please me?

DOÑA ANA: I'll please you in everything and anything.

DON LUIS: Then I'll watch over you till dawn.

DOÑA ANA: Yes, Don Luis.

DON LUIS: God bless you, Ana, for granting me this.

DOÑA ANA: Judge my sincerity—Mejia, I'll grant you everything!

DON LUIS: I'll come back later.

DOÑA ANA: Yes, do—at ten o'clock.

DON LUIS: Will you be waiting?

DOÑA ANA: Yes.

DON LUIS: Here?

DOÑA ANA: Don't be late.

DON LUIS: I won't.

DOÑA ANA: I'll get the key for you.

DON LUIS: Once I'm inside your house, let Tenorio come!

DOÑA ANA: Someone approaches. Be here at ten.

DON LUIS: I'll be here.

[DONA ANA *closes her window.* DON JUAN *moves forward.*]

DON LUIS: They're coming closer! Who goes there?

DON JUAN: Who? The one that's here.

DON LUIS: And what does that mean?

DON JUAN: Whatever you want to make of it.

DON LUIS: Do you want your tongue torn out?

DON JUAN: Make way.

DON LUIS: The street is closed.

DON JUAN: My hand is on my sword.

DON LUIS: Ask more courteously and you'll get by.

DON JUAN: Courtesy to whom?

DON LUIS: Don Luis Mejia.

DON JUAN: I want to get by!

DON LUIS: You know me?

DON JUAN: I do.

DON LUIS: Do I know you?

DON JUAN: You do.

DON LUIS: Then what are we arguing about?

DON JUAN: The street.

DON LUIS: Do you too intend to be master of it?

DON JUAN: Precisely.

DON LUIS: There's only one other man who would want to command this street at this moment.

DON JUAN: I know.

DON LUIS: Are you Don Juan?

DON JUAN: You've hit it! So here we are, the two of us—in the street.

DON LUIS: Didn't they arrest you?

DON JUAN: Just as they arrested you.

DON LUIS: Good God! You escaped!

DON JUAN: I followed your example. Now what?

DON LUIS: You'll lose.

DON JUAN: That remains to be seen.

DON LUIS: We'll see then.

DON JUAN: The lady has been gambled and you have lost.

DON LUIS: There's time.

DON JUAN: Your time is up.

DON LUIS: We'll see!

[DON LUIS *draws, but* CIUTTI, *who has entered stealthily with his men, pins him down.*]

DON JUAN: You see, Don Luis—I was right.

DON LUIS: A trick! Help!

DON JUAN: Gag him!

[*They gag him.*]

DON LUIS: Oh!

DON JUAN: Now his arms. [*They tie* DON LUIS' *arms.*] Tighter! And now, my dear Don Luis, I have the upper hand. [*To his men.*] Keep him under lock and key until morning. The wager is as good as won. What if the means are fair or foul—just so long as I win. Good evening, my dear Don Luis. [*Exeunt* CIUTTI *and men with* DON LUIS.]

DON JUAN: By God now. This is a good one! The kind of trick that makes me famous! While I'm stealing his bride away, he'll be locked in my wine cellar ripping his hair out by the roots! And she? She'll think that she's safe, nestled in the arms of Don Luis! [*He laughs.*] And there's no complaining—I've played it fair and square; I had him arrested—he got out; he had me arrested—I got out; that we were bound to meet here is obvious; we had to keep up our ends of the wager. Poor Mejia. He seems out of favor with lady luck and will lose this wager too. Nevertheless—just in case—it won't do any harm to make certain of Lucia, the maid. In matters like these no trifle is too small. . . . Oh, but here comes a large black shadow. Seems to be a woman! . . . Another adventure? Let's see.

[*Enter* BRIGIDA.]

BRIGIDA: Sir?

DON JUAN: Who's there?

BRIGIDA: Are you Don Juan?

DON JUAN: Good God, the duenna! I'd forgotten! Come, I'm Don Juan.

BRIGIDA: Are you alone?

DON JUAN: With the Devil.

BRIGIDA: Heavens!

DON JUAN: I mean, with you.

BRIGIDA: Am I the Devil, then?

DON JUAN: I should say so.

BRIGIDA: Oh, go on! The things you say! You're the one, you little devil, you —

DON JUAN: —who'll fill your purse for you—if you serve me well.

BRIGIDA: Try me and see.

DON JUAN: Unburden that bosom of yours and tell me what you've done.

BRIGIDA: Everything your page told me to—and what a nasty little creature he is too.

DON JUAN: Ciutti? What's he done?

BRIGIDA: Oh, he's a rogue, he is!

DON JUAN: Didn't he give you a purse and a paper?

BRIGIDA: Doña Ines is reading that paper at this very moment.

DON JUAN: You—ah—prepared her for it?

BRIGIDA: Prepared? I've convinced her so completely, she'll come to you as meek as a lamb.

DON JUAN: Was it that easy?

BRIGIDA: Bah! Like some poor bird in a cage, born in a cage, she doesn't know that there's more life and more space in which to fly. She's never seen her feathers shine in the sun—how can she be vain of their colors? She's only seventeen, the poor little thing, and a virgin even to the first impressions of love! She's never talked to a soul outside of her home and they've watched over her day and night. What with all those dreary years of solitude in the convent, they managed to bind her thought and cramp her mind until her whole world had shrunk to a mean little circle in which the cloister and the altar were her destiny and goal. "God is here," they said to her; "And here I worship," she replied. "This is the cloister and here's the choir." "And that's all there is to the world!" she thought. Without any illusions other than her own girlish dreams she managed to live through seventeen Aprils and never noticed a change.

DON JUAN: Is she lovely?

BRIGIDA: Oh! Like an angel.

DON JUAN: And you've told her—?

BRIGIDA: You judge for yourself if I haven't stuffed her head with an evil chaos! I talked to her of love. I told her of the world and the court. I described the pleasures—and told her how handsome you were and how prodigious with the women. I told her that you were the man her father had intended for her husband. I painted you dying for love of her, desperate for her, haunted by her, and deter- mined to risk your life for her. Well, to make a long story short, my sweet words, alighting in her ears, awakened her slumbering passions and stirred them into life. My words have kindled such a flame in her breast that she is now in love with you and can think of nothing else.

DON JUAN: Your provocative painting stirs my senses and fills my burning soul with a cruel passion of desire. It began with a bet and grew into a frenzy which later engendered desire—and now my heart is burning up. Getting into a cloister is nothing! I'd go down to Hell, if need be, and rip her from the arms of Satan himself! Oho! You lovely little flower still closed to the dews of love—wait till I transplant you into the garden of my heart. Brigida?

BRIGIDA: I've heard you and I'm amazed. I had thought you were a soulless, heartless rake!

DON JUAN: Don't be surprised. When the object of my passion is as noble as this one, then my effort and love must rise to the occasion.

BRIGIDA: You're right.

DON JUAN: Now—at what time do the nuns go to bed?

BRIGIDA: They're in bed already. Is everything ready?

DON JUAN: Everything.

BRIGIDA: Well, then, when you hear the bells tolling compline, vault the wall into the garden, then with the key I gave you you'll have no trouble getting into the convent. You'll find yourself in a dark and narrow cloister. Go straight ahead till you come to our cell.

DON JUAN: If I manage to make off with this treasure, I'll give you your weight in gold.

BRIGIDA: Oh! Now—really, Don Juan!

DON JUAN: Go now and wait for me.

BRIGIDA: I'm going. And I'll stop at the gate and talk to the door-keeper, Sister Marie—just to avoid suspicion. I'll see you soon!

[BRIGIDA *goes off. Some moments before her exit,* CIUTTI *returns and stands waiting to speak to* DON JUAN.]

DON JUAN: Well, sir! I've played many a game but I've never dealt a better hand. The cards are such that the game's worth the playing! Ciutti is waiting. Come here, you hound!

CIUTTI: Here, Sir.

DON JUAN: Don Luis?

CIUTTI: You're free of him for a day or so.

DON JUAN: Now I must speak to Lucia.

CIUTTI: And here's the place. [*He indicates the window at right.*] I'll call her, and when she comes to the window you can take over.

DON JUAN: Call her, then.

CIUTTI: Don't worry, she'll come. She knows my signal well.

DON JUAN: Well, if she comes, leave the rest to me.

[CIUTTI *calls.* LUCIA *comes to the window but is startled by the sight of Don Juan.*]

LUCIA: What do you want, Sir?

DON JUAN: I want—

LUCIA: Let's see—now what will it be?

DON JUAN: To see—

LUCIA: To see? What would you see at this hour of the night?

DON JUAN: Your mistress.

LUCIA: Ho! Run along, Sir, run along! Who do you think lives here?

DON JUAN: Doña Ana de Pantoja—and I wish to see her!

LUCIA: Don't you know she's getting married?

DON JUAN: Yes. Tomorrow.

LUCIA: Goodness! Unfaithful so soon!

DON JUAN: She will be.

LUCIA: But isn't she engaged to Don Luis Mejia?

DON JUAN: Ha! Unto each day—and tomorrow is another day, Lucia. Tonight *I* am to be with Doña Ana and if she marries tomorrow—well, let tomorrow take care of itself.

LUCIA: Oh! And is she expecting you?

DON JUAN: Perhaps.

LUCIA: And what am I to do for you?

DON JUAN: Open up.

LUCIA: Bah! What will open the castle's door?

DON JUAN: This purse.

LUCIA: Gold!

DON JUAN: You've a keen eye.

LUCIA: How much?

DON JUAN: More than a hundred.

LUCIA: Dear God!

DON JUAN: Count them—and then answer me. Can that purse open this house?

LUCIA: When the purse is fat enough.

DON JUAN: And shines yellow?

LUCIA: Yes. What name do you go by?

DON JUAN: Don Juan.

LUCIA: Does the surname have a luster?

DON JUAN: Tenorio.

LUCIA: Souls in Purgatory! You! Don Juan?

DON JUAN: Why fear me if you find me rich?

LUCIA: The lock squeaks.

DON JUAN: I'll take care of it.

LUCIA: And who'll take care of me?

DON JUAN: You will take care of yourself.

LUCIA: But how will I know what to do?

DON JUAN: Use your wits.

LUCIA: Bah! The devil take you!

DON JUAN: Double the gold.

LUCIA: That's more comforting.

DON JUAN: See, your wit takes care of everything.

LUCIA: But give me a little time.

DON JUAN: Till ten o'clock.

LUCIA: Where will I find you—or you me?

DON JUAN: Here.

LUCIA: Don't be late now.

DON JUAN: I won't.

LUCIA: I'll bring you a key.

DON JUAN: And I'll bring you another purse.

LUCIA: Don't fail me.

DON JUAN: Never fear. I'll be here at ten. Goodbye then, and trust in me.

LUCIA: And you in me, you handsome man, you!

DON JUAN: Until later, my —honest Lucia.

LUCIA: 'Till later, my—rich Don Juan.

[LUCIA *closes the window.* DON JUAN *makes a sign and* CIUTTI *comes to him.*]

DON JUAN [*laughing*]: Gold never fails. Ciutti, you know my plan. Nine at the convent and here at ten!

[*They go.*]

ACT III

Profanation

Doña Ines' cell. Doors left and upstage. DOÑA INES *and the* ABBESS *are talking.*

ABBESS: You understand me, don't you?

DOÑA INES: Yes, Mother.

ABBESS: It's fitting and proper; and, furthermore, it is your father's will. You are young and pure and good, and you've lived in this cloister ever since you were a child. There'll be no need to do penances and try your faith—as others do—in order to stay with us and take the vows. How fortunate you are, child—yes, lucky Ines! Never having known the world, you have no need to fear it. You happy child. Having stepped through the door of the cloister you'll never be tempted by what you've left behind. Worldly memories of riot and pleasure will never lure or trouble you. Since you're ignorant of all that lies beyond our holy wall, you will never feel a craving for it. Like a gentle dove that learned to eat at the hand of her master, reared in the shelter of an aviary, never having left your cage, you'll never feel the need to try your wings in the vault of space. You graceful lily, whose stem was stirred by the sweet breezes of the most flowerful month—those soft breezes will kiss you here and open out your petals —and here your leaves may wither gently and have their fall. Within our narrow confines and beneath the bit of sky that falls in through the bars you'll find a sweet repose and a blue veil joined to the very gates of Eden. Oh, I tell you true, my happy Doña Ines, I am jealous of your innocence and the virtue of your ignorance. But why so downhearted? Where's the cheerful answer you've given me before when I've broached the matter to you? A sigh? Oh, now I know. You miss your good nurse. But don't give it another thought. She went off to your father's at sundown and I'm sure she must be back by now. I'll send her to you since I must watch tonight. Well now, Doña Ines, make ready for bed. You mustn't set a bad example. My little novices have long since gone to sleep. Good night.

DOÑA INES: God be with you, Mother.

ABBESS: Good night, dear.

[*She exits.*]

DOÑA INES: She's gone. Oh, what's wrong with me? A thousand new thoughts are waging war within me—and all at once! How happily I've listened to her on other nights like these, and how comforting those gentle pictures she draws so well. Those quiet pleasures so simple and happy, that blessed calm, made me yearn for the solitude of the cloister and its holy rule. But how it was so hard to pay attention to her. When she wasn't annoying, she was, surely, very dull. And for some reason, when she told me that my vows would soon be upon me, I trembled! My heart began to pound and my face turned pale, I'm sure! Oh, dear me! My nurse—where is she? She at least amuses me now and then. How I miss her. Perhaps it's because I'm going to lose her when I take my vows, for then I'll give up everything I've loved. But I hear steps. Oh, it's she. I know her walk. She's here.

[*Enter* BRIGIDA.]

BRIGIDA: Good evening, Doña Ines.

DOÑA INES: Why are you late?

BRIGIDA: Let me close the door.

DOÑA INES: It's against the rule.

BRIGIDA: That's all very well for the other little novices who are going to take their vows, but not, Doña Ines, for you.

DOÑA INES: Brigida, you're breaking the rules of the convent; they won't let us—

BRIGIDA: Oh, fiddle faddle! It's more private this way and one can talk freely without interruptions. Have you looked at the book I brought you?

DoÑA INES: Oh, dear me! I forgot.

BRIGIDA: Well, I like that!

DoÑA INES: What could I do? The Abbess came right in.

BRIGIDA: The old busybody!

DoÑA INES: Why? Is it such a special book?

BRIGIDA: Special? Much good it did him, the poor beggar.

DoÑA INES: Who?

BRIGIDA: Don Juan.

DoÑA INES: Heaven preserve me! What are you saying? Did Don Juan send this book to me?

BRIGIDA: Of course.

DoÑA INES: Oh! I shouldn't even touch it!

BRIGIDA: The poor boy. He'd die if he heard you say that.

DoÑA INES: What do you mean?

BRIGIDA: If you don't accept that breviary, you'll upset him so that the poor dear will just take sick and die! I can see him—right now!

DoÑA INES: Oh, no, no! If you put it that way—I'll take it.

BRIGIDA: That's a good girl.

DoÑA INES: How lovely it is.

BRIGIDA: He's put himself out, believe me.

DoÑA INES: With its little gold latch, and so tiny, too. I wonder if it's complete and has the antiphonal responses? [*She opens it and a letter drops out.*] What's this?

BRIGIDA: A little piece of paper.

DoÑA INES: A letter!

BRIGIDA: It must be some sort of dedication, I'm sure.

DoÑA INES: What? You mean he wrote this himself?

BRIGIDA: My, how innocent! Well, of course. Since he gave you the book, it must come from him.

DoÑA INES: Oh, dear God!

BRIGIDA: What's the matter?

DoÑA INES: Nothing, Brigida—nothing.

BRIGIDA: No, no, you're quite altered, my dear. [*Aside.*] She's rising to the bait. Are you feeling better now?

DoÑA INES: Yes.

BRIGIDA: It was just a little dizzy spell.

DoÑA INES: Oh, just touching this letter sets my hand on fire.

BRIGIDA: Doña Ines! Heavens above! I've never seen you like this before. Child, you're trembling.

DoÑA INES: Oh, dear me!

BRIGIDA: What's troubling you?

DOÑA INES: I don't know—my mind seems full of a thousand shadows that trouble me. They have been haunting me for a long time now.

BRIGIDA: One of these shadows wouldn't resemble Don Juan, now, would it?

DOÑA INES: I can't tell. From the moment I saw him and you told me his name, he's been in my thoughts continually. I find myself thinking of him everywhere, and whenever I stop for an instant I find myself recalling him once more. I don't know why he should have such a hold over me to bend my mind and heart to him so constantly. Even here, or at my prayers—everywhere—I find myself thinking of Don Juan Tenorio.

BRIGIDA: Deliver me, God! My dear Doña Ines, from what you've told me I'm tempted to suspect that you've fallen in love.

DOÑA INES: Did you say love?

BRIGIDA: Yes, my sweet.

DOÑA INES: Oh, no, that couldn't be.

BRIGIDA: Even a simpleton could see it. But let's look at the letter. Why are you waiting? A sigh?

DOÑA INES: Oh, the more I look at it the less I dare to read it. [*She reads.*] "Doña Ines of my soul—" Holy Mary, Mother of God, what a salutation!

BRIGIDA: Sounds like verse. Though judging from the salutation it promises to be rather free.

DOÑA INES: "Oh light that feeds the sun; brave little dove deprived of flight, if you deign to turn your eyes upon these words, don't look away from them. Read them to the end."

BRIGIDA: How humble! How sensitive! What perfect submissiveness.

DOÑA INES: Brigida, I feel so strange.

BRIGIDA: Go on, go on reading.

DOÑA INES: "Our parents agreed to our engagement, for the heavens joined our destinies. Flattered by such smiling hopes, I have not since, my dear Ines, dreamt of a greater joy than you. My joy and my love struck a spark in my heart which was fanned into flame by time and cruel desire. And this flame, this inextinguishable flame, which feeds upon me, grows more fearsome every day, leaping voraciously—"

BRIGIDA: It's perfectly clear to me now. They let him hope to marry you and his love had taken deep roots when they tore you away from him. Continue.

DOÑA INES [*reading*]: "Time and absence have no power to harness the eruption of my passion, which now bursts forth. I'm struggling in the flames, torn hopelessly between the grave and my Ines—"

BRIGIDA: There, Ines, you see? Just think! If you'd sent that breviary back, they'd be wrapping the poor boy in his shroud this very instant.

DOÑA INES: Oh, I feel weak!

BRIGIDA: Courage.

DOÑA INES [*reading*]: "Ines, soul of my soul, lodestone of my heart, pearl cast out on the weeds of the sea, swan that never dreamt of flying from your nest to try your wings on the blue of heaven—if perchance from your cloister walls you look with longing on the world and sigh for its freedom, please remember, oh, please remember that waiting to save you, at the foot of your walls, are the arms of your Don Juan."

BRIGIDA [*Aside*.]: She's taken the hook. Well, let's on with it and hear the end.

DOÑA INES [*reading*]: "Take pity on the man who pines beneath your window from dawn to dark. Take pity on him who lives for you alone, my love, who would fly to you if you but called—"

BRIGIDA: You see, he'd come.

DOÑA INES: Here?

BRIGIDA: And throw himself at your feet.

DOÑA INES: Is it possible?

BRIGIDA: Oh, my, yes!

DOÑA INES: Dear heavens!

BRIGIDA: But let's hear the end, Doña Ines.

DOÑA INES [*reading*]: "Light of my eyes, farewell. Farewell, Ines of my soul. In God's name think long of what I've said. And should you hate that cloister which will become your tomb—send for him who'll dare to do all for your beauty. Don Juan." Oh, what poison's hidden in these words? It tears my heart apart! What hidden, sleeping thoughts these words uncover. What strange feelings they arouse. They cast a light upon me now like none I have ever seen before. What has sown my soul with such new and deep desire? Who has stolen my heart's rest?

BRIGIDA: Don Juan.

DOÑA INES: Don Juan! Is that man to haunt me wherever I go? Will I ever be able to hear any sound but his name? See any sight but his face? Oh, he spoke true! Heaven joined our destinies and planted this desire in my soul.

BRIGIDA: Sh! Dear God!

[*The evening bells chime out.*]

DOÑA INES: What?

BRIGIDA: Silence.

DOÑA INES: I'm trembling.

BRIGIDA: Don't you hear the bells, Ines?

DOÑA INES: Yes, just as always.

BRIGIDA: Well then, don't speak of him now!

DOÑA INES: Heaven help me, who?

BRIGIDA: Who do you think? That poor Don Juan you love so much, because he might suddenly appear before us.

DOÑA INES: Don't frighten me! Could he possibly make his way here?

BRIGIDA: Very likely—for the very echo of his name could reach his ears at this instant.

DOÑA INES: Oh dear! And—would he—?

BRIGIDA: Who knows?

DOÑA INES: Is he a ghost then?

BRIGIDA: No, but if he had a key—

DOÑA INES: Oh, my God!

BRIGIDA: Quiet! Doña Ines, do you hear those footsteps?

DOÑA INES: I hear nothing!

BRIGIDA: It's striking nine. Here they come—they're coming closer—Lady—he's here!

DOÑA INES: Who?

BRIGIDA: He.

DOÑA INES: Don Juan!

[*Enter* DON JUAN.]

DOÑA INES: What is this? I'm dreaming—I'm mad!

DON JUAN: Ines of my soul!

DOÑA INES: Is it true? Or are my eyes deceiving me? Hold me—I can't breathe—Oh, you—apparition, leave me! Take pity on me! [DOÑA INES *faints and* DON JUAN *catches her. Don Juan's letter remains on the floor where Doña Ines dropped it.*]

BRIGIDA: Your grand entrance bewitched her and her fright has discomposed her.

DON JUAN: That's just as well. She's cut my work in half. Well, let's not waste time gazing at her or we'll be lost! I mean to have her, and the sooner I take her into the cloister of my room, the better.

BRIGIDA: Oh! Do you mean to carry her off like that?

DON JUAN: Don't be an idiot. Having broken into this cloister, I don't mean to leave her here. My men are waiting outside. Follow me.

BRIGIDA: I'm frightened half to death! Oh, that man's a beast! He's afraid of nothing. All right, all right. You win!

[*Exeunt. Enter the* ABBESS.]

ABBESS: I could swear I heard footsteps. I've let Doña Ines stay up somewhat later than usual, and I fear . . . but they're gone! Why would the two of them leave the cell? Where would they go? I'll catch them before they make more trouble and stir up my novices. Yes, yes, that's it—but what's that? I hear steps. Who is it?

[*Enter* DOORKEEPER.]

DOORKEEPER: It's I, Mother.

ABBESS: In the cloister at this hour? What's the meaning of this, Sister?

DOORKEEPER: Oh, Mother, I've been searching for you.

ABBESS: What is it? Speak.

DOORKEEPER: An old gentleman wishes to speak with you.

ABBESS: Impossible.

DOORKEEPER: He says he's of the Order of Calatrava, and that his title permits him entry, and that the urgency of his case makes it necessary to speak with you.

ABBESS: Did he give you his name?

DOORKEEPER: Don Gonzalo Ulloa.

ABBESS: What could he want? Let him in. He's Commander of the Order. It grants him the right of entry.

[*Exit* DOORKEEPER.]

ABBESS: To come here? And at such an hour? What could it be? But it's just as well—when he finds that his daughter has strayed he'll scold her for me and teach her a lesson.

[DOORKEEPER *returns with* DON GONZALO.]

DON GONZALO: Forgive me, Mother, for disturbing you at such an hour, but my business is a question of honor and life itself!

ABBESS: Merciful God!

DON GONZALO: Hear me.

ABBESS: Go on.

DON GONZALO: Until today I've owned a treasure more precious than gold: my Ines.

ABBESS: Yes, well—

DON GONZALO: Listen. I've just been told that her nurse was seen not too long ago with the servant of a certain Don Juan whose ill fame surpasses any in the country. Some time ago he hoped to take my child in marriage, and today, when I denied her to him—he swore he'd steal her away! I don't doubt for a minute that her duenna is

already in league with the man. I have to be on my guard. One day
—one hour of careless supervision and that son of Satan will stain my
honor forever. You understand my fears—I come for the nurse. Doña
Ines must take her vows sooner than we thought.

ABBESS: You are a father and your worry is most laudable, my dear
Commander—but—you must see what a slight this is upon my honor.

DON GONZALO: You don't know Don Juan!

ABBESS: No matter how you paint him let me assure you that while
Ines is here with me, she is, Don Gonzalo, utterly safe.

DON GONZALO: I believe it. But enough talk. Give me the nurse and
forgive my worldly thoughts. While your words spring from your
virtue, mine have roots in my knowledge of the world and the cal-
lousness of youth.

ABBESS: So be it. Sister Doorkeeper, go find Doña Ines and her nurse.
[*The* DOORKEEPER *goes.*]

DON GONZALO: Now, Lady, tell me—either my memory has failed me,
or the hour is well past their bed time.

ABBESS: A while back I heard the two of them step out of the cell—I
don't know why.

DON GONZALO: Ha! Why do I tremble? [*Sees letter.*] But what's this?
Dear God, a letter. I knew it, I knew it! [*Reading*] "Doña Ines of my
soul—" and Don Juan's signature! Look—look—proof—and in writing! Read it. Oh, while you prayed for her to God, the devil stole
her away!
[*Enter* DOORKEEPER.]

DOORKEEPER: Lady—

ABBESS: What is it?

DOORKEEPER: Oh, it's killing me!

DON GONZALO: Out with it.

DOORKEEPER: I don't know how. I've just seen a man leap over the
walls of the cloister!

DON GONZALO: You see? Hurry! Oh, God!

ABBESS: Where to?

DON GONZALO: Fool! After my honor—which was stolen from you!

ACT IV

The Devil at the Gates of Heaven

Don Juan's country house near Seville, next to the Guadalquivir. There is a balcony upstage and a door at either side. BRIGIDA *and* CIUTTI *on stage.*

BRIGIDA: Oh my God, what a night. If I'd had the faintest notion, never in my life would I even think of serving such a hotheaded man! Ooh, Ciutti! I'm beaten to a pulp! I am absolutely black and blue.

CIUTTI: Well, where do you ache the most?

BRIGIDA: The most? It's my whole body, man! And my poor nerves have been whipped to a veritable lather.

CIUTTI: You're not used to riding horseback, that's all.

BRIGIDA: I came very near falling off at least a thousand times! Hoof! What confusion! What a fright! The trees seemed to fly past as though they'd taken wings in the middle of a hurricane! I was so frightened, so terrified, that if we hadn't stopped when we did I would have gone completely out of my mind.

CIUTTI: As long as you stay in this house you might as well get used to it. We have six such episodes per week.

BRIGIDA: Oh! Dear God!

CIUTTI: But the girl? Is she still unconscious?

BRIGIDA: And what on earth would bring her to?

CIUTTI: You're right. It's better for her to wake up in the arms of Don Juan.

BRIGIDA: Your master must have a devil for his very own.

CIUTTI: He's a devil in men's clothes, if you ask me. The only one I know that would dare stand up to him is Satan himself.

BRIGIDA: Oh! What a mad escapade!

CIUTTI: But he carried it off.

BRIGIDA: Breaking out of a convent! And right in the middle of a city like Seville.

CIUTTI: Only he could carry off an escapade like that. But what the devil, Ma'am, he's got luck at his side and failure seems to faint at his feet.

BRIGIDA: Oh, I believe you.

CIUTTI: I've never known a braver man. There is no danger too great for him! And once he's decided to do something, he'll never back down. He's game for anything. He never stops to question his deeds, seeks no advise. "There's an adventure," they say—and his answer is "There goes Don Juan." But he's late, by God.

BRIGIDA: It struck twelve some time ago.

CIUTTI: He should have been back by midnight.

BRIGIDA: Why didn't he come with us?

CIUTTI: He had a few things to do in the city.

BRIGIDA: For the journey?

CIUTTI: Of course—though tonight they might send him on his journey to Hell.

BRIGIDA: What a thing to say!

CIUTTI: And what would you call it? Do you think our little jaunt to-night was an errand of mercy? Although we'll be safe if he get's back.

BRIGIDA: Are you sure of that, Ciutti?

CIUTTI: Come to the balcony. Look, what do you see?

BRIGIDA: A vessel anchored in the river.

CIUTTI: Well, its captain knows no master but Don Juan, and what-ever happens he will take us safely to Italy.

BRIGIDA: You don't say?

CIUTTI: And don't you worry. It's the fastest ship on the sea.

BRIGIDA: Sh! I hear Doña Ines . . .

CIUTTI: I'll be going, then. Don Juan left orders that only you should speak with her.

BRIGIDA: That's shrewd of him. I know how to handle this.

CIUTTI: Goodbye then.

[*He exits.*]

BRIGIDA: Go in peace.

[DOÑA INES *enters.*]

DOÑA INES: Dear God—how I've dreamed! I must be out of my mind! What time is it? But what's this? Oh, me! I've never seen this place before. Who brought me here?

BRIGIDA: Don Juan.

DOÑA INES: It's always Don Juan—You here too, Brigida?

BRIGIDA: Yes, Doña Ines.

DOÑA INES: For God's sake, tell me where are we? This room—is it in the convent?

BRIGIDA: Not likely! That was just a dingy cubbyhole.

DOÑA INES: But then, where are we?

BRIGIDA: Look over that balcony and you'll see the difference between a convent and the estate of a man like Don Juan.

DOÑA INES: Does this house belong to Don Juan?

BRIGIDA: You might just as well say it belongs to you.

DOÑA INES: But I don't understand.

BRIGIDA: Listen to me. You were in the convent reading a letter from Don Juan when a terrible fire broke out.

DOÑA INES: Dear God!

BRIGIDA: Oh, it was frightful. The smoke was so thick you could cut it with a knife.

DOÑA INES: I don't remember—

BRIGIDA: The two of us—you reading, I listening—were absolutely carried away. It was so moving that we thought it was the letter that was overcoming us. We could scarcely breathe, and in the meantime the flames were licking at our beds. We would have choked to death when Don Juan, who adores you and was walking about the convent at the time, saw the devouring flames whipped up by the wind. With incredible courage, seeing that you were trapped in the flames, he came to your rescue as best he could. When you saw him burst into the cell that way, so suddenly—you fainted—quite naturally. And he, seeing you fall like that, took you into his arms and ran out. I followed him—and he saved us from the fire. Well, where were we to go at that hour? You still unconscious and I half choked to death? So he said, "You may stay in my house until morning." And so, Doña Ines, here we are.

DOÑA INES: So this is his house.

BRIGIDA: Yes.

DOÑA INES: To tell the truth, I don't remember a thing. But—in his house! Oh, we must leave instantly. I should be in my father's house.

BRIGIDA: I agree, but we—

DOÑA INES: What?

BRIGIDA: We can't leave now.

DOÑA INES: You amaze me.

BRIGIDA: We are some distance from Seville.

DOÑA INES: What?

BRIGIDA: Look for yourself. The Guadalquivir.

DOÑA INES: Aren't we in the city?

BRIGIDA: At least one mile beyond the walls.

DOÑA INES: We're lost!

BRIGIDA: Now, what makes you say that?

DOÑA INES: Don't confuse me, Brigida. I don't know what sort of net you have spread for me within these walls. I never left the convent and know nothing of the world. But I have my honor. I am of noble blood, Brigida, and I know that the house of Don Juan is no place for me. I know it. I don't know why, but I know it! Come, let's go.

BRIGIDA: Doña Ines, he saved your life.

DOÑA INES: Yes, but he's poisoned my heart.

BRIGIDA: You love him, don't you?

DOÑA INES: I don't know. But for pity's sake, help me flee that man whose very name draws my heart in his wake. Ah! You gave me his letter. You must have stuffed it with some evil spell. I've seen him only once through the shutters of a window and it was you who told me he was waiting there for me. You, Brigida, day and night, talking to me, making me remember his charms. You told me that my father had agreed to our engagement, and it was you who swore he loved me. You say I am in love with him? Very well, if this is love, then, yes, I do love him. But I know this love is my dishonor. If my poor heart can't help being dragged away by Don Juan, my honor and duty can pull it back. Come, let's go before he returns. If I come face to face with him I don't know if I'll have the strength to leave. Come, Brigida.

BRIGIDA: Wait. Listen.

DOÑA INES: What?

BRIGIDA: The sound of rowing.

DOÑA INES: You're right, we'll go back to the city in a boat.

BRIGIDA: Look, look, Doña Ines.

DOÑA INES: Stop talking and come with me.

BRIGIDA: We can't leave now.

DOÑA INES: For heaven's sake, why?

BRIGIDA: Because the man who's coming across the river in that little boat is Don Juan.

DOÑA INES: Oh! God give me strength.

BRIGIDA: He's here, he's stepped ashore. His men will take us home. But before we go we must take our leave of him.

DOÑA INES: Very well, but we must leave instantly. I don't want to see him ever again.

BRIGIDA [Aside.]: "If you see him again, you'll see him forever" is more like it. Come.

DOÑA INES: Let's go.

CIUTTI [Off stage.]: They're in here.

DOÑA INES: It's he.

[Enter DON JUAN.]

DON JUAN: Doña Ines, where are you going?

DOÑA INES: Don Juan, let me go.

DON JUAN: Let you go?

BRIGIDA: Sir, having heard of the fire in the convent, the Commander must be somewhat impatient to see his daughter.

DON JUAN: The fire? Oh! Please don't worry about Don Gonzalo. The message I've sent him will set his mind at rest.

DOÑA INES: You've told him—?

DON JUAN: That you were safe in my care, and that, at long last, you were breathing free the pure country air. [BRIGIDA goes.] Calm yourself, my love, rest a while, and for one moment forget the somber prison of your convent. Oh! It's true, now, isn't it, that on this isolated shore the moon shines more clearly and the air is pure and sweet? This breeze which has gathered up the fresh perfumes of the wild flowers that grow along the shore, that clear, still water flawlessly cut by the boat of the fisherman as he sings and waits for the dawn—my dove, they seem to breathe of love, don't they? That harmony the wind sets up in a thousand olive trees as it stirs their flowing branches; the trilling sweetness of the nightingale as it calls out for the dawn—my graceful gazelle, they seem to breathe of love, don't they? And these words of mine dissolving in your ears, ears which seem to cling upon the lips of your Don Juan, these words that strike the spark of fire in your heart—star of mine, they seem to breathe of love, don't they? And those two liquid pearls that fall from your radiant eyes, inviting me now to drink them up; seeming, lest I should see them, to evaporate in the warm glow that colors your cheeks. Oh, my beauty, they seem to breathe of love! Oh, yes! My exquisite Ines, light and mirror of my eyes, to listen to my words without reproach as you have done is nothing less than love. Behold here at your feet the pride of my deceitful heart that never dreamt of falling, but now surrenders worshipfully to the tyranny of your love.

DOÑA INES: In Heaven's name, be still, Don Juan! I can't bear much more of this emotion. Oh, be still for mercy's sake! When I hear you my brain is maddened and my heart begins to burn. Oh! You must have given me some infernal potion, a potion you use to conquer the virtue of women. Perhaps it is a fetish you keep upon your person that draws me to you like some pulling, irresistible magnet. Could Satan have given you his fascinating looks, his seductive voice, and the love that he denied to God? When you steal my heart away piece by piece what else can I do but fall into your arms? No, Don Juan,

I no longer have the strength to resist you. I come to you as certainly as that river is sucked into the sea. Your presence robs me of reason; your words cast a spell on me; your eyes entrance me, and your breath seems to poison me. Don Juan, Don Juan, in the name of your nobility, please take pity on me. Either tear out my heart or love me; for I adore you.

DON JUAN: Oh my soul! That one word alters my whole being and will comfort me till I open the gates of Eden. It's not Satan, Doña Ines, who plants this love in me, but God, who hopes, perhaps, to win me to Him through your love. No—the love I treasure in my heart is not the worldly one that I have felt before. It is no fleeting spark to be blown out by the first gust of wind that comes its way; it is a conflagration that devours all. So calm your fears, my lovely Doña Ines. At your feet I feel capable even of virtue. Yes, I'll go now and bend my pride before the good Commander. And either he will give you to me, or he'll have to take my life.

DOÑA INES: Don Juan of my soul!

DON JUAN: Be still; did you hear something?

DOÑA INES: What?

DON JUAN: Yes, a boat has just landed beneath the balcony. A masked man is jumping ashore. Brigida, come here. [BRIGIDA enters.] Go, both of you, into the next room and, forgive me, but I must handle this alone.

DOÑA INES: Will you be long?

DON JUAN: No, I won't.

DOÑA INES: Will I see my father?

DON JUAN: Yes, in the morning. Farewell.

[DOÑA INES and BRIGIDA leave. CIUTTI enters.]

CIUTTI: Sir.

DON JUAN: What is it, Ciutti?

CIUTTI: There's a masked man. He's determined to see you.

DON JUAN: Who is it?

CIUTTI: He says he will not reveal himself to any one but you and that his business is a question of life and death for both of you.

DON JUAN: Have you no clue to his identity?

CIUTTI: None. He's determined to see you.

DON JUAN: Is he alone.

CIUTTI: Except for the boatmen.

DON JUAN: Let him in. [CIUTTI goes.] Both he and I have placed our lives at stake. But if it's some other traitor who has followed me to my lair—he'll find me with weapons at my belt.

[*He puts on his sword and places two pistols in his belt, pistols which he deposited on the table on his entrance. After a moment* CIUTTI *ushers in* DON LUIS *who, covered up to his eyes, waits to be left alone with* DON JUAN. DON JUAN *motions* CIUTTI *out.* CIUTTI *goes.*]

DON JUAN [*Aside.*]: He carries himself well—Welcome, sir.

DON LUIS: Well met, sir.

DON JUAN: Speak without fear.

DON LUIS: I always do.

DON JUAN: Tell me, then, why come here at this hour and in such a state?

DON LUIS: Don Juan, I've come to kill you.

DON JUAN: I take it you're Don Luis?

DON LUIS: Your conscience must speak true. Let's not waste time, Don Juan, there's not room enough on this earth for both of us.

DON JUAN: In other words, Señor Mejia, you're suggesting that because I won the bet, the two of us must now end our revels in a fight.

DON LUIS: You're right. We wagered our lives, and now it's time to settle our debts.

DON JUAN: I agree wholeheartedly, but let me remind you that it's you who lost.

DON LUIS: That is why I'm here. I don't believe that a gentleman who carries a sword at his belt should ever die like a lamb led to slaughter.

DON JUAN: And I'm sure you've never found the slightest hint in my behavior to lead you to mistake me for a common butcher.

DON LUIS: Not the slightest. You see how much I trust you since I come to seek you out.

DON JUAN: You cannot trust me enough. And to prove it I ask you, Mejia, if there is anything I can do to satisfy your honor. I won the wager fairly, but since it's stung your pride so painfully, tell me what redress to make and I will do so.

DON LUIS: There is none, other than the one I have proposed. You put me in chains; you stole my place in Doña Ana's arms pretending to be me. You didn't win, Don Juan, having won in another man's name.

DON JUAN: Tricks of the game.

DON LUIS: I don't accept them, so now we must add our lives to the stakes.

DON JUAN: You risk yours to avenge Doña Ana de Pantoja?

DON LUIS: Yes, and my delay in wiping that stain clean increases my annoyance. Don Juan, I loved her—yes! But you've made her impossible for either one of us.

DON JUAN: Then why did you take on the wager?

DON LUIS: Because I couldn't believe that you would ever win her and —by all that's holy, let's get on with it!

DON JUAN: Let's go down to the riverside.

DON LUIS: No, here and now.

DON JUAN: Outside you fool. Don't you see that if we fought here they'd have to arrest the winner? You came in a small boat?

DON LUIS: Yes.

DON JUAN: Then let it return the winner to Seville.

DON LUIS: You're right. Outside, then.

DON JUAN: Wait.

DON LUIS: What is it?

DON JUAN: I hear something.

DON LUIS: Let's hurry.

[CIUTTI *enters.*]

CIUTTI: Sir, run for your life.

DON JUAN: What's happening?

CIUTTI: The Commander is here with some armed men.

DON JUAN: Let him in—but no one else.

CIUTTI: But sir—

DON JUAN: Do as I say.

[CIUTTI *goes.*]

DON JUAN: Don Luis, you have demonstrated your respect for me by coming here to my own house, so I don't hesitate to ask you—since you know something of my courage—to wait for me somewhat longer.

DON LUIS: I've never doubted your courage, but I certainly cannot trust you.

DON JUAN: Well, if you must know, remember that there were two parts to our wager—I have won them both.

DON LUIS: Simultaneously?

DON JUAN: Yes. The lady from the convent is here at this very moment. Since you've come to kill me, it's only fair that I should settle with the other claimant now. I should not leave unfinished business behind me.

DON LUIS: But it may just be that this interruption of our quarrel is a—

DON JUAN: What?

DON LUIS: An excuse for not fighting me.

DON JUAN: You cur! You alone can doubt the honor of Don Juan. But hide in here, by God. Suspend your hunger for revenge until I've settled my affair with this man. I swear that we will fight as soon as I have finished.

DON LUIS: But—

DON JUAN: An army of devils take you! Get in! I'm noble enough to give you satisfaction and some to spare! You're free to look and listen; the door is open. If you find my behavior suspicious, then open up.

DON LUIS: I will, if you take too long.

DON JUAN: You decide! But God in Heaven, there's time for everything.

[DON LUIS *goes into the room indicated by* DON JUAN.]

They're coming up.

[DON JUAN *listens. Enter* DON GONZALO.]

DON GONZALO: Where is the traitor?

DON JUAN: Here, Commander.

[*He kneels.*]

DON GONZALO: On your knees?

DON JUAN: At your feet.

DON GONZALO: You are low even in your crimes!

DON JUAN: Old man, hold your tongue and listen to me for a moment.

DON GONZALO: What could you say to erase this letter? You abomination! You take advantage of the candid simplicity of a girl who couldn't detect the poison of these words. To pollute her virgin soul with the gall of your own which is dry of virtue and faith!   To soil the honor of my crest as though it were some rag-picker's trash. Is that the measure of your courage? Is that the well-known daring that's struck fear into the whole country? Or do you save it up for young maidens and old men? And what for, by God? To lick my boots like this, showing yourself to be a stranger to both honor and courage!

DON JUAN: Commander!

DON GONZALO: Swine! You stole my daughter Ines from her convent and I've come to claim my honor and your life.

DON JUAN: I've never bowed my head to any man before, nor have I ever begged from anyone, not my father nor my king. And since I have not risen from my knees consider, Don Gonzalo, I must have some cause.

DON GONZALO: What you have is a fear of my revenge.

DON JUAN: God give me strength! Commander, you listen to me or I'll not be able to contain myself. Against my will, I'll be what I have always been.

DON GONZALO: Give me patience!

DON JUAN: I worship Doña Ines. I'm convinced that Heaven has granted her to me to turn my steps in the paths of righteousness. I didn't love her beauty nor did I worship her charms. Don Gonzalo, what I adore in Doña Ines is her goodness. That which judges and bishops could not bring me to with threats of jail and sermons was accomplished by her purity. Her love has transformed me into a new man; it has renewed my whole being. She can make an angel of one who was a devil. Listen well, Don Gonzalo, to what Don Juan is offering you at your feet. I will be your daughter's slave, live in your house, and let you rule my estates, and tell me what to do. I will go into retreat for whatever time you choose. Demand any trials of my daring and my pride; I'll agree to all with meekness. And when you judge me worthy of her I will make her a good husband, and she will lead me into Eden.

DON GONZALO: Enough, Don Juan! I don't know how I've endured so long these foul proofs of your villany. Don Juan, you are a coward, and when you are challenged there is no ruse too low for you, provided it gets you safely out.

DON JUAN: Don Gonzalo!

DON GONZALO: I am ashamed to see you begging at my feet for what you swore to take by force.

DON JUAN: It's the only way, the best solution.

DON GONZALO: Never! Never! Your wife? I'll kill her first. Come! Hand her over or I won't be able to restrain myself any longer. I'll run you through the chest while you kneel so falsely at my feet.

DON JUAN: Weigh what you say, Don Gonzalo. In losing her I may lose all hope of salvation.

DON GONZALO: What does your salvation mean to me?

DON JUAN: Commander, you are damning me!

DON GONZALO: My daughter!

DON JUAN: Remember that I tried by every means in my power to satisfy you—and with weapons at my waist! I suffered your insults while kneeling at your feet.

[DON LUIS *breaks in, with a mocking laugh.*]

DON LUIS: Very good, Don Juan.

DON JUAN: God!

DON GONZALO: Who is this man?

DON LUIS: A witness of his cowardice and your friend, Commander.

DON JUAN: Don Luis!

DON LUIS: I've seen enough, Don Juan, to know what use you make of courage. A man who strikes from behind and kneels when he's confronted is no better than a common thief who steals and runs.

DON JUAN: What more?

DON LUIS: As you can see, the wrath of God has joined the father of Doña Ines and the avenger of Doña Ana. Judge your fate when revenge overtakes you within and justice awaits you without.

DON GONZALO: Oh! Now I see—you're the one who—

DON LUIS: I am Don Luis Mejia, sent by God to second your revenge.

DON JUAN: Enough penance for one day. If my deeds and honor cannot convince you of my courage and honest sacrifice, nor the loyal solicitude with which I offer up all I can—then have at you, by God! For fear you'll besmirch my honor, I'll take the opportunity you offer me to show myself the Tenorio whose courage you have questioned.

DON LUIS: So be it—to fall at our feet, having at least earned your fame for courage.

DON JUAN: And let Hell win. Ulloa, since it's you who send me back to Hell, when God calls me to account, you'll have to answer for me. [*He shoots him.*]

DON GONZALO [*as he falls*]: Murderer!

DON JUAN: And you, thick-skinned fool, who called me a thief, defend yourself, for face to face I'm going to kill you.
[*They fight and* DON JUAN *stabs* DON LUIS.]

DON LUIS [*as he falls*]: Oh, God!

DON JUAN: A little late for your blind faith to call on God, Mejia. That's not my fault. But now the guard is here and by heaven they'll take my measure in steel.

CIUTTI [*Off stage.*]: Don Juan!

DON JUAN [*going to the balcony*]: Who is it?

CIUTTI: This way! Save yourself.

DON JUAN: Can we get out that way?

CIUTTI: Yes, jump.

DON JUAN: I'm coming. I called on Heaven and it did not answer. It closed its doors on me. Then let Heaven and not I answer for my steps on earth.
[*He jumps over the balcony. We hear him fall into the river and*

then the sound of oars as the boat casts off. Knocking at the doors. A few moments and two CONSTABLES *and soldiers enter.*]

FIRST CONSTABLE: The shot came from here.

SECOND CONSTABLE: There's still smoke in the air.

FIRST CONSTABLE: Good God! Here's a body.

SECOND CONSTABLE: Two of them.

FIRST CONSTABLE: And the murderer?

SECOND CONSTABLE: In there.

[*They open the door of the room in which Doña Ines and Brigida are hidden. They bring them on.* DOÑA INES *sees her father's corpse.*]

FIRST CONSTABLE: Two women!

DOÑA INES: Ah, how horrible! My father!

FIRST CONSTABLE: Is she his daughter?

BRIGIDA: Yes.

DOÑA INES: Oh! Where are you, Don Juan? How can you leave me here in such pain?

FIRST CONSTABLE: He murdered him.

DOÑA INES: Dear God! Did you hold this in store for me?

SECOND CONSTABLE: That devil must have jumped into the river through here.

FIRST CONSTABLE: See them? They're climbing aboard the Calabrian boat in the river.

ALL: Justice for Doña Ines!

DOÑA INES: But not against Don Juan.

PART TWO

ACT I

The Ghost of Doña Ines

The burial grounds of the Tenorio family. It is an impressive cemetery, beautifully landscaped as a garden. In the foreground are the tombs of Don Gonzalo de Ulloa, Doña Ines, and Don Luis Mejia, upon which rest stone sculptures of each figure. Don Gonzalo's tomb is at right. He is shown in a kneeling position. Don Luis' tomb is at left. He, too, is in a kneeling position. Doña Ines' tomb is at center and she is shown standing. Further back are two more tombs. In the background and raised is the tomb of Don Diego Tenorio which forms, as it were, the perspective apex of the tombs. A wall full of niches and carved markers surrounds the scene. There are two weeping willows at either side of Doña Ines' tomb, constructed to serve the technical demands of the action. Cypress trees and flowers enliven the scene which should not be in the least lugubrious. The action takes place on a quiet summer evening and is lit by bright moonlight. The SCULPTOR *is by the tomb of Don Diego.*

SCULPTOR [*preparing to leave*]:   Well, sir, that's that. Don Diego's soul can rest in peace now, as far as I'm concerned. The work is finished now with all the splendor he called for in his will. By God, not many rich men have their wills carried out so well. But it's time to go. It's all finished now; I'll leave Seville at the crack of dawn. Oh, my marble beauties, carved so lovingly with these hands. When Seville comes tomorrow, wide-eyed, to stare at your grand proportions and the beauty of this mausoleum, our age will earn the veneration of times to come. Men will come and go in the passing years, but you will stand firm—witnesses of my skill. Oh, children of my labor, stones I brought to life and for which I bowed under the beating sun, I, who gave you form and being—I am about to leave you. Stand there and witness the power of my art—you'll live longer than I. Who is coming?

[DON JUAN *enters with his face covered.*]

SCULPTOR: Sir—

DON JUAN: God rest you.

SCULPTOR: Your pardon, sir, but it's late and I—

DON JUAN: One moment please, I want you to explain—

SCULPTOR: Are you a foreigner?

DON JUAN: I've been abroad for years and was somewhat disturbed when I came here and found this place so changed.

SCULPTOR: I should think so! This used to be a palace and now it's turned into a mausoleum.

DON JUAN: The palace into a mausoleum?

SCULPTOR: That was the wish of its owner. The whole world was amazed.

DON JUAN: With good reason!

SCULPTOR: There's a famous story behind it all. I owe my fame to it.

DON JUAN: Would you tell it to me?

SCULPTOR: Yes, but I must be brief. They're waiting for me.

DON JUAN: All right.

SCULPTOR: Now this is the absolute truth.

DON JUAN: Don't keep me waiting.

SCULPTOR: Well, once there lived in this city—this palace—a gentleman, the owner, who was highly regarded for his nobility.

DON JUAN: Don Diego Tenorio.

SCULPTOR: The same. Well, this Don Diego had a son who was as wild as fire, an abortion of Hell itself, bloody, cruel, at war with Heaven and earth. There was absolutely nothing on this earth that he respected. A brawler, seducer, a great gambler—there was no honor, property, or life sacred to him. At least that's the way he's come down in history. And if the stories are true, then the old man certainly did the right thing to win himself a place in Heaven.

DON JUAN: What did he do?

SCULPTOR: He left all his estate to be converted into a splendid mausoleum; but with the condition that all those who fall beneath his son's cruel hand should be buried here. Look about and you'll see the graves of most of them.

DON JUAN: And you—are you the caretaker?

SCULPTOR: The sculptor in charge of making these statues.

DON JUAN: Ah! And are they finished?

SCULPTOR: They were finished a month ago. But I stayed on to see this grating installed to prevent vandalism by the crowds.

DON JUAN [looking about]: The old man got his money's worth.

SCULPTOR: I should think so! There he is.

DON JUAN: I see him.

SCULPTOR: Did you know him?

DON JUAN: Yes.

SCULPTOR: I took great pains to get a resemblance, I can tell you.

DON JUAN: Yes, they're wonderful.

SCULPTOR: Did you know the others?

DON JUAN: All of them.

SCULPTOR: And—do you find them true?

DON JUAN: Judging by the light of the stars, yes. They are very like.

SCULPTOR: Oh, they can be seen by the light of the moon almost as well as by day. This one's made of Carrara. [He points to the statue of Don Luis.]

DON JUAN: A good bust of Mejia, indeed. My! And here is the Commander. Very well.

SCULPTOR: I wanted to include a statue of the murderer amid his victims, as it were, but I couldn't lay my hands upon a likeness of him. They say that Don Juan Tenorio was a veritable Lucifer.

DON JUAN: Oh, very bad! But if it could speak, the statue of Don Gonzalo would have to say something in Juan's behalf.

SCULPTOR: Did you know Don Juan very well?

DON JUAN: Very well.

SCULPTOR: Don Diego disclaimed him—disinherited him, in fact.

DON JUAN: That didn't hurt him much. Good luck has followed him from the day he left his cradle.

SCULPTOR: They say he's dead.

DON JUAN: They're wrong. He's alive.

SCULPTOR: Where?

DON JUAN: Here—in Seville.

SCULPTOR: Isn't he afraid that public opinion—

DON JUAN: The seed of fear was never sown in him.

SCULPTOR: But when he sees what has happened to his family estate, I'm sure he won't want to stay in Seville.

DON JUAN: On the contrary, he'll welcome the opportunity of meeting these old friends of his in his home once more—since he has no hatred for any of them.

SCULPTOR: You think he'll dare to come here?

DON JUAN: Why not? Having been born here, I think it's quite proper that he should come back to die here, too. And since they've used his inheritance to pay the burial of these, it's only fair that they should bury him as well.

SCULPTOR: This mausoleum is open to everyone but him.

DON JUAN: Don Juan wields a very good sword. Who is going to stop him?

SCULPTOR: Dear God! Such desecration!

DON JUAN: Don Juan is the kind of man who—if it entered his head— would turn this mausoleum right back into a palace.

SCULPTOR: Do you mean to say he's still so wild he'd dare defy the dead?

DON JUAN: Why should he stand in awe of those that lay at his feet?

SCULPTOR: But has he no conscience? No soul?

DON JUAN: Perhaps not. He called to Heaven once in penitence, but Heaven answered him so rudely that right there on the spot he took the lives of two innocents in order to save his own.

SCULPTOR: God in Heaven, what a monster!

DON JUAN: Rest assured that God has wasted no love on him.

SCULPTOR: No wonder.

DON JUAN: He's a better man than you.

SCULPTOR [*Aside.*]: Who could it be, defending Don Juan so hotly?— Sir, I'm sorry but they are waiting for me and—

DON JUAN: Go on, then, hurry.

SCULPTOR: I must close up.

DON JUAN: Don't close up and do go!

SCULPTOR: But don't you see—

DON JUAN: I see a quiet night, and a comfortable place in which to enjoy it. Here I stay as long as I please, and all of Seville itself couldn't move me.

SCULPTOR [*Aside.*]: The man must be mad.

DON JUAN [*addressing the statues*]: Friends—I'm back.

SCULPTOR [*Aside.*]: What did I say? He *is* mad!

DON JUAN: But—oh, Heaven—what's this? My eyes are playing tricks on me—this must be Doña Ines!

SCULPTOR: You are right, sir.

DON JUAN: Is she dead, too?

SCULPTOR: They say she died of pain when she returned to the convent, abandoned by Don Juan.

DON JUAN: She lies here?

SCULPTOR: Yes.

DON JUAN: You saw her dead?

SCULPTOR: Yes.

DON JUAN: How did she look?

SCULPTOR: I could have sworn she was sleeping. Death was so gentle with her beauty that he left in her all the freshness of a rose.

DON JUAN: Ah! Death with its clumsy hand would have done ill to destroy the sovereign beauty of a face an angel would have envied. How lovely—and how true the sculpture. Oh, Doña Ines, what I'd do to bring you back to life! Is this the work of your chisel?

SCULPTOR: As well as the others.

DON JUAN: Such a likeness deserves something more. Here.

SCULPTOR: What is this, sir?

DON JUAN: What does it look like?

SCULPTOR: But—sir—why?—

DON JUAN: Because I want you to remember me.

SCULPTOR: But they're paid for.

DON JUAN: Not well enough.

SCULPTOR: Sir, let's leave. I must turn in the keys. I have to leave the city at dawn.

DON JUAN: Give me the keys and go.

SCULPTOR: To you?

DON JUAN: Yes. Why not?

SCULPTOR: Sir, I have not had the honor of—

DON JUAN: Sculptor, make an end.

SCULPTOR: If at least I knew your name—

DON JUAN: Heaven help me! Let Don Juan Tenorio keep vigil over the graves of his ancestors.

SCULPTOR: Don Juan Tenorio!

DON JUAN: Yes. And I swear to you if you don't do as I say, you'll be keeping your statues company from now on.

SCULPTOR [holding out the keys]: Here. [Aside.] I'm not one for losing my hide before my time. Let Seville settle the matter with him. [He goes.]

DON JUAN: So my good father spent all my inheritance in this. He did well. I would have staked it on a single card. [Pause.] You can't complain of me, my murdered ones. If I robbed you of the good life, I repaid you with a good burial. Really, it's a splendid idea, this mausoleum! And—my heart takes comfort in the solitude. Lovely night! . . . Oh, me . . . How many nights like this I've wasted in carousing. How often to the same glow of that lucid moon have I ripped life or honor from some innocent man. Yes, after so many years, the mere memory of which frightens me, I feel thoughts rising here [indicates his forehead] that are very strange to me. Perhaps they are heaven-sent—from that watchful soul that loves me well. [He approaches the statue of Doña Ines, addressing her with respect.] Marble in which Doña Ines lives on in form if not in spirit, let this poor soul weep at your feet awhile. Through a thousand misadventures I kept your image pure, and since it was Don Juan's foul fate that brought about your death, weigh well the love that brings him now to stand beside your grave. From the morning that he left you he has thought of nothing else. Having fled from here his only thought was to return. Don Juan's hope for happiness was bound up in you and now that he has returned in quest of your beauty, consider the poor beggar's pain, finding it in the grave. Oh, my innocent Doña Ines, whose lovely youth was sealed forever in that coffin by the man who weeps now at your feet—if you can see through those eyes of stone the anguish of my soul, find a space in your grave for him who loved you so. God created you for me. Because of you I learned of virtue, worshipped it and hungered for its holy reward. Yes, even now my hope is fastened upon you, for I hear a voice lulling my troubled soul to peace beside your grave. Oh, Doña Ines of my soul! If the voice I hear in my delirium is the last sigh of your eternal farewell—if the sigh which springs from you is raised on high to Heaven—and if—if there is a God behind that wide expanse of stars —tell him to look down upon Juan, weeping at your grave.

[*He leans on the grave and covers his face. He remains in this position while a mist rises and shrouds the statue of Doña Ines. When the mist recedes, the statue has vanished.* DON JUAN *rouses himself.*]

DON JUAN: This marble seems to sap my strength. I feel some unearthly presence surrounding me. But—Heaven help me! The statue is gone! What is this? That sculpture—was it all a dream?

[*The weeping willow and the flowers at left of Doña Ines' tomb alter in a scenic effect allowing us to see the glowing figure of* DOÑA INES' GHOST.]

GHOST: It was no dream. My spirit lingered in my tomb, waiting for your return.

DON JUAN [*on his knees*]: Doña Ines! Oh, spirit that I love, soul of my heart, if you have come to take my life, take it—don't drive me mad! If you're just a figment of my madness don't add to my misery by mocking my passion.

GHOST: Don Juan, I heard you in my grave. I am Doña Ines.

DON JUAN: Are you alive then?

GHOST: Alive for you—but I have my purgatory in that marble statue they carved upon my tomb. I offered God my soul in ransom for your sinful one. And God, beholding the tenderness of my love, replied, "Wait for Don Juan in your grave. Since you choose to be faithful to such a hell-inspired love, you'll earn your salvation with Juan, or with Juan you will lose it. Wait for him; and, if he should in his hardhearted madness cruelly disown the love you bear him and pursue his barbarous ways—let him claim your soul forever."

DON JUAN [*entranced*]: I must be dreaming in the shades of Eden!

GHOST: No. For if you choose well, you'll find me at your side; but if your choice is evil you'll bring us both eternal ruin. Think well on this, Don Juan. Tonight is all we are given to seek our final rest. Farewell, and in the terrible struggle that faces you listen to the voice of your sleeping conscience. For you must choose with skill and without subterfuge in the moment which will open the tomb to both of us, for either good or evil.

[*The* VISION *disappears. All remains as before except for the missing statue of Doña Ines.* DON JUAN *is stunned.*]

DON JUAN: Heaven! What have I heard? Even the dead leave their graves on my behalf! But . . . the ghost was no more than fancy. It was forged in my imagination. My brain gave it form and substance, and I blindly believed a thing that I invented myself. My reason's never played such tricks before. I've never fallen prey to my imagination. But I did sense a presence! That *was* the ghost of Doña Ines there among the branches! Oh—but that's the way all ghosts are supposed to look. What could be more subtle than the chimeras of a dream? What could be more pleasing and gentle? And it's well known that in our fevered exaltation our minds take the empty hope of our desire and make it real. Yes, by God, that's it! A delirium—no more! But her statue stood here. I know it did! I saw it; I touched it. I even gave that sculptor some money for his work. And now there's only the pedestal! Oh, God! Either I'm losing my mind or I'm struck down with some infernal dizziness. What was it she said? Oh, I heard her clearly. Her sad sweet voice gripped my heart. Ah yes! Our time was running out. No, no! It can't be! It must be a hallucination. My fever summoned Doña Ines. Out, away with you, sinister shades of my lost love and dead desires! Away, useless delirium of my stillborn love, and never again return to haunt me with that heavenly ghost of a woman! These nightmares are destroying me—they madden my brain. Now those statues seem to be moving! [*The* STATUES *turn their faces upon him.*] They are! They are! Their heads moved. Their features seem sharper than before. But Don Juan isn't frightened that easily! Come, ghosts, rise up and with my own hands I'll throw you back into your beds of stone! No, your cold faces don't frighten me. Nothing living or dead will ever humble my courage. I killed you both, that's well known; and if you are storing up a vengeance for me in your sepulchral palace, come then! Don Juan Tenorio is ready to meet you once more!

CENTELLAS [*Off stage.*]: Don Juan Tenorio?

DON JUAN [*as though coming to*]: What's that? Who calls me?

AVELLANEDA [*entering, to* CENTELLAS]: Do you see anyone?

CENTELLAS [*entering*]: Yes. There's a man over there.

DON JUAN: Who goes there?

AVELLANEDA: It's he!

CENTELLAS [*crossing to Don Juan*]: What a surprise! Don Juan!

AVELLANEDA: Tenorio!

DON JUAN: Get away from me, you ghosts!

CENTELLAS: Look again, sir, we're not ghosts but men, and men who hold your friendship dear. We made you out by starlight and have come to bid you welcome.

DON JUAN: Thank you, Centellas.

CENTELLAS: But what's wrong? By God, your arm is trembling—and your face is quite pale.

DON JUAN [*recovering his composure*]: Perhaps it's the moonlight.

AVELLANEDA: But what are you doing here, Don Juan? You know where you are, don't you?

DON JUAN: It's a mausoleum, isn't it?

CENTELLAS: And do you know who owns it?

DON JUAN: I do. Look about you and what do you see? Nothing but friends of my youth, witnesses of my daring and my courage.

CENTELLAS: Did you come here to insult them again?

DON JUAN: No, just to pay them a friendly visit. But I was struck by a sudden dizziness. It gave me a bad time, let me tell you. Those stone ghosts were threatening me so fiercely that if you hadn't come when you did—

CENTELLAS [*laughs*]: Don't tell me that Don Juan is afraid of the dead, like a common peasant.

DON JUAN: No, by God! Not while I've got air in my lungs and strength in my hands. If they were to come out of their tombs they'd be sent back the way they came—by my sword. Never forget, my dear Captain, Don Juan is always Don Juan and there is nothing that can make him feel fear. It was just a sudden fever that seized my brain. But it's over now, Centellas. We all have our moments.

AVELLANEDA *and* CENTELLAS: That's true.

DON JUAN: Let's leave.

CENTELLAS: Let's, and you can tell us of your third return to Seville.

DON JUAN: I will. If you want to hear my story, and it's a good one, believe me, it's best you hear it over a fine meal. What do you say?

AVELLANEDA *and* CENTELLAS: As you wish.

DON JUAN: Very well, you'll have supper with me at my house.

CENTELLAS: But I wouldn't want you to slight some guest for us. I'm sure you have something up your sleeve, haven't you?

DON JUAN: I've just arrived. No one will be present but yourselves.

CENTELLAS: Are you sure we won't force some lady to hide away in another room?

DON JUAN: No. Just the three of us will be there. Unless, of course—[*he indicates the statues on the tombs*]—one of these gentlemen wants to join us.

CENTELLAS: Don Juan, let them be; don't disturb their rest.

DON JUAN: Well, now you seem to be the one who's squeamish about the dead. You teased me first, and now, by God, I mean to show you how wrong you were. I will do everything in my power, and if you don't dine with the dead tonight, it won't be my fault. I am going to invite them.

AVELLANEDA: Stop these wild games.

DON JUAN: Do you question my courage? I'm man enough to eat out of their skulls. I fear nothing. [*He approaches the statue of Don Gonzalo which is nearest to him.*] You are the most deeply offended of them all, but if you are so disposed, Commander, I invite you to supper. I doubt that you can keep our engagement, and I'm sorry. But I at least will do my part and set a place for you. I will welcome you, because you can tell me whether there is another world beyond the one I live in—another life, in which, to tell the truth, I never have believed.

CENTELLAS: That is not courage, Don Juan. That's madness. That's raving.

DON JUAN: If you disapprove, so much the better; but I meet my obligations. Let's go. Commander, don't forget!

ACT II

The Statue of Don Gonzalo

Don Juan's room. There are two doors upstage left and right, fixed for the stage effects required by the action. There is another door in the flat at left and a window at right. When the curtain goes up, DON JUAN, CENTELLAS, *and* AVELLANEDA *are seated at the table. The table is sumptuously set; the table cloth is gathered in garlands of flowers. Don Juan sits at center with Avellaneda to the left of him and Centellas at right. There is one empty place at right.* CIUTTI *and a page are serving them.*

DON JUAN: And that's my story, gentlemen. Because of my courage, the Emperor himself offered to absolve me of my crimes. Even after he had heard all of my story, he said, "A man of such spirit deserves my help. Let him return to Spain whenever he wishes!" So here I am in Seville once more.

CENTELLAS: And with such pomp and luxury, too!

DON JUAN: He lives high who was made for heights.

CENTELLAS: To your return!

DON JUAN: Let's drink to that.

CENTELLAS: What I can't understand is how you could be so well established having just arrived yesterday.

DON JUAN: I took this house and all its finery because it was cheap—sold to pay the debtors. Since I returned to find myself disinherited, I could do no better.

CENTELLAS: Furnishings and all?

DON JUAN: That's right. Some fool or other who lost his wits over a woman lost his money as well and had to sell.

CENTELLAS: Did he sell all of his estate?

DON JUAN: Yes—and his soul to the devil.

CENTELLAS: Did he die?

DON JUAN: Quite suddenly. The courts, which were determined to settle the matter as promptly as possible, snatched up my offer, gave me the whole estate, and then threw a sop to the money lenders.

CENTELLAS: And the woman? What of her?

DON JUAN: A notary public was set on her trail, but she gave him the slip.

CENTELLAS: Was she young?

DON JUAN: And good looking, too.

CENTELLAS: She should have come along with the furniture.

DON JUAN: I don't like second-hand goods. I bought a house and a wine cellar; two things, which, believe me, are enough to guarantee good company. Your presence is ample proof. I hope you'll come often to enjoy both.

CENTELLAS: You do us a great honor.

DON JUAN: And you me. Ciutti—

CIUTTI: Sir.

DON JUAN: Serve the Commander some wine.

[*He points to the empty place.*]

CENTELLAS: Don Juan, are you serious?

DON JUAN: Yes, by God! Even if he doesn't come, I will have done my duty as a host.

CENTELLAS [*laughs*]: Señor Tenorio, I think you've had one drink too many.

DON JUAN: It's not like me—not my way at all—to invite a friend and not keep a place for him to the last minute. I have always done this and I don't mean to change. To tell the truth, seeing his empty place is very disappointing. But if the Commander is as tenacious in death as he was in life, he may still keep us company, eh?

CENTELLAS: Let's toast his memory and forget about him.

DON JUAN: Agreed.

CENTELLAS: A toast.

AVELLANEDA *and* CENTELLAS: A toast!

CENTELLAS: May he rest in God.

DON JUAN: But I don't believe in any rest other than the rest we take down here on earth. I couldn't drink that toast with conviction. . . . Well, all right, have it your way! I drink to his rest in God.

[*While they drink, a blow is heard off stage of someone striking on the front door of the house.*]

DON JUAN: Someone knocking.

CIUTTI: Yes sir.

DON JUAN: See who it is.

CIUTTI [*sticking his head out of the window*]: I can't see a soul. Who's there? . . . No answer.

CENTELLAS: Some trick or other.

AVELLANEDA: Probably some idiot who had nothing better to do.

DON JUAN [*to Ciutti*]: Close the window and pour some brandy. [*There is a louder knocking.*] What, again?

CIUTTI: Yes, sir.

DON JUAN: Go look.

CIUTTI: By God, I don't see anyone.

DON JUAN: Damn it! He won't get away with it again. Ciutti, the next time he knocks, shoot him with a pistol. [*More knocking, but nearer now.*] Again?

CIUTTI: Dear God!

AVELLANEDA *and* CENTELLAS: What's wrong?

CIUTTI: That wasn't at the front door, it came from the stairs.

AVELLANEDA *and* CENTELLAS [*getting to their feet in amazement*]: What do you mean?

CIUTTI: It's true! That knocking was inside the house.

DON JUAN: What's come over you? Do you think it's the ghost? I've loaded my pistols, gentlemen. Ciutti, go see who it is.

[*More knocking, closer still.*]

AVELLANEDA: Did you hear it?

CIUTTI: Saints preserve me! That one came from the antechamber.

DON JUAN: Now I have it! You knew about the Commander and so you rigged this little comedy yourselves!

AVELLANEDA: Don Juan. I swear—

CENTELLAS: We never—

DON JUAN: Hah! Any booby could see through this trick. And I'll bet that wretch of a Ciutti had a hand in it too!

AVELLANEDA: Don Juan, there is something mysterious going on here. [*The knocking is heard even closer.*]

CENTELLAS: There it goes again!

CIUTTI: It's from the salon this time!

DON JUAN: Enough! You've given my keys to this ghost—and a ghost that needs a key doesn't bother me. Your joke has misfired, gentlemen, and I don't intend to let your silly comedy interrupt my meal. [*He rises and goes to the door, bolts it, and returns to his place.*] There, the doors are bolted and if this spook wants to join us, he'll have to knock the doors down. But the minute he does, he can count himself dead and take his case to a higher court.

CENTELLAS: Oh, what the devil, you must be right!

DON JUAN: Then why are you trembling?

CENTELLAS: Well, I must confess that until you put it that way—I was a bit—apprehensive.

DON JUAN: You admit your share in the trick.

AVELLANEDA: I know nothing about it.

CENTELLAS: Neither do I.

DON JUAN: In any case, I've turned the joke on the joker. Shall we return to our supper? Be seated, gentlemen. We'll get to the bottom of this later.

AVELLANEDA: You're right.

DON JUAN [*pouring for Centellas*]: Cariñena wine—I know you're fond of it.

CENTELLAS: It comes from my part of the country.

DON JUAN [*to Avellaneda, pouring from another bottle*]: And sherry for the Sevillian, eh, Don Rafael?

AVELLANEDA: You've pleased us both. Now what wine will you drink?

DON JUAN: I'll do justice to both of them.

CENTELLAS: You always make a point of justice.

DON JUAN: On my faith, I do. Drink up.

AVELLANEDA *and* CENTELLAS: Drink up.

[*There is a knocking on the right door.*]

DON JUAN: The joke grows tiresome—but I'd like to see anyone interrupt our meal. [*To* CIUTTI, *who stands amazed.*] What are you standing there for, you rascal! Fetch us another dish. [CIUTTI *goes.*] But now that I think of it, we can get the better of those people out there by putting their wit to the test; just open the doors and let them in.

AVELLANEDA: Well said.

CENTELLAS: A good idea.

[*There is a loud knocking on the door upstage.*]

DON JUAN: Why knock gentlemen? Ghosts can walk through walls. Come in.

[*The STATUE of DON GONZALO comes through the door silently and without opening it.*]

CENTELLAS: Christ in Heaven!

AVELLANEDA: My God!

DON JUAN: What's this!

AVELLANEDA: I feel . . . faint.

[*He falls in a faint.*]

CENTELLAS: I'm dying.

[*He too falls.*]

DON JUAN: Fact or fancy, that is his shape—his manner too!

STATUE: Why fear a guest you invited to dine with you? A guest who comes especially for you?

DON JUAN: God! That's the voice of the Commander!

STATUE: I was sure you wouldn't wait for me.

DON JUAN: You lie. You see, I had them set a place for you. Sit down. For a moment I was taken by surprise. But even if you are Ulloa himself, you'll find I'm not afraid of you.

STATUE: You don't believe me?

DON JUAN: I don't know.

STATUE: You impious man, put your hand on the cold marble of my statue.

DON JUAN: I'll take your word for it. Let's eat. But . . .

STATUE: What?

DON JUAN: I warn you. If you are not dead now, you will be when you leave. [*To Centellas and Avellaneda*] Get up there!

STATUE: Let them be, Don Juan. They will not come to until I have gone. God's clemency to you needs no other witnesses than your own judgment and your conscience. In order to cast some light upon your soul, God has permitted me to accept the sacrilegious invitation that you issued at my tomb. I come in His name to teach you the truth. Listen. There is an eternity beyond the life of man. Your days are numbered. And tomorrow, Don Juan, you will die. But since you believe that all you have seen tonight is an illusion, God in His mercy has granted you this night to prepare your soul. And in order that you may know His infinite justice, I expect you to have the courage to return my call. Will you come, Don Juan?

DON JUAN: Yes, I'll come. But before you leave let me see how sound you are.

[*He picks up a pistol.*]

STATUE: Your idiotic pride is pushing you into madness. The heaviest bars and the thickest walls will give way before me. Look.

[*The* STATUE *disappears through the wall.*]

DON JUAN: Dear God! He fades into the wall as a water stain dries under the summer sun. Didn't he tell me to touch the marble of his statue? How can stone disappear like that? Impossible! It's all a dream. The former owner of this house must have poisoned the wine barrels, and the liquor now makes my head swim. But what if these illusions turn out to be spirits after all—sent by heavenly command to stir my conscience? Given my sins, what earthly use is the time allotted me for atonement? All God grants me is one single day! A real God would give me more time than that. "I will stand by you." Doña Ines said that to me! Well she isn't here now, so it must be a dream.

[*The wall becomes translucent and we see the* GHOST OF DOÑA INES.]

GHOST: I'm here.

DON JUAN: Heaven!

GHOST: Ponder well the words of the good Commander, and have the courage to keep your meeting with him. There is but one way of dying well. Choose it carefully, because tomorrow our bodies will sleep in the same tomb.

[*The* GHOST *disappears.*]

DON JUAN: Wait! Doña Ines, wait! If you love me, show me how to know fact from fancy! Some sign! . . . to help me prove the truth of these visions that I may go to my grave in peace. I've had enough chasing after shadows like a fool! . . . Oh! But all this could have been a joke made up by these two who have been pretending, all this while, to be unconscious. If that's the case, then by God, they'll have Don Juan to reckon with! Hey! Don Rafael! Captain! Enough! Get up!

[*He shakes* CENTELLAS *and* AVELLANEDA *who wake up as though aroused from a deep sleep.*]

CENTELLAS: Who's there?

DON JUAN: Get up.

AVELLANEDA: What is it? Oh! It's you!

CENTELLAS: Where are we?

DON JUAN: Gentlemen, let's be frank. I asked you here to my home—but I'm afraid you've engaged in some sort of wager to get the better of me and have a laugh at my expense. I've had my fill of fooling now! Enough is enough!

CENTELLAS: I don't understand.

AVELLANEDA: Nor do I.

DON JUAN: You mean to say you haven't heard anything or seen anything?

AVELLANEDA and CENTELLAS: Of what?

DON JUAN: Stop pretending!

CENTELLAS: Pretending what, Don Juan?

DON JUAN: It couldn't be true! Have the very stones come to life and joined forces against me—threatening to fix the span of my life? For God's sake, speak!

CENTELLAS: Ah! Now I see what you want!

DON JUAN: I want you to tell me what's been going on here or, by God, I swear I'll teach the pair of you that there's no one who can mock Don Juan!

CENTELLAS: Well, now that you put it that way, let me tell you, Don Juan, that it seems to me that it's you who are playing a trick on us!

DON JUAN: You insult me!

CENTELLAS: No, by God! But if you continue to insist that there have been ghosts about, I'll tell you how I explain it! I lost consciousness here in this room when I was completely sober—and there's only one way to explain that!

DON JUAN: Come—out with it.

CENTELLAS: You drugged the wine to make us fall into your trap.

DON JUAN: Centellas!

CENTELLAS: You invited the Commander to supper just to display your famous courage. And in order to claim that he accepted your grotesque invitation, you drugged the wine to make us sleep. Now a joke is all well and good; but when you take it that far it's intolerable!

AVELLANEDA: Agreed.

DON JUAN: You lie!

CENTELLAS: No, you do.

DON JUAN: What say you, Captain?

AVELLANEDA: Your accusation, Don Juan—

DON JUAN: I meant it. You lie! My courage doesn't need to be tested with false wonders, gentlemen. My daring meets my own standards and there is no better test than that.

AVELLANEDA *and* CENTELLAS: We'll see.

[*They lay their hands on their swords.*]

DON JUAN: Restrain your temper, gentlemen, until we step outside. I want no one to think I murdered you in my own house.

AVELLANEDA: Well said. But there are two of us.

CENTELLAS: We'll fight one after the other, if you agree.

DON JUAN: Or both at once, as you wish.

CENTELLAS: In a common brawl? Choose which one of us you'll fight first.

DON JUAN: You'll do.

CENTELLAS: Come.

DON JUAN: Come, Captain.

ACT III

The Mercy of God and the Apotheosis of Love

The mausoleum of the Tenorio family, exactly as it was in the first act of Part Two, except for the fact that Doña Ines' and Don Gonzalo's statues are missing. DON JUAN *walks in slowly, wearing a cloak. He seems distracted.*

DON JUAN: I am not to blame! Some sickly delirium drove me mad. I felt the need of victims to kindle the flame of my despairing faith. And finding them in my way, they fell under my madness. By God, I am not to blame! It was their own foolishness! They knew my swordsmanship and they knew my luck! Oh! My heart is seized by an infernal vertigo! My lost soul wanders over the desert of my life like a dry leaf whipped by the wind. I don't know—I'm afraid—I can't think! My brain seethes like a volcano. I move about aimlessly. A great mystery brings me low and I am frightened. [*A pause.*] Never in my pride have I recognized a greater worth than courage! —I thought death destroyed the soul along with the body. But now I'm not sure. I never believed in ghosts. Nonsense! But in spite of my courage, I keep hearing the heavy tread of that marble ghost wherever I go! Oh! Some mysterious power draws me to this place. [*He looks up and notices the absence of Don Gonzalo's statue.*] But what's this? His statue is missing now! Deliver me from this nightmare! I won't believe it! Out! Out of my brain you hallucination! You can't undermine my strength with childish tricks. If it's all illusion, and dream, no one can frighten me with cheap tricks. But if it's true, then it's foolish even to try to placate the anger of Heaven. No! Real or unreal, I must fight and conquer it or let it conquer me. But if Heaven is really trying to save my soul, it should do so with more honesty and regard. The image on that tomb asked me here to show me proofs of something I have obstinately refused to accept. . . . I am here. Commander, wake up!

[*He knocks at the tomb of Don Gonzalo. The tomb changes shape and becomes a horrible parody of the table in the preceding act. Instead of the garlands that gathered the table cloth into flounces, instead of the beautiful flowers and silverware, this table is decorated with snakes, bones, and fire. Placed upon the table are a large platter of ashes, a goblet of fire, and an hourglass. As this change occurs all the other graves open disgorging their skeletons wrapped in shrouds. Ghosts, skeletons, and spirits hover about in the background. Doña Ines' tomb remains unchanged. The* STATUE OF DON GONZALO *appears.*]

STATUE: Here I am, Don Juan—and with me are all those who clamor to God for your eternal damnation.

DON JUAN: Oh, dear Christ!

STATUE: Why so upset? If there's nothing that can frighten you—if, as you say, you're man enough to eat and drink from their skulls?

DON JUAN: Oh!

STATUE: What? Don't tell me you're losing your courage?

DON JUAN: I don't know! I may have been deceived! They aren't dreams; they're real! [*He looks at the Ghosts.*] A fear I have never known before attacks my soul! I don't lack courage—but I'm going mad!

STATUE: Because your life is coming to an end, Don Juan. The time allotted you is running out.

DON JUAN: What are you saying!

STATUE: What Doña Ines has already told you, what I have told you before, and what you have insanely rejected. But let me return your compliment. I've set a table especially for you. Come closer.

DON JUAN: What's that you're serving me?

STATUE: Fire, here—and here, ashes.

DON JUAN: My hair stands on end!

STATUE: I offer you what you will become.

DON JUAN: Am I to become fire and ashes, then?

STATUE: Exactly. Like those that you see around you now. Courage, youth, and power are all reduced to this.

DON JUAN: Ashes—I understand that—but fire?

STATUE: The fire of omnipotent anger in which you'll burn eternally for your blind and unbridled evil.

DON JUAN: So there is another life beyond our own, another world above our own. All that I refused to believe these many years is true! Oh deadly truth—it turns my blood to ice! Truth revealed to me at the brink of my perdition! . . . And that hourglass?

STATUE: To measure out your life.

DON JUAN: Is it running out?

STATUE: Yes. With each grain of sand you lose an instant of your life.

DON JUAN: And is that all that's left me?

STATUE: Yes.

DON JUAN: God, you are unjust! You discover your power to me now when I lack time to repent.

STATUE: Don Juan, a single act of contrition assures the soul's salvation. You still have time for that.

DON JUAN: Impossible! Erase thirty years of crime and sin in a single moment?

STATUE: Take advantage of it! And take care— [*The bells ring a funeral peal.*] —because your time will soon expire. Those bells are ringing for you, Don Juan. They are already digging your grave. [*We hear the Service for the Dead.*]

DON JUAN: Are they tolling for me?

STATUE: Yes.

DON JUAN: And that funeral music?

STATUE: The penitential psalms—sung for you. [*We see the light of torches flicker past at left and we hear the sound of praying off stage.*]

DON JUAN: And that funeral procession?

STATUE: Your own.

DON JUAN: Am I dead then?

STATUE: The Captain killed you in front of your house.

DON JUAN: The light of faith shines late upon my heart, for by this light I see nothing but my crimes. They strike terror in me now, and their number forces me to measure the wrath that God has stored up for me. Ah! Wherever I went I trod upon reason, scoffed at virtue, and laughed at the law. I poisoned everything I touched. I descended to the cottages, I scaled palace walls, and took convents by storm. There is no hope of pardon for me. [*To the Ghosts*] But there you are, waiting—obstinate and quiet! Let me die in peace! Let me bear my agony alone! That horrible calm of yours! You frightening shades —what more have you to tell me? What do you want?

STATUE: Your soul. They wait for you to die. Goodbye, Don Juan. Your life is at an end. All our efforts were in vain. Give me your hand in token of farewell.

DON JUAN: You show me friendship at a time like this?

STATUE: I do. I did you wrong, and God has commanded that I return to eternity your friend.

DON JUAN: Very well.

STATUE: And now, Don Juan, having spurned the moment that was granted you, you must come with me to Hell.

DON JUAN: Get away from me you treacherous stone! Let go! Let me go! There's still a grain of sand in that hourglass! Let me go! If it's true that a single act of contrition assures the soul's salvation, then— God in Heaven, I believe in you! If my sin defies description, your mercy is infinite! God, have mercy upon me!

STATUE: It is too late!

[DON JUAN *kneels, stretching the hand that the* STATUE *leaves free to Heaven. The skeletons and ghosts are about to fall upon him when the tomb of Doña Ines opens revealing her.* DOÑA INES *takes the hand that* DON JUAN *is holding up to Heaven.*]

DOÑA INES: No! I am here, Don Juan. And with my hand I support yours which raised itself to Heaven in passionate contrition. God forgives Don Juan at the foot of my grave.

DON JUAN: Merciful God! Doña Ines!

DOÑA INES: Spirits, disappear. His faith has saved us both. Return now to your graves. It is the will of God. Through my suffering I cleansed the impurity of his soul, and God has rewarded my yearning by saving Don Juan at the very foot of the grave.

DON JUAN: Ines of my soul!

DOÑA INES: I gave my soul for you, and because of me God has granted your salvation—an act beyond all understanding. Only the just in heaven will understand that love saved Don Juan at the foot of the grave. Let the songs of mourning end. [*The music and psalmody stop.*] And silence the funeral bells. [*The tolling ceases.*] Shades, return once more into your funeral urns. [*The skeletons return to their graves which close around them.*] You walking statues, climb once more onto your pedestals. [*The statues return to their places.*] And let the heavenly rewards enjoyed by the just begin now for Don Juan amid the graves themselves.

[*The flowers part and release several cherubim that surround* DOÑA INES *and* DON JUAN *and shower them with flowers and perfume. The light of dawn comes up to the tune of sweet and distant music.* DOÑA INES *falls on the carpet of flowers which has taken the place of her tomb.*]

DON JUAN: Merciful God, I praise Thee! All Seville will tremble tomorrow as they hear that Don Juan was killed by his own victims. It is just. And let this place forevermore remind the world that one act of contrition has won purgatory for me. The God of Don Juan Tenorio is the God of mercy.

[*He falls at the feet of Doña Ines. They die. Their souls issue from their mouths in the shape of flames that rise and disappear in space to the accompaniment of the music.*] *

*The usual representation of this play does not employ cherubim and omits the ascending souls. [*Translator's note.*]

The Second Half of the Century

In the year Zorrilla was writing and staging his *Don Juan,* the great Austro-Hungarian lyric poet Nikolas Lenau composed his own *Don Juan, ein dramatisches Gedicht.* Like Espronceda's version, this is a lyrical narrative rather than drama, with poetry of a very high order indeed. We get here a series of brief scenes in Don Juan's life, in which the hero is the only really visible figure. The scenes lack a connecting thread; they are rather isolated meditations, mostly elegiac but not devoid of humor. The work is not polished, for Lenau succumbed to insanity before he could give it a final revision.

Characteristically, Lenau's Don Juan tires of his dissipations. The fire of desire goes, indifference replaces it, and he is ready to die:

> Es war ein schöner Sturm, der mich getrieben,
> Er hat vertobt, und Stille ist geblieben—

"the storm that drove me was beautiful; it raged itself out, and silence remained." Not the possession, but desire made him happy: "If there is a heaven on the other side, it too must be most beautiful on its border":

> Wenn jenseits noch ein Himmel ist, so muss
> Auch er am schönsten sein an seiner Grenze.

In an episode which several later versions will repeat, Don Juan wearily allows himself to be killed by an avenger. Lenau's poem, incidentally, served as inspiration to Strauss' well-known *Don Juan.*

In or around 1850, Gustave Flaubert worked on a tale or novella which he entitled *Une nuit de Don Juan.* He never completed it and only a sketch remains, showing the influence of both Musset and Dumas. The novella would have deepened still further the pessimism of Lenau. I transcribe a few of the jottings, which look forward to several modern interpretations.

"Don Juan is weary."

"Don Juan would like to be pure, to be a virgin adolescent." (At the same time, the pure nun in the play secretly wishes to be a Don Juan: is this a hint for Puget's work?)[1]

"Don Juan's desire to define in his mind faces almost erased. What would he not give to recreate a clear notion of these images!" (The same curious anxiety will torture Rostand's protagonist.)

"Impossibility of perfect communion, however adhesive the kiss. Something hinders and makes a wall of itself."

"Don Juan is weary and ends up wanting to croak, the way you feel when you have thought too much, without solution."

And so forth.

Baudelaire too has a sketch, and it is a little more promising. His play might have borne some resemblance to *Axël*. There was going to be a "Don Juan who has reached boredom and melancholy," and who, unable to find satisfaction, envies the vulgar crowd; a servant described as "a rascal like Franklin" talking about economics and virtue; a son; a German princess; a Spanish king: apparently Baudelaire meant to work both the realistic and romantic sides of the street.

We do have, however, his poem, "Don Juan aux enfers" (1846). I give it in French, with a prose trot.

DON JUAN AUX ENFERS

Quand don Juan descendit vers l'onde souterraine
Et lorsqu'il eut donné son obole à Charon,
Un sombre mendiant, l'oeil fier comme Antisthène,
D'un bras vengeur et fort saisit chaque aviron.

Montrant leurs seins pendants et leurs robes ouvertes,
Des femmes se tordaient sous le noir firmament,
Et, comme un grand troupeau de victimes offertes,
Derrière lui traînaient un long mugissement.

Sganarelle en riant lui réclamait ses gages,
Tandis que don Luis avec un doigt tremblant
Montrait à tous les morts errant sur les rivages
Le fils audacieux qui railla son front blanc.

Frissonnant sous son deuil, la chaste et maigre Elvire,
Près de l'époux perfide et qui fut son amant,
Semblait lui réclamer un suprême sourire
Où brillât la douceur de son premier serment.

1. See page 671.

Tout droit dans son armure, un grand homme de pierre
Se tenait à la barre et coupait le flot noir:

Mais le calme héros, courbé sur sa rapière,
Regardait le sillage et ne daignait rien voir.

When Don Juan descended to the subterranean waters, and when he had given Charon his penny, a somber beggar, his eye as proud as that of Antisthenes, seized each oar, with a strong and avenging arm.

Showing their hanging breasts and their open dresses, women twisted under the black firmament, and trailed behind him, like a great herd of offered victims, a long bellowing.

Sganarelle demanded his wages with a laugh, while Don Luis, with a trembling finger, showed to all the dead who wandered on the shores the bold son who had mocked his white hair.

Shivering under her mourning, the chaste and thin Elvira seemed to demand of the perfidious husband who had been her lover a supreme smile glowing with the sweetness of his first oath.

Straight in his armor, a tall man of stone stood at the helm, cutting the black tide; but the calm hero stooped over his rapier, stared at the foam, and did not deign to see.[2]

Since the poem stands as a kind of epilogue to Molière's play, it would be instructive to read it immediately after finishing the latter. The outpouring of emotional phrases and adjectives would have been inconceivable to Molière's homely genius. Each classical tone is deepened; each emotion swollen. Now the beggar is *somber* and his eye is *as proud as that of Antisthenes*; the women are *twisting* under the black firmament and *bellowing*; Sganarelle *laughs* as he demands his wages; Don Luis' finger *trembles* as he exposes his son; and Elvire, chaste and *thin, shivers,* and asks of Don Juan the *supreme* smile of his first oath. Beyond this, the poem's oratory does not advance us a single step beyond Byron's more youthful exaltations. Here is the same rebel, defeated by "virtue" but indomitable, his lips thin and locked, the eternal aristocrat whose patent of nobility, now that society is no longer his, consists in the crimes he commits against it.

By mid-century, everything that the epoch had to say about Don Juan was said. Still, room should be made for Portugal's great poet,

2. "Regardait le sillage" is variously translated as looking at the foam, the wake, the water, the track. Baudelaire is unfortunately unclear at this point. It would be interesting to know whether he thought of his hero as merely looking absently into the water, or, with supreme disdain, showing his back to stare at the wake.

Abelio Guerra Junqueiro, who wrote early in his career a series of poems entitled *A Morte de Don João* (1874), in which Don Juan is represented as a scourge of society, and his women as innocent victims not without kinship to Dickens' Little Em'ly.[3] There is also a *Don Juan* by Aleksei K. Tolstoi, not as yet translated, which appears to be little more than a rebaking of Dumas' over-savory dish. I cannot assure the reader that no play, novel, story or poem of value was written on our subject in that period. Perhaps a masterpiece lies forgotten among the scores upon scores of versions which the bibliographers have unearthed. Had my hopes been greater, I would have searched longer.

All these years the puppet theatre was still flourishing and still obeying fashions set by the living drama of the day. Heroic and larmoyant melodrama, historical canvases and patriotic legends now took their places next to the as yet unexhausted *commedia dell' arte* plots. Here is a typical though rather serious repertory of a nineteenth-century German company: *The Robbers of the Western Wood; The Castle of Ghosts; The Knight of Falkenstein; Don Sebastian de Mongado, or the Struggle Between Honor and Love; The Marksman (der Freischütz); The Prodigal Son; Doctor Johann Faustus; A Storm over the Sea; The Burning of Moscow;* and *The Bombardment of Antwerp*—this one "with much noise and explosions of powder, for the delight of our dear young children."

Don Juan, who remained a popular figure on the puppet stage, followed suit. In *Marionette e Burattini* Roberto and Renata Leydi describe two scenarios (their exact dates cannot be determined), one from a famed puppet theatre in Turin, the other from Imola. The first is called *Il Convitato di pietra senza donne:* "The rather colorless and just a little tedious text offers us an unexpected Don Juan: already advanced in years though not yet old; tired and melancholy, with little amorous zest and no desire to catch fillies or to set traps for the ladies at night." In the Imolese *Don Giovanni* the hero is bored and out of sheer boredom he allows a disguised Arlecchino to take his place with Donna Eleonora. Repelled by (the supposed) Don Giovanni unaccountably transformed into a foul-smelling rustic, Eleonora seeks consolation in the arms of his handsome servant—none other than Don

3. Junqueiro's interests (and style) are those of Hugo envenomed by Baudelaire. He was a liberal fighting for social and political reform. Professor Weinstein mentions several versions of the later nineteenth century in which Don Juan is advised to turn to socially useful works (pp. 136–137).

Giovanni himself. The plot is old, but the spirit of both the Imolese and Turinese scenarios is that of the Romantic age.[4]

The nineteenth century had clung to a Don Juan defeated without but strong within, or else weary but still noble. These conceptions are still current: we must not exaggerate the difference between today and yesterday. But the twentieth century opened a new chapter as well by taking away from Don Juan time after time not only his happiness and his strength, but his dignity into the bargain. Our anti-human century adopted the coolness of the Classical age, but without its vigor, its elegance, its pride. The new Don Juan was to be a small man, carrying only a memory of the greatness bestowed on him by both his Classical and Romantic creators.

4. Roberto and Renata M. Leydi, *Marionette e burattini* (Milan: Collana del "Gallo Grande," 1958), pp. 260–266. The authors also reprint an excellent Milanese scenario (pp. 289–319), probably produced early in our own century, but obviously going back to a post-Mozartean time, as yet untouched by romanticism. The scenario is an extraordinarily pure, literate, and sophisticated reworking of classical sources from Tirso to Da Ponte.

Part III

THE MOLECULAR DON JUAN

Je mange l'herbe amère du rocher de
l'ennui. J'ai besogné Vénus avec rage,
puis avec malice et dégout. Aujourd'hui,
je lui tordrais le cou en baillant. . . .
Ah! comment le combler, ce gouffre de la
vie? Que faire?

O. V. DE LUBICZ-MILOSZ

Ich habe ausgeliebt.

MAX FRISCH

I have eaten the bitter grass of the rock of
boredom. I have belabored Venus with rage,
then with malice and disgust. Today I would
twist her neck with a yawn. . . . Oh, how
can the void of life be filled? What shall I do?

O. V. DE LUBICZ-MILOSZ

I have loved myself out.

MAX FRISCH

Twentieth-Century Views

(1903-1911)

G.B.S. and Don Juan

At the opening of the new century came the announcement that Don Juan was no more. The old rake might have replied that the news of his death was premature, but he would still have felt, I think, a premonitory pang in his bones. The obituary, which occurs in Shaw's splendid but elusive Preface to *Man and Superman,* is worth quoting at length:

Now it is all very well for you at the beginning of the XX century to ask me for a Don Juan play; but you will see from the foregoing survey that Don Juan is a full century out of date for you and for me; and if there are millions of less literate people who are still in the eighteenth century, have they not Molière and Mozart, upon whose art no human hand can improve? You would laugh at me if at this time of day I dealt in duels and ghosts and "womanly" women. As to mere libertinism, you would be the first to remind me that the Festin de Pierre of Molière is not a play for amorists, and that one bar of the voluptuous sentimentality of Gounod or Bizet would appear as a licentious stain on the score of Don Giovanni. Even the more abstract parts of the Don Juan play are dilapidated past use: for instance, Don Juan's supernatural antagonist hurled those who refuse to repent into lakes of burning brimstone, there to be tormented by devils with horns and tails. Of that antagonist, and of that conception of repentance, how much is left that could be used in a play by me dedicated to you? On the other hand, those forces of middle class public opinion which hardly existed for a Spanish nobleman in the days of the first Don Juan, are now triumphant everywhere. Civilized society is one huge bourgeoisie: no nobleman dares now shock his greengrocer. The women, "marchesane, principesse, cameriere, cittadine" and all, are become equally dangerous: the sex is aggressive, powerful: when women are wronged they do not group themselves pathetically to sing "Protegga il giusto cielo": they grasp formidable legal and social weapons, and retaliate. Political parties are wrecked and public careers undone by a single indiscretion. A man had better have all the statues in London to supper with him, ugly as they are, than be brought to the bar of the Nonconformist Conscience by Donna Elvira. Excommunication has become almost as serious a business as it was in the tenth century.

As a result, Man is no longer, like Don Juan, victor in the duel of sex. Whether he has ever really been may be doubted: at all events the enormous superiority of Woman's natural position in this matter is telling with greater and greater force. As to pulling the Nonconformist Conscience by the beard as Don Juan plucked the beard of the Commandant's statue in the convent of San Francisco, that is out of the question nowadays: prudence and good manners alike forbid it to a hero with any mind. Besides, it is Don Juan's own beard that is in danger of plucking. Far from relapsing into hypocrisy, as Sganarelle feared, he has unexpectedly discovered a moral in his immorality. The growing recognition of his new point of view is heaping responsibility on him. His former jests he has had to take as seriously as I have had to take some of the jests of Mr. W. S. Gilbert. His scepticism, once his least tolerated quality, has now triumphed so completely that he can no longer assert himself by witty negations, and must, to save himself from cipherdom, find an affirmative position. His thousand and three affairs of gallantry, after becoming, at most, two immature intrigues leading to sordid and prolonged complications and humiliations, have been discarded altogether as unworthy of his philosophic dignity and compromising to his newly acknowledged position as the founder of a school. Instead of pretending to read Ovid he does actually read Schopenhauer and Nietzsche, studies Westermarck, and is concerned for the future of the race instead of for the freedom of his own instincts. Thus his profligacy and his dare-devil airs have gone the way of his sword and mandoline into the rag shop of anachronisms and superstitions.[1]

Few writers, as it turned out, followed Shaw's suggestion that Don Juan would, or should, worry about the future of the race. That part of Shaw belonged to the world of William Morris and Karl Marx: a world in which it was a man's duty to bang the table for progress. Don Juan had never been much of a reformer, and the twentieth century proved to be a bad time to start in that direction. But two other guidelines of Shaw's were obeyed: doubts began to be cast on Don Juan as a lover, and Don Juan became a philosopher, thus confirming the adage that those who can, do, and those who can't, think.

I have not included Shaw's philosophical romp in this collection because it has really nothing of the Tenorio legend *in its action*. The fact that the legend suggested the idea of the play to Shaw touches only the process of inception, not the work as such. I do not deny that

---

1. *Man and Superman* (Baltimore: Penguin Books Inc., 1952), pp. xiii-xiv.

Hirschfeld's 1947 cartoon of Shaw as master puppeteer manipulating Maurice Evans and Frances Rowe in their respective roles of John Tanner (Don Juan) and Ann Whitefield (Dona Aña) in *Man and Superman*.

certain parallels can be made out—just enough so that, had the play been hard to come by, I should certainly have made room for it. 'Enry Straker might be Leporello; Ramsden might suggest the King in Tirso's play, or even the Statue; and of course there are Ann and Octavius, in whom we find Hoffmann's suggestions for these characters beautifully executed. But nothing is here which really needed the Tenorio matter to get itself invented. Were I told that Shaw thought of Don Juan after, rather than before, planning his play, I would not be surprised. In the end, the analogy between Don Juan and John Tanner rests on a singular syllogism which Shaw did not care to divulge in so many words, to wit: the essence of Don Juan is that Don Juan is a rebel against "virtue"; the Revolutionist (i.e. John Tanner) is a rebel against "virtue"; therefore Don Juan is the Revolutionist.[2] By this sleight-of-hand the modern Don Juan, that is to say, the modern rebel against the standard "virtues"—honor, romantic love, obedience to parents, and the like—is persuaded to turn from sex to the future of the race.

In fact, Shaw tells us, there never really was a pursuit of woman by man. Men invented the idea of this pursuit to shield themselves, for the pursuit always goes the other way around: the goose must chase the gander in order to propagate the race; the woman must "carry on Nature's most urgent work." In this task, to which she applies a thousand and one devious arts, she actually clashes with Don Juan— with the rebel. For the rebel is mind, is the vision of progress, is he through whom Nature is carrying on "the work of building up an intellectual consciousness of her own instinctive purpose," and for all this he must live an ascetic, dangerous, egotistic life where there is little room for women, and none for sentimental affairs of the heart. So then, step by semilogical step, we see Don Juan as rebel against society, hence as a fighter against the blunders and stupidities of the Life Force ("My brain is the organ by which Nature strives to understand itself"), hence as the enemy of cant and of empty pleasures (he calls beauty and pleasure "romantic mirages"), hence as the shunner of women, for unless they are themselves geniuses—like George Sand— they are merely looking for fathers to their children, hence finally as the quarry of the chase. The only hero is the Don Juan who escapes from women. [3]

2. See Section IV of "The Legend of Don Juan" in this volume.
3. Already in 1887, in a story entitled "Don Giovanni Explains," Shaw had presented Don Juan as a man who was irresistible against his will and who only wanted to be left alone.

It is hard to tell whether Shaw approves or disapproves of woman in her role of mother of the race, a role which forces her, for the time being, to be a flirt, coquette, liar, and trapper of men. It is hard to tell whether he is urging the man of genius to resist her to the end, or enjoying the sight of his surrender to her. Perhaps in this instance Shaw did not risk his whole view of the subject. We can, however, take the hint of John Tanner's enthusiastic response to the news that Violet is pregnant out of wedlock, as well as certain passages in the argument of the third act, to conclude that Shaw respects sheer fecundity, that is to say free love and unsentimental procreation. Flesh and blood he calls "those two greasy commonplaces"—but it may be supposed that they are so only when they are not steered by Nature's pilot, the philosopher. These are Shaw's own terms: "The philosopher," he says, "is Nature's pilot," and again—echoing Goethe—"To be in hell is to drift: to be in heaven is to steer."

Even though romantic love is one of Nature's tools for procreation, the proponents of romantic love are in Shaw's Hell, alongside all the other proponents of the "seven deadly virtues." Heaven is reserved for the rebel, the man of genius, the revolutionist. Don Juan has been assigned to Hell by a very natural mistake, considering his reputation of an amorist; and when we meet him, in the magnificent dream of Act III, he is wandering about like a fish out of water. The dream, as everyone knows, ends with the ascension of Don Juan to Heaven, which is his rightful seat.

I reproduce here the opening pages of the dream, those which precede the Socratic conversation. They show, among other things, how alive the true matter of Juan Tenorio still was after three centuries. A light touch and the cool glance of intellect could burst the overblown balloon of Romantic sentiment and propose a Don Juan sophisticated, civilized, modern, and still admirable: all this from a handful of pages, and with them our regret that Shaw gave us no more.

From *Man and Superman:* Act III

By George Bernard Shaw

Stillness settles on the Sierra; and the darkness deepens. The fire has again buried itself in white ash and ceased to glow. The peaks shew unfathomably dark against the starry firmament; but now the stars dim and vanish; and the sky seems to steal away out of the universe. Instead of the Sierra there is nothing: omnipresent nothing. No sky, no peaks, no light, no sound, no time nor space, utter void. Then somewhere the beginning of a pallor, and with it a faint throbbing buzz as of a ghostly violoncello palpitating on the same note endlessly. A couple of ghostly violins presently take advantage of this bass

and therewith the pallor reveals a man in the void, an incorporated but visible man, seated, absurdly enough, on nothing. For a moment he raises his head as the music passes him by. Then, with a heavy sigh, he drops in utter dejection; and the violins, discouraged, retrace their melody in despair and at last give it up, extinguished by wailings from uncanny wind instruments, thus:—

   It is all very odd. One recognizes the Mozartian strain; and on this hint, and by the aid of certain sparkles of violet light in the pallor, the man's costume explains itself as that of a Spanish nobleman of the XV–XVI century. Don Juan, of course; but where? why? how? Besides, in the brief lifting of his face, now hidden by his hat brim, there was a curious suggestion of Tanner. A more critical, fastidious, handsome face, paler and colder, without Tanner's impetuous credulity and enthusiasm, and without a touch of his modern plutocratic vulgarity, but still a resemblance, even an identity. The name too: Don Juan Tenorio, John Tanner. Where on earth—or elsewhere—have we got to from the XX century and the Sierra?

   Another pallor in the void, this time not violet, but a disagreeable smoky yellow. With it, the whisper of a ghostly clarionet turning this tune into infinite sadness:

The yellowish pallor moves: there is an old crone wandering in the void, bent and toothless; draped, as well as one can guess, in the coarse brown frock of some religious order. She wanders and wanders in her slow hopeless way, much as a wasp flies in its rapid busy way, until she blunders against the thing she seeks: companionship. With a sob of relief the poor old creature clutches at the presence of the man and addresses him in her dry unlovely voice, which can still express pride and resolution as well as suffering.

THE OLD WOMAN: Excuse me; but I am so lonely; and this place is so awful.

DON JUAN: A new comer?

THE OLD WOMAN: Yes: I suppose I died this morning. I confessed; I had extreme unction; I was in bed with my family about me and my eyes fixed on the cross. Then it grew dark; and when the light came back it was this light by which I walk seeing nothing. I have wandered for hours in horrible loneliness.

DON JUAN [*sighing*]: Ah! you have not yet lost the sense of time. One soon does, in eternity.

THE OLD WOMAN: Where are we?

DON JUAN: In hell.

THE OLD WOMAN [*proudly*]: Hell! I in hell! How dare you?

DON JUAN [*unimpressed*]: Why not, Señora?

THE OLD WOMAN: You do not know to whom you are speaking. I am a lady, and a faithful daughter of the Church.

DON JUAN: I do not doubt it.

THE OLD WOMAN: But how then can I be in hell? Purgatory, perhaps: I have not been perfect: who has? But hell! oh, you are lying.

DON JUAN: Hell, Señora, I assure you; hell at its best: that is, its most solitary—though perhaps you would prefer company.

THE OLD WOMAN: But I have sincerely repented; I have confessed—

DON JUAN: How much?

THE OLD WOMAN: More sins than I really committed. I loved confession.

DON JUAN: Ah, that is perhaps as bad as confessing too little. At all events, Señora, whether by oversight or intention, you are certainly damned, like myself; and there is nothing for it now but to make the best of it.

THE OLD WOMAN [*indignantly*]: Oh! and I might have been so much wickeder! All my good deeds wasted! It is unjust.

DON JUAN: No: you were fully and clearly warned. For your bad deeds, vicarious atonement, mercy without justice. For your good deeds, justice without mercy. We have many good people here.

THE OLD WOMAN: Were you a good man?

DON JUAN: I was a murderer.

THE OLD WOMAN: A murderer! Oh, how dare they send me to herd with murderers! I was not as bad as that: I was a good woman. There is some mistake: where can I have it set right?

DON JUAN: I do not know whether mistakes can be corrected here. Probably they will not admit a mistake even if they have made one.

THE OLD WOMAN: But whom can I ask?

DON JUAN: I should ask the Devil, Señora: he understands the ways of this place, which is more than I ever could.

THE OLD WOMAN: The Devil! *I* speak to the Devil!

DON JUAN: In hell, Señora, the Devil is the leader of the best society.

THE OLD WOMAN: I tell you, wretch, I know I am not in hell.

DON JUAN: How do you know?

THE OLD WOMAN: Because I feel no pain.

DON JUAN: Oh, then there is no mistake: you are intentionally damned.

THE OLD WOMAN: Why do you say that?

DON JUAN: Because hell, Señora, is a place for the wicked. The wicked are quite comfortable in it: it was made for them. You tell me you feel no pain. I conclude you are one of those for whom Hell exists.

THE OLD WOMAN: Do you feel no pain?

DON JUAN: I am not one of the wicked, Señora; therefore it bores me, bores me beyond description, beyond belief.

THE OLD WOMAN: Not one of the wicked! You said you were a murderer.

DON JUAN: Only a duel. I ran my sword through an old man who was trying to run his through me.

THE OLD WOMAN: If you were a gentleman, that was not a murder.

DON JUAN: The old man called it murder, because he was, he said, defending his daughter's honor. By this he means that because I foolishly fell in love with her and told her so, she screamed; and he tried to assassinate me after calling me insulting names.

THE OLD WOMAN: You were like all men. Libertines and murderers all, all, all!

DON JUAN: And yet we meet here, dear lady.

THE OLD WOMAN: Listen to me. My father was slain by just such a wretch as you, in just such a duel, for just such a cause. I screamed: it was my duty. My father drew on my assailant: his honor demanded it. He fell: that was the reward of honor. I am here: in hell, you tell me: that is the reward of duty. Is there justice in heaven?

DON JUAN: No; but there is justice in hell: heaven is far above such idle human personalities. You will be welcome in hell, Señora. Hell is the home of honor, duty, justice, and the rest of the seven deadly virtues. All the wickedness on earth is done in their name: where else but in hell should they have their reward? Have I not told you that the truly damned are those who are happy in hell?

THE OLD WOMAN: And are you happy here?

DON JUAN [*springing to his feet*]: No; and that is the enigma on which I ponder in darkness. Why am I here? I, who repudiated all duty, trampled honor underfoot, and laughed at justice!

THE OLD WOMAN: Oh, what do I care why you are here? Why am *I* here? I, who sacrificed all my inclinations to womanly virtue and propriety!

DON JUAN: Patience, lady: you will be perfectly happy and at home here. As saith the poet, "Hell is a city much like Seville."

THE OLD WOMAN: Happy! here! where I am nothing! where I am nobody!

DON JUAN: Not at all: you are a lady; and wherever ladies are is hell. Do not be surprised or terrified: you will find everything here that a lady can desire, including devils who will serve you from sheer love of servitude, and magnify your importance for the sake of dignifying their service—the best of servants.

THE OLD WOMAN: My servants will be devils!

DON JUAN: Have you ever had servants who were not devils?

THE OLD WOMAN: Never: they were devils, perfect devils, all of them. But that is only a manner of speaking. I thought you meant that my servants here would be real devils.

DON JUAN: No more real devils than you will be a real lady. Nothing is real here. That is the horror of damnation.

THE OLD WOMAN: Oh, this is all madness. This is worse than fire and the worm.

DON JUAN: For you, perhaps, there are consolations. For instance: how old were you when you changed from time to eternity?

THE OLD WOMAN: Do not ask me how old I was—as if I were a thing of the past. I am 77.

DON JUAN: A ripe age, Señora. But in hell old age is not tolerated. It is too real. Here we worship Love and Beauty. Our souls being entirely damned, we cultivate our hearts. As a lady of 77, you would not have a single acquaintance in hell.

THE OLD WOMAN: How can I help my age, man?

DON JUAN: You forget that you have left your age behind you in the realm of time. You are no more 77 than you are 7 or 17 or 27.

THE OLD WOMAN: Nonsense!

DON JUAN: Consider, Señora: was not this true even when you lived on earth? When you were 70, were you really older underneath your wrinkles and your grey hairs than when you were 30?

THE OLD WOMAN: No, younger: at 30 I was a fool. But of what use is it to feel younger and look older?

DON JUAN: You see, Señora, the look was only an illusion. Your wrinkles lied, just as the plump smooth skin of many a stupid girl of 17, with heavy spirits and decrepit ideas, lies about her age! Well, here we have no bodies: we see each other as bodies only because we learnt to think about one another under that aspect when we were alive; and we still think in that way, knowing no other. But we can appear to one another at what age we choose. You have but to will any of your old looks back, and back they will come.

THE OLD WOMAN: It cannot be true.

DON JUAN: Try.

THE OLD WOMAN: *Seventeen!*

DON JUAN: Stop. Before you decide, I had better tell you that these things are a matter of fashion. Occasionally we have a rage for 17; but it does not last long. Just at present the fashionable age is 40— or say 37; but there are signs of a change. If you were at all good-looking at 27, I should suggest your trying that, and setting a new fashion.

THE OLD WOMAN: I do not believe a word you are saying. However, 27 be it.

[*Whisk! the old woman becomes a young one, magnificently attired, and so handsome that in the radiance into which her dull yellow halo has suddenly lightened one might almost mistake her for Ann Whitefield.*]

DON JUAN: Doña Ana de Ulloa!

ANA: What? You know me!

DON JUAN: And you forget me!

ANA: I cannot see your face. [*He raises his hat.*] Don Juan Tenorio! Monster! You who slew my father! even here you pursue me.

DON JUAN: I protest I do not pursue you. Allow me to withdraw [*going*].

ANA [*seizing his arm*]: You shall not leave me alone in this dreadful place.

DON JUAN: Provided my staying be not interpreted as pursuit.

ANA [*releasing him*]: You may well wonder how I can endure your presence. My dear, dear father!

DON JUAN: Would you like to see him?

ANA: My father here!!!

DON JUAN: No: he is in heaven.

ANA: I knew it. My noble father! He is looking down on us now. What must he feel to see his daughter in this place, and in conversation with his murderer!

DON JUAN: By the way, if we should meet him—

ANA: How can we meet him? He is in heaven.

DON JUAN: He condescends to look in upon us here from time to time. Heaven bores him. So let me warn you that if you meet him he will be mortally offended if you speak of me as his murderer! He maintains that he was a much better swordsman than I, and that if his foot had not slipped he would have killed me. No doubt he is right: I was not a good fencer. I never dispute the point; so we are excellent friends.

ANA: It is no dishonor to a soldier to be proud of his skill in arms.

DON JUAN: You would rather not meet him, probably.

ANA: How dare you say that?

DON JUAN: Oh, that is the usual feeling here. You may remember that on earth—though of course we never confessed it—the death of anyone we knew, even those we liked best, was always mingled with a certain satisfaction at being finally done with them.

ANA: Monster! Never, never.

DON JUAN [*placidly*]: I see you recognize the feeling. Yes: a funeral was always a festivity in black, especially the funeral of a relative. At all events, family ties are rarely kept up here. Your father is quite accustomed to this: he will not expect any devotion from you.

ANA: Wretch: I wore mourning for him all my life.

DON JUAN: Yes: it became you. But a life of mourning is one thing: an eternity of it quite another. Besides, here you are as dead as he. Can anything be more ridiculous than one dead person mourning for another? Do not look shocked, my dear Ana; and do not be alarmed: there is plenty of humbug in hell (indeed there is hardly anything else); but the humbug of death and age and change is dropped because here we are all dead and all eternal. You will pick up our ways soon.

ANA: And will all the men call me their dear Ana?

DON JUAN: No. That was a slip of the tongue. I beg your pardon.

ANA [*almost tenderly*]: Juan: did you really love me when you behaved so disgracefully to me?

DON JUAN [*impatiently*]: Oh, I beg you not to begin talking about love. Here they talk of nothing else but love: its beauty, its holiness, its spirituality, its devil knows what!—excuse me; but it does so bore me. They don't know what they're talking about: I do. They think they have achieved the perfection of love because they have no bodies. Sheer imaginative debauchery! Faugh!

ANA: Has even death failed to refine your soul, Juan? Has the terrible judgment of which my father's statue was the minister taught you no reverence?

DON JUAN: How is that very flattering statue, by the way? Does it still come to supper with naughty people and cast them into this bottomless pit?

ANA: It has been a great expense to me. The boys in the monastery school would not let it alone: the mischievous ones broke it; and the studious ones wrote their names on it. Three new noses in two years, and fingers without end. I had to leave it to its fate at last; and now I fear it is shockingly mutilated. My poor father!

DON JUAN: Listen! [*Two great chords rolling on syncopated waves of sound break forth. D minor and its dominant: a sound of dreadful joy to all musicians.*] Ha! Mozart's statue music. It is your father. You had better disappear until I prepare him.

[*She vanishes.*]   (1903)

Extract from Act III of *Man and Superman*. Baltimore: Penguin Books Inc., 1952.

From *The Legend of Don Juan*
by Georges Gendarme de Bévotte

Translated by Frederick E. Conron

Gendarme de Bévotte's work on Don Juan is still the authoritative study in the field up to its own time, even though, as is to be expected, it is not the final word on every given version. Its two chief virtues are comprehensiveness and sanity. The opening chapter of the 1911 edition (the first half of the work, which took the legend from its origins to Romanticism, appeared in 1906) is a classic statement in which two questions are discussed and their interrelation established: namely, what the meaning of Don Juan is, and why Don Juan was born in the Renaissance. Gendarme de Bévotte probably exaggerates the freedom of the ancient Greeks (his is the picture of Greece-for-nineteenth-century-man rather than the historian's Greece), and the reasons he gives for Don Juan's absence from the medieval scene are forced. But his speculations have established themselves as standard points of reference, and Don Juan as the Great Liberal makes an attractive, if not quite credible, figure.—*The Editor*

The legend of Don Juan does not go back beyond the beginning of the seventeenth century and it owes its extraordinary diffusion in large part to the good fortune of having inspired one of Molière's chefs d'oeuvre. It owes it also to the fact that, born of a religious idea, it lost its original meaning early and was not slow in bringing about a particular conception of love. In it are expressed the feelings and the mores of a whole category of individuals who have their own way of understanding the relationship of man and woman. These individuals are innumerable and do not belong exclusively to any one country or time. They make up a separate type in humanity whose different characteristics were gathered together by literature for the first time in the person of a Spanish hero, Don Juan.

These characteristics found such vigorous and complete expression in that hero that since that time the term Don Juan has been naturally applied to all individuals of that kind. But, just as "tartufferie" was spread throughout the world before Tartuffe himself existed, "donjuanism" existed before having been formulated in the fable of the "Convive de pierre." This work merely gave it its name, but not life. "Donjuanism" is a general phenomenon; it was not born in any definite era and will not die in another. It is inherent in human nature;

the ancients were acquainted with it just as well as the moderns, and non-European civilizations are not unaware of it either.

Nevertheless, as universal as it is, it is not completely normal; it is the mark of a deviant physical and moral state. ,It interests psychologists and physiologists as a case whose frequency of recurrence does not diminish its originality. The moralist is troubled by it as a disorder brought into the social order. It is developed with the help of certain circumstances; to be born it needs favorable surroundings and it grows only in certain temperaments. Weak, anemic organisms, minds fond of rules, hearts capable of profound and durable sentiments are not good material for it. Likewise, worn out generations do not produce it. Inversely, there are some epochs in which the conditions of life and customs furnish it particularly fertile soil: the need for activity and expansion which in Italy created the "condottiere," in Spain the "conquistadores," is favorable to donjuanism.

But, if Don Juans are everywhere, if donjuanism is a natural human phenomenon, frequently observed in reality, how shall we explain why it took so many centuries to pass into literature? Literature is the reflection of life. Why did it neglect for such a long time a phenomenon from which dramatists, novelists, philosophers and poets were to draw interesting portraits of customs and wise moral lessons?

In order to understand this it is important to distinguish two elements in donjuanism. Don Juan is not solely a hunter after love, as the common man believes; he is the defender of natural laws and of individual rights against human and religious laws. The dissolute man who obeys his instincts spontaneously and who is commonly known by the vulgar but significant name of "lady's man" is not a complete Don Juan: he is only a sensualist.

This libertine existed in Greek society: a civilization that produced Epicureanism, and which proclaimed that truth consists in obedience to nature, was bound to beget men who live for love. In the eyes of the sage, virtue was nothing but the pursuit of happiness. The common man did not always take this rather vague definition in its higher moral sense; youth especially was inclined to lower it to mere physical pleasure. The esteem that surrounded the courtesans, the worship rendered Aphrodite and Eros, the very notion of beauty, stronger among the Greeks than any tenet, show the position that love held in Athenian life. It was the same somewhat later at Alexandria, whose licentious customs, under the Ptolemies, are well known. A volume could be written on Roman corruption. As for Byzantine profligacy, it has become proverbial.

In Greek and Roman literature lewdness is displayed with candor: there is not a single classic author whom our moral code would permit to be presented to the public at large without having first been expurgated. The gods themselves lived in adultery; the example comes from above and Zeus was, in a sense, the first Don Juan. He had six lawful wives before Juno, and an infinite number of mistresses. To come by them, he resorted to methods which the Burlador of Tirso was to take up later as well: corruption, pretense, deceit, abduction, and violence. One of the wisest of Athenian kings, one of the most glorious heroes of Greece, Theseus, could not in the course of his exploits encounter a woman without seducing her: he successively loved and abandoned Ariadne, Antiope, Helen, Phaedra, and legend even claims that his earthly successes were not sufficient for him; he descended into the underworld to abduct Proserpine. One English author somewhat facetiously tells the same story about Don Juan.

Thus, in ancient societies, love was omnipresent, in the heavens as upon the earth. Far from condemning it, philosophers proclaimed that there was no feeling more natural and, consequently, more legitimate, more sacred even. Men loved in complete freedom, without being stopped by scruples of conscience, by the restraining force of laws, by the dictates of customs. The union that no religious or legal rite had sanctioned was not a revolt either against religion or against the law. Don Juan being everywhere, there were, properly speaking, no Don Juans. It is clear then why ancient literature did not portray the seducer. He is a commonplace character who offers nothing to the curiosity of the moralist and the psychologist.

It might even be said that antiquity neglected Don Juan because, in spite of appearances, it did not truly know him. It knew of the lady's man and even of gods with propensities for many women, but if Don Juan is also and above all the champion of the right to love as opposed to religious and moral prohibitions, he can exist only in societies which proscribe the freedom of love, which make of it a reprehensible act or which authorize it only exceptionally under the dual control of the priest and the magistrate. The religion which first numbered among its commandments: "Thou shalt not desire the deeds of the flesh except in marriage alone" produced donjuanism.

Don Juan is the man goaded on by love, in a struggle against a God who forbids it. The day on which Christianity said to the lover of the flesh: thou shalt love in the spirit; the day on which the Fathers of the Church represented the female to the worshipper of feminine beauty as a corrupted and corrupting creature, donjuanism had to be born as a protest by the instincts.

But it was not born immediately. As long as Christianity held its faithful so docilely curbed by its laws that they did not dare to, nor even conceive of, revolt; as long as its dictates were accepted during the whole of the Middle Ages, Don Juan mortified himself, he became a monk, he strangled the desires of his concupiscence within the cloister.

It was with the coming of the Renaissance that Don Juan began to reason out his case, began wondering whether his sacrifice was rational, whether truth lay in immolation or in the exaltation of his natural inclinations. He no longer read only theological treatises which condemned the deeds of the flesh, but also the philosophical works of his time. In Italy, Valla's "De professione religiosorum" taught him the senselessness of the vow of chastity and the "De voluptate" even invited him to seek nothing but pleasure. One of the interlocutors of the dialogue, Beccadelli, presents virginity to him as a shameful torment and states that every woman ought to belong to every man. In France, he was tempted to enter a convent under the direction of Brother John where the rule "was but this proviso: do as you would like" and where no other women were admitted "except the beautiful, the well formed and those of good birth." Finally, with Montaigne he discovered that there was no better line of conduct than the impulses of Nature.

If the Church had subscribed to the new philosophy, or simply closed its eyes, he would have lived without revolting, living out his simple days in the abbey of Thélème, ignored by the public and unknown to himself. But the Church became disturbed: her dogmas, the basic principles of her morals were at stake. She immediately took up her battle positions and fought at first in the countries of the Inquisition. It was in Spain that for the first time a monk expressed the claim of the flesh to take precedence over the spirit, a bold affirmation of the right of Nature to invalidate the religious law of chastity. The danger seemed so great to her that she had recourse to the hand of God Himself. Don Juan was meted out a supernatural punishment. However, he did not concede defeat. Between him and his adversaries the struggle resumed across the nations and ages, and despite vain attempts at reconciliations, it will endure as long as Catholicism itself.

This is why donjuanism took so many centuries to be born. As long as man could satisfy his instinct for love without religious hindrances, Don Juan was nothing but a male a little more vigorous than others, fulfilling his normal function, obeying the laws of the species. Nothing essential distinguished him from the ordinary man and drew attention to him. No one revealed him to others and to himself but the light of day in which religion, provoking his temperament while claiming to curtail it, made of him a rebel.

Antiquity, which was as favorable to the demands of the flesh as to the aspirations of thought, could not know Don Juan any more than Faust. The one represents the body, the other the spirit which rebel when strangled. As long as this double restraint and the double revolt which resulted from it did not exist, there could be no intellectual or moral licentiousness. Faust and Don Juan were inconceivable. Both were born of Christianity, for similar reasons.

They are also the sons of modern thought. They are individualists: they are the enemies of the feelings, the ideas, the mores of the common man; their own thoughts, their instincts are the only law to which they claim to be responsible. They are antisocial beings. They do not melt into collectivity; they derive their rights from a personal ethic which is nothing more than the unimpeded development of their intellectual and physical energies.

Ancient civilization, which raised its children for the sake of the state, which formed citizens before forming men, was not favorable to the development of these independents, of these wilful outlaws, of these enemies of the accepted communal discipline. Nor could it be otherwise in the Middle Ages as long as the unity of belief and blind obedience to a faith considered as the universal basis of truth hindered man from drawing his principles of behavior from within himself.

Don Juan appeared the day that the "vir," the individual, frees himself from all collective restraint. He symbolizes the new spirit confronting tradition. He represents the philosophy of self, the independent ethical code opposed to the old rule of submission. He appears as the *libertin* [of the 17th century]. That is why the state and the Church unite to subdue him. But in vain: the power which animates him, once unleashed, will not permit itself to be imprisoned again. The individual conscious of his power, trying to accomplish his particular aims, no longer agrees to get back into line and become just another anonymous member of the herd.   (1911)

Excerpted from *La Légende de Don Juan*, 2 vols. Paris: Librairie Hachette, 1911.

Don Juan Unmasked (1921)

Edmond Rostand and *La Dernière nuit de Don Juan*

Shortly before World War I, Edmond Rostand wrote the last of his handful of plays, *La Dernière nuit de Don Juan*. For reasons as yet unknown, he failed to give the work its final touches, so that it appeared posthumously in 1921 with a few edges still rough. Rostand called his play a dramatic poem, but it is in effect another critical interpretation of Don Juan. Reviewers of the time immediately remarked on the play's bitterness. What had happened to Rostand's famous idealism and optimism? Why was Don Juan not another magnifico? And, in fact, no one could have foreseen that Rostand would attack and demolish Don Juan, who seemed the very figure to take his place in the happy playwright's heroic gallery. For if Rostand upset Romantic tradition and robbed Don Juan of a heart (not to speak of Heaven), he did so with conscious indignation, and not because the subject forced his hand.

And yet, in spite of this surprising turn, the play is consistent with Rostand's lifework. It is not a recantation. Rostand's persistent theme was not exactly "extravagant gallantry in pursuit of the unattainable," as Bacourt and Cunliffe typically assert;[1] rather, he was concerned all his life with the question of what happens either when reality secretes an illusion or when illusion is exposed by reality. Everything depends on whether the illusion is that of a noble mind or that of a villain, but Rostand did not lose track of his major question when he moved from Cyrano or Rudel to Don Juan.

Rostand's heroes are in effect reincarnations of Don Quixote, at least as Don Quixote was understood by Romantic readers. Sometimes they are themselves deceived by the ideal, like Chantecler, who believes that his crowing brings out the sun every day; sometimes they create the ideal deception for others, as Cyrano does. Noble illusions, in either case, breed noble deeds. They call out enthusiasm, purity, and above

1. *French Literature During the Last Half-Century* (New York: 1923), p. 227.

all love; and they have the capacity, illusions though they are, of refining reality. The "faraway Princess" is a weak woman in reality; but Rudel the troubadour has idealized her, and this vision has drawn him away from "vice, vain love-games, and the idle witty trifles of his little court." He has become a hero, and he has transfigured his rough crew, for idealism is contagious. Finally his vision succeeds even in sublimating the Princess herself. Thus Rostand at his most optimistic.

Rudel never has to face a reality unrefined by his illusion. But elsewhere Rostand did ask what happens to a hero, or to a villain, when he is forced to open his eyes. His answer is that the hero, like Don Quixote in his last lucidity, becomes even more superb in this defeat than he had been under the spell of his illusion. Chantecler, for example, returns to duty and to the love of "mankind" (the charming animals in the farmyard) even though he knows at last that the sun rises without him. The lovers in Rostand's first successful play, *Les Romanesques*, reaffirm their love when romantic illusion gives way to homespun reality.[2] And Roxane understands, in the end, that the really great man was Cyrano in spite of his ugly nose—Rostand's touching symbol for the ugly side of reality.

What, then, is Don Juan's place in this company? Here are illusions again, and here is reality stripping them off; but this time they are illusions of the heartless small man. Cyrano and the troubadour Rudel created illusions because they loved; l'Aiglon, to keep alive; Chantecler as an act of worship. But the scoundrel's illusions are lies to deceive himself and the world. When reality comes to him, it exposes, not greatness behind a dream, but pettiness behind a lie. The White Ghost offers Don Juan a last chance to meet reality with a gesture of love, but he casts her aside, and becomes the puppet he has always been.

In short, Rostand is looking at the old subject as it were from the nether side. The cynic had already appeared in the earlier plays, but always as a foil to the hero. Now he holds the stage by himself. Rostand chose not even to summon Octavio, who might have come riding in as the true lover. However, he was not renouncing true lovers when he exposed Don Juan. What perhaps he was suggesting in a bitter-gay parable is that the small souls are inheriting the earth.

It is quite possible that Rostand failed to polish the play because he

2. This play reappeared recently in a modern American adaptation as a tepid musical called *The Fantasticks*. The only notice anywhere of Rostand's paternity was in a minute acknowledgment in the printed program, where his play was miscalled *Les Romantiques*.

was repelled or alarmed by his own pessimism, or simply because the role of prosecutor depressed him. As the play stands, many of the lines and couplets shine with all the brilliance of his best work. Rostand has lost nothing of his genius in

> La femme, adorant mon reflet,
> Quand Don Juan n'est pas là couche avec son valet!

or in

> Car la barque jamais ne vaut la passerelle!

or in

> Il n'est pas de vertu, de science, ou de foi
> Qui ne soit le regret de ne pas être moi!

Other lines, I am sure, he would have mended or banished. Altogether, his buoyant verse keeps us clean of disgust or dejection. A lapidation carried out with so much elegance cannot be entirely dispiriting. Here, if ever, style triumphs over matter. In a word, the play firmly remains comedy. We are still at a happy distance from the deflated bladder of a Don Juan who is to appear in subsequent plays, speaking the unspeaking speech of molecular naturalism.

Edmond Rostand was born in Marseilles in 1868. Contemporaries were given to ascribing his sunny lyricism to the climate of his birthplace. More prosaically, his wealthy and prominent parents sent him to school in Paris. In 1890 he published a volume of poems which no one noticed. But he quickly achieved fame. Between 1894 and 1900 he produced five successful plays, to which Sarah Bernhardt and Coquelin contributed their talents. *Cyrano de Bergerac*, staged in 1897, made him the king of the French theatre. In 1901 he was admitted to the Academy, where he uttered the characteristic phrase: "Passion must be rehabilitated." It must be confessed that Rostand was a man who did not blush when he said *beauty, ideal, glory*, or *exalted feelings*. This is enough in itself to explain his eclipse in our own dry times. After 1900 he retired to a secluded residence in the Pyrenees and was silent until 1910, when he produced *Chantecler*. I take this play to be his second masterpiece, but it disappointed the public and has never established itself in the repertory. One of Rostand's most interesting works, it might be added, is a little-known fragment of a translation of *Faust*.

It must have been clear to Rostand in his last years that he was an outdated man. Had not *Ubu roi* appeared a year before *Cyrano?* In

1910, the year when Chantecler was singing his gorgeous hymn to the sun, Alban Berg was writing his third String Quartet. When Rostand died, in 1918, he was behind even the literary body which the avant-garde was leaving behind. But the great poet was neither attacked nor ridiculed. The other writers and critics just moved on.

Today *Cyrano de Bergerac* is as alive as ever, and other plays of Rostand's are occasionally performed (or read) as well. But for the sophisticated, he will remain a relic until the next revolution of taste. For our age is as incapable of understanding his genius as that of Victoria was of appreciating Alexander Pope, or Pope of doing justice to John Donne. The first collected edition of his plays and poetry made its long overdue appearance in 1962 (Fasquelle, 9 volumes), and it is to be hoped that this event will beget a comprehensive study of Rostand's achievement. No such study of any real value exists, and in any case the last one was attempted thirty years ago. No one has written a biography; no one has collected letters. In 1936 his widow published some cloying reminiscences, and since that year only one book concerning Rostand—and that one devoted entirely to *Cyrano*—has appeared. A few trivial articles, mostly chit-chat, complete the sad record. For information about the man and his work, we must turn to the profuse but often worthless literature of his own lifetime and of the decade after his death.[3] Needless to say, Rostand gets his paragraph in all the literary histories and handbooks, where he is always mentioned with polite good will.

3. A serviceable survey is that of Antoine Benoist, in *Le Théâtre d'aujourd'hui* (deuxième série; Paris: 1912).

EDMOND ROSTAND

The Last Night of Don Juan

(1921)

English Version by Dolores Bagley

EDITOR'S NOTE

According to a prefatory note in the original text: "The Prologue, reconstructed from a fragmentary rough draft with many erasures, can be considered only a sketch." Further, we are told that throughout the play it was necessary to amplify or to supply the description of settings and stage directions—entrances, exits, actions accompanying the dialogue, off-stage sounds, etc. The reader interested in finding out which of these "indications de scène" were in Rostand's own hand is referred to the original text, where all added material has been placed between brackets. For the sake of clarity, directions have been added in a few places in the present translation.

TEXT

Edmond Rostand, *La Dernière nuit de Don Juan: Poème dramatique en deux parties et un prologue*. Paris: Charpentier et Fasquelle, 1921.

Persons in the Play

Don Juan
The Statue of the Commander
The Devil
The Beggar
Sganarelle
The White Ghost
The Thousand and Three Ghosts

The Scenes

Prologue. The Stairway to Hell.
Parts I and II. A Venetian Palace.

PROLOGUE

We see nothing but a dimly lighted, narrow flight of stairs spiraling upward until lost from sight, and sinking below into an abyss. A green and sulfurous glow suffuses the base of the stairs. As the curtain opens, the STATUE OF THE COMMANDER *appears. He descends the stairs heavily, holding* DON JUAN, *magnificently calm, by his arm.*

DON JUAN: No need to clutch at me, I'll go alone.
[*With his every step he recites a name.*]
Nina ... Louise ... Agnes ... Joan ...
[*A dog's cries are heard in the distance. Don Juan listens.*]
Ah! My spaniel mourns for me, at least.
Now that's what I call an admirable beast.
　[*He continues his descent.*]
Amanda ... Elvira ...
[*He pauses.*]
　　　　　　　　Ah, sir! Lend an ear
To the cries of my faithful valet. He holds me dear,
Poor devil, he cannot bear to see me so!

VOICE OF SGANARELLE: My wages!

DON JUAN: 　　　　　　I beg you, Commander, let me go.
Permit me to give the poor wretch his due.

COMMANDER: Very well. I'll wait.

DON JUAN: 　　　　　　　　My thanks to you.
[DON JUAN *reascends the stairs, leaving the Commander alone. There is a pause.*]

COMMANDER: I'm a fool to trust him.
[*We hear the voice of Don Juan.*]

DON JUAN: 　　　　　　　　Scoundrel! Your wages!
A swift kick in the backside—that's for your rages.
　[DON JUAN *reappears.*]
He's gotten what he's earned.

COMMANDER: 　　　　　　　　So you're returning?

DON JUAN: That did me good. I'll think of it when I'm burning.

COMMANDER: You seem to be afraid of nothing, my son,
And courage is my weakness. I have done.
You've won an old knight's pardon. You are free.

DON JUAN: You should have said so sooner. Ouch! See?
              A monstrous claw is clutching at my cape.
              It's too late now, Commander. I can't escape.
              [*To the Claw*]
              The Devil, I presume. How do you do?

COMMANDER: Don Juan, I must be taking leave of you.
              The cock's metallic cries awake the dawn,
              My warning to return. Carry on;
              Do your best to escape.

DON JUAN: Don't worry! Oh—
              Would you leave the door ajar as you go?
              [*The* COMMANDER *leaves.* DON JUAN *begins to tug
              gently at his cloak, trying to free himself as he speaks.*]
              Now let's talk the whole thing over, old claw.
              That worthy marble gentleman you saw
              Has deigned to let me go scot free.
              Why shouldn't you do the same for me?
              Give me only five years! Ten would be more fair;
              I've still a pack of evil left to do up there.
              Ah! That moves you, eh? I must insist!
              I've still a score of ladies to add to my list.
              It might be worth your while to make a pact—
              You know I'm an expert in the evil act.
              Why, I'm the greatest sportman in your game;
              I'm devoted to sin. That's my key to fame.
              Not only that, but—Look here, old claw, let go!
              I'm no foolish Dr. Faust, you know,
              Asking no more than a little German peasant,
              And then—after making everything unpleasant
              By breeding a child—the ass!—trying to defend
              Himself by calling down an Angel at the end.
              Good Lord! Those blazing hooks have left five marks
              Upon my flesh. Oh, what ardent sparks
              This scar would strike from all the ladies' hearts!
              Release that scrap of cloth, sir, and I'll go far.
              Spain's Infanta watches the evening star,
              Lusting for my touch. Even you, sir,
              Must know that in my role of the seducer
              I'm practically your priest. Now let me go!
              [*The Claw releases its grip, and disappears.*]
              Finally!

Ten years, Your Deviltry, should see me through.
Only trust me, sir, as I trust you.
[*Again he ascends the stairs, reciting at every step.*]
Rosa . . . Lisa . . . Angelica . . . Annabelle . . .
[*His voice fades away. He is gone. After a moment we
can hear him shouting in the distance.*]
Ho there! Sganarelle! Sganarelle!

PART I

*Ten years have passed. The scene is a Venetian palace, a huge hall
opening on the Adriatic, into which descends a marble staircase. In the
center of the stage stands a table prepared for two, lighted by a gilded
candelabra.* SGANARELLE *is in attendance.* DON JUAN *enters.*

DON JUAN:	Lucy . . . Arabella . . . Dora . . . Lorelei . . .
SGANARELLE:	Your ten years are up, sir.
DON JUAN:	What a gorgeous sky!

I've just come back from the Grand Canal.

SGANARELLE:	So I see.
DON JUAN:	Every boat upon that rose and chocolate sea

Trails its watery carpet; while enviously,
Like Potiphar's wife, the lagoon tries to detain
Every craft by seizing its carpet of flame.
But here within this corner, green and deep,
The waters sleep their solitary sleep
Beneath a turquoise sky veined with brimstone,
As virtue slept before I made her moan.
I adore quiet waters. Do you know
Why the Adriatic compels me so?

SGANARELLE:	No.
DON JUAN:	She's married.
SGANARELLE:	Oh?
DON JUAN:	The Doge is her mate.

The Doge alone is master of her state.
As for me, I am her lover. I command you,
Deep lagoon. Only I can understand you.

SGANARELLE:	Obviously.
DON JUAN:	Now watch this sleeping sea

Awaken to debauch herself with me.
There!
[*He hurls a ring into the sea.*]
                    A ring for your left hand, my lass!

SGANARELLE [*With horror*]:
                    The ruby?

DON JUAN: No, you idiot! The glass.

SGANARELLE: Ah.

DON JUAN: Yes.

SGANARELLE: Hers? . . . That woman? . . . So fast?

DON JUAN: Of course.

SGANARELLE: Then—finished? Over? Past?

DON JUAN: Ah, Venice! The city of fragility—
Its plaster columns, its lacy walls,
Its liquid streets, its mirrored halls—
In Venice even when lovers exchange a ring
It has the sense to be a worthless thing.

SGANARELLE: Sir, ten years have passed, and you—

DON JUAN: I persevere.

SGANARELLE: But tonight—

DON JUAN: A ball.

SGANARELLE: Afterward you'll come back here?

DON JUAN: Oh, no. But stronger than mighty Hannibal
I'll cull the fruits of triumph after the ball.

SGANARELLE: Sir, if your final hour should arrive
Such joyous insolence will only contrive—
[*A clock strikes.*]

DON JUAN: Aha! Speak of the hour and it will peal.

SGANARELLE: Oh, dear.

DON JUAN: Listen: it bursts from the campanile.

SGANARELLE: How long must we stay here under Venice's sky
Listening to this racket? Must we die
Just for the pleasure of calling a clock a campanile?

DON JUAN: Those little white Venetian slippers have such appeal,
And a gondolier's a perfect go-between:
His music is romantic, his verses obscene.
And oh, the cedar scent in which the women bathe!
God! It would have made Hippolytus Phaedra's slave.
I adore Venice. Her lion is rather like me.
While a flock of doves adores him devotedly

He rejects his rule of the sea with sharp disdain,
Choosing to rule over love's eternal domain.
Oh, mad, profound city of perfection,
Wanting, like you, to exist on my reflection,
I build on water.

SGANARELLE: The city's mortal, you know.

DON JUAN: Yes; but even though that may be so,
Every rogue who reaches for the heights
Must come at last to taste of her delights.
And though to stay in Venice may mean to die
I cannot fly to some severer sky.
A city of love witnessed the hour of my birth;
A city of love shall see my last hour on earth.
One simple epitaph will mark my fall:
"Born in Seville; died in Venice." That's all.
Fool! I'm only trying to frighten you now.
I'm sure the Devil's forgotten us, anyhow.

SGANARELLE: Us?

DON JUAN: That's true, it's none of your affair.
And yet—you happen to be my only heir.

SGANARELLE: Why?

DON JUAN: Because you served Don Juan the Great
Your virtues will take on a greater weight:
Gentlemen will vie for you to discover
The secrets of the world's most famous lover.
And as for the ladies—

SGANARELLE: Yes?

DON JUAN: They'll shed a tear,
But you'll find other masters, never fear,
And other mistresses.

SGANARELLE: How do you know?

DON JUAN: Women have such a passion for Don Juan
They'll fight to sleep with his valet after he's gone.
Good auditor of maidenheads, what's the score?
A thousand—

SGANARELLE: And three, sir. We're coming to number four.

DON JUAN: I've never felt more virile, more unafraid!
I used to watch the gilders at their trade
As I combed the streets for caskets richly cast
To hold the billets-doux that I'd amassed.
And tonight I feel as if my heart were lacquered too,

Just like those gilders' caskets, in reddest hue
And finished with a golden filigree.
Let's eat! Everything is gilded here. You see?
Everything! . . . Even an oyster shell.
To speak the truth, rascal, who can tell,
Who knows if the Devil exists? As Tertullian said,
"Satan's day is over. The Devil is dead."
I see myself rushing from love to love,
Like fountain waters gushing from above
In these Venetian parks. My sword and mask!
The future is mine! I'm ready for any task.

VOICE [*in the distance*]:
        Burattini!

DON JUAN: Those old Venetian cries—they have such grace.

VOICE [*drawing nearer*]:
        Burattini!

DON JUAN: That voice seems bodiless, as if in space.

        [SGANARELLE *has gone to the window.*]

SGANARELLE: That old puppeteer with his touring show is on the
            stair—

DON JUAN: Have him come up.

SGANARELLE: —the one from the Slavonian square.

        [*He is signaling to the puppeteer.*]

DON JUAN: Punchinello! That's the one—that's the fellow!
Ah, I shall dine while watching Punchinello,
Like old Trimalchio who nibbled his sack
Of walnuts while he watched the Dancing Jack.

        [*The* PUPPETEER *enters, bowing obsequiously.*]

PUPPETEER: Burattini. . . . *Li far ballar.*

        [*Showing Don Juan a poster*]
                   Privileggio.

SGANARELLE: Four wooden posts, an old sack, and a screen—

PUPPETEER: My little castle. May I set the scene?

DON JUAN: By all means, do. Where do you come from, sir?

PUPPETEER: Everywhere. I'm quite a traveler.
I've met with writers—artists—every kind.
Why, once when I was in Holland who should I find
In front of me but Bayle himself?* That's right!

DON JUAN: I've traveled a bit myself, as a legend might.

*Bayle, Pierre (1647–1706). French rationalist philosopher whose followers acclaimed him as the "master of doubt." [*Editor's note.*]

Ah, little theatre, where I learned of life
And witnessed all the buffetings of strife,
You remind me of a tiny Grecian shrine—
Your little stage, your pillars, your strange design.
Ah, childhood . . .
[*To the Puppeteer*]
                         Come over here, old soul.

[*To himself*]
I can see him now, begging his dole—
"Remember Punchinello, sir?"—and then
Raising his eternal curtain again.
[*To Sganarelle*]
Go away; leave me with Punchinello.

[SGANARELLE *goes. The* PUPPETEER *enters the little guignol, in which we now see his puppets appearing, one by one.*]

PUNCHINELLO [*bursting onto the stage*]:
                 Ahratatat-Tat! Ahratatat-Tat!
DON JUAN: Ah, there he is. It's really he.
PUNCHINELLO: It's me, PUNCH! It's me, -IN! It's me, -NEL! It's me, -LO!
                 It's me, clumsy me! Now on with the show!
DON JUAN: Ah, this theatre used to be my delight! . . .
                 Why do you bump everything in sight?
PUNCHINELLO: Why does anyone?
                 Singing through my nose, I imitate a fife;
                 Striking mighty blows, I lead a hero's life.
                 Loud and long I sing a bawdy air
                 That someone taught me at a village fair.
                 [*He sings.*]
                 "It's me, the famous Mignolet,
                 A little Spanish martinet
                 Who makes the ladies melt."
                 [DON JUAN *tips his hat and continues the song*]
DON JUAN: "It's me, the famous Burlador,
                 Unlocking every maiden's door
                 With keys from his golden belt."
                 . . . I'm a poet, too.
PUNCHINELLO: If padded verse will do.
DON JUAN: Verses are like women: they must conceal

A certain amount of padding to appeal.

PUNCHINELLO: As always, Don Juan, your words smell of sin.

DON JUAN: You know my name?

PUNCHINELLO: Of course, brother. We're kin.

DON JUAN: In what capacity?

PUNCHINELLO: In lechery.

DON JUAN [*imitating him*]:   "In lechery."
As always, Punch, your words have no diplomacy.

PUNCHINELLO: I am redder than you; you are fatter than me.
But we'll look alike on Judgment Day, you'll see.

DON JUAN: Clown!
[PUNCHINELLO *rings a bell*.]
          What are you ringing?

PUNCHINELLO: The solemn bell-o
That faces poor Don Juan with Punchinello.

DON JUAN: Show some courtesy. Perform for me.

PUNCHINELLO: That I will, but not for courtesy.
I'll do it in honor of—polygamy.

DON JUAN: That's the word for those who hoard their mates.
I took my women and left them to their fates.
Come! Amuse me with your nasal wails.
Give me back my youth. Sing your scales.

PUNCHINELLO: Do . . . re . . . mi . . . fa . . . sol—

DON JUAN: That's it!

PUNCHINELLO: —la . . . ti . . . DOLT!

DON JUAN: I can see him now, a pale little boy
In a huge collar, frightened but filled with joy
To be in the theatre, next to—

PUNCHINELLO: Next to whom?

DON JUAN: The girls! Their joyous laughter filled the room
At all your antic peccadillos.
                    Do . . . re . . . mi—
[*The puppet* CASSANDRA* *appearing on puppet-box stage*]

CASSANDRA: You've seduced my daughter, you filthy pander!

PUNCHINELLO: You bore me.
[*He kills* CASSANDRA.]

DON JUAN: That was the Commander!

*The name does not allude to King Priam's daughter, but to the old dotard of early Italian comedy. [*Editor's note.*]

PUNCHINELLO: I'm in love with Charlotte.
               [*The puppet* PIERROT *appearing on stage*]
PIERROT: She's mine!
PUNCHINELLO: He bores me.
               Dullard!
               [*He kills* PIERROT.]
                       Let him live his own life!
               [*A dog appears, growls, and leaps at Punchinello.*]
                                        He roars me.
               Ha-ha . . . Ouch! He lives his own life—My nose!
               He's bitten my nose!
DON JUAN: How they laughed at your blows.
PUNCHINELLO: Who laughed?
DON JUAN: The girls—all of them so fair!
               I trembled at their beauty, sitting there
               Among their skirts—
PUNCHINELLO: Watching every knee!
DON JUAN: Be quiet!
PUNCHINELLO: Well, as for beauty, you know me.
               But Bayle, that thinking man from Rotterdam,
               As far as beauty was concerned, poor man,
               He didn't seem to be the least bit sure
               Of anyone's beauty, even Helen's.
DON JUAN: That boor!
               Great Helen's beauty? Why, it's the only thing
               Remaining in this world to which I cling.
               Ah, Helen! Helen! Where can she be?
               [*A tiny doll with blonde hair appears in the puppet
               theatre;* DON JUAN *utters a cry of delight.*]
PUNCHINELLO: Back from your Spartan voyage, I see.
DON JUAN: Unfortunately. Under the grizzled skies
               Of this stifling age, alas, great Helen dies.
               [*Contemplating the doll with admiration*]
               My! such a lovely star shedding its light
               On this undistinguished scene.
PUNCHINELLO: The very sight
               Of a stick of wood with a hank of bleached hair
               Is enough to drive away his great despair
               Over the loss of Helen. Well, brother,
               You see in what way we resemble each other?

[*To the Doll*]
I love you!

DON JUAN: We certainly haven't the same approach.

PUNCHINELLO: What's that?

DON JUAN: To say "I love you" now is gauche.

PUNCHINELLO: When *should* I?

DON JUAN: Neither too early—nor too late.
Let me see. You must—seduce her.

PUNCHINELLO: Now wait!
By doing what?

DON JUAN: My friend, that is an art.

PUNCHINELLO: Well, tell me what to do. How should I start?
With my feet?

DON JUAN: Too much. You look like a duck.

PUNCHINELLO: With my eyes?

DON JUAN: Worse! You look thunderstruck.

PUNCHINELLO: Well, how should I look?

DON JUAN: Like an abyss.

PUNCHINELLO: Watch me now—I'm getting deeper. Like this?

DON JUAN: She waits, knowing you're going to win her. You do.
And then you look elsewhere.

PUNCHINELLO: Yes, yes! How true!
Like this?

DON JUAN: Deceive as the horizon might,
Without a lie.

PUNCHINELLO: I'm fading away!

DON JUAN: That's right.
And the lady's prepared to embark. Ah, let us savor
That moment when the gangplank starts to quaver
Beneath her tiny foot. Because the trip,
My friend, is almost never worth the ship.

PUNCHINELLO: It doesn't work.

DON JUAN: Now what do you show her?

PUNCHINELLO: A dirty book?
                              What? Why, then you'll owe her
To Straparola* or Boccaccio.
Never!

---

*Straparola, Giovanni Francesco. Sixteenth-century Italian story writer whose most famous collection, *Tredici Piacevoli Notti* (1550–1553), served as a source for Shakespeare and others. [*Editor's note.*]

PUNCHINELLO [*to the Doll*]:

                Charlotte! Come over here. . . . No?

[*He hits her.*]

                                                Pow!

DON JUAN: We really differ in our methods now.

                One never hits a woman. One makes her suffer.

DOLL [*to Don Juan*]:

                Just a minute! How?

PUNCHINELLO: You filthy bluffer,

                You're trying to steal my doll! Dunderhead!

                [*He strikes the Doll.*]

                She's pure! She's pure!

DON JUAN: She's dead.

PUNCHINELLO: That's what I said!

                [*Throwing the Doll in the air*]

                Hoopla!

DON JUAN: The Devil's next?

PUNCHINELLO: No; the guard.

DON JUAN: Cut the scene with the guard.

PUNCHINELLO: What! Discard

                My best scene? . . . Oh, all right. Then the trial.

DON JUAN: Cut it.

PUNCHINELLO: What? You're ruining my style!

                Oh, very well. Then the execution.

DON JUAN: No.

PUNCHINELLO: If you're going to cut it all, I may as well go.

DON JUAN: You'll have to rearrange your masterpiece

                According to the fashion—and my caprice.

                I happen to think it might be very droll

                To see the Devil seizing someone's soul.

                [PUNCH *rings his bell.*]

DON JUAN: What are you ringing?

PUNCHINELLO: The bell that brings him running.

                [*Trembling*]

                Oh! I'm afraid! I can feel him coming!

                He's going to carry me away! Oh, dear!

DON JUAN: Where is he coming from, I pray? The rear?

                Why look behind you?

                [*Puppet Devil appears in the guignol.*]

DEVIL: Grrrr!

PUNCHINELLO [*hitting him*]:   Pow! Wait! My stick—
    It's broken! Filthy beast!
    [*The* DEVIL *disappears.*]
                            My other one—quick!

DEVIL [*reappearing*]:
    Grrrr!

PUNCHINELLO: Pow! It's impossible!

DON JUAN: Certainly.
    One should never hit the Devil, you see.

PUNCHINELLO: I suppose you want to make *him* suffer, too?

DON JUAN: But of course, stupid.

DEVIL: Just a minute, you!
    How?

DON JUAN: You shall see—when you are bigger.

DEVIL: Rat!

PUNCHINELLO: [*Hits the* DEVIL *with every word*]
    Pow! Another stick! Pow! Another! Take that!

DON JUAN: Control yourself.

PUNCHINELLO: But I'm afraid.

DON JUAN: That's wrong.
    Without fear, without remorse, and strong—

DEVIL: One lives his life.

DON JUAN: —and dies his death.
    [*The* DEVIL *has thrown* PUNCHINELLO *over his shoulder
    and is about to carry him away.*]

PUNCHINELLO: I don't care!
    What good is courage? I'm dying! It isn't fair!

DON JUAN [*to the Devil*]:
    Just like that, you carry off a soul?

DEVIL: Frightening, isn't it?

DON JUAN: No; it's rather droll.
    Strange, how badly he's taking it.

DEVIL: And you,
    I suppose, would take it very well?

DON JUAN: Quite true.

DEVIL: You would make me suffer?

DON JUAN: Naturally.
    Does that distress you?

DEVIL: No; it rather intrigues me.
    [*His voice changing suddenly*]

Let's toss this corpse aside for a moment or two.
[*He does so.*]
Now then, I'd like to know by what means you—

DON JUAN: Well, no more Italian accent, I see.

DEVIL: —would make me suffer?

DON JUAN: It's obvious to me
How much you suffer when you suspend a soul
Above the horrors of that smouldering hole
And he refuses to blanch. It gives you pause.
Oh, yes! When you have seized him in your claws
You'd prefer to see him clinging in despair
To every pillar, as you drag him by his hair.
The horns above that fire-breathing snout
Wait only for the sniveling, hopeless lout.
While *I*—even when you have undone me,
Fiend, you'll not have absolutely won me.

DEVIL: "Won" you? Oh—ha-ha-ha! I like that! "Won" you!

DON JUAN: To win me one would have to strike me down,
Have me raging and shouting like this clown,
Or heavy-lidded, pale and panting, out of breath,
As I had my women. Upright, I face my death!
Laughing, I stand beneath the door of Hell;
Dante's famous phrase is not for me.
Those blazing hooks of yours will never be
As burning as one memory. Like Nero,
I am what I am.

DEVIL: And that is—what?

DON JUAN: A hero
The greatest son of the Conquistadors—
And Woman is my Peru! I've fought my wars.
As brave as they but greedier, I always see
From conquered Indies *new* Indies beckoning me.
Those foolish speculators who believed
I would repent at the last are much deceived.
They have not seen me in my greatest hour,
Stealing from some conquered maiden's bower.
I am a monster with a mangled wing,
A black Archangel, scorning everything.
And if, when I pass, a sudden sigh should cause
A ruffled blouse to stir, it is because

I was not made like Punchinello here,
His coffin on his back.*

DEVIL: You have no fear?

DON JUAN: Neither of you, nor of yours. I'll persevere.

DEVIL: My flames?

DON JUAN: I can face them.

DEVIL: My horns?

DON JUAN: I embrace them.
The bravest of men are afraid. They used to say
That Marshal Trivulse** had a fit on the fatal day
At the mere sight of your imps. Not I, I trust!
I've never trembled at anything but lust.

DEVIL: You! You're going to squirm like a drowning rat.
I seize only the vanquished.

DON JUAN: Remember that
And I'm saved.

DEVIL [stretching out his hand]:
                          Agreed!

DON JUAN: Your hand on it!

DEVIL: Your hand!
[The DEVIL disappears.]

DON JUAN: What am I doing? I don't understand—
I only drank a drop. I feel quite steady.
What am I waiting for when now already
The time for my delightful ball is here?
Why did I—
[A clock strikes in the puppet theatre.]
                 That clock is striking. Queer.
[A searchlight on the sea goes out.]
That beacon on the water—it's gone out.
What on earth possessed me to babble about
My intimate affairs? The things I said!
Things I've never mentioned. I lost my head. . . .
Ah, well, Don Juan, let's go. Time for the ball.
You only lost a couplet; it's nothing at all.
There's not a moment to waste.
[At this moment the old puppeteer reappears. His dis-

*Alludes to Punchinello's humpback. [Editor's note.]
**Trivulse, Jean-Jacques (1448–1518), a prominent army commander during the reign of Louis XII. [Editor's note.]

guise is gone and we see him as he really is: no pup-
peteer, but the DEVIL *himself.*]
                                      Ah, it was you!
I understand my couplet now.

DEVIL: How do you do?
"Remember Punchinello, sir?"—A dole?

DON JUAN: What do you want?

DEVIL: Your soul, Don Juan, your soul!

DON JUAN: Adieu then, fickle women! Adieu!

DEVIL: The old puppeteer has come for you.
Tonight my sack is loaded with human pelf:
A judge, a king, a beggar, and now—yourself.
Profiting from a couple of lucky accidents,
I've swept two senators from their constituents.
Come into my sack?

DON JUAN: Thank you, no.
I'll walk.

DEVIL: The old puppeteer has a charming show—
In Hell.

DON JUAN: How clumsy! Age was my only fear.
The cruelest thing would be to leave me here.
Instead, you come for me now, raving of Hell,
And saving me from senility's dry farewell.
It's quite naïve; you've lost your strongest hold.

DEVIL: I know you better than that. You'd never grow old.

DON JUAN: Come, then. I've no objection to your claws.
Remove your gloves, take a moment's pause
And join me in a quiet little bite.

DEVIL: Ah, how gay! The bachelor's last rite.
Two velvet chairs?

DON JUAN: Always.

DEVIL: Two places laid?

DON JUAN: Always. I'm always prepared for the Devil, you see,
Or the Queen of the Nile. It's all the same to me.
Should the Queen arrive, *c'est bien!*
And should the Devil arrive—amen!
[*Music is heard playing softly.*]
My orchestra, in the distance.

DEVIL: Always?

DON JUAN: Always.
Not bad, eh?

DEVIL: Let's go.
DON JUAN: Good. No delays.
                        My coat. Like it?
DEVIL: Superb.
DON JUAN: It has to be.
                        Very important, that. Shall we go? You see—
                        Look at it carefully—notice the sleeve?
                        A little better cut than these, I believe.
                        [*Indicating the Devil's sleeves*]
                        Your gondola is waiting on the lagoon?
                        [*He calls out.*]
                        Charon! . . . It's always Charon, I presume?
DEVIL: I'll have to admit you have amazing gall.
DON JUAN: Oh, yes, I'm famous for it.
DEVIL: As I recall,
                        The weaker sex demands it.
DON JUAN: Shall we go?
DEVIL: Not yet.
DON JUAN: It vexes you to take me below
                        In such a pleasant fashion?
DEVIL: Let us dine.
DON JUAN: No doubt you're hoping that a glass of wine
                        Is going to weaken my head?
                        [*The two move toward the table.*]
DEVIL: We shall see.
DON JUAN [*indicating wine*]:
                        Dry or sweet?
DEVIL: Dry.
DON JUAN: Personally
                        I rather like these roses on the table.
                        Do you? I happen to be extremely able
                        At handling all these little details—and more.
DEVIL: Also very important?
DON JUAN: Note the decor.
                        The finest furniture—Brustolone!
DEVIL: Really? That furniture is still well known?
DON JUAN: This little bibelot's designed to embarrass
                        Even Venus.
DEVIL: You weave?
DON JUAN: Only an arras
                        For a bedroom. A little tapestry

Makes a charming background for adultery.
You like the menu?

DEVIL: You cook?

DON JUAN: Well, naturally!
Who could deny the value of the juices
That moisten the Romany hare, the lard that spruces
The Lombard quail? The proper food is a must.
One should have a painting or two, a bust,
A few of the latest books, strategically placed . . .
It's not so simple. A woman requires taste.

DEVIL: How interesting! You conduct, you cook, you weave!

DON JUAN: By heaven, you're incredibly naïve!
Sin must be intriguing, fascinating;
Even you must find it stimulating.
That reminds me: why are you in black?
It's absolutely wrong. Quite stupid, in fact.

DEVIL: Really?

DON JUAN: What caused this gloomy spectacle?

DEVIL: The inkwell peevish Luther threw at my skull.

DON JUAN: I liked you better in green.

DEVIL: You saw me?

DON JUAN: Before the Fall
In Eden, with Eve.

DEVIL: Then you—

DON JUAN: I was Adam.

DEVIL: You recall?

DON JUAN: In dreams. I still imagine I can see
The two of us beneath that gnarled tree.
What was the mystery you taught us then?
No one knew it. I was the first of men.
I bit into an apple and saw your twin
Undulating, supple and white, within,
As you were undulating, supple and green,
Above in the tree.

DEVIL: Ah, the worm. Unseen.

DON JUAN: I spat it out. You said to me: "Now then,
You must bite into another." But again
Within another fruit the same worm hid.
I spat. You said: "Try another." I did.
A worm! I bit. A worm! I bit. Another worm!

"Every beautiful fruit conceals a worm.
That secret's been revealed to no other man,"
You said. "Try to live with it, if you can."

DEVIL: Well, *try!*

DON JUAN: We did—and succeeded immediately!
The foliage which later gave her cover
Gave the female first of all—her lover.
We soon discovered other appetites,
And buried our taste for apples in other delights.

DEVIL: And thus—Don Juan!

DON JUAN: Thus the hero we know,
Avenging himself and shouting with every blow:
"On guard, Archangel! Defend thy Master's Paradise;
Protect the apples in which the maggot lies.
As for me, I renounce it. I'll joyfully replace
Jacob's ladder with a ladder of feminine lace.
I mock the Paradise reserved to the unstained."
And for one Paradise lost a thousand are regained.

DEVIL: A thousand and three. These diatribes that reek
Of Ecclesiastes aren't exactly unique.

DON JUAN: If everything is nothing—

DEVIL: Then it must follow
That nothing is everything. What logic! Bravo!

DON JUAN: Well, I knew how to create a substitute
More satisfying than that wormy fruit.

DEVIL: And what about Heaven?

DON JUAN: Heaven is the prize
That lies within a pair of loving eyes,
Waiting for my own specific uses.

DEVIL: And truth?

DON JUAN: Issuing from a well of excuses,
It is a woman.

DEVIL: And glory?

DON JUAN: There's only one:
That single, wordless victory which is won
Whenever Woman looses her tiny sandal.

DEVIL: Then you're delighted to have been—

DON JUAN: A vandal!
A hero to whom the whole of humanity looks
With admiration. Only read their books—

Look at their plays—listen to them sigh.
Virtue detests me, with such a gleam in her eye!
Every boorish lout prays for the power
To act as I do, if only for an hour.
Professors poke their analytic noses
Into each of my alluring poses.
Secretly they all admire me
For daring the kiss they are too cowardly
To dare. I represent the thing they miss.
There is no work—despite your adder's hiss—
No virtue, science, or faith that cannot be
Reduced to this: the wish to be like me.

DEVIL: And what is left to you?

DON JUAN: Whatever's left
In Alexander's ashes. Though bereft
He knows he was Alexander. I acted alone,
However, and having acted on my own
I possessed alone.

DEVIL: What is that?—"possess?"
"Possess." That's *their* word for it, I guess.
Well, then, tell me, dear immoralist,
What have you "possessed?"

DON JUAN: Sganarelle!

[SGANARELLE *enters; he is terrified at the sight of the Devil.*]

                                                 My list!

SGANARELLE: Heaven protect me!

DON JUAN: Here, take the ruby and go.

SGANARELLE [*to the Devil*]:
Get thee behind me!

    [*to Don Juan*]   Is that all?
No last requests?

DON JUAN: Not that I recall.

[SGANARELLE *goes.*]

DEVIL: No one? Not even a son?

DON JUAN: Not one heir.
Remember Silenus? After all his care
What thanks did he get? His son watered his wine.
To be betrayed like that by a son of mine?
Never! Curtain. *Finis.* Shall we go?

DEVIL: Not yet.
That word "possess"—it has me quite upset.
It has a meaning in the Devil's plan,
Of course, but what on earth does it mean to Man?
"Possess." Hmmmm. "Possess." If you don't mind,
I'd like to have that active verb defined.

DON JUAN: You old satyr! I can see obscenity
Glittering in your yellow eye.

DEVIL: Oh, pardon me!
Did I put my foot in it?

DON JUAN: Your hoof, you mean.

DEVIL: "And they all went to bed." I have seen
That phrase in Marlborough. It's rather flat.
Is *that* what it means—"possess"? No worse than that?

DON JUAN: "And then he knew her," as the Bible says.
To "know"—that is the meaning of "possess."
To know! To really know! And you can see
How terrible that kind of thing could be.

DEVIL: Ah, then one must "know" if one is to—

DON JUAN: Possess.

DEVIL: I see. And you have "known" them?

DON JUAN: Completely, yes!
I have pressed their naked souls against me.
No one better knows their ecstasy.
Who? Lauzun? Richelieu? Blunderers!
They couldn't touch me. They were amateurs,
While I, through years of practice, developed skill.
Ah, those hankies left behind on my sill,
Crumpled with rage. May I tear the list apart?

DEVIL: Of course. Destroy it.

DON JUAN: I know the names by heart.

DEVIL: By all means, tear it up. You're about to die.

DON JUAN: I know the name, the date, the reason, the lie.
Every secret is there. Here I stand
Toying with all the memories I command,
Dipping into nights and mornings in wonder,
A pensive victor toying with his plunder.
I'd tell you all there was to know, my friend,
If I thought you had the time to spend.
For any one of them to reappear

I've only to take her name and place it here
Between my lips, like a flower.

DEVIL: Let us destroy
These little fragments of your heart, my boy.
We'll put them in your hat.

DON JUAN: What's more, I swear,
There wasn't a tart among them anywhere.

DEVIL: Tear up the list! We'll make a thousand and three!

DON JUAN: Because I really wanted desperately
To feel remorse—

DEVIL: Tear it up, I said!

DON JUAN: And like the lion who never touches the dead,
I handled only flesh that smelled of soul. . . .
Together you and I shall destroy the whole.
Down with womankind!
[*They begin to tear up the list.*]

DEVIL: You've run the gamut, I see.
The entire alphabet, from A to Z.

DON JUAN: Z?—Ah, Zulma! Well, that ends the receipts.
Only a few B's—There! The four Brigittes.
That's it! Finished!

DEVIL: Now—
[*He produces a little violin, as if by magic, with a quick gesture of his hand.*]

DON JUAN: That's quite a trick.

DEVIL: Quite so. My fiddle—and my fiddlestick.
I always carry them about with me;
The old puppeteer's a ballet-master, you see,
Who causes even the sleeping leaves to spin.
[*To the violin*]
Sing for me now. Sing, little violin!
The Devil's going to play with you. Begin!
Fiddle made of wood, sing of the plight
Of lovers made of wood. Sing tonight,
Beneath my wooden bow, of maidenhood.
Sing a song of the great Don Juan of Wood.
[*He continues playing, murmuring softly, as if to conjure the torn scraps of paper that are strewn about the floor. And as he plays on, the scraps begin to move mysteriously.*]

DEVIL: Dance, little remains of a lecher's life! Be quick!

DON JUAN: What's wrong? You're dancing like a lunatic.

DEVIL: A gavotte! The Gavotte for a Torn List!—Shh!

[*He resumes playing.*]

Little souls, awakened by your names,

Like the phoenix, rise again in flames.

[*The little scraps of paper begin to move faster and faster, until as if caught up in a whirlwind, they fly into the air.*]

DON JUAN: What is it? Where are they going?

DEVIL: They're taking flight;

They're flying away. Ah! Fly! Into the night!

Away! Away with you, little butterflies,

You're all that remains of a life. Rise! Rise!

Fly away, white, white! Over the lagoon!

[*The tiny scraps, whirling wildly, scatter into the distance and fall like snow upon the lagoon.*]

And now the Devil's going to change his tune.

A farandole!

Over the water a sudden wind blows,

And every one of these tender morsels grows.

Holding its amorous name, each one begets

One of a thousand and three silhouettes:

A floating gondola—a gliding soul—

DON JUAN: What ghostly fleet is this?

DEVIL: A barcarolle!

These gondolas are like the loves you enjoyed,

Cradled, embraced, lulled, and then destroyed.

Watch them. Each is an alcove; each is a tomb.

DON JUAN: How quickly they seem to move beneath the moon.

DEVIL: See them darting back and forth. There—

Over the water. Sombre—sharp—spare—

DON JUAN: Still more of them are coming.

DEVIL: A thousand and one . . .

Two . . . three.

[*Calling to the gondolas now seen dimly in the distance*]

                  This way! Come! Come!

DON JUAN: Each one is a drifting star.

DEVIL: Over here!

My gesture is their only gondolier.
Would you like the one with the emerald flare
To bring its phantom to the foot of the stair?

DON JUAN [*shuddering*]:
What?

DEVIL: Or shall I hail that ruby glow?

DON JUAN: These floating fancies aren't empty?

DEVIL: Why, no.
Every gondola holds within its prow
The ghost of a former love, forgotten now,
A name from your list, floating on the sea.
I'm even stronger than Paracelsus, you see,
For I double the living, awaken the dead again.
Which of them would you like to see, then,
Rising from her cushion of black velour?
Which ghostly memory shall I conjure?
Which golden slipper shall rest upon the stair?

DON JUAN: Why . . . several.

DEVIL [*shouting to them*]:   Disembark! You there!
[*Taking the gilt candelabra from the table,* DON JUAN
stations himself at the head of the stairs, motionless.]

DON JUAN: The phantoms—they're ascending.
[*A few* GHOSTS *emerge from the shadows.*]

DEVIL: You will find
Every one of them concealed behind
A white Venetian mask.

DON JUAN: White slippers, your bloom
Overwhelms the marble with perfume.
[*Setting the candelabra down,* DON JUAN *throws himself into a chair. The* DEVIL *dances about, playing the
little violin.*]

DEVIL: You there! Over here!

GHOSTS: Good evening, Don Juan.

DEVIL: All ashore, ladies. Hurry along.
[*The* GHOSTS *continue to appear. All are masked and
wearing long cloaks. Each carries a fan and a rose.*]

DON JUAN: They keep appearing. Surely this must be
The way that Venus herself arose from the sea.

DEVIL: And—note—the luscious Venus Longhi painted,

Not the dowdy virgin Watteau sainted.
He doesn't exist any more, the sweet Watteau,
When one arrives on the other side, you know.

DON JUAN: Silver phantoms, rising from the sea—

DEVIL: And each of them is dressed identically.
There, swathed in frail attire, disguised,
The whole of womankind is symbolized:
Her rose, her cloak, her mask, and last, her fan.

DON JUAN: Yes . . . The rose, the cloak, the mask, and the fan.

MORE GHOSTS: Good evening, Don Juan.

DON JUAN: Ladies, will you take
A piece of luscious fruit? A little cake?
An ice, perhaps? You'll keep your fan and rose,
Of course, but may I help you to dispose
Of your cloaks and masks?
[*The* DEVIL *raps the violin with his bow.*]

DEVIL [*sharply*]:

                                          Oh no you don't, my man!
[DON JUAN *rises, looking at the Devil with surprise.*
The DEVIL *bows, and speaks more calmly.*]
Each must act according to my plan.
Wrapped in her cloak, hidden behind her fan,
And toying with the petals of her rose,
She'll whisper in your ear a phrase she chose
To reveal her identity. If you recall—
If you can say her name, her mask will fall.
[*A* GHOST *approaches Don Juan and whispers in his
ear.*]

GHOST: I . . .

DON JUAN: So low?

DEVIL: Unless you should find in the crowd
A woman who wishes to speak of it aloud.

DON JUAN [*caressing Ghost's hand*]:
                You—you—

DEVIL: Only her *soul*, don't forget.
Not her body.

DON JUAN: You say you always felt regret?
Every time? Your virtue was ironclad;
I always knew it. Lucille!

GHOST: Rogue!
DON JUAN: Not bad,
            Was it?
GHOST: Just by saying—
DON JUAN: Lucille! You see?
GHOST: You could almost convince me that I am she.
DON JUAN: You mean—
GHOST: No!
DON JUAN: But you—
SECOND GHOST: Now, let *me!*
            [*Whispers to him.*]
DON JUAN: You—
            [*Again* DON JUAN *tries to touch the* GHOST's *hand; the*
            DEVIL *raps him across the knuckles with his bow.*]
DEVIL: I said *forget* the body.
DON JUAN: —still the same.
            You—How could I ever forget your name?
            It's you! There were fireworks that night;
            Your mother and her dog were lost from sight.
SECOND GHOST: I'm afraid I was very bad.
DON JUAN: A silly fear.
            You were really very good, my dear
            —Suzanne!
SECOND GHOST: No!
DON JUAN: But these details!
DEVIL: Like others.
DON JUAN: Now that you mention it, there were many mothers
            And dogs . . . And fireworks.
THIRD GHOST: Let me try.
DON JUAN: Ahhh—you!
            [GHOST *whispers to him.*]
            What? A little disappointed? *Quite?*
            But no one could make love at such a height.
            Your highness, you were always too serene.
THIRD GHOST: No!
FOURTH GHOST: And I?
            [*Whispers*]
DON JUAN: Aha! The villa in Bellagio!
            Miss Ethel!
FOURTH GHOST: No!

DON JUAN: What's that?
DEVIL: Not Ethel at all.
          Only "Miss."
DON JUAN: Then wait. Let me try to recall
          Where did I know this tender heart? Let me see . . .
          Ah! The caretaker's daughter! The university!
FOURTH GHOST: No!
FIFTH GHOST: It's my turn.
          [*Whispers*]
DON JUAN: Ah, you I knew from the first.
          An evening at the bullfights—a heart that burst
          Like an enormous pink in bloom. Conchita!
FIFTH GHOST: No!
SIXTH GHOST: And I?
          [*Whispers*]   .
DON JUAN: Ah, this time—
DEVIL: Who is she?
DON JUAN: —I know!
          My aunt, who was so jealous of my niece.
SIXTH GHOST: No!
DON JUAN: You don't say!
          [SEVENTH GHOST *whispers to him.*]
                                I know this little piece!
          Your words betrayed you, little did you know.
          Unmask your Kalmuck nose, Princess Olga.
SEVENTH GHOST: No!
DON JUAN: What?
EIGHTH GHOST: And I?
          [*Whispers to him*]
DON JUAN: Ah, Lucy! You read Brantôme.*
EIGHTH GHOST: No!
          [DON JUAN *angrily pushes her away.*]
DON JUAN: Agh!
DEVIL: Leave my phantoms alone.
          Gently does it.
DON JUAN: But they're deceiving me.
DEVIL: They're telling you the truth.
DON JUAN: We shall see!

*The Abbé de Brantôme (c. 1540–1614), soldier, courtier, and author of intimate and chatty *Memoirs*. [*Editor's note.*]

[NINTH GHOST *approaches him.* DON JUAN *bends his head to listen. He turns to the* DEVIL.]
She said nothing.

DEVIL: That's what it was, obviously—
Nothing.

DON JUAN: Lucille . . . Anna . . . Emma . . . Zoe . . .

DEVIL: Search.

TENTH GHOST: Let *me* try.

DON JUAN: You! Help me!
He's turned his back. Quickly, take off your mask.
[*The* GHOST *unmasks, revealing another mask beneath the first.*]
Another?
[*As the* GHOST *continues to remove a succession of masks*]
                    Another? Another? An endless task!
What? Still another in its place?

DEVIL: She is one of those who has no face,
Only an everlasting series of masks.

DON JUAN: I can't be drunk—the wine's still in the flasks—
And yet I'm terrified of all these eyes.
The way they stare at me—they seem so wise.
That's it. Their eyes I have a right to control;
They don't belong to the body, but the soul.
These eyes are going to enlighten me.
No? My confusion's worse. They frighten me.
They used to be enigmatic—

DEVIL: That troubles you?

DON JUAN: It's hard to recognize them now.

DEVIL: Quite true.
Without flesh, without hair, and—worse—
Without a hat.

DON JUAN: They used to be so perverse,
Like the eyes of Bacchantes.

DEVIL: Well, never mind.
Perhaps Bacchantes aren't so easy to find,
After all.

DON JUAN: I've never seen them so clear.

DEVIL: Yes, tonight their eyes are quite sincere.
This is a gaze that men have never known,
A look every woman has when she's alone.

DON JUAN: You lie.
[Laughter from the GHOSTS.*]*
             Go ahead, laugh! I know your lies.
I knew you'd betray yourselves. I have eyes.
Your throats shook with laughter when you spoke.
[To the Devil]
What are they so amused at? Am I a joke?

DEVIL: This is the laughter women share together.
Not a single man has known it, ever.

DON JUAN: *I've* known it.

DEVIL: Does anyone really know?

DON JUAN: It's no use your making such a show,
Hopping about like a monkey. I'll conquer you;
I'll recognize them no matter what you do.
I'll take this torch, and—

ELEVENTH GHOST: Ha!

DON JUAN: That laugh I know.
It's Angela Tarabotti, from Monaco.

ELEVENTH GHOST:
     Sorry. No!
[A new contingent of GHOSTS *appears.]*
               Still more of them arise?

DEVIL: Over here! Disembark!

DON JUAN: By heaven, those eyes,
I know them! One of you I recognize.
Come, look at me—look at me, do you hear!
Don't laugh. Elvira's there with you, it's clear.
I recognized your voice, Elvira.

DEVIL: Then search.
[The DEVIL *laughs mockingly.]*

DON JUAN: Throughout the night, if I must, I'll scrutinize
Every single pair of mocking eyes.
I'll hold this light to every pallid brow
And probe those two abysses till, somehow,
I recognize one soul.

DEVIL: Sing, little violin!
[Furious, DON JUAN *turns on him with a cry of anger.]*
Why these rages? Search.

DON JUAN: Now, to begin—
Throughout the night, if I must. I'll conquer him.
My errors aren't important anyhow.

DON JUAN:
I'll begin again from the beginning. Now—
Those eyes, those dramatic eyes—Olga?

TWELFTH GHOST: No!

DON JUAN: Those romantic eyes. Lucy?

THIRTEENTH GHOST: No!

DON JUAN: Oh!
I must be calm. Begin again. . . . So—
From the beginning. Let's see. Over there . . .
I must be calm. Those eyes—so aware.
It is . . . It is . . . It is . . .
[*As the curtain closes, he is moving through the crowd
of phantoms, his torch held before him, murmuring
names.*]

PART II

Same scene. Dawn is beginning to break. DON JUAN *is still searching
the throng of Ghosts, muttering names as he goes.*

DEVIL: And so again,
Aurora will find you seeking Woman in vain,
O Diogenes, flushed by the candle's flame!

DON JUAN: Oh!
[*He flings the candelabra aside.*]
            To think I've tasted sleep in all these arms!

DEVIL: Yes.

DON JUAN: All night long I've scrutinized their charms,
Spouting names, searching this ghostly throng,
And still I—
[*He makes one last attempt.*]
                    Lucille?

GHOST: No.

DON JUAN: I'm always wrong.
All these names, swooping back and forth, distressed,
Like birds in frightened flight, never finding rest.
Did we really love?

GHOSTS: We loved.

DON JUAN: Like stone
I stand in the midst of a forest of souls, alone.
All of them are there—but I've sought! I've sought!

I spent my life on loves that came to naught,
Ignoring those that might have made me whole.
And now I die, not having known one soul.

DEVIL: Nothing is "possessed," my haughty friend,
Nothing is what you learned, nothing your end.

GHOST: Oh fisher, who lusts for pearls and never dives,
You took the easy and the quick—

DON JUAN: Your lies!

ANOTHER GHOST:
Did you ask for truth? No! Man requires,
With his every word, that women be liars.

ANOTHER GHOST:
A "blue stocking" chanced to be your current fad,
And so I spoke of Petrarch. Was that bad?

ANOTHER GHOST:
You wanted from me the strange, the exotic, somehow;
You wanted—I didn't know what, but I *did* know how!

ANOTHER GHOST:
You seemed to be looking around for a country lass:
To please you I minced and lisped, like a silly ass.

ANOTHER GHOST:
You happened to feel like stealing a rival's toy,
And so I played with my husband to give you joy.

ANOTHER GHOST:
The Delilahs and their kind were made by Man
And every clever woman knows the plan.
At the hour when Desire steals his wit
She returns to Man his little counterfeit:
Eternal Woman, delicate and pale . . .
Eternal Woman . . . masterpiece of the male!

DEVIL: Then your conquests were enigmas; I have good cause
To seize you now.

DON JUAN: No! Sheathe your claws!
Did my forebears conquer the Indies any the less
Because the Indians remained mysterious?

DEVIL: Then, to "possess"—

DON JUAN: —is to rule! My energy
Drove that spirit known to philosophy
As the Spirit of—of—

DEVIL: The Spirit of Power?

DON JUAN: Yes, I've dominated. I never cower.
              Half Machiavelli, half Aretino, free—
DEVIL: How jolly to have passed through Italy!
              Good little Andalusian, greedy and vain,
              Although you journeyed far from your domain,
              You merely stole from every nationality
              Some useless baggage from its sensuality.
DON JUAN: I corrupted!
DEVIL: Is that what you revel in?
              [*To the Ghosts*]
              Exactly when did you first taste your desire for sin?
GHOSTS: The first day!—The first night!—On seeing him!—
              Long before I saw him the thought was there!—
              After I singled him out he began to stare!
DON JUAN: But there were virgins—
DEVIL: So they're called, I know,
              The ones who make their choice without a show.
DON JUAN: But I seduced them—
GHOSTS: After we persuaded you!
DON JUAN: How?
GHOSTS: By the sign.
OTHER GHOSTS: Yes, the sign.
DON JUAN: That can't be true.
              There were noble ladies—
ANOTHER GHOST: They know the sign.
              With them it's just a little more refined.
DON JUAN: But I—
GHOSTS: Remember: Everything!—Nothing!—That perfume!—
              That baby suddenly embraced!—That crushed
                 bloom!—
              That nervous laugh, which falls like shattered glass—
DEVIL: —That sudden silence, during which I pass.
DON JUAN: But then—
GHOSTS: Remember?
DON JUAN: It isn't true! Liars!
A GHOST: You haughtily dictated our own desires.
DON JUAN: But those little Cinderellas that ran in fright?
DEVIL: With a touch of lost slipper in their flight!
ANOTHER GHOST:
              That ladder of feminine lace on which you climbed

Was only a ladder of cobwebs, you will find.

DON JUAN: But I spent my life—

DEVIL: Believing you were the first
To corrupt the hearts that I had already rehearsed!

DON JUAN: But my seductions—

DEVIL: "Oh, how I seduce,"
Says the iron to the magnet. It's no use!

ANOTHER GHOST:
You happened to be the only man in sight
Who offered his services, either day or night.

ANOTHER GHOST:
Oh, how we used to laugh at you, Don Juan!

ANOTHER GHOST:
What was he, really?

ANOTHER GHOST: A pawn! Only a pawn!

DON JUAN: I thought myself a wolf in a savage wood.
What was I? A ferret nesting in firewood!

ALL GHOSTS [*singing as they gather around Don Juan*]:
Through the wood, the savage wood,
The wolf will run, will run . . .
But in any wood, in any wood,
The ferret has his fun!

THE DEVIL [*tapping a Ghost over the heart with his bow*]:
He runs this way!
[*Tapping another*]
                              He runs that way!
[*And throwing himself suddenly upon Don Juan*]
Now I've got you! Deceived, betrayed, in pain—

DON JUAN [*shaking him off*]:
Not yet!

DEVIL [*recoiling, staring at him*]:
                    What further pride can you retain?

DON JUAN: There is still—

DEVIL: Ah! You continue to fight?

DON JUAN: Ah! You want to take away my right?
[*He staggers slightly, passing his hand across his perspiring brow, and then continues, almost to himself.*]
This is my greatest duel.

DEVIL: And your last!
What is this new pride?

DON JUAN: A pride that's cast
As iron is.

DEVIL: We'll file it down—and fast!

DON JUAN: Iron, sensing in itself some special thing,
Superior to others, which makes the magnet cling.

DEVIL: Ah, I see! Then this is your final plea,
Your pride in having pleased?

DON JUAN: Terribly!
When such a healthy number of women care,
How can any virile man despair?
What's more, I've given them all a world of pleasure.
And isn't pleasing another the greatest measure
Of any man's inherent worth?

DEVIL: *Chi lo sa?*
A foolish woman's disdain created Spinoza,
And Michelangelo's art was only a quirk
Until he broke his nose.

DON JUAN: An artist's work!
You see!

DEVIL: Very well; you pleased! But why?
Go and ask them why!

DON JUAN [*to one of the Ghosts*]: You there!

GHOST [*approaching, with a little laugh*]: I?

DON JUAN [*suddenly*]:
It might be better not to know.

DEVIL: Oh, excellent! He's trembling so!

DON JUAN: Tell me why.

GHOST: You had a certain perfume—

DON JUAN: Of mystery?

GHOST: —of tobacco and the fencing room.

ANOTHER GHOST:
For all the reasons that made the men abhor you.

ANOTHER GHOST:
Because we always used to blush before you.

ANOTHER GHOST:
Because we seemed to be your sole profession.

ANOTHER GHOST:
And then, you always seemed to give the impression
You had nothing else to do.

ANOTHER GHOST: Your audacity!

ANOTHER GHOST:
>   You had a most amazing capacity!

SEVERAL GHOSTS:
>   You had a way of removing our stays—and then
>   Such a gallant way of putting them on again!

ANOTHER GHOST:
>   For Woman enjoys Don Juan
>   As Man does his courtesan.

DEVIL:
>   Well, if it's satisfying to have been
>   Such a vile connoisseur of sin,
>   In your last hour, Prince Charming—

DON JUAN:
>   No, I detest it!

DEVIL:
>   But nothing else is left; you've confessed it.

DON JUAN:
>   There is still one thing. There is still . . .
>   Ahh—I can sense it. Little by little he'll kill
>   Everything that's left to me. It's absurd!

DEVIL:
>   I pluck his feathers, then I broil the Blue Bird!

DON JUAN:
>   There's still my courage! They took me for a fool
>   Because I mocked them. Damn their ridicule!
>   I was a shaker of the torch, I say!
>   They tricked me—but I was the first to run away.

GHOSTS:
>   "He runs this way! He runs that way!" *Très gai!*

DON JUAN:
>   What do you mean? I've always scorned the past,
>   Always leapt beyond myself . . . to the last.
>   I've followed every instinct ruthlessly,
>   Flirted dangerously with destiny,
>   Transgressing all their glib morality.
>   Don't you think I've lived courageously?
>   I've run my life without a law, without a rule—

DEVIL:
>   You've been reading what they write about you, fool!

DON JUAN:
>   I've pushed ahead throughout these ten long years,
>   Following my—

DEVIL:
>   No! You've run from your fears.

DON JUAN:
>   What? *I*—afraid?

DEVIL:
>   Of stopping, yes.

DON JUAN:
>   *I*—afraid?

DEVIL:
>   You fled from the distress
>   Of loving anyone, even for a day.
>   Ha! The hero of love was running away
>   From love itself.

DON JUAN: *Afraid!*

DEVIL: So you withdrew,
          Afraid to be the first to the rendezvous,
          Afraid of waiting—

DON JUAN: *I,* the joyous offender!

GHOSTS: Who positively trembled at being tender.

DON JUAN: When I made love, I used to sing like a lark.

GHOST: You were only whistling in the dark.

ANOTHER GHOST [*louder and louder*]:
          You ran from woman to woman constantly,
          As a man fleeing an archer he cannot see
          Will run in desperation from tree to tree.

ANOTHER GHOST [*in a piercing voice*]:
          From every body he touched, he stole some part
          To build a wall against some former heart.

ANOTHER GHOST:
          He was afraid!

ALL GHOSTS [*shouting*]:   He was afraid!

A GHOST [*gravely*]:   Of sorrow's toll.

ANOTHER GHOST:
          Afraid of sorrow's chisel, the sculptor of the soul,
          Something every man has the right to demand,
          But only from the touch of a woman's hand.

ANOTHER GHOST:
          Coward! You swindled Heaven by your abuse;
          You lived in a temple never marked by use.

ALL GHOSTS: Coward!

DON JUAN [*shaking his fist at them*]:
                    Spiteful females! That's what you say
          Because I was always the first to run away,
          And not yourselves.

DEVIL: Then that's your latest pride—
          That you were always the first to run and hide?

DON JUAN: No.

DEVIL: Then what *is?*

DON JUAN: Oh!

DEVIL [*shaking him, with a triumphant laugh*]:
          Can you possibly find another way
          To twist reality? What more can you say?
          Your life was nothing but a foolish game.

Search! Search! Does anything else remain?

DON JUAN: There is—

DEVIL: More agony?

DON JUAN [*getting to his feet, with despair*]:
                What?

DEVIL [*coldly*]:   *Agonia*, in Greek.

DON JUAN: My very agony reveals the pride I seek.

DEVIL [*smiling*]:
    You've found another stick, like Punchinello.

DON JUAN: I am what I always was, a daring fellow,
    Laughing at cuckoldry. There is no other
    Who can match me: the world's greatest lover!

DEVIL: Ha! The mention of a certain male
    Would be enough to make you go quite pale.

DON JUAN: Who?

HALF OF GHOSTS: Tristan!

OTHER HALF: Romeo!

DON JUAN: Be quiet, I say!

HALF OF GHOSTS: Tristan!

OTHER HALF: Romeo!

A GHOST: The real lovers were they!
    You only triumphed through the disarray
    Their names had left within our hearts. Pilferer!
    You did nothing but subdue the wounded, sir.

DON JUAN: Not so! My name is in your memory.

GHOSTS: Look inside our hearts; it's theirs you'll see.

DON JUAN: Oh!

GHOSTS: Tristan! Romeo!

A GHOST: They're the gods we cry for.
    We lie with you, but these are the men we'd die for.

GHOSTS: Tristan!

A GHOST: Go, hero! Kill them in a duel!

DON JUAN: Be quiet!

A GHOST: You suffer from the comparison
    Because you possessed every woman—and therefore
      none!

DON JUAN: At least I made them suffer in their love.

GHOST: A suffering you understood nothing of.

DON JUAN: What does it matter? Attila ravaged races
    He did not understand. I ravaged faces.

I'm still the scourge of the greatest gods, you know,
And therefore greater than Tristan—or Romeo.
What is love? The suffering of one lover;
The coldness of the other. Well, I was the other!
I watched the suffering weep—as cold as stone.

DEVIL: How jolly to be in a dear old English home!

DON JUAN: I know my worth, and you underestimate.

DEVIL: Then let us reckon it. Shall we pass the plate?

DON JUAN: What do you mean?

DEVIL: Take this frail bowl.
[*Handing Don Juan a cup from the table*]
The ghost of every loving woman's soul
Wears tonight at the corner of her mask,
Like a jewel, her purest tear. Here is your task:
Go. Gather every crystal tear. . . .

DON JUAN [*taking the bowl and starting to collect the tears*]:
Thank you.

DEVIL: Listen to them! Can you hear?
Like offerings they tinkle in your bowl.

DON JUAN: Alms for the soul of Don Juan, alms for the soul!
Thank you! . . . Thank you! . . . Give the Devil his
    due.

DEVIL: Here! Let me shorten the task for you.
[*With a magician's gesture to the tears*]
Come, tears!
[*At the Devil's gesture, the tears spill into the bowl all
at once.*]

DON JUAN: My bowl is filled to the brim!
How they shine! Ah moon, old partner in sin,
Gild my crystal fortune with your light!
All of these were plundered from women at night.
[*To the tears*]
Tell me—did you cry? Did you cry?
[*To the Devil*]
These will refresh me, even when I fry!
Every one of them was shed for me.

DEVIL: With these you hope to make your final plea?

DON JUAN: With these I win, Demon! What do you fear
Even more than holy water? A tear!

DEVIL: True, a single tear can scorch my hide.
                        [*He searches the pockets of his voluminous robe.*]
                        But only if I touch it!
                        [*He produces a large lens mounted in black steel.*]
DON JUAN: What's that?
DEVIL: My pride—
                        [*He begins to arrange the tears on the table.*]
                        A magnifying glass! With this I'll divide
                        The false ones from the true, the tears they feel.
                        The false ones over there; and here, the real.
DON JUAN [*with a start*]:
                        What do you mean, false?
DEVIL [*separating the tears with his magnifying glass*]:
                                                No good! No good!
                        No good! No good!
DON JUAN: And this one?
DEVIL: Misunderstood!
                        It soon dissolved in laughter with a maid.
DON JUAN: That large one there?
DEVIL: Oh, that one, I'm afraid,
                        Was shed for a lost hat, but applied to you
                        By a twist of feminine logic.
DON JUAN: And these two,
                        These long ones—are they real?
DEVIL: Not worth a peso!
DON JUAN: How do I know that? Only because you say so.
                        [*He suddenly seizes one of the tears.*]
                        What about these clear ones?
DEVIL: Secret tears.
DON JUAN [*indicating the one he holds*]:
                        Then look—a secret tear!
DEVIL: So it appears.
                        But I can touch it. You see? Only pretense.
                        I'm perfectly able to touch them all, it's plain,
                        Even the ones that held a world of pain.
GHOST: That's because they were all part of the show.
DON JUAN: What do you mean?
GHOST: But of course! Didn't you know?
                        One loves Don Juan, my sweet, to enjoy the luxury

                         Of knowing one is going to suffer dreadfully.
ANOTHER GHOST:
                         And to relish on his lips the taste of our tears.
ANOTHER GHOST:
                         It's really not so odd as it appears,
                         The Devil's touching them. They're worth their
                             weight in pleasure!
ANOTHER GHOST:
                         The tears that cruelty wrings from us we really
                             treasure.
                         Those are the tears—
ANOTHER GHOST: One savours!
DON JUAN: One devours!
DEVIL: Ovid pondered over that for hours,
                         Back in Caesar's day.
GHOST: All part of the show,
                         With the candy and flowers—
DEVIL: Tied with a red bow.
                         Well, the tears that one enjoys are hardly real.
                         What scepter of straw is left? What new appeal?
                         Search! Search!
DON JUAN: That cry! That constant cry
                         That cuts me to the heart is my reply.
                         My destiny is great because I seek!
                         I always dreamed that on some distant peak
                         A precious flower grew, destined for me—
DEVIL: How jolly to have passed through Germany!
DON JUAN: —and those who find it only end their dream.
DEVIL: Then, not having found it gives you your esteem?
DON JUAN: Yes!
DEVIL: Ouch!
DON JUAN: What is it?
DEVIL: I've burned my hand!
                         I rested it here on the table, and—
DON JUAN: Oh?
DEVIL: This is a real one, I swear!
DON JUAN: What?
DEVIL: A tear that's real, there!
DON JUAN: Look! Your hand is spattered with light!
DEVIL: Come over here, you'll see!

[*The two of them lean over to examine the tear.*]
                                        Ah, what a sight!
A subject for a Rembrandt! Here we are,
The damned, in tandem, bent upon a star. . . .

DON JUAN: You mean a woman shed this tear for me?

VOICE OF WHITE GHOST:
                 Yes.

DON JUAN: Really!
[*Another* GHOST, *whiter and purer than the others,
appears.*]

WHITE GHOST: This tear fell honestly
From the eyes of one who fell, herself, like a tear—

DON JUAN: A tear?

WHITE GHOST: Of pity.

DON JUAN: For your wounded virtue, my dear?

WHITE GHOST: No. For your agony.

DON JUAN: Really? For me?

WHITE GHOST: For you are nothing but an agony . . .
Only agony, despite your charms,
Agony which cries for loving arms.

DON JUAN: Who are you to set a star on your sin?

WHITE GHOST: She who speaks aloud of what she has been.

DON JUAN: And what were you?

WHITE GHOST: A heart.

DON JUAN: Your soul?

WHITE GHOST: My heart.

DON JUAN: Your meaning?

WHITE GHOST: Was contained within my heart.

DON JUAN: Who are you, Vision of Light?

WHITE GHOST: I am she
Who dares to speak her name, but quietly. . . .
[*She whispers her name in his ear.*]

DON JUAN: This graceful name escapes my memory.

WHITE GHOST: I am she who simply removes her mask.
[*She removes her mask.*]

DON JUAN: Where did I know this lovely face, may I ask?
Did you give yourself to me?

WHITE GHOST: Whenever you desired me.

DON JUAN: But on what day? In what country?
[*Automatically, he searches his doublet for the list.*]

                                              My list!
              I've torn it up!
DEVIL: Well, if you insist
              I happen to have a copy.
              [*Briskly, he reaches into one of the pockets of his vast
              robe and produces a strange portfolio from which his
              long fingers draw out another list, which he presents to
              Don Juan, with a bow.*]
DON JUAN [*seizing the list*]:   Give it to me!
              [*He begins to search the list.*]
              No? I've met her. She exists. . . . Let me see—
              She must be here, I'm sure. Her name—her name—
DEVIL: Search!
DON JUAN [*with mounting nervousness*]:
                   —her name is—No?
DEVIL: Ah, what a shame!
DON JUAN: The only name that isn't on my list!
DEVIL: You noted every name—but one you missed!
DON JUAN [*to the White Ghost*]:
              And it was yours?
WHITE GHOST: What can I do?
DEVIL: Well, now have I overpowered you.
              Seeker who finds and cannot recognize?
DON JUAN: Here on this list the least of them survives.
              And yet—when all these gondolas came to me,
              Born from their names, rising from the sea,
              How were you born?
WHITE GHOST: Your list had an empty space.
DON JUAN: The Ideal Woman's eluded my embrace!
              [*Drawing himself up suddenly.*]
              And yet, only once! Why should I be sad?
              One in a thousand and four is not so bad!
WHITE GHOST [*who has disappeared into the crowd of Ghosts on his
         left*]: Only once?
DON JUAN: She's slipped away!
WHITE GHOST [*crossing over to the right*]:
              Only once?
DON JUAN: Wait! Please stay!
              Her voice is almost lost . . . but we haven't begun!
              Why do you—

WHITE GHOST:	Only once?
DON JUAN:	—force me to run

WHITE GHOST: Only once?

DON JUAN: —force me to run
From woman to woman, pursuing every word,
As one who tries to follow the sound of a bird
Will run from tree to tree?

WHITE GHOST: So you will see—

DON JUAN: Where are you?

WHITE GHOST: —that you might have discovered me
By loving any one of them!

DON JUAN [seizing her]:   No!
You existed in only one. It isn't so!

WHITE GHOST: But I waited in them all. Though you were near,
Our heart beats only for those who try to hear.
You slept upon a heart you never heard.
Time after time we waited for your word,
The word that might have caused the Supreme Bride
To burst from each of us . . . had you but tried!

ANOTHER GHOST:
From myself, perhaps.

ANOTHER GHOST: Or from me.

ANOTHER GHOST: Or from me.

WHITE GHOST: She was in every one of them—don't you see?

DON JUAN: No!

WHITE GHOST [sadly]:
Yes.

ALL GHOSTS: Yes, Don Juan. Yes!

DON JUAN: What an enormous sob, drowning distress!
What a sea of arms, reaching to me,
Stretching out into infinity!

GHOSTS [together]:
She was in every one of us . . . in every one.
Don Juan! Ah, Giovanni! Johann! Don John!

DEVIL: This pity's going to rob me of their souls!
[Moving toward the Ghosts]
Back to your spite, wretches! Back to your holes!
Ah, how beautifully they would agree,
Eternal Man and Woman, but for me.

DON JUAN [to the White Ghost]:
I wanted to love you!

DEVIL: Die, knowing she exists!

WHITE GHOST: No! So long as the fire in my tear persists
                 Don Juan is free to find himself a heart.
DEVIL: Search! Should he find it, I'll happily depart.
WHITE GHOST: Love, if only for a moment, this Ghost of a kiss!
                 Take my head between your hands, like this.
                 Now say: "I want to braid—I want to braid—
                 To braid—every dreaming look that's laid
                 Upon this single chosen brow."
DON JUAN: "I want . . . to braid—"
DEVIL: It's too late now—
                 Too late! You've been the Adversary too long.
WHITE GHOST: Now say: "I belong to love. I belong . . ."
                 And hold me.
DON JUAN: "I belong to love—"
DEVIL: All wrong!
                 You fight like a buccaneer who wants to die
                 But parries, despite himself, to his last sigh.
DON JUAN: No! I carry her in my heart, at last—
                 A heart overflowing with joy—and faithful—
DEVIL: So fast?
GHOST: *Faithful!*
                 [*The* GHOSTS *remove their masks.*]
DON JUAN: Ah! Their masks have fallen. So!
                 I can see their faces!
WHITE GHOST: Let them go!
                 Remember! All of them have lied to you.
DON JUAN: All of them have lied—
GHOSTS: *Faithful!*
DON JUAN: —that's true!
                 Which means all of them are new! Well, then,
                 All of them must be seduced again.
                 No! I cannot concentrate on one.
                 The others disturb my equilibrium.
                 [*Laughter from the Ghosts*]
                 [*To the White Ghost*]
                 Go away!
                 [*To the other Ghosts*]
                                  Don't laugh; you haven't won.
                 I'm still invincible!
DEVIL: Then you had in mind

	A dream you didn't even want to find?
DON JUAN:	It's possible. If I had found what I sought
	I might have died of boredom. I wanted naught,
	Only the joy of searching—for myself, alone.
	Woman was only my tool. You haven't won!
	I took you to leap beyond, as anyone
	Might take a weapon, a goblet, or a staff,
	Or seize a torch.
DEVIL:	Is this your epitaph?
DON JUAN:	Yes!
	[*To the Ghosts*]
	You've merely been my catalysts!
A GHOST:	If that is true, Don Juan, then what exists
	Of all these stimulations?
DON JUAN:	But—
ANOTHER GHOST:	If, as you say,
	You took all this from us, where is it today?
	Well, Don Juan?
ANOTHER GHOST:	Well? . . . Reckon the score!
	What about that night you came ashore
	Swollen with pride, after a giddy night
	Of pleasure in my gondola?
ANOTHER GHOST:	That's right!
	Recount the daring exploits you achieved
	From all those stimulations you received
	Within my arms?
ALL GHOSTS:	Give us some report!
A GHOST:	If it's true that owing to our sport
	You leapt beyond—toward what? Our ecstasy
	Left what immortal gift to posterity?
ANOTHER GHOST:	
	Through what great Mona Lisa do I smile?
DON JUAN:	Quiet, all of you!
DEVIL:	Ah, that's my style.
	A cry of real pain! He's sealed his doom.
ANOTHER GHOST:	
	In what great epic does that rose now bloom—
	The one you used to gather from my trellis
	Of a morning, as you left me? Tell us!
DON JUAN:	Ah! You've hit upon my deepest wound!

ANOTHER GHOST:

As I succumbed to you I almost swooned:
"Do what you will—and where you please," I said.
And with what banners did you deck my bed?

DON JUAN: Silence!

ANOTHER GHOST: From our tender Sicilian hour,
What deed of might, of beauty, or of power?
What martial music made? What work of art?

DEVIL: Slash it with regrets, this haughty heart!

ANOTHER GHOST:

Women loved you! This verdant garden she holds
Bursting in her heart, when sudden love enfolds,
What have you done with it, you Boabdil?*
You squanderer of Alhambras! Razed it at will!

ANOTHER GHOST:

Because you always left us to our fate,
Men despised you. What did you create
From all their hatred?

ANOTHER GHOST: Remember, I was a queen!
What happened to my kiss, you libertine?
It should have made you king!

ANOTHER GHOST: I ruled the stage!
What have you done with the inspiration I gave,
Behind Electra's veils?

ALL GHOSTS: Don Juan! Don Juan!

DON JUAN: What is this? A spectral revolution?

ALL GHOSTS: If this is what we gave—

DEVIL: Your execution!
Stab the futile Caesar! Cut him down!

GHOSTS: What is your goblet worth, your weapon, your staff?
The torch you bore will light your epitaph!

WHITE GHOST: Don Juan—

DON JUAN: What? You turn against me, too?

WHITE GHOST: What have you done with my tear?

DON JUAN: Yes. You knew.
You sensed my agony. Your tear was real.
Hearts never know all the regrets they feel.
Oh, the opportunities I've missed!
What have I made of them? Only a list!

---

*Boabdil (Abu Abdullah), last Moorish king of Granada (1482–1492), who invaded Castile. He was finally driven from Granada by the Castilians. [*Editor's note.*]

DEVIL: On your knees on that list!

ALL GHOSTS: On his knees! His knees!
Let him stay there! He's degraded us.
In wanting only Woman he's made of us
A chain of women leading to no one!

DON JUAN: I'm cold!

A GHOST: The very love he scorns has made him bold.
He's made from moments filled with tender care
A chain of moments leading to despair.

DON JUAN: I don't regret it! Yet still these torments go on.
To think they call a victor a "Don Juan"—
Yet every other man has known one day
On which he felt at last that he could say:
"I am!" I've missed that day.

DEVIL: But you've had your nights!

DON JUAN: Ahhh . . . "Don Juan" . . . I regret my appetites
—a little. Why is it every dying man has need
To search his life, discover in his past some seed
That will flower in the future? Ahh, this fire!
Oh Death, do you covet life with such desire
That thus you take your vengeance this last day?
Must one collapse, like a runner by the way,
To burn in the flames of his own torch?

DEVIL: You see?
The worm! In every fruit—on every tree!

DON JUAN: Ah, if the will might sculpt some marble fruit,
Might mold but one immortal absolute,
To drive the worm from the fruit, and from the tomb!

DEVIL: Well, is it enough in your hour of doom
To have existed on your own reflection,
Like Venice? Eh?

DON JUAN: No! Man's one protection
Against mortality is his creation.
You cannot know the agony I feel.
[*The* DEVIL *laughs.*]
I've given life to nothing, for all my zeal.
From all my years of living—not one sigh.
Do you know what agony this is?

DEVIL: It's mine!
That is Hell. There's no creator there.

DON JUAN: Tell me, do you pity my despair?

DEVIL: I understand it. Pity is not in my power.
                Let's be going. Come, this is the hour.
                There's nothing more to say. I've won!
DON JUAN: Not yet. There still remains one deed, one word!
                That famous deed and word with which I stirred
                The cataclysm of the century!
                Remember that day? My mantle drawn across my face,
                The gendarmes at my heels, I fled to a rustic place,
                Where I met a beggar—
DEVIL: Let's discuss that fully.
DON JUAN: For the love of God he begged a sou of me.
                I gave the man a louis, and then, with a word,
                I set that golden coin afire. You heard!
                I said: "For the love of Humanity."
DEVIL: Humanity?
DON JUAN: I contributed that word to History!
DEVIL: How jolly to have passed through dear old France!
DON JUAN: Open that claw! I'm going to watch you dance!
                The future will owe me something, after all,
                Because one day I heard a beggar's call,
                And stripped him of his Christian resignation.
                Make way! Liberty owes her regeneration
                To libertines. My life was not in vain!
                I'll prove it; I can find that beggar again.
DEVIL: Speak to him, if you dare!
                [*The* BEGGAR *appears, moving slowly toward Don
                Juan, his hand outstretched.*]
DON JUAN: My gold's in his hand,
                Yet still he begs . . . I don't understand!
                What do you desire, Needy Ghost?
                What do you want?
BEGGAR: This, oh gracious host!
                [*Flinging the gold piece at Don Juan's head*]
                To pay you back!
DON JUAN [*staggering, his forehead wounded*]:
                                        Oh!
DEVIL: These alms will kill you!
DON JUAN [*to the Beggar, who strides toward him menacingly*]:
                Let me explain. Liberty—

BEGGAR: Be still, you!
This sudden concern of yours is much too grand.
DON JUAN: The people—
BEGGAR: The only thing you understand
Is the liberty of a petticoat.
DON JUAN: The future—
DEVIL [*to the Beggar*]:
Stifle in the liar's throat
His couplets and their socialistic taint.
Or has the lecher now become a saint?
DON JUAN: But I rebelled—
DEVIL: Not for the sake of another.
DON JUAN [*to the Beggar*]:
You're not going to—
BEGGAR: I'm going to choke you, "brother,"
For having had the crudity to slander
The word that held our hopes.
DON JUAN: A second Commander
Rolling up his sleeves?
BEGGAR: Because the first
Was much too dignified to do his worst,
And kill the hero of the idlers.
DON JUAN: Wait!
I'll help you, peasant, to improve your state—
WHITE GHOST: As long as there's a flame within this tear,
Don Juan is free to seek a heart, do you hear!
DEVIL: It's getting dimmer. It isn't going to last.
He'd better set about his labor—fast!
DON JUAN: I have audacity—
BEGGAR: Ah?
DON JUAN: —and cleverness—
BEGGAR: Ah?
DON JUAN: —a leader's eye—
BEGGAR: Yes?
DON JUAN: —destructiveness—
BEGGAR: Ah!
DON JUAN: If bloodshed should be necessary—
BEGGAR [*suddenly serious and frightening*]:
That, I'm afraid, will have to be.

DON JUAN: I'm ready to commit—
ALL GHOSTS [*throwing off their cloaks*]:   —a crime?
DON JUAN: I say!
                At last their silken cloaks have fallen away.
                As I was saying—
DEVIL: Search!
DON JUAN: You're stopping me!
BEGGAR: You spoke of committing—
GHOSTS: A crime?
DON JUAN: No, lechery.
                I cannot dream of serving Liberty,
                So long as a shoulder's fair or an eye amazes.
                Kill me!
DEVIL: Nothing sprouts where the he-goat grazes,
                That is all. The rest is cant. And now
                The mark of the satyr's horns is on your brow.
DON JUAN: Ah, let me bewail the rutting of the male!
                For that we betray all else, for that the mind
                That might have sought for something else is blind.
                And something else exists—I know it now.
                Oh, that a bit of shrouded flesh should be
                Enough to usurp the greatest mystery,
                That a heart fit to become an eagle's marrow
                Should have been only food for Lesbia's sparrow.
                Kill me, before I beg another thrill
                From these empty phantoms, like an imbecile!
                Or like a dog, returning to his—
DEVIL: Now, do I win?
                Have I peeled away that last layer of skin?
                There's that mind—
DON JUAN: Ah!
DEVIL: That great audacity—
DON JUAN: Ah!
DEVIL: That will—
DON JUAN: Ah!
DEVIL: That fine tenacity!
                Punchinello had the word—
DON JUAN: Quiet!
DEVIL [*in the voice of Punchinello*]:   Lechery!
DON JUAN: Oh, to have maintained at such expense

My noted reputation for insolence,
And then, after everything's been heard,
To have to give that puppet the last word!

WHITE GHOST: There's something else. Pride makes you conceal
Your one excuse, your only true appeal.

DON JUAN: No excuse!

WHITE GHOST: You could not love yourself, Don Juan!
So thus your self-respect depended on
The love of others!

DON JUAN: No excuse! I shall die
Without raising a hand, without one cry.
Give me my Hell!

DEVIL [to the Beggar]:   Bring that costume here,
That gaudy, vacant thing that makes them cheer.
I'm going to need it now.

DON JUAN: What for?

DEVIL: You'll see
How amusing your little hell is going to be!

DON JUAN: With monsters—Heliogabalus and Nero?

DEVIL: No, a canvas hell for a cardboard hero.
A tiny hell that's hauled about the land.

DON JUAN: That puppet theatre? . . . No! I want to be damned!

DEVIL: You'll be a puppet, acting out adultery
In one exacting little square, eternally.

DON JUAN: Please! Give me my eternal fire!

DEVIL: No! Eternal theatre! That's your pyre!

DON JUAN: No, I won't—I—

DEVIL [to the Beggar]:   Into the sack with him. Come!
That will keep him quiet.

DON JUAN: Let go, you scum!
I refuse, you hear! I demand—

DEVIL: No more demands!
Come to the old puppeteer's infernal hands!

DON JUAN: Please, not the theatre!

DEVIL: Quickly, let's begin!
The hour is striking. Ladies, please move in.
A little closer, please. Now! On with the show!

BEGGAR: Get a move on!

DON JUAN: I don't want the—Let go!

DEVIL: Drag him over here!

DON JUAN:	Not this hole!
	Give me something worthy of my soul—
	The fiery circle!
BEGGAR:	Come on!
DON JUAN:	I won't! I want to burn!
	I've never suffered. I've a right to learn.
	Give me my Hell.
DEVIL:	Hell is my affair.
	Every man has his own, and yours is there.
	Certain celebrities are put in stone;
	They suffer it in their statues. You alone
	Will suffer in your puppet.
DON JUAN:	Then I'll connive!
	I'll plague you! Stone is dead; a puppet is alive!
	If that's to be my Hell, well, then—
DEVIL:	You'll shine?
DON JUAN:	Yes! I'll make them laugh—
DEVIL:	Who, you swine?
DON JUAN:	The girls! I'll delight them with every antic
	Under their parents' noses—drive them frantic!
WHITE GHOST:	You, who might have had a great career!
DON JUAN:	I'll sing! I'll beat them with my stick! I'll leer . . .
WHITE GHOST:	You, who might have fought an epic war!
DON JUAN:	I'll sing: "It's me, the famous Burlador—"
WHITE GHOST:	Oh! The flame is gone!
BEGGAR [*pushing him into the guignol*]:	
	That's all!
DEVIL:	Be a puppet! Begone!
	You, who sought a noble destiny,
	You spent a lifetime imitating me!
DON JUAN [*reappearing on the little stage as a puppet*]:	
	"The famous Burlador—"
WHITE GHOST [*with infinite despair*]:	
	What a pity!
DON JUAN:	"Burlador . . . Burlador . . . Burlador!"

Twentieth-Century Views
(1922-1959)

Don Juan Analyzed

Analysis of Don Juan began, as we have seen, early in the nineteenth century, that is to say when Don Juan became a serious character again. In our own times, symptomatically, discussions have multiplied to the point where they have replaced the versions themselves as the most significant stage in the development of the legend. The Spanish world has been especially concerned with the hero who sprang up on its own soil. But comments from that world are sometimes marred by a rather comic chauvinism. A suggestion that Don Juan might have been born in Italy, or that he is essentially no more Spanish than he is anything else, is likely to be taken as an insult to the nation, and to be answered accordingly. The attribution of *El Burlador* to Tirso, too, is sometimes maintained with anger instead of evidence. Still, valuable essays have come to us from Spain and Spanish America. I have tried to sift out something of the best, not without including a few pages which are perhaps more amusing than instructive.

Our account of Don Juan would be incomplete without the psychoanalytic angle of vision, a hint of which has already been given in "The Legend of Don Juan." While Gregorio Marañón makes clear that he is dealing with the type of Don Juan found in reality, Otto Rank seems to be giving us an interpretation which we are to apply to our reading of the fiction itself. Whether we feel (or should feel) in Da Ponte's libretto, for example, that Anna or Elvira is a mother-substitute, and that the Statue is the manifestation of Don Juan's own feelings of guilt—for in killing the Commander he had really killed his father—many readers will allow themselves to doubt, even though they might agree with such a diagnosis if a real case were brought to their attention. The question of introducing our knowledge of reality to challenge the views and positions openly expressed in a literary text is a delicate one. Hoffmann had already asserted that Anna secretly loves Don Juan, without offering textual evidence for his point. Now, again without textual evidence, we are asked to believe that Don Juan—Da Ponte's Don Juan—embraces a mother-substitute every time he possesses a woman. What if we are convinced that this is indeed the motive of every *real* Don Juan? Are we to read the text in the light of this truth, or are we to obey the perhaps mediocre interpretation which the text taken by itself forces on us? Immediately the entire question of the extra-literary meanings, values, and consequences of literary texts opens before us, and at this point we take our prudent leave and let others come to blows.

No one, at any rate, will dismiss Rank's interpretation of Leporello when he calls him "die Kritik, die Angst und das Gewissen"—criticism, fear, and conscience: so much is made clear by the text itself. But when Rank adds "of the hero" to his sentence we may be more timid about following him. Because Don Juan uses Leporello a couple of times to impersonate him (Rank had already written an essay on the *Doppelgänger*), shall we conclude that Leporello incarnates *his* self-critique, *his* anguish, and *his* conscience?

If Leporello impersonates Don Juan, Don Juan himself impersonates Octavio and the Marquis de la Mota. This has led another wit in the psychoanalytic school to identify Don Juan with Zeus, who impersonated Amphytrion in order to enjoy Alcmene; with certain priests of the ancient Middle East who enjoyed first-night privileges with brides; and even with the Eskimos, who allow strangers to sleep with their wives. Don Juan's action is therefore a burlesque descendant of extremely serious ritual substitutions.[1] I mention this theory as a curiosity of our indefatigable century, which is never so content as when it proves that a thing is really another thing.

One of the most ingenious uses made of Don Juan is that of Albert Camus, in his chapter on Don Juanism in *The Myth of Sisyphus* (1940). Here Don Juan is the absurd man who, aware of the perfect meaninglessness of all phenomena, realizes in his life "an ethic of quantity." This much is left to man, to add, without consequence and without purpose, object to object to object, and to savor to its full each fraction of time as it offers itself to him. This is Shadwell's Don Juan all over again, given an up-to-date vocabulary to express the great Nothing of

1. Dallas Pratt, "The Don Juan Myth," *American Imago*, XVII (1960), 321–335.

the universe, but also—most significantly—bereft of the early hero's enthusiasm for the things of time.

The view that Don Juan is primarily a rebel whose method, so to speak, happens to be the seduction of women, is ably argued once more in an article written by Emile Capouya in 1959. Mr. Capouya attacks both the views that Don Juan is above all a lustful man and that he is a concealed homosexual. In his opinion, such interpretations are disguised symptoms of our political conservatism, since they neglect Don Juan's onslaught against society. "Lust alone," says Mr. Capouya, "is not an adequate object of contemplation for an adult audience." But must Don Juan be an iconoclast? Bertolt Brecht used him, quite on the contrary, as the libidinous figure which iconoclasts—revolutionaries —will have to break! The fact once more is that Don Juan can be indifferent, reactionary, or radical as far as politics is concerned—and every author can enlist him as he will—but he hardly can be deprived of his lust. Yet his lust, we are told, is not interesting to an adult audience. Is not this a very English or American objection? I think it gives us a clue to the failure of Don Juan to make himself at home in our literature.

From "The Don Juan Figure" by Otto Rank

Translated by Walter Bodlander

I

The immortal name of the Spanish lover involuntarily evokes in us, with its magical sound, a series of erotic images and expectations which seem to be indissolubly bound to it. We must therefore forewarn the reader that we plan to touch only slightly on this generally fascinating aspect of the Don Juan figure in the following reflections—prompted by a recent and outstanding performance of Mozart's masterpiece at the Vienna opera house (November 13, 1921). Even less do we plan to discuss Mozart himself, though he may have contributed even more to the immortalizing of our hero than would appear from the bare fact that his musical setting of a matter dear to poets is the only version which has remained thoroughly effective.

Since we happen to be preoccupied with psychoanalytic considerations, we propose rather to approach Mozart's opera from that point of view, omitting in part the conscious erotic aims of Don Juan. Thus we notice easily—though not without surprise—that the action deals not so much with an adventurer and his successful sexual exploits as with a poor sinner, who, pursued by misfortune, eventually gets his come-uppance in the fires of Christian hell. To envisage the happy and joyful hours of the actual Don Juan remains the prerogative of the listener's imagination—a prerogative of which it happily takes advantage—while the representation of the tragic traits in the Don Juan figure are left to the stage. And so we simply follow in the steps of tradition and poetry when we turn our analytic attention to that rather distressing side of Don Juan.

Let us then first direct our attention not so much to the final character but rather to its development. A quick survey of the numerous Don Juan stories tells us, however, that we can expect no answers there. For the type, as he was immortalized by Mozart, enters into literature already fully developed, whereas the type of the conqueror of women known in popular consciousness never existed in literary tradition. We can surely infer from this, that frivolous heartbreaking is not the key-note in the Don Juan figure, and that from the beginning legend and drama must have searched—and found—something else in it. The typical sensualist and lover—even one of this grand style—could have been easily and perhaps even better represented by a different figure. On the other hand, the drama of the Christian hell, loaded with all the guilt feelings of original sin, would by now seem as foreign and out-dated to us as all the other ecclesiastic medieval morality plays, were it not that so great a man and artist as Mozart liberated his Don Juan (as Goethe liberated Faust from the religious puppet-play concerning a magician, and Shakespeare liberated Hamlet from the ghost stories of his precursors) by recapturing the basic human values from a clutter of trivia, and expressing them in eternal symbols.

The past record clearly shows that the main motif in the Don Juan matter does not lie in the description of his unbounded sex urges. Indeed, sober historical proof of the non-existence of an actual Don Juan archetype is hardly needed to strengthen our assumption that in our hero's unchecked urge to conquer we can recognize the expression of poetic fantasy. Results of literary research fully confirm this assumption. The poet of the Burlador took from tradition only the taunted dead man's vengeance against the insolent scoffer ("burlador"). "It remained for the poet to turn the blasphemer into a seducer of women in the grand style, and in this respect he has the merit of having given his hero the thing for which he is most conspicuous to us. . . . In the Burlador the foundations are laid for the masterpiece of 150 years later, in which the Don Juan legend was to find its supreme expression: Mozart's *Don Giovanni*."[1]

Thus we see—again in accord with our thesis—that until Mozart the literary development of the Don Juan theme does not expand the seduction motif, so attractive to popular consciousness, but rather—as if pushed by a mysterious force—expands the ancient but painfully tragic motif of guilt and punishment. This is noticeable even on the surface. Most Don Juan stories up to the 18th century appear under the dual title of the first work of Tirso de Molina: "El Burlador de Sevilla y Convidado de Piedra." The name of our hero, so imposing to us, does not even appear in the title. If we adhere to literary tradition, in which this motif is the more important in the Don Juan theme, we will have narrowed the scope of our own investigation.

From our knowledge of psychoanalysis we are prepared to derive this overpowering guilt and punishment complex—coupled with sexual fantasies—from the Oedipus complex. It is clear that the serial form (Reihenbildung) so characteristic of the Don Juan type, together with the condition of the "injured third party," seems to confirm this psychoanalytic interpretation.[2] The many women whom Don Juan has to replace again and again represent to him the irreplaceable mother, while his adversaries, deceived, fought and eventually even killed, represent the unconquerable mortal enemy, the father. This is a basic psychological fact uncovered in individual analysis. Applied to an extra-analytical situation, however, it can be used only as a hypothesis to further our desire to understand; it is not a hypothesis whose correctness we are trying to prove. The change from a man who in his subconscious remained faithful to his untouchable mother to a cynical deserter of women, presupposes repressions, displacements and revaluations. To follow the dynamics and mechanism of these changes will be our principal and also our most interesting task. . . .

1. Hans Heckel, *Das Don Juan-Problem in der neueren Dichtung* (Stuttgart: 1915), pp. 7–8.

2. See Freud's pioneering study, "Über einen besonderen Typus der Objektwahl beim Manne," *Jahrbuch für Psychoanalyse*, vol. II (1910).

II

As, following our bent, we turn our attention away from the outstanding figure of Don Juan, we notice a trait in his famous servant Leporello which leads us by way of a small detour back again to our hero. This servant is on the one hand very much more—a friend and a confidant in Don Juan's many amours—while on the other hand he is no voluntary companion and accomplice but a cowardly and servile soul concerned only with his personal advantage. In his first character he feels free to make critical comments which are completely uncalled for ("the life you lead is that of a ne'er-do-well") and to ask—perhaps successfully—for part of the master's booty in kind. In his second personality he fearfully avoids all danger, constantly refuses his services and can be kept in line only by threats or money.[3] To complete the picture of the servant—he even steals food served at the banquet.

One could say: "like servant, like master" and point out that Don Juan allows him these liberties because he needs him. So for instance before the famous "aria of the list": when Donna Elvira confronts the hero, he extracts himself from this distressing situation by substituting Leporello. Before she knows just what happened, the clever adventurer has disappeared and in his stead Leporello recites the list with the pride of the servant which stems from identification with his master.

A motif is here being touched upon which is developed ever more clearly in the course of the action and which precedes the opera almost as a motto; at the beginning of the opera, Leporello's first words are: "I wish to play the master myself, I no longer want to be the servant." It is Leporello's tragedy that he is allowed to represent his master only in difficult and critical situations. This happens a second time, at the attempted seduction of Zerlina, when Don Juan pretends to punish his servant whom he represents as the one guilty of the deed.

Another time, however, a more pleasant adventure seems to await him. Here Don Juan exchanges hat and coat with him in order to win Donna Elvira's chambermaid while Leporello is to take on the abandoned mistress. But even this adventure, pleasant at first, turns into disaster for him; because the constantly growing band of avengers (Donna Anna, Octavio, Masetto, Zerlina) have pursued Don Juan into Donna Elvira's house and fall upon the presumed wrongdoer—who turns out to be Leporello. Insisting on his innocence, he begs for mercy.

---

3. Already in the first scene he is dissatisfied. In the second scene he says, "Don't count on me, master." In the third scene, "Now it would be wise to slip away." Etc.

The cleverness by which he gets out of this dangerous situation—he suddenly disappears—could give us the hint that he is more than an accomplished student of his master—that he might possibly be identical with him. Before we clarify what this means, we wish to refer to two scenes which respectively precede and follow the scene just discussed and in both of which the identity of master and servant is clearly indicated. In them we see that not only does Leporello occasionally represent Don Juan when the master might find a personal appearance distasteful, but indeed also that Don Juan plays occasionally the part of the servant. Thus the scene with Donna Elvira's maid and again a subsequent episode leading into the second part of the Don Juan material, namely the banquet. The action here is not shown on stage but is recounted. When master and servant meet in the graveyard after they have successfully completed their adventures in their respective disguises, Don Juan tells of still an additional affair which had occurred in the meantime and which he owed to his disguise as Leporello. The servant immediately suspects that it could have been only with his own wife and indeed so accuses his master, who thinks the situation most amusing. In fact, the latter makes a comment which discloses an uncovered reason for his action and which throws a strong light upon the reciprocity of master and servant: "I have merely gotten even for what you have done to me."[4] At that moment of wantonness a voice sounds from the statue of the commander: "Foolhardy man, grant the dead their rest"—and a second action begins: the banquet with the dead man which seems to be merely tacked on to the story of Don Juan. We shall postpone a discussion of this episode until we have delved into the question of what the identical aspect of the two figures, Don Juan and Leporello, really means and how that meaning can add to our understanding of the action, of the development of the characters and of the psychology of the poet as well as that of the spectator.

III

First of all, we must clearly understand that in verbalizing such a concept as the identity of Don Juan and Leporello, we leave the ground of common literary-aesthetic considerations completely aside

4. It is probable that this reply of Don Juan's occurred in the German version of the opera which Rank witnessed; but it does not occur in Da Ponte's libretto. Neither does the Statue's speech, as Rank quotes it. Da Ponte has "Before dawn your laughter will have ceased!" [*Editor's note.*]

and substitute for them a psychological concept which has nothing to do with the overt meanings and actions of the characters. Thus, in Heckel's fine description of Leporello we shall discover not so much the image of a total personality as a suggestion of the close psychological unity of the two heroes. "To see how this negative hero is chained to the bold seducer who fears neither death nor hell; how he wishes again and again to escape only to succumb to the spell of the stronger personality (?), how he constantly ends up as the scapegoat for the misdeeds of his master for which he bears no blame, produces in the final analysis an almost tragic effect" (Heckel, p. 24).

We cannot imagine Don Juan without his servant and helper, not only because of their real dependence on one another, but also—and much more—because we feel their psychological unity as a poetic product. By this we mean that the poet did not take the "anti-hero" from history, and that he did not invent him in order to enliven the action or as a means of contrast; but rather that the figure of Leporello is a necessary part of the artistic representation of Don Juan himself. It would indeed be an attractive task to show the universal validity of this mechanism in poetic constructions. One would no doubt find that the most beautiful examples come from the greatest poets of world literature. We are happy to point out that such an example is being mentioned in psychoanalytic research by Freud himself: In adding to a comment by L. Jekels, Freud says that Shakespeare frequently divides a character into two parts, each of which is incompletely understood so long as the two are not combined into a unity.[5] One finds this same psychological formation of personalities complementing each other in all the great poetic works, from an elementary expression in Cervantes, Balzac, Goethe and Dostoyevsky up to the modern psychological literature which attempts more or less consciously to use this artistic device. We are not concerned here with the banal concept that the poet projects parts of himself through his characters. Léon Daudet has recently attempted to prove the validity of this concept in his book L'Hérédo (Essai sur le drame intérieur, Paris 1916). We are interested in a very specialized, one might say secondary split of a character into two forms or parts which, united into one, results in a fully rounded and completely intelligible personality; as for instance Goethe's Tasso and Antonio, or Shakespeare's Othello, who can be so naïve and trustful because his own jealousy is split off in the person of Iago.

---

5. Freud, "Einige Charaktertypen aus der psychoanalytischen Arbeit," *Imago*, IV (1916), 327 ff.; and L. Jekels: "Shakespeare's Macbeth," *Imago*, vol. V (1917).

Similarly, the creation of a Don Juan figure with its carefree, frivolous, devil-may-care attitude would be impossible if the other part of Don Juan were not split off in the person of Leporello, who represents the disapproval, the fear and the conscience of the hero. This gives us the key to the question why Leporello must represent his master only in particularly difficult situations and why he is allowed to criticize him; he supplies, so to speak, the conscience which our hero lacks. On the other hand we can now better understand the magnitude of Don Juan's wickedness—made possible by the fact that the restraining elements of his personality have been split off.

If we look at the action from this point of view, we notice that Leporello not only substitutes for his master in the already mentioned scenes but that he represents in general the critical and rather fearful conscience of our hero. In the first part of the drama he appears as the critical power, he berates the loose life of his master and joins it only unwillingly. Starting with the scene in the house of Donna Elvira (Act II) when both the master's and the servant's lives are threatened, the guilt feeling becomes more pronounced. This mounts in intensity throughout the graveyard and banquet scenes, is joined by the most gruesome fear of the occult and leads finally to destruction. We are not merely using one of Freud's theories, if we recognize in Leporello a representation of Don Juan's ego-ideal—a specially formulated one, to be sure—but we will thus come closer to a deeper understanding of the dynamics of Don Juan's soul.

IV

By the ego-ideal Freud understands a combination of those critical and censoring functions in man which normally enact the repression of certain desires and which, through a function we call conscience, see to it that these bounds are not broken. This controlling organ of the soul consists of two factors which complement and regulate one another: An outer factor which represents the challenges of the world around us and an inner one which represents the demands of the self. More precisely, the ego-ideal is actually the representative of the inner demands which have already incorporated the demands of society. The heart of the ego-ideal is formed by that part of the primitive narcissism which the child has had to give up in order to conform—but which is preserved in the ego-ideal. The stimulus for the formation of the ego-ideal stems from the critical-pedagogic influence of the parents "to

which are added in the course of time the influences of teachers,
instructors and an unsurveyable multitude of other people in the
social structure in which the child is growing up (Society, Public
Opinion)."[6] . . .

At one point Freud tries to isolate the moment in the psychic development of mankind at which the individual took the great step from
mass psychology to personal psychology.[7] This progress came about
following the unsatisfactory commission of the arch-crime, parricide,
which brought remorse instead of fulfillment, and new and complicated inner restrictions instead of the desired freedom. This parricide
now occurred only in fantasy—and he who took that step was the first
epic poet. This poet changed reality to conform with his desires. He
invented the heroic myth. The hero was he who slew his father single-
handed—whereas up to then only the tribe as a whole had dared to
commit this arch-crime. Just as the father had been the first ideal of
the boy, the poet now created in the hero who wishes to replace the
father, the first ego-ideal. This hero, whose imagined deeds are
recounted by the poet to the masses, is basically of course none other
than the poet himself.

If we return now to the principal male characters in the Don Juan
story, we recognize in Leporello's broad urgings to amend, the critical-
ironic side of the ego-ideal; while in his fearful cowardice the conscience and guilt-feelings of the frivolous hero are split off. But at the
decisive tragic climax—the graveyard scene which introduces the collapse of Don Juan—the comic figure of Leporello which is mockingly
supposed to set aside the demands of the ego-ideal is replaced by a far
more powerful representative of the ego-ideal, namely the consciousness of guilt in the form of the statue of the commander, in which we
can easily recognize the immediate father image. This gradual sharp-
ening and strengthening of the demands of the ego-ideal, culminating
in the appearance of the "Stone Guest," might correspond, so to speak,
to a clarification of the critical voice of conscience, taken as the ideal-
formation stemming from the father complex. This psychological
clarification, shown in the opera like a dream, can be traced throughout the development of the Don Juan matter. In the Burlador, in
Molière and later in Zorrilla the warnings come from the father against
whom the hero acts aggressively. Indeed, the immediate precursors of

6. "Zur Einführung des Narzissmus," *Jahrbuch für Psychoanalyse,* vol. VI (1914).
7. Freud, "Zur Einführung des Narzissmus," pp. 124 ff.

Molière—Dorimon and de Villiers, have the hero commit atrocities against the father and these deeds are referred to in the titles of the pieces. In Molière's and later on again in Dumas père's play there is an argument about a will, and in the course of the action the hero shuns no crime—not even that of fratricide—in order to gain possession of the parental heritage. With Holtei, a post-Mozartian author, Don Juan kills a hermit in the course of an argument; the man turns out to be his father. "The fact that he has killed his father leaves Don Juan so completely unimpressed that shortly after the crime he plays a joke on the cowardly Leporello in the very hut of the victim and ends by hitting him" (Heckel, p. 42). It is notable also that in various puppet plays the hero stabs his father, who then appears as a ghost and summons him to hell. Thus in the plays from Ulm and Lower Austria *Don Juan the Wild,* or *The Nocturnal Tribunal,* or *Master Hans of Stone.*[8] . . .

Sometimes, instead of the father, it is a brother, sent by the father, who urges the hero to change his wicked ways. This happens, for example, in Lenau's work. Unlike his predecessors, Lenau does not attack Don Juan; instead, he lifts the conflict to the plane of a philosophic discussion between opposing points of view. But in the Don Juan of Dumas just mentioned, a duel occurs in which the brother is killed. Don Juan dies as well, killed by the shade of Sandoval (evidently a doublet of the brother) whom he had also killed in the course of a duel. Sandoval is, however, a clear doublet (Doppelgänger) of the hero himself: "A spiritually related knight . . . and both try to take away from each other the prize for wickedness" (Heckel, p. 55). The idea of the doublet goes so far that Sandoval bets and loses his sweetheart to Don Juan—though she kills herself in order not to become his booty. A similar doublet can be found in Zorrilla, in the figure of Don Luis Mejia. He and Don Juan bet to surpass one another in the number of seduced women and slain men and both come up with most impressive numbers (See also Leporello's one thousand and three). . . .

The close psychological relationship of the doublet motif to the ego-ideal explains why Leporello sometimes appears as a doublet of his master, especially when they substitute for one another with women (Amphytrion motif, father-identification). But the doublet motif seems to constitute a psychological refinement of the Don Juan matter and

8. See Kralik and Winter, *Deutsche Puppenspiele* (Vienna: 1885).

thus we find it only in the more modern works, most clearly in that by Sternheim (1909).[9] Here the hero has a genuine doublet who joins him after his servant has died and remains at his side until his own death. The doublet is recognized as the critical-ironical ego-figure, for he restrains the hero's deeds with sinister irony. In complete accord with our psychoanalytical interpretation, this tale of the *Doppelgänger*, like many others, rises to the point of actual madness.[10] In contrast to this psychological use of the doublet motif in literature is a related use which preserves the original meaning of the doublet, that of announcing the impending death of the hero: I refer to the participation of the living hero in his own funeral. Mérimée was the first to attach this motif to Don Juan, picking from folklore the old tale of the knight who saw his own funeral and thereupon repented. This motif leads us to the hero's weird end, so important in the entire tradition of Don Juan tales. . . .   (1922)

Extracted from *Imago*, VIII (1922), 142–155. An expanded version appeared under the title *Die Don Juan-Gestalt* (Vienna: Psychoanalytischer Verlag, 1924). This is available also in a French translation by S. Lautman, *Don Juan: une étude sur le double* (Paris: Denoël et Steele, 1932).

From *Don Juan or Power* by Ramiro de Maeztu

Translated by Lloyd D. Teale

The entire universe finds itself subject to the "Moira" of natural laws. "Moira" is the division, the classification, the partition, that is to say, the limits of each thing and each being. Over the gods of Olympus is "Moira." The gods themselves, the god of the sea, the god of the air, the god of fire, the god of wisdom, are nothing but specialized "Moirai." Each one will take care of his game and will be content with his space and his time. What existed cannot cease to have existed. What is in one place, is not in another. "Moira" is what establishes the boundaries and we must obey its orders. But could there be anything more beautiful than to leap over its barriers and change oneself into a law unto one's self? Life which passes and which is squandered cannot

9. Carl Sternheim, *Don Juan: eine Tragödie*. [*Editor's note.*]
10. Rank, "Der Doppelgänger," *Imago*, vol. III (1914).

be recovered. All of us are condemned to move through the world between high walls, like prison corridors, which deprive us of sight,
darken the air and paralyze our movement. But let the bugles sound.
Don Juan issues forth. There is no longer any past or future, or loneliness, or nostalgia: everything is present. There is no longer any thine
or mine: everything is mine. Barriers have fallen and the whole world
stretches out at our feet.

In addition to a "Moira" there is a "Dike." It is the moral law.
Society awaits our service. It says that we must pay it the cover charge
in the banquet of life. We are born debtors, because our parents have
worked for us. We are to pay our debt and we agree to play the part
which has been designated for each one of us, because the gods who
have kindled our lights can put them out, and those who give us
strength withdraw it and are inexorable toward the haughty. The
wheel of time cuts off the heads that rise too high. But here comes the
man who does not pay the bills that the world presents to him except
with the point of his sword. For him social boundaries are not in force
either: "Seville sometimes calls me / the Seducer, and the greatest /
pleasure that can exist for me / is to seduce a woman / and leave her
honorless," says Don Juan, according to Tirso. "No matter where I
went / I trampled reason underfoot, / virtue I ridiculed, / justice I
mocked, / and I was a traitor to women," he adds, according to Zorrilla. We men are condemned to be sheep in the public square, but
inside we also carry a wolf. Better a bull for a year than an ox for a
century, says a Russian proverb. Don Juan does not open his mouth
without overwhelming with joy the Bolshevik living within every man.

We are tired of reasoning and doing a thing in order to produce such
or such consequences. Laboring to fulfill our desires, working for
money, restraining ourselves for profit: these are the things that sad-
den life. What we like is to do something because we want to, to act
through impulse, to yield to caprice and scorn the consequences. There
is no happiness more intense than that of the madcap. Don Juan is
the perfect madcap. He will not be the one who makes secrets of the
results of his conduct. His motto, according to Tirso, is "If I still have
so much time to repent . . .!" Since the world ends every instant, he
will risk his future and eternity for a whim. "Tonight I am to enjoy
her," he exclaims, when he sees a different and appetizing woman. The
rest of us men live tormented by the consciousness of our own limitations or those which social laws impose on us, and by the anticipation
of the consequences of our acts. Natural law, social law and reason

oppress us: Moira, Dike and Logos. Don Juan hurdles the three. He has shaken off the three yokes. Reason and experience tell us that, among refined people at least, bragging and boastfulness gain no reward except scorn for the one who decides to let himself go. Nevertheless, is there anything we like to do so much as to force the truth down somebody's gullet and silence whoever dares to contradict? What has been the ideal of every bold child but to lead the life of a pirate? And when we played cops and robbers, why did we always prefer to be robbers, if not because a robber does whatever he takes a notion to do, while the policeman has to do whatever he is ordered to do?

The first known edition of *The Seducer from Seville* is that of Barcelona in 1630. The drama is earlier—1625? 1620? 1615? Was it written before or after the beginning of the Thirty Years' War, which was to end for Spain with the loss of the Netherlands? In any case it is subsequent to the appearance of the first part of *Don Quixote*. But when Cervantes was writing his work the Spanish soldiers scattered over the world already felt the earth on which they trod tremble under their feet. The process of decay has advanced in these years. Spain found itself a prisoner in its empire and engaged in a task which it could not avoid. It must stand guard in Portugal, in Flanders, in Germany, in Milan, in Naples, in the vastness of America and the vastness of the seas, which its galleons crossed. All was going to be lost sooner or later. It was no longer possible for Spain, as it had been a century before, to decide whether or not to undertake new adventures in faraway lands. This choice was now in the hands of these lands; the initiative belonged now to those who attacked Spain. Spain had to defend itself. If when they read *Don Quixote,* the Spaniards laughed at the adventures which they could no longer undertake, what must they have felt when Don Juan appeared? Don Juan represents liberty of movement, irresponsibility, infinite, inexhaustible energy. Just to dream of this freedom is paradise for the one who feels himself in water up to his neck. And a moment afterward life is only a dream, a lie, the flattery of the world, and the only truth is the one which the bells promise when they toll death.*

Don Juan uses his life poorly, but he has a strong life to use. Don Juan is strength, and strength is a treasure. Don Juan squanders his strength. Lord, Lord, we promise thee not to waste it, but give us

*That is to say, the works of Calderón follow those of Cervantes and Tirso. [*Editor's note.*]

strength to waste! whether for evil, for other goods, to ruin ourselves, or to follow thy footsteps; give us, Lord, strength, life, power, victory!

(1937)

Extracted from *Cincos ensayos sobre Don Juan*. Santiago de Chile: Editorial Cultura, 1937.

From *Don Juan* by Gregorio Marañón

Translated by Lloyd D. Teale

The Undifferentiated Instinct

Don Juan lives obsessed by women and he runs from one to another, without ever tarrying with any one of them; and not because none of them satisfy him, as some point out, confusing Don Juan with another sexual type which resembles him and which I have studied in my book on Amiel; but, on the contrary, because the primitive instinct of Don Juan is satisfied with any one of those women; with the princess as well as with the fisherwoman, as the Tenorio of the drama already tells us, so emphatically.

Now then; the typical characteristic of the perfect male is, precisely, the great differentiation of the loved object; its localization in a fixed feminine type capable of few modalities and often of none. The love of a perfect male is strictly monogamous or reduces its preference to a small repertory of women, generally resembling one another; in short, as I have said on another occasion, to a set of limited variations on one same theme.

Don Juan, on the contrary, is incapable of loving, even temporarily, a fixed type of woman. He seeks woman as a sex. A woman is for him only the means to arrive at sex. His attitude is, then, the same undifferentiated attitude as that of the adolescent, and also the attitude of the male of almost all the species of animals. Recent studies of the naturalists provide us with interesting illustrations of this theme which I can only suggest here.

From his appearance in the literary legend, in the first scene of the drama of Tirso de Molina, we see Don Juan violate the chastity of the duchess Isabela, presenting himself in the dark in her bedroom and pretending to be her betrothed. This is what Don Juan is; pure Don Juanesque essence. A differentiated man, a true male, demands, on the contrary, *to see his beloved* and to be seen by her; because the awareness of personality is an irrevocable condition for great love. When the king, attracted by the cries of the seduced duchess, asks what is going on, Don Juan, with deep biological exactitude, answers: "What can it be? A man and a woman"; that is to say, not two individuals, Don Juan and Isabela, but two sexes face to face. To Isabela herself, Don Juan replies when she hears him approach in the darkness and asks him who he is: "You ask who I am? A nameless man."

Here is definitively expressed, since his first literary version, the definition of Don Juan: a nameless man; that is to say, a sex and not an individual.

Don Juan's Physique

The physique of the genuine Don Juan confirms his indecisive male characteristics. Don Miguel de Mañara, considered as one of the human models of the Seducer, looks like a pretty girl in the portrait painted by Murillo. In the only authentic portrait that we know of him, Casanova—a notable Don Juan—has the perfection and delicacy of features of a woman. And almost all of the Don Juans that I have known were far from the energetic and hairy norm of the male prototype.

The morphology that fits men gifted with an extraordinary capacity for love is usually somewhat antiaesthetic: small stature, short legs, intensely pronounced physiognomical features, rough skin well provided with whiskers and fuzz. Not at all, in short, like the slender Don Juan, elegant, fine-skinned, wavy-haired and with beardless face or adorned with a light sharp-pointed beard, who passes through the salons or across the stage. The minutely precise care of his clothing, and at times its showy exaggeration, accentuate even more this indefiniteness of what is virile in Don Juan's morphology.

Jealousy. Trips

Our hero's inability to feel offended when jilted by a woman is also typical of his undifferentiated virility. Let us note the fact that *not a single case is known of a Don Juan saddened or irritated in the depth of his conscience*—although he may be in his vanity—*because he is abandoned or betrayed by any of his mistresses.* He is born with the lesson already learned that "he who kills by the sword dies by the sword." He is inaccessible to jealousy, which is a violent expression of the instinct of possession—a fleeting instinct in him. For Don Juan, once the woman is possessed, what is important is to abandon her and make sure she doesn't hinder his next conquest. If another man aids him by making love to the first woman, so much the better. Don Juan has rivals only before the possession of the desired woman; once she is possessed, the rival no longer exists for him.

The traveling instinct of the traditional Don Juan is related to this. In the immense and largely mobile population of the great modern cities, it is possible to live many years playing without danger the Don Juanesque game of conquering and forgetting women. But in the life of old, even that of famous capitals like Paris, Rome or Madrid, the life of a seducer could only be sustained for a very short time. The complications of each conquest and each desertion compelled him to look far away for a new place in which to indulge his instinct. . . .

Scandal. Deceptions

Another characteristic trait of the Don Juanesque instinct is the scandalous and deliberate parade of his amorous successes. He exaggerates them, or even invents them, as adolescents do. The indispensable condition of great love is, on the contrary, mystery. Only surrounded by mystery does true passion grow. Almost none of the truly deep things that have occurred between men and women have been known to other people; and for that reason we all know so little as yet about love. But Don Juan tells his conquests in the public square to anyone who will listen; partly because his shallow instinct enjoys the evil satisfaction of displaying his triumphs, the doubtful ones as well as the real ones; but, also, because scandal is the best weapon for his new adventures.

Finally, very typical of the classical Don Juan is his amorality in the game of love. Don Juan is fundamentally tricky. He never gives any consideration to the means he uses to win his women. Every misdeed or villainy seems a joke to him. His morality is the application to love of the Machiavellian maxim "the end justifies the means." The genuine Don Juan is not stopped by the normal inhibitions which protect women from an ordinary man—respect for innocence, the fact of being married, a different social level, religion, or the idea of causing harm or sorrow to others. But, of course, in times like ours, when morals are changing, and these inhibitions do not exist, Don Juan does not have to trample underfoot any prejudice or climb over convent walls; hence the present-day paleness of his personality.

Errors in the Interpretation of Don Juan

All these traits, among others which are not pertinent at this time, demonstrate the proximity between Don Juan's love and the undifferentiated love of the animal species; and in the human species between his love and that of adolescents and of the weak and the epicene; in short, his is far from the great, concealed and differentiated love of the true man.

Of all I have said on various occasions, what has reached the public most directly is the conclusion that Don Juan is an effeminate man, almost a homosexual. That is not exactly what I have meant. Don Juan possesses an immature, adolescent instinct, arrested in the generic stage, when face to face with the attraction of women, and not in the strictly individual stage, which is the perfect one. He loves women, but is incapable of loving *the woman*. The man most truly man, is the one who, like Dante, has been able to devote his entire male life to a single Beatrice; even when she is Dulcinea, that is to say when she is only a dream.

But the fact that a man may not attain this stage does not mean that he cannot be a respectable man. I swear now that I have never had the slightest desire to bother Don Juan, or any of the Don Juans; or anyone who believes himself to be one. What I protest against is that he should be considered the perfect male, because certainly he is not; I protest against anyone's speaking, as does Gendarme de Bévotte, of the "puissance superbe de sa virilité." His secret is something else.

We biologists measure the problem of equivocal sex with a much more generous criterion than that of uninformed people, who wink at each other on the sly when this subject is mentioned. But, besides, the fact that the undifferentiation of the instinct, so typical in Don Juan, does imply the *possibility* of wandering from the straight and narrow path (and reality proves this in the most unexpected cases), does not exclude the fact that there are many Don Juans who in their real lives follow, biologically, the right path without ever wandering from it.

Another of my commentators' errors which I have never succeeded in eradicating, despite my clarifications, is the following:

Neither I nor any of the critics of Don Juan consider a Don Juan every man who falls in and out of love with ease, and who is given to the sweet intercourse, more or less platonic, with the marvelous world that is women. There are many men who live by preference for love, aided by their charm or the resources of their experience, or by taking advantage of their social class—money, power or fame, which are and will be eternal magnets for feminine instinct. Because of any of these means they live a life of endless amorous triumphs.

These men may not be—and often are not—Don Juans. They are men gifted, perhaps, with a perfect instinct, but unfortunate in not finding the unique woman who, by her presence alone, eliminates the possibility of other women. If Dante had not met Beatrice one day at twilight, crossing a bridge, dressed in noble red velvet, it is possible that, with all his perfect manliness, he would have been seen many nights prowling furtively through the shady sections of Florence.

If, then, among the men who will read me there are some who feel offended by my opinions on Don Juan, I beg them to include themselves in this other group, in that of fortunate men who are not Don Juans, whose instincts the most puritanic souls would not reproach.

(1940)

Extracted from *Don Juan*. Colección Austral; Buenos Aires: Espasa-Calpe, 1944.

From *The Seducer Who Does Not Seduce*
by Jacinto Grau

Translated by Lloyd D. Teale

[*From the Preface*]

The Seducer Who Does Not Seduce, one of the last works which I assembled in manuscript form and which still has not reached the stage, is an act of recovery from the present decadence, which cannot conceive of any myth or vital force, without weakening it with subtleties, analyses stolen from science, or original emasculations of a hothouse psychology. The author of Zarathustra, a violent and gentle preacher, like a Christ in reverse, lets this spontaneous affirmation escape him: What is great is simple and only what is simple is great. The real Don Juan, whom I have brought forth into the world, unearthing him from the myth, is an insult and a challenge to all the cowardly prudence of an old morality and culture, indolent in the presence of boldness. Too many years of pontifical dignity, of conventionalism and of lukewarm hedonism weigh heavily on that morality and that culture. And when this is not the case, there prevails a sterile defensive scepticism. Don Juan is before anything else a magnificent blind instinct, but one that can force its way like those persons deprived of the sense of sight, by means of the sense of touch and with a cane. Since he lives intensely, he has no need of philosophizing. The few critiques that have reached my hands, among them a very long one published by Stanford University in California, in the review *Hispania,* have completely mistaken the Seducer, whom I have presented on the stage spiritually naked, as naked as a star. Current criticism, like husbands, is last to become aware of a truth so common that it has ceased to be talked about.

BEFORE THE FIGURE OF DON JUAN

Don Juan has been for a long time now an unexhausted literary myth. From the works of Tirso de Molina to the present time, many poets have brought the legendary seducer into the light from different points of view—some, the minority, humorous. This noisy lovemaker has not always given the approximate measure of the creative capacity of his revivers. If on some rare occasion he has occasioned masterpieces, most works about him have not been up to the evocative capacity of the author, because his expansive force, triumphant over all analyses, does not lend itself docilely to personal interpretations. However much critics dissect and study him under full light, applying to him the corrosive of reflection and examination, he remains always a blind vital impulse and a quality of emotion which understanding is incapable of capturing. Certain artistic zones and characters fall outside of a purely intellective function, however brilliant the latter may be, because they drag along with them an indubitably illogical element of passion which cannot be linked in any precise manner to what we commonly call "reason." Many things still escape not only a specific philosophy, but all the philosophies in the world. The sentence from *Hamlet,* even without being referred to a concrete person, is still true.

People have sifted and quibbled so much about the classic seducer, that this character has now come to be a phantom, a multiple symbol full of variants, some profoundly contradictory to one another. From the Don Juan of Kierkegaard, cold, perverse, the enemy of women and their cautious and expert ambusher, tinged by a morbid moral sadism, to a certain modern Don Juan, with emotion and love, who is no longer properly speaking Don Juan and whom I have tried to sketch in *Don Juan de Carillana,* there is a difference as essential as there is between the arrogant hero of Tirso and the Don Juan of Zorrilla. When Zorrilla's Don Juan contradicts his own character by falling deeply in love, with a love from the soul, he ceases to be what Don Juan is, since this figure is as dynamic as it is limited. In my judgment the deepest tragedy of Don Juan, which he is not aware of, is his invariable elemental nature, fixed in its structure, incapable of progress or regression, as long as the combination of atoms which integrates him does not change. For that reason, like the Greeks, he cannot feel remorse, even though he is a believer, as is Tirso, and is born in a Christian epoch; nor can he love in any other manner than as he loves: with intense and fleeting fury. To suppose in him complete coldness is not to know him. A cold Don Juan would have become bored with himself very soon, however moderate his reflexive action might be. Without lasciviousness concealed by a fleeting, violent and eloquent enthusiasm, without an intermittent and blind impulse, the boisterous Don Juan would not have been possible. . . .

Each person has *his* Don Juan. This customarily gives *each person* a very Catholic and very Spanish intolerance of the Don Juans created by others. The one who already has a Don Juan, for his own private use, will not be reconciled with the one in this work, for whom few scenic situations and very synthetical and obvious lines of the pencil suffice in order for him to reveal himself completely, midst the uproar and disaster that he produces. The latter are as indispensable to establish as the hero himself, whose soul adjusts itself with ease to that of the popular concept of that soul, the outline of which I have accentuated because for a clear and precise art it is the best way.

His tragedy is for what surrounds him and not for him, because he is stronger in himself than other men and more resistant to all the griefs which overwhelm other males to the point of transforming them.

The tragedy of Don Juan, for me, is not that he cannot love, since he loves in his own way. In *that way* is found all his idiosyncrasy. His eroticism, from the same source as that of all the men of his race, acquires an exaltation and infinite might, of such ardor that no one could breathe in his *hour of fire*. His reaction is also much greater than in an ordinary man. When he is not motivated by a new incentive that will kindle again his imagination and impetuous appetite, he becomes emptied of passion, and again he quickly becomes filled with it when in the presence of the enchantments of another woman. The immediate surfeit, common to all, is in him much greater, and his capacity for illusion and fantasy attain in him an extraordinary renovating vigor. He is, then, a great visionary and an insatiably greedy man, and because of that same facility of reviving his illusions and vehement cravings, his flamelike loves die out, freeing him of all anguish and regret. He only knows the uneasiness and the thirst of sexual enjoyment which fantasy embellishes for him, creating for him a real illusion of love, and since his conscience is deaf to everything that is not his ego, he passes in constant bewilderment through the sorrow that he produces. Regret is what his youth and exuberant virility least understand. He engenders grief in others, but frees himself from his own, since his absence of fear, of remorse and of tenderness, combined with his physical hardness, liberate him from all discouragement and sorrow. He is a hero and an archetype whose most vital energy is only directed toward sexual gratification. For that reason once he has enjoyed a woman, whoever she may be, his curiosity vanishes and he is left with indifference and insensibility. Custom and usage have calloused in him the interest of other men for the seduced virgin or for the exceptional woman. For him all are equal, once they have surrendered to him, and he does not leave any rancor in them, because his physical grace and his infinite charm produce in women a dazzle which they will never feel again. The rest of their lives seems empty to them after what they have felt. Unconsciously they desire the man who has shaken them so; he is still irresistible to them, even without the fascination of the legend, because he did not allow himself *to be enjoyed too much*. To take this fickleness of Don Juan for a keen subconscious desire to pursue an ideal is in my judgment an ingenious but not very convincing supposition. The Don Juan that I see always has his soul, his sex and his life on the surface of his skin. And this is the only Don Juan, very much ours, whom subsequent interpretations have distorted, making him, in my opinion, less great and more complex. As he is an extreme example of Nature, he is stronger than all the cosmetic put on him by a female psychology, unnerved by the fear of being deceived and by the dread of appearing to be too naïve, if it accepted what is simple as simple and not in some other way. Hence the artificial motivations of some Don Juans, or the simple-minded irony with which some interpreters of Don Juan have viewed him, missing his real greatness.

The famous Casanova does not have, except for his fondness for women, the slightest resemblance to Don Juan. Don Juan differs from all the Casanovas in that his feelings do not persist and also in the fact that he does not leave anguish in women's hearts, nor melancholy in their memories. He does not mature in life, and having the qualities of an exceptional hero, he is active only as a maximum lover. He is created by the instinct of the species as a representative specimen of the sheer male, born only to engender, and led by a vigorous faculty of illusion.

Hebbel, in the magnificent Holofernes of his *Judith,* gives life to a strange man of prey, an active, absolute vanquisher of all grief and dismay. Don Juan, with the same vigor and audacity, does not possess Holofernes' conscience and broad ambition, since the professional lover is not susceptible, like the warrior, of feeling the frightful anguish of solitude, nor of longing for a fellow creature in order to be able to struggle with him, or loving something on earth without despising it. Don Juan, equally a man of action, is a prisoner in his reduced orbit, but his enterprising impulse to satisfy his desire is equal to that of Holofernes, without his metaphysical anguish. The seducer's scorn for those around him is great, but it does not reach his inmost recesses. To return to the original lustful, reckless, Don Juan, unacquainted—not by design but by nature—with fear, it is best to stand before this figure just as one sees it, accumulating only those observations which have added to or explained something essential about its primitive character.

Many great objects and creations are sometimes more simple inside than they appear to be through distant perspective and legend. For me, Don Juan is no more or less than what with all possible sobriety is glimpsed in this play, in which care is taken principally to establish the character and the possibility of its reincarnation in any epoch. Like every great egotism, this one is fertile in deeds and consequences. The most elemental and uncomplicated beings follow their course with more daring and vehemence because nothing distracts them from themselves, and their integral simplicity gives an opportunity for a series of

complications in relation to other people. These complications are
generally perplexed by excessively subtle men, born to write com-
mentaries. Don Juan, like other vigorous and representative personages, has two lives: his own and the one attributed to him in successive
interpretations. We are dealing here with the Don Juan who seems to
me the true one, and it seems to me legitimate and natural that others
should differ from the way I understand him: but it seems foolish and
idle to give way to the frequent and ugly habit of reproaching the
author because he has not painted another figure than the one he
chose when he believes it to be the authentic and real one.   (1941)

Extracted from *El Burlador que no se burla*. Buenos Aires: Editorial Losada,
1947.

From *Don Juan and Don Juanism*
by Salvador de Madariaga
Translated by Lloyd D. Teale

I

Is Don Juan Masculine or Feminoid?

There is not in all western literature a more fertile theme than that
of Don Juan. It should be that way, however little you meditate on it,
since Don Juan is the quintessence of masculinity. This assertion, it
should be said, clashes head on with Gregorio Marañón's opinion, as
subtle as it is authoritative, that there is in Don Juan a feminine element. And it is obvious that, in dealing with subjects so closely related
to hormones, nobody will dare to argue with the great Spanish authority on hormones. Not I, at any rate—especially since, in fact, it is very
probable that Marañón is right when he suggests (as he does in his
monumental biography of Antonio Pérez) that the Don Juanesque type
of man, who flits from one woman to another, is usually not a man of
firm character, and always ends up by falling into the hands of a strong
and even manly woman who dominates him, and under whose domination he finally attains peace, equilibrium and stability.

But then, I will probably be asked, where does this leave us? Is Don
Juan not only fond of women but also an effeminate man, or is he the
prototype and the quintessence of masculinity? Everything depends on
agreeing first on what we are speaking about. Don Juan is one thing

and a Don Juanesque man is another. The one is a powerful literary symbol, perhaps the most powerful of the symbols of our art; the other is . . . Pérez, the fellow who lives in the house next door and Martínez the one across the street, and all those about whom the girls sing in chorus

> At midnight, at midnight,
> The rascal would leave, alas, alas, alas,
> The rascal would leave . . .

This rascal Pérez, as well as Martínez and the others of their ilk, are in effect, as Marañón points out, beings whose character is none too firm—beings incapable of achieving a balance within themselves, in need, then, of a complement to life, which they seek in women. More oriented toward what is generally called love, than toward what is generally called action, Don Juanesque men reveal in this the femininity which the physio-psychologists assign to them; because it appears in fact that women prefer love to action, and men action to love.

Byron, who was familiar with these things, puts it very clearly in his Don Juan—

> Man's love is of man's life a thing apart,
> 'Tis woman's whole existence.

It will be alleged, and not without grounds, that the second line is becoming less applicable, since women of action are becoming more and more numerous. There are only two possible answers to this: that the principle of love being the whole existence of a woman was still true in the times of Don Juan; and that it continues to be so in the essence of what is eternally feminine. Anyway it still remains unrefuted that the man who is too fond of love reveals through this fact a certain femininity.

But there is a great difference between a Don Juanesque man and Don Juan. They are so different that it is a pity that people have begun to call the *mujeriego* man Don Juanesque, because the symbol which Don Juan is and embodies is precisely the opposite of the *mujeriego* man. How? Patience. Patience, it will all come clear in time.

The *mujeriego* man likes women. He likes them not only carnally, but he also likes their company after enjoying them and their commerce before. Besides, he likes them in the plural. The *mujeriego* man lives among women as in a garden, sampling jasmines and roses and carnations, and enjoying this garden-like atmosphere; in his environment of femininity he takes recreation and he rests.

At his lowest level, the *mujeriego* man is the drone or brothel sluggard who spends his idle hours in the bawdyhouse, joking with "the girls," sometimes taking a beer, sometimes a whiskey, or a glass of wine—depending on the latitude and the fashion—and bathing in visual sensuality. At his highest level, the *mujeriego* man is an artist of life, with rich intuitive gifts, who enjoys, with fruition and an intellectual delight at the same time affective and sensual, the aromas of the feminine flowers that surround him. Women instinctively flock to him because they know that he will know how to appreciate them.

All this, although it is customarily called Don Juanesque, has nothing to do with Don Juan. It is, in fact, his true negation. Because woman in herself does not interest Don Juan: she only interests him as an object of possession. And the proof is that once he possesses her he abandons her. Zorrilla's Don Juan says it with all clarity, when to Don Luis Mejía's question, "How many days do you spend per seduction?" he answers with a boast which, even if it is a lie as such, is symbolically true: "One day to court 'em, one day to trap 'em, one day to jilt 'em, two to replace 'em, and an hour, more or less, to forget 'em." Here we are far from the complacency with which the *mujeriego* and "donjuanesque" man surrounds himself with women and dallies with them. The Marquis of Bradomin, for example, so artistic and so sentimental —Don Juanesque, but not Don Juan—is like a virtuoso whose spiritual hands strum delicate and melodic sonatas on the feminine souls which surrender themselves to him like musical instruments. But Don Juan is not at all sentimental.

Don Juan is the male; he is masculinity incarnate. He is the symbol of force which in nature attacks, subdues, enjoys and abandons—something similar to that *Urhunger* or *original hunger* of which Keyserling speaks.

II

Don Juan Is Elemental

This elemental and "brute" character of the force which Don Juan represents is what obliges all his creators—those who have understood him—to strip him of the scruples, the rules, the graces which constitute civilization. For Don Juan there cannot exist either religious, or moral or social law; but not because he examines them and then rejects them, but because these laws spring up into the human conscience at a later stage of its development than the one which he embodies; and, once sprung up, what is purely masculine, like brute force, dies, since with laws of a religious-moral-social nature it becomes embellished, conditioned, qualified, and consequently it ceases to be spontaneous.

Spontaneity is one of the essential traits of Don Juan. The Don Juan who stops to consider material or moral debit and credit of his adventures ceases to be Don Juan. Don Juan doesn't keep accounts; his accounts are stories to fascinate some woman who happens along the path of his imagination. But a bookkeeping Don Juan is an insoluble contradiction. No obstacles stop Don Juan. Like a spontaneous and masculine being he is impatient; he prefers climbing over walls to going around them, and forcing women to persuading them. More than the fruits of the conquest, perhaps, he enjoys the violence with which he obtains them, the broken wall, the mocked chastity.

All this explains that the great human symbol of what is masculine was born in Spain precisely when Spain was the capital of the religious, moral and social orb. There is no greater error in Don Juanesque literature than that of making of Don Juan an incredulous, immoral, unsocial character. What would Don Juan do without walls to scale, without virginities to violate? What would he do without religious, moral and social laws to transgress? No. Don Juan lives and breathes in a city which is marked by walls and rules. And of course he does not define it, analyze it or argue about it. It doesn't even interest him. He doesn't even realize that it exists as such. He takes it for granted, like air, like light. But he couldn't live without light, or air, or without the city with walls and laws which he leaps over and breaks; and whoever imagined that Don Juan, being a violator of the religious, moral and social laws, was a revolutionary denier of religion, of faith and of morality, did not observe that, if he pursued this line of reasoning he was obliged to postulate that Don Juan is a denier of women, since he also violates them.

No. Don Juan does not affirm or deny anything, because Don Juan *is*. To affirm and deny are forms of thinking; and thought is like a contemplative monk seated on the bank of the river of life. To think is to see; to live is to be—and (if I may quote myself)

> There is no deeper abyss
> Than the one which goes from being to seeing.

For the same reason, Don Juan, although apparently so active, is not a man of action. The difference between being and doing is the same as the difference between deeds and acts. And here I am going to quote myself again:

The deed is only an act
When before being done, it was an idea.

The deed is spontaneous. The act is performed. Don Juan brings forth deeds as the rosebush brings forth roses . . . and thorns; *just because.* And, like the roses on the rosebush, his deeds shoot forth independently and unrelatedly one to another. Thus is brute nature; and thus, in nature, is pure masculinity—force just because.

Shall I dare to say that Don Juan is chaste? Pure masculinity is always chaste. Concupiscence comes from the brain. The most virile animal is the bull; he is also the chastest: to fecundate the female he enters and leaves, and that is all. Don Juan—we have already heard Zorrilla say it—is equally rapid with women, through whose lives he passes like a meteor. Don Juan's chastity is due precisely to the fact that he does not think. Don Juan does not think, not because he is a brute, that is to say dull, but because he symbolizes brute virility, that is to say he is elemental.

For that reason, as I have noted in another place, Don Juan is the antithesis of Faust. And not because Faust is a feminine personage. Faust also, in his way, symbolizes man; but the man whose masculinity has been sublimated in intellectual ambition. Don Juan is sex without brains; Faust is brains without sex.

For that reason also Don Juan is more generous than Faust, because Don Juan does not calculate and Faust does. Don Juan breaks all the divine and human laws *just because;* because life does not recognize laws; and every moment he exposes his fully lived life, because the nature of life is to enjoy gambling with death. Faust signs a contract because he is in need of the devil. Don Juan doesn't sign anything because he doesn't need anybody. He doesn't keep accounts. He is rich. He throws money to the people by the bag-fulls. He is rich, not because his authors wish to solve the problem of making their character live in a perpetual dance of trips, parties and adventures; but because he symbolizes pure masculinity, which is nature's most inexhaustible force. Manuals of biology say that a single male ejection would suffice to fecundate all the women on earth. And Adam Smith has already said: "There is no other wealth than life."

That is why Don Juan is generous. He seduces women but he does not remain with them. He possesses them but he does not consider them as his property. On the other hand, in the man whose masculinity has been sublimated in intellectual ambition, the acquisitive spirit avidly awakens. Here also it is fitting to say that "there is no deeper abyss than the one from being to seeing"; because being is satisfied with itself, but seeing takes for itself everything it sees. Sight is a prolongation of the hand; and intellect is the prolongation of the eye. For that reason, so many words that express understanding are images of the manual act of taking possession of an object: in Spanish we have *percibir, comprender, aprehender, "pescar"* ["to hook"], *coger al vuelo, tomar;* in French, *saisir, comprendre, prendre au vol, percevoir, prendre;* in English: *get, seize, grasp, comprehend, apprehend;* in German, *begreifen, annehmen, auffassen;* and in all these languages the result of knowing is expressed by the domination of the one who knows over what is known: *dominer, dominar, master, beherrschen.*

Thus the dominating man is no longer Don Juan. He is more. Caesarean men have customarily been insufficient as males. If they won victories on the fields of battle, they were wont to lose them on other fields, to which Góngora alludes in his famous verse:

> For battles of love, a field of feathers.

The only general whom Napoleon did not succeed in impressing was Josephine de Beauharnais, who was quite a woman. Thence to considering Caesarism as a substitute which the insufficient male takes to console himself—dominating nations because he could not conquer women (although he does interest them), there is no more than a step; a step which is generally taken. Political power is then, in its extreme cases, the sublimation of sexual power. The dictator, a bad lover. Don Juan, a virile elemental force, is on the contrary indifferent to domination. He passes, and on to another.

III

The Universal Don Juan

This is precisely one of the causes of the universal popularity which Don Juan attained immediately. Popular among men, since he flattered masculinity by presenting it in its most unbridled form, he was also popular among women because of that feminine spirit of contradiction which incites them to seek the one who avoids them and to avoid the one who seeks them. Don Juan crosses Europe trampling on women's hearts, and the more he scorns them the more they surrender themselves to him. Women understand what is elemental better than men. All women realized at once that Don Juan incarnated the quintessence of masculinity: the wall scaler, the law breaker, the door breaker, the virtue wrecker, the Darer, the Seducer, the Destroyer, the Creator, the Renovator.

This is because women, precisely because they are the true mothers of civilization, of order, of law—in a word, of society—hunger for violence and for anarchy. And who is more violent and anarchic than Don Juan? The question is unnecessary, since Don Juan is precisely the symbol of violence and anarchy. He is the destroyer-creator principle, that is to say, the renovating principle of things. He is only present in the initial act of fecundation, a violating act of what was in existence, a creator of what will exist; but, through the natural law of his essence, he disappears and continues on his way when the moment, in the womb of the present, beats the life of the future.

IV

Don Juan Is Spanish

It is obvious that Don Juan had to be born in Spain, a bull-country. It is an unfortunate historical pun which, making of *Legión* León, gives to Spain for a heraldic symbol the most groomed, solemn and official animal of the forest. The escutcheon of the real Spain ought to display only a bull—as indeed the form of its territory indicates, the hide of a bull spread out to dry. The bull, a primordial, elemental, spontaneous, noble, impulsive animal, and a jumper of barriers, chaste and powerful, is the image of what is Spanish, as it is of what is purely masculine.

For that reason the literary symbol of masculinity was bound to be born in Spain; and was bound to bear the title of Don in all the countries of the world; a companion in his Spanish universality of the other immortal Don, the one from the Mancha, who, lacking a woman to love, created one in his own mind. Don Juan is so Spanish that, when the genius of Spain is imprinted on History, it is usually done in his style. Goya is a Don Juan of painting; and Picasso another—fecundating males from whose seed come forth many offspring. Another Don Juan is Lope de Vega, many of whose comedies

In twenty-four hours
Passed from the writing table to the theater,

with a velocity which recalls that of Don Juan Tenorio in seducing and forgetting women; as the "thousand and three" women seduced in Spain according to Leporello recalls the two thousand seven hundred comedies of Lope. And Cortés, Pizarro, Quesada, Balboa, what are they but various forms that Don Juan takes in history? This was soon divined by the language which named them *conquistadors* just as it calls Don Juan a *conquistador*. Because those men who made the great history of Spain went from one conquest to another, as Cortés went on to the unequaled feat of las Hibueras, after having subdued by force and violated Mexico; and they were in their conquests at the same time powerful and chaste like Don Juan, door breakers and wall scalers like Don Juan, respectful of the laws which they violated, like Don Juan of the women whom he violates; seducers, darers, destroyers and creators like Don Juan. And Bolivar is also a Don Juan, nothing more than Don Juanesque and a *mujeriego* man in his sensual life, but an Hispanic bull, swift seducer, destroyer, creator of nations in his public life.

Thus it had to be. Because when Don Juan was born in the mind of a friar of Mercy, Spain was giving law to Europe; and not only in politics but in the social order. The Spaniards brought to a Europe sunk in an outrageous social barbarity, to a Europe whose festivities, even the highest, ended in filthy pigpens, the feeling of sobriety, of dignity, of neatness which made social life possible. The Spaniards cleaned the salons of drunken brawls, of obscenities and of filth; they taught formality, imposed manners and respect for women. As, furthermore, in politics they traced over Europe the grillwork of a severe discipline, and in religion they were the supporters of a definite dogma, they became the architects of the city with walls and laws in which western civilization was going to live.

For that same reason, there came forth out of Spain one who would break all its laws and would leap over all its walls. Tirso, who as a friar knew about these matters, drew the character in outline but so infallibly that in all likelihood he did not create it—it just "sprang out of him." The work is like a series of waves of virile energy, which follow each other in vigorous and original rhythm, so that each scene no sooner ends than the following one already appears; as in the sea each falling wave reveals already the rising one which follows. There are in this work glimpses of modern ideas. The technique is almost that of the film; the lines

"May it please God that you are not lying"

or

"There is plenty of time to repent"

invent the *leitmotiv*.

Tirso is very careful not to make of Don Juan a denier. He is an impious blasphemer, of course. But not a denier. The very leitmotiv "There is plenty of time to repent" is a marvellous invention which situates Don Juan in full impiety, but not outside the circle of believers.

V

Don Juan in Europe

This error, which Tirso avoids, is precisely the one which Molière commits. Of course a French Don Juan is an intrinsic contradiction. He cannot exist. The Frenchman has to be a man of reason. It is his very essence. Spontaneity is not within his reach. Hence a Don Juan in French is impossible. Molière almost surely took his comedy from some Italian model, stripped by Italian wit of its Spanish bull-like character. Molière, with his brilliant stage sense, made above all a comedy for Paris. As a comedy, of course—it is a marvel; especially in the episodes which have nothing to do with the theme; like the one of the creditor's visit. But the Don Juan in himself is a failure; gone astray because of the typically French idea, *clear and mistaken* at the same time, that Don Juan violates the moral and social laws *because* he considers them wrong and wants to improve them (the truth being that he violates them *because he does*). Molière makes of Don Juan the first of the Voltairians and the predecessor of the Encyclopedists. Imagine anyone going to Don Juan with encyclopedias! He wouldn't even need them to enamor some bluestocking. She would soon forget all about her stockings!

Byron doesn't hit the nail on the head either. Not for the same reason, though nearly so; namely that at heart Byron isn't interested in Don Juan *per se;* he uses him to express everything that comes into his mind, and, in particular, all the impertinences that he longs to unleash against his fatherland. An ungovernable and ill-bred son of a haughty, rigid and demanding fatherland, Byron runs away from home slamming the door, sits down on the sidewalk across the street and begins to insult the hated (and yet loved) papa, disguised as a Spaniard. The disguise is not very good. Byron's Don Juan does not hide his insolent, ill-humored, haughty disposition of an Englishman tormented by his *spleen*. But he is too *blasé*, too *fin de siècle*, to harmonize with the symbol which our great friar created. He is not Don Juan. He is Sir John.

Just as Mozart's is not Don Juan but Don Giovanni. What a disaster for the history of the western spirit it is that this marvel of Mozart should come from the libretto of the skilful but superficial Da Ponte! Excellent for a character like Figaro, Da Ponte was incapable of understanding the theme of Don Juan; which, if it had been presented to Mozart in all its depth, would have inspired even greater music. But that peerless genius of our European music had to struggle with a libretto without greatness, common and at times even base; and with the deplorable custom of singers who forced the composer to find a place for arias and trills at the pleasure of the consumer. Still, Da Ponte-Mozart's Don Juan is less unfaithful to the type than the Don Juans of Molière and Byron; thanks perhaps to the fact that the narrow limits of the libretto did not permit Da Ponte to show off his philosophies and unload them on his character.

This Don Giovanni perforce turns out too civilized, because of his century, to incarnate elemental masculinity; and in this respect he falls also into the defect of Byron's Don Juan. How is a wigged Don Juan possible? Is there anything more contrary to spontaneity than a wig?

At the other end of Europe, Don Juan recovers his virile force in the Muscovite Don Juan of Pushkin. But the great Russian poet is too coarse. And this is so in spite of the fact that he seems to have taken for a model precisely Da Ponte's libretto, since he quotes it in an epigraph:

> LEPORELLO: *O statua gentilissima*
> *Del gran Commendatore!*
> *...Ah padrone!*

Pushkin, following Da Ponte, also adopts the name of Leporello for Don Juan's servant. But the Russian, perhaps instinctively impressed by the vigor which the character demands, soon falls into an error that northerners customarily make—that of confusing energy with brutality. Already in the first scene, Don Juan exhibits himself with this lack of restraint: *"Laura . . . I shall run straight to Laura . . . And if there is someone with her, I shall beg him courteously to leap through the window . . ."* No, Mr. Muscovite; that is not the way it goes. It is a still more serious error than that of making him tell Laura, on a Madrid balcony: *"The night is perfumed with the flower of the lemon tree and laurel."* No. That is not the way. Pushkin conceived a Don Juan in the Russian style, with episodes of an outrageous crudeness; a Don Juan who on the edge of the Commander's tomb makes love to Doña Ana, his widow, under a false name, and then invites the statue to guard Doña Ana's door the following night—that of his rendezvous with her. The Commander arrives when Don Juan, after revealing to Doña Ana his true identity, that of the murderer of her husband, obtains a kiss and a promise from her. The statue carries him off to hell. But . . . no, that is not it.

VI

Don Juan Returns to Spain

Only a bull of poetry, with more energy and intuition than conscious domination of things, only a Spanish poet could carry the symbol of Don Juan up to its last and perfect exposition. This is what Zorrilla did in his *Don Juan Tenorio*. The immense popularity of this work, which millions of people in both worlds know by heart, is due precisely to the fact that it expresses perfectly what is specifically Spanish in the quality of masculinity, in both its most superficial and deepest aspects. It particularly pleases the average Spaniard that after having lived a life of anarchy, free of all social or moral bonds, Don Juan is saved in a late repentance. As a matter of fact, in Zorrilla's work repentance is posthumous, when it no longer makes any difference, since by this time "the coal has been burned up."

It pleases the ordinary Spaniard exceedingly that Doña Inés takes care of the matter for him. This is perhaps—at this trivial level in which one *also* lives (because not all life is deep)—this is perhaps the most Spanish part of the work of Zorrilla: because the average Spaniard is accustomed to having the woman do everything for him, from taking care of his clothes and rearing the children to keeping the books for him and taking charge when moving—while he saves the country or wins the battle of Mukden or Sebastopol on the marble tops of the café tables. So that when Zorrilla presents a work in which the woman takes charge even of settling his accounts with God—and only God knows in what a bad state these accounts are—the average Spaniard howls with pleasure.

What more can be said for the popularity of a work? But Zorrilla contributes much more. In the first place, he contributes a feeling of defiance, a very Spanish attitude. One Sunday afternoon on a sultry summer day many years ago—so many that I was not twenty years old— I was looking out of a balcony window of a house in Alcalá de Henares which opened exactly above the kitchen window. The charcoal seller arrived, shaved and in his Sunday best, looking for the cook, and he gave three taps with his knuckles on the Persian blind—no doubt the agreed signal. Silence. The charcoal man knocked again, and again, and again—and finally, discouraged, he moved away down the deserted street (he hadn't seen me), exclaiming to himself, because he felt like it, "I called on heaven and it did not answer."* "That fellow," I said to myself off stage, "will take another woman." Defiance.

There is nothing more Spanish. Only to a Spaniard like Zorrilla could such an enormous blasphemy have occurred . . . and it is no wonder if one remembers that only believers can be blasphemous, and that for that reason, the more faith there is, the more scope and more vigor there is for the blasphemy. Only to a Spanish poet could the blasphemy occur of making Don Juan defiant toward God, and telling him, as he does tell him: "Well it is up to you! I am no longer responsible for my condemnation!"—only because his first minute of repentance after such a long life of crime does not produce at once a satisfactory reward: "I called on heaven and it did not answer. It closed its doors on me. Then let heaven and not me answer for my steps on earth."

The germ of this situation is already in Tirso; not in *The Seducer from Seville,* but in another work which has influenced the gestation of the Don Juan Tenorio of Zorrilla as deeply: *The Man Condemned for Lack of Trust.* In acts more than in words, the hermit Paulo becomes defiant toward heaven when he sees that Enrico with whose salvation his own has been linked turns out to be a bandit; and he becomes a bandit too. But in Zorrilla the situation acquires an unequalled plastic relief.

This plasticity of Zorrilla's Don Juan Tenorio is his most evident

*A line from Zorrilla's play, as quoted below. [*Editor's note.*]

virtue. But there are other deeper ones, and especially an almost mathematical exactitude in the situations that make of this wildly romantic,
graceful and excellent work a model of allegorical classicism. In substance, beginning with the second part, or, more exactly, with the last
verse of the first part, the Don Juan Tenorio of Zorrilla is the drama
of absolute love. Recall that final scene of the first part: The bodies
of Luis Mejía and the Commander are lying on the floor; Doña Inés
enters and exclaims: "My father!"—"Is she his daughter?" asks a constable; and Brigida answers: "Yes." And the dialogue continues:

DONA INES: Oh! Where are you, Don Juan? How can you leave me here in such
    pain?
FIRST CONSTABLE: He murdered him.
DONA INES: Good God! Did you hold this in store for me?
SECOND CONSTABLE: That devil must have jumped into the river through here.
FIRST CONSTABLE: See them? They're climbing aboard the Calabrian boat in
    the river.
ALL: Justice for Doña Inés.
DONA INES: But not against Don Juan.

    Here absolute love is defined with an unheard-of audacity. Doña
Inés protects with her love, against justice, the killer of her father.
Love which assumes such exorbitant rights necessarily must be justified
with obligations and sacrifices no less exorbitant. This is the way Doña
Inés does it, since she obtains the promise from the Lord that she will
be condemned or saved according to whether Don Juan is condemned
or saved—a reminiscence and transfiguration of the analogous bond
which joins the destinies of Paulo and of Enrico in *The Man Condemned for Lack of Trust*. But here the situation is much more fruitful, for the bond which unites the two destinies is eternal and real, and
not as in *The Man Condemned for Lack of Trust* a mere simulacrum
of the tempting demon. Because here Zorrilla ends his Don Juan by
saving him, not through his mere repentance *in articulo mortis,* but
through the miracle of the solidarity which the mystery of love establishes between two lovers.   (1948)

Extracted from *Don Juan y la Don-Juania.* Buenos Aires: Espasa-Calpe, 1950.

From "Apropos of Don Juan"

By Emile Capouya

As a counter of popular speech, Don Juan represents a man who is inordinately successful with the ladies. He has dash, charm and enough of the trappings of gallantry to make him an accomplished seducer. His specialty is sweeping women off their feet. The art or good fortune that might enable him to make them happy is not among his attributes; indeed, once the women have been swept off their feet, our imagination leaves them in that posture, not troubling to inquire how and in what condition they find themselves once more in contact with terra firma. Don Juan's personality (still in terms of popular speech) has the effect of annihilating the personalities of his mistresses. Oddly enough, he is not much resented for it. Men consider him a nuisance, but that is chiefly professional jealousy. Women deplore him in principle, but unless they happen to be his victims, deplore him only in that tone of caressing deprecation in which one says, "a handsome devil," "a gay dog."

All this does not add up to a character. In the popular mind Don Juan is not even the sketch of a personality, but simply the symbol for a fairly abstract notion: lust. Lust so uncomplicated by the traditional pieties, and so free of competing impulses directed toward traditional ambitions—for money, status, affection, security—that it has tremendous impetus and efficiency. It is so sincere that it is bound to be successful; the woman who resists or even hesitates incurs a certain onus as calling into question the principles of cosmic balance. There is, finally, a kind of beauty in the action of the naked impulse that is proper to Don Juan, the beauty as it were of a natural force—for of course beauty has no necessary connection with anything we may approve on moral grounds. The beautiful is more nearly what is direct, spontaneous—in Hamlet's phrase, "express in action"—so that artists struggle to achieve the appearance of directness and spontaneity in their works, actors in their persons, and athletes in their play, all by a concentrated labor of practice and forgetting. In reality, it is not his airs and graces but the beauty of express action that is seductive about Don Juan.

But this Don Juan *à l'état pur,* the Don Juan who is lust made animate and nothing more, is a far cry from the literary portraits that keep his name alive. He is very different from the Don Juan Tenorio conceived by Tirso de Molina, who is part *picaro,* the rogue and adventurer of Spanish tradition. He is only a distant relative of Mozart's Don Giovanni, or Molière's or Byron's or Shaw's Don Juan. Stendhal suggests that the tendencies incarnated in the literary Don Juan could only arise in an atmosphere of Counter Reformation; Stendhal worshipped strength of character, which he defined as the strength that allows a man to dispense with hypocrisy, and his portrait of Don Juan is basically that of a radical contemner of convention, extended to include all sanctions human and divine. It is with this hint that an understanding of the composite literary figure begins.

Don Juan was the character whom the Counter Reformation endowed with the sins it particularly feared. An iron orthodoxy and conservatism was its ideal. In morals, ethics, and social and political philosophy it opposed from their first vague adumbrations the tendencies that were to become the dominant themes of modern civilization: rationalism, romanticism, secularism, nationalism, democracy. Ribadeneira, who preached the Spanish crusade against England, particularly affected two terms of opprobrium. One was "heretic," the other *novedades,* or "novelties." Heresy and novelty were to the Counter Reformation what "agitator" and "anarchist" were to the era of the Palmer Raids, or "red" and "creeping socialism" today. The Don Juan of Molière and Mozart is more than an obsessed womanizer; he is an *esprit fort,* a freethinker, a rationalist, an agnostic, an atheist, a freemason—and, for all I know, an anabaptist, a single-taxer, and a follower of Silvio Gesell. Far from being in league with the devil, as was his predecessor, Faust, Don Juan is a man who does not believe in the devil—the appropriate punishment for such perversity is, of course, hellfire. What horrified and enthralled the audiences for whom Don Juan was first created was his openly proclaimed credo, *Ni Dieu ni maître.* The delicious terror of his revolt was rounded with a consummation in fire, representing with great dramatic effect those aspects of Hell that the spiritual exercises prescribed by Saint Ignatius Loyola commend to our attention in all physical immediacy—flame, heat, the brimstone stench, appalling noise.

Don Juan without the added dimensions of full-blown iconoclasm would be no fit instrument for the Counter Reformation morality play, even though it is his restless lust that supplies the chief impetus for the drama. Reduced to the bare principle of amatory conquest, he would be as skeletal as the idea of Don Juan that survives in popular speech. Indeed, whenever our attention is directed specifically to his priapic *raison d'être* in, say, Mozart's Don Giovanni, he immediately becomes mere caricature, and his mistresses puppets. His exploits with women are reduced to a comic statistic—*in Ispagna mila e tre*. Nor can our imagination make the sum come alive and represent a procession of ravished maids and deceived wives. If these women were real, we should be horrified by their fate, but we can no more take seriously the injury done them than we can believe in the tremendous blows dealt out in a Punch and Judy show. In his role of comic energumen, Don Juan destroys the idea of womankind, because in that role he is himself no man. It is for this reason that, when Donna Elvira, in Mozart's opera, belies her statistical past and actually appears on the stage, she comes trailing faint clouds of comedy, and we are ill at ease until familiarity at last persuades us that she is a wronged woman rather than a misplaced integer.

The Counter Reformation was wise in refusing to entertain the notion of a Don Juan reduced to a single principle. When all is said and done, lust alone is not an adequate object of contemplation for an adult audience. For one thing, unbridled desire, shown in unending pursuit and abandonment, is not very interesting. Faust accomplishes all that in one move by choosing Helen for his paramour. The quest, after all, is for the woman who will confer ineffable satisfactions— "Sweet Helen, make me immortal with a kiss"; with a melancholy persistence, the Don goes from one woman to the next, but Faust demands at once the face that launched a thousand ships.

It is significant, nevertheless, that the search for some supreme sexual fulfillment is common to the legends of Faust and Don Juan. It is of a piece with their colossal self-assurance that both heroes pretend to a license and satisfaction that cannot be reconciled with the facts of our conditional world. The Counter Reformation did not choose to believe that this fierce claim could be restricted to a single human concern. Instinct or logic suggested rather that a preoccupation with sexual conquest, in defiance of convention, implied further dangerous *novedades* that were inimical to the health of the established order. At the very least, it implied a sexual partner who was fully human, i.e., a woman, and not a parcel of real estate, a ward, a servant, a domestic animal, or any of the other sub-human avatars of womankind before the nineteenth century. Don Juan's womanizing may destroy shadow-women on the stage, and in quantities that run to four figures, but, offstage, an obsession with women admits them to *de facto* membership in the human race. *Sostegno e gloria d'umanità* ("the support and glory of mankind"), say Don Giovanni of woman, and there is a wicked possibility that he means it. Sexual license in Don Juan is part of a larger configuration of penchants, appetites and presuppositions that is bound to conflict at many points with the canons of a society that deliberately cleaves to a radical orthodoxy. Moreover, in the light of Freud's suggestion that the sexual instincts are ambivalently disruptive or cementing forces of great significance to society, it may seem particularly appropriate for a figure who threatens the social order with his advanced opinions and general cynicism and exuberance, to threaten it also by a display of outrageous libertinism. Individualism, the fragmentation of society into egotistic atoms, the modern sense of self, and the ground it provides for splendid independence or sordid irresponsibility—all these weighty consequences can follow in the train of a late-renaissance nobleman who sets no bounds to his carnal appetites. The Counter Reformation saw fit to make Don Juan carry that full weight of meaning. Our own age has chosen to devalue him—for characteristic reasons.

In a now-famous essay, Gregorio Marañón identifies a human prototype of the Don Juan of legend, and makes use of biographical evidence to support a general theory about compulsive libertinism. In brief, Marañón asserts that Don Juan's promiscuity is a mask for homosexuality and impotence. As psychological doctrine, some such thesis has long been current in countries that have been influenced by Freud's theories. To this day, however, Latin countries have been little affected by Freud, and Spain least of all; in this regard, Marañón must be something of a pioneer, and can probably lay claim to originality. In any case, the philosopher Unamuno is quoted, in a recent number of the New York magazine *Ibérica,* as agreeing with Marañón that Don Juan shows signs of "deficient virility." (Incidentally, Unamuno's historical prototype differed from Marañón's. Unamuno held that the best scholarship had established that Don Juan's name was not Tenorio but Tenoiro, and that, far from being a native of Seville, he had come originally from Galicia—in other words, that he was no aristocrat but the Spanish equivalent of a Yankee peddler.)

The question of whether or not promiscuity is connected with homosexuality and/or impotence is a technical one and, within the limits of definition, one of fact. It may be true, as a matter of clinical observation, or it may not. Debate on this point is the prerogative of the initiate, I take it, and the extent to which the idea has become a received truth of amateur psychology is neither here nor there. But I think that our imaginative strategy blunders badly when we apply the notion, whether clinical principle or popular cliché, to a legendary figure, to Don Juan.

Marañón deprecates promiscuous behavior—and I think we must all agree that in the present state of society it is plainly not a good thing, since its human consequences are so unpleasant—but then he goes on to say: Moreover, it is nothing but misdirected pederasty, or else impotence, or else both. Libertinism is bad, on this showing, because it is really something worse. It is a pity, in a way, that Marañón does not tell us for what realer, remoter horrors homosexuality and impotence are front-organizations.

Applying such human measure to the Don Juan of literature has the effect of devaluing what else is useful in the legend. It has the effect of denigrating and neutralizing the qualities that Shaw perceived in the character, and that led him to incarnate them in the revolutionist, John Tanner, in *Man and Superman*. In the last analysis, Marañón is out to geld Don Juan, and that his attempt should find favor in our eyes is a commentary on our times. The Counter Reformation dressed Don Juan in the gaudy robes of its most pressing fears. Our own age, so much more timid and tacit, undercuts the entire question of the necessity for revolution by declaring that the revolutionary is a defective. Lenin, Stalin, Hitler, Mussolini—our era has suffered so much from the actions of outsize personalities that it is ready to condemn out of hand any unorthodoxy, any originality, any exuberance, any protest. A homosexual and impotent age accuses its creative spirits of perversity and barrenness, even as it lays its frustrations at the door of woman (the *castrating female*—save the mark, we even have a technical term for the chimera that represents our excuse for not trying to change our castrating society). We like to be told that men are being molded to an innocuous, uncombative, asexual pattern, as Organization Men and members of the Lonely Crowd. It is easy to see why the notion that Don Juan is merely sick, sick, sick is congenial to a society that is made up of gelded men and altered women.

The shallow profundities that are the intellectual coin of our day are more dangerous than they seem. Conceived in fear, and bearing no relation to our real situation—which is that our political life is in a bad way and getting steadily worse—they reduce thought to the level of gossip. It will take a very different spirit to get us out of the woods; it is no help at all to look on artists as infants, statesmen as people with power drives. That way lies a madness for which there is as yet no name, but which informs the parables of our time, and shapes us all in its unlovely image.   (1959)

Extracted from "Apropos of Don Juan," *The Nation,* August 29, 1959.

Don Juan at Midcentury

From Rostand to Montherlant

Quite a few modern versions constitute defenses of Don Juan, in which his romantic position is maintained in the teeth of the attacks on him; others continue the Mañara tradition of saving his Christian soul; but the most typical, and also those which bring to the Tenorio matter a new note, present Don Juan as suffering from the irremediable anguish of molecular man. By this time there is scant contact with the episodes invented by Tirso and perpetuated by Mozart. Don Juan is likely to be given new adventures, but at the same time he often refers to the traditional episodes, or else the traditional episodes are somehow woven into the new pattern. Most of these plays suffer, as I have complained already, from over-cerebration. With the exception of Max Frisch's comedy, not one of them is quite worth the few pages from Shaw we have read already.

A *Miguel Mañara, Mystère en six tableaux,* written by Lubicz-Milosz around 1912, is little more than a Roman Catholic pamphlet.[1] After a scene in which the hero's misdeeds are heard by report, we find him redeemed by the insufferably pure Girolama, and after her death he becomes a living saint. "Have I not seen him," cries a fellow monk, "running toward the stone which a drunkard threw at him, picking it up, and tenderly kissing it?" The entire play is couched in the most suffocating style of modern French pietism.

It is very difficult to disengage aesthetic judgments from one's living doctrines, and I am far from sure that the attempt should even be made. I do not know how "reliable" I am, or for whom I speak, or whether my judgment is "objective" when I state once more that the Mañara legend, and any twist of the story by which Don Juan is made to repent and by which he is saved, enervate the Don Juan matter. If Don Juan is taken as the symbol of triumphant sensuality, or as the symbol of rebellion, the weakness of a conversion is obvious. But even

1. O. V. de Lubicz-Milosz: *Oeuvres complètes* (Paris: 1945), vol. III.

if he is looked at without a shred of philosophy, do not repentance, conversion, and salvation sentimentalize the indomitable toughness of Tirso's original conception? They are too patently compromises made for weak stomachs. Perhaps, then, I simply speak for the strong-stomach school when I deplore the admixture of any quantity of sugar to the Don Juan dish.

A case in point is Gregorio Martinez Sierra's very respectable *Don Juan de España,* subtitled a tragicomedy.[2] In the first three acts, we are face to face with the real Don Juan: young, dangerous, arrogant to men, polite and devastating to women, ticklish about his honor, perfectly self-possessed, totally fearless, and—pious. We follow him in new adventures in Italy, Flanders, and Paris. This Don Juan has boundless energy, no spark of which he dissipates in self-analysis. But in the fourth act he has aged. Now forty years old, he tries to seduce a young girl in an Aragonese inn. We draw a breath of relief when he fails, for it turns out that she is his daughter. Suddenly Don Juan is deflated beyond even what Rostand had imagined. Old, sad, ugly, he runs away, tail between his legs.[3] When we see him again, he is concerned with the same veiled lady we met in Espronceda's poem. He is now longing for death. He wants to rest his head on the lady's bosom. When he meets her in a cemetery, he falls and faints. In the sixth act Don Juan is in love with a gypsy girl who receives a fatal stabbing while protecting him. The veiled lady appears again and now reveals herself as Death. Don Juan is terrified and clamors for confession. In the final act, Don Juan is a monk. Martinez Sierra, however, has very sensibly kept him heroic and quarrelsome. A woman says of him, "Now he is a famous penitent, because he never could do anything except in style." When he dies from an accidental stabbing we are assured of his salvation.

This version has the virtues of being simple, entertaining, rapid, and colorful, but the latter episodes damage the fabric. Love, terror of death, veiled ladies, and salvation—all these take us too far from, not only the original Don Juan, but the Don Juan whom Martinez him-

2. G. Martinez Sierra, *Obras completas* (Madrid: 1921), vol. IX.
3. This is the deepest humiliation which the modern Don Juan has to suffer among his many humiliations. Martinez seems to have gotten his idea from an earlier play by Jacinto Grau, *Don Juan de Carillana* (1913) in which the aging hero likewise barely fails to seduce his own daughter. A less "Jacobean" anticipation of both occurs in an embarrassing playlet by Maurice Baring, *Don Juan's Failure* (1911), in which it is not his daughter but a little stranger who humiliates him. This situation, in turn, is taken up by Bataille in *L'Homme à la rose* (1920).

self has depicted in the opening scenes. Nevertheless, it must be granted that he has handled the weaker portions of the play without sentimentality, so that they retain our respect even while we condemn them.

Don Juan as a case in the psychiatrist's handbook reappears in one of the more interesting avatars of our theme, namely Henri-René Lenormand's *L'Homme et ses fantômes* (1924).[4] This play is an analogue, and yet it conserves a couple of elements from the original matter, namely the Tisbea-type, that is to say, the seduced country lass who seeks revenge; and the dinner invitation. The latter is handled most ingeniously. There is no Commander; but the dead girl herself appears at a séance to the hero (who is simply called The Man) and takes his hand; whereupon he invites her to dine with him. But the episode is vestigial, for the dinner does not take place.

Serious authors liked to flirt with spiritualism in those days. Nineteen twenty-four was the very year of *The Magic Mountain*, whose intellectual sanity is momentarily marred by a foolish visitation. But it must be confessed that the idea of converting the Statue into a Medium, and of unleashing the wrath of God through spirits evoked at a séance is a clever one. Although Lenormand conjures up the subconscious as well, and introduces a psychiatrist for whom these apparitions are mere projections from the Man's psychic depths, we are left in no doubt concerning the reality of Alberte's ghostly revenge. If this makes for good theatre—and who will refuse to let himself shiver when spirits rap in the dark?—it also imperils our intellectual respect for the work of art.

For Lenormand, as for Marañón, Don Juan is a veiled homosexual. From the beginning, we see him accompanied by his friend and alter ego, with whom he exchanges confidences. This friendship is more important to him than the passion of any woman. He has even a moment of intense jealousy when he suspects that this friend has leagued himself with a woman against him. The friend must reassure him: when he took the woman, he was laughing with the hero against her. Eventually the Man grows old and deteriorates, and before he dies in the ghostly arms of his mother (of course), he learns the secret—from the ghosts or from his subconscious, whichever the reader prefers: to wit, that he desired the death of all his women, and loved only his friend.

4. *Théâtre Complet* (Paris: 1925), vol. IV.

A certain toughness and alertness give the plays of Martinez Sierra and Lenormand an enduring, if not a permanent, appeal. So much cannot be said for the Don Juan play which the Machado brothers created in 1927.[5] Here is candy-Christianity at its worst. Don Juan is caught between an Elvira, seduced long ago and now a cold woman, a spy in the war (!) and the murderer of her villain of a husband; and Beatriz, the young thing about to enter a convent. This Don Juan has become a sentimentalist. He tries to redeem the fallen Elvira—to save her—to bring tenderness back to her soul. "I will be your dog to save you," he cries. And when he offers her marriage, even, if she wishes, without sex, we can only exclaim with her, "Juan, it is unbelievable how you have changed in so little time." Not much will be gained from the details of the naïve plot. Enough to say that after being stabbed by Beatriz, who has become a fury, he turns saint and marries her. As he goes on his rounds to visit the poor, a witness sees an angel accompanying him. He dies with both women at his side, in strong odor of sanctity, and not before having relieved himself of a great number of pious observations.

One of the most interesting of the modern plays is Henry Bataille's *L'Homme à la rose* (1920). Here, characteristically, is Don Juan aging, Don Juan writing his memoirs, Don Juan conscious of becoming a legend, Don Juan meeting again his old loves, Don Juan rejected by a young girl, Don Juan retired, and finally Don Juan humiliated in a country inn and following like a dog the first girl in his life who is asking him to pay for her favors. But Bataille has mixed his ingredients ingeniously, using elements of both the Tenorio and the Mañara legends. He has put to good use the most dramatic of the Mañara tales, that in which Juan (or Miguel) has a vision of his own funeral. A young man to whom Don Juan has graciously yielded a woman is killed in his stead by the furious husband and buried as Don Juan. This gives the latter the chance of really watching, in a sense, his own funeral service. The service takes up a third of the play, and it consists largely of a parade of Don Juan's former mistresses, including Elvira. Even the pauper who got the louis d'or in the name of humanity is there. And—could one not guess it?—so is the man who will be writing Don Juan's life. The play is full of these literary concerns, even down to Don Juan's worrying about his style. When the funeral is over, Don Juan accosts a little girl who calls him a disgusting old fellow (he is

5. Manuel and Antonio Machado, *Juan de Mañara* in *La Duquesa de Benameji* (Madrid: Colección Austral, 1942).

forty years old). Thereupon he decides to accept his "death" and to retire. In the third act Don Juan appears at an inn where he has been living under a false name. He is angrily reading his apocryphal life, which is written in a meretricious poetic style. We are reminded here of Don Quixote's indignation when he discovers that his unauthorized life is a best-seller. Don Juan decides to publish his true memoirs and to re-enter life in his own person. When, however, he tries to impress a widow with his real identity, he is basely ridiculed, first by her, and then by all the guests in the tavern.[6] The widow, besides, prefers the bad poetry of the apocryphal life to the dry realities of the true memoirs which Don Juan reads to her, and we may suspect that it is this literary defeat which really crushes the great lover. The final scene is the one in which Don Juan is reduced to paying ten *duros* for a girl. The play, then, is mostly memory, senescence, and literature; but it is at the same time charmingly unphilosophical and light, and such action as it has—especially in the first act, which has the superb pursuit and murder of the pseudo–Don Juan—presents all the grace and rapidity of the earliest versions. Had Bataille been less the self-conscious littérateur, he might have given our century its best Don Juan.

The rhetorical distention of the classics—not only of Shakespeare, Cervantes, Dante, as we all know, but of lesser men like Gabriel Téllez as well—was still a solvent enterprise in 1925, when the great critic and novelist "Azorín" published *Los Quinteros y otras páginas*, in which he wrote a little imaginative piece entitled *El Castigo de Don Juan*. Though Don Juan narratives are not our concern in this volume, "Azorín's" story is actually a commentary on the composition of *El Burlador*. In canorous and fastidious language he imagines Fray Gabriel hearing the confessions of several elegant ladies who have been deceived by too gay a lover. The friar listens with a certain degree of sophisticated amusement, gives proper advice to the peccant ladies, and returns to his cell, where he is working on *El Burlador*. How is he to punish Don Juan? Well, Fray Gabriel knows something about the ladies, and he is not about to deliver Don Juan to eternal fires for his little mistakes. Next time, however, Fray Gabriel hears the confession of a gaunt and shabby girl, accompanied by a hungry little boy. She

6. "Don Juan's conduct makes him ridiculous. Is this conceivable? In the case of this autumnal man, yes; in that of Don Juan Tenorio, no; for if Tenorio had reached his autumn, he would have been able to impose respect on his neighbor as he had at the age of twenty-five." Thus G. Torrente Ballester in *Teatro espanol contemporáneo* (Madrid: 1957), pp. 169–170, speaking of a Spanish play, but in words perfectly applicable here.

too was tricked by a rich lover, who left her with a child he refused to acknowledge. Now she is on the streets.

Fray Gabriel softly raises his head to the boy, and the boy looks at the friar with his sad eyes. There is a moment of deep emotion. . . . After he has contemplated the child awhile, the priest tenderly draws him to himself and kisses his cheek.

Fray Gabriel is back in his cell, writing again. In question once more is the conclusion of the third act. He pauses a moment.

A profound peace reigns in the cell. But at this moment something of extraordinary gravity will happen. Eternity, Eternity! Eternal suffering in the horrible abyss! The moment is of supreme consequence. Fray Gabriel is deeply moved. But he makes an effort to master himself, to master his pen, and slowly, carefully, imitating the printed letter, he writes"

—namely, the words of Don Juan's eternal damnation.[7] Here is the kind of romantico-academic rubbish which readers of Unamuno, who turned Don Quixote into a Christ, will recognize at once. As we have seen already, Spain has been reluctant to give up the "vibrant" image of Don Juan—or of anything else: of the artist, for example, usually shown (by the artist, of course) in photogenic attitudes of heroic fervor or compassionate meditation.

Jacinto Grau's *El Burlador que no se burla* (1930)[8] is secular, but it labors under the odd difficulty of being filled with discussions of, by, and around Don Juan tending to the point that Don Juan does not discuss himself. In the second act the hero appears in a girl's room late at night, woos and wins her, whereupon her sister bursts into the room and angrily accuses Don Juan of having wooed *her*, too. This dramatic situation is stopped while Don Juan defends his honesty and discusses his character, his relation to the myth, and his purpose in life. The third act is entirely given over to a discussion of Don Juan by strollers in the alameda on their way to hear a lecture on the subject of Don Juan at the Policultural center. The play has wit, and it does not lack amusing episodes, but it is so polemical that we actually do not see much of the hero himself on the stage.[9] In the end the poisoned Don Juan is interviewed by the Devil, Destiny, Life, and Death. The Epi-

7. The quoted passages are from the *Obras completas* (Madrid: Aguilar, 1948), IV, 640.

8. Buenos Aires: Editorial Losada, 1947. An excerpt from its introduction has already been given. See pp. 641–646.

9. Someone in the play asserts that only in a country dominated so long by Moslems could a hero be conceived who looks perpetually for a harem.

logue shows a number of women confessing. He never pretended to be constant to any of them—this is the jester who did not jest—yet they all wanted him and he made them all happy. Grau tells us that Don Juan furiously enjoyed himself and that the women loved it. More doing and less telling would have made this a better play.

Let us note the existence of a *Don Juan* by Ghelderode (1928) and another—*El hermano Juan*—by Unamuno (1934), because, although both plays are worthless, they come from the pen of extremely talented men.

In Puget's play, *Echec à Don Juan* (1941),[10] the hero is again forty years old, and though he is a fierce proud Spaniard, he is also a likable fellow. The play shows how ingenious construction, bright episodes, and linguistic sprightliness are helpless when the ordering intelligence at the center is weak. To exhibit a female opponent to Don Juan who decides to enslave him is pointlessly eccentric. But to have her fall in love with him, and he with her (on top of a series of disguises), is simply wearisome. Don Juan finally allows himself to be mortally wounded in a duel with the girl, and both declare their love before he dies. The play has also the rage for explanation which presses back to motives, purposes, and even childhood recollections; but its best scenes, in which the two protagonists play colossal practical jokes on each other, are well worth staging.

The Preface to Salvador de Madariaga's *Don Juan y la Don-Juania* (1948)[11] has already been seen. The play itself is an entirely negligible pasticcio in which the most famous Don Juans gather to have a critical chat.

Of André Obey's three attempts on the theme of Don Juan, I know only the last, *L'Homme de cendres*, produced at the Comédie Française, Salle Luxembourg, in 1949. It is, I believe, the only one of the three printed to date.[12] I have already quoted certain lines from the play, and I am afraid that they are characteristic. This version is not behind any other French play in its partiality to mere talk, but the talk here is particularly bathetic. "Who allows you," says this Don Juan to the innocent Elvira, "to mingle the childish lies of your hopefulness with the despair of dawn?" And Don Alvar, the military hero, Anna's erstwhile lover, and Don Juan's enemy, weeps out the

10. Claude-André Puget, *Théâtre* (Paris, 1943), vol. I.
11. Buenos Aires, 1950. The play is entitled *La Don-Juania o Seis Don Juanes y una dama.*
12. In *Opéra*, supplément théâtral, No. 16 (January 1950). See pp. 23–24.

following to the man whom he is about to kill: "Me, I was proud of you. . . . You were the hero of my adolescence. . . . But you don't know what admiration is, and devotion, and—the love of a young man! Ha! of a young man—virgin love! Go ahead! Sneer! [*Desperately*] Virgin! Virgin!"

Characteristically, we follow Don Juan's life from birth on. As an adult, he is an existentialist, "wrapped in bitterness and spitting sarcasms." He makes love and travels all over the world to find a reason for existence, and frightens everyone with his neo-Byronic platitudes ("there is nothing . . . nothing on earth; nothing in the sky"). Needless to say, he cannot find an answer through love, though he has tried with Anna. As for Elvira, who symbolizes joy in life, he abandons her on the morning of their wedding. All he really wants is death, and, like the Don Juan of Lenau and Puget, he allows himself to be killed in a duel.[13]

Of Montherlant's *Don Juan* (1956)[14] Professor Henri Peyre has recently said that it is the worst of all the bad versions of that legend. Alas, there are worse, but the play is a monstrosity which amply deserved its failure on the stage. "Tout ce qui est systématique est sot"— *All that is systematic is foolish*—wrote Montherlant in one of the many postscripts to his masterful *Malatesta;* but the incoherence which he admires and loves, the jets of absurdity in a character, the kaleidoscope of successive sincerities—all this explains but does not justify the ragged motley of his *Don Juan.* Without pretending to familiarity with Montherlant's whole oeuvre, I feel in this Don Juan the attempt of a humorless man to write comedy. The effect is painful and coarse. We discover Don Juan as an aging rake: he is sixty-six years old, tearing up his love-letters ("Mort aux jeunes!") and waiting for the fifteen-year-old Linda. He has a bunch of flowers for her, but not many, he says, because they are expensive. I cite this detail only to give an instance of the humor in this piece. As he waits, a pail of water is emptied over his head; then another; and then another: all this gravely footnoted by Montherlant (the humorless always explain themselves) as symbols of Don Juan's tenacious and absurd passion. The scene of the rendezvous which follows consists in a coarse exchange of insults.

13. Ronald Duncan's *The Death of Satan* (1954), feebly written though it is, deserves mention because it expresses the feeling that the modern world, having lost the concept of sin, provides Don Juan with nothing to defy, nothing to overcome. There is no God to challenge, married women are bold and willing, and husbands politely look the other way.

14. Paris: Gallimard, 1958.

Other scenes of the same caliber follow. A few are almost amusing. Throughout are the famous maxims, the brilliant dialogue, the dazzling comments, only not so brilliant and dazzling here as they once were; for example, "Whoever has thoroughly understood that all women are interchangeable thinks it is folly to fight in order to keep one of them," or "The horror of presently existing no more can be softened only by intense joys." Don Juan is represented as loving death, then avoiding it, then resigned to it. Here he speaks profoundly of existential anguish or of honor; there he has to fight with the fat Commander whom his wife is pricking on with a needle. Three Thinkers-Who-Have-Ideas-about-Don-Juan give us a farcical satirical discussion scene. A widow pursues Don Juan. The Statue speaks, but it is actually a gang of robbers trying to frighten Don Juan. Finally Don Juan puts on a mask to go chasing the girls of Seville; only the mask is a death's head. Shall we dare miss, in this farrago, the ancient satisfaction of a plot? Still, Montherlant's Don Juan is at least vivacious, and even though he is content to die, we see him going after pleasure, and not after an Ideal. But the wobble from farce to philosophy, and the waddle from good to bad taste, and the hopeless swipes at rollicking fun, must leave us sour in the end. I give an act of this play because Montherlant's Don Juan is very much the twentieth-century man we have been talking about: he is old; he dwells on death; he is small and cynical; he thinks and analyzes; he is mythically self-conscious; and he is alone in an empty universe.[15]

15. Professor Leo Weinstein, *The Metamorphoses of Don Juan* (Stanford: Stanford University Press, 1959), lists six motion pictures made on the subject of Don Juan since 1922, aside from filmings of Mozart's opera. Don Juan was interpreted by John Barrymore, Douglas Fairbanks, and Errol Flynn. In 1956 Fernandel played Sganarelle. I have unfortunately not seen any of these, but a recently released version made by Ingmar Bergman, entitled *The Devil's Eye*, exhibits Don Juan once more as a humiliated failure. Three centuries dead and damned, he is sent back to earth in order to seduce an obdurate virgin. His amorous maneuvers get him nowhere, but finally the fresh young girl offers herself to him—not out of love, but out of pity. Crushed, Don Juan returns to Hell, his mission unaccomplished.

HENRY DE MONTHERLANT

Don Juan

Act II

(1956)

Translated by Adrienne M. Schizzano

TEXT

Don Juan. Paris: Gallimard, 1958.

Characters

Don Juan Tenorio, *aged 66*
Alcacer, *his bastard son*
Don Felipe, *aged 26*
Count of Ulloa, *Commander of the Order of Calatrava, aged 60*
Marquis of Ventras, *fiftyish*
Don Basile, *fortyish*
First Thinker-who-has-some-ideas-on-Don Juan
Second Thinker-who-has-some-ideas-on-Don Juan
Third Thinker-who-has-some-ideas-on-Don Juan
Chief Float Builder*
Second Float Builder
Third Float Builder
First Policeman
Second Policeman
Some Passersby

Linda, *aged 15*
The Double Widow, *aged 45*
Anna of Ulloa, *aged 17*
Countess of Ulloa, *aged 60*
Women

The action takes place in Seville and in the countryside, about 1630.

Carnavalier in the original. M. de Montherlant informs me in a note that "this is a word peculiar to the French Midi, and notably to Nice, and designates the workers who make the cardboard heads worn by the maskers at the Carnival of Nice." [*Translator's note.*]

SYNOPSIS OF ACT ONE

N.B.: *Only an idea of the play can be given here. There are many scenes and conversations which cannot be sensibly fitted into a plot synopsis.*

A year before the play opens Don Juan, a man in his sixties, seduced the Count of Ulloa's sixteen-year-old daughter, Anna. Although suspicion did not fall on him, he left Seville. Now he has returned to the city and we find him awaiting Linda, a girl of fifteen with whom he has a rendezvous. Alcacer, his devoted bastard son, has made another assignation for him, this one with a hideously deformed girl at the Inn of the Three Rabbits. Alcacer urges his father not to linger in Seville. The aging Don Juan decides to break with his past. He tears up his love letters and throws them into the Guadalquivir, but the wind catches the scraps and spreads them over the city. When Linda arrives, Don Juan gives her a bouquet of flowers and a brooch. Although she accepts the presents, she repels his advances but promises to meet him again. Alcacer, by arrangement with Don Juan, accosts the girl, giving Don Juan a chance to come to her rescue. Afterwards Alcacer and Don Juan have a conversation about old age, women, religion, and Linda. In spite of the danger he faces now that the wind has scattered his letters, Don Juan decides to stay in Seville.

ACT II

The next day. A clearing in an olive grove in the outskirts of Seville. Enter the COMMANDER OF ULLOA *and the* MARQUIS OF VENTRAS.

COMMANDER: Let's rest here in the shade, Marquis, away from the heat of the road. We'll join my wife at the carriage in a little while. What a pity that I must travel with the shades down because of her horror of the countryside. The sight of exactly four trees puts her into a frenzy. She has to get fresh air with the windows closed—and that's very difficult! . . . Well—you'll see—ours is a lovely tomb. And as for the design, I don't mean to brag but it has a touch of genius. We've been working at it more than a year. Actually, only two months if we don't count the holidays. I stand on top of the tomb, seated, in an

678

attitude of meditation. I meditate on what I was not. One hand rests on the hip: that symbolizes human glory. The other hand hangs down open: that's the surrender to the will of God. My coat-of-arms is sculptured on the stone. As a matter of fact, it is the coat-of-arms of the elder branch of the family, and I have no right to it. My not having a right to it is two hundred years old more or less—so time has sanctified it. . . . The cross is sculptured above the coat-of-arms and runs through it—bars it, so to speak, to show that a cross can cancel it out and that a coat-of-arms means nothing. Do you gauge the depth of my intention?

MARQUIS: I gauge it. But is death so much on your mind that you are having your tomb built when you're barely sixty?

COMMANDER: I never think of death. All the gypsies of Triana looked at my hand, and they told me I had twenty years to live. But I want my monument to immortalize the fact that I knew I was nothing. I am ashes, dust, nothingness, rabbit dung. That is what I want people to remember in centuries to come.

MARQUIS: What dignity in your concept—and what scope!

COMMANDER: Oh dignity, my dear sir, dignity! The site of my tomb—you'll see—is very discreet. It stands about a hundred feet from the highway. Not *on* the highway—that would show a despicable pride —but travelers can reach it by a very short detour without being drawn to it by anything—except a billboard.

MARQUIS: I suppose you've also arranged for your funeral.

COMMANDER: I want my funeral to be conducted in the strictest intimacy, but there must be an enormous number of people present. A gift will be given to everyone attending: for the ladies a marvelous cosmetic case; for the gentlemen a pair of French boots made of the finest cowhide. With this, I think we can get all Andalucia to come. There will be no speeches; only a few deeply felt words. The Countess will be supported by Doña Maria de Villacabras, her oldest friend.

MARQUIS: If I outlive you, which is likely, I will be delighted to attend the sad ceremony. What bothers me is that I have no black gloves—but wait a moment—I'll buy a pair.

COMMANDER: Come along, Marquis, we've had enough fresh air. After admiring the monument, please join the Countess so that she doesn't get too bored behind her drawn blinds. For myself, I'll come back this way; the idea just crossed my mind that I could have another sign put here. One for the road traffic, the others for the dreamers of the forest. I would like to think a little more about it, and to consider in which spot the sign will be thoroughly visible. Always led by the same principle—humility and self-effacement.

[*Exeunt the* COMMANDER *and the* MARQUIS. *The* THREE FLOAT BUILDERS *emerge from hiding.*]

CHIEF FLOAT BUILDER: The fat one is the Commander of Ulloa. The big one is the Marquis of Ventras: just like the carnival figures we make out of papier maché to put on the floats. But the Marquis is my friend and I wouldn't want to hurt him, even if the two gentlemen were not better armed than we are. Besides, we're only three against two.

SECOND FLOAT BUILDER: The Marquis of Ventras is your friend?

CHIEF FLOAT BUILDER: Men can be divided into two kinds, bastards and trash. Bastards are bastards—you know that right off. Trash are the flabby types, rotten planks that have no honor and hurt you without thinking much about it, even without knowing it, and really without ill will. The Marquis of Ventras is trash—which means he's all right. That's why he's my friend. I love honest people.

THIRD FLOAT BUILDER: Bastards and trash—and you. What are you?

CHIEF FLOAT BUILDER: Me? A little of both.

SECOND FLOAT BUILDER: But—honestly—how did the Marquis become your friend?

THIRD FLOAT BUILDER [*who is particularly down-at-heels*]: I like to choose friends who are beneath me so I can keep on high ground.

CHIEF FLOAT BUILDER: One night a year ago I wanted to do a little job and I chose the Marquis' house. The eleven strokes of midnight were sounding at the village church—I say eleven because the clock was out of order. I entered the house of the Marquis—he was sleeping or dozing. I snuck up to his bed and that's when he let an enormous fart. Oh what a fart! A real mason's fart.

SECOND FLOAT BUILDER: There are places where the spirit blows.

CHIEF FLOAT BUILDER: Oh a poet! Well, I couldn't hold myself in any more and I burst out laughing. He woke up, jumped for his sword, I aimed my pistols. He was about to lunge when he stops and says, "One moment. Let me take off my ribbon of the Golden Fleece." He slept bare chested because of the heat, but with the ribbon of the Order of the Golden Fleece sticking to the hair of his tits. He quickly added that he despised the Golden Fleece and had only sought it to infuriate his friends. I asked him why the explanation. He said, "I could see right away with whom I was dealing." Now the ice was broken, you understand, so I told him, "Marquis, do you think I'm going to kill a man who farts like that? Let's sit down and have a drink." We ate a piece of old goat cheese he had on his nightstand. I can even reveal to you that he just eats the crust and leaves the rest; everybody to his taste! "Don't you want to take anything along?" he asked me when we finished. I refused, but he insisted and gave me a lot of silver and knickknacks. He even wanted to give me his wife's picture—and he made me take it in spite of all I could say. And that's how we became good friends. It's a mistake to say that something is wind when you mean it is nothing. Wind is a great deal when it comes at the right time.

SECOND FLOAT BUILDER: I hear steps again. Two other men are coming.

THIRD FLOAT BUILDER: Let's hide again.

[*They hide behind some trees.* DON JUAN *and* ALCACER *enter.*]

ALCACER: Linda won't come to the rendezvous. As I told you this morning, she was picked up at that old market place by a gentleman from Córdoba. Display a skirt in the market long enough and somebody will lift it.

DON JUAN: The gutter giveth and the gutter taketh away; let God's will be done. Whoever has understood that all women are interchangeable considers it folly—and a degrading kind of folly—to fight to keep one. He gives her up as soon as she is contested.

ALCACER: There goes our Toledo brooch.

DON JUAN: She must have given it to her mother; that touches me! Let's make mothers dance even when their daughters are not for us.

CHIEF FLOAT BUILDER [*hidden—in a whisper to Second Float Builder*]: You, the poet, compose on your guitar a slow waltz entitled "The Dance of the Mothers."

ALCACER: Don't let your teeth chatter. You sound like castanets. You know I don't like that.

DON JUAN: My teeth aren't chattering.

ALCACER: They are too. I can hear you.

DON JUAN: I don't know what it is—it's not me.

[*A pause.*]

ALCACER: Which still leaves the Inn of the Three Rabbits tomorrow night. I mean that anatomical marvel—but I've described her enough already. And here you are like a rat in a trap, hardly daring to leave this isolated house where you haven't come for a year, and which—to make matters worse—is near the Commander's tomb. Not to mention the float builders, who live near the stone masons' barracks and who aren't good for much.

[*The* FLOAT BUILDERS *react.*]

The float builders work from December to February. The other months they rest. They're dangerous when they rest.—My God! The Commander!

DON JUAN: Hide behind this rock, and don't interfere, come what may. I command it. Besides, you're unarmed.

ALCACER: Don't forget that he knows nothing.*

[*The* COMMANDER *enters.*]

COMMANDER: My dear Don Juan, what a joy to see you again!

DON JUAN: Dear Commander, our joy is mutual. [*They embrace.*] [*Aside.*] Keep it light; keep it easy.

COMMANDER: Do you know who's going to be happy? Anna. She really loves you, you know.

DON JUAN: How good of her.

COMMANDER: Did you hear about the trouble?

DON JUAN: What trouble?

COMMANDER: Anna's trouble. She has had trouble.

DON JUAN: Not unmentionable trouble, I hope.

COMMANDER: In her chamber—a man . . .

DON JUAN: Oh, the scoundrel!

COMMANDER: We identified him by the crimson belt he left in her room when he ran away. Only Duke Antonio wore a crimson belt. Neither of them confessed—but there was no doubt. Duke Antonio, that senseless and ridiculous ninny!

DON JUAN: I'm dumbfounded. And I thought I could tell from a face —I never would have believed that Anna—Why, she breathes innocence! You tell me neither of them confessed?

COMMANDER: The Duke hasn't stopped denying. As for Anna, when I bring up the subject she cries but says nothing.

DON JUAN: And did you punish the little whippersnapper?

COMMANDER: His family is too powerful. I beat a retreat. The truth is, I felt pity because of his age. But his father exiled him to the arid confines of their estate. Inactivity and the rugged climate are sapping his strength. I'm told they'll kill him.

DON JUAN: That bad? And all this in a year?

COMMANDER: Sometimes I'm sorry I didn't kill him. It would have been more comfortable for him and more honorable for me. Of course I'm not saying that if another chance came my way—

DON JUAN: Would you really do it?

* Alcacer means that the Commander does not know it was Don Juan who seduced his daughter. [*Translator's note.*]

COMMANDER: I'm not going to look for him, but if God should send him my way I don't think I could control myself.

[*A pause.*]

DON JUAN: Commander, Duke Antonio did not seduce your daughter.

COMMANDER: Come now!

DON JUAN: I swear I know the criminal.

COMMANDER: His name?

DON JUAN: I'm not going to betray a friend.

COMMANDER: The whole city accused the Duke.

DON JUAN: On what evidence?

COMMANDER: The crimson belt. He was the only one in Seville to wear such belts. You can't get them anywhere except in France and he was in the French war.

[*A pause.* DON JUAN *unbuttons his doublet and shows his belt, which is crimson.*]

COMMANDER: What! What do you mean?

DON JUAN: I was Anna's lover for four months.

CHIEF FLOAT BUILDER: Oh no, he's really an idiot.

SECOND FLOAT BUILDER: He's too much.

COMMANDER: You are lying. Why do you want to save the Duke?

[*All during the following speech the* FLOAT BUILDERS *repeat in a low voice: "What an imbecile! Oh no, what an imbecile!"*]

DON JUAN: At the beginning I met her in Doña Elvira's garden. Later in her own room. Should I describe it for you? The harpsichord to the right as you enter; to the left a chest, a closet, and in the closet her girdles and her nightgowns and other things I don't want to mention.

COMMANDER [*Drawing his sword*]: En garde, odious scoundrel, en garde! I'll have *your* life anyway!

DON JUAN: I see my family is not powerful.

[*He also draws his sword, but the* COMMANDER'S *sword pins him against a tree.* DON JUAN *lets his sword fall.*]

COMMANDER: Wretch! Ask God to forgive you for your crimes.

DON JUAN: I will not ask forgiveness of a nonexistent God for non-existent crimes.

COMMANDER: On your knees! Throw yourself on your knees! Show remorse, regret.

DON JUAN: I regret the things I dared not do. Whatever I dared not do is lost.

COMMANDER: Devil.

DON JUAN: I'm surrounded by devils—only *I* am not one.

COMMANDER: Don't you see I could kill you like an animal?

DON JUAN: Kill me, Commander, kill me. I'm tired of explanations.

COMMANDER: Do you want to go straight to Hell?

DON JUAN: I want to go straight into the void—not to feel myself any more. Kill me, Commander, for the love of the God that doesn't exist.

COMMANDER: I won't kill you. You want it too much—if you're sincere. But you probably aren't. You're unarmed, Don Juan. I'm not a murderer. I'm going to take you to the Governor and let him surrender you to the King's justice.

DON JUAN [*with scorn*]: The King's justice!

COMMANDER: What's that?

DON JUAN: Nothing. I lead too irregular a private life to allow myself political opinions.

COMMANDER: Justice in Heaven and on earth. Like action, like payment.

DON JUAN: No, no payment. For all eternity, no payment.

COMMANDER [*thinking*]: Really, when I said, "Like action, like payment," it's a sentence I blurted out, a sentence which is leading to something I didn't intend. You gave yourself up because Antonio is innocent. You were generous. I will not surrender you to the King. "Like action, like payment." [*He puts his sword back.*]

DON JUAN: I'll go to the King myself. I don't take a reward for being honest.

COMMANDER: Don't go to the King, Don Juan. You surrendered once; that's enough. You are free. Leave Seville for awhile. Only my wife and Anna and I will know what happened. I'll affirm to the King that I finally know the offender, but I'll refuse to mention any name. Duke Antonio will regain favor, even if I have to go myself to visit him in his desert and kiss his hands to convince the King.

DON JUAN: I see you're affected by good deeds, Commander. So before we part again I want to show you that I'm not the wretch and odious scoundrel you called me. You said, "Like action, like payment," and when you said it the first time it meant that I had to pay for something. But for what exactly? to pay for what? The pleasure I received or the wrong I did? If I must pay for the pleasure—so be it; I can never pay enough for it. The pleasure women have given me is the highest that human beings can give. But the wrong? What wrong have I done? I have made women happy. The married ones—why didn't their husbands satisfy them? As for the virgins—I'll say what warriors say when they plunder their countrymen's houses: If they hadn't done it, the enemy would have. As for the widows—I discreetly cared for the orphans. For the nuns—I filled their convents with offerings. For the spinsters—I gave illusions. For the young girls —I taught them to ripen; I was to them what the sun is to flowers. But my surest glory is that I never promised marriage. Deceive those dear unfortunate women? Really! . . . And if so many times husbands and mothers were my accomplices, it was because deep down these families really loved me. And something else. I—the so-called unfaithful lover—have been infinitely faithful. For years I have supported with money and care a crowd of persons with whom I no longer slept; because I desired them once, in my eyes they were sacred. Believe me, Commander, the trail I leave behind me on earth is a bright one. When I think of the incalculable number of women now alive that I haven't possessed, I consider myself an infant. But I am much better than an infant. I love the human race.

COMMANDER: Of course people love whatever they can.

DON JUAN: You're blaming me for something. What you are blaming me for is to have been sensitive. It's true that when I pronounce the word *goodness* I feel—well, I feel—I feel in a state which is flattering for a man of my age.

[*A very short pause.*]

COMMANDER: So you're always making love?

DON JUAN: What else should I be doing?

COMMANDER: And . . . you often pronounce the word *goodness?*

DON JUAN: Yes, often.

COMMANDER: And—with all deference to you—how old are you?

DON JUAN: With all deference to myself, I was sixty-six in February.

COMMANDER: And you want me to believe you get a lot of pleasure from sex?

DON JUAN: To tell the truth, I seek proof rather than pleasure.

COMMANDER: Proof of what?

DON JUAN: Let's say proof that I exist. All that doesn't throw me into ecstasy kills me. All that isn't love happens in another world, a world of shadows. What isn't love is a dream, a hideous dream. . . . Between one hour of love and the next hour of love, I make believe I'm alive, I move like a specter. If someone didn't hold me up, I would fall. I only become a man again when two arms enfold me. When they let me go I am a specter once more.

COMMANDER: A middle-aged blaze.

DON JUAN: You're too kind: an old man's spark.

COMMANDER: You are portrayed as a rebel against society.

DON JUAN: Society affords me too many comforts for me to rebel ever so little against it.

COMMANDER: I've also been told that you are avenging yourself for all the wickedness and absurdity of this world by evading human law. That's where your vengeance lies.

DON JUAN: I like human law, at least when I compare it to divine law. I'm wise enough to tip my hat at whatever the greatest number of people approve. If I hadn't chosen to be a lover, I would have become a judge.

[*Signs of indignation among the* FLOAT BUILDERS, *still behind the trees.*]

COMMANDER [*looking around*]: It's funny. I have an impression somebody is watching us.

DON JUAN [*looking in the same direction*]: No—let's see . . . We're in absolute seclusion.

[*The* FLOAT BUILDERS *are quite visible.*]

Last year I had a girl—

COMMANDER: Not a word about my daughter! You are forgetting yourself.

DON JUAN: It's not about your daughter. Her name was Concepçion. The name, thank God, didn't bring us bad luck. I think she was the stupidest girl I've ever had, and coming from me that's not slight praise.

COMMANDER: Of course—you loved a multitude of girls last year. What a fool I was to think that Anna's love meant something to you.

DON JUAN: Thousands of affections have meant something to me.

COMMANDER: Truth is found in a single being with whom you can achieve perfect harmony through affection, practice, and time. At least that's what I've read in books. Nothing resembles one skin more than another skin.

DON JUAN: Nothing differs more than one skin from another. Each one is completely original.

COMMANDER: Women are so much alike. Why should I be curious about new ones?

DON JUAN: Not a single one of them yields in exactly the same way as the others, even if before and after she is like the others. The world is so full of good things waiting for you, it is natural and reasonable to squeeze everything out of them. That's why I say—in all seriousness—that a husband who has no desire to deceive his wife is, as far as I'm concerned, a sick man.

COMMANDER: Oh dear! Don't say that word *sick*.

DON JUAN: Why?

COMMANDER: Nothing. But—you're not happy either. If you go from woman to woman it is because you find fulfillment in none of them.

DON JUAN: There are several women for whom I have real affection and with whom I savor the joys of security and duration when I take my pleasure with them. Besides, I have my ogling and my gallivanting. They are like the arpeggios played by one hand on the organ while the other does sostenutos. I pile up change and duration—and what I always seek in change is duration.

COMMANDER [*looking around*]: I still say that somebody is listening to us.

DON JUAN: Look for yourself. There's nobody.

[*The* FLOAT BUILDERS *are still visible.*]

COMMANDER: Affairs with girlies last as long as there are no suspicions. As soon as suspicions arise and they are questioned, they confess everything.

DON JUAN: Your daughter didn't confess.

COMMANDER: Anna loved you.

DON JUAN: I also loved her. Have—? [*He stops.*]

COMMANDER: Have what?

DON JUAN: Never mind.

CHIEF FLOAT BUILDER: I bet he wanted to ask him if her breasts have developed since last year.

COMMANDER: You were sixty-five and you soiled a little girl of sixteen!

DON JUAN: You don't soil when you give pleasure, and I can reassure you on that score. The first time—when I finished—she said to me, "Thank you."

COMMANDER: She's so well brought up. [*With a start*] Oh—I hadn't understood. Scumbum, aren't you ashamed?

DON JUAN: If love could be ashamed, it wouldn't have been painted naked. A few women don't understand that it gives them pleasure—but she—Oh—she's intelligent! The tree of science enfolded her with its foliage—that is to say, my arms. All my charity issued from my body like a sweat. As for my sixty-five years—her eyes were closed.

COMMANDER [*controlling his rage*]: Zooks! 'Sblood!

DON JUAN: As if tens of thousands of men my age didn't marry sixteen-year-old girls.

COMMANDER: The parents have blessed these unions.

DON JUAN: Why don't you say they had to? Anna at least is free.

COMMANDER: Where there is love there is no freedom.

DON JUAN: And should I insult a sweet young thing by not desiring her? That really wouldn't have been nice! People say girls are seduced when *they* do the seducing. The motto of my family is "Service for Honor and Pleasure." By serving your daughter I honored her and I gave us pleasure. Glory be to God in the highest!

COMMANDER: Gadsbud! I don't know how I can listen to you.

DON JUAN: I don't know either.

COMMANDER: I can't find words.

SECOND FLOAT BUILDER: If he can't find words it's because his vocabulary is very limited.

COMMANDER: You're swaggering—You've curled your mustache!

DON JUAN: I have not curled my mustache. I combed a hair of my nostril—that's all!

COMMANDER: Zounds! 'Sbody! Seducing her—that's one thing . . . But teaching her to lie to us! For six months she has been bathing in lies.

DON JUAN: When you were sixteen, didn't you lie to your parents too?

COMMANDER: I didn't have a stranger sixty-five years old teaching me how to lie.

DON JUAN: Sir, will you forgive me?

COMMANDER: Forgive? I should rather have to forget. Her sweet face— at the table—on the other side—so small—hiding her other world— silent—suppressed—hostile—her frightening other world: falsehood with an angel's face. Her forehead so pure where her crime should appear in red letters like the mark on galley slaves. We give the hussy everything and she gives everything to a transient. And the hussy would walk over my dead body to go to her filthy rendezvous— while she slips her arm through mine—and I feel like crying, "Don't touch me, viper!" Or *would* have felt, had I only known. In her eyes —I'm the show-off, the booby, the idiot cuckold father. And yet to love this monster as a lover—oh my God! You've never had a daughter.

DON JUAN: I have quite a few—but fortunately I've lost sight of them. And the picture you paint gives me no regrets. [*Very sincere*] Pox! Pawing my daughter—Bounder!—you'll answer for that. [*He draws, facing the audience.*]

COMMANDER: 'Sdeath! I stood by her cradle . . . [*He draws, facing the audience.*]

DON JUAN: The first one to touch my daughter . . . [*He thinks—then sheathes.*] After all . . . after all . . . A booby of a fop—but a ripe man—of good family—full of experience and of tact—who makes her avoid faux pas—well—well.

COMMANDER: I should hate you [*He sheathes*] and here I am paralyzed by the love my daughter has for you.

DON JUAN: For me it is like a light in my darkness.

COMMANDER: Your darkness? What darkness?

DON JUAN: I'm going to finish. Never again will I mold the moans of a woman under my mouth and in my mouth. At times—it's like a spear—piercing your heart—and you cry out. At other times—you can bear it. I'm forgetting the past. If only I could forget the future!

THIRD FLOAT BUILDER: Ha! Ha! Ha!

SECOND FLOAT BUILDER: Why are you laughing?

THIRD FLOAT BUILDER: Because it's sad.

COMMANDER: Come now! Everybody gets old.

DON JUAN: I'm the only one.

COMMANDER: Your memories should comfort you.

DON JUAN: I only remember the waiting and the unkept rendezvous. My dreams are not filled with faces I had—but with faces that have eluded me. I have everything to do and I've done nothing—everything is beginning—and everything is finished. What good is it to have lived—if I don't remember anything? It's as if I had never lived. Why look into my past—if I don't see anything?

COMMANDER: Unhappy wretch! You've lived in a world of illusions.

DON JUAN: There is the world of illusions and then—there is nothing. I've lived the dream that man calls love—one dream or another. . . . Listen—yesterday I threw my love letters into the Guadalquivir. Do you know what?—The moment I threw them it was as if I'd gone with them. And a man who has made this gesture tells himself he might just as well throw himself into the Guadalquivir.

COMMANDER: What!—a Christian—flinging himself into the river. If he wants to die—it's so simple—let's see—he can slap an armed stranger and refuse to defend himself.

DON JUAN: By killing oneself—one shows unquestionably to all men his disbelief in God.

COMMANDER: I didn't know you were so unhappy.

DON JUAN: But I'm not unhappy.

COMMANDER: Not unhappy after what you've just told me?

DON JUAN: It's not my kind of life that makes me unhappy—that's exactly what prevents me from being unhappy. —At my age—my experience of the world fills me with horror—and it's only in the act of amorous pursuit and possession that the horror is forgotten. On all sides—I find only the black night; the hours of love are for me the stars of that night. They are the only light. But as I have no memory—I have said that happiness writes in white ink on white pages.

COMMANDER: Happiness . . . white ink on white pages—magnificent formula! Do you mind if I give it to my confessor, Father Aranda? What a weapon this would be in the church's hands. No more happiness. You've butchered it.

DON JUAN [feigning]: All right—I confess—my life is nothing but misery.

COMMANDER: Well—finally! You don't know how happy you make me by recognizing your misery. I feel twenty years younger. Don Juan unhappy—what a victory for us all! Now tell me the truth—don't you have a taste of ashes in your mouth?

DON JUAN: That's just what I was going to tell you: a taste of ashes in my mouth. Look! My tongue is full of them. [He shows his tongue.]

COMMANDER: I'll call you "Brother wolf"—the way St. Francis used to speak to the wolf—you who have a painful hunger for new women and suffer from having to devour them.

DON JUAN [Aside.]: What is he driving at? [Aloud.]: Yes—yes—suffering —always suffering.

COMMANDER: Leave the country, brother wolf. I won't surrender you to the King. I pity you. My pity is punishment enough. Others will punish you differently.

DON JUAN: And why should your pity punish me? Do I refuse the women who give themselves to me because of pity? What a mistake not to want pity! At times—to be pitied is as necessary as to be despised. Better pitied than envied.

COMMANDER [very interested]: On your word, do you really believe what you're saying, sir?

DON JUAN: On my word, I do indeed!

COMMANDER: Here's something I hear for the first time.

DON JUAN: And how do you like it?

COMMANDER: My God . . .

DON JUAN: I would certainly be glad to please you in some way—I owe you that at least.

COMMANDER: Everyone has to pocket affronts—I won't conceal from you that my age . . . the Countess . . .

DON JUAN: Sh . . . I guessed everything. There's *always* a woman who can cure you. It's only a question of finding her.

COMMANDER: Exactly.

DON JUAN: There are the nymphettes and the experts. The nymphettes—I know you have theories about them. Then there is—let's say —just as an example—Madame Bélisaine. Do you want me to test the ground—without mentioning your name of course?

COMMANDER: Yes—No—hm . . . I'm going to ask my confessor.

DON JUAN: No—don't ask your confessor. I'll see Madame Bélisaine tonight and tomorrow you'll know what's what. Dine with me tomorrow. At eight o'clock one of my men will wait at the crossroads of the Cuatro Caminos and will take you to my secret residence— which isn't far from there.

COMMANDER: The password?

DON JUAN: The password? "Death to the young!"

COMMANDER: "Death to the young"—that's easy to remember. Oh! I must be dreaming. Now I don't believe at all that this sort of thing leaves a taste of ashes in your mouth.—Who spreads those nasty rumors anyway?

DON JUAN: You curled your mustache. Not so fast!

COMMANDER: I accept your dinner invitation—but on one condition: no peas. I hate peas.

DON JUAN: Just imagine—I do too! We were made for each other. I promise—no peas.

COMMANDER: Also—I must warn you: I eat sloppily; it's a family tradition. I dirty everything.

DON JUAN: Don't worry—I'll be a good host—I'll do the same. [*Feeling the* COMMANDER's *stomach*] What have you got there? Your wallet?

COMMANDER [*pitiful*]: It's my stomach.

DON JUAN: That will have to go. [*Taking his hand*] And why those dirty nails?

COMMANDER: Dirty nails are distinguished.

DON JUAN: I'm afraid you'll have to clean them.

COMMANDER: What—clean nails? Quite clean?—The things I'm learning! Oh my dear Don Juan—it's so nice to have you as a friend.

DON JUAN: That's what your . . .

A WOMAN'S VOICE [*off-stage*]: Where are you, Gonzalo? What's delaying you?

COMMANDER: My wife! I'll tell her everything.

DON JUAN: Tell her what?

COMMANDER: Your abject action and your noble action.

DON JUAN: She'll only think of her daughter—and we'll see what we'll see.

COMMANDER: The Countess is a noble soul. Your chivalry will impress her—and she will forgive you as I have forgiven you. Women love anything that exalts them.

DON JUAN: You're putting me in a difficult situation.

COMMANDER: Look here—don't I know my wife—my companion of forty-three years?

[*The Countess appears. She is monumental.*]

DON JUAN [*Aside.*]: Keep it light! Keep it easy!

COUNTESS: Don Juan! What a happy surprise!

COMMANDER [*Aside to Don Juan.*]: Throw yourself at her feet!

DON JUAN [*Aside.*]: One moment, please! [*He kisses the* COUNTESS' *hand.*]

COMMANDER: Countess—I present to you the worst and the best man in the world. He was with Anna that unhappy night—and he now confessed it—of his own free will—to exonerate Antonio.

COUNTESS: He—with Anna? The crimson belt—

COMMANDER: It's his. [*To Don Juan*] Show your belt, let's see it.

COUNTESS: And you stand there—doing nothing—kill him! Somebody —get him!

COMMANDER [*to Don Juan*]: Throw yourself at her feet. What are you waiting for?

COUNTESS: Ho there—Marquis! Ho! My people! Help, help!

COMMANDER: Countess, he's under my protection. You don't know the favor he was about to do me.

COUNTESS: Come closer, monster—so I can dig your eyes out. [*She menaces him with one of her hair pins.* DON JUAN *covers himself, then draws his sword.*] He draws his sword against a weak woman! Coward! Poltroon! Seize him, Gonzalo. He drew his sword against me.

COMMANDER [*drawing his sword*]: Defend yourself, Don Juan. You see —we have to fight now. My wife commands it—my companion of forty-three years.

[*They fight.*]

COUNTESS: Sink of corruption!

DON JUAN: Madame—show some respect—a father of thirty children!

COUNTESS: Animal! Revolting lecher! [*With her hair pin she pricks his buttocks.*]

DON JUAN: Commander—you're a witness. The Countess is pricking my behind! [*They fight. The* FLOAT BUILDERS *from behind their trees support them with gestures of sport fans.* DON JUAN *defends himself apathetically. With a very quick movement, the* COMMANDER *throws himself on* DON JUAN's *sword and falls transpierced.* DON JUAN *runs away crying to* ALCACER]: To horse! On to Cadiz!

COUNTESS [*kneeling at the side of the corpse*]: Amor de mi alma. Is his heart still beating? [*She puts her hand on the right side of the* COM- MANDER's *chest.*] Oh no! That was the wrong side. [*She puts her hand on the left side.*] Nothing to the right, nothing to the left. He's dead on all sides. Amor de mi alma! I will stab myself over your grave. I'm tearing off my Talavera comb! I'm tearing off my mantilla! I'm tearing off my beautiful sixteenth-century shawl that cost three thousand five hundred duros plus one thousand duros for the lining! I'm tearing my hair out and I'm letting my beard grow! [*She throws her wig just as she has thrown the other objects one by one.*] Pobre- cito, que la Virgen de las Lagrimas te lleva de la tierra y te haga subir al cielo! I'm plundering my brassiere. I'm scratching my nipples! [*She does so*] Ay de mi! Señor, tu que eres justo! Mi vida por la suya! Que no puede el amor!

[*The* FLOAT BUILDERS *have come out of their hiding place and sur- round the corpse.*]

CHIEF FLOAT BUILDER: Gentlemen—your hats! [*They put their hands to the hats they don't have.*] This is truly Spanish grief!

COUNTESS: Angelillo del Cielo, permite que yo ponga mis labios de terciopelo carmesi [*to the audience*] "let me put my red velvet lips" en tu frente purisima. Unidos! siempre unidos [*To the audience*]— that of course means "United! united forever!"

CHIEF FLOAT BUILDER: Let's play a funereal tune—but—to conform to the well-known modesty of the deceased, let's do it with the utmost reserve and discretion.

[*They begin by scratching very softly on their guitars with a deeply affected look to suit the occasion. Then they get excited and finish with a frightening uproar, accompanied by grimaces inherent in the "cuadro flamenco."*]

SYNOPSIS OF ACT THREE

In spite of what has happened Don Juan remains in the vicinity of Seville. Alcacer begs him to leave, but Don Juan lives for his pleasure and refuses to be a coward. He is besieged in his hiding place by the ugly Widow who is accompanied by three Thinkers. These pedants offer foolish analyses of Don Juan—here Montherlant is satirizing the critical literature on the subject—before Alcacer draws his sword and chases them away. Having eluded the Widow, Don Juan considers where he can hide; there is no one he can trust. Anna appears. More loyal to Don Juan than to her father, she urges him to fly. He suddenly falls in love with her and promises to marry her, meaning it, when he returns. He declares that he will deserve her; she in turn tells him that "it is you who have made a woman of me." She leaves. Don Juan insists that he has been sincere. He has changed his mind about infidelity, but then "Man is made to do what pleases him." Thereupon the Commander's statue appears, manipulated and supported by the three Float Builders. They hope to frighten Don Juan and to rob the house, but he unmasks them. Braced by his own defiance of illusion, he again changes his mind and decides to return to the pursuit of women in Seville. The mask he puts on is a death mask. He cannot tear it from his face, but he is off to Seville undaunted.

Max Frisch and *Don Juan oder die Liebe zur Geometrie*

No one, I think, can read through the Don Juan versions written this century without a feeling of discouragement. Excellent authors have attempted the legend; why has it consistently defeated them? My diagnosis is implicit in the remedy I have already proposed: simplify, lighten, do not psychologize, go politely fantastic, let the symbol dance, and dance at a distance, and above all, make Don Juan a strong man.[1] I have mentioned *Felix Krull* and *Les Caves du Vatican* as models to follow, for Don Juan's blood is picaresque. He does not have to be successful—that is asking too much of a contemporary writer—but the pícaro was often a failure too, and so was Don Quixote. One can fail with a bang or a whimper, and Don Juan ought never to fail with a whimper. Fortunately, rumors to the contrary notwithstanding, the opportunities of being strong have not vanished. In the postscript to his play, Montherlant mentions the opposition of other men, of the tribunals, of Don Juan's own self; elsewhere I have suggested that the complex of barbed wires known as modern civilization has been placed everywhere across the course of frivolity. If Don Juan were to symbolize the spirit of gaiety, he would find more obstacles in our world to leap over or run down than Tirso's hero did in Catholic Spain. And why should not this gaiety consist in the enjoyment of sex? What, in spite of psychoanalysis, is more natural, more likely?

While we await the appearance of a worthy new Don Juan, our hopes are supported, and our palates satisfied, by the presence of two anti-Don Juan plays which make use of the legend, namely the tantalizing fragment in *Man and Superman* and a remarkable work by the Swiss playwright and novelist, Max Frisch, entitled *Don Juan, or the Love of Geometry*. This play was first produced in Zürich and Berlin in 1953. Recently it was published in a revised version, from which the final two acts are given here. Frisch's play is a philosophical quasi-comedy—light and acerb—which rehandles the traditional mate-

1. "And here we have Don Juan's ultimate predicament in the twentieth century—psychology. . . . Don Juan could pull the beard of the Commander of Calatrava; he cannot, or has not yet learned, to pull Sigmund Freud's beard. He thrives on being called a villain, a damned soul; he can even stand ridicule; but he cannot stand the earnest admonition that he is immature, neurotic, compulsive." Thus H. A. Grunwald in an attractive article, "The Disappearance of Don Juan," *Horizon*, IV (January 1962), p. 64.

rials with a deep elegance. The author has read widely in the literature. He alludes to the old ballads, to Tirso, to Molière, and he is
clearly indebted to the Mañara legend, to Rostand, to Shaw, and
perhaps to Bataille; but the literature does not sink him; quite on the
contrary, it is the wave on which he sails.

In this *Don Juan,* the pieces of the legend play a role which every
reader of Camus' *The Stranger* will recognize. Frisch's reluctant lover
is a cousin to Shaw's John Tanner and to Mirabell in Fletcher's *Wild-
Goose Chase;* but a cousin who has waded the swamps of Existential-
ism. For him, life is only a series of sensations. Like Camus' Meursault,
he rejects *patterns* and *deeper meanings,* though he does so with
patrician dash. Not only religion, but "eternal" love, honor, friendship, obligations, fidelity—all these are *Schwindel,* humbug. While Don
Gonzalo, the professional hero, resists the lures of an entire harem
because of his Christian faithfulness to his wife, his wife deceives him
with a priest and then again with Don Juan. Miranda, the whore, falls
in love with Don Juan and yet cannot really distinguish him from the
bumbling Don Roderigo. All Spain unites in fobbing off the clearest
evidence to the contrary in order to believe that Don Juan has been
swallowed by Hell. People are too weak to live without humbug. They
need the orthodox patterns, and they need to believe that Heaven
designed them. They are sentimentalists. Encouraged by religion and
literature, they gush feelings over the humbug of patriotism, self-
sacrifice, romantic love, or any "ideal" that comes their way. Only in
the bordello, where one woman is like another and experience is without meaning or consequence, do they touch truth. "Here," says
Celestina, "men recuperate from their false feelings."

Against all this stands Don Juan, strong and honest. He is disloyal
to religion, to the crusades, to holy wedlock, to father and friend,
and to honor. He has only one moment of what we might call bourgeois idealism, namely in a curious (and perhaps unsatisfactory) scene
in which he does fall in love with the disguised Miranda, believing her
to be Donna Anna. But the universe laughs at human sentiment:
Donna Anna has drowned herself and Don Juan is wooing a prostitute.
For that matter, the prostitute turns up as a duchess in the end. There
are no neat arrangements made for the benefit of man. The human
world is unkempt.

But Don Juan is not simply another Meursault. He has a desire. He
desires to make human life imitate the exactness, limpidity, dependa-
bility of the cosmos. And if not this, he desires to be rid of human

concerns altogether in order to contemplate the geometry of the physical world, where "what is valid today is valid tomorrow, and valid when I no longer breathe, without me and without you." But this world is denied to him, because he is a man; it is not a world meant for mankind. He ends his days in the Castle of Imperfection, subject to the "morass of our moods," loving against his will a woman who loves him but who never comes to dinner on time (a charming symbol), and even begetting, of all useless objects, an heir. Sex is the inescapable irrationality. But Don Juan must make himself as comfortable in the shoddy human world as is humanly possible. He remains comically suspended between rebellion and submission, or at the center of a triangle formed by anger, love, and despair.

Solemnity would have undone this play. But like Figaro, Frisch laughs at the world lest he must weep over it. His argument always moves from pathos to a somewhat clinical amusement, from moments of philosophical insistence to unrepentant farce. We get both moods in the final two acts and the intermezzo between (the latter severely and unjustly shortened by Frisch himself in the revised version): the fourth act with its magnificently comical reworking of Tirso's great scene, and the fifth with its long closing dusk, neither day nor night: Don Juan imprisoned in a luxurious jail (forty-four rooms!) and sitting down at a meal with Woman, his perpetual reminder that humanity will not be geometrical.

MAX FRISCH

Don Juan

or

The Love of Geometry

A Comedy in Five Acts

ACTS IV AND V

(1962)

Translated by James L. Rosenberg

TEXT

Don Juan oder die Liebe zur Geometrie. Frankfurt-am-Main: Suhr-kamp Verlag, 1962.

Characters

Don Juan
Tenorio, *his father*
Miranda
Don Gonzalo, *Commander of Seville*
Donna Elvira, *his wife*
Donna Anna, *their child*
Father Diego
Don Roderigo, *friend to Don Juan*
Donna Inez
Celestina, *the bordello-keeper*
Don Balthazar Lopez, *a married man*
Leporello
Widows of Seville
Three Dueling Nephews
Musicians

Place: A theatrical Seville

Time: A costume period

SYNOPSIS OF ACTS ONE, TWO, AND THREE

As the play opens, preparations are going forward for the wedding of Don Juan and Donna Anna. The twenty-year-old Juan is described from several points of view. We hear accounts from his father, who is in despair because his son is not interested in women; from Miranda, a prostitute with whom Don Juan has played chess at Celestina's bordello, and who has fallen in love with him; from his close friend Roderigo; and from Don Gonzalo, his prospective father-in-law, who tells of Don Juan's surprising heroism against the Moors during the siege of Cordoba. Don Juan slips in under cover of darkness; he has spent a night of passionate love on an island with an unknown girl (who will turn out to be Donna Anna herself). In a conversation with Roderigo, Don Juan confides his terror of the approaching marriage. We also learn that his ideal is "geometry," and that he brought about the fall of Cordoba by mathematical calculation, not heroism.

In Act Two the marriage arrangements continue under the supervision of Donna Elvira (in this version Donna Anna's mother) and Father Diego, Elvira's former lover, later Bishop of Cordoba. After a scene in which Don Gonzalo confesses to Father Diego the temptation he felt while visiting a Moorish harem, the wedding ceremony begins. Anna recognizes her lover of the night on the island, and Don Juan scandalously refuses to answer yes to the priest's question. He flees pursued by the outraged Don Gonzalo and members of his family. The elder Tenorio suffers a heart attack and dies.

The time of Act Three is the following morning. We learn that Don Juan has interrupted his flight for life long enough to enjoy the favors not only of Donna Elvira, the wife of his pursuer and mother of his bride-to-be, but also of Donna Inez, wife of his friend Roderigo. Near the end of the act Juan is finally surrounded by Don Gonzalo and his followers. In a brief duel with Don Gonzalo, Don Juan fatally wounds him. He then hears in rapid succession of the suicides of Roderigo, whose wife he has violated, and of Donna Anna, driven to madness by his having jilted her at the altar, and of the death of his father.

Act Four opens some thirteen years later. Don Juan is now a romantic legend in his own despite, besieged by women (including the former prostitute Miranda, now the Duchess of Ronda). He has acquired a servant, Leporello, and a new enemy, Don Balthazar Lopez, another aggrieved husband. Preparing an escape from the prison of his fame to "geometry," Don Juan has the help of an accomplice, Celestina, proprietress of the bordello and Spain's proverbial go-between.

ACT IV

A drawing room. DON JUAN, *now a thirty-three-year-old man, stands before a festive table decorated with silver and candles. He is inspecting the arrangements. His servant* LEPORELLO *is placing carafes on the table.* THREE MUSICIANS *stand nearby, awaiting instructions. In the background, a large tapestry.*

DON JUAN: You will remain in this adjoining room. Understand? Now as for the Hallelujah Chorus: remember, if something extraordinary should happen, an accident—for example, suppose, say, I were swallowed up by Hell—

MUSICIAN: Sir?!!

DON JUAN: —simply go on playing. Understand? Keep on playing the Hallelujah Chorus until there's no one left in the room. [*He removes his white gloves as he continues to examine the banquet table.*] All right. Get ready.

MUSICIAN: And our wages?

DON JUAN: Later! Later!

MUSICIAN: Later? When there's no one left in the room?

DON JUAN: Gentlemen, I am expecting thirteen ladies for dinner—thirteen ladies who all maintain that I have seduced them. And as if that weren't enough, I am also expecting the Bishop of Cordoba, who happens to share the ladies' opinion. And as if *that* weren't enough, I am expecting to entertain a statue, one whom I have invited for this occasion—a stone guest, as it were. . . . Gentlemen, I am sure you understand—my nerves—my nerves are in no condition for a discussion of wages. [*The* MUSICIANS *withdraw.*] Are you sure everything is ready?

LEPORELLO: The wine will never last, sir; there's barely enough for one small glass per person.

DON JUAN: That will be enough. I have a feeling they'll lose their taste for wine—at least, by the time the stone guest arrives.

LEPORELLO: Sir—

DON JUAN: We are bankrupt. I know. [*A bell rings off-stage.*] Where are the place cards?

LEPORELLO: But, sir, you don't really believe he'll come, do you? Him with the granite pedestal?

DON JUAN: Do *you* really believe it?

LEPORELLO: Me? [LEPORELLO *attempts a scornful laugh which dies in his throat as the doorbell rings a second time.*] Maybe that's him! [DON JUAN *starts to put out the place cards.*] Sir . . .

DON JUAN: If that's the veiled lady again, tell her I never—on principle —receive veiled ladies. We know all that business. She wants to save my soul, hoping in this way to entice me into seducing her. Tell the lady we are well acquainted with this little trick and are, as a matter of fact, weary of it. [LEPORELLO *goes out fearfully. Offstage the musicians begin to test their instruments—a strange commingling of various melodies—while* DON JUAN *continues laying out the place cards; he comes to the last card and pauses, studying it.*] You, more living than all the rest combined, you will not come. You, the only one that I ever loved, the first, the last, beloved and yet unrecognized. . . .* [*He burns the card in a candle flame.*] Ashes.

[LEPORELLO *returns.*]

LEPORELLO: The Bishop of Cordoba.

DON JUAN: Blow these ashes off the table and ask the Bishop of Cordoba to wait. But politely! This Bishop isn't exactly a religious man —not that I blame him. However, I can use him. Remember, Leporello, without the Church there is no Hell.

LEPORELLO: Sir—

DON JUAN: Why do you keep on shaking like that?

LEPORELLO: Sir—enough is enough, sir, don't push things too far—I mean, to invite a monument to dinner! I must say—an absolutely dead man, who has been dead and mouldering since—well, what I mean to say, sir, is: I'm as big a rascal as the next fellow, as long as it pays off—I'll do anything if the price is right—on my honor, I'm no coward; but yesterday in the graveyard, sir—inviting a monument to dinner. . . . No.—No, sir, count me out.

A VOICE: Don Juan?

LEPORELLO: Holy Joseph and Mary!

A VOICE: Don Juan?

DON JUAN: One moment.

LEPORELLO: My God! He's coming!

*A reference to Donna Anna. [*Editor's note.*]

DON JUAN: "One moment," I said. "One moment."

LEPORELLO: Mercy, I beg of you! I am innocent, I have a family—God in Heaven—five children and a wife! [*He falls to his knees.*] Mercy!

DON JUAN: If you want to pray, get out of here.

LEPORELLO: He called you, I heard him!

DON JUAN: Stand up. [LEPORELLO *rises.*] Now do as I tell you. Tell the Bishop of Cordoba I will see him now. But say it with lots of words and gestures—you know. I need three minutes alone here.

LEPORELLO: Mary and Joseph . . .

DON JUAN: And don't forget to kneel—where it's appropriate. [LEPO-RELLO *goes out.*] Well—what's the matter back there?

[*He goes to the tapestry in the background and* CELESTINA *steps out. She is dressed as the statue; only her head is uncovered.*]

CELESTINA: This helmet's too tight for me.

DON JUAN: No one will notice that.

CELESTINA: *I* will! [DON JUAN *gestures for her to go back into hiding.*] I've been thinking it over—

DON JUAN: And . . . ?

CELESTINA: A thousand is the least I'll do it for. After all, if I sell you to the Duchess of Ronda, I'll get my thousand pesos from her—cash on the barrelhead.*

DON JUAN: This is absolute extortion.

CELESTINA: I don't care what you call it. Names don't bother me. All I care about is the money—and, frankly, five hundred is just not enough.

DON JUAN: I don't have any more.

CELESTINA: Then count me out. [DON JUAN *tears something from around his neck.*] What's this? An amulet?

DON JUAN: The last one I have. Now disappear! If my descent into Hell doesn't come off now, I'm lost—forever.

CELESTINA: Well, it's not my fault, you know, that you're bankrupt. Why don't you just listen to my offer? You would be richer than the Bishop of Cordoba! I'm telling you: a castle with forty-four rooms—

DON JUAN: I don't want to hear any more about it, do you hear?

CELESTINA: But now is the time.

DON JUAN: Will you please spare me your damned meddling match-making! All Spain knows it, and now I tell you once more, for the last time: I will never marry!

CELESTINA: Many a man has said that.

*The Duchess is Miranda, the former prostitute, who fell in love with Don Juan thirteen years before. [*Editor's note.*]

DON JUAN: Oh, shut up! [CELESTINA *disappears behind the tapestry;* DON JUAN *turns expectantly—but it is only the terrified* LEPORELLO *who re-enters.*] What's the matter?

LEPORELLO: Sir—I've forgotten what I'm supposed to say, sir. He—he's so stately, sir, and he strolls back and forth there in the hall in that grand way—as though he can hardly wait for the heavens to smash us down!

DON JUAN: Tell him I will be happy to see him now.

[LEPORELLO *goes out, leaving the swinging doors open.* DON JUAN, *preparing himself to receive the Bishop, draws a large armchair to the side, practices just how and where he will kneel, then nods to the Musicians. They begin to play a religious-sounding air.* DON JUAN *stands before the mirror, arranging his clothing, as through the door the* VEILED LADY *enters slowly; he sees her in the mirror and starts, without turning around.*]

THE LADY: Why are you afraid?

DON JUAN: Because I know the only thing in this world worth knowing—that you are not Donna Anna, for Donna Anna is dead. Why are you veiled? [*He turns around.*] Who are you?

THE LADY: You refused to see me. Then suddenly I found this door open—

DON JUAN: What can I do for you?

THE LADY: I loved you once, long ago, because you found a game of chess more irresistably attractive than a woman. And because you passed through my life like a man with a goal. Do you still have one? It used to be geometry. Long, long ago. Now I see your life, Juan—full of women but empty of geometry.

DON JUAN: Who are you?

THE LADY: I am the Duchess of Ronda.

DON JUAN: Black as death, Duchess—that's how you entered my mirror just now. But you didn't need black to frighten me—the more blooming women look, the more they remind me of death.

THE LADY: I am dressed in black because I am a widow.

DON JUAN: Through me?

THE LADY: No.

DON JUAN: Well, then—what is it you want, Duchess of Ronda?

THE LADY: I want to save you.

DON JUAN: Ah, yes, you are the lady who wants to marry me. You are the castle with forty-four rooms. Your perseverance is astonishing, Duchess. And of course you are quite right: although chess entices me much more powerfully than women do, my life is full of women. And yet you're mistaken about one thing! No woman has ever conquered me, and I would rather rush straight to Hell than into the arms of marriage—

THE LADY: I do not come as a woman.

DON JUAN: You shame me, Duchess.

THE LADY: I have had more men than I knew what to do with, each one overflowing with smiles; and one of them, who thought he couldn't live without my smiles, made me his duchess, whereupon he died.

DON JUAN: I see.

THE LADY: Now I have this castle in Ronda—

DON JUAN: I've heard about it.

DUCHESS: And so I thought: you could live in the left wing, I could go on living in the right wing. There's a big courtyard in between. The coolness and quiet of fountains. There would be no need for our ever meeting—unless, of course, one of us felt a need to talk. And with all this, there would be a certain amount of wealth and power —perhaps not great enough to completely wipe out your stupid guilt, but enough to silence the courts of this world which accuse you of murder. To put it in so many words: as long as you live in Ronda, no man will ever be able to drive you out of your geometry.

DON JUAN: But . . . ?

THE LADY: No buts.

DON JUAN: Your understanding of men, I'll grant you, is extraordinary. But what will this rescue operation cost me?

THE LADY: All you need do is accept it, Juan.

DON JUAN: Nothing more?

THE LADY: It may be I still love you, but you needn't be afraid. I have discovered I don't need you to be happy, and that is what I can offer you above all. I am the one woman who is free of the illusion that she can't live without you. [*Pause.*] Think it over. [*Pause.*] You have always loved yourself, and so you have never found yourself. That's why you hate us. You have always taken us as women, never as wives. We were episodes to you. Each of us. Yet these episodes have somehow swallowed up your whole life. Why have you never put your faith in one woman, Juan, one time? It's the only path, Juan, to your geometry. [LEPORELLO *shows in the* BISHOP OF CORDOBA.]

LEPORELLO: His Excellency.

DON JUAN: Ah—you will forgive me, Duchess of Ronda. His Excellency and I must talk business; but I hope to see you soon at dinner—un-veiled!

THE LADY: In Ronda, Juan!

[*The* LADY *draws her cloak about her, makes a deep curtsy before the Bishop, then goes out followed by* LEPORELLO, *who closes the door.*]

DON JUAN: You see how it is, Your Excellency, I don't have a mo-ment's peace. They all want to save me by marrying me . . . Your Excellency! [*He kneels.*] Thank God you have come.

BISHOP: Rise.

DON JUAN: For twelve years the Spanish Church has been persecuting me. I'm not kneeling, God knows, out of force of habit, but out of a very real sense of gratitude. Oh, how I have longed, Your Excel-lency, to talk with a *man* for a change!

BISHOP: Rise. [DON JUAN *rises.*] What is it you wish?

DON JUAN: Will Your Excellency be seated? [*The* BISHOP *sits.*] Your Excellency, I can no longer bear either to see or hear another woman. Frankly, I don't understand God's creation at all. Was it really necessary to make two sexes? I have thought a great deal about that—about men and women, about the incurable wound of sex, about the species and the individual—yes, about that particularly: the lost position of the individual.

BISHOP: Let us come to the point. [DON JUAN *sits.*] What is it you wish?

DON JUAN: To put it briefly: I want to create a myth.

BISHOP: I beg your pardon?

DON JUAN: I want to create a myth. [*He reaches for a carafe.*] I'm sorry, Your Excellency; I forgot to offer you something to drink. [*The* BISHOP *waves it away.*] We don't have much time before the ladies descend upon us, so—with your permission—I'll come straight to the point.

BISHOP: Please do.

DON JUAN: My proposition is clear and simple: Don Juan Tenorio, who by this time has attained the rank of a sort of popular archfiend, yet who sits here before you in the full glory of his manhood and resolved to become immortal, to become, if you will, a myth—Don Juan Tenorio, I say, is both ready and determined to die—this very day.

BISHOP: To die?

DON JUAN: With—er—certain conditions.

BISHOP: Of what sort?

DON JUAN: Your Excellency, we are quite alone here. Let us speak frankly. You, the Spanish Church, will give me a modest allowance—nothing more—a small cell in a monastery somewhere—not *too* small, of course—and one which I can leave from time to time, if I wish to, and, if possible, with a view of the Andalusian mountains; there let me live forever on bread and wine, nameless, safe from women, quiet, satisfied with my peaceful geometry.

BISHOP: Hm.

DON JUAN: And to you, Bishop of Cordoba, I offer that which the Spanish Church needs more than money itself: the myth of the blasphemer's descent into Hell. [*Pause.*] Well—what do you say?

BISHOP: Hm.

DON JUAN: Your Excellency, for twelve years now that statue has been standing there with its painful inscription: *May Heaven destroy the blasphemer!* And for twelve years I, Don Juan Tenorio, have gone strolling past it, whenever I'm in Seville, as undestroyed as any other man in the city. How long, Your Excellency, how long am I to go on this way? Seductions, murders, laughter . . . [*He stands up.*] Something has got to happen to stop it.

BISHOP: Something will.

DON JUAN: What sort of an example am I for the youth of today? They take me as their model, their ideal—I can see it coming, I can see a whole era coming, an era of young men rushing into the abyss as I have done—and why? Because they have seen that there *is* no Divine Justice—a generation of idlers and mockers, who think that they are like me, empty, scornful, stupid to the point of despair—oh, Your Excellency, I can see it coming!

BISHOP: Hm.

DON JUAN: Don't you? [*The* BISHOP *takes the carafe and pours himself a glass.*] Understand me correctly, Bishop of Cordoba, it's not just that I am weary of women. I am weary of blasphemy—believe me. Twelve years of irretrievable life, wasted in this childish challenging of the empty blue air that men are pleased to call Heaven! What a waste of time! I have shrunk from nothing in all this time, I have thumbed my nose at Heaven at every opportunity, and you yourself have seen what has happened: It has simply made me famous. [*The* BISHOP *takes a drink.*] I am in despair. [*The* BISHOP *takes a drink.*] For thirty-three years now I have shared the fate of so many famous men: all the world knows our deeds, but no one knows our souls. I tell you, I shudder when I hear people talking about me. As though I ever cared anything about women!

BISHOP: Nevertheless . . .

DON JUAN: Oh, in the beginning, I'll admit, it was amusing. My hands, they said, were like divining rods—able to find what husbands had never found in ten years of searching for the springs of pleasure.

BISHOP: You are thinking of the worthy Lopez?

DON JUAN: If you don't mind, Your Excellency, I'd rather not name any names.

BISHOP: Don Balthazar Lopez.

DON JUAN: I was ready for almost anything, Your Excellency, but not for this horrible boredom. Their enraptured lips, their dewy eyes, narrowed with voluptuousness, I can't stand them any longer! Even you, Bishop of Cordoba, you enhance my fame as much as anyone else—it's a joke. They come out of your sermons against me dreaming about me, and then their worthy husbands draw their swords, before I've even glanced at their wives; the result is, I'm always fighting, everywhere I go—and what can I do? Practice makes perfect. The first thing you know—another dead husband, and the widow is hanging on my neck, sobbing, even before I can put my sword back in its sheath. And then I must comfort her. What else is left for me, I ask you, what other act appropriate to my fame, except to become a sacrifice to my fame? And, incidentally, notice that nobody talks about how the women pursue *me*—oh, no! Or—suppose I simply let the widow lie there, and turn on my heel and go on about my business? What do you suppose will happen then? We all know the unquenchable vengeance of the woman who has hoped to be seduced, but in vain— [*A knock on the door.*] One moment! [*Another knock on the door.*]

BISHOP: Why do you look at me like that?

DON JUAN: Remarkable.

BISHOP: What is remarkable?

DON JUAN: For the first time I see you close at hand, Bishop. Weren't you always considerably fatter?

BISHOP: You are probably thinking of my predecessor.

DON JUAN: Perhaps. Nevertheless, I suddenly have the strange feeling I know your face. Where have we met before? [*A knock at the door.*] Very peculiar— [*Still another knock at the door.*] But I was speaking about my proposition.

BISHOP: Marriages disgraced, families destroyed, daughters seduced, fathers murdered—not to mention the husbands who must somehow survive their disgrace—and you, who have been guilty of all this, you, Don Juan Tenorio, you dare to speak of your own problems!

DON JUAN: You're trembling.

BISHOP: Throughout the entire world, to be laughed at and jeered at as a cuckolded husband—do you have any idea what that is like?

DON JUAN: Do *you,* Your Excellency?

BISHOP: A good man like this worthy Lopez—

DON JUAN: Your Excellency seems almost obsessed with this man, the way you constantly return to him—this worthy Lopez, as you call him—who has, I know, given half his fortune to aid the Spanish Church in its persecution of me and now has even gone so far as to surround my house with his own hired henchmen. You turn pale, Your Excellency, but it's quite true—I can no longer leave my house without having to stab someone en route—it *is* a problem, Your Excellency, a real problem. [LEPORELLO *comes in.*] Don't disturb us now! [LEPORELLO *withdraws.*]

BISHOP: To come back to the issue under discussion . . .

DON JUAN: Yes.

BISHOP: The creation of a myth.

DON JUAN: You need only say "yes" and the legend is created. I have hired someone to play the role of the dead Commander, and the ladies, never fear, will scream like mad when they hear the voice from the grave. Nothing can go wrong. First, a sort of sneering laugh from me, so that chills run up and down their spines, then an explosion at the right moment, so that the ladies hide their faces—Your Excellency will notice this clever machine under the table here!— suddenly the room stinks of sulphur and smoke. All this very fast, you understand. Surprise is the mother of miracles. And you, I thought, might say something appropriate *en passant,* the sort of thing you do so well, you know—something about the inevitability of Heavenly justice; my musicians play the Hallelujah Chorus, as arranged, and—curtain!

BISHOP: And you?

DON JUAN: Safely tucked away in the cellar—Your Excellency will notice this cleverly concealed trap door in the floor! I leap down into it, naturally with an appropriately terrifying cry—one that will arouse the proper pity and terror in the best Aristotelian tradition! In the cellar a brown monk's robe awaits me, and a sharp knife—to cut off my all-too-famous mustache, and *voilà!*—there wanders forth upon the dusty highway a harmless friar.

BISHOP: I see.

DON JUAN: One condition: We both guard this secret. Otherwise neither of us will get what he wants. My descent into Hell—the report of it will spread like wildfire, and the fewer the eyewitnesses, the more firmly it will be believed by all those who weren't present and who will *want* to believe it—my descent into Hell will satisfy and comfort the ladies, their husbands, all my youthful disciples—in short, everyone will be satisfied and fulfilled. What could be more perfect?

BISHOP: I see.

DON JUAN: Don Juan is dead. I have my geometry and my peace. And you, the Church, have a proof of the justice of Heaven, which otherwise you can never find in all of Spain.

BISHOP: I see.

[LEPORELLO *enters once again.*]

LEPORELLO: Sir—?

DON JUAN: Yes. What is it?

LEPORELLO: The ladies are here.

DON JUAN: Where?

LEPORELLO: In the patio. And all very excited. Each one of them is thinking: "Just Juan and I," and so on and so forth. In fact, if I hadn't bolted the doors they might all have flown the coop by now. They're chattering and cackling out there like a barnyard full of Andalusian hens.

DON JUAN: Good.

LEPORELLO: Which is to say, everything is going the way my master likes it—all of them sashaying about, watching each other and fanning themselves—like this.

DON JUAN: Let them in. [*After a glance at the* BISHOP] In—let's say—five minutes.

[LEPORELLO *goes.*]

DON JUAN: Your Excellency, tell me which monastery will be mine.

BISHOP: You are very sure about all this.

DON JUAN: Naturally the Church is only interested in a myth which succeeds; I realize this. I understand your hesitation. But don't worry; the story is quite credible, in no way original, an old folkloristic theme, really—a statue striking down the murderer—that goes back to antiquity; the man who jeers at a death's-head, only to be hauled off into eternity as a result—just consider some of those old Breton ballads that our soldiers sing. Your Excellency, we're working in a great tradition— [*The* BISHOP *removes his robes and his dark glasses, revealing his face for the first time.*] Don Balthazar Lopez?

LOPEZ: Yes.

DON JUAN: I see.

LOPEZ: We *did* see each other one time, Don Juan, for a brief moment. A white curtain billowed out into the candle-flame as I opened the door and found you with my wife; a sudden tongue of red flame, you remember—I had to put out the fire . . .

DON JUAN: Quite correct.

LOPEZ: There was no time for sword-play then. [DON JUAN *draws his sword.*] Now that I have discovered what you are up to in an attempt to escape our vengeance, it will give me the greatest pleasure, I assure you, to unmask your blasphemous legend. Bring in the ladies! You will remain here on this earth, Don Juan Tenorio, just like the rest of us, and I promise you I will not rest until I see my vengeance fulfilled—until I see you, Don Juan Tenorio, married!

DON JUAN: Ha!

LOPEZ: Yes—and to my wife!

[LEPORELLO *enters.*]

LEPORELLO: The ladies!

LOPEZ: Even a master chess-player, it seems, can sometimes move the wrong piece and, confident of his cleverness, suddenly find himself in checkmate.

DON JUAN: We shall see.

[SIX WOMEN *burst in, a babble of noisy indignation, then pause and fall silent before the seeming Bishop,* LOPEZ *having replaced his bishop's robes. The ladies kiss the hem of his robe. This, very solemnly; then:*]

DONNA ELVIRA: Your Excellency, we have been betrayed—!

DONNA BELISA: Shamelessly betrayed—!

DONNA ELVIRA: I thought he was on his death-bed—!

DONNA ISABEL: So did I—!

DONNA VIOLA: We all did—!

DONNA ELVIRA: Otherwise, I would never have *dreamed* of coming—on my honor—!

DONNA FERNANDA: None of us would—!

DONNA ELVIRA: I, the Commander's widow—!

DONNA FERNANDA: I was told he was on his death-bed—!

DONNA INEZ: So was I, so was I—!

DONNA ELVIRA: I thought he wanted to repent—!

DONNA BELISA: We all did—!

DONNA ISABEL: *I* thought he wanted to atone—!

DONNA VIOLA: Yes. What else—?

DONNA ELVIRA: Your Excellency, I am a lady—!

DONNA BELISA: Oh? And what are *we?*

BISHOP: Donna Belisa . . .

DONNA BELISA: Aren't we ladies, too, Your Excellency?

BISHOP: Calm yourself, Donna Belisa. I know, you are the wife of the worthy Lopez.

DONNA BELISA: Please. Don't mention his name to me.

BISHOP: Why not?

DONNA BELISA: The worthy Lopez!—as he always calls himself—and not once has he ever fought for me, not once has he dared to draw his sword! All the other husbands, Your Excellency, have fought at least *one* duel for their wives; I am the only one of these ladies who does not have the honor of being a widow.

BISHOP: Control yourself, madam!

DONNA BELISA: The worthy Lopez!

DONNA ELVIRA: I was prepared for anything, Your Excellency, but not for this parade of—of soiled adultresses, who seem to feel, for some reason, that I am one of them.

THE LADIES: Oh!

DONNA ELVIRA: Oh, cackle away, you pack of chattering hypocrites, fan yourselves and lower your eyes—I know well enough why you are all here in this accursed house!

DONNA BELISA: And you?

DONNA ELVIRA: Where is he, this great lover of yours? Show him to me, so I can scratch his eyes out!

DON JUAN: I am here. [DON JUAN *steps into the circle of women like a torero.*] I thank you, my darlings, for coming here, all of you—not quite all, to be sure—some are missing—but enough, enough to celebrate my descent into Hell.

LEPORELLO: Sir—!

DON JUAN: My darlings, shall we be seated? [*The ladies remain standing, motionless; even their fans stop fluttering.*] I tell you, it's not every day that you see all your sweethearts gathered together in one room—not every day. You know, I have tried to imagine what this little scene would be like—but in vain—and I didn't know how I would speak to you in this solemn moment when I would see you all together, strangers, united only through me—and yet alienated from me, so that none of you will look me in the face—[*The ladies fan themselves.*] My darlings, once we loved each other. [*One of the ladies spits at his feet.*] I am astonished, Donna Viola, how little remains of that love—

DONNA ISABEL: My name isn't Viola!

DON JUAN: I beg your pardon.

DONNA VIOLA: He calls *her* Viola!

DON JUAN: I beg *your* pardon, too.

DONNA VIOLA: I won't stand for this!

DON JUAN: How fleeting are the emotions which carry us so near to eternity that they blind us! Yes, Donna Fernanda, it is a bitter truth.

DONNA ISABEL: I am *not* Donna Fernanda!

DON JUAN: My darling—

DONNA ISABEL: That's what you've called all of us: my darling!

DON JUAN: I didn't mean it personally, Donna Isabel—ah, now I re-member: Donna Isabel! Yes, you with the soul that was always over-flowing—why haven't you started crying by this time? [*To the Bishop*] The memory of man is strange—you're right; we know only the immediate small circumstances: a white curtain blowing into a candle-flame . . .

DONNA BELISA: Oh, God.

DON JUAN: Another time, there was a rustling in the reeds and, terri-fied as I was, I drew my sword . . . it was only a duck in the moonlight.

DONNA VIOLA: Oh, God.

DON JUAN: The things that remain in the memory are details, tiny details: a tasteless vase, slippers, a porcelain crucifix. And odors: the perfume of fading myrtle blossoms—

DONNA ISABEL: Oh, God.

DON JUAN: And so forth and so forth. And far in the distance of my youth—which was so very short—I hear the baying of a pack of hounds in a nocturnal park—

DONNA ELVIRA: Oh, God.

DONNA CLARA: Oh, God.

DONNA INEZ: Oh, God.

DON JUAN: And—that's all that I can remember. [LEPORELLO *lights the candles.*] I don't know if I am really different from other men. Do they really remember their nights with their women? I shudder when

I look back over my life: I see myself as a swimmer up a long stream, leaving no trace on the water. Don't you? And if a young man asks me: What's it like, being with a woman? I don't know what to tell him. I forget it all, the way I forget food and sorrow and joy, and then, when it's there again, I remember: Ah, yes, this is how it is, this is how it always was . . . [LEPORELLO *has finished lighting the candles.*] I don't know, Don Balthazar, whether you would like to unmask now or later.

DONNA BELISA: What did he say?

[*The* BISHOP *takes off his disguise.*]

LOPEZ: My name is Lopez.

DONNA BELISA: You?

LOPEZ: Don Balthazar Lopez.

DON JUAN: Chancellor of the Exchequer of Toledo, if I mistake not, holder of various orders and medals, as you can see, Don Balthazar has unselfishly taken upon himself the rather odious task of defending the cuckolded husbands of the world.

LOPEZ: Your mockery is at an end, Don Juan.

[*A muffled rumbling sound is heard.*]

DON JUAN: Silence! [*More rumbling*] Don Balthazar of Toledo has the floor.

[*A deeper rumbling noise*]

LOPEZ: Don't be afraid, ladies; I know all about the little game that is being played here. Listen to me!

LEPORELLO: Sir—

DON JUAN: Quiet.

LEPORELLO: The doors are locked.

[*The ladies scream.*]

LOPEZ: Listen to me!

[*The ladies run to the doors and find them locked.* DON JUAN *meanwhile seats himself at the table and pours himself a glass of wine.*]

DON JUAN: Listen to him.

LOPEZ: Ladies—!

DON JUAN: You'll forgive me if I drink while you're talking? I'm very thirsty. [*He drinks.*] Now, then—Go right ahead.

LOPEZ: He will not leave this house, ladies, not without the punishment that is due him. I have taken care of that. The hour of judgment is here, the cup of his blasphemy is full to overflowing.

DON JUAN: Hasn't it been for a long time now? [*He drinks.*] And yet nothing happens—that's the joke. Yesterday in the graveyard,

Leporello, didn't we do everything possible to taunt the dead Commander into some sort of action?

LEPORELLO: Sir—

DON JUAN: Didn't I even invite him here to dinner?

DONNA ELVIRA: My husband?!

DON JUAN: My worthy servant saw it with his own eyes, how he nodded with his stone head, your husband, evidently as a sign that his social calendar was open today. Why doesn't he come, then? It's past midnight. What must I do to get your Heaven to destroy me?

[*Again, the heavy rumbling from below.*]

LOPEZ: Be calm, Donna Elvira, be calm! [*Rumbling again, louder.*] This is not true—it's all a hoax—listen to me, he's trying to make fools out of all of you! Here! Look! See this clever machine under the table? The explosion and the smoke are supposed to terrify you out of your senses, so that you will believe that Don Juan has been taken down into Hell as a judgment of Heaven, but it's all nothing but theatre—a final unparalleled blasphemy whereby he escapes his punishment here on earth! To make fools out of all Spain, that's his plan—to create a myth, so that he can escape his proper punishment, that's all it is! It's all theatre, nothing but theatre— [DON JUAN *laughs.*] Do you deny it?

DON JUAN: Not at all.

LOPEZ: You hear him, ladies! Nothing but theatre.

DON JUAN: What else? [*He laughs.*] That's what I've said for twelve years: There is no real Hell, no Eternity, no Judgment of Heaven. Don Balthazar is absolutely correct: Nothing but theatre.

LOPEZ: You hear him, ladies?

DON JUAN: Here! [*He rises, goes to the tapestry in the background and draws it aside, revealing the theatrical-looking* STATUE OF THE COMMANDER. *The ladies shriek.*] Why do you tremble?

VOICE: Don Juan!

LEPORELLO: Sir—sir—!

VOICE: Don Juan!

DON JUAN: Nothing but theatre.

VOICE: Don Juan!

LEPORELLO: Sir—look—he's stretching out his arm—!

DON JUAN: I'm not afraid, my darlings. Look, I seize his stone hand!

[DON JUAN *takes the hand of the Statue. Explosion. Smoke.* DON JUAN *and the* STATUE *disappear through the trapdoor. The musicians start to play the Hallelujah Chorus.*]

LOPEZ: It's not true, ladies, it's not true, I swear it—please! Stop! don't cross yourselves! [*The ladies are all kneeling and crossing themselves.*] Women—! [*All the doors open, a guard at every door.*] You! Why didn't you stay at your posts?

GUARD: Where is he?

LOPEZ: He has won.

INTERMEZZO

[CELESTINA *and* LEPORELLO *appear in front of the curtain.*]

CELESTINA: I want to talk with her alone. You stay here with the coach. I know you: a little convent garden, some vesper bells, and all of a sudden you go all weak. The next thing I know, *you'll* be believing he's in Hell, too. [*A* NUN *appears.*] Sister Elvira? [LEPORELLO *goes out.*] I have come, Sister Elvira, because I have a guilty conscience. Because of the past. I didn't want to do it. When I look about me and see what I have done, I can't help reproaching myself—believe me—when I see how you pray here day in and day out, all because you were taken in by that foolish hoax about the Stone Guest. Honestly, I never thought anyone would really believe it. Word of honor! And now all Spain believes it. It's gotten so a person can't speak the truth in public. This unhappy Lopez! You've heard about him, of course: banished from the country because he dared to say that a swindler had played the role of the Commander's ghost. Sister Elvira, *I* was the one who played the Stone Guest—me, no one but me. This unhappy Lopez! You've heard the rest, of course: how he went and hanged himself over there in Morocco, after he'd given all his fortune to the Spanish Church—and now not even the Church believes him. Why is it that truth has such a hard time of it here in Spain? Sister Elvira, I've just traveled three hours in order to speak the truth, the bitter truth. Are you listening to me? I am the last witness left in all this stupid business, and I tell you, it's been weighing on my soul since I heard that you had entered the convent here —on my account. Mind you, I have nothing against the convent. But, just between the two of us, Sister Elvira: He is not in Hell. Believe me! I know where he is, although I can't tell you; I was bribed, you know—otherwise I couldn't have hired his servant. But—Sister Elvira, as one woman to another, Don Juan is alive; I've seen him with my own eyes, and I assure you, where he is has nothing to do with Hell!

You can pray for him all you want to, but it's a waste of breath. [*Vesper bells. The* NUN *walks away, praying.*] No use. [LEPORELLO *returns.*] Let's go! I have no time for people who turn to faith because they don't want to be bothered with the truth. Cross yourself!

LEPORELLO: Celestina—

CELESTINA: You heard. He is in Hell.

LEPORELLO: And my wages? What about my wages?

CELESTINA: Never mind! Let's go! March!

ACT V

[*A loggia. In the foreground, a table, set for two.* DON JUAN *is waiting, evidently for the other person. After a while, his patience grows thin, and he rings with a small handbell. A* SERVANT *enters.*]

DON JUAN: I have asked—repeatedly—not to be called away from my work until we are really ready to eat. I have been waiting here exactly one-half hour. Aren't my days short enough as it is? Oh, I know, Alonso, it's not your fault. [*Picks up a book.*] But where *is* she, anyway? [*The* SERVANT *shrugs.*] I'm sorry. Go on about your work. And —Alonso—forget I said anything.

[*The* SERVANT *withdraws.* DON JUAN *attempts to read his book, but then suddenly hurls it into a corner and calls:*] Alonso! If, as, and when we are finally ready to eat dinner, I will be in my study!

[*He starts to go, but just then the plump* BISHOP OF CORDOBA— *formerly our old friend Father Diego—comes up out of the garden, an aster in his hand.**]

BISHOP: Where are you off to in such a hurry, my young friend?

DON JUAN: Ah!

BISHOP: We've been awaiting you in the garden, dear boy. What a charming evening it is! And how sorry I am that I can't stay here with you today! Down there, under the arcades, where one looks out over the Vale of Ronda, the last sun is shining on the glowing asters, red and violet, and the cool valley below is so blue where it lies in the early evening shadows . . . . Every time I see it, I think: Here indeed is Paradise lying at my feet.

DON JUAN: I know.

BISHOP: But autumn is coming . . .

*Father Diego was the lover of Donna Elvira, wife of his excellent friend Don Gonzalo and mother of Donna Anna. [*Editor's note.*]

DON JUAN: Can I offer you a glass of wine, Diego?

BISHOP: With pleasure. [*As* DON JUAN *takes a carafe and pours two glasses of wine*] I was thinking: The old Moors who built these lovely gardens—what a talent they must have had for living life to the brim. All these courtyards, vista upon vista, these cool, cosy terraces—and the silence within them is not like the silence of the grave, no, it is a silence of secrets, delicious, deep-blue secrets behind enticing shutters and swaying curtains; one wanders about, bathing himself in the shadows, yet warmed by the golden reflection of the sunlight off a wall. How beautifully and tenderly all this has been made! Not to mention the fountains. What art, what pure art, to let creation play, as it were, upon the instrument of our senses, what mastery, to capture the evanescent, to become, as it were, pure beauty, pure spirit—what culture! [*He sniffs at the aster.*] The Duchess will be here in a moment.

DON JUAN: Oh? Will she, indeed?

BISHOP: She said she didn't feel altogether well. [DON JUAN *hands over the filled glass.*] And how is the geometry coming along?

DON JUAN: All right.

BISHOP: You know, I've been doing a lot of thinking about what you told me last time—that story about the dimensions, you remember, and how geometry too eventually comes to a truth beyond which one can no longer proceed. Isn't that what you said? Line, Surface, Space—ah, but what is the fourth dimension? And yet you can prove, intellectually, that there must be one. [DON JUAN *knocks over his glass.*] Don Juan, what is the matter with you?

DON JUAN: With me? Nothing. Why do you ask? Nothing at all. [*He refills his glass.*] Forget it. [*He knocks over his glass again.*] Why should anything be the matter?

BISHOP: Your health.

DON JUAN: Your health. [*He fills his glass for the third time.*] Every day I repeat the same request—that I shall not be called to the table until dinner is ready! Useless! First it was the gong, which the Duchess couldn't seem to hear if the crickets were chirping too loud —so I ordered another one, loud enough to reverberate through the whole damned valley! Oh, I tell you, all Ronda knew when we were having dinner up here! But not the Duchess. I ordered my servant to seek out the Duchess personally and to find her and to tender her my personal damned invitation to dinner and not to call me until the Duchess had actually appeared in the courtyard. You're laughing! It's petty, I know, ridiculous—but that's exactly why it's such torture. What am I to do? I'm her prisoner, you know—don't forget that—I can't leave this castle. If anyone were to see me outside these walls, my legend would be destroyed—which means I would have to go back to living the rest of my life as Don Juan— [*He knocks over his glass for the third time.*] Let's not talk about it any more!

BISHOP: A delicious sherry. [DON JUAN *sulks in silence.*] I said—a delicious sherry. I congratulate you.

DON JUAN: I'm sorry. [*He fills the* BISHOP's *glass again.*] Forget that I said anything.

BISHOP: Your health.

DON JUAN: Your health.

BISHOP: The Duchess is a wonderful woman. [*He sips.*] She is sweet-tempered, yet clever; she knows very well that you, her husband, are not happy, and that, incidentally, is the only thing that she has ever complained of in talking to me.

DON JUAN: She can't help it, I know.

BISHOP: But?

DON JUAN: Let's not talk about it! [*The* BISHOP *sips.*] Every day, as I come into this loggia, every day, day in and day out, three times a day, I get the sudden, blazing feeling that I can't stand it any longer! Trifles! But I can't tolerate them! And then, when she finally arrives, I act as if they really were nothing but trifles. We sit down at the table, and I say, very politely: Would you pass the bread, please?

BISHOP: She loves you.

DON JUAN: That's got nothing to do with it. If she stays in Seville for a week, to have her hair dyed or some such thing, I won't go so far as to say that I miss her—

BISHOP: But she misses you.

DON JUAN: Yes.

BISHOP: It is not good for man to live alone—as the Scriptures say—and so God created Woman.

DON JUAN: And did He think *that* was a solution? [*The* SERVANT *appears with a silver tray.*] We're not ready yet. [*The* SERVANT *goes out again.*] No, seriously, my dissatisfaction with a Creator who split us into man and woman grows greater day by day. I tremble before every meal. What a horrible thing, that a man alone is not complete! And the greater is his longing to be complete, the more accursedly he stands there, bleeding, torn off, separated from the opposite sex. What has man done to deserve this? And yet I should be thankful

for this, I know. I have only the fairly simple choice—to be dead or
to be here. Thankful for this prison in paradise!

BISHOP: My friend—

DON JUAN: It *is* a prison!

BISHOP: With forty-four rooms. Think of all those who have only a
tiny hut to live in.

DON JUAN: I envy them.

BISHOP: Why?

DON JUAN: They will go mad, perhaps, and then they will notice nothing. . . . Why didn't you leave me in the monastery?

BISHOP: Not everyone can live in the monastery.

DON JUAN: Be fruitful and multiply!

BISHOP: Thus it is written.

DON JUAN: No churchly ban, you know, and no worldly sword ever
made me tremble; but she, a woman, she brings me to it twenty
times a day! And how? Because I see that somehow I can no longer
laugh at laughable things. Because I find myself satisfied in a world
where no satisfaction really exists! She is a woman—to be sure, the
best of all possible women—but still a woman; and I am a man. And
there is nothing that can be done about that, Your Excellency, even
with the best of good will. It becomes a wrestling match in which we
shame each other with good will. Oh, you should see us and hear us
when we're alone. Not a raised voice! We are idyllic. Once I threw
a glass against the wall, that's true—but only once! We have come to
a sort of murderous politeness; we are sorry when the other one is
unhappy. What more do you want to make a marriage complete?
[*Pause.*] All that remains now is for sex to throw one last rope around
my neck. . . .

BISHOP: And that would be—?

DON JUAN: To make me a father. What could I do? *She* couldn't help
it, God knows. We would simply sit down at the table as always and
say: Please pass the bread.

[MIRANDA, *the Duchess of Ronda, appears.*]

MIRANDA: Am I interrupting you?

BISHOP: Not at all, my dear Miranda. We were just chatting about
Don Juan's descent into Hell. Have you seen the new play about it
in Seville, by the way? It's playing now.

DON JUAN: I never go to Seville.

MIRANDA: A play?

BISHOP: "The Trickster of Seville," it's called, or "The Stone Guest."

I had to go see it, you see, because it's rumored it was written by our prior, Gabriel Téllez.

MIRANDA: How is it?

BISHOP: Rather witty. Don Juan actually goes to Hell, and the audience cheers and shudders pleasantly. You really should see it, Juan.

DON JUAN: My descent into Hell?

BISHOP: What else can the theatre show? Truth cannot be shown, only experienced. Just imagine an audience seeing the real Don Juan, here in this autumnal castle in Ronda! The women would preen themselves and on the way home they would say: You see? And the husbands would gloat and rub their hands: Don Juan in carpet-slippers! Ha! There always comes a point where the unusual seems all too usual. And then where—as my secretary is fond of saying— where is the punishment? Not to consider this question would be a grave mistake. And then some young fool, who prides himself on being a pessimist, would explain: Marriage, you see—that is the true hell! and Heaven knows how many other idiotic platitudes—No, it would be horrible to listen to the reactions of an audience which sees only reality. [*He extends his hand.*] Farewell, Duchess of Ronda!

MIRANDA: Must you really go?

BISHOP: I must, I must. [*Extending his hand to* DON JUAN] Farewell, Trickster of Seville!

DON JUAN: Will it be printed?

BISHOP: I suppose so. People enjoy it immensely, you know, to see a man on the stage doing the things they'd all like to do, and then atoning for them.

MIRANDA: But don't I appear in it, Diego?

BISHOP: No.

MIRANDA: Thank Heaven.

BISHOP: Thank Heaven, I don't either—otherwise we would have had to ban it, and the theatre needs all the good plays it can get. Yet I doubt if it is really by Tirso de Molina; it's much too artless, it seems to me, and stylistically far beneath his earlier plays. [*He places the aster on the table.*] God bless your table!

[*He goes out, accompanied by* DON JUAN. MIRANDA *is alone for a moment or two; she sways slightly, as if unwell. Then she finds the book on the floor.* DON JUAN *returns.*]

MIRANDA: How did this book get here?

DON JUAN: I—I don't know.

MIRANDA: Did you throw it down?

DON JUAN: What is it, anyway?

MIRANDA: You asked if it were to be printed. This is it: "The Trickster of Seville and the Stone Guest."

DON JUAN: He must have brought it with him.

MIRANDA: Why did you throw it away? [DON JUAN *holds her chair for her.*] Is it time to eat? [*She sits down.*] Are you angry? [DON JUAN *sits down.*] You are unfair, Juan . . .

DON JUAN: Of course, my dear, of course . . .

MIRANDA: I think I'm going to have to lie down for a moment.

DON JUAN: Do you want some wine?

MIRANDA: No, thank you.

DON JUAN: Why not?

MIRANDA: Suddenly I was so dizzy. Juan, I think we're going to have a child.

DON JUAN: A child—? [*The* SERVANT *comes in.*] So. We have come this far. Yes, Alonso, we are ready. [*The* SERVANT *goes out.*]

MIRANDA: You don't have to say that it makes you happy, Juan, not yet—but it will make me happy if I see some day that it makes you happy. [*The* SERVANT *returns with the silver tray and serves them.*]

DON JUAN: Will you pass the bread, please?

[*She does so. They begin to eat in silence. The curtain falls very slowly.*]

Bibliography

Several excellent bibliographies provide the titles of a multitude of Don Juan versions and analogues, as well as titles of numerous studies devoted to this subject. Basic is Armand E. Singer's "A Bibliography of the Don Juan Theme," *West Virginia University Bulletin*, 1954, with three supplements to date in *West Virginia University Philological Papers*, 1956, 1958, and 1959. Another useful list is Everett W. Hesse's *Catálogo bibliográfico de Tirso de Molina* (Madrid: Publicaciones de la Revista Estudios, 1949), which has a section devoted to the Don Juan matter. Professor Hesse has published several supplements to this catalogue in various issues of *Estudios* (Madrid). Another excellent bibliography is provided in Leo Weinstein's study of Don Juan (see below).

The basic study of the Don Juan matter is that of Georges Gendarme de Bévotte, *La Légende de Don Juan*, 2 vols. (Paris: Librairie Hachette, 1911). Other useful treatments, in chronological order, are Karl Engel, *Die Don-Juan Sage auf der Bühne* (Oldenburg and Dresden: Schulze, 1887); Arturo Farinelli, *Don Giovanni* (Milan: Fratelli Bocca, 1946)—a reprint, with valuable additional notes, of a monograph published in 1896; Theodor A. Schröder, "Die dramatischen Bearbeitungen der Don-Juan Sage . . . bis auf Molière einschliesslich," in *Beihefte zur Zeitschrift für Romanische Philologie*, XXXVI (1912), 1–215; Hans Heckel, *Das Don-Juan Problem in der neuere Dichtung* (Stuttgart: J. B. Metzler, 1915); John Austen, *The Story of Don Juan* (London: Martin Secker, 1939); Esther van Loo, *Le Vrai Don Juan: Miguel de Mañara* (Paris: SFELT, 1950); Leo Weinstein, *The Metamorphoses of Don Juan* (Stanford: Stanford University Press, 1959).

For the folklore sources, consult Victor Said Armesto, *La leyenda de Don Juan* (Madrid: Sucesores de Hernando, 1908); and Dorothy E. MacKay, *The Double Invitation in the Legend of Don Juan* (Stanford: Stanford University Press, 1943).

Other titles consulted or cited in this compilation are as follows:

"Azorín." *El Castigo de Don Juan* in *Los Quinteros y otros páginas; Obras completas.* Madrid: Aguilar, 1948.
Bacourt and Cunliffe. *French Literature During the Last Half-Century.* New York: 1923.

Baring, Maurice. *Don Juan's Failure.* 1911.

Bataille, Henry. *L'Homme à la rose.* 1920.

Bennett, Arnold. *Don Juan de Maraña.* 1913.

Benoist, Antoine. *Le Théâtre d'aujourd'hui.* Deuxième série; Paris: 1912.

Bergman, Ingmar. *The Devil's Eye.* 1961.

Bergmann, A. (ed). *Christian Dietrich Grabbe: Werke.* Göttinger Akademie Ausgabe; Emsdetten: Verlag Lechte, 1960.

Borgman, A. S. *Thomas Shadwell: His Life and Comedies.* New York: New York University Press, 1928.

Bragaglia, A. G. *Pulcinella.* Rome: G. Cassini, 1953.

Brecht, Bertolt. Notes to an adaptation of Molière's *Don Juan. Stücke,* vol. 12. Frankfurt-am-Main: Suhrkamp, 1959.

Bushee, Alice H. *Three Centuries of Tirso de Molina.* Philadelphia: University of Pennsylvania Press, 1939.

Byron, Lord. *Don Juan.* 1818–1823.

Camus, Albert. *The Myth of Sisyphus.* New York: Alfred A. Knopf, 1940.

Campardon, E. *Les Spectacles de la foire.* Paris: 1877.

Casalduero, J. "Contribución al estudio del tema de Don Juan en al teatro español." *Smith College Studies in Modern Languages,* XIX (1938).

Castro, Americo (ed). *Tirso de Molina: Obras.* Clásicos Castellanos; Madrid, Espasa-Calpe, 1932.

Chekhov, Anton. *Platonov.*

Cheney, Sheldon. *The Theatre.* London: Longmans, Green, 1929.

Coleridge, Samuel Taylor. *Biographia Literaria.* 1817.

Collier, Jeremy. *Short View of the Immorality and Profaneness of the English Stage.* 1698.

Córdoba y Maldonado, Alonso de. *La Venganza en el sepulcro.*

Corneille, Thomas. *Festin de Pierre.* 1677.

Cotarelo y Mori, Emelio (ed.). *Comedias de Tirso de Molina.* Madrid: Bailly-Baillere, 1907.

Croce, Benedetto. *Aneddoti di varia letteratura.* Naples: 1943.

Da Ponte, Lorenzo. *Memoirs.* Translated by Elizabeth Abbott. New York: Orion, 1959.

Dent, Edward J. *Mozart's Operas.* 2nd ed.; New York: Oxford University Press. 1947.

Despois and Mesnard (ed.). *Molière: Oeuvres.* Paris: 1912.

Diaz-Plaja, Guillermo. *Nuevo asedio a Don Juan.* Buenos Aires: Editorial Sudamerica, 1947.

Dibdin, Thomas J. *Don Giovanni; or, A Spectre on Horseback!* 1817.

Dumas, Alexandre (père). *Don Juan de Maraña, ou la chute d'un Ange.* 1836.

Duncan, Ronald. *The Death of Satan.* 1954.

Espronceda, José de. *El Estudiante de Salamanca.* 1840.

Fenichel, Otto. *The Psychoanalytic Theory of Neuroses.* New York: W. W. Norton, 1945.

Fitzlyon, April. *The Libertine Librettist*. London: John Calder, 1955.

Flaubert, Gustave. *Une nuit de Don Juan*. Ca. 1850.

Fletcher, John. *The Wild-Goose Chase*. 1621.

Fournel, V. (ed.). *Les Contemporains de Molière*. Paris: 1875.

Fry, Christopher. *Venus Observed*. Oxford: University of Oxford Press, 1950.

Fucilla, J. G. "El Convidado de Piedra in Naples in 1625," *Bulletin of the Comediantes*, X (Spring 1958).

Gautier, Théophile. *La Comédie de la Mort*. 1838.

Gendarme de Bévotte, G. (ed.). *Le Festin de Pierre avant Molière*. Paris: Conelly et Cie., 1907.

Genest, John. *Some Account of the English Stage from the Restoration in 1660 to 1820*. Bath: 1832.

Ghelderode, Michel de. *Don Juan*, in *Théâtre*. Paris: 1955.

Goldoni, Carlo. *Don Giovanni Tenorio*. 1736.

Grau, Jacinto. *Don Juan de Carillana*. 1913.

———. *El Burlador que no se burla*. Buenos Aires: Editorial Losada, 1947.

Green, John Richard. *History of the English People*. New York and London: Harper, n.d.

Grunwald, H. A. "The Disappearance of Don Juan," *Horizon*, IV (January 1962).

Junqueiro, Abelio Guerra. *A Morte de D. João*. 1874.

Kennedy, Ruth L. In *Hispanic Review*, X, XI, XII (1942–1944).

Lazare, Christopher (ed.). *Tales from Hoffmann*. New York: A. A. Wyn, 1946.

Lenau, Nikolas. *Don Juan, ein dramatisches Gedicht*. 1844.

Lenormand, Henri-René. *L'Homme et ses fantômes* in *Théâtre Complet*. Paris: 1925.

Leydi, Roberto and Renata M. *Marionette e burattini*. Milan: Collana del "Gallo Grande," 1958.

Lida de Malkiel, M. R. "Sobre la priordad de ¿Tan Largo me lo fiáis?" *Hispanic Review*, XXX (October 1932).

Lubicz-Milosz, O. V. *Miguel Mañara, Mystère en six tableaux* in *Oeuvres complètes*. Paris: 1955.

Machado, Manuel and Antonio. *Juan de Mañara* in *La Duquesa de Benamejí*. Madrid: Colección Austral, 1942.

Madariaga, Salvador de. *La Don-Juania o Seis Don Juanes y una dama*. Buenos Aires: Espasa-Calpe, 1950.

Maeztu, Ramiro de. *Cincos ensayos sobre Don Juan*. Santiago de Chile: Editorial Cultura, 1937.

Magnin, Charles. *Histoire des marionettes en Europe*. Paris: 1862.

Mandel, Oscar. "Molière and Turgenev: The Literature of No-Judgment," *Comparative Literature*, XI (Summer 1959).

Manning, C. A. "Russian Versions of Don Juan." *PMLA*, XXXVIII (1923).

Martinez Sierra, Gregorio. *Don Juan de España* in *Obras completas*. Madrid: 1921.

Maurois, André. "Don Juan," *L'Illustration*, CII (1928).

Mérimée, Prosper. *Les Ames du purgatoire*. 1834.

Meynieux, André. "Pouchkine et Don Juan," *La Table Ronde*, No. 119 (November 1957).

Moncrieff, William Thomas. *Giovanni in the Country*. 1820.

Musset, Alfred de. *Un Spectacle dans un fauteuil*. 1832.

――――. *À Quoi rêvent les jeunes filles*. 1840.

Nicoll, Allardyce. *History of English Drama, 1660–1900*. 6 vols.; Cambridge: Cambridge University Press, 1952.

Obey, André. *L'Homme de cendres* in *Opéra*, supplément théâtral, No. 16 (January 1950).

Petraccone, E. (ed.). *La Commedia dell' Arte*. Naples: 1927.

Pinto, Vivian de Sola. *Enthusiast in Wit: A Portrait of John Wilmot Earl of Rochester, 1647–1680*. Lincoln: University of Nebraska Press, 1962.

Pí y Margall, F. "Observaciones sobre el carácter de D. Juan Tenorio," *Colección de libros españoles raros y curiosos*. Madrid: 1878.

Pratt, Dallas. "The Don Juan Myth," *American Imago*, XVII (1960).

Puget, Claude-André. *Echec à Don Juan* in *Théâtre*. Paris: 1943.

Pushkin, Aleksandr. *The Stone Guest* in *Poems, Prose and Plays*. New York: Modern Library, 1943.

Rank, Otto. *Die Don Juan-Gestalt*. Vienna: Psychoanalytischer Verlag, 1924.

Rennert, Hugo A. *The Spanish Stage in the Time of Lope de Vega*. New York: Hispanic Society of America, 1909.

Richardson, Samuel. *Clarissa*. 1747–1748.

Rios, Blanca de los (ed.). *Obras de Tirso de Molina*. Madrid: Aguilar, 1946, 1952, 1958.

Rosimond, Claude La Rose, Sieur de. *Le nouveau Festin de Pierre, ou l'Athée foudroyé*. 1669.

Rougemont, Denis de. "Don Juan," *Nouvelle Revue Française*, LIII (1959).

Scheible, J. *Das Kloster*. Stuttgart: 1856.

Shaw, George Bernard. "Don Giovanni Explains." 1887.

Singer, Armand E. "Don Juan in America," *Kentucky Foreign Language Quarterly*, VII (1960).

Speaight, George. *History of the English Puppet Theatre*. London: Harrap, 1955.

Steffan, T. Guy. *Byron's Don Juan, the Making of a Masterpiece*. Dallas: University of Texas Press, 1957.

Steigner, August. *Thomas Shadwell's "Libertine."* Berne: 1904.

Thackeray, William Makepeace. *Paris Sketchbook*. 1841.

Tolstoi, Aleksei K. *Don Juan*.

Torrente Ballester, G. *Teatro español contemporáneo*. Madrid: 1957.

Unamuno, Miguel de. *El hermano Juan*. 1934.

Valbuena Prat, Angel. *Historia de la literatura* española. 6th ed.; Barcelona: Gustavo Gili, 1960.

Varey, J. E. *Historia de los Títeres en España.* Madrid: Revista de Braganza, 1957.

Viardot, Louis. *Etudes sur l'histoire des institutions, de la littérature, du théâtre et des beaux-arts en Espagne.* 1835.

Vogt, Nicolas. *Der Farberhof oder die Buchdrükerei in Mainz.* 1809.

Wade, Gerald E. "Tirso de Molina," *Hispania (A Teachers' Journal),* XXXIII (May 1949).

Wade, G. E. and E. J. Mayberry. "Tan Largo Me Lo Fiais and El Burlador . . . ," *Bulletin of the Comediantes,* XIV (Spring 1962).

Werner, R. M. (ed.). *Der Laufner Don Juan.* Hamburg and Leipzig: 1891.

Young, G. M. (ed.). *Early Victorian England.* London: Oxford University Press, 1934.

Zamora, Antonio de. *No hay plazo que no se cumpla ni deuda que no se paga.* 1714.

Acknowledgments

I extend my thanks to a number of persons who have facilitated and some-times rectified this work: to Professors Gerald E. Wade, Eric Bentley, and Robert E. Knoll; to Professors Leo Weinstein, Joseph G. Fucilla, Germaine Brée, and Armand E. Singer; to the library staff of the University of California, Los Angeles, and in particular to Mr. Edmond Mignon; and to Messrs. Richard Greene and John March. Some have patiently read and offered their comments on this collection; some have replied to one or twenty queries; some have guided me to sources I might have overlooked; and to all I owe a debt of gratitude.

Four libraries have been drawn upon for materials in the course of my work: that of the University of California, Los Angeles; the Harvard College Library; the University of Nebraska Library; and the Henry E. Huntington Library. I am thankful for the unfailing courtesy extended to me by all these institutions.

A particular acknowledgment must go to Professor Boyd Carter, who pro-posed the idea of a collection of Don Juan plays to the University of Nebraska Press.

Finally, I acknowledge with thanks the kindness of the following persons and publishers for granting permission to reprint or translate copyrighted material:

Hill and Wang, Inc. for a selection from *Tales of Hoffmann,* edited by Christopher Lazare. Copyright © 1946 by Hill and Wang, Inc.

Princeton University Press for a selection from *Either/Or* by Søren Kierke-gaard, translated by David F. Swenson and Lillian Marvin Swenson. Copy-right 1944 by the Princeton University Press. Copyright © 1959 by Doubleday & Co., Inc.

The Huntington Library, San Marino, California, for permission to repro-duce *Giovanni in London* by W. T. Moncrieff.

The Public Trustee and The Society of Authors (England) for selections from *Man and Superman* by George Bernard Shaw. Copyright 1903 by George Bernard Shaw. Renewal copyright 1931 by George Bernard Shaw.

M. Jean Rostand for permission to translate *La Dernière nuit de Don Juan* by Edmond Rostand. Copyright 1921 by Eugene Fasquelle.

Dr. Helene Rank Veltfort and Mme. Pierre Simon for a selection from "Die Don-Juan Gestalt" by Otto Rank.

Senora Herminia Peñaranda de Grau for a selection from *El Burlador que no se burla* by Jacinto Grau. Copyright 1941 by Editorial Losada, S.A. Buenos Aires.

The heirs of Gregorio Marañón for a selection from *Don Juan* by Gregorio Marañón. Copyright 1944 by Cía. Editora Espasa-Calpe Argentina, S.A. Buenos Aires.

Don Salvador de Madariaga for a selection from his *Don Juan y la Don-Juanía*. Copyright 1950, Editorial Sudamerica Sociedad Anoníma, calle Alsina 500, Buenos Aires.

Emile Capouya and *The Nation* for a selection from "Apropos of Don Juan." Copyright 1959 by *The Nation*.

Henry de Montherlant for a selection from his *Don Juan*. Copyright 1958 by Librairie Gallimard.

Max Frisch and Suhrkamp Verlag, Frankfurt-am-Main, for selections from his *Don Juan oder die Liebe zur Geometrie*. Copyright 1953. © 1962 by Suhrkamp Verlag.

Librairie Hachette for a selection from *La Légende de Don Juan* by Georges Gendarme de Bévotte. Copyright 1911 by Librairie Hachette.

Al Hirschfeld and *The New York Times* for permission to reprint the "Man and Superman" cartoon. Copyright by The New York Times.